THE
Winn Rosch
HARDWARE
BIBLE

THE
Winn Rosch
HARDWARE
BIBLE

WINN L. ROSCH

BRADY
NEW YORK

Brady

Simon & Schuster, Inc.
Gulf + Western Building
One Gulf + Western Plaza
New York, NY 10023

Distributed by Prentice Hall Trade
Manufactured in the United States of America

1 2 3 4 5 6 7 8 9 10

Library of Congress Cataloging-in-Publication Data

Rosch, Winn L.
  The hardware bible / by Winn L. Rosch.
    p. cm.
  Includes index.
  1. Microcomputers—Handbooks, manuals, etc. I. Title.
TK7888.3.R67 1988
621.391 '6—dc19   88-29176
                                             CIP

ISBN 0-13-160979-3

TO MY FATHER

CONTENTS

Acknowledgments   xi

1 **Introduction   1**

2 **Background to an Industry Standard   7**
Origins of the PC   9
Computer Competitors   10
The IBM Strategy   13

3 **The Motherboard   21**
System Board Common Features   26
Motherboard Functions   34

4 **Microprocessors   37**
Microprocessor Family Tree   42
The 8086 Family   44
The Second Generation, the 80286   48
Sixteen Megabytes   49
State of the Art: The 80386   50
How Microprocessors Work   57
Programming Languages   58
Chip Packaging and Identification   59

5 **Coprocessors   65**
Numeric Coprocessor Types   70
Adding a Numeric Coprocessor   76

6 **Memory   81**
Memory Architectures   89
Logical Memory Organization   93
Memory Expansion   98
Expansion Board Memory   106
Memory Errors   110

7 The Expansion Bus   115
Electrical Function of the PC Bus   **119**
The 16-bit AT Bus Extension   **123**
32-bit Bus Technologies   **129**
Micro Channel Architecture   **136**
How the Micro Channel Works   **149**
EISA   **152**

8 The Basic Input/Output System   157
PC BIOS Basics   **161**
PS/2 BIOS Innovations   **174**

9 Support Circuitry   179
Clocks and Oscillators   **181**
PC Oscillators and Timers   **182**
AT Oscillator/Timer   **184**
PS/2 Oscillators and Timer   **188**
Interrupt Controllers   **189**
Direct Memory Access   **194**

10 The Power Supply   199
Power Supply Types   **201**
Practical PC Power Supplies   **202**
Power Supply Replacement   **204**
Power Protection   **208**

11 Cases   217
Radio Frequency Emission   **219**
Cooling   **221**
Hardware Considerations   **224**
Device Mounting   **226**

12 Input Devices   237
The Keyboard   **239**
Keyboard Technologies   **243**
Key Layouts   **246**
Keyboard Use   **249**
Mice   **257**
Light Pens   **264**
Touch Screens   **265**

13 Display System Basics   267
Block Graphics   **277**
Bit-Mapped Graphics   **278**

Memory to Screen   **280**
Graphics Coprocessors   **283**
The Intel 82786   **287**
Texas Instruments' TMS34010   **290**

14 Video Adapters   293
The Monochrome Display Adapter   **295**
The Color Graphics Adapter   **298**
Hercules Graphics   **307**
The Enhanced Graphics Adapter   **309**
The Video Graphics Array   **314**
The Memory Controller Gate Array   **324**
EGA Plus   **326**
8514/A   **327**
Display Adapter Setup   **330**

15 Computer Displays   335
IBM Monitor Types   **355**

16 Parallel Port   365
Parallel Communications   **369**
Parallel Port Signals and Connections   **371**

17 Printers   377
Printer Mechanics   **379**
Image-Forming Methods   **383**
Paper Handling   **391**
Printer Control   **396**

18 Serial Ports   409
Synchronous and Asynchronous Communication   **411**
Serial Connections   **417**
Non-Standard Serial Connections   **421**
PC-Based Serial Ports   **426**
Diagnosing Serial Communication Problems   **428**

19 Modems   435
Modem Operating Principles   **438**
Channel Limits   **440**
Modem Modulation Methods   **444**
Modems Faster Than 300 Bits Per Second   **446**
High Speed Modems   **448**
Modem Control   **452**
Modem Features   **463**

Other Modem Considerations   **469**
Connecting and Using a Modem   **471**

20 Magnetic and Mass Storage   475
Introduction to Magnetic Media   **477**
Data Coding   **482**
Sequential and Random Access Media   **485**
Device Controllers   **491**
Device Interfaces   **493**
Physical Aspects of Mass Storage Devices   **499**

21 Floppy Disks   503
The 5 1/4-Inch Disk   **507**
3 1/2-Inch Floppies   **515**
Floppy Disk Drives   **517**
Floppy Disk Controllers   **519**
Installing Floppy Disk Drives   **523**
Cabling considerations   **526**
Terminating Resistor Networks   **527**

22 Hard Disks   533
Naming Conventions   **535**
Understanding Hard Disks   **537**
IBM Disk Formats and Capacity Limits   **545**
Disk Performance Issues   **550**
Configuring a Hard Disk   **560**
External Hard Disks   **563**
Hard Disk Cards   **565**
Hard Disk Cabling   **569**
Hard Disk Setup   **575**
Hard Disk Formatting   **583**

23 Tape   587
Open-Reel Tape   **590**
3480 Cartridges   **593**
Cassette Tape   **594**
Cartridge Tape   **598**
QIC-40   **606**
QIC-100   **611**
Nonstandard Tape Systems   **612**
Tape Backup Systems   **615**

Index   621

ACKNOWLEDGMENTS

This book would not have been possible without the aid of the following people:

Bernie Wu, Archive Corporation; Rainer Schulz, CAE/SAR Systems; Bob Root and Sam Thompson, Carlyle Memory Products Group; Stephanie Campbell, Compaq Computer Corp.; John Simonds, Core International; Marty Alpert, Cumulus Corporation; Michael Dell and Ron Leonard, Dell Computer Corporation; Bob Goligoski, Grid Systems; Ken Plotkin, Hauppauge Computer Works; Jill Liscom and Mona Roberto, Hewlett-Packard, Inc.; Bobbie Crowell, Intel Corporation; Chet Heath, Jim Monahan, and Carey Ziter, IBM Corporation; John Klonick, Maxtor Corporation; Jennifer Roney, Miniscribe Corp.; Richard L. Sager, Mitsubishi Electric America; Kim Warnock, NCR Corporation; Dick Reiser, Priam Corporation; Catherine Hartsog, Quantum; Tim Mahoney and Debra Diamond, Rodime, Inc.; Dave Williams, Storage Dimensions, Inc.; Kathy Botz and Bob Flynn, Tecmar, Inc.; Philip Hage, 3M Company; Burt Gabriel and Ozzievelt Owens, Brady Books; and The Bookmakers, Incorporated.

Limits of Liability and Disclaimer of Warranty

1

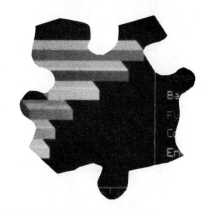

INTRODUCTION

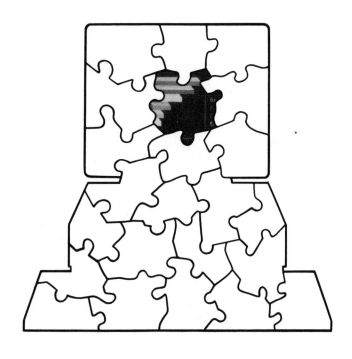

Computers strike fear in the hearts of the meek and strong alike. Tinkering with them is often held in the same awe as open-heart surgery—except that cardiovascular surgeons are as apprehensive as the rest of us about tweaking around the insides of a computer. But computers are merely machines, made by people, meant to be used by people, and capable of being understood by people.

As with other machines, they are only unapproachable by those inexperienced with them. An automobile mechanic may reel at the sight of a sewing machine. The seamstress or tailor may throw up his hands at the thought of tuning his car. Working on the computer is no different. In fact, today's personal computer is purposely designed to be easy to take apart and put back together, to change and modify, and is generally invincible except at the hands of the foolish or purposely destructive. As machines go, the personal computer is sturdy and trouble-free. Changing a card in a computer is safer and more certain of success than fixing a simple home appliance such as a toaster.

The mystique surrounding the computer probably has its roots in several troubling aspects of the machine. First and foremost, the computer is a *thinking* machine—and that one word implies all sorts of preposterous nonsense. The thinking machine could be a devious machine, hatching plots against you as it sits on your desk, thinking of evil deeds that will cause you endless frustration. A thinking machine has a brain, therefore opening it and working inside is brain surgery, and the electronic patient is as likely as the human to suffer irreversible damage at the hands of an unskilled operator. A thinking machine must work the same unfathomable way as the human mind—something so complicated that, in thousands of years of attempts by the best geniuses, no one has satisfactorily explained it.

But computers don't think—at least not in the same way you do or Albert Einstein did. The computer has no emotions or motivations. The impulses traveling through it are no odd mixture of chemicals and electrical activity, of activation and repression. The computer deals in simple pulses of electricity, well understood and carefully controlled. The intimate workings of the computer are probably better understood than the seemingly simple flame inhabiting the internal combustion engine inside your car. Nothing mysterious lurks inside the thinking machine called the computer.

Computers are considered fearsome because they are based on electrical circuits. Electricity can be dangerous, as the ashes of anyone struck by lightning will attest. But inside the computer the danger is low. At its worst it measures twelve volts, which makes the inside of a computer as safe as playing with an electric train. Nothing that's readily accessible inside the computer will shock you, straighten your hair, or shorten your life. The personal computer is designed that way, it's designed for tinkering, adding in accessories, and taking them out.

Computers are thought delicate because they are built from supposedly delicate electronic circuits, the same ones that warn about holding a cold water pipe before touching them, the same ones costing $500 each. In fact, the one variety of electronic component that is particularly delicate requires extreme protection only when it's not installed where it belongs. Pulses of static electricity do the damage, but circuitry in which the component is installed naturally keeps the static under control. Certainly a bolt of lightning or a good spark of static can still do harm, but the risk of either can be minimized simply. In most situations and workplaces you should have little fear of damaging the circuits inside your computer.

Most people don't want to deal with the insides of their computers because the machines are complex and confusing. In truth they are and they aren't. It all depends on how you look at them. Watching a movie on videotape is hardly a mental challenge but understanding the whirring heads inside the machine and how the image is synchronized and the hi-fi sound is recorded is something that will spin your brain for hours. Similarly, changing a board or adding a disk drive to a computer is simple. Understanding the Boolean logic controlling the digital gates on the disk drive is perhaps more difficult.

Most of what you may want to do with your computer requires no arcane knowledge of electronics; nor will you need great technical or mechanical skill. Enhancing a computer is a matter of fitting connectors together and, at most, operating a screwdriver—almost anyone can do it, and that includes you.

Although you don't need skill or an in-depth knowledge of computer or data processing theory, you do need to know what you want to accomplish and what you can accomplish, the how and why of working with, expanding, even building a personal computer system.

And that's the purpose of this book. It's a dual-purpose book: The text is written to give you an overview of what makes up a computer system. It will give you enough grounding in how the machine works so you can understand what you're doing if you want to dig in and expand or upgrade your system. At the same time, the charts and tables will provide you with the reference materials you need to put your new knowledge to work. As a whole, this book will help you install, setup, and take advantage of your computer, its peripherals, and all their power.

The computer is nothing to fear and it need not be a mystery. It is a machine, and a straightforward one at that.

2

BACKGROUND
TO AN
INDUSTRY
STANDARD

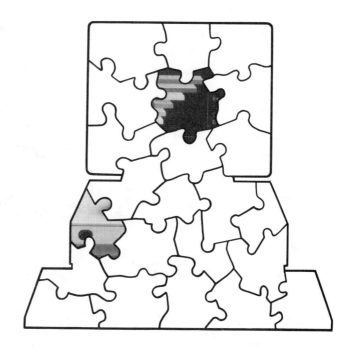

The personal computer can be defined in a couple of ways: It is a computer that's meant to be used by one person instead of shared among a number of operators, or it can be the IBM Personal Computer, the PC that moved the personal computer from the hobbyist's fascination to a mass market business tool. In many situations, the two definitions of personal computer are one and the same. The IBM PC is the embodiment of the idea of the personal computer. Only recently has it been superseded by new machines from IBM—the so-called Personal Systems— and challenged by other designs like Apple Computer's Macintosh. Nevertheless, the IBM PC is the foundation of personal computer technology as it is now known. It is the system that set the first standards, standards that helped other brands of personal computers earn success, standards that have locked computer design into past technology and slowed progress.

Origins of the PC

This book would not exist, nor would the personal computer industry in its present form, were it not for a number of seemingly arbitrary but practical decisions made at the IBM Corporation Entry Systems Division in Boca Raton, Florida, just as the decade of the 1980's was dawning. The culmination of that decision-making came on August 12, 1981, with the introduction of the IBM PC. Today, all personal computer hardware benefits and suffers from the effects and ramifications of the original design.

A full understanding of how a personal computer works, how it can be augmented, how it can be altered must begin with a recognition of the underlying concepts implicit in that initial design. All too often, elements of the design of a personal computer seem overly restricting without real purpose.

One thing is for certain, the PC did not spring as a fully armed product for the head of the Entry Systems Division. In fact, even after the first machines had been ushered into the bright daylight of public scrutiny, even IBM did not know what it had wrought. The immediate success of the PC led to demand outrunning supply, shortages, and an unbelievable windfall to authorized IBM dealers who found a little silicon could be worth its weight in gold.

Opportunist Design

Exactly how this wildly successful design came about can only be conjectured. The true motivations and design decisions underlying the first PC are forever the secret of IBM. The best guess is that the success of the PC stemmed from equal measures of serendipity and hard-nosed bottom-line-oriented decision-making. IBM wanted to cash in on the success small computers were having among hobbyists and, increasingly, small businesses. The desktop computer presented a tremendous opportunity—one IBM did not want to miss as it had with minicomputers. (Most industry analysts attribute the astounding success of number two computer-maker Digital Equipment Corporation (DEC) to IBM's failure to move into the minicomputer field quickly.)

To create IBM's first true desktop machine, the company's engineers carefully pruned and grafted the ideas embodied in other small computers then on the market to make their new product stand out. They then put together a computer made mostly from off-the-shelf parts and components crafted by other manufacturers so that if the product misfired, losses would not be great, and IBM could go on to other, more important products in its bread-and-butter mainframe line.

Computer Competitors

To understand why particular elements were chosen for the design of the PC, you need to remember what was happening in the small computer marketplace at the time.

In 1980 the term personal computer was still evolving, and there was no lack of hardware choices. In fact, most of the available small computers could be divided into one of three major groups. Each of two of these were dominated by a single manufacturer. The other was unified by an operating system.

Apple Computer

The most important desktop computer competitor, in terms of longevity and acceptance, that has survived the longest with the least alteration, was (and is) the original *Apple II*. (Its predecessor Apple was more a design effort than a commercial product.) The design of the Apple II was innovative and clever, and it introduced features and technologies which will soon become familiar in the discussion of the implementation of the IBM PC.

The original Apple II blazed a path as one of the first *single-board computers* that also featured a dedicated *expansion bus* into which accessories (and some necessities) could be attached. The keyboard was combined into the housing for the electronics—a simple, practical, and cost-effective approach.

The central processing unit of the Apple II was a *microprocessor* that bore the designation *6502,* at the time a respectable chip choice, and could perform 8-bit calculations at an operating speed of about one million cycles per second (MHz).

The straightforward original design of the Apple II made no provision for lower case letters, could put only 40 columns of text across the screen, and could be bought with as little as 8 kilobytes of memory. For more permanent storage it could route data from its electronic memory onto magnetic tape using a conventional audio cassette machine.

Later additions to the Apple II repertory included lower case characters in 80 columns, *bit-mapped graphics,* and disk storage controlled by *Apple DOS* (Disk Operating System). Some of these potential additions were neither foreseen nor allowed for in the original design, and as a consequence, required some clever engineering (which was duly provided). These design alterations resulted in some workable but odd adaptations, particularly in memory structure in which alternate characters on the screen, for example, were separated into different blocks of memory.

Tandy/Radio Shack

Design camp number two rallied under the *Radio Shack* flag. The familiar corner-store vendor of everything from batteries and toys to watches and telephones added small computers to its wide range of offerings by producing a number of machines based on different technologies, microprocessors, and operating systems.

The wide variety of the Radio Shack products was intended to appeal to the widest market. The leader at the time of the introduction of IBM's first machine was the TRS-80, a desktop computer combining monitor, keyboard, and electronics into a single box, all built around a Z80 microprocessor. Both cassette and floppy disk storage was available, the later using the TRS-DOS (widely known as Trash DOS to both its friends and detractors).

The nickname applied to the model designation is one of the reasons this computer brand has officially disappeared from the market. After years of trashy jokes, Radio Shack's corporate parent Tandy Corporation elected to pull not only the TRS designation, but also the Radio Shack label from its computer products, and instead substituted its own name and less allusive model numbers.

Among the virtues of the TRS-80 were its ability to show 80-column text in upper and lower case characters. Among its biggest drawbacks were its styling, which was of the sort that appealed to those who found aesthetic ecstasy in the Cadillac tail-fins of a generation earlier. It was all rounded curves and metalized plastic, styling that might appeal more to Buck Rogers than to a businessman.

CP/M

The third group of small computers huddled around the CP/M operating system, an acronym for Control Program for Microcomputers. CP/M linked the popular and powerful 8080 and Z80 microprocessors with flexible disk drives. Its low cost and usefulness led to its wide use and its emergence as a standard.

CP/M-based computers typically allowed the use of 80-column text with lowercase characters in a text-oriented display that usually ran through a *teletype interface*. The teletype interface was designed for computers constructed from separate terminals and central processing units which communicated through thin wires one bit at a time (serially).

The combination of microprocessor and operating system yielded enough power to handle many business chores, from word processing to bookkeeping. It was exactly what was needed in business, and consequently CP/M computers emerged as the business standard among desktop machines. In the early 80's more business oriented software (which often consisted of little more than a few dozen lines of BASIC code) was available for CP/M than that of any other computer operating environment.

The IBM Strategy

This environment provided IBM with the incentive for creating the PC. By then the small computer market had grown to tens of thousands of machines per year, clearly too large to ignore—especially since much of the growing base was among business users. Business, remember, is IBM's middle name.

Misstep Avoidance

Added to this incentive was IBM's generation-old minicomputer misstep. When IBM ignored the bottom rung of computer power because the market was small and profits were minuscule in comparison to those of producing mainframes, DEC gained a toehold and developed a loyal following in small computers. As DEC users graduated to higher power computers, DEC followed by producing what they required, and grew until the company had become IBM's chief rival.

Faced with the new flush of small computers, IBM decided to enter the market quickly but with minimum risk.

The Acquisition Angle

Perhaps the best way of accomplishing their goals would be with the straightforward strategy of acquisition. IBM could simply buy a manufacturer of small computers and integrate the company and its products into the IBM corporate monolith (much as IBM later strode into the communications business by buying *Rolm Corporation* and gradually sucked the company into the Big Blue mainstream).

The obvious choice would have been Apple. However, Apple was not IBM's type of target. Apple had not yet aimed its products at business applications. It was still supplying hobbyists, not an IBM market.

Nor did Apple have much of a track record as a company and computer manufacturer. Of course, the same could be said about any company that had begun its life by building small computers. The industry itself was not that old, so the companies in the industry were necessarily young. Nevertheless, Apple was a small start-up company with no track record and, according to normal business sense, a dubious future. Moreover, its sole product, the Apple II, just wasn't a very good design.

Acquiring Radio Shack was never an alternative. Although Radio Shack and its parent Tandy Corporation had a proven track record of profits, computers had little to do with that. At the time, computers were a small part of the sales of the mass retailer. In simple terms, IBM would have had to buy a restaurant to get a cup of coffee.

The other makers of small computers were even less attractive. IBM really didn't need to own someone's garage optimistically called a microcomputer factory.

The Roll-Your-Own Strategy

Developing its own machine was not quite so far-fetched. IBM had already made small computers in the guise of its transportable (by a stretch of the imagination and arm) *Model 5100*. Built without benefit of such innovations as floppy disk drives, the 5100 primarily found use within IBM, but never did much as a commercial product.

Microprocessor Choice

There could be no doubt the IBM machine would be based on a microprocessor. The smart chips were what had originally made small computers practical and the industry possible. The question was which chip to use.

Apple's choice, the 6502, would have been considered dated even in 1981. An 8-bit chip, the 6502 both processed and referenced data in memory just 8 bits at a time, and operated at a clock speed of about one megahertz. Its processing throughput paled in comparison to that achieved by the CP/M machines and their Z80 microprocessor.

Although the Z80 is also an 8-bit data engine, it is more efficient in handling code and can run faster than the 6502. Weighing more heavily in favor of the Z80 was the huge CP/M software library.

IBM would face a marketing problem in designing a machine around the Z80 microprocessor, however. Such a product would hardly stand out from the pack of existing CP/M machines. An IBM CP/M computer would have no advantage—however tenuous—over the hardware available from other manufacturers, hooks for the IBM salesforce to use in marketing the machine.

The Intel 8088

The Intel 8088 on the other hand, was similar enough to the Z80 that software could be easily converted to run on it, at least in theory. Moreover, the 8088 differed from the Z80 in two significant ways: It had wider internal *registers* and a greater memory addressing range.

The 8088 was truly an 8-bit processor in that information moved in and out of the chip 8 bits at a time, its internal processing at times performed 16 bits at a time, and while the Z80 could only address 65,536 bytes of memory, the 8088 could handle 16 times as much, 1,048,576 bytes. Potentially the 8088 was a more formidable microprocessor.

Even in the early 80s, more powerful chips were available, however. For example, the bigger and older brother of the 8088, the *8086*, for instance, had the same 16-bit internal architecture, the same wide addressing range, and also used 16-bit connections with the outside world. The difference potentially made the 8086 twice as fast as the 8088 even when operating at the same speed.

IBM had one good reason for foregoing the full 16-bit power of the 8086, however. In the early 80's, the price of microprocessor support chips, as well as memory, was much higher than today. Using a full 16-bit bus structure would add substantially to the cost of the computer using it.

Going with a 16-bit architecture probably did not make sense to IBM's PC designers as a marketing move, particularly since the 16-bit internal nature of the 8088 would still allow IBM to advertise the erstwhile 8-bit PC as a 16-bit computer. However, power was not a real issue. Although the 8086 brain would have resulted in a superior machine, the marketplace placed no demands on performance. After all, having a computer was vastly better than not having one, and in comparison the performance difference between 8- and 16-bit designs was insignificant. An 8-bit design would be easier, and faster, to implement, had no relative market disadvantage, and was less costly (a powerful advantage). The 8088 won out over the 8086.

Other chips were out of the running. The *Motorola 6800,* a full 16-bit chip, lost partly for the same reason as the full 16-bit 8086, and partly because it lacked easy CP/M translatability. The *Texas Instruments* family of microprocessors lost out for the same reason. As a result, the 8088 was chosen—not quite an arbitrary or capricious decision, but one that lacked the foresight to see performance arising as a major issue in microcomputers.

Memory Issues

Once the microprocessor had been decided upon, the next choices were of memory. Several aspects had to be considered. The working memory of the computer system must be designed both physically (what sort of chips should be used and how they should be connected) and logically (what uses should the various memory locations be put to). In addition, mass storage (the holding zone for programs and data) must also be decided upon.

The first part of the physical memory question—the hardware to use—was easily solved. At the time the PC was first designed, memory chips holding 16,384 bytes (16K) were the most plentiful and cost-effective. They were also the basis of most competing computers.

The least expensive and most popular of these stored their bytes in a one dimensional array, giving 16,384 places to store a single memory bit. (Other chips might store four bits at a location, half a byte or a nibble at a time.) A minimum of eight chips of these one dimensional chips are required to hold a byte of information because of their one dimensional architecture.

IBM added one more chip to the basic and minimal eight. In the mainframe business, data integrity is extremely important, so large computers use complex schemes for detecting and possibly correcting memory errors. IBM decided to include a form of memory quality insurance in the PC, a system that would randomly detect if a memory bit should fail.

The simplest possible detection scheme involves adding up all the bits in the byte, then adding in a special parity bit to insure the total is always even. If one bit changes, the total comes out odd, and an error must have occurred. The extra parity-check bit requires one additional RAM chip. Consequently, the PC was equipped with nine memory chips.

With a bit of prescience (the knowledge that most programs won't run with so little memory as 16K) IBM provided places for adding more memory. A total of 27 empty sockets allowed you to plug up to 64 kilobytes of memory into the PC. With an eye to the future, IBM even made provisions for installing boards containing extra RAM, allowing the system to be expanded up to 512K—at the time more than any program could possibly require.

The IBM engineers reserved the other half of the addressing range of the 8088 for special purposes. Some locations were used for video memory, others for the permanently-recorded programs in ROM that are collectively called the *Basic Input/Output System*. Only a small fraction of this reserved memory area was actually put to use, but IBM made sure it was there should it ever be needed. In fact, only about 20K were initially used—4K for video memory and 16K for the BIOS.

In mass storage IBM almost indiscriminately exploited the same options other personal computer makers had used. Miniature (for the time) 5 ¼-inch floppy disks were a natural, both because of their use in other small computers and because of IBM's experience with their larger cousins, 8-inch drives, in other IBM products such as its *Display-Writer* word processor.

Again, no one at the time foresaw a need for huge amounts of mass storage, so IBM elected to use only one side of the potentially two-sided disks, limiting capacity to 160 kilobytes. Although puny by today's standards, that capacity was substantially greater than the 80 to 130 kilobytes used in other small computers at the time.

IBM also hedged its mass storage bet by including a cassette port as part of the first PC. Instead of buying a $500 floppy disk drive, you could use your tape recorder to remember programs and data, even exchange files with your friends. Cassette tape is, of course, slow and inconvenient, a particularly poor match for the PC. But should hobbyists actually be the major market for the somewhat undirected PC, the cassette port would undoubtedly find users.

All computers need a programming language, and IBM gave the PC *BASIC*, the Beginners' All-purpose Symbolic Instruction Code. Weighing in favor of IBM's including BASIC in its PC was the acceptance of the language in the small computer industry and among hobbyists, the small size of the language that made it usable on machines with limited memory, and IBM's own experience with BASIC in the 5100. Another programming language, *APL* (short for A Programming Language), was also used on the 5100 and in many cases preferred by the users of the computer. However, BASIC won out.

Much to the consternation of compatible makers ever since, IBM stuffed a rudimentary form of BASIC into the ROM chips (unchangeable hardware) of the PC. Because mass storage was essentially optional in the first PCs, the machines would have been little more than vegetables without an internal programming language. BASIC was always there waiting for you even if you had no disk drive, ready to save and load programs from cassette tape.

The Display System

Every computer needs a display system. IBM designed one for its personal computer with experience won in the office and in making computer terminals. It had to have sharp, easy to read characters and no annoying flicker.

Experience with mainframe and the typical implementation of CP/M computers might have led IBM to use so-called *teletype* video where the computer sends characters to a terminal and the terminal then displays them. The terminal circuitry does most of the worrying where text will appear on the screen.

Apple, however, used a different technique called *character-mapping*. A character-mapped display is divided into a matrix of character positions and each character position is assigned a memory location. The display system matches the character designation in the map with the dot-pattern of the character that is stored elsewhere in a font library (which can be either RAM or ROM). Independently of the host microprocessor, the video system sends the appropriate dot information from the font library to the screen.

The advantage of this arrangement is that it is fast and efficient from the microprocessor and memory point of view. It needs to deal with only efficient character codes. Only two kilobytes of data need to be moved or stored for a full 80-column by 25-row screen of text. It also eliminates much of the cost of a terminal. Making it work requires only a display—essentially a picture tube and its control circuitry—instead of a complete terminal.

IBM added an extra byte for each character of the display to hold attribute information—whether the character was dim, highlighted, underlined, or shown in reverse video on the screen. IBM also chose to put the character and attribute bytes for each on-screen cell adjacent to one another, using a total of four kilobytes of memory area.

The Keyboard

A keyboard was required for user input and controlling the computer. Instead of following the Apple technique of making the keyboard part of the computer, IBM also relied on its office experience to tether the keyboard on a cord so it could be positioned to better suit the user.

In overall design, IBM took the best ideas of the machines on the marketplace, refined them, and put them together in a single, clever computer. The IBM PC was a single-board microcomputer—all of its essential circuitry was located on one large printed circuit board. Like Apple and many other computer makers, IBM provided expansion slots for adding accessories.

IBM might have made the PC a *bus-oriented computer,* one in which even the main brain is itself on an expansion board. Logic ruled against such a strategy, however. All the circuitry required would not have fit on a single expansion board, so IBM designed the PC with a large master circuit board holding the bulk of the system's circuits (the system board) and allowed for the addition of other expansion on it.

The bottom line was that the IBM PC was designed around a lot of practical constraints at an almost totally unfocused market. It was almost as if IBM put the machine in stores to see who, if anyone, would buy it.

Much to the surprise of everyone, including IBM, people did buy it. Small businesses did. Huge corporations did. PCs sold so quickly that IBM couldn't make them fast enough.

The PC touched off a revolution. It spawned several succeeding and more powerful models. Its logical and practical design set the standard for a new industry. Dozens of manufacturers—from one-man-and-a-soldering-iron garage operations to multibillion-dollar megacorporations—created their own versions of the PC, each designed to be as compatible as possible with the IBM original.

These machines changed the way people worked and even the way they thought.

3

THE
MOTHERBOARD

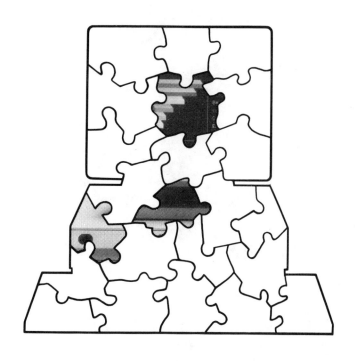

The centerpiece of any small computer system is the printed circuit board which holds the machine's microprocessor and its support circuitry. In most cases this circuit board is made from a flat sheet of a green compound called *glass-epoxy* because it has a woven fiber glass base that's filled and reinforced with an epoxy plastic. Other colors are used (a fireproof red, for example) but are not common in computers. The actual circuitry is etched from two or more layers of conductive copper that form *traces* which map out the flow of electricity between the electronic components soldered to the board.

Single-Board Computers

This glass-epoxy central circuit board can take many functional forms. In some cases one such board contains all the electronics necessary for making an entire computer system and is called, appropriately, the *single-board computer.*

Bus-Oriented Computers

The opposite of the single-board design technique puts only a minimum of computer circuitry on this one board, dividing up the various computer functions between many circuit boards. The most common implementation in this style is the *bus-oriented computer,* so called because a number of parallel conductors termed a *bus* links the various constituents of the computer together. Like a Greyhound, all the signals of the bus travel together and make the same stops at the same connectors along the way.

Mother and Daughterboards

The circuit board holding the connectors that allow attachment to the bus circuitry is termed the *motherboard*. The cards that plug in electronically suckling on the motherboard—are *daughterboards,* the term probably chosen for its mellifluousness rather than any overt sexism. Neither "son-board" nor the more generic "offspring-board" roll off the tongue as sweetly.

System Board

The original IBM PC and its successors XT and AT, as well as many clones, incorporate elements of both of these basic designs. Most of the necessities of the single-board computer are present on the large motherboard that lines the bottom of the cases of all the products in the IBM PC family. IBM terms this composite multifunctional assembly the *system board*.

Expansion Boards

The system board approach differs from the single-board computer in that it does not quite produce a complete computer in itself. The system board alone lacks a video adapter, some form of mass storage, and a means of communicating with accessories. These functions are added to the system board by plugging daughterboards into the expansion bus which is part of the system board. In the IBM environment, these add-in cards are usually called *expansion boards,* cleverly sidestepping the issue of son-daughter sexism.

Planar Boards

In the Personal System/2 line, the motherboard is much more like a true single-board microcomputer which has an added expansion bus, one so radically different from its predecessors that IBM describes its expansion bus as a *channel*. To the functions contained on PC-style system boards, the PS/2 adds video circuitry, input and output ports, and floppy disk-control circuitry.

IBM highlights the updates and upgrades that separate the PS/2 motherboards from those of previous computers by referring to the motherboards of PS/2s as *planar* boards, often dropping the surname. The new term is both descriptive—the flat board is topologically a plane—and in common use to describe similar assemblies in other electronic applications (as well as other computers). The term was sometimes used by IBM to describe the system boards of previous computers, and the term "system board" is occasionally used to describe PS/2 mother-boards. Planar appears to be the consistently preferred choice for PS/2 motherboards, however.

Although labeled by just two descriptive terms, IBM motherboards are quite diverse. Every PS/2 model, including those with similar electronic abilities like the Models 50 and 60 has a distinctively different planar. Even those machines with the same model number may have different system boards. For instance, each of IBM's three Models 70 has its own planar board design. PCs, too, use variant system boards for each model except one, only the XT and Portable Personal Computer share an identical system board. PCs, on the other hand, have gone through two major design changes.

PC-1 and -2

The original IBM PC, introduced in August, 1981, is often called the *PC-1* and was upgraded with a new system board into the *PC-2* in 1983. The PC-1 was able to hold a maximum memory of 64 kilobytes without using expansion boards; however, the PC-2 stretched that to 256 kilobytes. A more important distinction involves the factory programming of the two boards. Without being updated, the PC-1 system board is unable to handle most of the more powerful expansion accessories, such as hard disks and advanced video adapters.

IBM has made other, more minor upgrades in its various system boards as the PC has evolved. For example, the XT system board was upgraded from holding 256 kilobytes of memory to 640K. None, however, has been as much a watershed as that first revision.

OEM Boardmakers and System Integrators

The system boards wrought by other companies are both more and less diverse because of the nature of the industry. When it comes to the system boards inside their products, compatible computer makers fall into two types. Those who design and manufacture their own system boards and those who act as *Original Equipment Manufacturers* or *OEM*s. This meaningless term describes companies fabricating their products from the products of other companies. Some invest as little time and effort as it takes to put a nameplate on a finished product produced by someone else. Others incorporate subassemblies into more powerful products and submit them to thorough testing. These latter companies are also termed *system integrators*.

The difference between the OEM and the company that produces its own products is that you're likely to find the same system board inside many computers bearing the names of different OEMs. In many instances you'll find nothing to distinguish them but the case or the label. Such computers are essentially interchangeable, termed by economists as *commodities;* and as with all commodities, the best of these look-alike-inside off-the-shelf computers is the one with the lowest price.

System Board Common Features

Because there are so many makers of compatible computers, different system board designs number into the hundreds, therefore, they would be difficult to discuss with any depth. However, understanding compatibles becomes more manageable once you understand that one of the biggest segments of the industry are the companies that serve as OEMs. There are fewer system boards designs in use than you might suspect. Moreover, all of them owe a great tribute to the IBM products from which they are mostly copied.

Physical Aspects

In mainstream, first-generation IBM personal computers (that is, the PC, XT, and AT) motherboards fit one of three different sizes, each defined by the machine's initials. In the past, the motherboards of all PCs measured about 8 1/2 by 11 inches. The XT stretched nearly an inch longer. The AT, in need of more space for more circuitry, extended all the way to 12 by 13 1/2 inches. Lower-priced commodity computers generally followed the same scheme, allowing for board manufacturers and case makers to offer compatible products. You can be sure that a clone of an XT motherboard will fit an XT clone case. IBM set the pattern, compatible makers merely followed it.

Major compatible manufacturers—Compaq, Epson, Leading Edge, Tandy, and so on—control the manufacture of both system board and case. They have the freedom to vary dimensions as may be required. For example, the original Compaq Portable motherboard was somewhat larger than that of the PC.

System Board Replacement

You'd have little reason to care about how big your motherboard is. Size has little influence on performance on the motherboard level (in mainframes and microchips, size does count). The issue is physical compatibility. Should you ever want to upgrade the performance of your computer by replacing its motherboard—the best possible upgrade outside of replacing the entire computer—board size will determine what will fit in your case. If you are daring and want to save a few hundred dollars by getting a real lesson about how really simple PCs are by building one yourself, you'll need to know what size box to put everything in. Once you know motherboards are different sizes, the rule is intuitively obvious—if you have an XT-size case, you'll need an XT-size motherboard.

System Board Screws

Mere size is not the only factor determining the physical compatibility of system boards, however. Otherwise you might consider putting a smaller board into the box made for a larger one. Waiting to frustrate you are the magical moving screw holes. Although the PC and XT system boards are nearly the same size, the patterns of their mounting holes do not match. The variations often amount only to a fraction of an inch, but they are enough to prevent the easy substitution of one board for another.

IBM is amazingly frugal in the hardware used to hold its system boards inside their cases. As few as two screws hold them in place. (There are good electrical reasons for this miserliness with the hardware, proper grounding being paramount among them.) The balance of the mounting holes in the IBM's system boards are devoted to nylon fasteners which insulate the boards from the metal chassis while holding them in place.

Mechanically, the screws hold the IBM system boards in place. The nylon fasteners are designed to space the board vertically and fit special channels in the metal work of the case, allowing the boards to slide into place.

IBM carried this same hardware frugality over to its PS/2 line. Although PS/2 planar boards wildly differ in shape and size between the various models, they share the same parsimonious use of screws to hold them in place.

IBM System Board Removal

To remove an IBM system board from its case, simply remove the two or three screws holding it in place (after you've removed all the expansion boards from their slots and disconnected all the wires plugged into the system board). Then, slide the board about one inch to the left, freeing the nylon fasteners from their channel. You should then be able to remove the board from the case by lifting its left edge above the rim of the case and continuing to slide it to the left.

Planar boards in PS/2s don't require the left-shift when they are removed because they are simply held in place by their mounting screws. Once you've removed the screws holding the planar down, you should be able to lift it free.

IBM System Board Installation

Installing an IBM system board is just the reserve of the above. Slide the board into the case from the left at a slight angle. When the left edge of the board clears the edge of the case, lower it until it sits—flat in the case. Finally, slide it over to the right flat in the bottom of the computer—until it stops. You might have to push it back a bit to the left to make the screw holes line up so you can fasten the board into place.

Before you can reinsert the system board, you must have the nylon fasteners locked into their proper holes, which are indistinguishable from those to be used by the screws. Figure 3.1 shows the size and proper screw and fastener placement of the IBM PC system board; Figure 3.2, the XT system board; and Figure 3.3, the AT system board.

Planar board installation is nothing more than properly aligning the board with the stanchions molded in the case, dropping it in place, and securing the screws.

System Board Spacers

Should you upgrade the system board of your computer, you may have to transfer the nylon fasteners from your old system board to the new one. They can be removed by pinching together the two wings at the top (use long-nosed pliers) so that they will clear the mounting hold, then pushing the fastener down through the hole backwards. Once the bottoms of the wings have been forced through the hole, you can release your

Figure 3.1 **PC system board size screw placement**

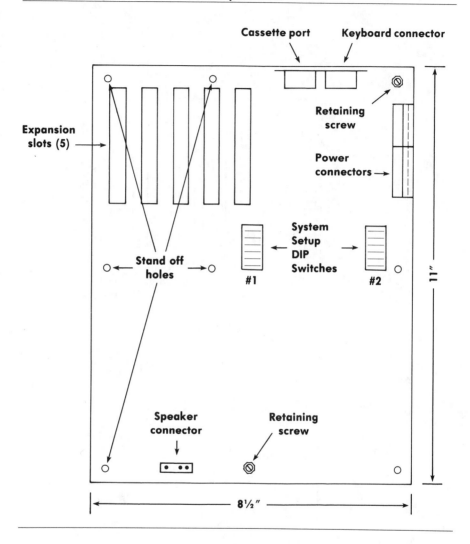

pliers' grip and press them into place with a finger. (See Figure 3.4.)

Insertion is even easier. Just press the pointed end of the fastener into the appropriate hole from the bottom of the system board (the size without electronic components on it). Push the fastener up until its two wings snap out and hold the fastener in place.

Figure 3.2 **XT system board size screw placement**

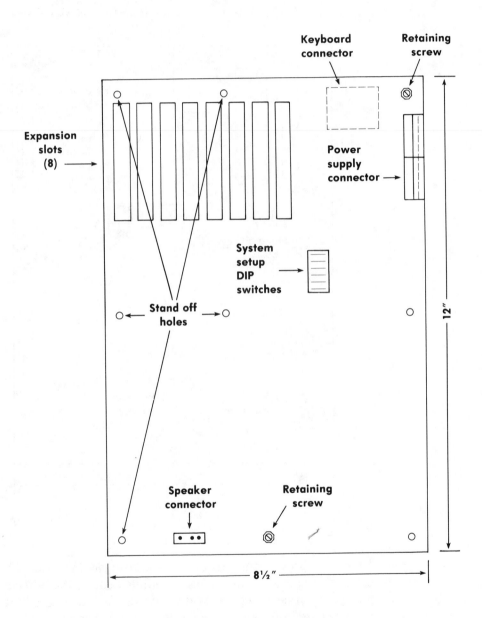

Figure 3.3 **AT system board and screw placement**

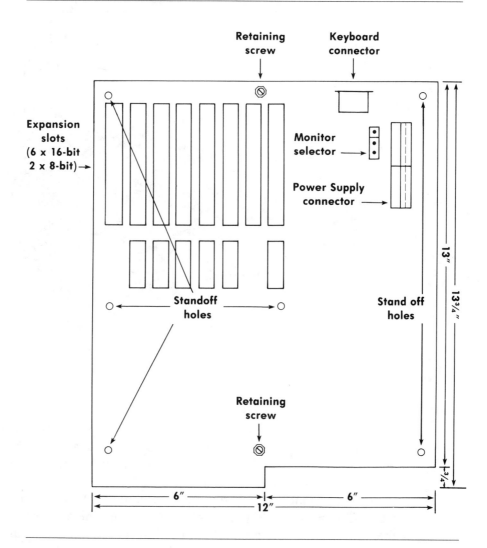

Nonstandard Mounting

Some replacement computer cases do not use the normal IBM mounting scheme for motherboards. These aftermarket manufacturers save the cost of welding the fastener mounting channels in place by drilling a few holds in the bottom of the case and supplying you with a number of

Figure 3.4 **Spacer used by IBM to mount system board and removal technique**

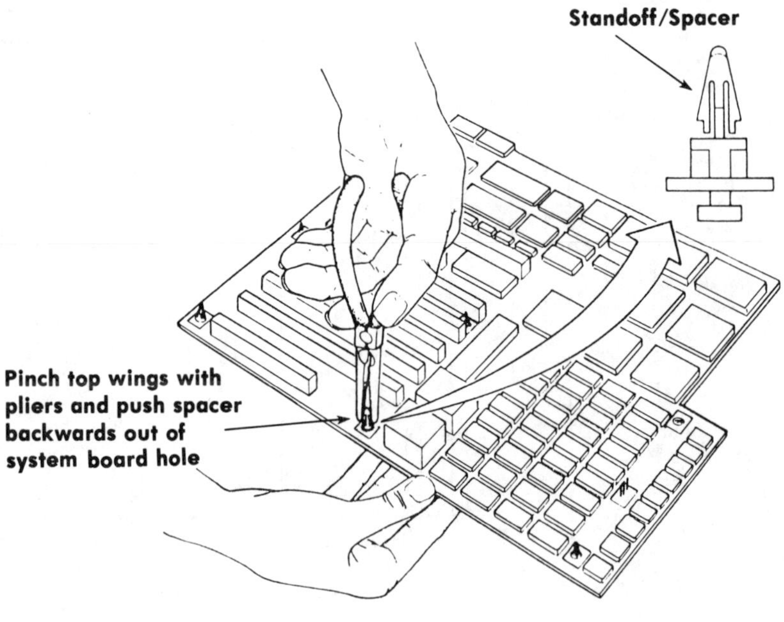

Standoff/Spacer

Pinch top wings with pliers and push spacer backwards out of system board hole

threaded metal or plastic spacers (usually nothing more than small nylon tubes) and screws. (See Figure 3.5.) These spacers are meant to hold the system board the same height about the bottom of the chassis as would the IBM-style fasteners.

You could handle this kind of motherboard installation in one of two ways: Either screw the spacers into the case, put the motherboard atop them, then screw the motherboard to the spacers; or you could screw the motherboard to the spacers and then try to get the spacers to fit the holes in the bottom of the case. Neither method is very satisfactory because you're faced with getting ten or so holes and screws to line up which, owing to the general lack of precision exercised by cut-rate manufacturers in making these cases, they never do. The best thing to do is compromise. Attach the spacers loosely to the motherboard, then try to get the screws at the bottom of the spacers to line up with the holes in the case. You should be able to wiggle them into the holes.

Figure 3.5 **Do-it-yourself system board spacers**

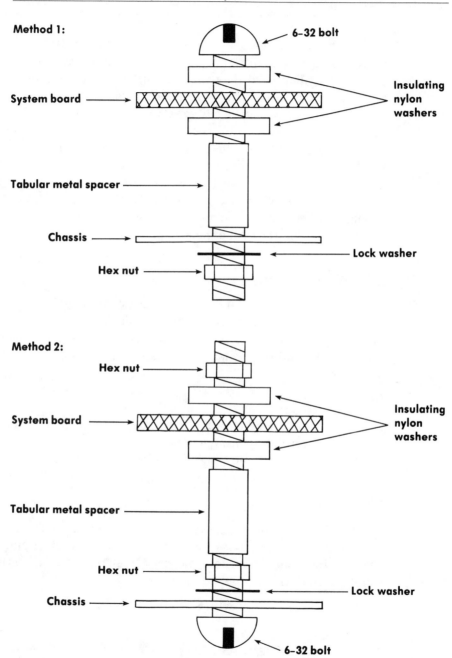

Motherboard Functions

The motherboard of any computer that follows the IBM design scheme performs several major functions. At the most basic level, it is the physical foundation of the computer. It holds the expansion boards in place, provides firm territory to attach connections to external circuit elements, and provides the base of support for the central electronics of the computer. Electrically, the circuitry etched upon it includes the brain of the computer and the most important elements required to nourish that brain. This circuitry determines the entire personality of the computer— how it functions, how it reacts to your every keystroke, what it does.

No one part of the system board completely defines a computer's personality. Its essence is spread throughout the circuit traces and components. Among these, the most important include:

The Microprocessor

Which does the actual thinking inside the computer. Which microprocessor is used of the dozens currently available determines not only the processing power of the computer but also what software language it understands (and thus what programs it can run).

Coprocessors

An adjunct to the microprocessor, the coprocessor permits a computer to carry out certain operations much faster. A coprocessor can make a computer run five to ten times faster in some operations.

Memory

Required by the microprocessor to carry out its calculations, the amount and architecture of the memory of a system determines how it can be programmed and, to some extent, the level of complexity of the problems that it can work upon.

BIOS

The *Basic Input/Output System* or *BIOS* of a computer is a set of permanently recorded program routines that give the system its fundamental operational characteristics. It determines what the computer can do without loading a program from disk and how the computer reacts to specific instructions that are part of those disk-based programs.

Expansion Slots

They act as portals that allow new signals to enter the computer and directly react with its circuitry. Expansion slots allow new features and enhancements to be added to the system as well as permitting the quick and easy alteration of certain computer prerequisites, such as video adapters.

Support Circuitry

A microprocessor, although the essence of a computer, is not a computer in itself (if it were it would be called a computer). It requires a number of additional circuits to bring it to life: clocks, controllers, and signal converters. Each of these support circuits has its own way of reacting to programs, and thus helps determine how the computer works.

4

MICROPROCESSORS

All personal computers and a growing number of more powerful machines are based on a special type of electronic circuits called the *microprocessor*. Often termed "a computer on a chip," today's microprocessor is a single slice of silicon that has been carefully grown as an extremely pure crystal, sawed thin with great precision, then heinously polluted by subjecting it to high temperatures in ovens containing gaseous mixtures of impurities.

Semiconductors

The recipe calls for atoms of the impurities wedging themselves into the crystal's microscopic lattice structure without destroying its intricate design. These impurities affect how the silicon conducts electricity, and changes the metal silicon into a new class of materials called *semiconductors*. The term refers to the altered silicon resisting electrical current flow more than *conductors* (like the copper in wires) but not as much as *insulators* (like the plastic wrapped around the wires).

Doping

Although this subtle transformation might seem more the meat of a minor footnote in a metallurgists' textbook, these electrically mediocre materials showed the promise of revolutionizing electronics from their inception. In 1947 scientists at Bell Laboratories carefully added impurities to silicon crystals, a process they called *doping,* to divide the lattice into three thin layers, a sandwich alternating slices of silicon infused with atoms of one element with another.

Transistors

The result was the first *transistor,* a tiny fleck of silvery silicon with the ability to let one electrical current, applied to one layer of impure silicon, alter another larger current flowing between the other two layers.

Transistors were a break with the past because the entire flow of current in them was through solid material. In contrast, the previous technology, the vacuum tube, electrical currents passed through the rarefied gases inside the tubes. Because of this distinction, semiconductor-based circuits are sometimes called *solid-state.*

Analog and Digital Circuits

These electrical alterations can take two forms. The changes in a small signal can be magnified and intensified into a larger signal exactly duplicating every fluctuation of the original. This process, called *amplification,* results in every change in the large signal being analogous to each one in the small signal. These signals are called *analog* because their intensity can be used to represent another value, for instance a sound level, so the signal in an analogy is what it represents.

Alternately, a small signal can cause a larger one to switch from off to on, or on to off, ignoring the more subtle variations. The result is a series of pulses which can be used to code values not by strength but by numbers. For example, a series of seven pulses might represent the numeral 7. In that information can be coded as groups of such numbers (digits), electrical devices using this technology are described as *digital.*

Digital Logic

By itself, one current switching another might appear minimally useful. However, a transistor can be switched by combinations of signals as well as by individual currents. For instance, a transistor circuit can be designed that will switch one current on only when both of two other currents are present. A slightly different circuit might turn a third current on only when neither current is on, or when at least one of two or more currents are present. Such circuits are called *logic gates.* They earned this name because, like a garden gate, they swing open to allow a current to pass and their functions can be made to correspond to the basic decision-making operations of formal logic.

The first computers were made from logic gates; however, those were based on different technologies than those of the transistor. Both vacuum tubes and relays can operate as logic gates. Transistors have the advantage of being smaller and faster. So small, in fact, that dozens, hundreds, thousands, or hundreds of thousands can be squeezed onto a chip of silicon the size of a thumbnail.

Integrated Circuits

A microprocessor is nothing but an elaborate arrangement of such miniature transistors, called an *integrated circuit* or *IC* because they operate like many discrete transistors and other devices integrated and implemented on a single small slab of silicon. Sometimes abbreviated IC, integrated circuits are often called simply *chips* because of their construction from a single small piece of silicon, a chip off the crystal.

The microprocessor is just one device in the much larger family of integrated circuits that do everything from amplify audio to track feeding time at the zoo. In a microprocessor, the thousands of integrated transistors, as well as similar silicon-based electronic circuits, are interconnected in such a way that certain patterns of signal going in will cause other patterns to come out. Microprocessors differ from other integrated circuits built from similar arrays of transistors in that the electrical changes made in accordance to the input signals may occur entirely within the microprocessor.

Inside the Microprocessor

Most microprocessors have special built-in memory areas called *registers* in which they perform all their data manipulations and calculations. For instance, to add two numbers, one number is first moved into the register, then the other number is added to it, leaving the sum inside the register.

The signals going into the microprocessor consist of a collection of digital pulses arriving nearly simultaneously—in parallel—on several wires. Each pattern is a command that elicits a certain function from the microprocessor, and is assigned a name to identify it. The entire repertory of these functions and their names is called the *command set* of the microprocessor.

The internal silicon wiring of the microprocessor determines what it does in response to each command. In effect, it is a computer program for the microprocessor built into its hardware. This program is called the microprocessor's *microcode*.

Microprocessor Connections

Besides internal storage and manipulation of digital bits, microprocessors also need some way to move data in and out of themselves so the
answers they get can be put to work. These connections make up the
microprocessor's *data bus*.

In addition, the microprocessor needs some method of locating data
that is stored in memory outside the chip itself. Microprocessors use
another bus called the *address bus* to indicate to the rest of the computer which memory areas it needs to access.

Microprocessors differ in the resources they devote to each of these
facilities, and this in turn influences the speed that the microprocessor
can find answers. Not only do microprocessors have differing numbers
of registers, but the registers may be of different sizes. Registers are
measured by the number of bits they can work with at one time. For example, a 16-bit microprocessor should have one or more registers that
each holds 16 bits of data at a time.

Bus Width

The number of bits in the data bus of a microprocessor directly influences how quickly it can move information. The more bits a chip can
use at a time, the faster it is. Microprocessors with 8-, 16-, and 32-bit data
buses are all used in various IBM personal computers.

The number of bits available on the address bus influences how much
memory a microprocessor can address. For instance, a microprocessor
with 16 address lines can directly work with 2^{16} addresses, that is 65,536
(or 64K) different memory locations.

Microprocessor Family Tree

The history of microprocessor development has been chiefly a matter of
increasing bus width and register size. With each new generation of
microprocessor, the number and size of its registers increases while data
and address buses become wider. As a result, personal computers have
become increasingly powerful.

Four-Bit Thinking

The first true general purpose microprocessor was manufactured by Intel Corporation in 1971. As might be deduced from its manufacturer's designation *4004,* this groundbreaking chip had registers capable of handling four bits at a time. Puny by today's standards, those four bits—enough to code all numerals from zero to nine as well as other symbols—was useful enough to make calculations. It could add, subtract, and multiply just as capably (but hardly as fast) as the much larger computers of the time.

In fact, this is how to 4004 originated. The chip was conceived by Ted Hoff of Intel Corporation in response to a 1969 request by a now-defunct Japanese calculator company, Busicom. The original proposal comprised some 12 chips to be used in different types of calculators. The small volumes of each design would have made development costs prohibitive. Hoff, however, envisioned creating one general purpose device that would satisfy the needs of all the calculators. It worked. The 4004 proved to be a success, ushering in the age of the low-cost calculators and giving designers a single solid-state programmable device for the first time.

Eight-Bit Chips

Larger computers work not only with numbers but also with alphabetic symbols and text, something beyond the ken of the 4004. Making the microprocessor into a more general purpose device required expanding the size of the chip's registers so it could handle representations of all the letters of the alphabet and more. While 6 bits could accommodate all upper and lowercase letters as well as numbers (2^6 bits can code 64 symbols) it would leave little room to spare for punctuation marks and such niceties as control codes. In addition, the emergence of the 8-bit byte as the standard measure of digital data resulted in it being chosen as the register size of the next generation of microprocessor, Intel's *8008* introduced in 1972.

The 8008 was, however, just an update of the 4004 with more bits in each register at heart. It was an interesting and workable chip, and it found application in some initial stabs at building personal computers.

Intel continued development (as did other integrated circuit manufacturers) and in 1974 created a rather more drastic revision, the *8080*. Planned from the start for byte-size data, the 8080 had a richer command set, one that embraced all the commands of the 8008 but went farther. With them, the 8080 was among the first chips with the inherent ability to serve as the foundation of a small computer.

A few engineers had even better ideas for improving the 8080 and left Intel to develop these improvements on their own. After forming Zilog Corporation, they unveiled the Z80 microprocessor to the world. In truth, the Z80 was an evolutionary development, an 8080 with more instructions, and it began a revolution by unlocking the power of the first widely accepted standard small computer operating system.

Developed by what is now Digital Research, this operating system, a special program that linked programs, the microprocessor, and its related hardware such as storage devices, was called the Control Program for Microcomputers or *CP/M*. It was patterned after operating systems for larger computers but shrunk down to a size that would work on a microprocessor chip. Though hardly perfect, it worked well enough that it became the standard for many small computers used in business. Its familiarity helped programmers of larger computers to adapt to it, and they threw their support behind it. Although CP/M was designed to run on the 8080, the Z80 chip offered more power, and it became the platform of choice to make the system work.

Meanwhile, Intel continued to work on the 8-bit 8008 design. One effort was the *8085*, a further elaboration on the 8080 which was designed to use a single 5-volt power supply and use fewer peripheral chips than its predecessor. Included in its design were vectored interrupts and a serial input/output port. Alas, it never won the favor of the small computer industry. A few small computers, now almost entirely forgotten, were designed around it.

The 8086 Family

Sixteen Bits

In 1978 Intel pushed technology forward with its *8086*, a microprocessor that doubled the size of its registers again to 16 bits and promised ten times the performance of the 8080. The 8086 also improved on the 8080 by doubling the size of the data bus to 16 bits to move information in and out twice as fast. It also had a substantially larger address bus, 20 bits wide, that allowed the 8086 to directly control over one million bytes, a megabyte, of memory.

As a direct descendant of the 8080 and cousin of the Z80, the 8086 shared much of the command set of the earlier chips. Just as the 8080 elaborated on the commands of the 8008, the 8086 embellished those of the 8080. The registers of the 8086 were cleverly arranged so they could be manipulated either at their full 16-bit width or as two separate 8-bit registers exactly like those of the 8080.

Segmented Memory

The memory of the 8086 was also arranged to be a superset of that of the 8080. Instead of being one vast megabyte romping ground for data, it was divided up into 16 *segments* that contained 64 kilobytes each. In effect, the memory of the 8086 was a group of 8080 memories linked together. The 8086 looked at each segment individually and did not permit a single large data structure to span across segments—at least not easily.

In some ways, the 8086 was ahead of its time. Small computers were based on 8-bit architectures, memory was expensive (that is why a megabyte seemed more than enough), and few other chips were designed to handle 16 bits at a time. Using the 8086 forced engineers to design full 16-bit devices which were not entirely cost-effective at the time.

The 8088 Downgrade

Consequently, a year after the introduction of the 8086, Intel introduced the *8088*. The 8088 was identical to the 8086 in every way—16-bit registers, 20 address lines, the same command set—except one: Its data bus was reduced to 8 bits, allowing the 8088 to exploit readily available 8-bit support hardware.

As a backward step in chip design, the 8088 might have been lost to history much like the 8085 had not IBM begun to covertly design its first personal computer around it. IBM's intent was, evidently, to cash in on the 8088 design. Its 8-bit data bus allowed the use of inexpensive off-the-shelf support chips. Its 16-bit internal design gave the PC an important edge in advertising over the 8-bit small computers already available. And its 8080-based ancestry hinted that the wealth of CP/M programs then available might easily be converted to the new hardware. In the long run, of course, these advantages have proven either temporary or illusory. Sixteen-bit support chips have become not only available but cheap. The IBM name proved more valuable than the 16-bit registers of the 8088, and few CP/M programs were ever directly adapted to the PC.

What was important is the lame 8088 microprocessor became the basis of a generation of small computers. The fast track to making compatible computers was paved with 8088s.

The 8086 is potentially twice as fast and almost completely compatible with the 8088. Consequently, manufacturers intent on selling performance engaged in the extra effort to design around the 8086. Even IBM chose the older yet more powerful 8086 to power its low-end PS/2s.

As compatible as they are, the 8088 and 8086 are not interchangeable. The need for 8 additional data bits going into the chip requires 8 more data lines or leads. The connections made to each of the two chips are thus different. The 8088 and 8086 are not identical pin-for-pin and are not plug-compatible. Computers must be designed for one chip or the other.

Low Power Designs

The typical microprocessor requires a few watts of electricity to perform its functions. When the electrical supply is drawn from a wall outlet, the amount of power is almost insignificant. A typical home has 10,000 watts or so at its disposal and an outlet can supply about 2000. Batteries, however, aren't so munificent. An AA battery cell, for instance, might be expected to deliver 20 milliwatts (thousandths of a watt) or so. Switching to battery power to make a truly portable computer thus requires a drastic downward revision in the amount of power required for running the microprocessor.

The typical microprocessor is built from a technology called *NMOS*, which stands for *N-channel Metal Oxide Semiconductor*, the method by which the logic gates in the circuitry are fabricated. NMOS circuitry is distinguished by design simplicity, small size (even on a microchip level), and a need for power. NMOS circuits constantly sip electricity whether they are thinking (active) or not. Even idle, current flows through them.

CMOS (Complementary Metal Oxide Semiconductor)

CMOS technology is much more frugal with its source of power than NMOS. Its name derives from each of its logic gates actually being two-in-one—when one gate switches on, its twin switches off. Large currents flow through these dual circuits only when they change states. During an idle, almost no power is required. Although more complicated, CMOS technology can duplicate every logic function made with NMOS, but with a substantial saving of electricity (with some increase in manufacturing costs).

Laptop computers, for which low power requirements are mandatory, are thus often built around CMOS equivalents of popular microprocessors. Both 8088 and 8086 versions are available, distinguished by embedding a "C" in their names, as in *80C88* and *80C86*.

Higher Integration

Just as the microprocessor incorporates thousands of discrete logic components on its tiny sliver of silicon, it's possible to build more functions into a single chip. Besides a microprocessor, a number of other special circuits are typically used in building a small computer, such as interrupt controllers, timing generators, and bus controllers. All of these functions can be designed to fit onto the same chip as the microprocessor circuitry.

Normally, all this extra circuitry would not be included because a microprocessor is a general purpose device, not necessarily committed to becoming the basic of a desktop computer system. The additional circuitry might be wasted in something like an industrial process controller.

As the small computer industry grew, however, the market for circuits optimized for this purpose reached a point where Intel felt safe in creating a more complete computer chip—an 8086—with most of its support circuitry on one substrate. Introduced in 1982 as the *80186*, this chip has served as the basis for a number of compatible computers and at least one turbo board. Intel also offers the *80188*, essentially an 8088 blessed with more on-chip support, much like the 80186.

Foreign Competition

Two chips are directly interchangeable with the 8088 and 8086, Nippon Electric Company's (NEC) *V20* and *V30*, respectively. The V20 can be used to replace a 8088; the V30 replaces the 8086. Although the NEC chips use the same command set as the Intel devices, they are not identical. Much of their microcode is different—more efficient because the NEC chips were designed with the benefit of hindsight. Replacing an 8088 with a V20 or 8086 with a V30 can improve overall microprocessor throughput, and thus the speed of the computer around which it is based, from 10 to 30 percent.

Years of research and development go into the design of every integrated circuit. All of that work can be avoided in copying someone else's effort by *reverse-engineering,* coming up with the design from the product itself instead of the product from the design. To prevent other companies from copying their chip designs, most makers of integrated circuits use all the legal protections available to them such as patents, copyrights, and secrecy.

Sometimes they will license other makers to use the *masks* they have designed to lay down the silicon circuitry of a chip to provide a *second source* for a product. This licensing or "second-sourcing" earns the original designer a royalty and, often, greater acceptance of the chip because buyers of integrated circuits look askance at any product with a single source of supply. Second sources insulate against labor or manufacturing troubles and can sometimes reduce costs through competition. Intel licenses Advanced Micro Devices and IBM to produce many of its chips.

NEC was not licensed to use Intel designs. In a lawsuit between the two companies, Intel has alleged that NEC copied more than 25 percent of its 8086 microcode through reverse engineering.

The Second Generation, the 80286

The introduction of IBM's Personal Computer AT in 1984 immediately focused attention on another of the Intel microprocessor family, the *80286,* which itself was introduced in 1982. Compared to its immediate forerunner, the 8086, the 80286 was endowed with several features that made it superior for personal computers. It used a full 16-bit data bus with 16-bit internal registers. It was designed to run faster—initially at 6 MHz, which quickly rose to 8, then 10. Versions that operate at 12.5, 16, and even 20 MHz have also become available. Moreover, for its clock speed it functions more efficiently, giving it even more of a performance advantage than its faster speed would imply. For example, although the first AT ran only 25 percent faster than the PC, it achieved throughput about five times greater.

Sixteen Megabytes

Most important of all in the long run, was the superior memory-handling ability of the 80286. Instead of the 20 address lines of the 8088/8086, the 80286 had 24. The four extra lines increase the maximum amount of memory the chip is able to address by 15 megabytes, up to a total of 16 megabytes.

Virtual Memory

The 80286 also allowed the use of *virtual memory*. As the name implies, virtual memory is not made up of real, physical memory chips. Rather, it is information stored elsewhere, in a mass storage system, that can be transferred into physical memory when it needs to be worked upon. The 80286 has special provisions for distinguishing each memory byte that is in real and virtual memory, although it requires additional circuitry to handle the actual swapping of bytes. The chip can track up to one gigabyte (1024 megabytes or a billion bytes) of total memory—16 megabytes physical, 1008 megabytes of virtual memory.

In theory, the upgraded memory-handling of the 80286 should have made the 1-megabyte addressing barrier faced by earlier Intel microprocessors a thing of the past. In reality and as a practical matter, the improvement was not realized.

The problem was partly a matter of compatibility, partly of tradition. By the time the 80286 was being readied for the market, the success of the IBM PC had already been assured. A substantial software base had been built for the 8088 and 8086 microprocessors. Taking advantage of that software would speed the acceptance of the improved chip.

Real Mode

To maintain compatibility with the earlier chips, Intel's engineers endowed the 80286 with two operating modes: *Real mode* was designed to be nearly an exact duplicate of the way the 8086 operated. The copying followed the 8086 so closely (as it had to to assure compatibility) that real mode brought along with it all the barriers of using the 8086, including the 1 megabyte limit on memory. The limit was necessarily imposed because the 80286 had to be able to recognize memory addresses just as an 8086 would.

Protected Mode

To take advantage of the improved memory handling of the 80286 architecture, Intel created *Protected mode.* Although not compatible with existing 8086 programs, protected mode allows all 16 megabytes of real and the gigabyte of virtual memory to be actively used by programs written specifically to take advantage of it.

As a faster 8086 with the ability to handle more memory, the 80286 proved immensely successful. However, protected mode did not win favor with programmers very quickly. Almost three years elapsed between the time of the introduction of the AT and the availability of an IBM-endorsed protected mode operating system, *OS/2.*

80286 Downside

Two reasons underly the slow, begrudging support of the protected mode. For programmers working under the constraints of DOS, the problem was shifting between real mode and protected mode. Intel designed the process to be a one-way affair. After all, once you have tasted 16 megabytes, why would you want to go back to a measly one? Although the 80286 readily shifted gears from real to protected mode (the upshift was necessary because the chip starts functioning *only* in real mode) downshifting was not possible. Once in protected mode, the only way to regain real mode control was to reset the microprocessor, equivalent to rebooting a computer.

In addition, protected mode was only a partial fulfillment of the dreams of programmers. Although it did allow more memory to be used, it still operated with memory segments of 64 kilobytes. Instead of a free romping ground for their software, programmers got a bunch of little boxes that they had to shift their numbers between.

State of the Art: The 80386

Unlike the 80286, which was seemingly aimed at a brave new world beyond DOS, the next generation of Intel microprocessor opened its arms to DOS and the $16 billion dollar software library built around it.

The *80386,* introduced in 1985, combines the hard lessons won with the 80286 with the needs and dreams of programmers. It brought more speed, more power, and more versatility than ever before available in an Intel microprocessor. It is able to handle nearly every chore of an 8088, 8086, and 80286 yet leap beyond them in features and power.

The enlightenment embodied by the 80386 makes the 80286 look like a misfire—too late and too bad. Some former Intel employees have dismissed the shortcomings of the 80286 as a result of its design having been started earlier than even the 8086. The 80286 was the original idea of a chip to follow on the heels of the 8080, but may have proved too ambitious. The 8086 was born from a reappraisal of design objectives. Only later was the original idea marketed as the 80286.

In contrast, the 80386 was created in full awareness of the personal computer and microprocessor marketplace. Consequently, it had to accommodate all the features that were making other Intel processors sell. For example, its *instruction set* (the bit patterns it recognizes as commands to perform its various functions) is a superset of that of the 80286, so older software will run on the chip without a hitch. At the same time, the 80386 had to be designed to bring new features to the table so it would be accepted in new designs, maybe even lure engineers away from the microprocessors made by other manufacturers who did not suffer from the handicap of segmented memory.

32-bit Power

First and foremost, the 80386 was a leap ahead in raw power. It doubled the size of its registers and data buses to a full 32 bits. Information could be moved into the chip and processed twice as fast as with 16-bit chips like the 80286.

Faster Clocks

The 80386 was designed from the beginning to be a fast chip, perhaps a product of the speed wars among AT-compatible computers. Using a semiconductor technology called *CHMOS,* the first 80386 chips to be marketed started where the 80286 left off. Two ratings of 80386 were initially available, 12.5 and 16 MHz, with the former pretty much ignored by speed-hungry computer designers. Shortly thereafter, a 20 MHz version became available. In 1988 the limit became 25 MHz, and currently, chips rated at up to 32 MHz (and probably beyond) are in development.

Temperature Limit

Note that some computer makers often operate chips (and not just 80386s) beyond the manufacturer's rating. This tactic works because there may be few differences between the designs of chips rated at different speeds. One major problem arises, however: Higher speed operation generates more heat because every logical thought involves a digital switching operation. Even with low-power HCMOS circuitry, each digital switch requires a burst of current which heats the chip. Faster operation means more current bursts in a given period, heating the chip more.

Heat is the biggest enemy of semiconductor circuits. It can make them unreliable, and, if severe, it can destroy them. A small increase in clock speed can lead to a substantial, even surprising, increase in chip temperature. Running a microprocessor beyond its speed rating can make it unreliable or even ruin it forever. Heat sinks (finned metal plates mechanically in contact with the chip) help cool the chip down by radiating the heat and may actually help improve reliability at higher speeds.

Improved Memory Architecture

Complementing the expansion of the data bus of the 80386 to 32 bits, the number of available address lines was also increased to 32. By itself, that expansion allows the 80386 to directly address up to four gigabytes of physical memory. In addition, the chip can handle up to 16 terabytes (trillion bytes) of virtual memory. The chip has full facilities for managing all this memory built into its circuitry.

The big breakthrough in the 80386 is the way this memory is organized. All of it can be addressed as one contiguous section, equivalent to the great open prairie for programs. Programs or data structures can be as large as the full memory capacity of the chip.

Dividing this memory into segments is possible but optional. Segments are not, however, arbitrarily limited to 64 kilobytes in length. They can be virtually any size that is convenient for a program or programmer to work with (as long as it is smaller than four gigabytes, which is not an insubstantial limit).

In addition, the 80386 incorporates 16 bytes of *pre-fetch cache memory*. This special built-in memory area is used to store the next few instructions of the program the chip is executing. Independently of the calculating portion of the chip, special circuitry loads software code into this memory before it is actually needed. This small cache helps the 80386 run more smoothly, with less waiting as code is retrieved from system memory.

Multiple Modes

To maintain compatibility with previous Intel microprocessors, and thus with the library of DOS programs, the 80386 was designed to be as compatible as possible with the 8086 and 80286. As with both, the 80386 has a Real mode, complete with one megabyte addressing limit. The chip boots up in this mode and operates, for all intents and programs, as if it were one of its older siblings.

From Real mode, the chip can be switched into Protected mode where it functions like a 80286, except it has more memory at its disposal and it has more flexibility in manipulating it because of its variable segment size. In contrast with the 80286, the 80386 can switch modes without being reset using simple software commands.

DOS Accommodations

A new mode called *Virtual 8086 mode* gives the 80386 particular freedom in running DOS programs. In this mode, the chip simulates not just one 8086 but an almost unlimited number of them, all at the same time. This mode allows a single 80386 microprocessor to divide its memory up into many virtual machines, each one acting like it is an entirely separate computer equipped with an 8086 microprocessor.

Each of these virtual machines can run its own program, totally isolated from the rest of the virtual computers. That means you can simultaneously run several DOS programs on one computer. While this kind of multitasking was possible without the exotic architecture of the 80386, such systems were either complex or shaky, and most required that software be specially written to proprietary standards to effect multitasking operation. The 80386, on the other hand, makes multitasking control software almost trivial because all the hard work is done in hardware. Off-the-shelf DOS programs work without modification in most 80386-based multitasking environments.

If the 80386 were perfect, you would probably expect to find it in every PC-compatible computer. Choosing another chip is taking a step backward. In fact, only two practical considerations keep other chips viable in the overall personal computer market: One of them is the cost of the chips themselves. When introduced, a single 80386 cost upwards of $500, compared to the $10 or less of an 8086. You could almost buy an entire PC-compatible computer for the price of a single chip. Because Intel has chosen not to license other companies (except IBM) to make the 80386, they can pretty much dictate whatever price they want for the chip, basing their decision on such market forces as supply and demand. Or, in other words, they can charge whatever the market will bear. Understandably, 80386-based system will necessarily be more expensive than those based on lesser chips.

Original Sin

The 80386 has suffered more severe teething pains than most microprocessors. Shortly after it was originally released, design errors were found that caused inaccuracies when the chip performed 32-bit mathematical operations. The problem was undiscovered in the first PC-compatible computers to use the chip because DOS uses only 16-bit operations. The random errors occur only when the software uses the 32-bit modes of the 80386.

The problem was quickly discovered and corrected, and 80386 chips manufactured after April, 1987, do not have the problem. According to Intel, all 80386 chips manufactured after the correction was made are labeled with a *double-sigma* symbol. (See Figure 4.1.) Some, but not all, earlier chips with potential problems were recalled before being delivered to users and have been stamped "For 16-bit Operations Only" by Intel. These chips will work with all 16-bit versions of DOS (which include all versions to date, up to DOS 3.3), and the initial releases of OS/2 (Versions 1.0 and 1.1) which do not use 32-bit mathematics.

Intel does not have a return policy for end-users except for those buying products made by its Personal Computer Enhancement Operation, specifically the Intel Inboard 386. If you find a potentially bad chip in your 80386-based PC, you should contact the manufacturer of the computer. If you find an aged and possibly error-generating 80386 in your Inboard 386, you should contact Intel Corporation's Personal Computer Enhancement Operation Customer Support in Hillsboro, Oregon for its replacement. The telephone numbers there in 1988 are (800) 538-3373 in the United States or Canada, or (503) 629-7354 in other countries.

Figure 4.1 **Pin-grid array socket (with PGA chip)**

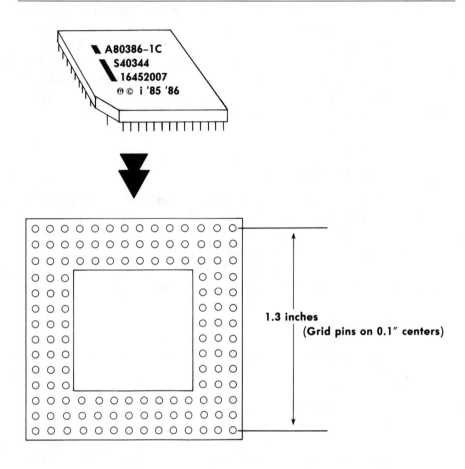

The 80386SX

Which virtue of the 80386 is best depends on what you want to do with the chip. For many, speed is the main consideration. Many users want to roar through calculations lickety-split—a second saved on the recalculation of a spreadsheet or the drawing of a blueprint is an extra dollar earned. For these people, 32-bit power is the essence of the 80386.

But the other strengths of the 80386 make it a more exciting chip to people who want to take advantage of its multiuser and multitasking power. The virtual 8086 mode alone is worth the premium price of 80386 silicon to them, and the extensive memory handling abilities of the chip make it all the more valuable. Although the speed of the 80386 may be exciting, for them it is unnecessary, an extra priced option for which they are forced to foot the bill, particularly considering the modest performance increase the 32-bit chip brings to standard 16-bit software like DOS and OS/2 Versions 1.0 and 1.1.

Ultimate Compromise

For exactly this sort of person, Intel created the ultimate compromise, the 80386SX, a scaled-down 80386 that loses power but not features. Just as the 8088 was derived from the 8086 to facilitate the use of cheaper 8-bit components, Intel created the 80386SX as a little sister to the 80386. Internally, the 80386SX is nearly identical to the 80386 with full 32-bit registers and all of its operating modes, just as the 8088 is a 16-bit chip like the 8086 inside its epoxy case.

Only two differences of major import separate the 80386 from the SX: Instead of interfacing to a 32-bit memory bus, the 80386SX is designed for a 16-bit bus. Its 32-bit registers must be filled in two steps from a 16-bit I/O channel, and the 80386SX is cheaper by about $100, a bargain of sorts for those who prefer a more leisurely pace.

But the 80386SX is no sluggard. Its initial version operated at a full 16 MHz, almost 33 percent faster than Intel's quickest 80286. Despite its 16-bit I/O channel, the 80386SX still races along faster than an 80286 with an equivalent speed rating because it can process instructions twice as fast.

In addition, the 80386SX understands the same 32-bit instructions as the 80386. Just like the 80386, it is backwardly compatible with the 16-and 8-bit instructions of previous Intel microprocessors.

A Brief History

Long before its introduction in June of 1988, the creation of the 80386SX had been rumored in the computer industry. It was known mostly under its code name *P9*. Its final designation is probably an effort by Intel to cash in on the overwhelmingly favorable publicity garnered by the 80386 microprocessor.

The P9 was long rumored to be a plug-compatible upgrade for the

80286. In theory, you could pop out the old chip and pop in 80386 power using the P9. However, with the final 80386SX design, that direct conversion is not possible.

Different Package

The 80386SX is packaged entirely different than the 80286, and the two chips will not fit the same sockets. The main reason is that the 80286 multiplexes its bus connections (so fewer physical wires are needed for a larger number of connections) while those of the 80386SX are not multiplexed. As a result, the 80386SX requires simpler interface circuitry than the 80286, facilitating its application in lower-cost computers.

Future Play

A small adapter card with auxiliary multiplexing circuitry can convert the 80386SX to an 80286 socket, however. Such an adapter promises to be a low cost way of adding 80386 features to existing computers.

On the other hand, the 80386SX does demand a slight price premium over the 80286, and, when operating at its rated speed it requires faster, more expensive memory. Computers based on the 80386SX are likely to be more expensive than their 80286-equipped equivalents. In the long run, however, there is no compelling reason to settle for 80286 technology. As the number of software products requiring 80386 features increases, the more desirable the 80386SX—and the more obsolete 80286-based machines. Buy a computer equipped with an 80386SX if you have an eye to the future; an 80286 will only mire you in the past.

How Microprocessors Work

Reduced to its fundamental principles, the microprocessor is not difficult to understand. It's simply the electronic equivalent of a knee-jerk. Every time you hit the microprocessor with an electronic hammer blow—the proper digital input—it reacts by performing a specific something, always the same thing for the same input. For example, the bit pattern 0010110 tells an Intel 8086-family microprocessor to subtract.

Of course, the microprocessor needs to know what to subtract from what, and it needs to know what to do with the result. The first question is handled by variations of the subtract instruction, of which there are about seven (depending on what you regard as subtraction because each particular instruction tells the microprocessor to take numbers from differing places and compute the difference in slightly different manners).

The numbers to be worked on can be located in one of three places—in one of the microprocessor's registers, in ordinary RAM memory, or in the code of the instruction itself. The result is always stored in a register. (If the information to be worked on is stored on disk it must first be transferred to RAM.)

Other microprocessor instructions tell the chip to put numbers in its registers to be worked on later and to move information from a register to somewhere else, for example to the memory or an output port. The example instruction tells the microprocessor to subtract an immediate number from the *accumulator,* a particular microprocessor register that is favored for calculations.

Everything the microprocessor does consists of nothing more than a series of these one-step-a-time instructions. Simple subtraction or addition of two numbers may entail dozens of steps, including the conversion of the numbers from decimal to the binary (ones and zeros) notation that the microprocessor understands. Computer programs are complex because they must reduce processes that people think of as one step in itself—adding numbers, typing a letter, moving a block of graphics—into a long and complex series of tiny, incremental steps.

Programming Languages

To make the manipulation of bytes by microprocessors easier for human minds to grasp, programming languages of various types were created. These range from the simplest, machine language, to high level languages such as BASIC, Pascal, C, COBOL, and FORTRAN.

Machine Language

Machine language is simply the bit patterns of the microprocessor instructions expressed in more familiar hexadecimal form. That is, the 0010110 subtraction instruction becomes 16(hex).

Assembly Language

A slight improvement on machine language is *assembly language,* which for the most part merely gives mnemonic names to the numbers of each instruction, for example, SUB for 16. Every command given to the microprocessor, every step of its operation, must be coded in assembly-language instructions.

Most *assemblers,* (programs that convert assembly language) into machine language, also have meta-instructions which look like assembly language commands, but are translated by the language program into a series of machine-language commands. These meta-instructions break the onerous one-to-one correspondence between the programmer's careful coding and what the microprocessor does.

Higher Level Languages

Higher level languages go even further by allowing programs to be written in individual steps corresponding more closely to the human way of thinking. Instead of dealing with each movement of a byte of information, high level commands let the programmer deal with problems as decimal numbers, words, or graphic elements. The language program takes each higher-level instruction and converts it into a lengthy series of digital-code microprocessor commands in machine language.

No matter how high the level of the programming language, no matter what you see on your computer screen, no matter what you type to make your machine do its daily work, everything the microprocessor inside does is reduced to a pattern of digital pulses to which it reacts in knee-jerk fashion.

What the microprocessor does cannot be considered magic. In fact, it doesn't even have to be electronic. A series of gears, cams, and levers or pipes, valves, and pans could execute similar programs based on knee-jerk type reactions. Mechanical and hydraulic computers have, in fact, been built. The advantage of electronics and the microprocessor is speed. Electrical signals travel at the speed of light; microprocessors carry out their instructions at rates up to several million per second.

Without this speed, elaborate programs would never have been written because executing one with a stream-driven computing engine might have taken lifetimes. The speed of the microprocessor makes it the miracle that it is.

Chip Packaging and Identification

You will probably never need to see or touch a microprocessor. As long as your computer works—and considering the reliability most have demonstrated, this will be a long, long time—you really need have no concern over your microprocessor except to know it is inside your computer doing its job.

If you're curious, however, you can easily locate and identify the chip in its native turf inside your system unit. As a general rule, all you have to look for is the largest integrated circuit chip on your computer's motherboard—almost invariably it will be the microprocessor. This is only fitting because the microprocessor is also the most important chip in the computer.

If you find several large chips on your system board, odds are one of them is the microprocessor. Others are equally large because they have elaborate functions and need to make many connections with the system board, which means they need relatively large packages to accommodate their many leads.

8086-Family Chips

The Intel 8088 and 8086—as well as the plug-compatible NEC V20 and V30—are packed in dual in-line pin (DIP) packages. That is, they are black epoxy plastic rectangles about two inches long and half-an-inch wide. A row of connecting pins (a total of 40) line both long sides of the chip package like the legs of a shortchanged centipede. The number one pin is on the same end of the chip as its orientation notch, on the left row when viewed from the top of the chip. Intel puts a dot-like indentation in the black epoxy, just above pin one to help in its identification.

Intel identifies these chips with a plain, silk-screen label, white on the black plastic case. A large lowercase "i" indicates Intel Corporation was the manufacturer. Advanced Micro Devices labels its chips with the initials AMD. On Intel chips, the top line of the chip label reveals its designation, often following the preface letter "P."

8088/8086 Speed Rating

These chips are available in two speed ratings, 5 and 8 MHz. Those labeled merely with their model designation (for instance, 8088) have the lower speed rating. Those with their model designations followed by a "-2" are rated at the higher speed. An 8088-2, for example, is rated to operate at up to 8 MHz.

On NEC microprocessors, the number following the chip designation represents the chip's speed rating in MHz. In other words, a V20-8 would be rated at 8 MHz.

The second line of the chip designation contains coded manufacturing information, including the week during which the chip was manufactured.

The 80286

Three styles of 80286 microprocessor packages are likely to be found in personal computers. IBM and a few compatible makers use a *Pin Grid Array* or *PGA* chip that is roughly two inches square and has two rows of pins parallel to each edge of the chip, and dropping down from its bottom. The 68 pins of the chip are arrayed as one square inside another. Actually, the pins are spaced as if they were laid out on a checkerboard, all evenly spaced, with the central block of pins (and those at each of the four corners) eliminated. (See Figure 4.2.)

Figure 4.2 **Leadless Chip Carrier, bottom view and top view**

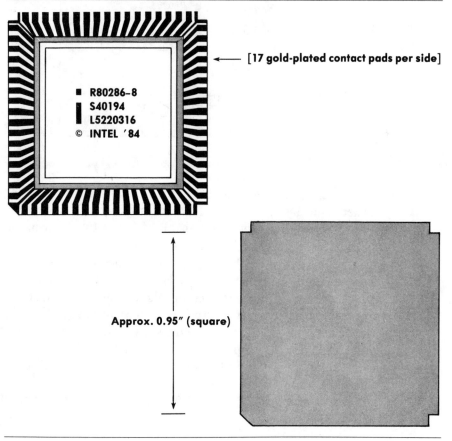

R80286-8
S40194
L5220316
© INTEL '84

← [17 gold-plated contact pads per side]

Approx. 0.95" (square)

Figure 4.3 **Plastic Leadless Chip Carrier package**

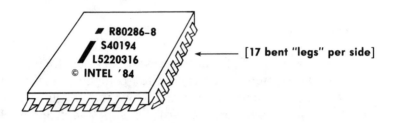

R80286-8
S40194
L5220316
© INTEL '84

← ——— [17 bent "legs" per side]

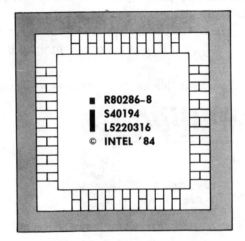

R80286-8
S40194
L5220316
© INTEL '84

Another style of 80286 plugs into a *Leadless Chip Carrier,* or *LCC* socket. The chip itself may be hidden invisibly in its socket under a heat sink, or only its top may be visible, framed by the four sides of the socket. (See Figure 4.3.)

The chip is held in place by a pivoting metal wire—pull the wire off the chip, and the chip pops up. Hold the chip in your hand (do this carefully because like most computer circuits, the 80286 is extremely vulnerable to damage from static electricity discharges). It will resemble a small ceramic tile. Its bottom edges will be dotted with bright flecks of gold; these are the chip's electrical contacts, which are held in tightly against matching pads in the socket to link the chip with the rest of the computer's circuitry.

A newer case design, the Plastic Leadless Chip Carrier or PLCC case is replacing both the PGA and LCC designs because it is less expensive to make. The PLCC design trims the costs of the other packages by using plastic construction instead of the combined metal and ceramic used by the LCC, and by eliminating gold contact pads or pins. Instead of these, the PLCC has a single row of bent contact pins on each of its four perimeter edges. (See Figure 4.3.)

A PLCC chip is also easy to work with. It simply pushes into its mating socket and can be quickly pried out. The pressure of its legs against the sides of the socket holds the chip in place.

The package the chip is housed in has no effect on its performance, however, it can be important when you want to enhance your 80286-based computer with a higher performance 80386-based turbo card. Many of these products require that you replace your system's microprocessor with an adapter cable, which is connected to the card. Cables fit but one type of socket.

80286 Speed Ratings

The speed ratings of 80286 chips are plainly marked after the model designation. The figure given there is the chip's maximum rated operating speed in MHz. Hence, a chip marked 80286-10 would be rated to operate at 10 MHz.

The 80386

Because it has twice the number of data lines and 25 percent more address lines, the 80386 naturally requires more connections than an 80286. Consequently, it is available packaged in a ceramic PGA-style housing with 132 pins projected from its bottom. These pins are arranged in three squares of increasing size, arranged on a 14 x 14 grid with 0.100-inch spacing with the central pins removed. Pin one is closest to the cut-off corner of the case.

80386 Speed Ratings

As with the 80286, the speed ratings of 80386 chips are plainly marked after the model designation of the chip. The figure given there is the chip's maximum rated operating speed in MHz. Hence, a chip marked 80386-25 would be rated to operate at 25 MHz.

The 80386SX

Because of its unique input and output configuration, the 80386SX uses
its own package. Speed ratings are given on the chip in the same way as
the 80286 and 80386—as a number representing the rated speed in MHz
following the chip designation.

5

COPROCESSORS

A *coprocessor* is a special integrated circuit that works cooperatively with your microprocessor. Usually the coprocessor is optimized to handle a specific operation—for example, number crunching or making images on your display screen—and it can handle its particular functions many times faster than can the microprocessor itself. In effect, the coprocessor relieves the microprocessor from having to handle the hard stuff.

Special Purpose Microprocessors

At heart, a coprocessor is a microprocessor but it is not usually a *general purpose* microprocessor like those of the Intel 8086 family. Usually the coprocessor is dedicated to its specific function as a special purpose device. Because its repertory is somewhat limited, it can concentrate on being best in its field.

As microprocessors, coprocessors work just like all other microprocessors. They simply run programs consisting of a series of instructions. Unlike the main microprocessor in a PC, however, the coprocessor may not directly control the bulk of the machine. Instead, its lifeline is through the main microprocessor, which may send the coprocessor the program instructions it requires and then carry away the results.

In normal operation, the microprocessor handles all the functions of running the computer. However, when it encounters a task best handled by the coprocessor, it passes the data and instructions over and patiently awaits the answers.

Coprocessor Instruction Sets

Coprocessors do not share the same instruction set with the microprocessors that they complement. They have their own special command sets. Consequently, programs must be specially written to take advantage of coprocessors. They must use the special coprocessor instructions if they want the coprocessor to do anything. Programs that are not written to use the coprocessor will not benefit by its availability.

The rule is worth repeating: By itself, a coprocessor will not improve the performance of your computer. You need to run software that has been specially written to include coprocessor instructions to take advantage of the speed and power of the coprocessor. Programs that do use the coprocessor can often run many times faster, a speed-up on the same order of magnitude as moving from a PC to an AT or PS/2.

The coprocessor will not automatically kick in when a tough problem crops up. Moreover, not only must an application be written to use a numeric coprocessor, but it must also match a particular coprocessor. Although all of the coprocessors made by Intel corporation for enhancing the mathematical performance of PCs recognize most of the same instruction set, there are a number of subtle incompatibilities between the various chips. Another coprocessor used by some 80386-based PCs made by Weitek Corporation is completely incompatible with programs written for Intel chips.

If an application does not include coprocessor instructions that match those recognized by the coprocessor, the numeric coprocessor will not do a thing. The only way to be sure the coprocessor will be active during the execution of a specific program is to check for an explicit statement from the program's publisher to that effect. There is no easy way to tell whether the coprocessor is working other than comparing performance with and without the chip.

Although somewhat expensive (the little sliver of silicon you slide into your computer can cost several hundred dollars), the coprocessor can be one of the most cost-effective performance improvements you can add to your computer.

Numeric Coprocessors

The coprocessors most commonly used with PCs are *numeric* coprocessors. As numbers specialists, they excel at multiplying and dividing numbers. (They hardly speed up simple adding and subtracting at all, functions which are handled quite capably by an ordinary microprocessor.)

Numeric coprocessors are occasionally termed *floating-point processors* because they deal best with floating-point numbers, that is, figures expressed in scientific notation with a mantissa of a given number of digits and an ordinate (the power of ten) determining where the decimal point floats to.

Coprocessor Benefits

The benefit won by adding a numeric coprocessor depends on the kind of work you do with your computer. According to Intel, a coprocessor can cut processing time on mathematical operations such as multiplication, determining standard deviations, and exponential operation by 80 percent or more. Yet simple math, such as ordinary addition and subtraction, may not benefit at all.

As a practical matter, your system's performance and responsiveness in word processing and database management, which involve no complex mathematics, will not improve with a numeric coprocessor. Spreadsheet recalculations may show some improvement depending on the relationship of formulae-rated cells to one another.

The software most likely to benefit from a numeric coprocessor include engineering applications, scientific programs, statistical analysis procedures, and anything that displays graphics (computing graphic images is a numerically intensive activity).

Speed Independence

Coprocessors do not have to operate at the same speed as the microprocessors they work with. They can operate from the same clock that drives the microprocessor or from one dedicated to the coprocessor.

When the two clocks of the separate microprocessor and coprocessor are related by harmonic relation (one clock being two, three, or another whole number times the rate of the other), they operate *synchronously,* and can carry out their own operations and transfer data between each other optimally. Nonsynchronous operation requires one or the other to wait a fraction of a cycle for the other to catch up, imposing slight but measurable waiting periods.

Even then the coprocessor runs more slowly. However, the combined power of two brains is still much more than that of the main microprocessor alone because the coprocessor can be so much more efficient at handling its own chores. When you have your choice a faster coprocessor will, of course, improve your system's performance more than a slower one.

Numeric Coprocessor Types

The Intel family comprises four principal numeric coprocessor chips, the *8087,* the *80287,* the *80387,* and the *80387SX.* Each is designed to work with a particular microprocessor in the Intel 8086 family.

Each of this quartet shares some common traits. Beyond the 8-, 16-, and 32-bit processors you're used to dealing with, the Intel coprocessors work *80* bits at a time. Each uniformly has eight 80-bit registers in which to perform their calculations. They work with 32-, 64 or 80 bit floating point numbers, 32 or 64-bit integers, and 18-digit *binary coded decimal* (BCD) numbers. (Binary Coded Decimal numbers simply use a specific four-bit digital code to represent each of the decimal digits between zero and nine.) The Intel numeric coprocessors also add new abilities to those native to the host microprocessor, such as tangent and logarithmic functions.

Instead of simply working with the resident microprocessor in your computer, the Intel coprocessors work as an extension of it. They connect to the address and data lines of your PC and execute the instructions meant for them as they arise within programs. They can carry out their calculations at the same time as the microprocessor, so both chips can be thinking at the same time. Because they read their instructions directly from the bus, they impose no microprocessor overhead to set them rolling on a problem.

The 8087

Designed as a complement to the 8086, 8088, 80186, and 80188 microprocessors, the 8087 shares the same addressing and data handling abilities of those chips. To match both the 8- and 16-bit data buses used by the 8088 and 8086 families, the 8087 automatically adapts itself as necessary, detecting the size of the data bus. It fits into a standard 40-pin DIP socket and adds 68 new machine language instructions to your computer's repertory.

Three different versions of the 8087 are available: The plain *8087* operates at system-clock speeds up to 5 MHz; the *8087-2* operates at speeds up to 8 MHz; and the *8087-1* operates at up to 10 MHz.

Other than the rated speed, there is little difference between these chips. They understand the same commands and run the same software. The faster chips will just produce results faster *in a faster computer.*

Although a higher speed 8087 will work at a clock rate slower than its rating, there is no advantage to doing so. The speed of the system clock determines how fast the chip calculates. The rating of the chip only determines how fast a system the chip will work in.

All IBM PCs, XTs, 8086-based PS/2s, and nearly all compatible computers have sockets designed to accommodate the 8087. The IBM PC and XT line need nothing more exotic than the ordinary 8087. PS/2s and higher speed (so-called Turbo XT) compatibles generally require the 8087-2.

The 80287

Just as the 80286 is an upgrade of the 8086, the *80287* is an improvement upon the 8087. The chief distinction of the 80287 is its ability to deal with both the real and protected modes of the 80286 processor, enabling the 80287 to address the full 16-megabyte range of its host.

The 80287 is almost completely backwardly compatible with the 8087 and will execute most of the same software. The primary functional differences between the two processor chips appear in error handling. When errors occur during the execution programs, the two chips may act differently. Software can compensate for these idiosyncrasies and can be written to run interchangeably on either coprocessor.

The 8087 is packaged in a 40-pin DIP socket similar to the 8087. Unlike the 8087, the 80287 does not necessarily operate at the same speed as its host microprocessor. While it can be connected directly to the same clock that runs the microprocessor, an internal divider slows down the 80287 to operate at one-third the clock speed.

Note that the 80287 divides down the crystal oscillator speed, not the microprocessor speed. The crystal oscillator found in 80286-based computers delivers a frequency twice that at which the microprocessor operates, so the coprocessor will operate at two-thirds the microprocessor speed. In an 8 MHz IBM AT, for example, the 80287 coprocessor runs at 5.33 MHz.

The 80287 may also be used with a dedicated clock of its own. Using a dedicated clock can boost the data throughput of the 80287 substantially.

Four versions of the 80287 are available: The plain *80287* or *80287-3* operates at up to 5 MHz; the *80287-6* runs at up to 6 MHz; the *80287-8* runs at up to *8* MHz; and the *80287-10* goes all the way to 10 MHz. The four chips can be used interchangeably as long as the clock rate is within operating range. There is no advantage to using a chip rated faster than the clock when a slower 80287 will work—and the prices for quicker chips tend toward the stratosphere.

All IBM ATs and the XT Model 286 put minimal demands on the numeric coprocessor, so an ordinary 80287 is quite sufficient for them. Micro Channel PS/2s (Models 50, 50Z, and 60) and the Model 30–286 run the coprocessor at the same speed as the main microprocessor, 10 MHz, so an 80287-10 is required. Compatibles are difficult to characterize because the latest machines drive their coprocessors from dedicated oscillators and may operate with nearly any speed rating. (Table 5.1 lists 80287 compatibilities of several compatible computers.)

The 80287 is also compatible with the 80386 microprocessor. However, the 80287 is not capable of operating at the same speeds as the 80386 and requires special interface designs to match it to the data bus used by the 80386. Moreover, because the 80287 is essentially a 16-bit chip, all communications between it and a host 80386 must be handled in 16-bit words, a potential (but not substantial) performance roadblock.

The 80387 and 80387SX

Just as Intel learned its lessons and made the 80386 into a dream microprocessor, its cousin the *80387* numeric coprocessor improves the capabilities of its predecessor, the 80287. While remaining essentially code-compatible with the 80287, the 80387 manages to squeeze out five to seven times the data throughput. Some minor differences exist, again in error handling. In addition, the abilities of the 80387 are greater, spanning a full range of transcendental operations and include sine, cosine, tangent, arctangent, and logarithmic functions.

The *80387SX* is essentially the same chip as the 80387 but is designed to work with the 16-bit bus of the 80386SX instead of a full 32-bit data bus.

While the 80387 and 80387SX should be able to run all programs written for the 80287, the reverse is not necessarily true. Programs that take advantage of all the power of the 80387 or 80387SX may not run on the lesser chip. On certain problems the 80387 or 80387SX may, in fact, deliver slightly different answers than would a 80287—not to the extent of simply adding two and two and getting six, but deriving transcendental functions that may differ in the far right decimal place. Not that either microprocessor is wrong; the 80387 and 80387SX just conform better to floating-point calculation standards promulgated by the Institute of Electrical and Electronic Engineers (IEEE) and round figures a bit differently. In general, however, code meant for the 8087 and 80287 will run on either the 80387 or 80387SX.

Table 5.1 **Coprocessor Compatibility**

Manufacturer	Model	Recommended Coprocessor
Amax Engineering Corp.	386 Business System	80287–6, –8, or –10
American Logic Research	386/2	80287–10
American Logic Research	FlexCache 20386	80387–20
American Research Corp.	ARC 386i	80287–10
AT&T	6300	8087–2
AT&T	6300 Plus	80287 or 80287–6
AT&T	6386 Work Group System	80387–20
CAE/SAR	386	80287–10
CAE/SAR	CAE/SAR II	80387–25
Chicago Computer Conn.	CCC–386c	80287–6, –8, or –10
Commodore	PC–10	8087 or 8087–3
Compaq	Deskpro 286 (8 Mhz)	80287 or 80287–6
Compaq	Deskpro 286 (12 Mhz)	80287–8
Compaq	Deskpro 386 (early)	80287–6 or –8
Compaq	Deskpro 386/16	80387–16
Compaq	Deskpro 386/20	80387–20
Compaq	Deskpro 86	8087–2
Compaq	Portable II	80287 or 80287–6
Compaq	Portable III	80287–8
Compaq	Portable 386	80387–20
Computer Classified Corp	ST–386	80287–6, –8, or –10
Computer Components Corp	Heritage 386 (early)	80287–10
Computer Components Corp	Heritage 386 (late)	80387–20
Computer Dynamics	Micro System 386	80387–16
Core	ATomizer	80287–6
Corvus	386	80387–16
Dell	310	80387–20
Epson	Equity III	80287 or 80287–6
Everex	Step 386/20	80387–20
Herko Electronics	HEI Turbo 386 Tower	80287–10 or 80387–20
Hewlett-Packard	Vectra R5/20	80387–20
IDR	386 Workstation	80387–20
IBM	AT (6 or 8 Mhz)	80287 or 80287–6
IBM	PC	8087 or 8087–3
IBM	PS/2 Model 30	8087–2
IBM	PS/2 Model 30 286	80287–10
IBM	PS/2 Model 50	80287–10
IBM	PS/2 Model 60	80287–10
IBM	PS/2 Model 70 (16 Mhz)	80387–16
IBM	PS/2 Model 70 (20 Mhz)	80387–20
IBM	PS/2 Model 70 (25 Mhz)	80387–25
IBM	PS/2 Model 80 (16 Mhz)	80387–16
IBM	PS/2 Model 80 (20 Mhz)	80387–20

Table 5.1 (continued)

Manufacturer	Model	Recommended Coprocessor
IBM	XT	8087 or 8087–3
IBM	XT Model 286	80287 or 80287–6
IBM	Portable PC	8087 or 8087–3
IBM	3270 AT	80287 or 80287–6
Intel	Inboard 386	80387–16
Intel	Inboard 386/PC	80387–16
Kaypro	386	80287–10 or 80387–16
Laser Digital	Pacer-386	80287–10
Micro 1	386 PC	80387–16
Mitsubishi	MP 386	80287–8 or 80387–16
NEC	APV-IV	80287 or 80287–6
NCR	PC4	8087 or 8087–3
NCR	916	80287–10 or 80387–16
Northgate Computer Sys.	386/20 Northgate Power	80387–20
Osicom Technologies	Osicom 386	80287–10 or 80387–16
Pan United Corp.	Micro Lab 386	80287–8, –10 or 80387–20
PC Designs	GV 386	80287–6, –8, or –10
PC Link	386/20	80387–20
PC's Limited	386/16	80387–16
Proteus Technology	286 Standard	80287–10
Proteus Technology	386A	80287–10
Sperry	PC/microIT	80287 or 80287–6
Tandon	PCA	80287 or 80287–6
Tandy	3000	80287 or 80287–6
Tandy	4000 (early models)	80287–8
Tandy	4000 (later models)	80387–16
Televideo	Tele/386	80287–10 or 80387–16
Toshiba	T5100	80387–20
VIPC	386 Colossus	80387–20
VIPC	System Micro 386	80287–8, –10 or 80387–20
Wang	380	80287–10
Whole Earth	386 Tower	80387–20
Wyse	pc286	80287–10
Wyse	pc386	80387–16 or 80287–6, –8, or –10
Wyse	1400	8087 or 8087–3
Wyse	1500	8087 or 8087–3
Zenith	148	8087–2
Zenith	150	8087 or 8087–3
Zenith	158	8087–2
Zenith	160	8087 or 8087–3
Zenith	386	80287–6, –8, or –10 or 80387–16
Zenith	Z200	80287 or 80287–6

The 80387 operates at the same speed as the 80386 with which it is installed. Available versions have tracked the speed of the 80386 as it has been improved, all the way up to 25 MHz. The speed rating of the chip is given in MHz following the part number, thus, an 80387-20 is rated to operate at 20 MHz.

The 80387 even looks like an 80386, only smaller. Its square 68-pin PGA case has the same slate-like appearance as the microprocessor. It can use either a 68-pin socket which exactly matches its package, or it can use a larger socket with 114-pins like that of the 80387. The latter socket is designed to allow the use of other processors as well as the 80387. Only the central two squares of pins of the three are used by the 80387.

The Weitek WTL 1167

Unlike other coprocessors, the *WTL 1167,* made by Weitek Corporation, Sunnyvale, California, is not a single chip but a multiple chip assembly on a small L-shaped printed circuit board. Three Weitek proprietary VLSI modules (the 1163, 1164, and 1165) give the WTL 1167 its basic power. In addition, the adapter board provides space for an Intel 80387, allowing you to put both chips in one system to reap the benefits of both. Note, however, that the two coprocessors do not interact or work with one another. Instead, each one runs only the code designed specifically for it.

Although odd-looking and expensive, the WTL 1167 has one great strength—it delivers even higher performance than the 80387 on numeric operations, CAD in particular. Because of its power some computer makers, notably Compaq, have incorporated compatibility with the 1167 in their top-of-the-line machines.

According to Weitek Corporation, the WTL 1167 can deliver from three to four times the performance of an 80387 in machines designed to handle it. Note, however, that it differs from the Intel design in that it delivers its performance improvement purely through inherent speed, not through an exotic command set. In fact, it lacks both the rich command repertory and wider register width of the Intel chips.

A 32-bit numeric coprocessor, the WTL 1167 handles addition, subtraction, multiplication, division, negation, absolute value, comparison testing, data movement, and format conversion functions. Transcendental functions are available through a subroutine library.

One result of the big difference in operation between the WTL 1167 and Intel coprocessors is that it is *not* code compatible with Intel-numeric coprocessors or software written solely to use Intel coprocessors. The WTL 1167 uses not only its own commands, but its own way of communicating those instructions to the chip. Programs written for the Intel chips will not work with the WTL 1167. To take advantage of it, you will need programs written specifically for it.

As with Intel coprocessors, the WTL 1167 relies on special instructions passed to it by its host microprocessor, but those instructions are passed in a different manner entirely. The Weitek coprocessor instructions cause the host microprocessor to address certain areas of memory, well outside the range used by DOS or OS/2 programs. The addressing action itself, that is, the activation of certain patterns of these special address lines, tells the Weitek processor what operation to carry out.

The WTL 1167 works only with the 80386 microprocessor. Versions rated at various speeds are available to match the speed ratings of the host microprocessor.

The WTL 1167 plugs into a special 121-pin socket with a pinout using a superset of that used by the 80387. Thus, either an 80387 or WTL 1167 often can be slipped into computers that use this socket. A socket on the WTL 1167 board provides a home for the expatriated 80387.

Adding a Numeric Coprocessor

The relatively easy operation of sliding a coprocessor chip into its socket is complicated by two factors: Usually the pins of a new chip won't fit and when they do, you've got your choice of two possible orientations. If you put the chip in backwards, the result is not just a failure to operate but a destruction of a chip which may have set you back several hundred dollars. If you know the tricks, however, you can make the surgical implant in a few minutes without gnawing your fingernails off in worry.

Making the Coprocessor Fit

First, the pins. Chips in dual in-line packages like the 8087 and 80287 are naturally delivered with their two rows of legs somewhat spread apart. Getting these ornery legs to fit in a socket merely requires pushing them closer together. Don't worry. It's easy.

After taking the grounding precautions advised by Intel, take hold of the chip by its two narrow ends and rest one row of leads (legs) against a

Figure 5.1 **A notch and/or indented dot indicates pin one of a Dual In-line Package device**

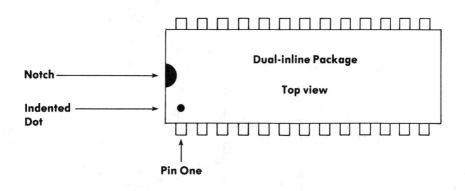

hard surface, such as a table top. With even, steady pressure, push down on the chip until the legs are bent perpendicular to the plastic case of the chip—don't bend them at the edge of the case but where they naturally fold about 1/16 inch out. Flip the chip over, and repeat this operation for the other side. When both sets of leads are perpendicular to the case, (parallel to each other) they should firmly slide into the socket.

Coprocessor Orientation

Before you slide the chip in, you must be certain it is oriented properly— that the right end points in the right direction, and pin one on the chip goes into the socket hole meant for pin one.

Normally, you should not have a problem. A notch at the end of the chip indicates the pin one end, and a corresponding notch at the end of the socket indicates its pin one end. (See Figure 5.1.)

However, some of IBM's early ATs were manufactured with the coprocessor socket oriented backwards. The sockets were put on their system boards by machines that had neither the eyes to detect a difference, nor the motivation to care whether there was one. Consequently, if by chance you have such an AT and you have followed the standard notch code, your expensive coprocessor could still go up in smoke.

Figure 5.2 **In the IBM AT, the notch in the 80287 coprocessor chip should always be oriented toward the front of the chassis. In some early models, the 80287 socket was inadvertently installed backwards**

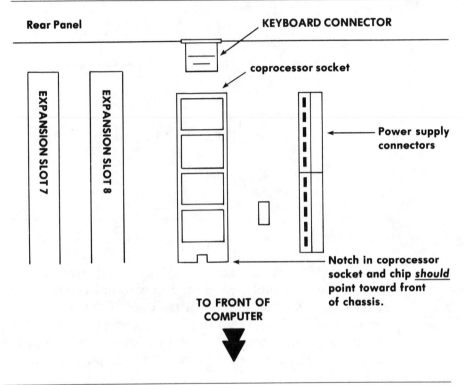

Here's how to know you're inserting your coprocessor correctly: The silk screening on the system board (when it is visible) shows the correct orientation with the notch in the correct position. The blind insertion machine could not alter the silk-screened image. In ATs, this means that the socket *should* have its notch at its end toward the front of the system unit. Make sure the notch on the top of your 80287 also points toward the front of the computer case. (See Figure 5.2.)

Note that PCs and XTs are just the opposite of ATs: The notch of the 8087 should face toward the rear of these 8088-based computers.

Coprocessor System Setup

Even after you install a numeric coprocessor in your PC, it may not do you any good until you indicate to your computer that the chips are there. Although a coprocessor can be found using only software, IBM

Figure 5.3 **Coprocessor switch settings—In the PC, switch 2 of DIP switch bank one controls the coprocessor. In the XT, switch 2 of the only DIP switch bank controls it. In either case, the OFF position indicates the presence of a coprocessor**

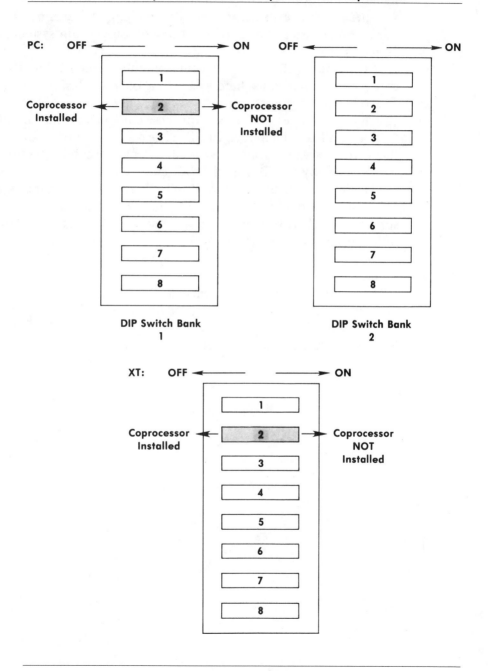

had tried to make coprocessor detection easier. Programs can avoid testing for a coprocessor by checking an *equipment flag* (a special memory location where system information is stored), to determine whether a coprocessor is present. The equipment flag is not set to indicate the presence of a coprocessor unless you tell your system that the chip is there.

Depending on the model of your computer, you can tell it about a coprocessor either with a hardware setting or through software. The PC and XT require you to throw a switch. (The location of the proper switch and the direction to set it for these computers is shown in Figure 5.3.) The AT and all models of PS/2 learn about coprocessors through the software setup routine. In general, compatible computers follow the scheme used by the IBM model they emulate.

Machines designed to use the Weitek WTL 1167 make a special provision for it, either a DIP-switch setting or a special entry during software-controlled setup. Simply make the correct adjustment to reflect installation of the WTL 1167 board. If you install an 80387 on the WTL 1167 board, you'll have to indicate its presence to your computer, too.

Once you make the adjustments to your computer to show that you have installed a coprocessor, you need not repeat the process (unless the setup memory of your AT or PS/2 loses power, in which case you'll have to go through the entire setup process).

6

MEMORY

All computers require memory of some sort. Memory holds all the steps of a program so the microprocessor can pull out each one as it needs it. Memory holds both the raw data that needs to be processed and the results of the processing. Memory is often used for communicating with peripherals and even maintains the image you see on your monitor screen.

Primary and Secondary Storage

Computer memory systems are often divided into two types, *primary storage* and *secondary storage*. Primary storage is that which is immediately accessible by the computer or microprocessor. Anything kept in primary storage is immediately accessible and ready to be used. This form of memory is called *on-line* storage because it is always connected to the computer. It may be directly accessible through the address lines of a microprocessor or through the I/O ports of the computer. Because any specific part of this memory, any random byte, can be instantly found and retrieved, primary storage is often termed *Random Access Memory* or *RAM*.

Regardless of its name, primary storage is, in effect, the short term memory of the computer. It's easy to get at but tends to be limited in capacity.

Long-term computer memory is termed secondary storage. Not only does this form of memory maintain information that must be kept for a long time, but it also holds the bulk of the information the computer deals with. Secondary storage may be tens, hundreds, or thousands of times larger than primary storage, and because of its bulk is often termed *mass storage*. These data are held off-line and is not directly accessible by the computer. To be used, it must be transferred from secondary storage into primary storage.

Saving States

In digital computer systems, memory operates on a very simple concept. In principal, all computer memory needs to do is preserve a single *bit* of information so it can be later recalled. Bit, an abbreviation for binary digit, is the smallest possible piece of information. It simply indicates whether something is or isn't—on or off, up or down, something (one) or nothing (zero). By storing as many single bits as needed in duplicative memory units, any amount of information can be retained.

To remember a single bit computer memory needs only to preserve a state, that is, whether something is true or false, positive or negative, a binary one or zero. Almost anything can suffice to remember a single state; the only need is that the memory unit has two possible states and it will maintain itself in one of them once it is put there. Should a memory element change on its own, randomly, it would be useless because it does not preserve the information it is charged to keep. The possibilities of what can be used for remembering a single state are nearly endless—whether a switch is turned on or off, whether a marble is on the shelf or on the floor, whether you have a string tied around your finger.

In digital computers it is helpful to store a state electrically so the machine doesn't need eyes or hands to check the string or marble. Possible candidates for electrical state-saving systems include those that depend on whether an electrical charge is present or whether a current will flow. Both of these techniques are used in computer memories for primary storage, however.

The analog of electricity, magnetism, is also used. Formerly the domain of all computer memory, magnetic storage is now generally reserved for mass storage.

Dynamic Memory

The most common memory inside today's personal computers relies on electrical charges to remember memory states. Charges are stored in small *capacitors*. The archetypical capacitor comprises two metal plates separated by a small distance that is filled with an electrical insulator. A positive charge can be applied to one plate and, because opposite charges attract, it draws a negative charge to the other nearby plate. The insulator separating the plates prevents the charges from mingling and neutralizing each other.

The capacitor can function as memory because a computer can control whether the charge is applied to, or removed from, one of the capacitor plates. The charge on the plates can thus store a single state and a single bit of digital information.

In a perfect world, the charges on the two plates of a capacitor would forever hold themselves in place. However, as one of many imperfections of the world, no insulator is perfect—the circuitry that charges and discharges the capacitor also allows some of the charge to leak off.

This system seems to violate the primary principal of memory—it won't reliably retain information for very long. Fortunately, it can retain information long enough to be useful—a few milliseconds—long enough that practical circuits can be designed to periodically recharge the capacitor and *refresh* the memory. Because the changing nature of this form of memory and its need to be actively maintained by refreshing, it is termed *dynamic* memory.

In actual personal computer memories, special semiconductor circuits are used instead of actual capacitors. A large number of these circuits are combined together to make a dynamic memory chip. As with true capacitors, however, dynamic memory of this type must be periodically refreshed.

Static Memory

While dynamic memory tries to trap evanescent electricity and hold it in place, *static* memory allows the current flow to continue on its way. It alters the path taken by the power, using one of two possible courses of travel to mark the state being remembered. Static memory operates as a switch that potentially allows or halts the flow of electricity.

A simple mechanical switch will, in fact, suffice as a form of static memory. It, alas, has the handicap that it must be manually toggled from one position to another. A switch that can be itself controlled by electricity is called a *relay,* and this technology was one of the first used for computer memories.

The typical relay circuit provided a *latch.* Applying a voltage to the relay energizes it, causing it to snap from preventing electricity from flowing to allowing it. Part of the electrical flow could be used to keep the relay itself energized which would, in turn, maintain the electrical flow. Like a door latch, this kind of relay circuit stays locked until some force or signal causes it to change, opening the door or the circuit.

Transistors, which can behave as switches, can also be wired to act as latches. A large number of these circuits combined together make a static memory chip.

Volatility

Note that both the relay and the transistor latch must have a constant source of electricity to maintain their latched state. If the current supplying them falters, the latch will relax and the circuit will forget. Similarly, if dynamic memory is not constantly refreshed, it too forgets. When the electricity is removed from either type of memory circuit, the information it held simply evaporates, leaving nothing behind. Consequently, these electrically-dependent memory systems are called *volatile*. A constant supply of electricity is necessary for them to maintain their integrity.

Read-Only Memory

Not all memory must be endowed with the ability to be changed. Just as there are many memories that you would like to retain—your first love, the names of all the stars in the Zodiac, the answers to the chemistry exam—a computer is better off when it can remember particularly important information without regard to the vagaries of the power line. Perhaps the most important of these more permanent recollections is the program code that tells a microprocessor that it is actually part of a computer and how it should carry out its duties.

In the old-fashioned world of relays, you could permanently set memory in one position or another by careful application of a hammer, and with enough assurance and impact, you could guarantee the system would never forget.

In the world of solid-state the principle is the same, but the programming instrument is somewhat different. All you need is switches that do not switch—or, more accurately, switch once and jam.

This permanent kind of memory is so valuable in computers that a whole family of devices called *Read-Only Memory* or *ROM* chips has developed. They are called read-only because the computer that they are installed in cannot write or rewrite new code and store it in them. Only what is already there can be read from the memory.

In contrast, the other kind of memory, to which the microprocessor can write as well as read, is logically termed *Read-Write Memory*. This term is, however, rarely used. Instead, read-write memory is generally called RAM even though ROM also allows random access.

If ROM chips cannot be written by the computer, the information inside must come from somewhere. In one kind of chip, the *mask* ROM, the information is built into the memory chip at the time it is fabricated.

The mask is a master pattern used to draw the various circuit elements on the chip during fabrication. When the circuit elements of the chip are grown on the silicon substrate, the pattern includes the information that will be read in the final device. Nothing, other than a hammer blow or its equivalent, can alter what is contained in this sort of memory.

Mask ROMs are not common in personal computers because they require their programming be carried out when the chips are manufactured; changes are not easy to make and the quantities that must be manufactured to make production affordable are daunting.

One alternative is the *Programmable* Read-Only Memory chip or *PROM*. This style of circuit consists of an array of elements that work like fuses. Normally, the fuses conduct electricity. However, like fuses, these circuit elements can be blown, which stops the electrical flow. PROM chips are manufactured and delivered with all of their fuses intact. A special machine—called a PROM programmer or PROM burner— is used to blow the fuses one-by-one according to the needs of the software to be coded inside the chip. This process is usually termed "burning" the PROM.

As with most conflagrations, the effects of burning a PROM are permanent. The chip cannot be changed to update or revise the program inside. PROMs are definitely not something for people who can't make up their minds—or a fast changing industry.

Happily, technology has brought an alternative, the *Erasable* Programmable Read-Only Memory chip or *EPROM*. EPROMS are almost self-healing semiconductors because the data inside an EPROM can be erased and the chip reused for other data or programs.

EPROM chips are easy to spot because they have a clear window in the center of the top of their packages. Invariably, this window is covered with a label of some kind, and with good reason. The chip is erased by shining high-intensity ultraviolet light through the window. If stray light should leak through the window, the chip could be inadvertently erased. (Normal room light won't erase the chip because it contains very little ultraviolet. Bright sunshine does, however, and can erase EPROMs.) Because of their versatility, permanent memory, and easy reprogrammability, EPROMs are ubiquitous inside personal computers.

RAM Chips

The evolution of the RAM chip has closely followed the development of the personal computer. The success of the small computer fueled demand for memory chips. At the same time, the capacity of memory chips has increased and, except for a temporary rise following the plummet of the dollar, their price has tumbled.

At the time the first PC was introduced the standard RAM chip could store 16 kilobits of information, that is, 16,384 bits or 2048 bytes. The memory cells (where each bit is stored) was assigned its own address so bits were individually retrievable.

These were the smallest capacity memory chips used by any PC-compatible computer. Besides the original IBM PC, they were also used on some accessories, such as memory expansion boards and video adapters. Today these chips are expensive because relatively few new devices use them and their rarity has made manufacturing, distributing, and storing of these chips uneconomical.

By the time the XT was introduced, about a year later, chips with a larger capacity proved to be more cost-effective. Although able to store four times the data, 64-kilobit chips then began to cost less than four times the price of 16-kilobit chips. The PC system board was revised to accommodate the better memory buy and the XT was designed to accept them. In a few years, 64-kilobit chips became so popular that their price fell below that of 16-kilobit chips.

By 1984, the best value in memory had become the next step larger, the 256-kilobit chip, and RAM chips of this size were chosen for the original AT. Now chips with one megabit capacity are becoming popular.

Shadow Memory

The latest 32-bit computers often provide for accessing memory through 8, 16, or 32-bit data buses. It is often most convenient to use a 16-bit data path for ROM BIOS memory (so only two expensive EPROM chips are needed instead of the four required by a 32-bit path). Many expansion cards which may have on-board BIOS extensions, connect to their computer hosts through eight-bit data buses. As a result, these memory areas cannot be accessed nearly as fast as the host system's 32-bit RAM. This problem is compounded because BIOS routines, particularly those used by the display adapter, are among the most frequently used code in the computer.

To break through this speed barrier, many designers of 80386 computers use *shadow memory*. They copy the ROM routines into fast 32-bit RAM and use the memory-mapping abilities of the 80386 to switch the RAM into the address range used by the ROM. Execution of BIOS routines can then be speeded up by a factor of four or more (more because greater wait states are often imposed when accessing slower

ROM memory). Of course, the shadow memory is volatile and must be loaded with BIOS routines every time the computer is booted up. In most (but not all) 80386-based computers, BIOS routines are automatically loaded into shadow memory each time the computer is turned on.

Memory Architectures

The original PC had a rather ordinary memory arrangement, at least when it is viewed from the perspective of the latest high-speed hardware. The PC's memory was simply arranged as a block where any byte of information was directly available by calling its address. The address lines on the 8088 microprocessor simply connected to some circuitry, collectively called *address decoder logic,* which translated the address numbers requested by the microprocessor to the matrix arrangement of the memory chips.

The memory chips themselves were arranged in banks of nine using either 16-kilobit (on the earliest PCs) or 64-kilobit chips. Eight chips each provided one bit of a byte of information with each of the bits held in a different chip, but at the same memory address. The ninth chip held a *parity check bit* which was set at either a logical one or zero in such a way that the total of all nine bits at one address was always odd. Every time memory was read, this total was computed by special circuitry. If ever an even total was discovered for a byte held in system board memory, the circuitry would interrupt the system and blast the ominous message *Parity Check 1* on the screen, freezing the computer. An even total on a memory expansion board would elicit a *Parity Check 2* error with the same fatal failing.

Memory Speed

When the 80286 microprocessor was adopted for the AT and subsequent computers, a problem arose with this simple architecture. Ordinary memory chips could not keep pace with the speed of the microprocessor. The 80286 could request bytes in such short order that memory was unable to respond. Consequently, *wait states* were added when the microprocessor requested information for memory. A wait state is exactly what it sounds like; the microprocessor suspends whatever its doing for one or more clock cycles to give the memory circuits a chance to catch up. At normal 80286 operating speeds, up to 12 MHz, one wait state was usually all that was necessary. All ATs and the PS/2 Models

50 and 60 impose one wait state. Because it uses faster memory chip and a slower microprocessor (6 MHz) the XT Model 286 required no memory wait states. With the Model 50Z, IBM upgraded system memory so that no-wait states were required even at IO MHz.

Dynamic memory chips are speed-rated, usually with a number emblazoned on the chip following its model designation. This number reflects the *access time* of the chip given in nanoseconds with the right-most zero left off to make the expression a little more compact. Hence, a chip that has a -12 labeled on it has an access time of 120 nanoseconds.

If this were the number of merit for chip speed, even the fastest of to-day's computers would have no problem. At 16 MHz, for example, one clock cycle is 62.5 nanoseconds and the 80386 chip requires at least two cycles between memory operations, a total of 125 nanoseconds. Chips rated at 120 nanoseconds are readily available and relatively inexpensive.

The access time is not the only—or the most important—figure to describe a memory chip, however. More relevant is the *cycle time,* which measures how quickly two back to back accesses can be made to the chip. The cycle time is generally about two to three times the access time of the chip. Hence, even an 80-nanosecond DRAM chip is not capable of reliably serving a 16 MHz 80386. Static RAM chips, however, have cycle times equal to their access times (because there is no need to refresh memory). Static RAM rated at 80 seconds could, in fact, service the 16 MHz 80386 (or a 20 MHz 80386 for that matter). However, these chips are much more expensive.

To cope with the speed limitations of affordable memory chips, a number of memory architectures have been used. The most straightfor-ward of these are simply uses ordinary memory and imposes as many wait states as necessary. With this simple design, the only way of in-creasing speed is to use faster memory chips, either expensive DRAM or static RAM.

Memory Caching

A clever alternative is to use a high speed cache instead of filling their whole machine with fast RAM. Most memory access are made within a limited block of memory, and by keeping the most memory addresses most likely to be used in the cache, the microprocessor can read them there without any wait states.

Not all memory caches are created equal, however. A major factor determining how successful the cache will be is how much information it contains. The larger the cache, the more data that will be in it, and the more likely any needed byte will be there when it is needed. Obviously, the best cache is one that is equal in size and duplicates the entirety of system memory. It is also absurd—you could use the cache as primary memory and forget the rest. The smallest cache would be a byte, also an absurd situation because it guarantees the next read is not in the cache. Practical caches range from a couple of kilobytes to 64K with the 16–64K size being most favored.

Actual caching systems are not as simple as they sound in the abstract. Microprocessors not only must be able to read from the memory but also write to it as well. What happens if the microprocessor writes a new byte to the cache just as the cache is reloading from the area where the byte was supposed to go? Will the old information overwrite the new in the cache? To insure that the new information makes it to real memory, sometimes *write-through caches* are used. Memory writes bypass or go right through the cache to the underlying regular memory. Of course, this slows down the memory because writes are no longer cached. Worse, the microprocessor might call for the information it has just written— before it gets loaded into the cache. Memory integrity is one of the principal problems faced by the cache designer.

One preferred solution is to delegate all responsibilities for supervising the cache to dedicated circuits designed for that purpose. In the PC environment, the most illustrious of these is Intel's *82385* cache controller.

Among its other powers, the 82385 has a "snooping" capability, that is, it hunts around in main memory to determine when bytes are altered. For example, when a hard disk is read and information is transferred into memory through a control system that does not involve the microprocessor, *Direct Memory Access* or DMA, the 82385 ensures those changes made in main memory aren't missed when the microprocessor next draws those bytes from the same location inside the cache.

In addition, the 82385 has the capability to buffer memory writes as well as reads. After the memory write is made to the cache, the 82385 diligently copies the changes to system RAM without the intervention of the microprocessor. Consequently, the 82385 allows the system to run with zero wait states for both reading and writing.

Page-Mode RAM

Another memory architecture breaks the whole memory of a computer system into a number of individual sections that each operate as if it were a small cache. The high speed access to a limited memory area is a function of some very special memory chips that allow part, but not all, of their endowment to be read without wait states. This memory speed-up technique requires special RAM chips that divide their address ranges into pages or a group of rows and columns. Operating with what is called *page-mode* access, these special chips allow very fast access in one of the two directions of their organization. As long as sequential reads or writes require access to the same page as the last memory operation, no wait states are encountered. When memory access requires crossing the boundary between memory pages, however, wait states are required.

The special chips required by this technique are called *static-column* RAM and *page-mode* RAM. Although technically these two terms describe distinct chip technologies, most practical applications yield exactly the same results. In the static column RAM arrangement memory is logically laid out as a two-dimensional array and sequential memory bits are organized in adjacent rows within a single column. Page-mode RAM chips break the total chip capacity into a number of pages, usually containing two kilobits.

As with true caching, the performance of static-column or page-mode memory systems depends on the page or column size that is used. The larger the page, the more likely the next bit of memory will be inside it and the better the chances of reading it without wait states. The performance improvement can be dramatic. Most programs execute within the limits of a 2K page most of the time, so overall system performance is boosted to near what it would be were system RAM entirely static. For example, the static-column RAM of the original (but now discontinued) Compaq Deskpro 386-16 reduced the two wait states ordinary memory would impose to about 0.8 when running typical software.

Banked Memory

Another clever technique, called *interleaved memory,* is like page-mode RAM in that it picks up speed on sequential memory accesses, but it does not suffer the limitation of small page sizes. Interleaved memory works by dividing the total RAM of a system into two or more banks. Sequential bits are held in alternate banks, so the microprocessor goes back and forth between banks when it reads sequential bytes. While one bank is being read, the other is cycling, so the microprocessor does not have to wait. Of course, if the microprocessor must read logically non-contiguous bits, whether it encounters wait states is governed by the laws of probability.

In a typical interleaved memory system, system RAM will be divided into two banks so the probability of encountering a wait state is about 50 percent. A four-way interleave can reduce wait-states by 75 percent.

Because interleaved memory does not require special memory chips, it is perhaps the most affordable method of speeding up system operation. Memory interleaving can also be combined with page-mode memory chips to further enhance system performance.

Logical Memory Organization

Although it may be made from the same kind of chips, not all memory in an IBM-standard personal computer is the same; not all of it can be used by programs, and some must be accessed entirely differently from the rest. Part of the reason for this divergence has to do with some arbitrary design decisions made by IBM. Part is a result of the design of the various microprocessors used in IBM-style computers, and the efforts made by hardware and software companies to overcome those limitations.

Base Memory

Arbitrary decisions were made when the PC was originally designed. To be used by the 8088 microprocessor, memory must be addressable, which means it must fall within the one megabyte addressing range of the chip. IBM's engineers decided to assign and reserve certain parts of the PC's memory to specific purposes that required its accessibility by the 8088. They drew up a map of what memory could be used for what purposes and what areas were reserved. The resulting chart is called a *memory map*.

In the initial design of the PC, just over half of its memory was reserved. The top half of the 8088 address range, 512K, was given over to providing an addressing range for the system's BIOS code and direct microprocessor access to the memory used by the video system. The first few kilobytes were reserved for specific hardware and operation system functions, to provide space for remembering information about the system and the location of certain sections of code that are executed when specific software interrupts are made. (See Figure 6.1.)

These last memory locations are called *interrupt vectors* because like the arrow used to schematically represent a vector, they point to where the software routine begins. The function of this program code is said to *service the interrupt*.

Figure 6.1 **Memory map of the PC and XT**

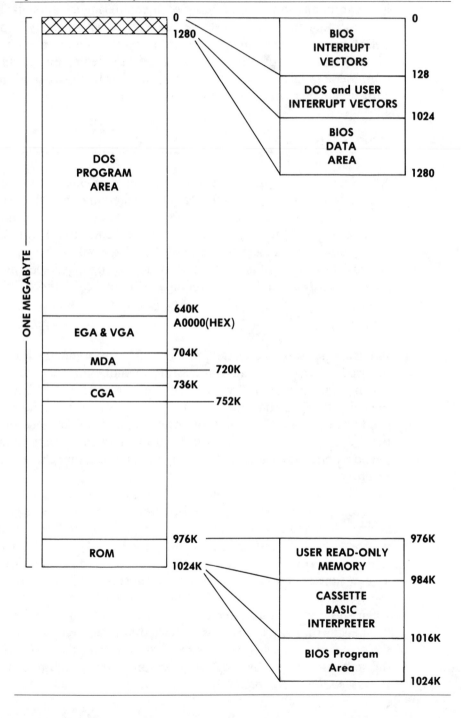

Also included in these bytes at the bottom of the address range are the *keyboard buffer*—nominally 16 bytes of storage which hold the code of the last 16 characters you pressed on the keyboard. This temporary storage allows the computer to accept your typing while it is temporarily busy with other tasks—it can then go back and process your characters when it is not as busy. The angry beeping your PC sometimes makes when you hold down one key for too long is the machine's way of complaining that the keyboard buffer is full and that it has no place to put the latest characters, which it will steadfastly refuse to accept until it can free up some buffer space.

In addition, various system *flags,* indicators of internal system conditions that can be equated to the code of semaphore flags, are stored in this low memory range.

Even though 512K seemed generous in the days when 64K was the most other popular computers could use, the wastefulness of the original limit soon became apparent. IBM engineers figured the 128K could safely be reassigned to program access, leaving 384K at the upper end of the address range for use by video memory and BIOS routines.

This division persists, leaving us with 640K of *DOS Memory Area,* the maximum contiguous memory area within the addressing range of the 8088 microprocessor that can be used for program execution. At times this 640K is also called *base memory* because it is the standard foundation on which all IBM-compatible systems must be built. Programs written for the PC-DOS or MS-DOS operating systems are able to use only this memory and are, in most cases, constrained by this 640K limit. Note, however, that a few memory boards and some special software for the 80386 microprocessor (*386Max* from Qualitas Software, for example) can add more bytes to the DOS area by cutting unused slivers out of the upper 384K addressing range of the 8088.

Extended Memory

Memory beyond the megabyte addressable by the 8088, which can be accessed through the protected mode of the 80286 and 80386 microprocessors, is generally termed *extended memory* (although IBM sometimes calls it expanded memory, a term reserved by most writers for another type of memory). Up to 15 megabytes of extended memory can be added to an 80286-based computer, four gigabytes to an 80386. The most important distinguishing characteristic between extended and base memory is that programs that run in real mode cannot execute in extended memory. DOS is written for the real mode, so it is limited to base memory.

This is not to say extended memory is inaccessible in real mode. Programs don't know how to address its extra bytes. Although extended memory can be used for data storage, software must be particularly written to take advantage of it. Few DOS-based programs are. The primary example of a program that is the VDISK floppy-disk emulator included with DOS 3.0 or later. Although the program code for VDISK executes in normal DOS memory in real mode, it can use extended memory for data storage.

Because OS/2 can operate in protected mode, it can take full advantage of extended memory. Note, however, that when its compatibility box is used to run old-fashioned DOS applications, OS/2 shifts back to real mode and is constrained by the 640K memory limit in executing them.

Expanded Memory

In April, 1985—months after the AT was introduced with its multiple megabytes of extended memory range—a major software publisher, Lotus Development Corporation, and a hardware maker, Intel Corporation, formulated their own method for overcoming the 640K limit of older DOS computers based on the 8088 microprocessor. A few months later they were joined by Microsoft Corporations, and the development was termed the *Lotus-Intel-Microsoft Expanded Memory Specification* (for its originators), or *LIM memory,* or *EMS,* or simply *expanded* memory. The initial Version was numbered as EMS Version 3.0 to indicate its compatibility with then-current DOS 3.0. When Microsoft joined, the spec was slightly revised and denominated as Version 3.2.

The new memory system differed from either base memory or extended memory in not being within the normal address range of its host microprocessor, instead, it relied on hardware circuitry to switch banks of memory within the normal address range of the 8088 microprocessor where the chip can read and write to it. This technique, called *bankswitching,* was neither novel nor unusual, for it has been applied to CP/M computers based on the Z80 microprocessor to break through their inherent 64K addressing limit. Only the cooperative effort at standardization by oftentimes competing corporations was surprising.

The original EMS specification dealt with its expanded memory in banks of 16 kilobytes. It mapped out a 64K range in the non-DOS memory area above the bytes used for display memory to switch these banks, up to four at a time, into the address range of the 8088. Up to eight megabytes of 16K banks of expanded memory could be installed in a system.

The Expanded Memory Specification included the definition of several function calls—predefined software routines contained in special EMS software called the *Expanded Memory Manager*—that were to be used by programs to manipulate the expanded memory. Because the memory areas beyond the DOS 640K range had been assigned various purposes by IBM, were the bank-switching area assigned an arbitrary location, it could potentially conflict with the operation of other system expansion. Consequently, the specification allows several address locations for the bank-switching area within the range 784K to 960K.

Because programs had to be specially written to include the function calls provided by the EMS drivers, expanded memory does not allow ordinary software to stretch beyond the DOS limit. Moreover, the original Expanded Memory Specification put a burdensome limit on the uses of this additional memory because it could only be used for data storage—program code could not execute in the EMS area. Adding EMS memory to your system also necessitated special expansion boards with the required bank switching hardware built into them. You couldn't just buy a handful of AST Six-Paks and expect to put all their bytes to work.

The introduction of the AT and its potential of 16 megabytes of addressability overshadowed EMS until the hard reality of the inaccessibility of extended memory hit home. Even the few available programs that could take advantage of EMS were more useful than the VDISK driver, which was the only DOS-compatible product to use extended memory. In fact, until the announcement of OS/2, the most valuable application for the extended memory of the AT was as expanded memory using an expanded memory emulation driver, such as *V-EMM* from Fort's Software.

These software-only EMS products can be divided into two classes, those that take advantage of the paged-virtual memory-mapping abilities built into the 80386 microprocessor and those that copy 16K banks of memory from extended into base memory. Although both types of software have been used effectively, Lotus claims the 80386-based systems are truly compatible with EMS and the block-copying programs cannot provide full, correct EMS functionality.

Enhanced Expanded Memory Specification

Shortly after the introduction of EMS, a competing system was proposed by another cooperative association of otherwise competing computer products companies, AST Research, Quadram, and Ashton-Tate. Called the *Enhanced Expanded Memory Specification* or *EEMS,* it was an elaboration of the EMS idea—a superset of EMS—that allowed program execution and multitasking in the expanded memory area. Its design enhancements included the ability to switch banks of up to 64K in size, as well as utilizing part of the DOS 640K area for the switch. EEMS, too, required a special driver, special hardware, and software written to take advantage of its refinements—all different from those created for EMS.

EMS Version 4.0

In August, 1987, the two systems (EMS and EEMS) were brought together with the adoption of *EMS Version 4.0*. Because both EMS and EEMS are subsets of Version 4.0, software written for either system can run under it. Beyond the previous standards, Version 4.0 supports up to 32 megabytes of bank-switched memory (all of which can support program execution and multitasking) and provided more than double the number of function calls to aid programmers in creating products to take advantage of it. While EMS 4.0 is compatible with previous hardware designs, it requires new memory management software to bring it to life. Although applications must be specially written to use its advanced function calls, those written for previous EMS or EEMS standards will operate within the limits of the specification for which they were originally designed.

According to its creators, the purpose of EMS 4.0 is to extend the life of 8088-and 8086-based computers. Although it may be an alternative to OS/2 in some cases (Lotus 1-2-3 Release 3 will be available in separate versions to operate under OS/2 and EMS 4.0, for example), EMS 4.0 is not an operating system in itself. It merely affords facilities to software and operating system developers and requires an EMM program to be used effectively as a multitasking environment.

Memory Expansion

The most common circuit-level modification that is made to personal computers is increasing its memory endowment. Although in many cases memory expansion requires you to handle delicate, static-sensitive integrated circuits, the operation is not difficult, and if you're properly careful, you run little risk of damaging chips or your computer.

Before you can add memory to your computer, you will have to identify the type of add-in memory it requires. If the owner's manual of your machine does not identify the memory type it uses, you should still be able to determine the memory type by removing the case from your computer and examining the parts inside.

System designers can choose between two ways of installing memory into their systems, either as *discrete chips* or as *memory modules*. While the first choice allows greater versatility and a wider selection of parts, the second is more compact and easier to work with and design around.

If the instruction materials accompanying your computer did not specify the type of memory it uses, you can tell by taking a quick look. Discrete memory chips are nearly always located in a rectangular array on the system board, typically in multiple rows (usually four) of nine chips each, although some machines may use 18-chip rows or more than four rows. Some of the rows may be vacant sockets, allowing for the memory expansion you wish to accomplish.

The giveaway in identifying a computer that uses discrete memory chips is that all the chips in its chip array are identical—all usually will have the same identifying numbers on their cases. It is possible, however, for black sheep chips to appear because different chip manufacturers use different part numbers. Moreover, some computers may use different chip types in different rows of memory. Nevertheless, an array of multiple, similar chips is a good indicator of discrete memory.

You can tell if your computer is equipped with memory modules of some type by looking for several tiny circuit boards sticking up from your system board, usually at a right angle. A few computer designers spread out the memory modules, perhaps placing them between expansion slots. Usually, however, they're all located together in about a 4-inch-square patch.

Discrete Chips

When adding memory to a system based on discrete memory chips, you need to consider several chip characteristics even before you order the add-in memory from your dealer or mail-order supplier. Among the more important considerations are:

Capacity The fundamental difference between memory chips is the amount of data they store. In RAM chips, this value is almost universally given in bits rather than bytes. Commonly available chip capacities range from 16 kilobits to 1 megabit. The standard intermediate sizes are 64 kilobits and 256 kilobits, perhaps the most common size today. The initial 6 MHz AT used special 128K memory modules, which, unlike SIMMs and SIPPs, were essentially just two discrete 64K chips soldered to one another.

In general, only one capacity of memory chip will work in a given socket in a computer. However, a few machines and accessories can be setup (through jumpers or DIP switches) to accept two or more sizes in their sockets.

Case   As mundane as it sounds, the black epoxy package of a memory chip is important when making a purchase. Chips are available in several different package styles including the common *Dual In-line Pin (DIP), Single In-line Pin (SIP),* and *Zig-zag In-line Pin (ZIP)*. DIP chips have two rows of pins in two parallel rows on either side of the case. In general, the pins are spaced 1/10 inch apart and the rows are separated by 4/10 inch. SIPs put all the pins on one row, all 1/10 inch apart. ZIPs use two parallel rows of pins 1/10 inch apart with the individual pins also separated from the others in the same row by 1/10 inch. The pins in the two rows are offset from one another by half the spacing between the pins to create a zig-zag pattern.

Memory chips are also available in surface-mount packages, tiny (½-inch) square blocks of epoxy which are designed to be soldered in place. These cannot be used for expanding system board memory because they won't fit into any standard socket.

Speed   All memory chips are speed-rated by access time, which is measured in nanoseconds. Faster computers require quicker chips with a lower nanosecond rating. The veteran PC was slow enough to get away with using the cheapest, most laggardly memory available which were chips rated at 250 nanoseconds. Many 80386 machines are constrained even by quick, 80-nanosecond chips.

In general, you'll do no harm installing quicker chips than a computer requires—putting 150 nanosecond ICs into a PC, for example. Slower chips may not work, or will more likely work sporadically, leaving you vulnerable to parity check errors at unexpected times.

Access   Even discounting all the differences mentioned above, all memory chips are not created equal. Though two chips have the same capacity, packaging, and access time, they can provide different means of accessing the bits they store. The typical computer memory chip stores information in a series of addresses, typically about 256,000, one bit wide. The same capacity can be split four ways, so each address stores four bits. In this way, a 256-kilobit memory chip would store four bits at each of about 64,000 addresses. This style of chip, growing in popularity in display adapters and a few computer systems (such as the XT Model 256) is called a 4 x 64-kilobit chip, distinguishing it from the 1 x 256-kilobit conventional chip, although both can be legitimately called 256-kilobit chips.

Video systems and some performance-enhancing turbo boards use memory chips with a different design twist. They provide two paths for getting to memory bits. In turbo boards, this *dual-ported memory* allows the turbo processor to share information with its host computer by loading and unloading data through memory. The memory acts like a warehouse with two doors—one processor pushes bytes into the warehouse through one door while the other can pull them out through another. Special *video memory* chips work similarly, although with more restrictions. A microprocessor can load information into one side of the memory while the video graphics controller can pull individual bits out the other side. While the microprocessor may have full read and write random access, the video side only needs to be read sequentially.

To improve the performance of 80386-based computers, a number of different chips, styles are used. Besides static memory chips which are incompatible with dynamic RAM and cannot be used interchangeably, these systems may also use *static-column* or *page-mode* memory chips. However, these chips are not compatible with standard memory chips, either. They cannot be used to expand computers requiring normal DRAM chips nor can DRAM chips be used where these varieties are called for.

The only certain way of identifying memory chips is through the manufacturer's designation stenciled onto the top of the chip case.

Generic Memory

Most computers use a style of memory chip that's so ubiquitous they are nearly generic—bit-wide, dynamic RAM chips in DIP packages. The odds are your computer, too, uses this kind of memory. If so, your only concern is the capacity of the individual chips, whether it is 64-kilobit, 256-kilobit, or one megabit. To confound you, every manufacturer uses its own nomenclature for this garden-variety kind of memory chip. (Table 6.1 lists the part numbers used by many major manufacturers.)

Table 6.1 Equivalency Chart for Popular DRAM Chips

Note that these chips may also be available in different speed ratings, differing only in suffix. For example, 120-nanosecond chips designations end with -12, 150 nanosecond with -15.

64K × 1 bit chips, DIP package:		*64K × 4 chips, DIP package:*	
Fujitsu	MBM8264-15	Fujitsu	MB81464-15P
Intel	P2164B-15	Hitachi	HM50464P-15
Mitsubishi	M5K4164P-15	Micron	MT4067-15
Motorola	MCM4164BP-15	NEC	UPD41464C-15
Oki	MSM3764-15	Samsung	KM41464PA-15
Panasonic	MN4164P-15	Texas Instru.	TMS4464-15NL
Samsung	KM4164A-15		
Texas Instru.	TMS4164-15n1		

256K × 1 chips, DIP package:		*1024K (one megabyte) × 1 chips, DIP package:*	
Fujitsu	MB 81256P-15		
Hitachii	HM50256P-15	Hitachi	HM511000-12
Intel	P21256-15	Micron	MT4C1024DJ-12
Mitsubishi	M5M4256P-15	NEC	UPD421000LP-12
Motorola	MCM6256AP-15	Samsung	KM41C1000-12
NEC	UPD41256C-15	Toshiba	TC511000-12
Oki	M41256-15		
Samsung	KM41256-15		
Texas Instru.	TMS4256-15		
Toshiba	TMM41256P-15		

SINGLE IN-LINE MEMORY MODULES

256K × 9 SIMMs:		*1024K (one megabyte) × 9 SIMMs:*	
Fujitsu	MB85227-12PDPB	Hitachi	HB56100BB-120
Hitachi	HB561003B-12	Kanamatsu Gosho	KG10009-C120
Micron	MT9259M-12	Micron	MT8C904M-12
Mitsubishi	HM25609J-12	NEC	UPD421000L-12
Oki	MSC2305-12YS9	Oki	MSC2310-12YS9
Samsung	KMM59256-12	Toshiba	THM91000L-12
Texas Instru.	TM4256GU9-12L	Toyocom	TH3C1009-120
Toyocom	TH32569-N12		

The major exception to the generic memory rule are the few 80386-based machines that use more exotic chips to achieve greater performance than DRAM can deliver. If you're not certain of the memory technology which your 80386-based computer uses, compare the legends on its memory chips to those listed in Table 6.1. If you find a match, you're probably safe with expanding your system's memory with that chip or its equivalent.

Memory Modules

Memory modules are simply a second step in integration. They combine a number of discrete chips, usually nine, on a small printed circuit board that plugs in as a single assembly. (Some IBM modules use four special proprietary chips.) In general, memory modules are designed to provide a given number of *bytes* of memory rather than discrete bits. Standard sizes in common use include 256 kilobyte and one megabyte modules. Although physically similar, some machines are particular about what capacity modules you install. Others allow you to use either size, providing you fill an entire bank (either two or four modules for 16 or 32-bit computers, respectively) with the same capacity modules and set the system up properly.

Two incompatible styles of package are generally available, *Single In-line Memory Modules (SIMMs)* and *Single In-line Pin Package* memory modules *(SIPPs)*. The difference arises from the form of connector used—SIMMs use PC card-edge connectors, SIPPs use header pins. The two are not interchangeable so you must be certain about the correct style when adding memory to a given computer.

Memory Module Identification

Beside a group of memory modules, you should also find a number of empty sockets for them. If you can't find any vacant sockets, then there's no room left on the system board for expansion. If you find vacant sockets, a cursory examination will reveal if they are designed for SIMMs or SIPPs: SIMMs fit into a groove in a socket lined with gold fingers on either side, while SIPPs use pins that slip into matching holes.

The manufacturer's part number given to a memory module is often stenciled on the side of the board opposite the one carrying the individual memory chips. If it's not there, or anywhere else as is often the case, you can identify the memory module from the nomenclature on its chip components. For example, a module made from nine 256-kilobit chips rated at 80 nanoseconds is a 256 *kilobyte,* 80 nanosecond memory module. Note that memory modules are available in the same profusion of types as are the discrete chips from which they are made: static, dynamic, page-mode, and all the rest. You must match any memory modules you use in expansion to the type that your computer requires.

For a better look when attempting to identify memory modules, you may want to pop the module from its socket. For SIPPs, the process is easy—just pull it out by applying even pressure. SIMMs are more difficult.

Removing SIMMs

Normally SIMMs are latched into place by plastic fingers at either end of the slot in their connectors. Look closely and you'll see that the plastic of the socket has two latching fingers at each end. You must carefully pry these away from the SIMM before you can pull it out. You can then lean the SIMM over a bit and pull it out. When you re-insert the SIMM, you must press it firmly in place until the fingers lock it down again and little round tabs appear in the latching holes in the SIMM near the fingers.

Memory Expansion Rules

No matter the physical embodiment of the memory used by your computer, your memory expansion effort must be governed by a few rules.

Full Banks Only   All computers deal with memory as banks rather than as individual chips. A bank of memory chips or memory modules comprises enough chips to store a memory word at each address. That is, an 8-bit computer requires a bank of nine chips, eight for the data bits in each word plus one for parity; a 16-bit computer needs 18 chips per bank, 16 for data bits and two for parity; a 32-bit computer needs 36 chips per bank, 32 for data bits and four for parity.

Memory modules, which are a byte wide and include parity, must be added in a manner similar to discrete chips. For an 8-bit computer, one memory module constitutes a full bank of memory. Two memory modules are required to complete a 16-bit bank and four for a 32-bit bank. You'll need at least that many chips or modules to add any expansion memory to a PC.

Chips Within a Bank Must Match   Although some computers accept combinations of different capacities of memory chips, no computer allows you to combine different chip capacities within a memory bank. All of the chips (or memory modules) within a bank must be of the same capacity. Access times are not so critical, however, and you can mix chips with different access times within a bank providing all chips are at least as quick as the computer requires.

Orientation Is Important   As with coprocessors or any other chips you might install inside your computer, memory chips must be properly aligned in their sockets. That is, pin number one of the chip must fit into the corresponding pin-1 hole of the socket.

All chips have some means of identifying either pin-1 or the end of the chip at which pin-1 is located. Usually the pin-1 end of the chip is notched. Occasionally, a small circular depression—an indented dot—is located directly adjacent to pin-1. The end of the chip that is so marked is oriented to match the notch in the chip socket. Sometimes pin-1 of the socket is also identified with a silk-screened legend on the circuit board. Occasionally all the pins in a socket will be denoted with numbers molded into the plastic of the socket itself.

An improperly oriented chip will likely fail immediately when you power up your computer. In fact, the backwards chip may short out and prevent your computer from booting at all. To avoid such disasters, double-check the orientation of every chip before switching on your computer after adding any chips.

All Leads Must Engage   Sliding chips into sockets is not foolproof. The legs of ICs have a nasty tendency to go exactly where you don't want them: Sometimes they fold outward and slide down outside the socket instead of making a connection; and sometimes they bend underneath the chip and don't make a connection. If a chip leg misses its place, you will encounter memory errors when you boot up your computer, although the bent pin is unlikely to cause other damage to your system. Avoid such problems by carefully investigating each leg of every chip you install. Make certain it fits properly into the hold provided in its socket.

If you discover a leg that is misplaced, simply pry the chip out of the socket, straighten the pin as best you can (don't flex the leg too much because they break off easily), and re-insert the chip.

Beware of Static Electricity   Although it takes electricity to power a computer, the same force can be the worst enemy for your memory. A shuffle across a wool rug can charge you up to 20,000 volts just rarin' to zap a memory chip designed to operate on five. While taking all the recommended precautions may be overkill—you don't have to ground yourself to a cold water pipe—there's no sense in taking chances. Grounding can be simply a matter of touching the case of your PC, or even touching the plastic tube or foam your memory chips come in before you begin. The key move is to make yourself, your computer, and the memory chips at the same potential, which simply means linking them all together before you actually touch the legs of the memory chip.

A few companies recommend you leave the power cord plugged into your computer to ground it while making the installation. You'll be safer ignoring this advice and unplug *all* cables from your computer before you begin. This way you can't accidentally try to install memory chips while the computer is running, an exercise guaranteed to be fatal to the memory chips.

Set Up the Computer to Recognize the Additional Memory   Once you've installed your expansion memory, you need to tell your computer about it. Sharing the word requires different actions for different computers.

PCs, XTs, and most 8-bit compatibles require you to set DIP switches, or jumpers, or both to indicate to the machine how much memory you have installed. If you don't adjust the switches, your machine will never know it has extra memory and will never try to use it. (Table 6.2 shows the settings required for PC, XT, and some compatible computers.)

ATs, the XT Model 256, and all PS/2s use a software setup procedure using the *Reference Disk* supplied with the computer system. Most compatibles using the BIOS written by Phoenix Technology use a similar setup disk. Those using the BIOS written by American Megatrends, Inc., have the necessary setup routines built into the BIOS itself.

Expansion Board Memory

Once you have the system board of your PC or XT filled with memory, you can still add more RAM to your system by plugging in memory expansion boards. Because of their greater flexibility in addressing memory, ATs, many 80386-based computers, and some PS/2s allow the use of expansion board memory even when their motherboard sockets are not completely filled.

Of course, installing additional memory requires some adjustments to your system, just as it did when the memory is installed on your motherboard. The hardware setup procedure of the PC and XT—that is, DIP switch settings—requires you to make adjustments to reflect the total amount of memory installed on the system board and any expansion boards.

Installing extended memory in AT and XT Model 256 systems often requires setting a switch on the memory expansion board used. This set-

Table 6.2 **PC and XT Memory Switch Settings**

KEY:
I means switch is set ON
0 means switch is set OFF
– means switch is not used for setting memory

PC-1 (64K system board):

Total Memory	Switch #1								Switch #2							
	1	2	3	4	5	6	7	8	1	2	3	4	5	6	7	8
16K	–	–	I	I	–	–	–	–	I	I	I	I	I	–	–	–
32K	–	–	0	I	–	–	–	–	I	I	I	I	I	–	–	–
48K	–	–	I	0	–	–	–	–	I	I	I	I	I	–	–	–
64K	–	–	0	0	–	–	–	–	I	I	I	I	I	–	–	–
96K	–	–	0	0	–	–	–	–	0	I	I	I	I	–	–	–
128K	–	–	0	0	–	–	–	–	I	0	I	I	I	–	–	–
160K	–	–	0	0	–	–	–	–	0	0	I	I	I	–	–	–
192K	–	–	0	0	–	–	–	–	I	I	0	I	I	–	–	–
224K	–	–	0	0	–	–	–	–	0	I	0	I	I	–	–	–
256K	–	–	0	0	–	–	–	–	I	0	0	I	I	–	–	–
288K	–	–	0	0	–	–	–	–	0	0	0	I	I	–	–	–
320K	–	–	0	0	–	–	–	–	I	I	I	0	I	–	–	–
352K	–	–	0	0	–	–	–	–	0	I	I	0	I	–	–	–
384K	–	–	0	0	–	–	–	–	I	0	I	0	I	–	–	–
416K	–	–	0	0	–	–	–	–	0	0	I	0	I	–	–	–
448K	–	–	0	0	–	–	–	–	I	I	0	0	I	–	–	–
480K	–	–	0	0	–	–	–	–	0	I	0	0	I	–	–	–
512K	–	–	0	0	–	–	–	–	I	0	0	0	I	–	–	–
544K	–	–	0	0	–	–	–	–	0	0	0	0	I	–	–	–
576K	–	–	0	0	–	–	–	–	I	I	I	I	0	–	–	–
608K	–	–	0	0	–	–	–	–	0	I	I	I	0	–	–	–
640K	–	–	0	0	–	–	–	–	I	0	I	I	0	–	–	–

PC-2 (256K system board):

Total Memory	Switch #1								Switch #2							
	1	2	3	4	5	6	7	8	1	2	3	4	5	6	7	8
64K	–	–	0	0	–	–	–	–	I	I	I	I	I	–	–	–
128K	–	–	0	0	–	–	–	–	I	0	I	I	I	–	–	–

Table 6.2 (continued)

PC-2 (256K system board):

Total		Switch #1								Switch #2						
Memory	1	2	3	4	5	6	7	8	1	2	3	4	5	6	7	8
192K	–	–	0	0	–	–	–	–	I	I	0	I	I	–	–	–
256K	–	–	0	0	–	–	–	–	I	0	0	I	I	–	–	–
288K	–	–	0	0	–	–	–	–	0	0	0	I	I	–	–	–
320K	–	–	0	0	–	–	–	–	I	I	I	0	I	–	–	–
352K	–	–	0	0	–	–	–	–	0	I	I	0	I	–	–	–
384K	–	–	0	0	–	–	–	–	I	0	I	0	I	–	–	–
416K	–	–	0	0	–	–	–	–	0	0	I	0	I	–	–	–
448K	–	–	0	0	–	–	–	–	I	I	0	0	I	–	–	–
480K	–	–	0	0	–	–	–	–	0	I	0	0	I	–	–	–
512K	–	–	0	0	–	–	–	–	I	0	0	0	I	–	–	–
544K	–	–	0	0	–	–	–	–	0	0	0	0	I	–	–	–
576K	–	–	0	0	–	–	–	–	I	I	I	I	0	–	–	–
608K	–	–	0	0	–	–	–	–	0	I	I	I	0	–	–	–
640K	–	–	0	0	–	–	–	–	I	0	I	I	0	–	–	–

XT (256K system board):

System Board		Switch Setting						
Memory	1	2	3	4	5	6	7	8
64K	–	–	I	I	–	–	–	–
128K	–	–	0	I	–	–	–	–
192K	–	–	I	0	–	–	–	–
256K	–	–	0	0	–	–	–	–

ting does not tell the host computer how much memory is present, rather, it sets the address that the board assigns to its memory. This bother of dealing with such switches is actually a blessing because it lets you add more than one board of the same brand and manufacturer to your computer. You can assign the memory address of each board to start where the precious memory left off. You must make that range of memory addresses continuous because the memory installed in ATs must be contiguous—that is, it must appear as one big block without empty areas in it.

Setting these switches does not relieve you from the responsibility for configuring your system's equipment flags. You'll still need to run the normal setup program for the new memory to be recognized, no matter the address you assign it.

Except for the Model 30 286 non-Micro Channel PS/2s do not support extended memory because their microprocessors (8086s) cannot operate in protected mode and address areas beyond the one megabyte of base memory. Because all of these systems come completely equipped with their maximal 640K DOS memory endowment, you won't have to worry about adding more bytes of ordinary memory to them.

The Micro Channel PS/2 models and the Model 30 286 require your running the setup utilities found on the Reference Disk when you add more memory in the expansion channel. The Micro Channel procedure also demands you copy hardware identification files from the disk sent with the memory board to a copy of your Reference Disk so you can properly configure the system. These files contain descriptive information about the memory board you are installing, including information about the addresses used by the memory on the board. Expansion boards that properly implement the Micro Channel Architecture specification will need no hardware setup procedure.

Adding Expanded Memory Boards

Installing EMS expanded memory in your system normally requires the use of expansion boards because of the need for hardware support of its paging features. However, 80386-based computers and the Micro Channel PS/2 have built-in bank-switching abilities and, using the proper software, can make use of their extended memory as expanded memory.

A hardware-implemented expanded memory system (the add-in expanded memory board) requires its own setup through adjusting on-board DIP switches and jumpers as well as running the normal EMS drivers. This procedure is a function of the add-in expanded memory board, not your computer. Because IBM did not officially recognize this form of memory until the introduction of DOS 4.0, installing this form of memory generally does not require resetting system board switches (on PCs and XTs) or running setup again (on the XT Model 286 and AT).

In Micro Channel PS/2s all memory is the same. No special expansion boards are needed to implement EMS. To bring their EMS functions to life, memory boards for Micro Channel PS/2s require you to run the system setup procedure to reassign conventional memory to the expanded memory area.

Memory Errors

Memory chips (and memory modules) sadly seem to be the most likely solid-state part of your computer to fail. They can fail in one of two ways—with *soft errors* or *hard errors*.

Soft Errors

For memory chips, a soft error is a transient change. One bit in a chip may suddenly, randomly change state. Typically one of the slightly radioactive atoms in the epoxy case of the chip will spontaneously decay and shoot out an alpha or beta particle into the chip. (There are a number of radioactive atoms in just about everything. They don't amount to very much but they are there.) If the particle hits a memory cell in the chip, the particle can cause cell to change state, blasting the memory bit it contains.

This error can be detected thanks to the parity-check bit assigned to each byte of memory. As soon as the error is detected, your machine shuts down with a parity error. However, the chip itself has suffered no damage from the particle blast and as soon as you reboot your computer, the error will be gone. Because such radioactive decay is rare and unpredictable, you machine is likely to resume processing and not have an error again for a long time.

There's nothing you can do to prevent soft errors, and there's nothing to do after they occur. The best you can hope for is to understand them.

Hard Errors

When some part of a memory chip actually fails, the result is a hard error. For example, a jolt of static electricity can wipe out one or more memory cells. The initial symptom is the same as a soft error—a parity failure and your computer shuts down. The difference is that a hard error recurs. Your machine may not pass its memory test when you try to reboot it, or you may encounter repeated, random errors when a memory cell hovers between life and death.

Hard errors require attention—the chip in which the error originates should be replaced.

IBM facilitates finding the error by providing diagnostic messages.

These numbers will appear during the *Power On Self-Test* procedure that your system goes through every time you turn it on. Sometimes they will appear during a parity error, either briefly before the parity error message appears or accompanying it. Armed with the information provided by the IBM memory tests, you can zero-in on the bad chip (or chips) and replace them.

Alas, the memory failure messages, and almost all other diagnostic messages provided by IBM computers, are designed for service technicians and not normal people. They are given in a numeric code that must be translated to zero in on the defective chip.

The secret IBM code deals with system RAM in terms of banks and chips within the bank using binary notation.

Finding a Bad Bank

The first step is to narrow down your search for the bad chips to a specific memory bank. The bank location procedure differs with various types of motherboard, although most compatible manufacturers follow the IBM numbering scheme.

With PC-2s and XTs, the left digit of the error code, should it be from 0 to 3, indicates which system board bank contains the bad chip. Banks are numbered starting with bank zero, which is the rearmost of the four on the system board. (See Figure 6.2.)

PC1s requires examination of the left two digits. 00 indicates a failure in the first bank (the rearmost); 04 the second bank; 08 the third bank; and 0C the bank nearest the front panel of the machine. (See Figure 6.3.)

In ATs take the left two digits of the error code. A number from 00 to 03 indicates the failure was in system board bank zero; from 04 to 07 indicates an error in bank one. Each bank comprises two rows of nine chips, starting with bank zero at the front of the machine. In ATs the lower numbers chips are also toward the front of the machine. (See Figure 6.4.)

Expansion boards in either kind of system complicate matters, but a little math will help sort things out. In any style system, the first two digits indicate the bad bank by its memory address. You must convert these hexadecimal numbers into a memory address, then multiply by an appropriate factor. The bad bank begins with the address corresponding to that number of kilobytes. For 8-bit PCs the multiplication factor is four; for 16-bit machines, the factor is 64.

For example, to determine the bad bank in an XT that produced the

Figure 6.2 **PC-2 and XT memory bank numbers and chip number designations**

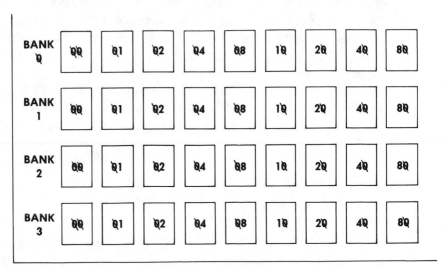

FRONT OF CHASSIS

Figure 6.3 **PC-2 memory bank and chip designations**

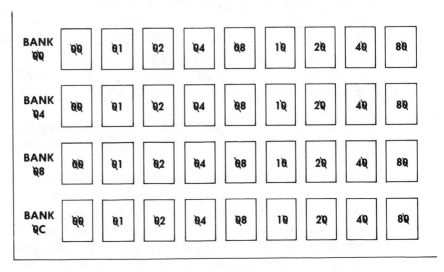

FRONT OF CHASSIS

Figure 6.4 **AT memory bank and chip designations**

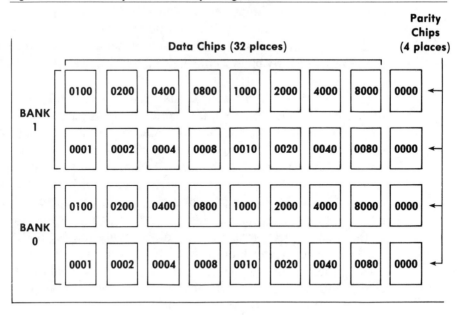

FRONT OF CHASSIS

error code beginning with the digits 18: First convert the hexadecimal 18 into decimal ($16 + 8 = 24$), then multiply by 4. The result is 64K, indicating the error is in the second bank (which starts at 64K because each bank contains 64K).

Finding Bad Chips

In 8-bit PCs, the last two digits code the bad chip or chips. To find it, convert the last two digits displayed by the error code from hexadecimal into binary notation. The location of the 1's in the resulting number indicates the position of the bad chip. The complication is that on the system board you start counting from right to left.

There is yet another complication: Converting two digits of hexadecimal into binary results in eight digits. There are nine chips in a bank. The first chip (the one on the left) on 8-bit system boards is the parity check chip, and it is not included in the position-indicating error code. If the parity check chip is bad, the last two digits of the error code will be zeros.

For example, if you get an error code of 0420, convert the last two digits (20) into the binary equivalent (00100000), so you would count three chips over from the right to find the bad chip.

If, you get more than 1 in the resulting binary code after you make the hexadecimal to binary conversion, *both* indicated chips should be replaced.

In 16-bit PCs the last four digits represent the chip code. Convert these from hexadecimal to binary, and you'll have a display of two 8-bit rows of chips with the bad one indicated by the 1 or 1's that appear in the number.

On AT system boards, the map is backwards just as there are for PC and XTs. In addition, of the two eight-digit binary pairs you get from converting the four hexadecimal digits, the last indicates the chip row toward the front of the computer. However, the chips on the far right (rather than the left) are the parity chips and are skipped in the counting.

The two parity-check chips in each bank are not distinguished from one another in this scheme. If the last four hexadecimal digits of the AT error code come up all zeros, either parity chip in that bank could be bad. You'll have to replace them both.

For Micro Channel PS/2s the pragmatic approach can be much quicker than tangling with math. After all, with the Model 50, where you have two memory modules and you know you have to replace one, why not just pop in the replacement? If it fixes the problem, you've avoided the brain strain. If it doesn't work switch the module you've pulled out with the one you haven't changed, and your problem should go away. The Model 60, and others with four-system-board banks, complicates things with its four modules, but not much.

7

THE
EXPANSION BUS

The expansion bus of a computer has a straightforward purpose: It allows you to plug things into the machine and, you hope, enhance its operation. The design of the expansion bus of a computer is one of the primary determinants of what enhancement products will work with it—whether they are compatible. The design of the expansion bus also sets certain limits on how the system performs and what may be its ultimate capabilities.

Although the concept is simple, the expansion bus itself is not. It represents a complex system of design choices, some made by necessity, many picked pragmatically.

Most important of the necessities are the connections needed for moving data between the add-in circuits, the microprocessor, and the rest of the computer. Among these connections are all the data and address lines from the microprocessor. In addition, special signals are required to synchronize the thoughts of the add-in circuitry with those of the host computer.

Pragmatic concerns involve how these connections are arranged, what connector is used to link system to add-in, and even the physical size of add-in products. Although some of the choices are constrained (you need sufficient connections for the required circuits) the choice of connectors should be made from actual products that are commercially available—the possibilities are almost limitless. Little wonder, then, that so many bus designs have been created and used by various incompatible computer systems.

One of the biggest blessings for the small computer industry was the expansion bus of the original PC. It offered a single standard where none seemingly existed before. At least there was a compelling reason to choose and use it—it was backed by the prestige of IBM, the standard setter in the large computer industry. Compared to other expansion buses used up to that time, the PC bus was nothing remarkable. In fact, it may be regarded as a step back. The *S-100* standard that teetered near universal acceptance only to be steamrollered by the IBM bandwagon, at least allowed for 16 data lines. The new PC bus only accommodated eight. Yet everything needed was there. The expansion bus was entirely workable, and the IBM PC became a runaway success.

In essence, the PC bus was designed to be little more than an extension of the connections on the microprocessor itself. Only a few electrical characteristics needed to be changed. All the connections to the chip are not assigned separate pins on the chip package. A few are combined together (multiplexed) to give the 8088 more legroom. These connections must be demultiplexed before they can be used by the computer's other circuits. These demultiplexed connections are then extended to the PC bus. In addition, the 8088 chip itself is not designed to supply enough power to run the numerous devices that might be plugged into an expansion slot. Consequently, the microprocessor connections are repowered—run through a digital amplifier called a buffer that boosts the current available for running accessories.

Because the bus of the IBM PC (and the XT and Portable Personal Computer as well) are nearly direct connections to the microprocessor, they operate in lock-step with the chip, that is, the clock that controls the PC bus operates at exactly the same speed as the one operating the microprocessor. In fact, it is exactly the same clock, controlled by the same vibrating quartz crystal.

With the advent of the AT, IBM modified the PC bus. The big physical difference was the addition of a second connector to carry more data and address lines, four more address lines and eight data, for a total of 16 data lines and 24 address lines, enough to handle 16 megabytes, the physical addressing limit of the 80286 chip. To make up for some of the shortcomings of the PC which limited its expandability, the new AT bus also included several new interrupt and DMA control lines. In addition, IBM added a few novel connections: One in particular helps make expansion boards compatible across the 8 and 16-bit lines of IBM Personal Computer. It signals to the host that the card in the socket uses the PC or AT bus.

The AT design also made it possible to sever the nearly direct connection between microprocessor and bus. As a result, a separate clock can be used for the microprocessor and the expansion bus (as well as the system timers). This change allows expansion boards to operate at speeds different from that of the microprocessor. Although IBM never took advantage of this capability in any PC (including the AT), this ability is exploited in many high-speed AT compatible computers, which may run their expansion buses more slowly than the microprocessor to permit the use of the system expansion option that might not be able to keep up with a 12 or 16-MHz clock rate. A notable exception is PC's Limited (now Dell Computer Corp.), which, in its early 80286-based PC models, locked the bus speed to that of the microprocessor. Although some expansion boards may not work with higher speed models using this architecture, those that do get an automatic speed enhancement.

All 80386-based computers sever the connection between microprocessor and bus clocks because no expansion boards will operate at the 16 MHz or more that gives the 80386 its performance edge. Even IBM runs the Micro Channel expansion bus of the PS/2 Model 80 at a speed slower than the microprocessor speed.

The bus speed does not need to be a fraction of the microprocessor clock, but keeping it there allows the two to be *synchronized*. That makes it easier to transfer information between the chip and the bus. Moreover, because of synchronizing problems, there is little speed advantage to coaxing a bit more performance from the bus by speeding it up. The microprocessor will only accept bytes when it coincides with its own clock, so the data sits idle while the next microprocessor cycle comes around.

Electrical Function of the PC Bus

Perhaps all of this discussion makes the bus of a computer sound complex. It's not. For all of its connections, the PC bus is actually a simple creature. The 62 pins it uses comprise three grounds, five lines to supply the various voltages needed around the computer—one each -5, 12, -5, -12 volt direct current (VDC), and 2 ground, twenty address lines, eight data lines, ten lines devoted to interrupts, and several special purpose connections to bring it all to life.

Although the list of bus functions is complicated by a wealth of specialized terminology that makes it look as forbidding as the list of ingredients on a candy bar, everything is completely straightforward.

The *Oscillator* line supplies a signal derived directly from the crystal oscillator that runs all the clocks and timers inside the computer. Operating at 14.31818 MHz, it's the frequency standard of the entire computer.

The odd frequency on which PCs were based was actually derived from a very practical consideration. It's exactly three times the speed at which the microprocessor operates and four times the frequency to which televisions (and inexpensive computer monitors) use to lock their color signals. This one oscillator can serve multiple purposes through simple frequency dividers, running both the microprocessor and display system.

The *Clock* line on the bus is one of those signals derived from the Oscillator. It is the one electrically divided by four, to 4.77 MHz, and supplied to the microprocessor and other system circuitry to time and synchronize all logical operations.

The *I/O Channel Check* line provides the microprocessor with an integrity check of the memory and devices connected to the PC bus. If the signal on this line is interrupted, it indicates to the microprocessor that a parity check error has occurred. Grounding this line will effectively crash the system.

Supplying a pulse to the *Reset Driver* line of the PC bus instructs the whole system to reset or initialize itself. A signal is generated on this line whenever the system is turned on, or power is interrupted.

The *Data Lines* carry digital information in parallel form throughout the computer. These same lines are used to move information to and from both memory and input/output devices. Eight data lines are used in the PC, identified with numbers from 0 to 7 with 0 indicating the line carrying the least significant bit of each digital word of information.

The *Address Lines* are used for specifying locations in memory to and from which bytes of information are moved. The twenty total lines are identified with numbers 0 through 19, again with line zero being the least significant.

Microprocessor Bus Control

To read or write memory, the microprocessor sends the memory address that it wants to use down the address lines, then pulses a special line called the *Address Latch Enable* to indicate to devices connected to the bus that it has sent a valid address and that the devices should remember it (by "latching"—electronically locking their circuits to that address). Finally the microprocessor sends a signals down the *Memory Read Command* line which tells the memory controller to put the data at the indicated address on the data lines. Alternately, the microprocessor can send a signal down the *Memory Write Command* line, which indicates that the microprocessor itself has put a byte of information on the data lines and that the memory controller should store that information at the indicated addresses.

The same data lines are used for moving bytes to input/output devices through other special purpose lines on the bus. The *I/O Read Command* line tells a device to move information from an input port onto the data lines so the microprocessor can read it into its registers. The *I/O Write Command* line instructs an input/output device to take the information on the data lines, placed there by the microprocessor, and move it to its output port.

Because the microprocessor can generate or demand data quicker than an input/output device or even memory might be able to handle, the PC bus also includes a provision for making the microprocessor wait while the other part of the system catches up. By removing the "ready" signal from the *I/O Channel Ready* line, the memory controller or input/output device tells the microprocessor to pause for one or more clock cycles.

If the microprocessor does not find a ready signal on this line at the beginning of a clock cycle when it tries to use the bus, it waits till the start of the next clock cycle before trying again, and it continues to wait as long as the ready signal is not present. IBM specifications do not allow these delays to extend for longer than ten clock cycles.

Direct Memory Access Bus Control

Information can be moved from one place in a PC to another much faster under DMA control rather than through the use of the microprocessor. To make those moves, however, the DMA controller must take command of both the address and data lines. In addition, devices connected to the bus must be able to signal to the DMA controller to make those moves, and the controller needs to be able to signal back to the system when it is done. Several bus lines are used for these functions.

The *Address Enable* line is used to tell the DMA controller that the microprocessor has disconnected itself from the bus to let the DMA controller take command. Once this signal is asserted, the DMA controller has charge of the address and data lines in addition to the memory and input/output read and write control lines.

At the end of a DMA memory move, a pulse is sent down the *Terminal Count* line. It is called that because the pulse represents the termination (end) of a count of the number of bytes moved in the DMA transfer. (The number of bytes to be moved must be declared before the transfer begins so they can be appropriately counted.)

Devices indicate to the DMA controller that they wish to make DMA transfers by sending signals down one of the three *DMA Request* lines.

Each line is assigned a priority level corresponding to its numerical designation, with one having the highest priority, three the lowest.

To indicate a request has been received by the DMA controller as well as provide the rest of the system with an acknowledgment of the DMA request, four *DMA Acknowledge* lines are provided. Three are used to confirm the DMA requests across the bus itself, designated by numbers corresponding to the request acknowledged. The fourth, designated 0, acknowledges memory refreshing (which also deprives other devices access to the PC bus).

Finally, the PC bus provides for five *Interrupt Request* lines, which are used for hardware signals from various devices to the microprocessor to capture its attention and temporarily divert it to a different process. The Interrupt Request lines are designated with numbers 2 through 7, in order of decreasing priority.

Interrupts 0 and 1 are not available on the bus but are used internally by the PC in its system board circuitry. The former is controlled by the system timer and generates a periodic interrupt at a rate of 18.2 per second. The other is devoted to servicing the keyboard, generating an interrupt with each keypress. In addition a special interrupt called the *Non-Maskable Interrupt* or *NMI* because it cannot be masked or switched off in the normal operation of the system through software, is used to signal the microprocessor about parity errors.

Note that the NMI can be switched off through the *NMI Mask Registers,* which are available at I/O port 0A0(hex) in the PC and XT. (Similar functions are available in other IBM computers but at different ports.) By loading 00(hex) into this register, the NMI can be masked off and the computer will *not* shut down on parity errors. Loading 80(hex) to this register turns the NMI back on. (Table 7.1 gives an example of how to accomplish this using the DOS program Debug.)

XT Slot Eight

Normally, all the connectors on a bus have exactly the same signals available at the same positions. In the IBM environment that congruency is normally the rule, but like all rules it has an exception: Slot eight, the short slot nearest the power supply in IBM XT system units differs electrically from all other 8-bit IBM PC-bus slots. One connection, which was noted as reserved in the original PC bus, is devoted to a *card selected* function.

Unlike other expansion slots, XT slot eight is electrically separated from the others. In ordinary operation, system board drivers pay no at-

Table 7.1 **Turning NMI Off Using DEBUG**

To turn NMI off and prevent system halting with parity errors:

DEBUG	; Load the Debug program
−rax	; Read the AX register
AX 0000	; System responds with current AX value
:0a	; Load the register with the port number, 0A(hex)
−o 00	; Output 00(hex) to the port in AX
−q	; Quit Debug to return to DOS

To turn NMI on and halt system upon detection of parity errors:

DEBUG	; Load the Debug program
−rax	; Read the AX register
AX 0000	; System responds with current AX value
:0a	; Load the register with the port number, 0A(hex)
−o 80	; Output 80(hex) to the port in AX
−q	; Quit Debug to return to DOS

Note: Port 0A(Hex) applies to PC-class machines. AT-class computers control NMI through port 070(Hex). Substitute this port number when using this routine on AT-style computers.

tention to slot eight—only when the card selected line is activated does the system board respond and link up to the circuitry on the card. The card itself controls its isolation. This feature is designed to be taken advantage of by special purpose adapters, for example the multi-board emulation facility of the 3270 PC.

If you slide an expansion board that makes no special provision for slot eight into that slot, it won't work properly. A few products will not function in slot eight, and their instructions usually warn of that fact. Many vendors of short PC-bus expansion cards (the only ones fitting into slot eight) include a jumper or DIP switch on their boards to allow them to adapt to this special expansion slot. Before you use this slot, check the compatibility of the board you want to put there and modify its setup if necessary.

(Table 7.2 shows the standard XT expansion bus pin-out.)

The 16-bit AT Bus Extension

In the three years between the PC and the advent of the AT, the deficiencies of the original bus design had become apparent. Not only was the bus limited in its memory handling and the width of its data path, but many of the available system services were in short supply for

Table 7.2 **Pin-out of the Standard 8-bit PC Bus Used by PC, XT, Portable Personal Computer, and Most Compatibles**

Pin	Signal Name	Pin	Signal
B1	Ground	A1	Input/Output Channel Check
B2	Reset Driver	A2	Data 7
B3	+5 VDC	A3	Data 6
B4	Interrupt Request 2	A4	Data 5
B5	−5 VDC	A5	Data 4
B6	DMA Request 2	A6	Data 3
B7	−12 VDC	A7	Data 2
B8	Card Selected (XT Only)	A8	Data 1
B9	+12 VDC	A9	Data 0
B10	Ground	A10	Input/Output Channel Ready
B11	Memory Write	A11	Address Enable
B12	Memory Read	A12	Address 19
B13	Input/Output Write	A13	Address 18
B14	Input/Output Read	A14	Address 17
B15	DMA Acknowledge 3	A15	Address 16
B16	DMA Request 3	A16	Address 15
B17	DMA Acknowledge 1	A17	Address 14
B18	DMA Request 1	A18	Address 13
B19	DMA Acknowledge 0	A19	Address 12
B20	Clock	A20	Address 11
B21	Interrupt Request 7	A21	Address 10
B22	Interrupt Request 6	A22	Address 9
B23	Interrupt Request 5	A23	Address 8
B24	Interrupt Request 4	A24	Address 7
B25	Interrupt Request 3	A25	Address 6
B26	DMA Acknowledge 2	A26	Address 5
B27	Terminal Count	A27	Address 4
B28	Address Latch Enable	A28	Address 3
B29	+5 VDC	A29	Address 2
B30	Oscillator	A30	Address 1
B31	Ground	A31	Address 0

growth of the PC beyond a desktop platform for simple, single-minded jobs. At the same time, engineers were faced by the profusion of PC bus-based expansion products, many of those made by IBM, which would be rendered incompatible if the bus were radically changed. A complete redesign would require creating an entirely new line of expansion products for IBM and the compatibles industry, probably creating an outcry loud enough to weaken the IBM standard.

As a result of balancing these conflicting needs, the new AT bus was born a hybrid. It retains compatibility with most previous PC expansion products while adding functionality needed to push forward into full 16-bit technology. In addition, it contains new ideas (at least for PC-compatible computers) that hint at, and perhaps even foretell, the Micro Channel. Inherent in the AT bus but almost entirely unused are provisions for cohabitating microprocessors able to take control and share resources inside the system.

Maintaining physical compatibility with the previous PC bus was accomplished with the simple but masterful stroke of adding the required new bus connections on a supplementary connector rather than redesigning the already entrenched 62-pin connector. Expansion cards that only required an 8-bit interface and needed no access to protected mode memory locations or the advanced system services of the AT could be designed to be compatible with the full line of 8 and 16-bit IBM-standard computers. Those needing the speed or power of the AT could get it through the supplemental connector. The design even allows cards to use either 8 or 16-bit expansion depending on the host in which they are installed. (For example, the MSC Corporation bus-mouse adapter makes such provisions. Although it works in 8-bit PCs, it can take advantage of some AT facilities when installed in a 16-bit slot.)

(Table 7.3 shows the complete pin-out of the 16-bit AT bus.)

16-bit Data Bus Width

The obvious addition required when moving from 8 to 16-data bits is eight additional data lines. These eight new lines, designated Data 8 through 15, complete the sequence started with the first eight, increasing in significance with their designations.

Because both 8 and 16-bit devices may be present in one computer, some provision must be made to indicate how many bits are actually to be used for each memory and input/output operation. IBM uses several signals to facilitate such matters. One of these is called *System Bus High Enable,* and it must be active for 16-bit data transfers to take place. In addition, expansion cards indicate to the host system that the data transfer taking place is a 16-bit operation with the *Memory 16-bit Chip Select* and *I/O 16-bit Chip Select* signals depending on whether the transfer is from, or to, memory, or an input/output device.

Table 7.3 **Pin-out of the Standard 16-bit AT Expansion Bus Used by AT, XT Model 286, and Most 16-bit Compatibles**

Pin	Signal Name	Pin	Signal
B1	Ground	A1	Input/Output Channel Check
B2	Reset Driver	A2	Data 7
B3	+5 VDC	A3	Data 6
B4	Interrupt Request 9	A4	Data 5
B5	−5 VDC	A5	Data 4
B6	DMA Request 2	A6	Data 3
B7	−12 VDC	A7	Data 2
B8	Zero Wait State	A8	Data 1
B9	+12 VDC	A9	Data 0
B10	Ground	A10	Input/Output Channel Ready
B11	Real Memory Write	A11	Address Enable
B12	Real Memory Read	A12	Address 19
B13	Input/Output Write	A13	Address 18
B14	Input/Output Read	A14	Address 17
B15	DMA Acknowledge 3	A15	Address 16
B16	DMA Request 3	A16	Address 15
B17	DMA Acknowledge 1	A17	Address 14
B18	DMA Request 1	A18	Address 13
B19	Refresh	A19	Address 12
B20	Clock	A20	Address 11
B21	Interrupt Request 7	A21	Address 10
B22	Interrupt Request 6	A22	Address 9
B23	Interrupt Request 5	A23	Address 8
B24	Interrupt Request 4	A24	Address 7
B25	Interrupt Request 3	A25	Address 6
B26	DMA Acknowledge 2	A26	Address 5
B27	Terminal Count	A27	Address 4
B28	Address Latch Enable	A28	Address 3
B29	+5 VDC	A29	Address 2
B30	Oscillator	A30	Address 1
B31	Ground	A31	Address 0
D1	Memory 16-bit Chip Select	C1	System Bus High Enable
D2	I/O 16-bit Chip Select	C2	Unlatched Address 23
D3	Interrupt Request 10	C3	Unlatched Address 22
D4	Interrupt Request 11	C4	Unlatched Address 21
D5	Interrupt Request 12	C5	Unlatched Address 20

Table 7.3 (continued)

Pin	Signal Name	Pin	Signal
D6	Interrupt Request 15	C6	Unlatched Address 19
D7	Interrupt Request 14	C7	Unlatched Address 18
D8	DMA Acknowledge 0	C8	Unlatched Address 17
D9	DMA Request 0	C9	Memory Read
D10	DMA Acknowledge 5	C10	Memory Write
D11	DMA Request 5	C11	Data 8
D12	DMA Acknowledge 6	C12	Data 9
D13	DMA Request 6	C13	Data 10
D14	DMA Acknowledge 7	C14	Data 11
D15	DMA Request 7	C15	Data 12
D16	+5 VDC	C16	Data 13
D17	Master	C17	Data 14
D18	Ground	C18	Data 15

Besides slowing down memory access with the *I/O Channel Ready* signal, the AT bus also provides for a speedup signal. The *Zero Wait State* signal indicates the current bus cycle can be completed without wait states.

24-bit Addressing

To accommodate the full 16-megabyte physical address range of the 80286 microprocessor used in the AT, IBM expanded the number of memory address lines to 24. Instead of adding just four new lines, however, IBM elected to add eight.

The new address lines differ from the old in that they do not latch, that is, their value is not held by the system board throughout the memory cycle. Instead, they are asserted only until the memory read or write command is given at which point their value becomes undefined. The expansion board is charged with the responsibility for remembering the address for any longer period needed. This technique can allow faster operation on the bus.

The *Memory Read* and *Memory Write* functions of the AT bus are shifted to the supplementary connector while the bus connections at the positions used by the Memory Read and Memory Write functions of the original (8-bit) PC bus are devoted only to operation on real mode memory.

Memory transfers within the 1-megabyte real addressing range require both the new and old memory read or write lines be activated. When a read or write request is made to the area above the one megabyte limit of real memory, however, only the supplementary connector Memory Read or Write lines are activated. An 8-bit card will thus never receive a command (or be able to issue one) that it cannot act upon.

Added System Services

To make up for the shortages of interrupts and DMA channels that often occur in PCs and XTs when multiple serial ports, hard disks, tape systems, and other peripherals are installed, IBM virtually doubled the number of each. Two sets of DMA controllers are available, one that yields four 8-bit channels, one with four 16-bit channels of which one is reserved for use only on the system board. The operation and priorities assigned to DMA channels follow the pattern set with the PC. DMA channel 0 has the highest priority and DMA channel 7 the lowest.

The number of interrupts was also nearly doubled in the AT—from eight to a total of 15. Not all of these appear on the expansion bus, however. Five interrupts are reserved for the system board: interrupts 0, 1, 2, 8, and 13. In addition, the AT makes provisions for interrupt sharing so that one interrupt can be used for several functions.

Bus Sharing with Other Microprocessors

With the XT's slot eight, IBM made a token effort toward adding more power on the PC bus. With the AT, specific support is given to running more than one microprocessor on the bus.

The bus sharing works like a DMA cycle. The expansion card containing the visiting microprocessor first activates a DMA request and receives back an acknowledgment. Once it has its acknowledgment, the visiting microprocessor activates the *Master* line on the bus, which gives the chip complete control of all address, data, and control lines of the bus. For a short period, it is the master in charge of the computer.

The short period is delimited by memory refreshing, which requires host-system access to RAM. If the visiting microprocessor tries to steal more than 15 microseconds at a time from the bus, the host may lose its memory and mind because the chip gets *total* control and the host isn't even able to refresh its own memory.

To prevent unwanted interruptions during memory refresh cycles, the

AT bus also provides for a *Refresh* signal, which serves as a warning indicator.

32-bit Bus Technologies

While IBM was able to set the standard for 8-bit personal computers by starting the revolution by adding new legitimacy to the product area and for 16-bit PCs by aggressively introducing the AT, its entry into the 32-bit marketplace was delayed more than a year. In fallow fields chaos grows, and in 32-bit anarchy was rampant. Nearly every manufacturer that created a 32-bit computer based on the 80386 microprocessor also designed its own 32-bit expansion provisions. Only the 32-bit Extended Industry Standard Architecture (EISA) bus offers hope, yet even it is questionable.

The results of this free-for-all are both good and bad. In practical terms, the lack of standardization means that your high speed expansion choices in 80386-based PCs are very limited. You are only likely to be able to buy 32-bit expansion products made by the original computer manufacturer. Buy a 80386-based PC and you become a hostage to whatever prices for which the manufacturer chooses to gouge you.

On the other hand, in an effort to make faster 32-bit computers, manufacturers have exploited different bus techniques to extract more speed from what is essentially an outdated architecture—all the while retaining some form of PC compatibility. By using proprietary expansion, manufacturers have pushed performance well beyond the level at which the PC or AT bus is able to operate.

(Table 7.4 shows some examples of the pin-outs of some proprietary 32-bit extensions to the standard AT bus.)

Although nearly every 80386-based personal computer uses a different expansion architecture, the various products can be lumped into several groups, each defined by the technology used for its 32-bit expansion bus. Among these are:

No 32-bit Expansion Bus Since no 32-bit expansion products (other than computer manufacturers proprietary memory boards) were available at the time most early 80386-based PCs were designed, little reason existed to provide a 32-bit bus connector. Only memory expansion was required and if enough space was provided to accommodate a good amount of system-board memory, no 32-bit expansion slots would be

Table 7.4 **Proprietary Bus Pin-outs**

Compaq Deskpro 386 (Original 16 MHz machine) 32-bit Memory Bus

Pin	Purpose	Pin	Purpose
E01	+ 5 VDC	F01	Ground
E02	Data 0	F02	Data 1
E03	Data 2	F03	Data 3
E04	Data 4	F04	Data 5
E05	Data 6	F05	Data 7
E06	Data 8	F06	Data 9
E07	Data 10	F07	Data 11
E08	Data 12	F08	Data 13
E09	Data 14	F09	Data 15
E10	Data 16	F10	Data 17
E11	Data 18	F11	Data 19
E12	Data 20	F12	Data 21
E13	Data 22	F13	Data 23
E14	Data 24	F14	Data 25
E15	Data 26	F15	Data 27
E16	Data 28	F16	Data 29
E17	Data 30	F17	Data 31
E18	Address 2	F18	Address 3
E19	Address 4	F19	Address 5
E20	Address 6	F20	Address 7
E21	Address 8	F21	Address 9
E22	Address 10	F22	Address 11
E23	Address 12	F23	Address 13
E24	Address 14	F24	Address 15
E25	Address 16	F25	Address 17
E26	Address 18	F26	Address 19
E27	Address 20	F27	Address 21
E28	Address 22	F28	Address 23
E29	BE3–	F29	BE2–
E30	BE1–	F30	BE0–
E31	ADS–	F31	MI/O
E32	D/C	F32	W/R
E33	CLK32	F33	CLK16–
E34	MRDY–	F34	M32–
E35	LOWA20	F35	RST–

Table 7.4 (continued)

Pin	Purpose	Pin	Purpose
E36	Address 31	F36	BHLDA
E37	NA–	F37	READY–
E38	Parity	F38	NAM–
E39	+ 5 VDC	F39	Ground
E40	+ 5 VDC	F40	Ground

Compaq Deskpro 386/20E 32-bit Memory Bus

Pin	Purpose	Pin	Purpose
1	Address 00	51	Ground
2	Address 01	52	Address 02
3 +	5 VDC	53	Address 03
4	Address 04	54	Address 05
5	Address 06	55	Ground
6	Address 08	56	Address 07
7	+ 5 VDC	57	Address 09
8	Address 23	58	Address 22
9	Address 21	59	Ground
10	Err0*	60	Address 20
11	+ 5 VDC	61	Err1*
12	Err2*	62	Err3*
13	STB*	63	Ground
14	Address 19	64	Enable
15	+ 5 VDC	65	Address 18
16	Address 17	66	CSEO*
17	CSE1*	67	Ground
18	CSE3*	68	CSE2*
19	+ 5 VDC	69	RASA*
20	RASB*	70	Ground
21	MCAS*	71	Ground
22	MWE*	72	MRD*
23	+ 5 VDC	73	Ground
24	REF*	74	EN1M*
25	System 1Address4	75	Ground
26	4MB0*	76	1MB0*
27	+ 5 VDC	77	1MB1*
28	4MB1*	78	1MB2*
29	4MB2*	79	Ground

Table 7.4 (continued)

Pin	Purpose	Pin	Purpose
30	Data 00	80	SPD100*
31	+ 5 VDC	81	Data 01
32	Data 02	82	Data 03
33	Data 04	83	Ground
34	Data 06	84	Data 05
35	+ 5 VDC	85	Data 07
36	Data 08	86	Data 09
37	Data 10	87	Ground
38	Data 12	88	Data 11
39	+ 5 VDC	89	Data 13
40	Data 14	90	Data 15
41	Data 16	91	Ground
42	Data 18	92	Data 17
43	Data 20	93	Data 19
44	Data 21	94	Data 22
45	Data 23	95	Ground
46	Data 25	96	Data 24
47	Data 27	97	Data 26
48	Data 29	98	Data 28
49	Data 31	99	Ground
50	Ground	100	Data 30

Intel iSBC 386AT System Board 32-bit RAM Expansion Bus Extension:

Pin	Function	Pin	Function
1	Address 3	2	Data 0
3	Address 4	4	Data 1
5	Address 5	6	Data 2
7	Ground	8	Data 3
9	Address 6	10	Data 4
11	Address 7	12	Data 5
13	Address 11	14	Data 6
15	Address 12	16	Data 7
17	Address 13	18	+ 5 VDC
19	Ground	20	Data 8
21	Address 14	22	Data 9
23	Address 15	24	Data 10
25	Address 16	26	Data 11

Table 7.4 (continued)

Pin	Function	Pin	Function
27	Address 17	28	Data 12
29	Address 18	30	Data 13
31	+ 5 VDC	32	Data 14
33	Address 19	34	Data 15
35	Address 20	36	No connection
37	Address 8	38	Data 16
39	Address 9	40	Data 17
41	Address 10	42	Data 18
43	Ground	44	Data 19
45	Address 21	46	Data 20
47	PI 0__7	48	Data 21
49	PO 0__7	50	Data 22
51	PI 8__15	52	Data 23
53	PO 8__15	54	Data 24
55	Ground	56	Data 25
57	PI 16__23	58	Data 26
59	PO 16__23	60	Data 27
61	PI 24__31	62	Data 28
63	PO 24__31	64	Data 29
65	Address 22	66	Data 30
67	Ground	68	Data 31
69	Address 23	70	+ 5 VDC
71	No connection	72	LA19B0
73	No connection	74	LA21B0
75	SLEB0	76	LA19B1
77	SLEB1	78	LA21B1
79	Ground	80	WE__0
81	RMSEL0	82	WE__1
83	RMSEL1	84	WE__2
85	MEMREF	86	WE__3

needed at all. Several manufacturers have followed this philosophy, offering system board capacities from one to eight megabytes. Products from IDR Systems and PC Designs use this nonexpansion expansion scheme.

If you don't need to go beyond the maximum provided by the system-board facilities, these AT-bus-only machines will work well. Remember, however, that OS/2 and other advanced operating systems (if they will otherwise work on a 80386-based clone computer) will require substantial memory—at least two megabytes for OS/2. Should you want to jump into OS/2 with your boots on, you'll need at least that much RAM.

32-bit Memory Expansion Only   A number of manufacturers offer special 32-bit slots on their 80386-based PCs that accommodate memory expansion boards only. These are usually based on a proprietary memory architecture and are understandably incompatible with other products on the market. For example, the Compaq Deskpro 386 uses a static-column RAM board; the PC's Limited 386[16] and Model 300 use static memory. Often (and in the two examples given) these special expansion boards supply all of the system's memory with none present on the motherboard.

The advantages of this technique are, of course, expandability and future flexibility. You're not limited by the finite capacity of the system-board-memory sockets. In addition, you can take advantage of new memory technologies, such as bigger chips, when they become available. On the other hand, practical realizations of this technique yield only one 32-bit slot, which must be used for memory; there is no possibility of 32-bit expansion products beside that.

32-bit Extension to the AT-bus   The logical way of moving from 16-bit expansion to 32-bit would be to try to fit your shoes into IBM's footsteps, extrapolate from the 8 to 16-bit PC to AT move made back in 1984. With any luck, you could hit upon what IBM will do when they finally move off first base. That is what Intel did in designing its first 80386-system board, made as an OEM product (one that other companies can package inside their own cases and sell as their own work and label with their own name brands). The Intel system board features a combination of 8, 16, and 32-bit expansion slots, which allow downward compatibility just like the AT, that is, 8-bit cards fit anywhere and 16-bit cards fit both 16 and 32-bit slots. This design holds the potential of making available real 32-bit expansion products such as screamingly quick hard disk systems, faster-than-lightning display adapters, and the like.

Unfortunately, the odds aren't in your favor when you try to predict what IBM might do with a 32-bit bus, just the 16 additional data lines allow for something over twenty trillion different bus arrangements. Then again, IBM might abandon the PC-bus style entirely and go on to something entirely new—like the Micro Channel.

If there were to be a standard 32-bit expansion addition to the 16-bit AT bus, the Intel choice is among the best ways to go. Alas, even Intel with its second generation 80386-based OEM system board abandoned its own original 32-bit bus design.

Bifurcating the Bus   This technique is a variation of the memory-only bus method, and it is a result of the primary problem facing the designers of really fast computers: To get the most speed out of a machine, you want its microprocessor and memory to race along as fast as possible, but you can't just jazz up the whole system because you'll outrun the cards you plug into the expansion bus. The answer is, of course, a divorcing of memory and input/output functions.

Just as the microprocessor and the expansion bus need not run at the same speeds, there is no real need (other than design ease) to throttle memory down to I/O speed. You can split the expansion bus in two at the bus controller level, providing parallel data paths to memory and the input/output expansion bus. Memory can run at whatever ridiculous speed you can buy chips to operate at. The expansion bus can be kept down to eight or so MHz so off-the-shelf expansion components run reliably.

The very fastest 80386-based PCs all use this technique; for example, Advanced Logic Research in the FlexCache 20386, Compaq in the Deskpro 386/20, and Everex Systems in its STEP 386/20. Run your favorite bench-mark programs on one of these computers, and you'll get some truly astounding numbers.

While the speeds you'll see are accurate and reflect the outstanding calculating performance these machines can turn in, they ignore one reality—the majority of personal computer applications rely on the expansion bus for a lot of what they do. Many applications are disk intensive, others flash images on the screen. The slower expansion bus tugs like an anchor dangling behind the high-speed microprocessor and memory. As a result, boosting microprocessor speed does not commensurately speed up your work (unless you are primarily involved in heavy-duty statistical analysis and other calculation-intensive applications) because no matter how fast the microprocessor runs, it will still be held back by the low speed on the expansion bus required for compatibility with aftermarket-expansion products.

To really break this last performance barrier requires a radical step, a complete redesign of the expansion bus that eliminates the need for, and worries about, backward compatibility with aging PC-bus expansion products. When IBM introduced its version of the breakthrough, however, no one was quite sure what they were getting, let alone whether they were getting what was wanted.

Intel, in its 25 MHz OEM system board provides one method for breaking the speed limit imposed by conventional expansion cards: The Intel board incorporates two special 32-bit expansion slots with the ability to change speeds depending on the kind of card that was plugged in. While the slots were both physically and electrically compatible with PC and AT expansion boards, running at 8 MHz, when special 32-bit Intel bus cards are plugged in the slots run at full microprocessor speed, 25 MHz. The high speed 32-bit interface promises the quickest data transfers of any currently available bus. However, it faces stiff competition from IBM in the guise of the other high-speed standard, the Micro Channel.

Micro Channel Architecture

The new bus that the high end of the Personal System/2 line of personal computers was built around was so radically different from the PC and AT buses that IBM coined a new name for it, *Micro Channel Architecture,* which is a registered trademark of IBM.

The Micro Channel may be the most misunderstood innovation since the beginnings of the personal computer. It is misunderstood because it was unexpected, unanticipated and, in many instances, unwanted. Before the PS/2 introduction, what everyone wanted seemed to be a 32-bit expansion standard to rally around, one that would continue in the mold of the PC bus, an extension of the status quo. After all, everyone—both user and manufacturer—had a substantial investment in hardware built around the PC bus, and abandoning that standard could not help but be costly. If you had money tied up in a production line to manufacture PC-bus based computers or a thousand PC-bus expansion cards, moving to a new standard is definitely unadvisable.

If you think beyond merely monetary matters, however, it should be obvious that the PC bus had to go. The slow speed of the bus (required for backward compatibility) is the biggest performance limit on 80386-based computers which use the PC bus. Even the Intel 25 MHz slot is similar to a band-aid because it does not alter some of the design problems (such as the generation of interference) of the PC bus that limit its high speed operation.

Sever the link with the past and system performance is unfettered. IBM, the creator of the PC bus, was perhaps the only organization in the world that could come up with a replacement for that standard, or at least create a replacement that might be taken seriously.

Examine the Micro Channel and its history, however, and you'll discover performance may not be the major motivation behind its creation. According to IBM, work began on the Micro Channel as early as 1983; this was even before the AT with its extended PC bus went on sale. Little wonder, then, that there are hints of the Micro Channel in the AT.

The Micro Channel Standard

The Micro Channel came along at the same time IBM made the move to 32-bit processing, but it was not required for the upgrade. Rather, the Micro Channel merely marks a rethinking of the computer expansion slot and an improvement to match state-of-the-art technology. It endows the upper end of the PS/2 line, 16-bit as well as 32-bit machines, with powerful new abilities which fundamentally alter the way personal computers work, and make them similar to more powerful mainframe computers.

Not all PS/2s use the Micro Channel, however. Micro Channel models start with the Model 50 and work their way up. The PS/2 Models 25 and 30 use a slightly modified PC bus, one differing from the original primarily by having been physically flipped on its side. Electrically, it is the same old story. The Model 30 286 treats the 16-bit AT bus similarly.

The Micro Channel is a many splendored thing, nothing you can put your finger on, hold in your hand, or even classify in one sentence—it is a jargon term that gives you a single handle to describe a wide collection of specifications and technologies; it is a set of redefined standards for linking various circuit elements and internal peripherals in the more powerful PS/2s.

In those specifications, you'll find the term Micro-Channel Architecture defines the size and physical arrangement of the bus connectors used in the more powerful PS/2s, the electrical signals they carry, and the logical function that dictates how the entire system works.

(Table 7.5 lists the pinout of the 16-bit Micro Channel and its variations for its 32-bit, video, and Matched Memory extensions.)

New Connectors

Some of the more obvious changes from the familiar PC bus seem so obvious it is almost trivial. It uses physically different (smaller) connectors from those used by the aging PC bus—that is fact alone makes

Table 7.5 **The Micro Channel and Its Extensions**

Micro Channel Basic 8-bit Section:

Pin	Function	Pin	Function
A01	Card Setup	B01	Audio Ground
A02	Made 24	B02	Audio
A03	Ground	B03	Ground
A04	Address 11	B04	14.3 MHz Oscillator
A05	Address 10	B05	Ground
A06	Address 09	B06	Address 23
A07	+5 VDC	B07	Address 22
A08	Address 08	B08	Address 21
A09	Address 07	B09	Ground
A10	Address 06	B10	Address 20
A11	+5 VDC	B11	Address 19
A12	Address 05	B12	Address 18
A13	Address 04	B13	Ground
A14	Address 03	B14	Address 17
A15	+5 VDC	B15	Address 16
A16	Address 02	B16	Address 15
A17	Address 01	B17	Ground
A18	Address 00	B18	Address 14
A19	+12 VDC	B19	Address 13
A20	Address Decode Latch	B20	Address 12
A21	Preempt	B21	Ground
A22	Burst	B22	Interrupt 09
A23	–12 VDC	B23	Interrupt 03
A24	Arbitration 00	B24	Interrupt 04
A25	Arbitration 01	B25	Ground
A26	Arbitration 02	B26	Interrupt 05
A27	–12 VDC	B27	Interrupt 06
A28	Arbitration 03	B28	Interrupt 07
A29	Arbitration Grant	B29	Ground
A30	Terminal Count	B30	Reserved
A31	+5 VDC	B31	Reserved
A32	Status Bit 0	B32	Channel Check
A33	Status Bit 1	B33	Ground
A34	Memory/Input Output	B34	Command
A35	+12 VDC	B35	Channel Ready Return

Table 7.5 (continued)

Micro Channel Basic 8-bit Section:

Pin	Function	Pin	Function
A36	Card Ready	B36	Card Selected Feedback
A37	Data line 00	B37	Ground
A38	Data line 02	B38	Data line 01
A39	+5 VDC	B39	Data line 03
A40	Data line 05	B40	Data line 04
A41	Data line 06	B41	Ground
A42	Data line 07	B42	Channel Reset
A43	Ground	B43	Reserved
A44	Data Size 16 Return	B44	Reserved
A45	Refresh	B45	Ground
A46	Key (No Contact)	B46	Key (No Contact)

Micro Channel 16-Bit Extension:

Pin	Function	Pin	Function
A47	Key (No Contact)	B47	Key (No Contact)
A48	+5 VDC	B48	Data line 08
A49	Data line 10	B49	Data line 09
A50	Data line 11	B50	Ground
A51	Data line 13	B51	Data line 12
A52	+12 VDC	B52	Data line 14
A53	Reserved	B53	Data line 15
A54	Status Byte High Enable	B54	Ground
A55	Card Data Size 16	B55	Interrupt 10
A56	+5 VDC	B56	Interrupt 11
A57	Interrupt 14	B57	Interrupt 12
A58	Interrupt 15	B58	Ground

Micro Channel 32-Bit Extension:

Pin	Function	Pin	Function
A59	Reserved	B59	Reserved
A60	Reserved	B60	Reserved
A61	Ground	B61	Reserved
A62	Reserved	B62	Reserved
A63	Reserved	B63	Ground
A64	Reserved	B64	Data line 16

Table 7.5 (continued)

Micro Channel 16-Bit Extension:

Pin	Function	Pin	Function
A65	+ 12 VDC	B65	Data line 17
A66	Data line 19	B66	Data line 18
A67	Data line 20	B67	Ground
A68	Data line 21	B68	Data line 22
A69	+ 5 VDC	B69	Data line 23
A70	Data line 24	B70	Reserved
A71	Data line 25	B71	Ground
A72	Data line 26	B72	Data line 27
A73	+ 5 VDC	B73	Data line 28
A74	Data line 30	B74	Data line 29
A75	Data line 31	B75	Ground
A76	Reserved	B76	Byte Enable 0
A77	+ 12 VDC	B77	Byte Enable 1
A78	Byte Enable 3	B78	Byte Enable 2
A79	Data Size 32 Return	B79	Ground
A80	Card Data Size 32	B80	Translate 32
A81	+ 12 VDC	B81	Address 24
A82	Address 26	B82	Address 25
A83	Address 27	B83	Ground
A84	Address 28	B84	Address 29
A85	+ 5 VDC	B85	Address 30
A86	Reserved	B86	Address 31
A87	Reserved	B87	Ground
A88	Reserved	B88	Reserved
A89	Ground	B89	Reserved

Micro Channel Auxiliary Video Extension:

Pin	Function	Pin	Function
AV10	Vertical Sync	BV10	ESYNC
AV09	Horizontal Sync	BV09	Ground
AV08	Blanking	BV08	Video data 5
AV07	Ground	BV07	Video data 4
AV06	Video data 6	BV06	Video data 3
AV05	ED Clock	BV05	Ground
AV04	Dot Clock	BV04	Video data 2

Table 7.5 (continued)

Micro Channel 32-Bit Extension:

Pin	Function	Pin	Function
AV03	Ground	BV03	Video data 1
AV02	Video data 7	BV02	Video data 0
AV01	E Video	BV01	Ground
AV00	Key (No Contact)	BV00	Key (No Contact)

Micro Channel 32-bit Matched Memory Extension:

Pin	Function	Pin	Function
AM04	Reserved	BM04	Ground
AM03	Matched Mem Cyc Command	BM03	Reserved
AM02	Ground	BM02	Matched Mem Cyc Request
AM01	Matched Memory Cycle	BM01	Reserved

hardware meant for the PC bus incompatible with the Micro Channel.

The new connector choice seemed almost devious. In effect, IBM rendered all third-party peripherals obsolete in one bold stroke. The company earned itself an instant head start against all other vendors in the design of enhancements for the more profitable top end of the PS/2 line.

If you didn't have a few million dollars tied up in PC-expansion inventory and product designs you might see a bright side to the adoption of miniaturization connectors. For one, they make it easier to engineer expansion boards based on *surface mount components,* miniaturized microchips that pack more functions into less space than ever before. Because the pin spacing on the new Micro Channel connectors, in increments of 0.050 inch, corresponds to that of surface mount circuit components, the job of the layout artists (or drafting machine) is easier. On the negative side, they aren't amenable to garage-based engineering because soldering them to circuit boards demands special equipment.

Miniaturization

IBM complemented the smaller connectors and smaller surface-mount components by reducing the size of expansion boards, from the 4.75 x 13.5 of AT boards to 3.5 x 11.5 inches. (See Figure 7.1.) Surface-mount components also help in this size reduction because they require less power and thus produce less heat, allowing more miniaturization. For people who just use computers and don't have to worry about designing

Figure 7.1 **Expansion card dimensions (approximate) compared**

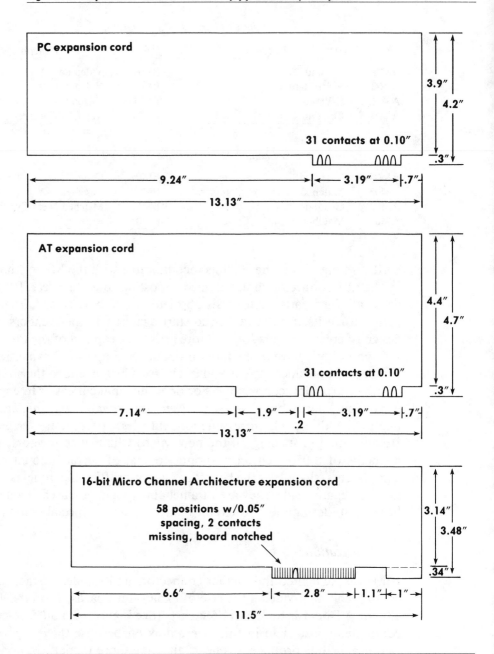

and building them, the smaller connectors, surface mount components, and smaller expansion cards was good news because less of your desk needs to be overrun by rampaging computer equipment.

Unfortunately, much of the promise of miniaturization was slow to be fulfilled. Of all the Micro Channel computers that IBM introduced in the first year the new bus was available, one, the Model 50 for example, took advantage of the potentials of pygmy packaging. The other early Micro Channel computers, the Models 60 and 80, were actually larger than the original PC.

Smaller boards help manufacturers cut costs, at least after the price for developing new designs is paid. They require less in the way of the glass-epoxy base materials the boards are built from. This is only a small advantage, however, because the cost of components, development, and labor far outweigh the price of the glass-epoxy that makes up the board substrate.

Less Interference

On the interference front, the Micro Channel marks a quantum improvement over the PC-bus design. The radically altered arrangement of signals on the Micro Channel puts an electrical ground on every fourth pin. The many grounds and their proximity to the high frequency digital signals on the bus help reduce interference more than would be possible in PCs or ATs. This, in turn, makes achieving FCC certification less of a headache, giving designers one less thing to sit up nights worrying about. Independent lab tests show that the Micro Channel can operate as fast as 80 MHz without interference problems. The AT cannot go much faster than one-third that speed.

More Speed

The better arrangement of signals in the Micro Channel also aids in increasing the maximum speed at which expansion boards can operate because it increases the bandwidth of the bus. That means higher frequencies and higher data rates are possible. The first Micro Channels broke through the old IBM 8 MHz barrier and pushed the limit up to ten. Even the 20 MHz Model 80-111 operates its expansion bus at 10 MHz. The Micro Channel design does not impose 10 MHz as an absolute speed limit, however. Undoubtedly, faster systems will be released.

Signal Enhancements

Rearranging signals and changing connectors were only a small part of the Micro Channel innovation. The new bus design adds extra data lines, more address lines, and several unexpected refinements such as channels for audio and video information:

More Data

The most expected and most awaited enhancements of the Micro Channel were its specification of 16 new-data lines, stretching the width of the bus data path to 32-bits. The wider data path means that memory, input/output devices, and anything connected to the bus can be accessed twice as fast, all else being equal. The Micro Channel is the only IBM-endorsed standard for a 32-bit data bus.

More Addresses   However, the Micro Channel extended more than the data lines. It also goes beyond third party AT-compatible 80386 designs by extending the address bus by eight more bits, raising the total number of address lines from 24 to 32. This extension pushes the maximum addressable memory of the bus from 16 megabytes (same as the AT) to 4 gigabytes (billion bytes).

More Music   Other extensions made for both the 16- and 32-bit Micro Channel designs allow for integrating a single channel analog audio signal of medium fidelity, for instance, synthesized voice or music, with the IBM bus structure. Audio quality is designed to be nearly as good as FM radio, though potenially noisy, with a frequency range up to about 10 KHz. (Technically, the response is 50 Hz to 10 KHz +/− 3 dB.)

The *Audio* signal is the only analog signal on the Micro Channel. The Micro Channel specification allows an analog noise level of up to 50 millivolts, against a maximum analog signal of 2,500 millivolts, an inauspicious signal-to-noise ratio of about 32 dB.

Because this audio channel is incorporated as extension to the bus, the Micro Channel allows expansion cards on the channel to exchange and independently process audio signals.

Video Extension   The video extension to the Micro Channel (a small auxiliary connector, generally only on one slot in each PS/2) allows expansion cards to access the Video-Graphics Array circuitry that is built into the high-end PS/2s. You can plug in a video coprocessor card, which will enhance the performance of the VGA but will connect to your monitor through the video connector on the chassis.

The video extension uses several important signals: There are horizontal and vertical synchronizing signals plus a special control line called *ESYNC* or *Enable Sync*. This line determines whether the synchronizing signals used in the video-system original on the planar board, or from an adapter plugged into the Micro Channel. ESYNC is normally held to logical high, but bringing it low enables the system to use the synchronizing signals from the Micro Channel adapter.

Video data is transferred across the Micro Channel video extension in digital form using eight *Video Data Lines*. The data in this location is used to drive the VGA Digital-to-Analog converter on the system board.

Two clock signals and a special *blanking* signal are also provided. The last switches off the output VGA Digital-to-Analog converter to blank the screen. When this signal is high, the screen remains lit; a low darkens the screen.

Bus Arbitration   The Micro Channel's biggest break with traditional PC design is in its hardware-mediated bus arbitration scheme, a move which puts the high-end PS/2 on par with minicomputers. While the PC bus was created solely for handling the needs of a single microprocessor working on one job at a time, Micro Channel PS/2s allow multiple microprocessors and ancillary devices to share the bus in an organized manner, permitting not only multitasking but also parallel processing.

The key words are hardware-mediated. The AT allowed bus sharing, but required special software to control the system. All prioritizing had to be accomplished through programming, and little support was given to the programmer. Only the implementation of this hardware-mediation is new, however. The idea was borrowed from mainframe computers, an area in which IBM has some expertise.

The current PS/2 implementation of hardware bus arbitration allows up to eight microprocessors and eight other devices such as DMA controllers all to share the single data bus of the Micro Channel without interfering with one another and without the need for elaborate software control systems. Engineers can add in coprocessors, advanced communications, and high resolution graphics subsystems to a PS/2 almost with impunity—and without worrying whether programmers will deliver the necessary code in time.

This hardware arbitration scheme could not be added to PCs or ATs without sacrificing backward compatibility, however. For the system to work properly, all expansion cards—even those that do not exploit bus arbitration to take control—must implement its circuitry. Even if the bus were not modified, the expansion card would have to be. This fact alone would require an entire redesign of expansion card circuitry. As long as the cards were being redesigned, of course, adding the rest of the Micro Channel features was effortless.

New Configuration Procedure   Another indication of this conceptual shift is the Micro Channel's *Programmable Option Select* or *POS* feature, designed to make installation and expansion of system enhancements much easier and less confusing that in previous PCs. POS does away with all the DIP switches, jumpers, and headers that made configuring a system a slightly less arcane ritual than an exorcism.

Using low-power, battery-backed-up CMOS memory much like the AT uses for storing its disk drive types and memory endowment, each PS/2 can remember its own hardware configuration. That includes which board is supposed to be in each of its expansion slots and how that board is supposed to function in relation to the rest of the system.

Every different expansion board designed for the Micro Channel is assigned a unique identifying number that is coded into its firmware. When the system boots up, the PS/2 compares the installed options with its CMOS memory and files stored on its disk drive to detect changes to insure the integrity of its setup. The identifying numbers also serve to link each Micro Channel board data files holding information on using and installing the option. The setup files are automatically incorporated into the software setup procedure on the system *Reference Disk* so you see one seamless installation procedure. That way one simple and familiar installation procedure can take care of any expansion board, no matter its origins.

The PS/2 even eliminates the single switch in every AT and nearly every compatible (including 80386-based models)—the one which selects the default monitor type. The VGA system renders it unnecessary because signals in the monitor cable cause the VGA adapter to automatically adjust for either monochrome or color displays.

Level-Sensitive Interrupts

The Micro Channel also changes how many of the familiar signals carried over from the traditional PC bus work. For example, interrupts, which are edge-triggered on the PC bus, are level-sensitive on the Micro Channel. Systems based on the technology of the old PC means sense interrupts only at the instant when the interrupt request changes state.

In the Micro Channel design the interrupt signal remains active during the interrupt.

While either edge-triggering or level-sensing works for interrupt signals, the latter design confers several benefits in computers in which interrupts are shared. The computer knows an interrupt is active just by examining a level-sensitive interrupt line. It must *remember* that an edge-triggered line has been set. As a result, level-sensing simplifies the design of the logic-sharing circuitry on expansion boards. It reduces the sensitivity of the interrupt controller to noise and transients, and it allows for a mixture of sharing and nonsharing hardware on the same interrupt level.

New Signals

In addition, some new signals have been defined on the Micro Channel bus (besides those used by the new hardware arbitration feature). For example, *Card Selected Feedback* provides an indication from an expansion card to the host that the card is at the address it is supposed to be. It's primary use is during setup and diagnostics to help the system decipher what options are installed in it.

The *Channel Ready* line differs substantially from the I/O Channel Ready line of the PC bus. In the Micro Channel, it is used by devices connected to the bus to signal that more time is needed to complete an operation, not to exceed 3.5 microseconds. Each connector has its own independent signal that is not bussed together with those from other connectors. All of the signals from every connector are combined logically, and if they all indicate that no additional time is needed, another special signal, *Channel Ready Return* is created to make monitoring the condition of the bus easier.

Each connector in the Micro Channel also has its own *Card Setup* line, which is used during setup and error recovery procedures. Activating this signal allows the configuration data space on the expansion board in the connector to be read.

Instead of using separate lines for memory and input/output operations as does the PC bus, the Micro Channel uses a combination of three signals—*Memory/Input-Output, Status Bit One,* and *Status Bit Two* to define the type of bus cycle to be made.

Like the I/O Channel Check line of the PC bus, the *Channel Check* line of the Micro Channel is used to indicate serious error conditions such as parity check errors.

The Micro Channel uses special signals to indicate the bus width of each card inserted into a connector. *Card Data Size* 16 is generated by devices connected to the bus to tell expansion cards that 16-bit information is available to them. The card signals back on *Data Size 16 Return* that it is able to handle 16-bit data. Similarly the signals *Card Data Size 32* and *Data Size 32 Return* indicate and confirm 32-bit operations in 80386-equipped PS/2s such as the Models 70 and 80.

Byte Enable Bits 0 through 3 are used to identify the type of data transfer carried across the bus. They permit Micro Channel components to move information 8, 16, 24, or 32-bits at a time without ambiguity. This aids Micro Channel adapters in using any bus width that is an even multiple of a byte so 8, 16, and 32-bit expansion accessories can be mixed in the same computer.

Memory Address Enable 24, when not turned on, indicates the microprocessor or other device on the bus is using the extended 32-bit addressing range of the 80386 microprocessor instead of the 24-bit range of the 80286.

Matched Memory Cycles

In addition to the wider 32-bit bus and the faster allowable clock speed of the Micro Channel, 32-bit versions of the system allow for a new data transfer mode. Called *Matched Memory,* this mode endows the Micro Channel with the potential of further quickening the pulse of data transfers between the planar board and expansion cards. The new signals take the form of another extension to the 32-bit bus that indicate to the 80386 that the data moving between devices can be synchronized at a higher rate. When memory or a 16 or 32-bit internal peripheral is capable of operating at this higher speed, it can use the Matched Memory provisions of the Micro Channel to speed each information transfer by 25 percent, from 250 nanoseconds per cycle to 187.

The Matched Memory extension to the Micro Channel adds eight possible connections, three of which are reserved for future use and two of which are grounds. The *Matched Memory Cycle* signal is activated by the host microprocessor to indicate that it is capable of handling matched memory transfers. The *Matched Memory Cycle Request* line is actively driven by a device on the bus to indicate that it wants transfers to be made in the faster Matched Memory mode, either as 16 or 32-bit data. A third signal, *Matched Memory Command* indicates a Matched Memory cycle is active.

How the Micro Channel Works

As forbidding as the new Micro Standard seems to system designers, the operation of its most important feature, hardware bus arbitration, is actually easy to conceptualize. It's just a system of several signals that serve as semaphores to let each device sharing the bus know when its turn to share the data bus has come up. Enough controls are provided so up to 16 different devices inside the host computer can share, with each assigned it own level of priority.

To provide a familiar analog to the Micro Channel, IBM relied on the metaphor of a superhighway in its initial explanations. Like the Interstate, the Micro Channel provides, according to IBM, multiple lanes going in every direction at the highest possible safe speed. Because it has more lanes it can handle more traffic, speeding the flow of data around inside the system.

It's a good metaphor and could only be better were it to actually describe how the Micro Channel works. At best, however, it's misleading. The Micro Channel only provides two parallel paths for high speed traffic running next to its (up to) 32 bits of data—one for its auxiliary audio signal and one for analog video information.

A more appropriate and descriptive highway analogy for the Micro Channel would be a Manhattan thoroughfare—one lined with traffic lights, kamikaze taxicabs, pedestrians, and a propensity for gridlock.

The Micro Channel works like the humble traffic cop, breaking up gridlock with a mixture of nerve, willpower, and guts. Just as the officer, armed with nought but his white gloves, keep hacks and hitchhikers out of harms way and keeps traffic flowing, the Micro Channel's hardware bus arbitration gives all the processors sharing the bus its own turn, assuring that nothing bogs down. Data processing flows along in as orderly and efficient a manner as possible. Like the cop, the Micro Channel monitors the highways and gives signals to provide alternate data paths or eliminate waiting. It just keeps everything under control and orderly, preventing collisions and accidents.

Micro Channel bus arbitration accomplishes this task by specifying the hierarchy of signals that each device must use to gain access to the data bus of the PS/2 that it's running in. The arbitration scheme also provides a means of resolving conflicting claims, when two or more devices demand their right to ride the bus. Hardware arbitration prevents the confusion of two devices from trying to appropriate control of the Micro Channel at the same time.

New Lines

To implement this arbitration strategy, the Micro Channel adds several new lines to the old PC bus. Four of these, called *Arbitration Bus Priority Levels 0 through 3,* carry signals that code the level of priority assigned to each device that wants to take control of the Micro Channel, allowing for its 16 levels of priority.

In addition, two additional levels of priority are used by the devices on the system board of the PS/2 and do not appear on the Micro Channel. These special levels are used to assign the absolute top priority to memory refreshing (which preserves data integrity) and the non-maskable interrupt (the familiar parity check error signal).

Bus arbitration involves three additional signals: One, called *Pre-empt,* is used by expansion cards to indicate they require access to the Micro Channel. Another, *Arbitrate/Grant,* is sent out from the Micro Channel *Central Arbitration Control Point* (which manages use of the bus) to start a haggling process for bus access. A final signal, *Burst,* allows Micro Channel devices to retain control while they transfer multiple blocks of related data so they don't have to go through arbitration until the entire transfer is complete. It's a "Do Not Disturb" sign for block-data transfers.

In Arbitration

The arbitration process begins when one or more devices want to take control of the Micro Channel and send that message to the Central Arbitration Point. Once a pause appears on the data bus, the Arbitrator signals all devices connected to the Micro Channel that they should start bidding for control.

Each Micro Channel device wanting bus access then sends out its assigned priority level on the four Arbitration Bus Priority Level lines. Each Micro Channel expansion card checks these signals and ceases its efforts if it finds a higher priority level is being asserted. Conflicting claims of the same priority level should never appear because the Micro Channel design does not allow two devices to be assigned the same priority.

These priority levels are assigned during the configuration process of each Micro Channel board and are stored on disk in the Adapter Description Files, disk files that are associated with each Micro

Channel device during the Programmable Option Select process.

Hardware bus arbitration holds several advantages over the alternative technique, pure software control. With traditional PC architecture, however, such a software arbitration scheme would have to be governed by the host microprocessor, which necessarily handles all software instructions. This microprocessor-mediated process would involve substantial software overhead—the microprocessor monitoring every request from every device and deciding which one should get control. Whenever the microprocessor must take a break from its normal duties to oversee such housekeeping, system performance suffers. In addition, the microprocessor would always be tied up because it would have to constantly monitor the bus; it could not be sent on its own chores while some other device peeked and poked through the system memory.

The Micro Channel breaks the connection between bus and microprocessor. No software is necessary because all of the bus arbitration functions are built into the hardware of the expansion cards. It's a faster and, in the end, a cleaner system.

Turbo Example

One application, perhaps unimportant today, that shows the advantage of Micro Channel hardware bus arbitration is the coprocessor card like the turbo boards used for enhancing the performance of older computers.

In a traditional PC-bus system, handling video (or any I/O) signals becomes a complex, software-intensive chore for a turbo-board coprocessor. One of the most vexing complications is handling the display. Many programs write directly to the screen by pushing bytes of information into video memory. When these run on a coprocessor board, they write to its memory rather than the video RAM of the computer host, so nothing appears on the display. The coprocessor must simulate that video memory in its own address range, accept the data that's written there, then transfer that information to the ordinary video memory of the host.

No matter how adroitly this operation double-writing and shift process is handled (and over the years turbo boards have improved immeasurably in their video handling) video updates always take substantially longer because of the heavy overhead of dealing with two distinct memory systems.

On the Micro Channel, however, this operation is trivial. A coprocessor board would merely map the normal video memory of its computer host into its own address range. When a program writes directly to video memory, the coprocessor board merely takes control of the Micro Channel and routes the display information exactly where it belongs. Overhead is trivial and performance can be extraordinary.

Some coprocessors allow communication with their hosts using expensive dual-ported memory. The coprocessor writes to one port of the memory, and the host pulls the data out the other. With the Micro Channel data can be shared directly in any memory location, and ordinary RAM chips serve the purpose.

One of the most intriguing promises of the Micro Channel is parallel processing, breaking tough problems into small pieces that are simultaneously solved by multiple microprocessors. A single Model 80, for example, might house eight 80386 microprocessors and deliver correspondingly fast performance—about on par with a VAX cluster (considering that a single 80386/80387 combination has nearly the same raw processing horsepower as a VAX 8600).

This parallel processing would, of course, require entirely new software. It's not a technology of today, but it is one that is showing great promise in breaking the bottlenecks in mainframe processing. The Micro Channel makes those same potentials possible in a desktop computer.

EISA

Extended Industry Standard Architecture

To give the personal computer industry a 32-bit bus standard that avoids reliance on the IBM Micro Channel design, an industry consortium lead by Compaq Computer Corporation announced its own standard on September 13, 1988. Called the *Extended Industry Standard Architecture* or *EISA*, the new standard added features to the AT bus that bear a strong resemblance to those offered by the Micro Channel but used a very different implementation.

EISA extends the AT bus with its prime focus on backward compatibility. It's designed to allow the use of any PC or AT expansion board that's capable of running at its 8 (or 8.33) MHz clock rate.

Expansion Boards

To maintain backward compatibility with AT expansion products, EISA clings to the AT standard for board size and available power. It adds its new 32-bit capabilities and bus arbitration through an auxiliary connector installed between the ordinary 16-bit connectors in expansion slots. A special connector extends out of the board to the new bus jacks.

The choice of the side-by-side connector, instead of adding more contacts in-line with the existing AT jack, was probably motivated by two physical issues. Putting all extra connections in line would have created a connector that runs nearly the full length of the expansion card. Little room would have been left on the system board for electrical components. In addition, many proprietary memory cards of existing computers have added contacts on the bottom of cards beyond the 16-bit AT edge connectors. By putting the EISA connector to the side, the new bus remains physically compatible with these specialized memory boards in addition to all AT and PC boards.

Bus Arbitration

While the PC and AT buses were created solely for handling the operation of a single microprocessor working on one job at a time—single-tasking—the needs of computers have grown beyond that minimum. Multitasking operating systems and multiprocessor computers need the ability to allow multiple microprocessors and other ancillary devices to share the bus in an organized manner. EISA adds hardware to allow different devices to take turns using the bus, giving them complete and independent control. The big difference is that the change in control is hardware-mediated. Special circuits organize the operation of the bus. In the PC and AT, those chores are left to the microprocessor itself. While adding extra work to the microprocessor inevitably slows the system down, the hardware circuitry of EISA can handle the multitasking provisions without holding the system back.

The facility for doing this is called *bus arbitration*. EISA centralizes control of the bus in a special *Application-Specific Integrated Circuit* (ASIC) called the *Centralized Arbitration Control* unit. Each of the six devices that EISA allows to take control of the bus is assigned its own exclusive priority level. It sends and receives signals to ask for control of the bus over special bus lines that run from the CAC to the expansion device with the given priority level. A device that wants control signals its desires to the CAC. If more than one device wants control at a given time, the CAC unit resolves any conflicts, then signals down one of the six acknowledgement lines to the device to which it grants bus control.

In the EISA scheme, arbitration levels are fixed. Certain housekeeping functions—memory refresh and Direct Memory Access—get top priority. The next priority goes to the microprocessor. Finally, the six arbitration levels, in fixed order, are given the claim to bus access.

Dual Buses

According to Compaq, EISA earns an advantage in that cache memory is regarded as an intrinsic part of the architecture. The cache allows the microprocessor to continue working even when normal memory is beyond the chip's reach because another device has priority on the bus.

In effect, the EISA system has two buses: one for input and output devices (the actual EISA bus) and a separate bus for memory. This two-bus approach can deliver a tremendous performance increase on multitasking applications.

EISA Memory

This two-bus approach is actually a result of one disadvantage of the EISA design. To maintain compatibility with old expansion cards, EISA must operate too slowly to handle memory at the rate required by high speed microprocessors. EISA thus requires a separation of buses for performance reasons.

As a result, the standardization that EISA brings does not extend to memory expansion. The situation with 32-bit memory cards under EISA is the same as it currently is among 80386-based computers. Every machine will have its own proprietary memory expansion cards. At least the chips for them are somewhat standardized. Channel scheme, however, and the 25 MHz Model 70-A21 implements such a memory cache.

In regard to the advantages of memory caching, the two architectures are equal in their capabilities. In bus arbitration, however, the more flexible, more expandable, and potentially faster Micro Channel holds a substantial edge.

Burst Mode

To move information between expansion cards on the EISA bus and the rest of the system, EISA allows the use of a *burst mode*. Normally, bytes are wrangled between devices one at a time. A special device called a *Direct Memory Access* (DMA) controller negotiates for the bus, sends a byte, then returns the bus to its previous condition, all without microprocessor intervention. Burst mode allows the DMA controller to avoid the setup and shutdown operation between sending sequential bytes. As a result, transfers of blocks of data can be accomplished more quickly.

In addition, EISA supports four different speeds for moving byte with DMA control, each speed based on the needs of the expansion board moving the memory and the technology it uses.

For compatibility with old-fashioned expansion cards designed for PC- and AT-style computers, the default operation of the EISA DMA channels matches that of the AT. Three higher speed modes are also allowed: Type A, Type B, and Type C. The timing that any particular device requires is specified by sending a setup byte to the DMA controller.

The standard AT-compatible mode requres nine clock cycles to set up each burst transfer, then cycles to move each byte. At an 8 MHz bus speed and eight cycles per transfer, this mode can move one megabyte of data in a second, about the same rate as an AT. The first access of a Type A transfer requires seven cycles, then six cycles for each subsequent transfer, moving bytes at a 1.33 per second rate. Type B first needs six cycles, then four for subsequent transfers for a two megabyte per second rate. Type C requires four cycles to set up and one for each transfer.

This last rate is actually faster than DMA transfer should be able to occur because they usually require a minimum of two cycles. EISA transfers, keying the transfers to both the leading and trailing edge of the bus clock. This allows for an eight megabyte per second rate.

Because the EISA specification allows for DMA transfers of 8, 16, and 32 bits at a time, the above transfer rates could be quadrupled in compatible software. DOS, however, uses only 8-bit transfers, so the lower rates mentioned apply for data moves with most software.

EISA Interrupts

While PCs and ATs use edge-triggered interrupts and Micro Channel uses level sensitive interrupts, EISA uses a combination of the two. To retain compatibility with existing expansion boards, it defaults to edge-triggered operation. But it permits each interrupt channel to be reprogrammed for level-sensitive operation for use with devices that support interrupt sharing. A level-sensitive and an edge-triggered device cannot share the same interrupt, however. Moreover, to take advantage of interrupt sharing, any device must be redesigned to use level-sensitive interrupts.

I/O Port Assignment

EISA is designed to prevent one of the most common problems in expanding PC and AT computer systems, port conflicts. To do so, it uses a novel scheme for assigning I/O ports to devices. Each expansion slot is assigned a 4K range of addresses out of a possible 64K, and the slot itself supplies the first digit of the four used in the hexadecimal identification of the ports assigned ot that slot. For instance, slot one uses the addressing range 1000(hex) through 1FFF(Hex); slot two, the range 2000(Hex) to 2FFF(Hex). The identifying number of each expansion board is readable at I/O port xC80(Hex), with the x corresponding to the slot in which it is installed (for instance, 1C80(Hex) for slot one).

Device Identification Numbers

EISA also permits the devices in its slots to be uniquely identified by code numbers that can be read by the computer when it boots up. The computer can use the number to check an adapter description file to find out about the options that the device uses. The device identifying number is located at the same I/O port for each EISA expansion card. The host system can query each expansion board independently to find its number using the slot addressing system.

Identifying numbers are set partly by the EISA organization and partly by the board maker. At the time an option board maker signs up to use the EISA standard, it is assigned a unique three character manufacturer's code. This code serves as the prefix for all the identifying numbers of that company's products. Three other characters can be used to specify individual products, the actual characters selectable by the manufacturer.

8

THE BASIC INPUT/OUTPUT SYSTEM

The *Basic Input/Output System* or *BIOS* of a computer is like the mythical man-beast Minotaur, half hardware and half software. More than that, it's the missing link that connects the two and helps them work together. Like software, the BIOS is a set of instructions to the computer's microprocessor. Like hardware, however, these special instructions are not evanescent, rather, they are coded into the silicon of PROM chips. Because the twilight state of programs like the BIOS, existing in the netherworld between hardware and software, such PROM-based programs are often termed *firmware*.

The BIOS of a IBM or compatible computer is very special firmware, comprising routines that test the computer, others that give it its personality, more to help other programs more smoothly mesh with the electronics of the system, and in computers made by IBM only, a programming language to allow you to use the machine without any other software (or even a disk drive to load it).

BIOS Compatibility

The goal of the compatible computer manufacturer is to match the BIOS used by his machine to that inside the IBM. The match cannot be perfect, however. The code used by IBM is protected by copyrights which forbid others from legally duplicating it. Instead, compatible makers are charged with writing their own BIOS routines without copying IBM's. Many companies seek to do that job themselves, others buy the necessary firmware from specialist firms such as American Megatrends, Inc., Award Software, or Phoenix Technologies, Ltd.

The distinct parts of the BIOS work separately and distinctly even though the code for each is contained inside the same silicon chips. It operates like a set of small *terminate and stay resident programs* (like SideKick or ProKey) that are always in memory and at your beck and call. In this case, they are always in memory because you can't get them out. Such is the nature of nonvolatility.

The one function of the BIOS that's essential to the compatibility of a computer is its software to hardware link of its resident routines.

BIOS Purpose

The design of any computer requires that many of the hardware elements of the machine be located at specific addresses within the range of the input/output ports of the computer. Other computer components have many registers of their own that are used in their control. Because of the number of separate components inside any computer, the potential number of possible variations is limitless. Software that attempts to control any of this hardware must properly reach out to these registers. As long as all computers are crafted exactly the same, with the same ports used for exactly the same hardware with exactly the same registers, there should be no problem.

With the first PC, however, IBM reserved the right to alter the hardware at will. It made no guarantee that any of the ports or registers of the PC would be the same in any later computer. In the well-ordered world envisioned by IBM, programs would never need to directly address hardware. Instead, it would call up a software routine in the BIOS which would have the addressing part of the instruction permanently set in its code. Later computers with different hardware arrangements would use BIOS routines that worked like the old ones and were indistinguishable from the old ones when used by application software. The addresses inside the routines would be changed, however, to match the updated hardware. The same software could thus work with a wide variety of hardware designs.

BIOS Shortcomings

The problem with BIOS routines is that no finite number (or at least no reasonable number) of routines could possibly cover all situations and software needs optimally. Consequently, using BIOS routines is sometimes advantageous but sometimes a bother. In particular, BIOS routines can make many computer functions slow, and performance problems are most evident in the video display. For example, all IBM BIOS routines are designed for putting information on the video display one character at a time. Text can be blasted onto the screen much faster by directly manipulating the hardware.

Another limitation imposed by handling all system operations through the BIOS is that the computer can't do anything that the BIOS doesn't know about. Take, for example, floppy disk drives: when operated in their standard modes, the BIOS routines function well and allow you to read, write, and format floppy disks using the standard IBM disk formats. At the same time, however, they impose limits on what the drives can do. Controlled through the BIOS, drives act exactly like IBM products. However, floppy disk drives are more versatile than the BIOS gives them credit for: They can read and write the disk formats used by other computer systems and others can be used for copy-protecting diskettes.

Direct Hardware Control

The way to make video faster or control floppy disks with the most dexterity is to bypass the BIOS and write programs that directly address the system hardware. At heart, such a concept is forbidden by the IBM dream and could result in compatibility. However, so many software writers have taken liberties with direct hardware control that many of the hardware features of personal computers are more standardized than the BIOS. Most compatibles do an exact job of mimicking all the hardware of a PC. The BIOS's they use, however, are bound to be somewhat different because of the demands of copyright laws. Hardware is actually more standardized (in many respects) than is the BIOS firmware. Even IBM, in effect, admitted some of the shortcomings of the BIOS-only restriction in conceding that the hardware memory locations used by the video display will be supported for as long as possible.

Nevertheless, the BIOS offers other advantages to programmers. In many cases their use can simplify the writing of a program. Certain system operations are always available and can be easily accessed through software. They are reasonably well documented and well-understood, removing many of the concerns and worries of the programmer.

PC BIOS Basics

The IBM BIOS made its debut with the first PC. From this point on it was probably the most copied set of software routines in the world. All PC-compatible computers must duplicate the operation of the PC BIOS without copying IBM's code. The PC BIOS is thus the point of departure for all compatible computer developers. Every compatible BIOS is patterned after the way it operates.

BIOS Operation

The IBM BIOS is designed to work through a system of *software inter-rupts*. To activate a routine, a program issues the appropriate interrupt, a special instruction to the microprocessor. (Table 8.1 lists the BIOS in-terrupts and their functions.)

The software interrupt causes the microprocessor to stop what it is do-ing and start a new routine. It does this by suspending the execution of the code that it is working on, saving its place, and looking in a table held in memory that lists *interrupt vectors*. Each interrupt vector is a pointer telling the microprocessor the location where the code associated with the interrupt is located. The microprocessor reads the value of the vector and starts executing the code located at the value stored in the vector.

The table of interrupt vectors begins at the very start of the micro-processor's memory, address 00000(Hex). Each vector comprises four bytes, and all vectors are stored in increasing order. The default values for each vector are loaded into RAM from the ROM containing the BIOS when your computer boots up. Programs can alter these vectors to change the meaning of software interrupts. Typically, *terminate-and-stay-resident programs (TSRs* are pop-up programs like SideKick, and background programs like Pro-Key) make such modifications for their own purposes.

Because there are many fewer interrupts available than functions you might want the BIOS to carry out different functions are available for many of the interrupts. These separate functions are indentified by *parameter passing.* That is, information is handed over to the BIOS routine as a parameter, a value held in one or more of the registers at the time the software interrupt is issued. The BIOS routine may also achieve some result and pass it back to the program.

PC BIOS Change

The watershed differece between the first IBM PC, the machine with a maximum memory capacity of 64K on its system board, and the PC-2 which has a system board with 256K capacity, is the BIOS. The original IBM PC BIOS was written before such things as hard disks were to become an expected part of a personal computer system. No provisions were made in the BIOS for automatically adding extra code to it. It was *nonextensible.*

Table 8.1 **BIOS Interrupts and Functions**

00(Hex)	Divide by Zero
01(Hex)	Single Step
02(Hex)	Nonmaskable interrupt
03(Hex)	Breakp[oint
04(Hex)	Overflow
05(Hex)	Print Screen
06(Hex)	Reserved
07(hex)	Reserved
08(Hex)	System Timer
09(Hex)	Keyboard
0A(Hex)	Reserved
0B(Hex)	Reserved
0C(Hex)	Reserved
0D(Hex)	Reserved
0E(Hex)	Diskette
0F(Hex)	Reserved
10(Hex)	Video
11(Hex)	Equipment determination
12(Hex)	Memory Size Determination
13(Hex)	Diskette
14(Hex)	Asynchronous Communications
15(Hex)	System Services
16(Hex)	Keyboard
17(Hex)	Printer
19(Hex)	Bootstrap loader
1A(Hex)	System Timer and Real-Time Clock Services
1B(Hex)	Keyboard Break
1C(Hex)	User Timer Tick
1D(Hex)	Video Parameters
1E(Hex)	Diskette Parameters
1F(Hex)	Video Graphics Characters
20(Hex) to 3F(Hex)	Reserved for DOS
40(Hex)	Diskette BIOS Revector
41(Hex)	Hard Disk Parameters
42(Hex)	Reserved
43(Hex)	Reserved
44(Hex)	Reserved
45(Hex)	Reserved
46(Hex)	Hard Disk Parameters
47(Hex)	Reserved
48(Hex)	Reserved
49(Hex)	Reserved
4A(Hex)	User Alarm

Table 8.1 (continued)

4B(Hex) to 5F(Hex)	Reserved
60(Hex) to 67(Hex)	Reserved for User Program Interrupts
68(Hex) to 6F(Hex)	Reserved
70(Hex)	Real-time Clock Interrupt
71(Hex) to 74(Hex)	Reserved
75(Hex)	Redirect to Nonmaskable Interrupt
76(Hex) to 7F(Hex)	Reserved
80(Hex) to 85(Hex)	Reserved for BASIC
86(Hex) to F0(Hex)	Used by BASIC Interpreter When Running BASIC
F1(Hex) to FF(Hex)	Reserved for User Program Interrupts

The PC-2 BIOS (and that of the XT, released at the same time, as well as all later IBM and compatible computers) solved the problem by adding special code to the BIOS routines which makes the machine, as the last step of the boot-up process, look for extra pieces of BIOS code.

The line of demarcation between the two versions of the PC BIOS is October 27, 1982. A BIOS dated earlier than that is not extensible.

Determining the BIOS Date

PC-1 computers are easiest to identify by their memory endowment. Any IBM-manufactured machine that can accept only 16-kilobit memory chips and allows only a total of 64 kilobytes on its system board is a PC-1. If you have such a PC, chances are the BIOS is not extensible.

This method is not foolproof, however. You might not be able to tell one kind of memory chip from another, or you might not want to pop open the case of your PC just to find out the type of memory chips it uses. Moreover, if you didn't buy a new machine new, if someone else set it up for you, or if you do not recall, the BIOS in your machine may have been updated without your knowledge. IBM sold a now-discontinued upgrade BIOS for these early machines that added extensibility to them.

The one sure-fire way to be certain of the date of your PC's BIOS without opening the lid is to examine its BIOS code using the DEBUG program supplied with DOS.

To check the BIOS date of your PC or any other computer (this procedure works on nearly all models), simply run the DEBUG program.

At the hyphen prompt, type the following instruction:

```
D F000:FFF0
```

A mysterious-looking line of numbers and letters should appear on your screen. This line is divided horizontally in three parts. At left is the label of a memory location at which the display of 16 bytes begins—in this case, 0FFFF0(Hex). The central block of characters shows you the individual contents of each of those 16 bytes of memory. The right block gives the ASCII representation of those values (if the value is a printable character). You should be able to read the date of the BIOS directly as it appears in the right column. (See Figure 8.1.)

Other BIOS Revisions

Beyond the PC-2 update, the IBM BIOS has been updated several times, usually to take advantage of new computers or new system boards inside existing computer models. The most radical of these was the addition of the new Advanced BIOS to Micro Channel PS/2s, which added new protected mode capabilities to the natural endowment of those machines. (Table 8.2 lists many of the revision dates of the IBM BIOS.)

BIOS Extensions

Every BIOS since the PC-1 is *extendable*. During boot-up, the host computer can read the extra sections of code contained in add-in boards and add their instructions to its repertory. For example, new interrupt routines may be added or the function of existing routines may be changed.

Figure 8.1 **Reading BIOS date from the screen**

Run the Debug program that comes with most versions of DOS. You'll need to have the program DEBUG.COM in the currently logged disk and directory or accessible through the path command. Then, type

    DEBUG

Once the Debug program loads, you'll see a hyphen prompt on the screen. Type the following command in response to the prompt:

    D F000:FFF0

Debug will respond with a display like that shown below; the BIOS date appears in the right column:

    F000:FFF0   EA AC 86 00 F0 20 30 39-2F 32 33 2F 38 37 FC 45   ..... 09/23/87.E

To exit Debug, at the hyphen prompt type the Quit command, simply the letter Q, as shown below:

    -Q

Debug will then return you to the DOS prompt.

During the Power On Self Test, after interrupt vectors have been loaded into RAM, the resident BIOS code then instructs the computer to check through its ROM memory for the occurrence of the preamble bytes in the address range 0C8000(Hex) to 0F4000(Hex). Should it find them, it verifies the subsequent section of code is a legitimate BIOS extension by performing a form of cyclical redundancy check on the specified number of 512-byte blocks. The values of each byte in the block are totalled using Modulo 0100(Hex) addition. The effect is dividing the sum by 4096. A remainder of zero indicates that the extension BIOS contains valid code.

The additional sections of code are marked by having certain code bytes as their preamble, 055(Hex) followed by 0AA(Hex). Immediately following the two-byte preamble is a third byte that quantifies the length of the additional BIOS. The number represents the number of block, 512 bytes long, needed to hold the extra code.

Once a valid section of code is identified, system control (BIOS pro-

Table 8.2 **IBM BIOS Revision Dates**

PC-1 (64K system board)	4–24–81
PC-2 (256K system board)	10–19–81
PC (latest)	10–27–82
XT	11–08–82
	11–10–86
	5–09–86
PCjr	5–01–83
AT (6 Mhz)	1–10–84
AT (8 Mhz)	6–10–85
	11–15–85
XT Model 286	4–21–86
PC Convertible	9–13–85
PS/2 Model 30	9–02–86
PS/2 Model 50	
PS/2 Model 60	

gram execution) jumps to the fourth byte in the extension BIOS and performs any functions specified there in machine language. Finally, when the instructions in the extension BIOS are completed, control returns to the resident BIOS. The system then continues to search for additional blocks of extension BIOS. When it finally completes its search all the way to 0F4000(Hex), it starts the process of booting up your computer from disk.

External Additions

The ROM chips containing this extra BIOS code do not have to be present on the system board. The memory locations used are also accessible on the expansion bus. This feature allows new ROM chips that add to the BIOS to be part of expansion boards that can be slid into the computer. The code necessary to control the expansion accessory thus loads automatically whenever the system boots up.

Multiple sections of this add-on code will fit into any computer, limited only by the address range available. One complication is that no two sections of code can occupy the same memory area. Consequently, most expansion board makers for the PC-series incorporate jumpers or DIP switches on their products to allow you to reassign the addresses used by their BIOS extensions to avoid conflicts. That's part of the justification for the complicated steps required in setting up expansion boards.

ROM BASIC

One section of code contained in the Read-Only Memories of all IBM computers is not, strictly speaking, part of the IBM BIOS. Nor do compatible computer makers attempt to duplicate it because it is not only protected by copyright law but also undocumented as to function and entry points. This section of code is actually a primitive programming language called *Cassette BASIC* or sometimes ROM BASIC.

The original purpose of the Cassette BASIC language was to enable the first IBM computer to do something—anything—without the need for a floppy disk drive. When you boot up without a system disk in one of your boot drives (hard or floppy), an IBM computer starts the Cassette BASIC language executing.

At the time the IBM PC was introduced, floppy disks were by no means a standard. Many small computers got along fine using only cassette recorders for mass storage. Cassette BASIC enabled the PC to boot up and load a program from tape (as well as run simple BASIC programs).

A more advanced version of the BASIC language was included with PC DOS. However, this BASIC code was designed to augment the Cassette BASIC already in an IBM computer's ROM. Since the code was already in the machine, there was no compelling need to duplicate it

Table 8.3 **IBM Model and Submodel Identification**

System	Model Byte	Submodel Byte	Revision
PC	FF	none	none
XT	FE	none	none
Portable PC	FE	none	none
XT (1-10-86)	FB	00	01
XT (5-9-86)	FB	00	02
PCjr	FD	none	none
AT (original)	FC	none	none
AT (6-10-85)	FC	00	01
AT (11-15-85)	FC	01	00
XT Model 256	FC	02	00
PC Convertible	F9	00	00
PS/2 Model 30	FA	00	00
PS/2 Model 50	FC	04	00
PS/2 Model 60	FC	05	00
PS/2 Model 80	F8	00	00
PS/2 Model 80	F8	01	00

on the DOS disk. Loading BASIC or BASICA from disk simple adds new routines that augment Cassette BASIC.

Non-IBM computers do not have Cassette BASIC built into their ROMs. When a disk is not ready when you boot them up, nothing happens. Worse, when you try to run the BASIC or BASICA language program that is included with PC DOS they are likely to crash. The crash occurs because BASIC or BASICA cannot find the ROM code that it needs to make itself into a complete language. It and your machine lose their minds.

The GWBASIC language sold directly by Microsoft as well as the BASIC interpreter languages that accompany many compatible computers do not need the ROM-based BIM Cassette BASIC to work, so those languages run on virtually any PC-compatible computer.

System Identification Bytes

Also a part of the IBM ROM, but not strictly part of the BIOS, are IBM's *System Identification Bytes.* These two bytes of code can be read by programs so the program will know what kind of computer or system board that it is attempting to run on.

Originally, IBM assigned one byte to this purpose. Starting with the XT Model 286, however, IBM added a second byte to permit more specific identification. In IBM nomenclature, these are called the *Model Byte* and the *Submodel Byte.*

The Model Byte is located at absolute memory address 0FFFFE(hex) and the Submodel byte follows it. (Table 8.3 lists the Model and Submodel Byte values for various IBM computers.) Compatible computers generally use the byte value of the system to which they are the closest match.

BIOS Data Area

Once the BIOS code starts executing, it makes use of part of the host system's memory to store parameter values important to its operation. Included among the data that it stores are *equipment flags,* the base addresses of input/output adapters, keyboard characters, and operating modes. This *BIOS data area* comprises 256 bytes of memory, starting at absolute memory location 0000400(Hex). (Table 8.4 lists the definition of some of the more important (and interesting) bytes in the BIOS data area.)

Table 8.4 **Important BIOS Data Area Assignments**

Address	Function
0400	Base address of first RS232 adapter (COM1)
0402	Base address of second RS232 adapter (COM2)
0404	Base address of third RS232 adapter (COM3) PS/2s only
0406	Base address of fourth RS232 adapter (COM4) PS/2s only
0408	Base address of first printer adapter (LPT1)
040A	Base address of second printer adapter (LPT2)
040C	Base address of third printer adapter (LPT3)
0410	Installed hardware flags
	Bit 0 = IPL diskette
	Bit 1 = Numeric coprocessor
	Bit 2 = Pointing device (except PC, XT, AT, and Convertible)
	Bit 4,5 = Video mode
	01 = 40 × 25 color; 10 = 80 × 25 color; 11 = 80 × 25 mono
	Bit 6,7 = Number of floppy disk drives
	Bits 9,10,11 = Number of serial ports
	Bit 13 = Internal model (Convertible only)
	Bits 14,15 = Number of printer adapters
0412	Initialization flags
0413	Base memory size in kilobytes (0 to 640)
0417	Keyboard status flags
	Bit 0 = Right shift key pressed
	Bit 1 = Left shift key pressed
	Bit 2 = Ctrl key pressed
	Bit 3 = Alt key pressed
	Bit 4 = Scroll Lock locked
	Bit 5 = Num Lock locked
	Bit 6 = Caps Lock locked
	Bit 7 = Insert locked
0418	Additional keyboard status flags
	Bit 0 = Left Ctrl key pressed
	Bit 1 = Left Alt key pressed
	Bit 2 = Sys Req key pressed
	Bit 3 = Pause locked
	Bit 4 = Scroll Lock key pressed
	Bit 5 = Num Lock key pressed
	Bit 6 = Caps Lock key pressed
	Bit 7 = Insert key pressed
0419	Storage for alternate keypad entry

Table 8.4 (continued)

Address	Function
041A	Pointer to head of keyboard buffer
041C	Pointer to tail of keyboard buffer
041E to 042D	Keyboard buffer
043E	Diskette drive seek status Bit 0 = Recalibrate drive 0 Bit 1 = Recalibrate drive 1 Bit 2 = Recalibrate drive 2 Bit 3 = Recalibrate drive 3 Bit 7 = Interrupt flag
043F	Diskette drive motor status Bit 0 = Drive 0 motor on status Bit 1 = Drive 1 motor on status Bit 2 = Drive 2 motor on status Bit 3 = Drive 3 motor on status Bits 4,5 = Drive selected 00 = Drive 0; 01 = Drive 1; 10 = Drive 2; 11 = Drive 3 Bit 7 Write/Read operation flag
0440	Diskette drive motor count
0441	Last diskette drive operation status flag 00 = No error 01 = Invalid diskette drive parameter 02 = Address mark not found 03 = Write-protect error 04 = Requested sector not found 06 = Diskette change line active 08 = DMA overrun on operation 09 = Attempted DMA access across a 64K boundary 0C = Media type not found 10 = Cyclical Redundancy Check error on diskette read 20 = General controller failure 40 = Seek operation failure 80 = Diskette drive not ready
0449	Current video mode
044A	Number of columns displayed on monitor screen
044C	Length of regen buffer in bytes
044E	Starting address in regen buffer

Table 8.4 (continued)

Address	Function
0450 to 045F	Current cursor position for up to 8 pages
0460	Cursor mode setting
0462	Current page being displayed
0463	Base address for active video adapter board
0465	Current setting of the 3X8 register
0466	Current setting of the 3X9 register (video palette)
046C to	Current timer count046F
0470	Flag indicating timer has rolled over since last read
0471	Flag indicating that Break key has been pressed
0472	Reset flag 1234 = Bypass memory test 4321 = Preserve memory on reset (Micro Channel PS/2s only) 5678 = System suspended (Convertible only) 9ABC = Manufacturing test mode (Convertible only) ABCD = System POST loop mode (Convertible only)
0474	Hard disk status flag (results of last operation) 00 = No error 01 = Invalid function request 02 = Address mark not found 03 = Write protect error 04 = Sector not found 05 = Reset failure 07 = Drive parameter activity failure 08 = DMA overrun on an operation 09 = Data boundary error 0A = Bad sector flag detected 0B = Bad track detected 0D = Invalid number of sectors on format 0E = Control data address mark detected 0F = DMA arbitration level out of range 10 = Uncorrectable ECC or CRC error 11 = ECC corrected data error 20 = General controller failure 40 = Seek operation failure 80 = Time out

Table 8.4 (continued)

Address	Function
	AA = Drive not ready
	BB = Undefined error occurred
	CC = Write fault on selected drive
	E0 = Status error
	FF = Sense operation failed
0475	Number of hard disks installed
0476	Fiuuxed disk drive controller port (XT only)
0478	Timeout counter for LPT1 printer response
0479	Timeout counter for LPT2 printer response
047A	Timeout counter for LPT3 printer response
047C	Timeout counter for COM1 serial device response
047D	Timeout counter for COM2 serial device response
047E	Timeout counter for COM3 serial device response
047F	Timeout counter for COM4 serial device response
0480	Base address of beginning of keyboard buffer
0482	Base address of end of keyboard buffer
0484	Rows displayed on monitor (less one)
0485	Character height (bits per character, EGA and thereafter)
0488	Feature bit switches
048B	Flag indicating last diskette data rate selected Bits 6,7: 00 = 500Kbyte/sec; 01 = 300Kbytes/sec; 10 = 250Kbytes/sec
048C	Status register flag
048D	Error register flag
048E	Hard disk interrupt flay

0490	Drive A media state flag
	Bits 1,2,3:
	    000 = 360K diskette/360K drive not established
	    001 = 360K diskette/1.2M drive not established
	    010 = 1.2M diskette/1.2M drive not established
	    011 = 360K diskette/360K drive established
	    100 = 360K diskette/1.2M drive established
	    101 = 1.2M diskette/1.2M drive established
	    111 = None of the above
	Bit 4 = Media established
	Bit 5 = Double-stepping required (360K disk in 1.2M drive)
	Bits 6,7: 00 = 500Kbyte/sec; 01 = 300Kbytes/sec; 10 = 250Kbytes/sec

Table 8.4 (continued)

Address	Function
0491	Drive B media state flag
	Same as above
0492	Drive A operation start state flag
0493	Drive Boperation state state flag
0494	Drive A present cylinder flag
0495	Drive B present cylinder flag
0496	Keyboard mode state and type flags
	Bit 0 = Last code was E1 hidden code
	Bit 1 = Last code was E0 hidden code
	Bit 2 = Right Ctrl key pressed
	Bit 3 = Right Alt key pressed
	Bit 4 = 101/102-key (Advanced) keyboard installed
	Bit 5 = Force Num Lock if read ID and KBX
	Bit 6 = LAst character was First ID character
	Bit 7 = Read ID in progress
0497	Keyboard LED flags
	Bit 0 = Scroll Lock on
	Bit 1 = Num Lock on
	Bit 2 = Caps Lock on
	Bit 3 = Reserved (must be 0)
	Bit 4 = Acknowledgement received
	Bit 5 = Resend receive flag
	Bit 6 = Mode indicator update
	Bit 7 = Keyboard transmit error flag
04CE	Calendar (count of days since January 1, 1980)
0500	Print screen status flag
	00 = Ready/okay
	01 = Print screen in progress
	FF = Error

PS/2 BIOS Innovations

Because the PS/2 is an entirely new kind of computer, IBM had to revise many aspects of its BIOS to handle its added functions. The result was that BIOS firmware was more tightly integrated with the rest of the system than ever before. The BIOS was part of a complete system that included new system board hardware and special software for aiding in setup. The additions help the computer better adjust itself for the options and accessories that you install inside it.

Programmable Option Select

The *Programmable Option Select* or *POS* of the Micro Channel removes the need for jumpers and DIP switches entirely because all configuration is handled through software. Setup information is stored both in CMOS memory and in special disk files. The PS/2 BIOS automatically loads the stored configuration information into each expansion board every time the system is booted up. The BIOS also insures the integrity of the setup information.

The Programmable Option Select process is keyed to adapter identification numbers, unique designations assigned to each model of Micro Channel adapter. These identification numbers are coded as four digits and stored as two bytes of data. Every Micro Channel expansion board must have such a number. Although IBM acts as a clearinghouse and attempts to prevent conflicts, some makers of Micro Channel accessories may invent their own numbers, creating the possibility of conflicts, or may copy the numbers used by IBM for similar adapters, perhaps to add legitimacy or an aura of compatibility to their products. Neither strategy is recommended in that there is no dearth of identifying numbers. The two byte approach makes 65,536 numbers possible, so assigning a unique number to each expansion product will likely be possible for a long time to come.

The Programmable-Option-Select process begins by individually selecting each expansion slot and querying it about the presence of an adapter. If no adapter resides in the slot, no response will be forthcoming. If an adapter is present, the POS procedure queries it for its adapter identification number. This number is compared to the value stored in CMOS memory assigned to that slot.

Adapter Description Files

If the two numbers match, the POS looks for an *Adapter Description File* on the boot disk. This special file contains setup information for configuring the associated adapter. If the file is found, its values are read and the card is set up, then the next slot is queried.

If the identifying number read from the card does not match the number stored in CMOS or if the Adapter Description File is not found, an error results and you have the honor of running the system configuration utility again.

IBM prescribes the exact contents and arrangement of the Adapter Description File because its contents are used by the configuration utility on the PS/2 Reference Diskette. All the prompts and option choices are listed in the file. These are read into and displayed by the configuration menu.

An Adapter Configuration File can be recognized by its filename extension .ADF. The four numbers in the file name are the same as the identifying number assigned to the associated adapter.

Before a Micro Channel expansion board can be properly configured, its associated .ADF file must be transferred to your working copy of your Reference Diskette. The configuration procedure provides an option for carrying out this copying process as the menu selection, "Copy an option diskette."

Some Micro Channel options also include *diagnostic code modules* and *Power-On Self-Test Error Message Files.* These can be identified by their filenames, which are keyed to the identifying number of the option and should also be transfered to the working copy of your Reference Diskette.

PS/2 Advanced BIOS

With the introduction of the Micro Channel PS/2, IBM revised its standard BIOS with the addition of new protected mode routines designed to facilitate the use of OS/2 and other advanced applications. Instead of integrating them into the existing BIOS, IBM chose to make the new routines a separate entity so the PS/2 BIOS consists of two sections that take up nearly 128K of Read-Only Memory.

The first is called the *Compatibility BIOS* or *CBIOS*. it addresses only the first megabyte of system memory and is used by PC DOS. It is fully compatibile with the previous IBM BIOS, hence its designation.

The second section of BIOS code is all new. Called the *Advanced BIOS* or *ABIOS,* it can address all the memory within the 16-megabyte range of the 80286 microprocessor in its protected mode. The ABIOS is specifically designed to provide support for multitasking systems which include, of course, OS/2.

The way the ABIOS work differs substantially from the operation of the CBIOS. Instead of using software interupts and parameter passing for accessing hardware devices, it is based on a call system that is meant to integrate with programming language subroutines. To make use of an ABIOS routine, a program just transfers control to a subroutine, which sends control back to the program once the routine is completed.

Unlike the CBIOS, the ABIOS is reentrant. This feature allows it to issue a second call while waiting for the results of the first call. For example, a program may request that the ABIOS read a cluster of data from the system's floppy disk drive. However, the disk might not be ready to transfer data. The ABIOS routine would let you know that the disk wasn't ready but would continue to keep trying to read the disk. Because the ABIOS routine is reentrant, the underlying program can issue a second call, such as to another disk drive. This reentrant ability permits the ABIOS of Micro Channel PS/2s to operate in a true multitasking mode.

9

SUPPORT
CIRCUITRY

Making a computer requires more than a mere microprocessor, otherwise a microprocessor *would* be a computer. However, a computer requires a number of support functions to make the microprocessor useful—and make the microprocessor work.

Clocks and Oscillators

Today's personal computers are built using a circuit design known as *clocked logic*. All the logic elements in the computer are designed to operate synchronously. They carry out their designated operations one step at a time and each circuit makes one step at the same time like all the rest of the circuits in the computer. This synchronous operation helps the machine keep track of every bit that it processes, assuring that nothing slips between the cracks.

The system *clock* is the conductor who beats the time that all the circuits follow. The clock, however, must get its cues from somewhere, either its own internal sense of timing or some kind of metronome.

An electronic circuit that accurately and continuously beats time is termed an *oscillator*. Most oscillators work on a simple feedback principle. Like the microphone that picks up its own sounds from public address speakers too near or turned up too high, the oscillator, too, listens to what it says. As with the acoustic feedback squeal the public address system complains with, the oscillator, too, generates it own howl. Because the feedback circuit is much shorter, however, the signal need not travel as far and their frequency is higher, perhaps by several thousand fold.

The oscillator takes its output as its input, then amplifies the signal, sends it to its output where it goes back to the input again in an endless and out of control loop. By taming the oscillator by adding impediments to the feedback loop, and by adding special electronic components between the oscillator's output and its input, the feedback and its frequency can be brought under control.

Increasingly a carefully crafted *crystal* of quartz is used as this control element. Quartz is one of many piezoelectric compounds. Piezoelectric materials have an interesting property—if you bend one, it makes a tiny voltage, or if you apply a voltage to a it in the right way, the piezoelectric material will bend.

Quartz crystals do this exactly. More importantly, however, by stringently controlling the size and shape of a quartz crystal, it can be made to resonate at a specific frequency. The frequency of this resonance is extremely stable and very reliable—so much so that it can help an electric watch keep time to within seconds a month.

PC Oscillators and Timers

The PC, XT, Portable PC, and PCjr are all built around one such oscillator that uses a crystal that resonates at 14.31818 MHz. The odd frequency was chosen for a particular reason—it's exactly four times the subcarrier frequency used in color television signals (3.58 MHz), and the engineers who created the original PC thought compatibility with televisions would be an important design element of the PC.

This actual oscillator is made from a special integrated circuit, type 8284A, and a crystal that resonates at 14.31818 MHz. An output of that frequency is routed to the bus. Another output is divided down by an auxiliary chip to create the 1.19 MHz that feeds the timer/counter circuit. This chip also divides the fundamental crystal frequency by three to produce the 4.77 MHz. This signal is the actual clock used by the PC to synchronize all the logic operations inside the PC and other IBM 8-bit bus computers. It also determines the operating speed of the system microprocessor.

PC System Timer

One of the logic circuits driven by the PC system clock is a type *8253 timer/counter* chip. Actually three 16-bit timers in one, the 8253 derives several important signals from the system clock. One of its outputs controls the time-of-day clock inside the PC, another controls the Direct Memory Access circuitry of the computer, and the third is used to operate the speaker.

The timer operates by counting the clock pulses it receives, reducing the value it holds in an internal register by one each time it receives a pulse. In the PC series of computers, the signal it uses for this timing function is the system clock that has been divided again by four, to about 1.19 MHz.

The 8253 can be set up (through I/O ports in the PC) to work in any of six different modes, two of which can only be used on the speaker channel. In the most straightforward, Mode 2, it operates as a frequency divider or rate generator. You load its register with a number, and it counts to that number. When it reaches it, it outputs a pulse and starts all over again. Load the 8253 register with 2 and it will send out a pulse at half the frequency of the input. Load it with one thousand, and the output will be 1/1000th the input.

(The six modes and their function and programming are given in Table 9.1.)

The time-of-day signal uses the timer to count out the longest increment it can, 65,535 clock pulses. The output pulse occurs 18.2 times per second. The pulses cause an interrupt, and the PC counts the interrupts to keep track of the time. These interrupts can also be used by programs that need to regularly investigate what the computer is doing, for exam-

Table 9.1 **Operating Modes of 8253 Timer/Counter Chip**

Mode 0—Interrupt on Terminal Count
   Operation: Timer is loaded with a value and counts down from that value to zero, one count per clock pulse.

Mode 1—Hardware Retriggerable One-Shot
   Operation: A trigger pulse causes timer output to go low; when the counter reaches zero, the output goes high and stays high until reset. The process repeats every time triggered. Pulse length set by writing a control word and initial count to chip before first cycle.

Mode 2—Rate Generator
   Operation: Timer divides incoming frequency by the value of the initial count loaded into it.

Mode 3—Square Wave
   Operation: Produces a series of squares waves with a period (measured in clock pulses) equal to the value loaded into the timer.

Mode 4—Software Retriggerable Strobe
   Operation: Timer counts down the number of clock cycles loaded into it, then pulses its output. Software starts the next cycle.

Mode 5—Hardware Retiggerable Strobe
   Operation: Timer counts down the number of clock cycles loaded into it, then pulses its output. Hardware-generated pulse initiates the next cycle.

ple, checking the hour to see if it is time to dial up a distant computer.

The speaker section of the 8253 works the same way, only it generates a waveform that is used to power the speaker and make sounds. Programs can modify any of its settings to change the sound of the speaker. Likewise, programs can modify the other two channels of the 8253. While modifying the first channel can be useful in some programs, it can also result in your PC keeping bad time. Modifying the channel that drives the DMA controller will likely crash your computer.

Bad Speed-Up Strategy

Because the 14.31818 crystal determines the speed at which a PC or related computer operates, an easy way to boost the performance of the system would seem to be replacing the crystal with one operating at a higher frequency. While this strategy will actually work, it is not a good idea for several reasons.

One problem is easily solved. Although the standard 8088 microprocessor in the PC is rated at only 5 MHz, you can swap it out for one that will handle a faster clock—an 8088-2 or NEC V-20, for example. But other parts of the PC must be brought up to speed, too. You will have to upgrade system memory so it can be on par with the higher clock rate, for instance. In addition, changing the crystal itself will be more work than you realize because the crystal is soldered in place, and the multi-layer construction of the PC system board makes desoldering the crystal a delicate job.

Those obstacles pale when compared to the dubious result you'll get. Because all timings throughout the whole PC system are locked to that one oscillator, odd things will happen—the system clock won't keep very good time, perennially kept in a high speed time warp; software depending on system timings may crash; and even your floppy disks may operate erratically with some software.

The moral is: The oscillator and clock circuitry of the PC and related computers were designed to run solely at a single and predefined speed. Don't mess with them.

AT Oscillator/Timer

The seeming goal in the oscillator/clock design of the PC was crystal frugality. Those systems generate one master frequency that gets cut, chopped, minced, and diced into whatever else is needed in the computer. It is perhaps a worthy goal if you want to save the dollar or so a crystal costs (and if you want to insure everything in the computer operates synchronously), but such a design does limit flexibility.

AT Oscillators

The more enlightened AT design broke the system clock free from the bondage of the timer and its oscillator. Instead of just one crystal and oscillator, the AT uses three. One is used to drive the system clock for synchronizing the bus, microprocessor, and related circuits. Another operates at 14.31818 MHz and provides input to a timer/counter chip and a 14.31818 bus signal for compatibility with the PC. The third oscillator controls the CMOS time-of-day clock that runs on battery power even when the computer is switched off.

The oscillator of the AT is much the same as that of the PC, even based on the same 8284A timer chip and 14.31818 MHz crystal. Its output is routed to the bus. Another output is divided down to the 1.19 MHz that feeds the timer/counter circuit.

AT Timer/Counter

The timer/counter of the AT is similar to that of earlier IBM computers except it is based on an 8254-2 chip. It provides three outputs: One generates the 18.2 per second pulse that drives the time-of-day signal and interrupt; the second provides a trigger for memory refresh cycles, fixed in the case of the AT to produce a signal with a period of 15 milliseconds; and the third drives the speaker. Controls for these operate in the same way as those for the related PC functions and are found at the same I/O ports.

AT System Clock

The AT dedicates a special circuit to generating its system clock signal, a type *82284 System Clock Generator* chip. The clock frequency is governed by a crystal associated with this chip. The 82284 divides the crystal frequency in half to produce the clock that controls the speed of the microprocessor, bus, and associated circuitry.

AT Speed-Up

The first AT model used a 12 MHz crystal to produce an operating frequency of 6 MHz. Later AT models used a 16 MHz crystal which produced an 8 MHz operation.

The 6 MHz speed of the first AT generated considerable debate in the user community. Many people felt the performance of the machine was artificially limited, that its circuitry and constituent parts were capable of faster operation.

The point was easily proved because the clock crystal of the AT is mounted in a socket and can readily and easily be changed. Although higher speed operation in 6 MHz ATs is not officially sanctioned by IBM, most experimenters reported their ATs operated flawlessly at 8 MHz. Many ventured further into the unknown, to 9 MHz and beyond, but found that their machines become somewhat temperamental and sometimes temperature sensitive.

If you have a 6 MHz AT and are curious or want the absolute most from your computing investment, you can easily replace its clock-controlling crystal yourself. The job requires no tools other than a screwdriver or nutdriver needed to get inside your system unit.

Once you have access to the system board, the crystal is easy to find. It's a small, (3/16 of an inch wide, half an inch long and slightly taller (silver can located in the right rear quadrant of the AT system board. Because of its socket, you can readily slide it out and another one in without soldering. Crystals are available at the corner Radio Shack or through mail order suppliers. Some companies even offer synthesized multi-speed oscillators with selector switches that allow you to choose any operating frequency from about 8 to 14 MHz.

Note that Radio Shack crystals are not guaranteed to work in your AT and probably won't be a perfect fit. The diameter of their leads is usually smaller than what the socket in the AT is designed to accept. You may have to bend the leads of the Radio Shack crystal double to make good contact. Remember that you'll need a crystal rated for *twice* the frequency at which you want your machine to operate.

Should you choose to move your 6 MHz AT into high performance territory, remember the microprocessor is not the only speed-sensitive component in the AT. The rest of its circuitry will be stretched to its limits, too. In particular, you'll probably want to upgrade its RAM from IBM's stock 150-nanosecond chips to 120, 100, or 90-nanosecond chips.

AT Speed Limit

When IBM upgraded the AT to 8-MHz operation, a subtle change was made to the system BIOS. When the machine boots up, the BIOS checks the clock rate of the computer (by comparing microprocessor speed to the system timer). If the machine is operating at a speed other than the one for which it was designed—that is, should someone have tried to soup up its performance with a new, higher speed crystal—the AT won't boot. The intent behind this BIOS change can only be inferred because IBM keeps the reasons behind its decision-making its own secret. The change was definitely meant to thwart anyone changing the crystal in his PC. Rather than force slow speeds on the tinker, it was probably aimed as an aid to IBM's service force. High speed crystals inside ATs can lead to their working intermittently, causing them to crash for no reason. The preventive scheme is sour medicine, but it's for your own good. It prevents you from getting in trouble—and blaming IBM for your deviltry.

Some tinkers appreciate a challenge, and this AT speed-up situation provided a good one. A number of products have been developed to coax more performance from the AT: They work on a simple principle. They keep the clock speed down to the stock rate while the system is booting up, for once the BIOS speed test is over, they kick into high gear.

While these products do work, one important speed-up caveat still applies: Push your AT too close to the edge, and it may slip over the brink and crash. Any modification pushes your AT dangerously closer to its limits, and a speed boost is more dangerous than most.

XT Model 286 Oscillator/Timer

IBM's half-breed computer, the XT Model 286, is essentially an AT in an XT case (with a slow hard disk). Its oscillator and timing circuitry is much like that of the 8-MHz AT, with the exception of its 6-MHz system clock. As with the later AT, the XT Model 286 resists performance boosts through crystal upgrades. Its BIOS confirms its clock speed before it allows the system to boot up.

PS/2 Oscillators and Timer

As with other aspects of IBM's PS/2 line, the oscillator and timer circuits of the new machines break with the past but go to great lengths to remain compatible with previous IBM hardware. Much of the support circuitry on the various PS/2 planar boards has been integrated into the VLSI gate arrays that dominate the planar boards. The oscillator and system clock are among these newly integrated functions.

Models 25 and 30

The timer, oscillator, and clock functions of the PS/2 Models 25 and 30 are built into two VLSI chips, the *System Support Gate Array* and the *I/O Support Gate Array* as well as some familiar discrete circuitry.

The former circuit generates the system clock, starting with the output of a 48 MHz external oscillator. The System Support Gate Array divides this frequency down by a factor of 6 to achieve the 8 MHz that serves as the system clock. It also controls the refreshing of system memory without using a channel of the system timer. In addition to these functions, the System Support Gate Array also controls which functions and devices (microprocessor, coprocessor, DMA controller, and so on) have command of the system bus.

The I/O Support Gate Array controls the serial and parallel port, the floppy and hard disk controllers, the video system, and the real-time clock, but does not contain the full circuitry for these functions. It also generates the 1.19 MHz signal used by the system timer.

The timer itself is a separate circuit, an 8253 as in IBM's previous PCs and XTs, and the timer is accessed and controlled through the same ports with the same commands. It differs, however, in the assignment of its three outputs. Another still generates the 18.2 per second pulses to serve as the system timer, and another controls the speaker. The other channel, used for memory refresh operations in PC and XTs, is only used for diagnostics in the Models 25 and 30. Its output is unconnected. Its former refresh function is handled by the System Support Gate Array.

Micro Channel PS/2 Timers

Micro Channel models in the IBM PS/2 line also integrate their oscillator and timing functions into VLSI chips while striving to maintain compatibility with previous models. System timer functions have been revised somewhat to help forestall disasters in two ways.

As with the Models 25 and 30, the system timer has been freed of its duty to refresh system memory, this chore being handled by a gate array. The timer channel and I/O port address, 041(Hex), nominally assigned to that function are undefined in Micro Channel PS/2s.

These machines do have a third timer channel, however, one assigned to serve as a "watchdog." This timer channel monitors the 18.2 times per second time-of-day interrupt. It counts the number of these interrupts that do not arrive on schedule. Should the total number of missed interrupts reach a critical value, it reports an error to the system. If a program goes awry and interferes with proper operation of the system interrupts, the watchdog reports an error, allowing corrective action to be taken.

In a single-user, single-tasking system, the watchdog is of dubious value. When the interrupts go away, both the executing program and the machine have effectively crashed. In a multitasking system, however, the watchdog gives the system a chance to save properly executing applications from the effects of one that crashes.

The watchdog can be defeated or its timing values adjusted through the I/O ports that control the timer (as listed in Table 9.2).

Interrupt Controllers

Intel microprocessors understand two kinds of interrupts—software and hardware. A software interrupt is simply a special instruction in a program that is controlling the microprocessor. Instead of adding, subtraction, or whatever, the software interrupt causes program execution to temporarily shift to another section of code in memory.

A hardware interrupt causes the same effect but is controlled by special signals outside of the normal data stream. The only problem is that the microprocessors recognize far fewer interrupts than would be useful—only two interrupt signal lines are provided. One of these is a special case, the Non-Maskable Interrupt. The other line is shared by all system interrupts.

IBM's personal computer architecture nevertheless allows for several levels of interrupt which are prioritized—a more important interrupt takes priority over one of lesser importance.

Table 9.2 **Registers and Control of 8253 Timer**

Register I/O Port Address	Function
040(Hex)	Timer 0 count
041(Hex)	Timer 1 count
042(Hex)	Timer 2 count
043(Hex)	8253 Control Register

Bit 0 - 0 = Binary counter 16-bits
　　　1 = Binary-Coded Decimal (BCD) counter (four decades)

Bits 1 to 3—Mode select in binary form

Bit 3	Bit 2	Bit 1	Mode
0	0	0	0
0	0	1	1
X	1	0	2
X	1	1	3
1	0	0	4
1	0	1	5

Bits 4 and 5—Read/load

Bit 5	Bit 4	Function
0	0	Counter latching operation
0	1	Read/load least significant byte only
1	0	Read/load most significant byte only
1	1	Read/load least significant byte first, then the most significant byte

Bits 6 and 7—Select counter

Bit 7	Bit 6	Function
0	0	Select counter 0
0	1	Select counter 1
1	0	Select counter 2
1	1	Illegal instruction

PC and XT Interrupt Control

To organize the hardware interrupts of the PC-series of computers, IBM selected the *8259 Interrupt Controller*. This chip handles eight interrupt signals, numbered zero through seven, assigning each one a decreasing priority as the numeric designation increases. (Table 9.3 lists

Table 9.3 **Interrupt Assignments for the PC, XT, and Portable PC**

Number	Function
NMI	Parity errors
0	System timer
1	Keyboard
2	EGA display PC Network 3278/79 adapter
3	COM2 PC Network (Alternate) 3278/79 adapter (Alternate) SDLC communications BSC communications Cluster adapter
4	COM1 SDLC communications BSC communications Voice communications adapter (Preferred)
5	Hard disk
6	Diskette
7	Printer Cluster adapter (Alternate)

the interrupt assignments of the PC, XT, Portable PC, and PCjr computers.)

AT Interrupt Control

Eight hardware interrupts, of which but six were available on the expansion bus, quickly proved inadequate for complex systems so IBM nearly doubled the number of them in the AT. The arrangement, assignment, and interplay of these interrupts was altered substantially from the PC design.

The near-doubling of interrupts was accomplished by adding a second interrupt controller chip (another 8259A) to the system architecture by cascading it to the first. That is, the new chip is connected to another which, in turn, connects to the microprocessor. The chip closest to the microprocessor operates essentially as the single interrupt controller in a PC or XT. However, its interrupt 2 input is no longer connected to the PC bus. Instead, it receives the output of the second 8259A chip.

The interrupt channel on the bus that formerly led to the interrupt 2 input is now connected to interrupt 9 on the second chip. This interrupt works similarly, only the signal itself must traverse two controllers before action is taken. Despite its new number, AT interrupt 9 functions just like PC interrupt 2, with the same priority activated by the same control line.

While the 8259A controllers each still handles individual interrupts on a priority level corresponding to the reverse of the numerical designation of their inputs, the cascaded arrangement of the two controllers results in an unusual priority system. Top priority is given to interrupts 0 and 1 on the first chip. However, because the second chip is cascaded to interrupt 2 on the new chip, the new, higher numbered interrupts that go through this connection get the next highest priority. In fact, interrupt 9 (which, remember, is actually the interrupt 0 input of the second 8259A controller) gets top priority of all interrupts available on the expansion bus. The rest of the interrupts connected to the second controller receive the next priority levels in ascending order up to interrupt 15. Finally, the remaining interrupts on the first chip follow in priority, from interrupt 3 up to interrupt 7.

(AT interrupt assignments are listed in Table 9.4.)

AT Interrupt Sharing

Just in case the 15 available interrupts (16 counting the special nonmaskable interrupt) still don't stretch far enough, the AT bus makes provisions for *interrupt sharing*. IBM does not, however, implement interrupt sharing i this is left up to the designers of add-in componentry. It involves designing device hardware to allow interrupt sharing and writing not only the code for the software routines that get carried out as a result of the interrupt but program code to sort through the shared possibilities, arbitrate conflicting interrupt calls, and put everything back together again at the end of the interrupt. Best done in assembly language, it's not stuff that timid programmers play with.

Table 9.4 **Interrupt Assignments for the AT and its clones**

Number	Function
NMI	Parity errors
0	System timer
1	Keyboard
2	Cascade input for second interrupt controller
3	COM2 PC Network (Alternate) SDLC communications BSC communications
4	COM1 SDLC communications BSC communications
5	LPT2
6	Diskette controller Hard and diskette drive
7	LPT1 Data Acquisition Adapter General Purpose Interface Bus Adapter Voice Communications Adapter (Preferred)
8	Realtime clock interrupt
9	Software redirected to Interrupt 0A(Hex) PC Network
10	Reserved
11	Reserved
12	Reserved
13	Coprocessor
14	Hard disk controller
15	Reserved

Model 25 and 30 Interrupt Control

The advance to PS/2 design at first appears to be a backward step for the interrupt structure of the Models 25 and 30. Like the PC and XT, these computers support only a total of eight interrupts. However, in these machines IBM not only allows interrupt sharing but also takes advantage of it. Interrupt 1, assigned solely to the keyboard in PC-style computers, is shared among the keyboard, the pointing device (mouse), and the time-of-day clock in the Models 25 and 30.

Micro Channel Interrupt Control

While the level-sensitive interrupts of the Micro Channel work differently from, and are incompatible with, the edge-triggered interrupts used in previous IBM personal computers, the circuitry that controls them is familiar indeed. Micro Channel PS/2s use two 8259A interrupt controllers—the same chips as other IBM personal computers—arranged exactly as are those in an ordinary AT. That is, the second 8259A is cascaded to the interrupt two channel of the first. Interrupt priorities are the same in both the AT and Micro Channel designs.

The 8259A chip is capable of either edge-triggered or level-sensitive operation. In Micro Channel computers, the chips are initialized in level-sensitive mode. Circuits external to the 8259A chips prevent their being set up in edge-triggered mode.

Direct Memory Access

The best way to speed up system performance is to relieve the host microprocessor of all of its housekeeping chores. One of the more time consuming of these is moving blocks of memory around inside the computer, for example, shifting bytes from a hard disk (where they are stored) through its controller into main memory (where the microprocessor can use it). The memory moving chores can be handled by a special device called a *Direct Memory Access* or *DMA* controller.

This specialized chip only needs to know the base location of where bytes are to be moved from, the address to where they should go, and the number of bytes to move. Once it has received that information from the microprocessor, the DMA controller take command and does all the dirty work itself. The DMA controller used in all IBM computers is completely programmable and operated through a series of I/O registers.

PC and XT DMA

IBM first chose the 8237A-5 DMA controller for the PC and used the same chip in all later personal computers up to Micro Channel PS/2 models. The -5 in the designation is the speed rating of the chip, 5 MHz, which closely matches the one and only clock in the PC and XT, 4.77 MHz. Each transfer of a byte under DMA control requires five cycles of the system clock, a total of 1,050 nanoseconds.

The 8237A-5 affords these computers four separate DMA channels which can be used independently for memory moves. The PC design reserves one of these channels for refreshing system memory. The other three channels are available on the I/O bus.

In most IBM software only one DMA channel is used at a time. Only on rare occasions are two channels needed. One such case is backing up a hard disk. It is convenient to pull data from the hard disk and immediately write it to the backup device. Many floppy disk-based backup systems do, in fact, use two DMA channels simultaneously for this purpose.

PC Two-Channel Problem

Normally, such operations should cause no problems, however in 10–15 percent of the original PCs such operations will not work properly because of defective 8237A chips. The chip errors don't normally show up (and didn't in the testing of the chips) because only one channel is typically used at a time.

The only sure cure for this problem is to replace the chip should its symptoms be noted. As this replacement is not easy—the ailing chip is soldered in place—and the error is likely only to occur with a few backup programs, the procedure usually is not worthwhile. The better and more affordable strategy is to live with the bad chip, which won't otherwise misbehave, and avoid the software that causes the problem.

This problem does not occur with other computers because the design of the 8237A chip has been revised to eliminate it.

AT DMA

The AT and the XT Model 286 use the same DMA chip as the PC and XT, the 8237A-5, but they double it. Because one of the eight DMA channels available on the two chips is used to cascade the other four channels of the other chip to the microprocessor, the net yield to the system is seven DMA channels. Each of these channels can address the full 16-megabyte range of the 80286 microprocessor. The PC and XT DMA can address only one megabyte, the maximum memory of those systems.

Four of these DMA channels are 8 bits wide and operate identically to those of the PC and XT. The other three channels on the second chip are a full 16-bits wide.

In the AT, each of the DMA controllers operates at one-half the microprocessor speed to stay within its speed rating. That is, in a 6 MHz AT, the 8237A-5 operates at 3 MHz. In an 8 MHz AT, the 8237A-5 operates at 4 MHz. Because each DMA cycle requires five clocks, each takes 1,666 nanoseconds in a 6-MHz machine or 1,250 nanoseconds in an 8-MHz machine. Note that even in an 8-MHz AT in 8-bit mode, DMA transfers actually occur more slowly in the AT than in the PC. In 16-bit mode, however, AT DMA transfers are faster because the wider bus width permits more data to move through the controller.

PC DOS was written in the days before 16-bit DMA transfers became possible, so DOS cannot make use of the 16-bit DMA mode of the AT. In order to keep the performance of AT hard disks commensurate with the high-speed microprocessors used by the system, IBM reworked the AT to avoid its slow 8-bit transfers for hard disk data moves. The AT transfers data to and from hard disk by giving string move instructions to the microprocessor. These instructions are able to take advantage of the full 16-bit data path of the AT and take advantage of its speed. PS/2s revert back to using their DMA channels for hard disk data transfers that its hard disk transfers do not use.

Non-Micro Channel PS/2 DMA

The lesser PS/2s, those lacking Micro Channel Architecture, use an 8-bit DMA arrangement similar to that of the PC and XT. However, in these computers the 8237A DMA chip operates at 4 MHz. In addition, each DMA cycle requires six cycles of that clock rather than the five used in PC, XT, and AT systems. Each cycle of a DMA transfer thus requires about 1,500 nanoseconds.

Micro Channel PS/2 DMA

In IBM's Micro Channel Architecture, the DMA controller is incorporated into one of the very large-scale integrated circuits on the system board. The design is functionally compatible with that of the AT, and can mimic the operation of a pair of 8237A chips. However, the Micro Channel machines make an additional DMA channel available and offer a additional extended command set for control.

In a Micro Channel machine, DMA timing is essentially independent of the system clock. In general, each DMA cycle requires 600 naoseconds from system board memory or 500 from an expansion board on the Micro Channel. Another few hundred nanoseconds of overhead is required to setup the entire transfer (which may consist of up to 64K cycles). Transfers can be either 8 or 16-bits at a time. Overall, Micro Channel DMA transfers are more than twice as fast as those of the AT, giving the newer computers a substantial performance advantage.

10

THE
POWER
SUPPLY

All practical computers made today operate electronically. Their thought processes are made from pulses of electricity that move from one circuit to another. This electricity does not arise spontaneously but must be derived from an outside source. Conveniently, nearly every home in America is equipped with its own electrical supply that the computer can tap into. Such is the wonder of civilization.

The solid-state semiconductor circuits of today's computers cannot directly use the electricity supplied by your favorite utility company, however. For economic reasons, commercial power is transmitted between you and the utility company as *alternating current,* the familiar *AC* found everywhere, because it is easy to generate and adapts readily between voltages (including very high voltages that make long distance tranmission efficient). Computer circuits almost universally use low voltage *direct current* because it is easier to control.

The computer power supply is the intermediary that translates AC you have to the DC that your computer's circuits need. In the process it attempts to make the direct current that is supplied to your computer as pure as possible and kept as close as is possible to the exact voltages used by your computer.

Power Supply Types

In electronic gear, two kinds of power supplies are commonly used— *linear* power supplies and *switching* power supplies.

Linear Regulation

The former earn their name because they use standard linear (analog) semiconductor circuits. In a linear power supply, the raw electricity from the power line is first sent through a *transformer,* which reduces its voltage to a value slightly higher than is required by the computer's circuits. Next, one or several *rectifiers,* usually semiconductor diodes, convert the now low voltage AC to DC. Finally this DC is sent through the *linear voltage regulator,* which supplies the carefully controlled DC to your computer's circuits.

Most linear voltage regulators work simply by absorbing the excess voltage made by the transformer, turning it into heat. The regulator adjusts the amount of power it dissipates to constantly supply the same voltage even if the power line voltage varies as much as 10 to 20 percent.

Switching Regulation

Although more complex, switching power supplies are more efficient and often less expensive than their linear kin. While designs vary, the typical switching supply first converts the incoming 60 Hz utility power to a much higher frequency of pulses, in the range of 20,000 Hz. At the same time the power is increased in frequency, it is regulated using a digital technique called *pulse-width modulation.* The duration of each power pulse is varied in response to the needs of the computer circuitry being supplied. The width of the pulses is controlled by electronically switching the current flow on and off, hence the name of the technique. The pulses are reduced in voltage by a transformer and turned into pure direct current by rectification and filtering.

Switching power supplies earn their efficiency and lower cost in two ways: Switching regulation is more efficient because less power is turned into heat. Instead of dissipating energy, the switching regulator switches all current flow off. In addition, high frequencies require smaller, less expensive transformers and filtering circuits. Nearly all of today's personal computers use switching power supplies.

Practical PC Power Supplies

The power supplies used by all full-size IBM personal computers and PS/2s produce four distinct voltages that are used by the machines. Nearly all of today's digital circuitry, from microprocessor to memory, requires 5 volts of direct current. The motors of most disk drives use 12 volts. Serial ports and some other I/O devices require both a positive and negative 12-volt supply. A few components and peripherals also requires a negative 5-volt supply.

Voltages and Ratings

Each of these four voltages is available from PC power supplies in different quantities (amperages). Typically the power supply is rated as the sum of all the power, measured in watts, that it makes available. The power rating can be calculated by individually multiplying the current rating of each of the four voltages supplied and summing the results. The power supplies in IBM computers range from 63.5 watts to 220; compatibles cover a similar range.

How much power you need depends on what you want to fill your computer with. A system board may require 15–25 watts; a floppy disk drive, 10–20; a hard disk, 10–50; a memory or multifunction expansion board, 5–10. In a short time, you can come up with a pretty hefty total.

Supply Voltage

Most power supplies are designed to operate from a certain line voltage and frequency. In this country, utility power is supplied at a nominal 115 volts and 60 Hz. In other nations, the supply voltage and frequency may be different. In Europe, for example, a 230-volt, 50-Hz standard prevails.

Most switching power supplies are willing to operate at either frequency, so that shouldn't be a worry when traveling. (Before you travel, however, check the ratings on your power supply to be sure.)

Many computers have switchable power supplies. That is, a small switch on the rear panel selects the operating voltage. Ensure that the switch is in the proper position for the power available before turning on your computer.

When traveling in a foreign land, always use this power supply switch to adjust for different voltages. Do not use inexpensive voltage converters. Often these devices are nothing more than rectifiers that clip half of the incoming waveform. Although that strategy may work for lightbulbs, it can be disastrous to electronic circuitry and using such a device can destroy your computer. It's not recommended procedure.

Most IBM computers introduced since the XT Model 286 have had auto-adjusting power supplies that automatically adjust themselves to the prevailing voltage and frequency. (Notably, the PS/2 Model 30 286 does not have an autoadjusting power supply.) If you have a computer with such a power supply, all you need to do is plug the computer in and it should work properly.

PC Power Inadequacies

Although it's hard to peg exactly how much power any particular computer might require, one generalization can be made reliably—the 63.5 watts of the original PC-series is clearly inadequate for a contemporary personal computer. A workable rule-of-thumb is that a 63.5 watt PC has enough expansion power for running two of the three following internal peripherals: a multifunction card, an internal modem, and a hard disk card. However, if you're careful about the products you choose, you may be able to squeak by with all three. For example, select a low power consumption hard disk card (such as the now-discontinued 5-watt 10-megabyte Western Digital FileCard or an 8-watt Plus Development HardCard) and a frugal modem (best to stick with a 1200 bit per second half-length card).

The Power-Good Signal

Beside the voltages and currents that the computer needs to operate, IBM power supplies also provide another signal called *Power-Good*. Its purpose is just to tell the computer that all is well with the power supply and the computer can operate normally. If the Power-Good signal is not present, the computer shuts down. The Power-Good signal prevents the computer from attempting to operate on oddball voltages (those caused by a brown-out for example) and damaging itself.

Power Supply Replacement

The sure cure for a deficiency of wattage is radical surgery, the power supply transplant. The same strategy applies should the juice generator in your computer is ailing.

Power Supply Selection

The first step is finding a power supply to slide into the chassis of your computer. A variety of advertised units abound in the nether pages of most computer magazines. Alas, getting the right unit is more than a matter of buying the right number of watts. You'll find two broad classes of power supplies with many subtle variations within them.

The classes are the generic and the glamorous. The generic power supplies make no claim except that they deliver the volts and amps you need. They likely originate in some part of the Far East that you can't pronounce and even less imagine. They're cheap—prices as low as the $50 range—and they work, at least for a while. In fact, many are likely to be the same units that nestle themselves in your favorite compatible computers.

The glamorous watt-makers promise some grand advantage over their generic siblings (more watts, less noise, more wind, whatever). The glamor demands a premium price and may earn a premium guarantee, but whether you need one depends on your sensibilities and motivations. If an extra $50–100 brings you a dozen decibels of additional quiet, your ears may overrule your budgetary sense.

The variations on a theme all have to do with packaging. The simple matter is that you must match the physical size and packaging of a power supply to the computer you have. AT power supplies are taller and wider than PC models. While it's obvious that the AT power supply won't fit into the smaller XT-size chassis, you may be surprised to discover that the smaller XT power supply also won't fit properly into an AT chassis. The placement of screws and other functional parts is different enough that the little box won't fit right into the big box.

Other variations may frustrate your power supply replacement efforts. Some offbeat units vary so far from the normal IBM theme that they dispense with the big red paddle power switch on the right side. Instead, they may substitute a rocker switch on the rear panel, which may butt against the rear panel of your computer's chassis, unreachable from the outside.

As a rule, when you buy a replacement power supply, you must explicitly specify what computer you want to slide it into when you purchase it. PS/2, Compaq, and other compatible computers use power supplies packaged far differently, making replacement units hard, if not impossible, to find.

Power Supply Removal

Removing a power supply from a PC, XT, or AT is easy. In all cases, the big chrome power supply box is held in place by four screws in the back panel of the computer. Once you remove the top of your computer's case and locate the power supply, you'll see that four of the screws in the rear panel roughly coincide with the four corners of the

Figure 10.1 **Power supply rear panel screws**

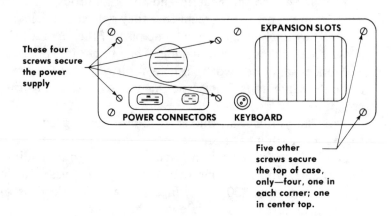

backside of the power supply. When you face the rear of the computer, the four screws will be on the left half of the rear panel, arranged roughly in a rectangle. (See Figure 10.1.)

Remove these screws and the power supply will be loose inside the chassis. Before you attempt to lift it out, remove the power supply connectors from each disk drive and the two connectors from the system board. Finally, slide the power supply box about one inch forward in the chassis till it bumps lightly against the rear of the disk drive bay or disk drives. The power supply should then lift out of the chassis without further ado.

Power Supply Installation

Installing a power supply is equally easy. The first step is to properly orient the supply so that the power switch protrudes through the notch cut in the top of the chassis; then lower the power supply straight down into the chassis into the empty space left by the old power supply.

Before attempting to screw the new power supply into place, push it toward the front of the chassis and lightly into the drive bays; then, while pressing it down, push it back toward the rear panel of the chassis. This front-then-back slide should slip the two steel fingers on the computer chassis through slots at the bottom of the power supply to hold it in place. You may also want to attach the power-supply connectors before you screw the power supply down.

Finally, screw the power supply into place: Start all four screws but give them no more than two full turns before you have all four started. This will allow you to move the power supply slightly to line up all four holes. If you tighten one screw first, you may find that the rest of the holes in the power supply won't line up with those in the chassis. Once all four screws have been started, drive them all home.

Connector Orientation

All IBM-standard PC, XT, and AT power supplies have two kinds of connectors dangling from them: Two of them go to the system board; the rest are designed to mate with tape and disk drives.

The tape and disk drive connectors supply 5 and 12 volts to operate those devices. The connectors are polarized, in other words, they are not rectangular but have two of their corners truncated so they fit in the sockets on the drive in only one orientation. If a drive connector doesn't seem to fit, don't force it! Instead, rotate it 180 degrees and try again. It will likely slide into place. (Figure 10.2 shows this connector and the voltages present on each of its four pins.)

The two system board connectors are not identical. Each has its own repertory of voltages. Normally, these connectors are labeled *P8* and *P9*. The lower number attaches to the mating connector at the rear of the chassis.

The connectors are supposed to be keyed so you cannot put one in the wrong place. Unfortunately, many replacement power supplies are shipped without being keyed.

If you examine the power connectors meant to attach to the system board, you'll see that one side of the connector has one or more small tabs sticking out. If just one is longer than the rest, the connector is keyed. If all are the same length, the connector has not been keyed. You can key it by cutting off all but the one right tab using a pair of diagonal cutters. (Figure 10.3 shows the proper keying of these connectors.)

Another way of being sure the system board connectors are in their proper positions is by the color codes of the wires. Proper installation puts black wires in the middle—that is, the black wires on the connectors adjoin one another.

PS/2s eliminte the possiblity on inadvertently swapping connectors by combining the two into a single, long connector on a large, wide connector.

Figure 10.2 **Mass storage device power connector**

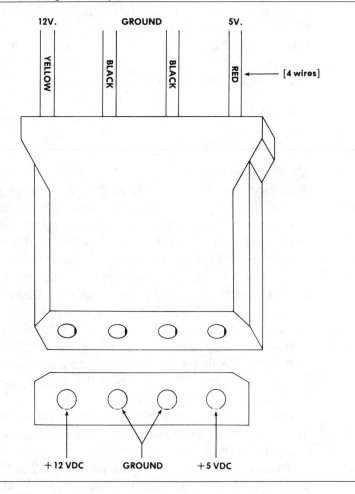

Power Protection

Normal line voltage is often far from the 115-volt alternating current you pay for. It can be a rather inhospitable mixture of aberrations like spikes and surges mixed with noise, dips, and interruptions. Some of these aberrations can be powerful enough to cause errors to your data or damage to your computer.

Power line problems can be broadly classed into basic categories: overvoltage, undervoltage and noise. Each of the problems has its own distinct causes and requires a particular kind of protection.

Figure 10.3 **Keying of system board power connectors**

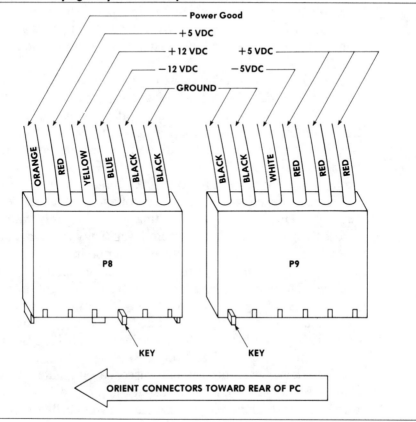

Overvoltage

The deadliest power line pollution is *overvoltage,* lightning-like high potential spikes that sneak into your PC and actually melt down its silicon circuitry. Often the damage is invisible, except for the very visible lack of image on your monitor. Other times, you can actually see charred remains inside your computer as a result of the overvoltage.

As its name implies, an overvoltage is gushing more voltage into your PC than the equipment is designed to handle. In general and in the long run your utility supplies power that's very close to the ideal, usually within about 10 percent of its rated value. If it always stayed within that range, the internal voltage regulation circuitry of your PC could take its fluctuations in stride.

Short duration overvoltages larger than that may occur too quickly for your utility's equipment to compensate, however. Moreover, many overvoltages are generated nearby, possibly within your home or office, and your utility has no control over them. Brief peaks as high as 25,000 volts have been measured on normal lines, usually due to nearby lightning strikes.

Overvoltages are usually classed into short duration phenomena called *spikes* or *transients,* which may last from a nanosecond (billionth of a second) to a microsecond (one millionth of a second) and longer duration overvoltages called *surges,* which can stretch into milliseconds.

Spike and surge protectors are designed to prevent such overvoltage from reaching your PC. They absorb excess voltages before they can travel down the power line to your computer.

Perhaps the most common overvoltage protection devices are the *varistors.* They work by conducting electricity only when the voltage across their leads exceeds a certain level. They can short out the excess voltage in spikes and surges before it can pop into your PC. The voltage at which the varistor starts clipping spikes is termed its *clamping voltage.* The excess energy doesn't disappear but turns into heat, possibly destroying the varistor. It may give its life to protect your computer. Varistors can potentially start fires as they succumb in the line of duty. This possibility may be the prime reason IBM does not include varistors in its PC and PS/2 power supplies.

Other devices are occasionally used to eliminate overvoltages, including semiconductors, ionized spark-gaps, and ferro-resonant transformers. Most of these devices function much like varistors but use different operating principles.

The most important characteristics of overvoltage protection devices are how fast they work and how much energy they can dissipate. Generally, a faster *response time* or *clamping speed* is better. Response times can be as short as picoseconds—trillionths of a second. The larger the energy handling capacity of a protection device, the better. Energy handling capacities are measured in watt-seconds or joules. Devices claiming the ability to handle millions of watts are not unusual.

Undervoltage

An undervoltage is simply less voltage than you expect to get. They can range from *sags,* which are dips of but a few volts, to complete outages or *blackouts.* Durations can vary from nearly instantaneous to hours, or even days, if you haven't paid your light bill recently.

Very short dips, sags, and even blackouts are not a problem. As long as they are less than a few dozen milliseconds—about the blink of an eye—your computer should purr along as if nothing happened. The only exceptions are a few computers that have power supplies with very sensitive Power Good signals. A short blackout may switch off the Power Good signal, shutting down your computer even though enough electricity is available.

Most PCs are designed to withstand prolonged voltage dips of about 20 percent without shutting down. Deeper dips or blackout will result in shut down.

Three devices help your computer deal with undervoltages. *Voltage regulators* keep varying voltages within the range that will run your PC but offer no protection against steep sags or blackouts. The *standby power system* and *uninterruptible power system* (or *UPS*) fights against blackouts.

Voltage regulators are the same devices that your utility uses to try to keep the voltage it supplies at a constant level. These giant regulators consist of large tranformers with a number of *taps* or *windings,* outputs set at different voltage levels. Motors connected to the regulators move switches which select the taps that will supply the voltage that most nearly approximates normal line voltage. These mechanical regulators are gargantuan devices. Even the smallest of them is probably big enough to handle an entire office. In addition, they are inherently slow on the electrical time scale, and they may allow voltage dips long enough for data to be lost.

Solid-state voltage regulators use semiconductors to compensate for line voltage variations. They work much like the power supply inside your computer but can compensate over a wider range.

The *saturable reactor* regulator applies a DC control current to an extra control coil on the transformer, enough to "saturate" the transformer core. Once saturation is achieved, no additional power can pass through the transformer. Regulating the DC control current adjusts the output of the transformer. These devices are inherently inefficient because they must throw away power throughout their entire regulating range.

Ferroresonant transformer regulators are "tuned" into saturation much in the same way as a radio is tuned—using a capacitor in conjunction with an extra winding. This tuning makes the transformer naturally resist any change in the voltage or frequency of its output. In effect, it becomes a big box of electrical inertia that not only regulates but also supresses voltage spikes and reduces line noise.

The measure of quality of a voltage regulator is its *regulation,* which specifies how close to the desired voltage the regulator maintains its output. Regulation is usually expressed as the output variation for a given change in input. The *input range* of a regulator indicates how wide a variation in voltage variation that it can compenstate for. This range should exceed whatever variations in voltage you expect to occur at your electrical outlets.

Blackout Protection

Both standby and uninterruptible power systems provide blackout protection in the same manner. They are built around powerful batteries that store substantial current. An *inverter* converts the direct current from the batteries into alternating current that can be used by your computer. A battery-charger built into the system keeps the reserve power supply fully charged at all times.

Because they are so similar, the term UPS is often improperly used to describe both standby and uninterruptible power systems. They differ in one fundamental operating principal and may yield a different level of protection for your personal computer, particularly if it is sensitive to very short interruptions in its supply of electricity.

Standby Power Systems

As the name implies, the standby power system constantly stands by, waiting for the power to fail so it can leap into action. Under normal conditions—that is, when utility power is available—its battery charger draws only a slight current to keep its source of emergency energy topped off. The AC power line that the standby supply feeds from is directly connected to its output, and then to the computer. The batteries are out of the loop.

When the power fails, the standby supply switches into action—*switch* being the key word. The current-carrying wires inside the standby power supply that lead to the computer are physically switched from the utility line to the current coming from the battery-powered inverter.

The switching process requires a small but measurable amount of time. First, the failure of the electrical supply must be sensed. Even the fastest electronic voltage sensors take a finite time to detect a power failure. Even after a power failure is detected, there is another slight pause before the computer receives its fresh supply of electricity while the switching action itself takes place. Most standby power systems switch quickly enough that your computer never notices the lapse. A few particularly unfavorable combinations of standby power systems and computer, however, may result in the computer shutting down during the switch.

Uninterruptible Power Systems

The name of the uninterruptible power system is self-explanatory. Its output is never interrupted because it does not need to switch its output from line power to battery. Rather, its battery is constantly and continuously connected to the output of the system through its inverter. It's always supplying power from the batteries to your computer. Your computer is thus completely independent of the vagaries of the AC electrical line.

While the AC power is available to the uninterruptible power system, its batteries are kept from discharging from the constant current drain of powering your computer by a large charger. When the power fails, the charger stops charging but the battery, without making a switch, keeps the electricity flowing to the connected computer.

In effect, the UPS is the computer's own generating station, only inches away from the machine it serves, keeping it safe from the polluting effects of lightning and load transients. Dips and surges can never reach the computer; instead, it gets a genuinely smooth, constant electrical supply exactly like the one it was designed for.

Backup Power System Specifications

The most important specification to investigate before purchasing any backup power device is its *capacity* as measured in volt-amperes (VA) or watts. This number should always be greater than the rating of the equipment the backup device is to be connected to.

Standby and uninterruptible power systems are also rated as to how long they can supply battery power. These time ratings may vary with the VA the backup device must supply, and, because of the efficiencies and inefficiencies of the inverter circuitry, the ratings may seem to vary inconsistently.

You probably won't need a lot of time from a backup power system. In most cases, five minutes or less of backup time should be sufficient because the point of a backup supply is not to keep a system running forever; instead, the backup power system is designed to give you a chance to shut down your computer without losing your work. Shutting down shouldn't take more than a minute or two.

Different backup-power systems also vary as to their output waveform. The perfect waveform is one that matches that from utility power, the *sine wave*. Sine waves are also the most difficult to generate, so most backup power system actually generate *square waves* or *modified square waves* that approximate sine waves. (Figure 10.4 shows the shapes of these different waveforms.)

The least desirable is the ordinary square wave, which may cause overheating of your PC's power supply. Because they power your computer from batteries only for a short time, the output waveform from standby power systems is less critical than that from an uninterruptible power system.

Zenith Power Problems

Short switching times for standby power systems are most critical for one particular model of computer—the IBM XT equipped with a power supply made in Mexico by Zenith Electronics. These are early XTs, made between the introduction of the XT itself and 1985. While most personal computers operate unflinchingly through power failure or switching time 20–40 milliseconds long, these Zenith-equipped XTs may shut down (losing all data in memory) during power outages as short as a few milliseconds.

The underlying problem is the Power-Good connection. The actual DC output from all PC power supplies (including the Zenith) continues for about 30–45 milliseconds after utility-supplied electricity fails because of the filtering circuitry inside the power supply. With all PCs other than Zenith-equipped XTs, the Power-Good line remains valid for 10–15 milliseconds after line voltage fails, so shorter interruptions won't affect the computer. The Power-Good line in Zenith power supplies almost immediately becomes invalid. As a result, the computer quickly shuts down even though power may still be available inside the power supply.

Because of this inordinate sensitivity, most standby power systems cannot protect a Zenith-equipped XT. If you have such a computer, you have three options in assuring blackout protection: buying an uninterruptible power system instead of a standby power system; buying one of the few standby supplies that switch fast enough for the XT;

Figure 10.4 **Power supply wave forms**

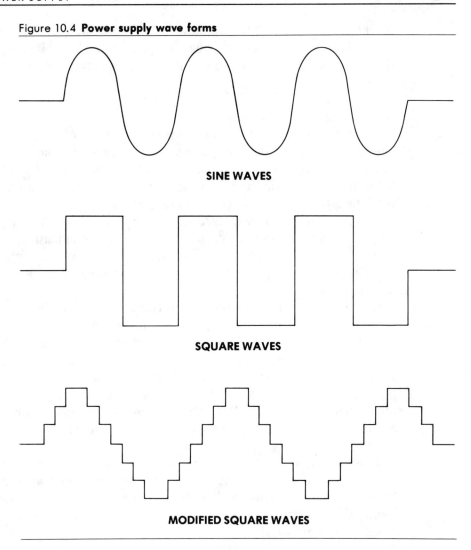

SINE WAVES

SQUARE WAVES

MODIFIED SQUARE WAVES

or installing a new power supply into the XT without the Power-Good problem. This last option is the least expensive and often the easiest.

According to American Power Conversion Corporation, which makes a special standby power supply model to handle the needs of more tempermental XTs, Zenith power supplies can be identified in two ways: By looking slightly upward through the ventillation slots in the rear of the computer, a small white sticker that says "Made in Mexico"

can be seen in the Zenith supplies. In addition, the receptacle for the
power line cord on Zenith power supplies is held in place by black
rivets. On Aztec power supplies, silver or green rivets are used.

Noise

Noise is a nagging problem in the power supplies of most electronic
devices. It comprises all the spurious signals that wires pick up as they
run through electromagnetic fields. In many cases, these signals can
sneak through the filtering circuitry of the power supply and interfere
with the signals inside the electrical device.

For example, the power cord of a tape recorder might act like an
antenna and pick up a strong radio signal. The broadcast could then
sneak through the circuitry of the recorder and mix with the music that
it's supposed to be playing. As a result, you might hear a CB radio
maven croaking over your Mozart.

In computers, these spurious signals could confuse the digital thought
coursing through the circuitry of the machine. As a practical matter,
they don't. All better computers are designed to minimize the leakage
of their signals from inside their case into the outside world to avoid
your computer's interference with your radio and television. The same
protection against signals getting out works extremmly well against
other signals getting in. Personal computers are thus well-protected
against line noise. You probably won't need a noise filter to protect
your computer.

Then again, noise filtering doesn't hurt. Most power protection
devices have noise filtering built into them because it's cheap and it can
be an extra selling point (particularly to people who believe they need it).
Think of it as a bonus. You can take advantage of its added protection—
but don't go out of your way to get it.

11

CASES

Some of the primary purposes of the case of a computer are easy to understand. It's meant to keep in what's inside and out what's outside. The chief evil on the inside is electrical energy that can cause interference to radios, televisions, and other electronic devices. On the outside all sorts of nastiness continually attempts to get in, such as young children, hot coffee, errant paperclips, to wreak their havoc with the delicate electronics of your computer.

But the computer's case must be selective. Some of what's inside has got to get out—heat, for example, and some of what's outside needs to get in, such as signals from the keyboard and power from your electrical outlets. In addition, the computer case must form a solid foundation upon which your system can be built. It must give disk drives a firm base and hold electrical assemblies out of harm's way. Overall, the simple case may not be as simple as you think.

Radio Frequency Emission

All electrical circuits share one property: Every flow of electrical energy sets up an electromagnetic field that radiates away. Radio and television stations push kilowatts of energy through their antennae so they will radiate over the countryside, eventually to be hauled in by a radio or television set for your enjoyment or disgruntlement.

Radio Frequency Interference

The electrical circuits inside all computers work the same way but on a smaller scale. They radiate electromagnetic energy whenever the computer is turned on, and when the thinking gets tense, so does the radiation.

A problem arises because the radiation from the computer circuitry occurs at a wide variety of frequencies, including the range occupied by your favorite radio and television stations, aviation navigation systems, and the eavesdropping equipment some initialed government agency has buried in your walls. Unchecked, these untamed radiations from within your computer will compete with broadcast signals not only for the ears of your radio but that of your neighbors. These radio-like signals emitted by the computer generate what is termed *radio frequency interference* or *RFI,* so called because they interfere with other signals in the radio spectrum.

FCC Certification

The government agency charged with oversight of the chaos of the airwaves, the *Federal Communications Commission,* has developed regulations that limit the allowable extraneous radiation from any electrical device, including the computer. Before it can be legally sold, any equipment with the potential for generating interference must be certified by the FCC to keep its radiation within certain set limits.

The FCC has two levels of certification: *FCC Class A* certification pertains to equipment designed to be used in business; and *FCC Class B* certification is required for electrical devices meant for consumer use at home. Of the two, Class B is the more stringent, allowing substantially less radiation to escape from the equipment, one-tenth the level that is permissible under Class A certification. The feeling here is that interference is more likely to be bothersome in a residential neighborhood in which couch potatoes are the primary crop.

The heavy steel case of the typical PC, XT, AT, or compatible computer does a reasonable job of limiting RFI. However, as the frequencies inside the computer increase, the spurious radiation becomes more pernicious. Any crack in the case may allow too much radio energy to leak out. If different parts of the chassis and the lid of the case are not electrically connected together, RFI can leak out. In addition, any cable attached to the computer potentially can act as an antenna, sending out signals as effectively as a radio station.

A number of design elements help reduce RFI. Special metal fingers on the edge of the case and its lid insure that the two pieces are in good electrical contact. Cables can be shielded. RFI absorbing *ferrite beads* can be wrapped around wires before they leave the chassis to suck up excess energy before it leaks out. Every one of these cures adds a bit to the cost of the computer, both for the materials and for their fabrication and installation. Moreover, it can take a substantial time to track down all the leaks and plug them. Consequently, achieving an FCC Class A rating is cheaper and can be accomplished faster.

PS/2 Emission Reduction

The PS/2 series of computers were designed by IBM from the ground up to be inherently low in radio frequency emissions. Their system boards and the Micro Channel are designed in such a way that spurious radiation is at a minimum. The outer layers of the planar boards consist primarily of ground layers, which shield the high frequency signals within the inner layers of the circuit board. Ground wires alternate with every few active conductors on the Micro Channel to partially shield the bus.

The plastic cases of the PS/2s that have them are covered with a silver-rich paint that is conductive and shields the computer much like the full metal jacket of other computers.

Cooling

Another by-product of any electrical current flow is heat. Some of the electricity in any circuit (except one that superconducts) is turned into heat by the unavoidable resistance of the circuit. Heat is also generated whenever an element of a computer circuit changes state. In fact, nearly all of the electricity consumed by a computer eventually turns into heat.

Inside the protective case of the computer, heat builds up, driving up the temperature. Heat is the worst enemy of semiconductor circuits; it can shorten their lives considerably or even cause their catastrophic failure. Some means of escape must be provided for the excess heat.

Passive Convection

The obvious solution is to punch holes in the computer case to let the heat out, but to keep the holes small enough so other things such as mice and milkshakes can't get in. In due time, *passive convection* will let the excess thermal energy drift out of the case.

Active Cooling

Unfortunately, all IBM-standard computers (except for some laptops) produce heat faster than passive convection can rid it from the case. These machines need some form of *active cooling*. The means of choice is the fan.

Figure 11.1 **XT cooling update**

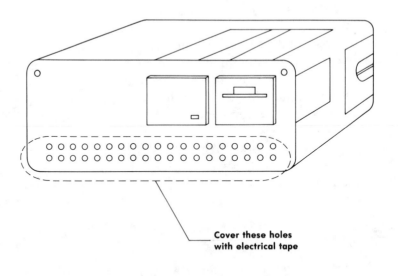

Cover these holes
with electrical tape

Usually tucked inside the power supply, the computer's fan forces air
to circulate both inside the power supply and the computer. It sucks
cool air in to circulate and blows the heated air out.

The cooling systems of early PCs were particularly ill-conceived,
however. The fans were designed mostly to cool off the heat-generating
circuitry inside the power supply itself and only incidentally cool the inside of the computer. Moreover, the chance design of the system resulted
in most of the cool air getting sucked in through the floppy disk-drive
slots. Along with the air, all the dust and grime floating around in the
environment was also sucked in, polluting whatever media you had sitting in the drive. At least enough air coursed through the machine to
cool off the small amount of circuitry that the meager power supply of
the PC could provide.

The XT added more electricity from the power supply but no better
ventilation. And this brought its own problem. The airflow around expansion cards and the rest of the computer was insufficient (actually too
ill-placed) to keep the temperature throughout the machine down to an
acceptable level. As a correction to later models of the XT, IBM
eliminated a series of ventilation holes at the bottom of the front of the

chassis. The absence of these holes actually improves the air circulation through the system unit and keeps things cooler.

Early Model XT Cooling Fix

Early model XTs can be brought up to this newer cooling standard simply by blocking these anti-cooling holes with electrical tape. Although it's easier to do with the cover off your machine, you can actually make the upgrade without popping the lid on your XT. The holes in question will be found tucked underneath the front bezel. They are small perforations, about 1/8 inch diameter each, in several rows totaling about 3/4 an inch wide and running across the width of the machine.

If your machine lacks these holes, you need do nothing. If you find holes here, just cover them over with tape—black vinyl electrical tape works well but in a pinch duct tape or what have you will suffice. You shouldn't notice any difference, but your expansion boards will. (See Figure 11.1.)

Advanced Cooling

Cooling problems are unlikely in the AT, which seems capable of handling most expanded configurations. The PS/2 series features exemplary cooling. In fact, much of the space in the floorstanding models is devoted to ducting area around the expansion area before it gets sucked through the power supply.

That's not to say that the cooling inside a PC, XT, or AT should be taken for granted or cannot be improved. Booster fans that clamp on the rear panel of the computer and power supplies with beefed-up fans are available. These do, in fact, increase air circulation through the system unit, potentially lowering the internal temperature and prolonging the lives of components. Unless you stuff every conceivable accessory into your machine, however, you're unlikely to need such a device except for the added measure of peace of mind it provides.

On the other hand, blocking the airpath of the cooling system of any PC can be fatal, allowing too much heat to build up inside the chassis. Never locate a PC or PS/2 in cramped quarters that lacks air circulation (like a desk drawer or a shelf on which it just fits). Never block the cooling slots or holes of a computer case.

Fan Failure

The fan inside a computer is a necessity, not a luxury. If it fails to operate, your computer won't falter—at least not at first, but temperatures will build up inside the case. The machine may even fail catastrophically from overheating.

The symptoms of fan failure are subtle but hard to miss. You'll be able to hear the difference in the noise your system makes. You may even be able to smell components warming past their safe operating temperature.

Should you detect either symptom, hold your hand near the area the air usually emerges from your computer. (On PCs and ATs, this is near the big round opening that the fan peers through.) If you feel no breeze, you can be certain your fan is no longer doing its job.

A fan failure constitutes an emergency. If it happens to your system, immediately save your work and shut the machine off. Although you can safely use it for short periods, the better strategy is to replace the fan or power supply as soon as you possibly can.

Hardware Considerations

Physical Aspects

In general, you'll never need to worry about such things as the size of your system board, where its mounting screws go in the case, or other such mechanical matters. However, if you ever decide to update your system board with a high performance replacement or you want to customize or even just improve the appearance of what you have, the physical aspects of the package will assume tremendous importance to you.

IBM matches its system boards to its cases more closely than you might think. For example, as similar as they look the cases of the PC and XT are not the same. The two system boards are different sizes, they mount with screws in different places, and they have differing numbers and spacings of their expansion slots. You cannot put the system board of one into the case meant for the other—at least not without some clever mechanical work. Know which style you need before you buy, and be sure you get it.

The AT system board, although it uses the same expansion slot spacing as the XT, is a different size again.

Pygmy PCs

So-called *mini-AT* cases are better termed maxi-XT cases. They are designed to accommodate not AT system boards but those that fit the XT-form factor. Sometimes the styling is the only thing that matches the AT. Usually, though, the mini-AT case also matches AT system units in height so you can use taller expansion boards.

True *small footprint* computers can go to great length to shrink the size of their cases. Many reduce their overall height by installing expansion cards on their sides, horizontally, and restricting both their number and the space devoted to disk-drive bays. As long as such a small footprint machine can accommodate full-length expansion cards and all the expansion options you want now and forever into the future, there is no reason to avoid them and every reason to covet one for your desktop.

Foreshortened computers with expansion slots that are ten or eleven inches long instead of the normal thirteen should be avoided unless you are absolutely certain you'll never need to install a full-length expansion board. Such computers make your choice expansion product more critical and may limit the selection available to you. For example, few hard disk cards will fit foreshortened expansion slots.

The Flip-Top Case

In the XT replacement (or original) case arena, you'll have your choice of cases that follow the standard PC/XT configuration with covers that slide forward and off or the so-called flip-top case. This latter unit at first appears compelling—you can get easy access to what's inside your computer simply by lifting the lid as if your were opening the hood of your car—but in the long run it may not be as desirable as you think. You still must pull whatever's atop the machine off to get inside. Worse yet, you may have to pull the plug on some of the peripherals that you've connected to the expansion slots because the pivoting back end of the lid shears down upon them. You've either got to pull the plugs or you can access your expansion boards. I've tried both and prefer the good, old IBM style.

Tower-Style Cases

The AT brought legitimacy to installing personal computers on edge, a mounting scheme developed for somewhat bulkier minicomputers. The method used for the AT was more of an afterthought—a cocoon to enclose the machine on its edge.

The tower-style PS/2s were the first IBM personal computers designed to operate edgewise from the start. In fact, many of the design features of these vertical computers are reminiscent of minicomputer packaging, particularly in hard-disk mounting hardware (which is discussed below.)

Compatible computers took to towers for one very good reason: they are generally more commodious because they are not restricted by the amount of desk space they might occupy. The greater volume of the tower often equates to more space for disk drives. Some offer bays for eight or more half-height disk drives.

Vertically mounting computer components causes no problems—electronic circuits don't know which way is up, anyhow. The only part of a computer that may complain about vertical installation is the hard disk, and any such problems can be cured by low-level formatting the hard disk in its vertical mounting. You probably won't even face this problems because most towers keep their disk drives aligned on a horizontal plane.

Choose a tower for its greater physical capacity for internal peripherals and its flexibility of installation wherever there are a few vacant feet of floorspace.

Device Mounting

The chassis of a personal computer also provides a mounting area for its power supply and mass storage devices. The power supply needs only a vacant area in the right rear of the chassis (generally). Mass storage devices require an installation area in the form of one or more drive bays. The bay simply provides space for the mass storage device and some means of mounting it.

Matching the Power Supply

An important consideration when scratch building or replacing your PC's case is matching your power supply. Most power supplies follow the IBM style and put the on/off switch on an extension bracket to the right of the box. A few cases are designed to use power supplies with rear-panel-power switches. Usually the company selling one variety of case offers power supplies that match, and vice versa. But if you're just replacing the case *or* the power supply, you'll have to be careful.

Don't forget that PC/XT and AT power supplies are different sizes and one will not fit in a case meant for the other. It's an obvious problem but one that can be eliminated if it's anticipated. (See Chapter 10 for power supply installation instructions.)

Mass Storage Device Installation

Internal installation of any mass storage device in a drive bay is actually quite simple. Most disk and tape drives are held in place by two to four screws that can be removed and replaced with a couple of twists. Anyone who knows the right end of a screwdriver to grab is qualified to physically install or remove a device from a drive bay.

PC and XT Floppy Disk Bays

The floppy disk drives of the original PC and XT were mounted inside a relatively simple mounting tray. The sides of the tray were bent upward and holes were provided to match the two tapped mounting holes on each side of the standard full-height 5 1/4-inch floppy disk drive. These screws are visible on the right side of drives in the right drive bay and the left side of drives in the left bay. Gaining access to the latter may require removing the expansion cards inside the computer.

Removing a drive requires only extracting the screws, unplugging the cables from the drive, and sliding the drive forward and out of the chassis. Installation is the reverse—slide the drive in part way, attach the cables, then twist in the screws. Before tightening the first screw all the way, start the second screw and adjust the drive so that its front panel aligns with that of the other drive or blank panel in your computer.

PC and XT Hard Disks

While the two-screw mounting technique is more than adequate for full-height floppy disk drives and tape transports, it is not a recommended mounting scheme for hard disks. The unfastened side of the disk is left to flap in the breeze. Jarring or dropping the machine, as is quite likely in shipping, can cause the drive to pivot around its fastened side, the loose side jumping up and down. As a result, the disk could suffer irreparable damage.

IBM prevents XT hard disks from flapping by using a third screw to hold the drive down. In that a screw cannot be driven into the free side of the drive because of the design of the drive bay, IBM elected to pop a third screw into the drive from the bottom of the chassis. To remove the XT hard disk, you'll have to remove this screw. In fact, it should be the first screw you remove so you don't accidentally drop the drive from the chassis when removing it. The two side screws will hold the drive in place so you don't have to worry about your expensive hard disk flopping about like a fish in its death-throes on your desktop.

PCs don't make a provision for this third screw. If you are gentle with your system and don't plan on shipping it, you may not miss this extra fastener. But should your PC be in contention for joining the jet set, you may want to add the extra hole and screw for securing your disk drive or remove your hard disk drive from your PC before consigning it to your favorite shipper.

Half-Height Drives in PCs and XTs

The drive shelves of the IBM PC and XT were not designed for half-height devices, so only a single set of screw holes is available in each full-height position for drive-mounting. You can install a single half-height drive in each slot simply by using these mounting holes and filling the empty space above the drive with a blank half-height panel.

Of course, that solution is hardly satisfactory if your intention is expanding the mass storage space in your PC or XT. What you really want to do is install two half-height devices in over-under fashion in a single slot. To do so, you need a pair of *adapter plates*. Basically adapter plates are just thin pieces of steel with a number of slots or holes in them which allow you to assemble two half-height drives into a single unit that will install into a full-height drive bay. (Figure 11.2 shows one form of adapter plate that is easily fabricated.)

Figure 11.2 **Half-height drive adapter plate**

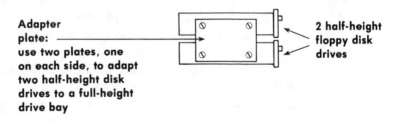

Adapter plate: use two plates, one on each side, to adapt two half-height disk drives to a full-height drive bay

2 half-height floppy disk drives

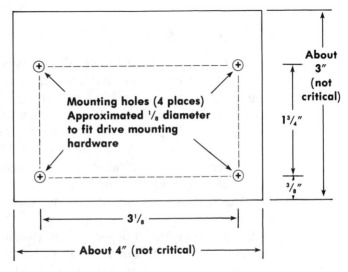

Sheet metal stock, preferrably as thin steel as possible

Mounting holes (4 places) Approximated $1/_8$ diameter to fit drive mounting hardware

About 3" (not critical)

$1^3/_4$"

$3/_8$"

$3^1/_8$

About 4" (not critical)

Installing drives with these adapters is more difficult than you may think. You can't just connect two drives with them and slide the whole assembly into the drive bay—the screw heads (and maybe the plates themselves) make the drive package too wide to slide through the front panel opening in the chassis.

The first step to a double-half-height installation is to connect the two drives together on the side opposite that which attaches the mounting tray. Once one plate is installed, you should be able to slide the drive stack into the computer as a single piece.

Once the two-drive stack is in its proper place, but while you can still maneuver the drives in and out of the bay, install all the cables to both drives. When everything is plugged in, slip the other mounting plate between the drives and the side of the drive bay. Secure this mounting plate and the drive by screwing through the two holes in the bay, through the mounting plate, and into the screw holes in the bottom drive. Finally, finish your work by screwing the top drive into place.

Most PC and XT-compatible computers use a variation on the PC drive-mounting scheme. Their drive mounting trays are usually drilled to accommodate two half-height devices in a full-height slot. You can install half-height drives directly into these bays without adapters; just secure the drives with two screws on the side to which you have open access.

AT Drive Installation

The inadequacies of the PC and XT drive mounting arrangement was probably part of the motivation behind IBM's improved AT drive-mounting scheme. In the AT, mass storage devices are secured on both sides by sturdy mounting rails that slide into channels on either side of the drive bay. The two-sided mounting prevents the drive in the bay from bouncing or rattling around during shipment.

Drive removal and installation is relatively easy, providing you have hands small enough or skin tough enough so you don't bloody your knuckles reaching behind the drive to connect or disconnect its various cables.

AT mounting rails are secured by two brackets that screw into the front panel of the chassis. Most of the brackets are L-shaped, but one is U-shaped. The arm or arms of the bracket that projects backward presses against the drive-mounting rail and secures it at the end of its travel in its channel.

To remove an AT drive, simply remove the two brackets holding either mounting rail in place, then pull the drive slightly forward. When you have adequate room behind the drive, remove the cables (including the ground wire). Once the drive is free, slide it straight forward and out of the chassis.

Installing a drive is simply the reverse. Before sliding the drive into the bay, make sure no cables protrude in the way of the drive. Slide the drive about two-thirds of the way in, then connect its associated cables. Push the drive back as far as it will go. Position one of the brackets over its associated screw hole, hold its arm against the end of the drive rail, and drive the screw home to hold the bracket in place. Make sure the bracket does not twist out of place as you screw it in.

Installing AT Mounting Rails

When mounting a new drive you'll need rails for it. Many products come with the rails already installed, Others come with loose rails left for you to install. Some come without rails, leaving you to find a pair of your own.

All sorts of rails are available. Official IBM rails are different for the right and left side of the drive and have only two installation holes. Point the tapered end of the rail toward the rear of the drive. The screws to hold the rails in place then go into the lower pair of the two sets of mounting holes on the drive.

Third-party mounting rails are usually made to be interchangeable between the left and right sides of the drive. They have four holes, which combined with the four mounting holes in the drive itself, give you four installation permutations, only one of which will work. Only two screws should be used to hold the drive to the rail. In general, the lower holes on the rail (when its tapered is pointed toward the rear of the drive) should mate with the lower holes in the drive.

Note that some odd rails may have holes in different positions. If you install rails on a new drive, make sure that the drive lines up in the proper vertical position before you secure its mounting brackets and try to reinstall the lid of the case.

AT-compatible computers may use AT rails, some variation of rail mounting, or ordinary XT-like screws-in-the-side-of-the-bay installation. For example, full-size AT-compatible computers from Dell Computer Corporation use wider rails that are held in place by screws in the side of the bay. The two rails keep the drive from jostling in the bay, while the screws keep the rails from sliding out of the computer. (Figure 11.3 shows the dimensions of the standard AT drive-mounting rail and the similar rail used by Compaq.)

Better manufacturers will include spare rails with the computer when you buy it should it use a proprietary rail size. Otherwise, you'll have to try to get special rails directly from the manufacturer of the computer.

Figure 11.3 **IBM AT and Compaq drive mounting rails**

A. IBM Personal Computer AT mounting rail:

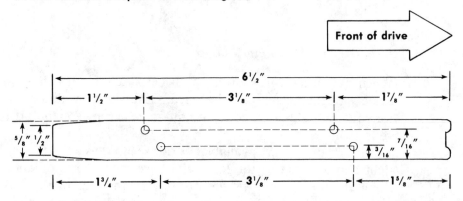

Left rail shown; right rail is mirror image

Use upper holes for full-height drive in internal bay
Use lower holes for half-height drive in half-height bays

B. Compaq drive mounting rail

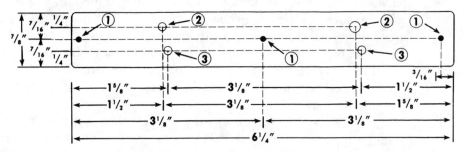

① = Hole for securing rail to computer
② = Hole for securing rail to disk drive
③ = Not used (make rail symmetrical so that it
      can be used on other side of drive

PS/2 Floppy Installation

In the PS/2 series of computers, IBM refined its floppy disk mounting scheme so that drives can be installed or removed from the computer without tools. Drives mount in special plastic sleds (which might some-

Figure 11.4 **PS/2 3.5" hard disk mounting sled (dimensions approximate)**

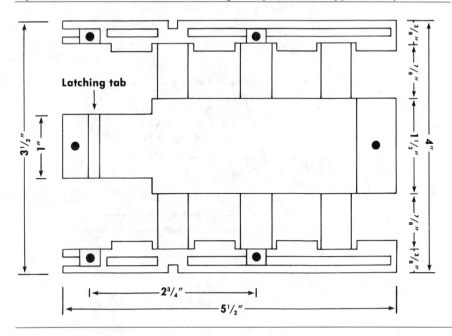

day become an integral part of the drive case) which slide into the molded bays of the PS/2. (See Figure 11.4.)

To access the drive bay to install or remove one of these sleds, you'll have to remove the front fascia panel from your PS/2. These are secured by plastic snaps molded into the fascia. Just pry the front panel free at the seam running around it about half-an-inch behind its face. You should be able to pull it off using no tools other than your fingers.

A "floating" connector (one with some freedom of movement) at the rear of the bay automatically mates with an edge connector on the drive. Besides carrying the signals, this connector also supplies power to the drive, eliminating the need for a separate power connector.

Once the drive is pushed fully into its bay, a latch at the bottom of the drive snaps down, locking the drive securely in place. To remove the drive this latch must be released. To do so, simply lift up on the tab that's centered under the drive. Firmly pull the drive forward while lifting the tab to release the latch. After the initial effort required to pull the drive from the connector at the back of the bay, the drive will pull easily and smoothly from the bay.

Figure 11.5 **Internal hard disk rails for tower-style computers**

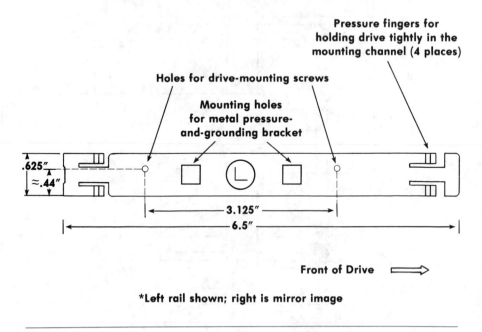

*Left rail shown; right is mirror image

PS/2 Internal 3 1/2-Inch Hard Disks

A similar mounting scheme prevails for 3 1/2-inch hard disks mounted in the internal bays of PS/2s that accommodate them. The sled is of a different design but uses the same plastic latch technique to secure itself in place. (See Figure 11.4.) Drives simply slide into place. (Note that Model 50 internal hard disks and those of the Model 50Z and Model 70 are not interchangeable due to interfacing differences. Don't try to exchange them without the proper adapters! IBM supplies a full kit with its hard disk upgrades for PS/2s.)

PS/2 Internal 5 1/4-Inch Drive Mounting

Tower-style PS/2 systems, like the Models 60 and 80, allow for the internal installation of standard 5 1/4-inch drives using a rail mounting system. Instead of the simple steel channels of the AT, however, these machines use a sturdy cage to hold the drive. One or two drives fit into the cage, one of which can peek out the front panel of the computer, and are held down by screw pressure. Big blue daisy-like knobs of plastic turn the screws, designed to be spun without tools by firm pressure from the palm of your hand. (Figure 11.5 shows the dimension of the rails of PS/2 tower-style computers.)

Drive installation in single-drive systems simply requires lowering the drive decked out in its mounting rails through the open center of the cage. The drive should be oriented so the connectors at its rear will end up nearest the center of the chassis once the drive is positioned. Once you've lowered the drive into the cage, simply push it to the end of its travel and tighten down the blue daisies.

Two-drive systems require a more complicated installation because one drive will block access to the central open area of the chassis. The drive to be located at the rear of the chassis should be inserted first, as for a single drive installation. The second drive can then be slid into the cage through the opening in the front of the chassis. You'll want to snap out the front panel bezel to gain access. The front-mounted drive is tightened into place just like the rear unit.

12

INPUT
DEVICES

The input devices are the means by which you move information into your PC, the primary means by which you interact with your personal computer. The various available devices span an entire range of technologies, from the tactile to the vocal. Although they work in different ways, all accomplish the same task, allowing you to communicate with your computer.

The Keyboard

The primary input device for most computer systems is the keyboard, and until the time-voice recognition systems are perfected to the point they can recognize continuous speech, the dominance of the keyboard is not likely to change. As long as you're stuck with it, you might as well understand how it works.

IBM has offered at least eight different keyboards with its variety of personal computers. Four really weren't mainstream products because two designs were meant only for the PCjr, one fit the Portable PC, one was designed particularly for the 3270 PC. Three of the others marked a progression of adjustments in key layout and convenience features. The last gives a smaller, more convenient alternative for crowded desks.

The PC/XT Keyboard

Complaints began with the original PC/XT keyboard, introduced with the first PC (shown in Figure 12.1). Despite a vociferous outcry (primarily from the press) this design was kept as the IBM standard through the introduction of the AT, equipped as it was with a total of 83 keys. It put two vertical rows of function keys at the left of the main alphanumeric keypad, and forced cursor controls to share the same keypad with a calculator-style array of numbers for direct data entry.

Figure 12.1 **Layout of original IBM PC and XT keyboard**

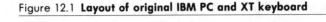

Figure 12.2 **Original IBM AT keyboard layout**

The Enter key was small and ambiguously identified with a bent arrow legend, and no indicators were provided for the three locking shift keys (Caps Lock, Num Lock, and Scroll Lock).

The complaints about the original design concerned mainly the layout of peripheral keys. The lefthand function keys did not correspond to the bottom-of-the-screen listings of function key assignments used by most programs. The lack of indicators led to a lot of mistypings of numbers for cursor movements and capital letters for lower case. Spreadsheets needed both a numeric keypad and cursor control keys. Also, the Enter key was too small.

The AT Keyboard

After years of complaints in the press, IBM took heed and introduced a new keyboard layout with the AT: It had an additional key (Sys Req, designed primarily for use with multiuser applications); enter was made bigger, Selectric-size; and indicators were provided for the locking shift keys. (See Figure 12.2.)

In fact, the differences went much deeper. Unlike the PC keyboard, the AT keyboard was made programmable and was given its own set of commands, which could be relayed to it through the system unit. This fact alone made the AT keyboard incompatible with PC and XT system units. Although the connectors are the same, a PC/XT keyboard won't work when plugged into an AT and an AT keyboard won't work when plugged into a PC or XT.

The IBM Advanced Keyboard

With the introduction of the upgraded AT, IBM also unleashed another new keyboard, termed the *Advanced Keyboard* by IBM but commonly also called the *Enhanced Keyboard*. Although electrically similar to the original AT product (to the extent they can be plugged in interchangeably and remains incompatible with PCs and XTs) the layout was altered again. The advance it made was a greater endowment of keys, to a total of 101 in the standard United States model. In international models it gains one more. (See Figure 12.3.)

The key additions were several. A new, dedicated cursor-control pad was provided, separate from the combined numeric and cursor pad, and several other control keys were duplicated in another small pad. Two new function keys (F11 and F12) were added, and the whole dozen were moved to a top row, above and slightly separated from the alphanumeric area. Duplicate Ctrl and Alt keys were provided at either side of the space bar, and Caps Lock was moved to the former location of the Ctrl key.

Figure 12.3 **IBM advanced keyboard layout**

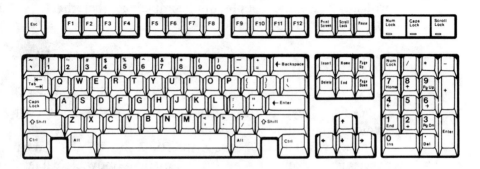

Figure 12.4 **IBM Compact keyboard layout**

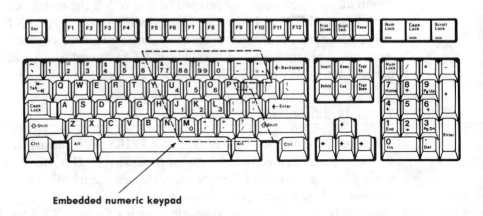

Embedded numeric keypad

One supposed blessing provided by the advanced design, the top row function keys, was demanded by computer writers since the introduction of the PC. Finally, the function keys corresponded to the positions of on-screen key labels. The complainers soon learned that the left twin rows of function keys were much more convenient to use, particularly when needed in combination with Alt or Ctrl. What once could be done with one hand now required two.

Moreover, the relocated function keys proved to be more cumbersome to use. The smaller Enter key of the new design was more apt to be missed in fast typing. All in all, the keyboard was designed more for hunt-and-peck key bangers than proficient typists—probably the exact people who complained most loudly about the previous designs. In fact, probably the same people who complained that the letters are not arranged in alphabetic order.

PS/2 Keyboards

The PS/2 line universally uses the IBM Advanced Keyboard or a special reduced-size keyboard designed primarily for the tiny Model 25. (The layout of the latter is shown in Figure 12.4.)

The only difference between the PS/2 and XT/AT Advanced Keyboards is the connector at the end of the removable cable. The PS/2 cable simply uses a miniature DIN connector in place of the standard

DIN connector on PC/XT/AT keyboards. This cable is also removable so you or IBM can substitute the proper cable to match the system you have.

Compatible Keyboards

Compatible computer makers have striven to keep pace with IBM and have adapted their keyboards to the prevailing standard. Thus they have followed suit in adopting the advanced design, its drawbacks not-withstanding. Some manufacturers have compounded the confusion created by IBM's troika of key layouts by adding their own subtle refinements, a complete elaboration of which would probably require a book of its own—"The Mystery of the Moving Keys." Anything out of the normal alphanumeric contingent is a candidate for roving anywhere around the keyboard.

One improvement made by many compatibles manufacturers is the inclusion of a compatibility switch, usually located on the bottom of the keyboard. The two positions of this switch allow you to select the electrical compatibility of the keyboard between the PC/XT and AT standards. One keyboard can thus be used with either type of system unit, providing you've put the switch in the correct position.

Several keyboards also include extra key caps to allow you to swap the position of the lefthand Ctrl and Caps Lock keys so Ctrl falls in its more familiar position. The electrical relocation is handled either through another keyboard switch or through software that you must run on the host computer. Although these features cannot be added to an existing keyboard, they are worth looking for when buying a replacement.

Keyboard Technologies

No matter how their keys are arranged, all keyboards have the same function, detecting the keys pressed down by your fingers and relaying this information to your computer. Even though two keyboards may look identical, they may differ considerably in the manner in which they detect the motion of your fingers. The technology used for this process—how the keyboard works electrically—can affect the sturdiness and longevity of the keyboard.

Several technologies have been used for keyboards, ranging from the exotic (Hall-Effect switches, for example) to the mundane (switches that actually just switch). The two most common designs in PCs are the *capacitive* and *hard contact* keyboards.

Capacitive Keyboards

All the mainstream IBM keyboards—and those of the Portable PC and 3270 PC as well—are united by the sharing of a common mechanism: All operate using capacitive keyboard technology.

Capacitive keyboards are generally built around an etched circuit board. Two large areas of tin and nickel-plated copper form pads under each every switch *station* (in keyboard terminology, each key is called a station). The pads of each pair are neither physically nor electrically connected to one another.

Pushing down any key on the keyboard forces a circle of metalized-plastic down, separating a pair of pads that lie just below the key plunger. Although the plastic backing of the circle prevents making a connection that would allow electricity to flow between the pads, the initial proximity of the pads results in a capacity change. Separating them causes a decrease in this capacitance—a change on the order of 20 to 24 picofarads decreasing to 2 to 6 picofarads. The reduction of capacitance causes a small but detectable current flow in the circuitry leading to the pads.

Some compatible capacitive keyboards do the opposite of the IBM design. Pressing the key pushes capacitive pads together and increases the capacitance. This backward process has the same effect, however. It alters the flow of current in a way that can be detected by the keyboard.

A spring mechanism gives the IBM keyboard its tactile feel and delivers the infamous click of every keypress. The spring mechanism also returns the key to the top of its travel at the end of each keystroke. So called soft-touch keyboards often use foam as a spring mechanism and for cushioning the end of each keystroke.

Under control of a microprocessor (generally an 8048-series device in the most popular keyboards), all of the pads of the keyboard are scanned for current changes every few microseconds, and the minute current flow caused by a keystroke can be detected. Because there is a slight chance random noise could cause a current pulse similar to that generated by a keystroke, keyboards may require that the increased current flow be detected during two or more consecutive scans of the keyboard. (Although you might think scanning twice would slow things down, the entire check and verification operation occurs so quickly that some keyboards are capable of handling typing as fast as 300 characters per second—somewhat faster than the typical programmer or even the most rapid typist.)

Once a keystroke has been detected, the microprocessor built into the keyboard then generates a scan code which indicates which key was struck. The scan code is then converted to serial data and relayed to the microprocessor in the computers system unit.

Hard Contact Keyboards

The mechanism and electronics of the capacitive keyboard are relatively complicated and correspondingly expensive. A lower cost alternative is the hard contact design, such as was used in the two PCjr keyboard designs. In those products, each key operated as an individual switch. When you press down on a key, hard contact is made between the two poles of a switch. The connection conducts electricity which, detected through a matrix array, indicates which key was pressed.

The hard contact design requires simpler circuitry to detect each keystroke, but still requires a microprocessor to assign scan codes and serialize the data for transmission to the system unit.

The specific hard contact design of the PCjr keyboard is a marvel of simplicity. It's based on a molded rubber sheet which provides the spring action needed to return the keys to their rest positions as well as holding one of the contacts required for switching. This rubber is carefully tailored into domes which collapse under pressure in a controlled manner that gives a positive over-center action and feel to each key.

Many of the keyboards used by today's compatible computers are of a very similar hard contact design. Their advantage is low cost. Their primary disadvantage is they may not last as long as capacitive keyboards. A common problem is that one key may deteriorate and suddenly get much stiffer, requiring greater pressure for activation than the rest. The solution to this problem is to get another keyboard.

Keytops

The most damning design aspect of the PCjr was probably its original keyboard which used small, tab-like keys termed *chicklets* (for the resemblance of the keys to the small, white, pillow-shaped, sugar-coated pieces of gum) by the derisive press. IBM's excuse for the radical design was that it allowed the use of templates with the keyboard, plastic or cardboard overlays which could be used to identify each key. Coincidentally, the smaller keys made the PCjr keyboard more difficult to type upon and eliminated any possibility that the low cost PCjr might replace the more expensive PC in business applications.

The updated PCjr keyboard, which was made available as a free upgrade from the dealer who sold the PCjr and its original keyboard to unwitting consumers, is electrically and mechanically identical to the original model. The only change was an increase in size of the keytops.

As with all other IBM designs, these keytops feature a concave cylindrical profile. A few non-IBM keyboards, primarily European products, have round, dish-shaped depressions in their keytops. The only difference is what feels best to you—and usually whatever is the most familiar feels best.

Cordless Keyboards

As a styling gimmick, IBM designed the PCjr keyboard to operate wirelessly. Two infrared-emitting LEDs on the rear edge of the keyboard send out scan codes optically, which are then received by a photodetector embedded in the front panel of the PCjr system unit. When the keyboard is used in its wireless mode, it requires four type-AA cells for power. IBM recommends the use of alkaline batteries, which should last several months under normal usage.

For more reliable operation, you'll probably prefer to use IBM's optional keyboard cable for the PCjr. When the cable is plugged into the keyboard, it switches off the battery supply (preserving the life of the batteries) and supplies power to the keyboard from the system unit.

The PCjr keyboard cable uses a telephone-style modular connector at the keyboard end and a Berg connector at the system-unit end. The Berg connector is difficult to obtain, thus making the manufacture of your own keyboard cable impractical. However, you can add extra length to it should your application (or desk arrangement) require simply plugging in one or more standard telephone extension cables between the IBM cable and keyboard.

Key Layouts

QWERTY

Anyone new to typing will be amazed and perplexed at the seemingly nonsensical arrangement of letters on the keys of the typical computer keyboard. Even the name given to this esoteric layout has the ring of some kind of black magic or odd cabala —*QWERTY*. Simply a list of the first six characters of the top row of the nominal arrangement, the absurdity harks back to the keyboard of the first practical typewriter.

Actually, the first typewriter had its keys arranged alphabetically. But within a year of his invention, Christopher Sholes discovered what he viewed as a superior arrangement, the QWERTY system which is known and hated today.

Legend Debunked

A legend surrounds the QWERTY arrangements. According to the common myth, QWERTY came about because typists pounded on keys faster than the simple mechanisms of the first typewriters could handle the chore. The keys jammed. The odd QWERTY arrangement slowed down the typists and prevented the jams.

Sholes left no record of how he came upon the QWERTY arrangement, but it certainly was not to slow down speedy typists. High typing rates imply modern-day touch typing, ten fingers flying across the keyboard. This style of typing did not arise until about ten years after Sholes had settled on the QWERTY arrangement.

Other arguments about the QWERTY placement also lead to dead-ends. For instance, breaking a strict alphabetic order to separate the keys and prevent the type bars (the levers which swing up to strike letters on paper) from jamming doesn't make sense because the arrangement of the typebars has no direct relationship to the arrangement of keys.

There is no doubt that the standard arrangement is the not only possible ordering of the alphabet—in fact, there are 26! (or 26 factorial, exactly 403,291,461,126,605,635,584,000,000) different possible arrangements of letters alone, not to mention the further complications of using rows of different lengths and non-alphabetics keys. But not only is QWERTY not the only possible layout, it's probably not the best.

Dvorak-Dealey Keyboard

The most familiar challenger to QWERTY, one that crawls in a distant second in popularity and use, is the *Dvorak-Dealey* letter arrangement, named for its developers, August Dvorak and William L. Dealey. The name is often shortened to Dvorak.

The Dvorak-Dealey design incorporates several ideas that should lead to faster typing. A basic goal is to foster the alternation of hands in typing—after you strike one letter with a key under a finger of your left

Figure 12.5 **The Dvorak-Dealey key layout (as implemented in the PC-compatible Key Tronic KB 5150D)**

hand, the next key you'll want to press will likely be under a righthand finger. This hand alternation is a faster typing strategy. To make hand alternation more likely, the Dvorak-Dealey arrangement put all vowels in the home row under the lefthand's fingertips and the consonants used most often in the right hand's home row. Note that the Dvorak-Dealey arrangement was developed for speed and does nothing to make the keyboard more alphabetic or learning to use it easier. (See Figure 12.5.)

The first publication of the Dvorak-Dealey keyboard was in the 1936 book *Typewriting Behavior,* authored by the developers of the new letter arrangement. To back up the philosophic and theoretical advantages attributed to the Dvorak-Dealey arrangement, tests were conducted in the Thirties on mechanical typewriters, amounting to typing races between the QWERTY and Dvorak-Dealey key arrangements. Dvorak and Dealey ran the tests, and —not surprisingly—they came out the winner by factors as large as 30 percent.

Dvorak believed in both his keyboard and his test results and wrote papers promoting his ideas. Alas, the more he wrote, the greater his claims became. Articles like ''There Is a Better Typewriter Keyboard'' in the December, 1943, issue of *National Business Education Quarterly* has been called by some experts ''full of factual errors.'' Tests run by the U. S. Navy and the General Accounting Office reported much more modest results for Dvorak.

Notwithstanding the exaggerated claims, the Dvorak layout does offer some potential advantages in typing speed, at least after you've become skilled in its use. The penalty for its increased typing throughput is increased difficulty in typing when confronted with a QWERTY keyboard.

The design of the PC makes converting to Dvorak relatively easy. While typewriters have to be redesigned for the new key arrangement, you can just plug a new keyboard into your PC. Commercial Dvorak keyboards are often available by special order.

In fact, if you don't mind your keytop legend bearing no likeness to the characters that actually appear on your screen (and in your files), you can simply reprogram your PC to think that it has a Dvorak keyboard by intercepting the signals sent by the keyboard to your computer and converting them on the fly.

Keyboard Use

Scan Codes

The internal microprocessor in all IBM keyboards identifies the keys that are pressed and converts the information so derived into scan codes, which are then sent serially to the host computer. Each press of a key generates two different scan codes—one when the key is pushed down and another when it pops back up. The two-code technique allows your computer system unit to tell when a key is pressed and held down—for example, when you hold down the Alt key while pressing a function key.

Each key generates a unique scan code. Even if the same legend appears on two keys, such as the duplicate number keys in the alphanumeric and numeric-and-cursor keypads, the individual keys generate the same codes. The code for a given key is the same whether the Caps Lock or other shift key is in effect. (Table 12.1 shows the scan codes sent by the keys of the different IBM keyboards.)

Your computer receives these scan codes at a special I/O port. When a scan code is received by your computer, the keyboard controller chip notifies the microprocessor that a scan code is available to be read by issuing an interrupt. When that happens, your computer sorts through the scan codes and figures out which keys are pressed and in which combination. The program code for doing this is part of your system's BIOS. The computer remembers the condition of the locking shift keys by changing special memory locations, called *status bytes* to reflect each change made in their condition.

Normally you do not have to deal with scan codes. The computer makes the translation to numbers and letters automatically and in-

Table 12.1 **Scan Codes on U.S. Keyboards**

Alphanumeric Key Area (all keyboards)

Key	Make Code	Break Code
A	1E	9E
B	30	B0
C	2E	AE
D	20	A0
E	12	92
F	21	A1
G	22	A2
H	23	A3
I	17	97
J	24	A4
K	25	A5
L	26	A6
M	32	B2
N	31	B1
O	18	98
P	19	99
Q	10	90
R	13	93
S	1F	9F
T	14	94
U	16	96
V	2F	AF
W	11	91
X	2D	AD
Y	15	95
Z	2C	AC
0 or)	0B	8B
1 or !	02	82
2 or @	03	83
3 or #	04	84
4 or $	05	85
5 or %	06	86
6 or ©	07	87
7 or &	08	88
8 or *	09	89
9 or (	0A	8A
0 or)	0B	8B
° or ™	29	A9
- or __	0C	8C
= or +	0D	8D
[or §	1A	9A

Table 12.1 (continued)

Alphanumeric Key Area (all keyboards)

Key	Make Code	Break Code
] or †	1B	9B
¶ or ®	2B	AB
; or :	27	A7
' or "	28	A8
, or <	33	B3
/ or ?	35	B5
Left Shift	2A	AA
Left Ctrl	1D	9D
Left Alt	38	B8
Right Shift	36	B6
Right Alt	E0 38	E0 B8
Right Ctrl	E0 1D	E0 9D
Caps Lock	3A	BA
Backspace	0E	8E
Tab	0F	8F
Spacebar	39	B9
Enter	1C	9C

Numeric/Cursor Keypad

Key	Make Code	Break Code
Scroll Lock	46	C6
Num Lock	45	C5
*	37	B7
-	4A	CA
+	4E	CE
Enter	E0 1C	E0 9C
1 or End	4F	CF
2	50	D0
3 or Pg Dn	51	D1
4	4B	CB
5	4C	CC
6	4D	CD
7 or Home	47	C7
8	48	C8
9 or Pg Up	49	C9
0 or Ins	52	D2
Num Lock	E0 35	E0 B5

*Note: When the keyboard is in a shifted state, the make code of the Num Lock key changes to AA E0 35 and the break code to E0 B5 2A.

Table 12.1 (continued)

Function Keys (F11 and F12 on Advanced and Compact keyboards only)

Key	Make Code	Break Code
Esc	01	81
F1	3B	BB
F2	3C	BC
F3	3D	BD
F4	3E	BE
F5	3F	BF
F6	40	C0
F7	41	C1
F8	42	C2
F9	43	C3
F10	44	C4
F11	57	D7
F12	58	D8

Dedicated Cursor Area and Related Keys (Advanced and Compact Keyboards)

Key	Make Code	Break Code
Up arrow	E0 48	E0 C8
Down arrow	E0 50	E0 D0
Left arrow	E0 4B	E0 CB
Right arrow	E0 4D	E0 CD
Insert	E0 52	E0 D2
Home	E0 47	E0 C7
Page Up	E0 49	E0 C9
Delete	E0 53	E0 D3
End	E0 4F	E0 CF

*Note: The keys send out different scan codes in when the keyboard is in a shifted or Num Lock condition, effeectively cancelling the effect of the locked shift. That is, when the key is shifted, its scan code is preceded by E0 AA, mimicking the effect of pressing shift before the key and temporarily nullifying the shift. The break code is followed by E0 2A, restoring the keyboard back to its shifted condition. Similarly, when the keyboard is in Num Lock state, the make codes of these keys are preceded by E0 2A and the break codes are followed by E0 AA.

Page Down	E0 51	E0 D1
Scroll Lock	46	C6
Pause	E1 1D E1 9D C5	[None — Make only]
Print Screen	E0 2A E0 37	E0 B7 E0 AA

*Note: When the keyboard is in a shifted state or the Ctrl key is held down when the Print Screen key is pressed, it sends out a make code of E0 37 and a break code of E0

Table 12.1 (continued)

Dedicated Cursor Area and Related Keys (Advanced and Compact Keyboards)

B7. When the Alt key is held down, the make code of print screen becomes 54 and the break code D4. The Pause key also acts differently in the shifted or Ctrl state, sending out the make code E0 46 E0 C6.

Embedded Cursor Keypad (Compact keyboard only)

When shift is active, the Scroll Lock key sends a scan code of 45 C5, which switches on the embedded numeric keypad on the Compact Keyboard. The scan keys of the following keys change to the indicated values during this state:

Key	Make Code	Break Code
; or : or *	37	B7
-or __ or -	4A	CA
= or +	4E	CE
J or 1	4F	CF
K or 2	50	D0
L or 3	51	D1
U or 4	4B	CB
I or 5	4C	CC
O or 6	4D	CD
7 or &	47	C7
8 or *	48	C8
9 or (	49	C9
0 or)	52	D2

visibly. The converted information is used in generating the information that appears on your monitor screen, and it is also made available to the applications you run and even the programs you write. Sometimes, however, when you write your own programs, it is useful to detect every key change. You may, for example, want to cause something to happen when a certain key combination is pressed. Your program only needs to read the keyboard-input port and compare what it finds there to a scan-code chart.

Keyboard Cabling

The scan codes are sent from the keyboard to your computer serially so only one wire conductor is needed to convey the *keyboard data* information. A second conductor is required to serve as a return path for the data signal, and, as a *ground,* it serves as common return for all the other circuits in the keyboard cable. To synchronize the logic in the

Figure 12.6 **IBM PC, XT, AT keyboard connectors, 5-pin DIN connector**

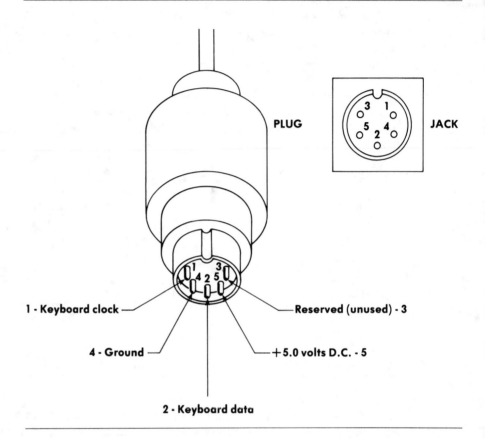

PLUG   JACK

1 - Keyboard clock ————————————————————— Reserved (unused) - 3

4 - Ground ——————————————————— +5.0 volts D.C. - 5

2 - Keyboard data

keyboard with that in your computer, a separate wire is used for a
keyboard clock signal. A fourth and final wire is used to supply the
keyboard with the five-volt direct current power that it needs to
operate. These four conductors are all that is necessary to link keyboard
to computer.

All PCs use standard five-pin DIN connectors for their keyboard
connection. Pin 1 is assigned the keyboard clock; 2, keyboard data; 4,
the ground; 5, the five volt electrical supply. One of the connections
provided by the keyboard plug (pin 3) is assigned to carry a signal to
reset the keyboard, but it is normally not used and need not be connected in normal keyboard cabling. (See Figure 12.6.)

Advanced keyboards use a modular (AMP) connector on the rear of
the keyboard, allowing the cable itself to be easily replaced. The

Figure 12.7 **Connector for IBM Advanced Keyboards SDL (Modular) connector**

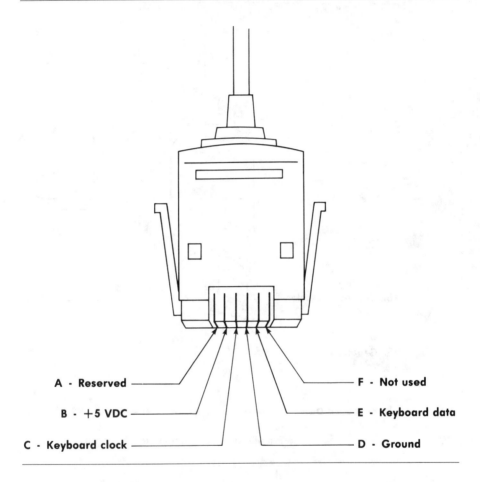

A - Reserved   F - Not used

B - +5 VDC   E - Keyboard data

C - Keyboard clock   D - Ground

removable cable also allows one keyboard to serve both the old AT line and the new PS/2 line, which use different system-board input connectors. (The pinout for this connector is shown in Figure 12.7.) It has the following assignments: A, reserved; B, keyboard data; C, ground; D, keyboard clock; E, five volts; and F, reserved. When looking at the gold contacts of the connector, the contacts are labeled in reverse alphabetical order from left to right.

PS/2s use different wire assignment in their six pin miniature DIN connectors: Pin 1 is assigned keyboard data; pin 3, ground; pin 4, five volts; and pin 5, keyboard clock. Pins 2 and 6 are reserved, and the shield is attached as a chassis ground. (See Figure 12.8.)

Figure 12.8 **IBM PS/2 keyboard connector**

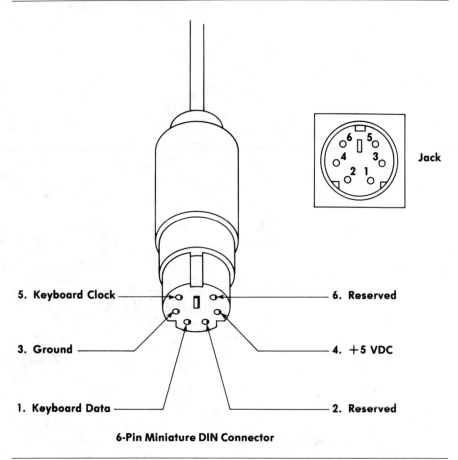

Jack

5. Keyboard Clock —————————— 6. Reserved

3. Ground —————————— 4. +5 VDC

1. Keyboard Data —————————— 2. Reserved

6-Pin Miniature DIN Connector

Making a Keyboard Extension Cable

If you want to get away from your computer, you can lengthen the cable running between it and the keyboard that you've got to keep under your hands. Such *keyboard extension cables* are available in various lengths, already assembled, for prices that range from reasonable to outrageous.

If you can find a length that you want or refuse to pay five times what it would cost you to make your own extension cable, you can manufacture your own without much trouble. The 5-pin DIN connectors are available at Radio Shack. The part numbers are as follows: 5-pin plug (male), 274-003; 5-pin in-line jack (female), 274-006; and 5-pin chassis-mounting jack (female), 274-005.

Although almost any wire will work, a shielded cable will reduce radio interference; one that uses stranded (as opposed to solid) conductors is recommended because stranded conductors withstand repeated flexure much better than solid wires.

You can cut the amount of soldering you must do in half and get exactly the right shielded, stranded cable by using Radio Shack's molded DIN patch cord (part number 42-2151) for your keyboard extension wiring. Although this cable has a male connector at each end, you can simply lop off one end of the cable and solder a female connector in its stead. These patch cords also work well as MIDI (Musical Instrument Digital Interface) cables.

Making extension cables for PS/2s is more difficult because miniature DIN plugs are not yet widely available.

Because IBM keyboards were not designed to be frugal with power—the Advanced Keyboard, for instance, consumes 275 milliamps—the length of extension cable you can add is somewhat limited no matter the style of keyboard you're working with. The smaller gauge the cable (the higher the gauge number), the shorter the extension cable must be. Telephone cables have very little current capacity and their range is the most limited. Should the cable be too long, your keyboard will work erratically or not at all. If you want to make a really long cable, you'll have to experiment to prove its reliability.

Mice

For many people, the keyboard is the most formidable and forbidding aspect of a PC. It, as well as the uninformative and unforgiving user interface of DOS and OS/2 Version 1.0, are the major elements that alienate new PC users.

In an effort to make the computer more accessible, Douglas C. Engelbert of the Augmentation Research Center of the Stanford Research Laboratory developed a graphical/menu-driven on-screen user interface coupled to a special pointing device between 1957 and 1977. The pointing device allowed the user to indicate which menu selection he wanted by physically moving the device, which caused a corresponding on-screen movement of the cursor. One or more buttons atop the device allowed the user to indicate he wished to select a menu item.

The device was small enough to fit under the palm of a hand with the button under a fingertip. With a cord connecting the device to its computer host trailing like a tail, and the device's characteristic scurrying around the desktop to carry out its function, it quickly earned the name *mouse*. The whole process of moving the mouse and its on-screen representation is termed *dragging* the mouse.

The mouse idea was further developed by the Palo Alto Research Center of Xerox Corporation during the 1970s. Apple Computer, understanding the need to make computers easier to use to make them more accessible, incorporated the best of the Palo Alto ideas into its Macintosh, including the mouse, in 1983. IBM, more performance than ease-of-entry oriented, only made the mouse a built-in feature of its personal computers with the introduction of the Micro Channel PS/2 line, each machine of which incorporates a special *mouse port* in its planar board circuitry.

Mice can be distinguished by three chief differences—the number of buttons, the technology they use, and the manner in which they connect with their computer hosts.

Mouse Buttons

In purest form, the mouse has exactly one pushbutton. Movement of the mouse determines the position of the on-screen cursor, but a selection is made only when that button is pressed, preventing any menu selections that the mouse is inadvertently dragged across from being chosen.

One button is the least confusing arrangement and the minimum necessary to carry out mouse functions. Operating the computer is reduced to nothing more than whether you press the button or not. Carefully tailored menu selections will allow the single button to suffice in controlling all computer functions.

Two buttons allow more flexibility, however. For instance, one can be given a "Do" function and a second, an "Undo" function. In a drawing program, one might "lower" the pen analog that traces lines across the screen while the other "lifts" the pen.

Of course, three buttons would be even better because the programmer would have more flexibility still. Or, possibly, four buttons would—but as the number of mouse buttons rises, the mouse becomes increasingly like a keyboard. It becomes a more formidable device with a more rigorous learning curve. A profusion of mouse buttons is counterproductive.

Three buttons is the practical limit because three positions are available for index, middle, and ring fingers while the thumb and pinkie grab the sides of the mouse. Most applications use two or fewer buttons, and the most popular mice are the two-button variety. There's nothing wrong with three-button mice—they can do everything two-button mice can and more—but most applications don't require the extra button.

The buttons you press as well as the movement of the mouse are relayed to your computer as a series of codes. (Figure 12.9 shows the codes used by many popular mice.)

Mechanical Mice

The first mouse was a mechanical design. It was based on a small ball that protruded through its bottom and rotated as the mouse was pushed along a surface. Switches inside the mouse detected the movement and relayed the direction of the ball's rotation to the host computer.

Although the ball is free to rotate in any direction, only four directions are detected, corresponding to two axes of a two-dimensional coordinate system. The movement in each of the four directions is quantified (in hundredths of an inch) and sent to the host as a discrete signal for each discrete increment of movement.

The mechanical mouse works on just about any surface. In general, the rotating ball has a coarse texture and is made from a rubbery compound that even gets a grip on smooth surfaces. In fact, you can even pick up a mechanical mouse and spin the ball with your finger (although you'll then have difficulty fingering the pushbuttons!)

On the other hand, the mechanical mouse requires that you move it across a surface of *some* kind, and all too many desks don't have enough free space to give the mouse a good run. (Of course, if all else fails, you can run a mechanical mouse across your pants leg or skirt, but you're likely to get some odd looks.) In addition, mechanical parts can break. A mechanical mouse tends to pick up dirt and lint that can impede its proper operation. You'll want to regularly clean your mechanical mouse even if you think your desktop is spotless.

Mechanical mice are made and sold by a number of companies, including IBM, Logitech, and Microsoft.

Optical Mice

The alternative technology to the mechanical mouse is the optical mouse. Instead of a rotating ball, the optical mouse uses a light beam to detect movement across a specially patterned *mouse pad*. No moving parts means that the optical mouse has less to get dirty or break.

Figure 12.9 **Mouse control codes (Courtesy MSC Technologies, Inc)**

THREE-BYTE / TWO-BUTTON (Microsoft) Protocol:

Data is transmitted only when a mouse state changes, for instance a switch turning on or off or when the mouse is moved in any direction. The description of each position is in two's complement form; the data rate is 1200 bits per second using seven-bit words.

BYTE ONE:

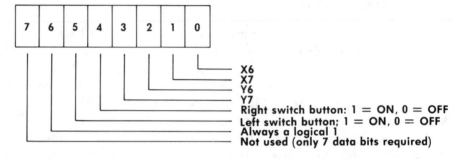

BYTE TWO:

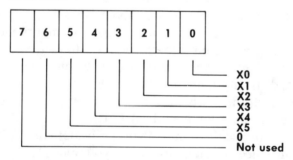

BYTE THREE:

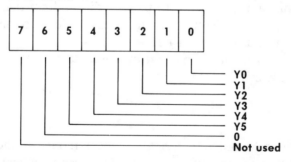

X0 through X7 = Eight-bit binary count of change in X-position. When positive, movement is to the right; negative, to the left.

Figure 12.9 **Mouse control codes (Courtesy MSC Technologies, Inc)**

Y0 through Y7 = Eight-bit binary count of change in Y-position. When positive, movement is downward; negative indicates upward.

FIVE-BYTE / THREE-BUTTON (MSC Technologies) Protocol:

Five bytes are used as a data block. The beginning of the data block is indicated by a sync byte the first five bits of which are always 10000 (binary). The remaining three bits code the state of the three mouse pushbuttons. The next four bytes encode the change in the mouse's position since the last data block. The second and third bytes encode the change in the X- and Y-positions of the mouse since the last data block; the fourth and fifth byte encode the change in X- and Y-positions since the readings given in the second and third bytes. In effect, each data block encodes two changes of mouse position as two's complement, 8-bit binary numbers.

X7 and Y7 define the direction of mouse travel. When X7 is 0, it indicates motion to the right; Y7 at 0 indicates motion upward or in the direction of the mouse cord.

Codes are transmitted as eight-bit words at 1200 bits per second with no parity.

BYTE ONE:

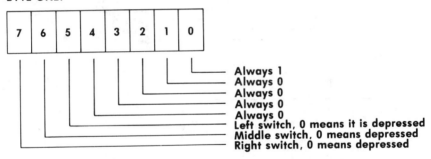

BYTE TWO:

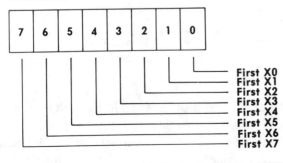

Figure 12.9 **Mouse control codes (Courtesy MSC Technologies, Inc)**

BYTE THREE:

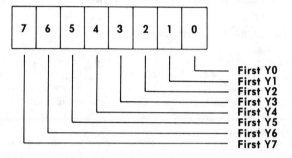

BYTE FOUR:

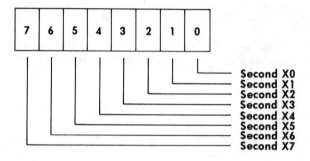

BYTE FIVE:

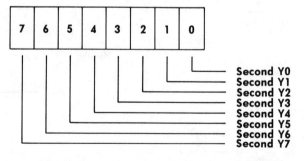

The most popular optical mouse is made by MSC Corporation (at one time Mouse Systems Corporation, hence the name). The MSC mouse uses two pair of LEDs and photodetectors on its bottom, one pair oriented at right angles to the other. Its matching mouse pad is coated with an overlapped pattern of blue and yellow grids. Each pair of LEDs and photodetectors detects motion in either direction across one axis of the grid. A felt-like covering on the bottom of the mouse makes it easy to slide across the plastic-coated mouse pad.

The big disadvantage of the optical mouse is that it does require you to use its special mouse pad. You have to put the pad somewhere, so you always have a place for your mouse to run. The pad itself can get dirty and can be damaged. The plastic coating can stick to your bare forearm on a humid day and lift off in sheets. In a normal, air-conditioned office environment, however, it should prove long-lasting and trouble-free.

Serial Mice

In order to communicate its codes to your computer, the mouse must in some way be connected. Micro Channel PS/2s make the connection easy by providing a dedicated mouse port. PC and compatibles, however, have no such provision.

Most mice adapt to a port that is generally available, the standard serial port. Called *serial mice,* they simply plug in and deliver their movement codes to the serial port. Driver software for operating the mouse can give the mouse priority by generating an interrupt whenever a new mouse movement code appears at the port. The driver then passes along the mouse code to the software that is in control.

Bus Mice

This connection works very well except for one problem: PCs that face a two-serial port limit may not have enough connections available to bring a mouse to life. The alternative is attaching the mouse to a dedicated mouse adapter that plugs into your computer's expansion bus. These so-called *bus mice* work identically with serial mice except they may use their own dedicated ports.

In most cases, these special mouse ports conform to the RS-232 standard and act just like serial ports except that they cannot be directly accessed by DOS because the operating system doesn't know what I/O addresses the port is assigned to. Otherwise, a bus mouse is just like any other mouse. It can use optical or mechanical technology and have any number of buttons.

If you have a spare serial port, you'll probably want a serial mouse because you pay extra for the bus mouse's adapter card. If you're short on serial ports, however, you'll likely want a bus mouse. The IBM PS/2 mouse is simply a bus mouse with the adapter built into the host computer.

Light Pens

Sometimes what you want to do with your computer is so obvious you could just point at the screen. If only you could move things around by pointing at them, you'd have instant, easy control.

A *light pen* lets you do exactly that. Shaped like a pen but trailing a cord, the lightpen lets your computer register positions on the screen by your pointing at them. The trick is inside the pen: At the tip is a photodetector that can detect changes in brightness; the picture tube in a computer monitor is lit by a scanning electron beam that lights tiny patches on the screen by scanning them back-and-forth and top-to-bottom. As each patch of the screen is struck by the beam, it briefly glows. The beam repeats its scan of the tube face so quickly—50 to 70 times a second—that it appears continuously lit to you, but not to the sharp eye of the light pen.

The light pen registers the instant the patch on the screen lights up, then signals to your computer at that instant. Your computer can figure out exactly where the pen is because it knows where the scanning electron beam is all the time. From the light pen, then, the computer can tell where you are pointing on the screen.

You can use the light pen for anything that requires pointing. For example, with a painting program, you can draw on your monitor screen with a light pen as if it were filled with ink and the screen were paper. The light pen is used in graphic editing so artists need only point to the screen or circle design elements they want to change or move.

All in all, the light pen is a wonderful idea but one that is inefficient, of low resolution limited to the sharpness that your monitor can display. It also makes your arm tired when you stretch it toward the screen all day long.

IBM provides an interface for a light pen on its graphics display adapters used with PCs, XTs, and ATs. The connector is simply a header on the card itself, requiring you to route a cable from inside the computer outside to the light pen. The light pen interface is not included on the IBM Monochrome Display Adapter because most light pens won't work with the IBM monochrome display. The lingering glow of the IBM green screens does not give the sharp on-off transition that the light pen needs to detect its position on the screen.

By itself, the light pen does little that's useful. It simply provides a signal at an input/output port, and it's up to your software to figure out what to do with the signal. To make a light pen useful, you'll need a special software driver or an application that is specifically written to use a light pen.

Touch Screens

Pointing is so natural (if impolite) that other technologies have been developed to exploit this human ability to data processing control. The most natural pointing device is, of course, the index finger and, in decreasing order of preference, the other four digits. Giving the computer some means of detecting what a finger is aiming at would turn the humble appendage into a true digital interface.

The *touch screen* is designed for exactly that purpose. This technology can detect the presence and location of a finger on or near the display screen of the computer. At least two methods of finger-detection have been employed. One form relies on actual contact with the surface of the screen to capacitively detect the presence of the finger. Another, used by Hewlett-Packard's Touch-Screen system, uses a special frame around the screen. This frame lines two perpendicular sides of the screen with LEDs emitting invisible light and on the two sides opposite with photodetectors. A finger approaching the screen breaks the constant light beam and allows the computer to determine its location.

Although a very natural interface, touch screen technology suffers its own logistical problems. As with light pens, reaching to the screen to perform normal daily work is a great way to build biceps and triceps, and otherwise tire yourself out. You're also apt to cover your screen with oily smudges, and if you share your computer with others less kempt than yourself, unknown contaminants and organisms.

The biggest problem with touch screen is the very practical matter of accuracy. Whereas light pens can zero in on any given pixel, the touch screen is much patchier in its pointing abilities. The screen is divided into a checkerboard pattern with resolution of about 16 × 16. While the touch screen can be used for making menu choices, it is hardly adequate for drawing or graphic editing on screen.

Touch screens have been effectively used to interface computers with a general public not versed in the intricacies of computing, enabling them to point at the function they wish to carry out. However, for a skilled computer user, the touch screen is an exotic aberration.

13

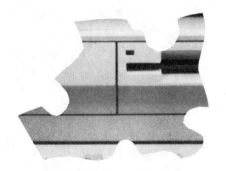

DISPLAY
SYSTEM
BASICS

If you couldn't see the results of your calculations or language manipulations, the personal computer would be worthless as a tool. You need some way of viewing the output of the computer system to know what it has done and whether you're wasting your time feeding it data. Today's choice for viewing data from your computer is the video display, a device similar to a television that substitutes a cable to your CPU for an antenna.

Video was not always the primary output for thinking machines. Computers existed even before there was television, at least commercial television as we know it. These first data processors shared the same output device that was used by their predecessor the mechanical adding machine—printed output. Before video, computers directly operated printers of some kind to show their results to an almost disbelieving world.

Teletype Output

The printer of choice was the *teletype* machine, long used to convey words and numbers across continents. These early computers fed characters to the teletype printer as if they had begun at some different keyboard—one character at a time in a long series.

Video Terminals

Although the teletype has reached a status somewhere between endangered species and museum piece, the method of data transmission and display that it used still does service to today's high-tech toys. Instead of hammering away at paper, however, these machines send their character strings at the electronic equivalent of the teletype, the *computer terminal*. These terminals are often called *Video Data Terminals* (at other times they are called Video Display Terminals, or *VDTs*) because they rely on video displays to make their presentations to you.

They are terminal because they reside at the end of the communications line, in front of your eyes.

A terminal at its most rudimentary is the classic *dumb terminal* which merely displays each character exactly as it is received, on a phosphor coated screen instead of paper. The refinements are few—instead of rattling off the edge of the paper, a too-long electronic line more likely will "wrap" down to the line below. The terminal never runs out of paper for it seemingly has a fresh supply of blank screen below that rolls upward as necessary to receive each additional line. Alas, the output it generates is even more tenuous than the flimsiest tissue and disappears at the top of the screen, perchance never to be seen again.

A *smart terminal,* on the other hand, has the data processing abilities of a computer, recognizes special commands for formatting its display, but often may work like and be used as a dumb terminal.

A few other characteristics also distinguish the mechanical teletype. Its paper travels in but one direction. It can never go backwards because like a stock ticker, it merely churns out an unending string of text. The teletype cannot type over something it did before, and it can jump ahead without patiently rolling its paper forward as if it has printed so many blank lines.

In the electronic form of the computer terminal, the teletype method of text handling means that when one character changes on the screen, a whole new screen full of text must be generated and set to the terminal. The system cannot backup to change the one character, so it must rush headlong forward, reworking the whole display along the way.

Mammoth primeval computers and rattling teletypes might seem to share little in common with the quiet and well-behaved PC sitting on your desk. However, the simplest of programs still retain this most primitive way of communicating with your video screen. They generate characters and send them one by one to the video display, only instead of traveling across the globe, the text merely shuffles from one place in memory to another inside the machine. These programs in effect operate as if the video system of your computer was the screen of a terminal.

Many computers are limited to this form of video imagery, which, understandably, is often called a *teletype display*. For IBM standard computers, from the first PC onward, teletype displays are only a vestige of their ancestry that's used only by rudimentary programs. However, teletype-type output is the highest level of support provided by the IBM system BIOS.

Character Mapping

The standard means for display text on a PC or PS/2 is the *character-mapped display*. A special section of memory is reserved for storing the image that will appear on the screen, and programs write text on the screen by pushing characters into that memory. The screen is divided into a matrix that is most often 80 characters wide and 25 high, and a memory location is assigned to each character cell of the matrix. Programs can push characters into any screen location in any order that they please—top, bottom, left, or right, even lobbing one letter atop another, overwriting its transitory existence.

This character-mapped display is obviously more versatile than the teletype method, and it can be faster. Instead of rewriting an entire screen just to change one character in the middle, the change can simply be poked into the proper memory location.

In the IBM scheme of things, the teletype method is even slower because each character must be individually manipulated by software. The system BIOS includes commands for taking each charcter from a program and squeezing it into the next video memory location. Each character thus requires the execution of a short program, and even the shortest program takes time. Directly writing to the memory used by the screen saves the time required to run this video BIOS program.

Character Boxes

The actual patterns of each character that appears on the screen are stored in a special ROM chip that is part of the video circuitry of the computer. The byte that defines the character is used by the video circuitry to look up the character pattern matching it. The pattern is then sent to the screen in its appointed place.

Each on-screen character is made from an array of dots, much like the text output of a teletype or dot-matrix printer. The several video standards used by IBM and other manufacturers build individual characters out of different size dot arrays. The framework in which the dots of an individual character are laid out, called the character box, is a matrix like a crossword puzzle. The *character box* is measured by the number of dots comprising its width and its height. For example, a 9 × 14 character box would be nine dots wide and fourteen dots high.

Individual characters do not necessarily take up the entire area that a character box affords. For example, text characters on IBM monochrome displays keep one row of dots above and one below those used by each character to provide visible separation between two adjacent lines of text on the screen.

Video RAM Assignments

IBM assigned not one but four memory locations for its video map: Two of the locations were assigned to the video systems of the first PC and XT: Another came along with the PCjr; and a fourth is used for IBM's more advanced display systems.

The first two PC video systems were assigned different memory locations so they could operate simultaneously. In this way, you can plug to displays into your computer at the same time. One of the two memory maps is nominally assigned to monochrome displays; and the other is given over to color. The memory locations are the same for each mode no matter which display-adapter system is used. Monochrome screen memory is located at B0000(hex); color, at B8000(hex). For compatibility reasons, all newer IBM video systems are also capable of operating through these same addresses even though they may store additional video information elsewhere.

PCjr Video Memory

Among IBM and compatible computers, the one that varied widest from this standard was the PCjr. For no particularly good reason IBM chose to locate its video memory—which is unchangeably built into the system board using the Color Graphics Adapter standard—at a location of 20000(hex). To maintain compatibility with programs that wrote directly to video memory, IBM had to build in special circuitry to trap and move information written at the normal video memory location to the PCjr location. To cope with the weird IBM approach, after-market memory suppliers had to supply special programs to let the PCjr access add-in memory.

Video Mode Flags

Programs that write to the screen must know which video memory is available to use. They can find out by reading a special byte in memory, a *video mode flag*. Originally called the the *video equipment flag* by

IBM, it was designed to keep track of what kind of display adapter was inside the computer and being actively used. It allowed the computer to know whether it was using a monochrome or color display.

This byte is still used to indicate whether a monochrome or color display is attached to the computer and active, even in the case of video adapters that can handle either kind of display. The memory byte is located near the beginning of your PC's RAM at 0463(hex). To code the active display mode, it uses the byte 0B4(hex) to indicate the monochrome adapter is active, 0D4(hex) for color.

Video Attributes

The character-mapped displays of the IBM standard do not store each letter adjacent to the next. Instead, each on-screen character position corresponds to every other byte of memory; the intervening bytes are assigned as *attribute bytes.* Even numbered bytes store character information; odd bytes, attributes.

The attribute byte determines the highlighting or color of displayed character that's stored in the preceding memory byte. Monochrome and color attributes use different codes. Monochrome characters are allowed the following attributes: normal, highlighted (brighter on-screen characters), underlined, and reserve-video characters (dark on light instead of the normal light on dark). The different attributes can be combined. Note, however, that highlighted reverse-video characters make the character background brighter instead of highlighting the character shape itself. (Monochrome display attributes are shown is Figure 13.1.)

Color systems store two individual character hues in the attribute byte. The first half of the byte (the most significant bits of the digital code of the byte) code the color of the character itself. The latter half of the attribute (the least significant bits) code the background color. (Color display attributes are shown in Figure 13.2.)

Because each character on the screen requires two bytes of storage, a full 80-character column by 25-character row of text (a total of 2000 characters) requires 4000 bytes of storage. In the basic IBM monochrome video system, 16 kilobytes are allotted to storing character information. The basic (and basically obsolete) color system reserved 64 kilobytes for this purpose. The basic IBM display adapters don't use all the memory this is allotted, however.

Figure 13.1 **Monochrome text display attributes**

EVEN-BYTE: ASCII character value

7	6	5	4	3	2	1	0

ODD BYTE: Display attribute

	7	6	5	4	3	2	1	0
Non-blinking characters	0	x	x	x	x	x	x	x
Blinking characters	1	x	x	x	x	x	x	x
Non-display	x	0	0	0	x	0	0	0
Underline	x	0	0	0	x	0	0	1
White-on-black	x	0	0	0	x	1	1	1
Reverse video	x	1	1	1	x	0	0	0
Normal intensity	x	x	x	x	0	x	x	x
High intensity (bright)	x	x	x	x	1	x	x	x

Key: x=don't care
       0=binary 0
       1=binary 1

Video Pages

The additional memory does not go to waste, however. It can be used to store more than one screen of text at a time, with each separate screen called a *video page*. Either basic video system is designed to quickly switch between these video pages so on-screen images can be changed almost instantly. Switching quickly allows a limited degree of animation.

The basic IBM color system also has a special mode in which it displays text in 40 columns across the screen, an accommodation to people trying to use televisions instead of computer monitors as displays. Televisions are not as sharp as computer monitors, therefore fine, 80-column characters blur together on their screens. Half as many columns requires half as much storage, which in turns allows twice as many pages of video text.

Through the years, IBM has refined the quality of the display systems and increased the amount of memory devoted to video. In character-based displays, this additional memory has been put to work by offering new video modes that put more rows of text on the screen (up to 43)

Figure 13.2 **Color text display attributes**

EVEN BYTE: ASCII character value   **ODD BYTE: Display attribute**

7	6	5	4	3	2	1	0

7	6	5	4	3	2	1	0

FOREGROUND COLOR:

	7	6	5	4	3	2	1	0
Black	x	x	x	x	0	0	0	0
Blue	x	x	x	x	0	0	1	0
Green	x	x	x	x	0	0	1	0
Cyan	x	x	x	x	0	0	1	1
Red	x	x	x	x	0	1	0	0
Magenta	x	x	x	x	0	1	0	1
Brown	x	x	x	x	0	1	0	1
Light grey	x	x	x	x	0	1	1	1
Dark grey	x	x	x	x	1	0	0	0
Bright blue	x	x	x	x	1	0	0	1
Bright green	x	x	x	x	1	0	1	0
Bright cyan	x	x	x	x	1	0	1	1
Bright red	x	x	x	x	1	1	0	0
Bright magenta	x	x	x	x	1	1	0	1
Yellow	x	x	x	x	1	1	1	0
White	x	x	x	x	1	1	1	1

BACKGROUND COLOR:

	7	6	5	4	3	2	1	0
Black	x	0	0	0	x	x	x	x
Blue	x	0	0	1	x	x	x	x
Green	x	0	1	0	x	x	x	x
Cyan	x	0	1	1	x	x	x	x
Red	x	1	0	0	x	x	x	x
Magenta	x	1	0	1	x	x	x	x
Brown	x	1	1	0	x	x	x	x
White (light grey)	x	1	1	1	x	x	x	x
Non-blinking characters	0	x	x	x	x	x	x	x
Blinking characters	1	x	x	x	x	x	x	x

Key: x = don't care
          0 = binary 0
          1 = binary 1

and by allowing an increased number of video pages. Third party video system may add their own text modes that permit up to 60 rows of text and 132 columns of characters on a single screen in text mode.

Block Graphics

Graphics are actually quite easy to display in any character-mapped text mode. Because one byte can encode 256 different characters, and the alphabet and other symbols total far short of that number, IBM assigned some special characters to some of the higher-numbered bytes in its character set. Many of these extra characters are designed for drawing graphic images from blocks that entirely fill in the character matrix as well as many partially filled-in areas of different patterns.

Graphic images can be made by strategically locating these character blocks on the screen so they form larger shapes. Other extra characters comprise a number of single and double lines as well as corners and intersections of them to draw borders around text areas. The characters are building blocks of the graphics images, and consequently this form of graphics is termed *block graphics*. (Table 13.1 shows the block graphic characters used in IBM-standard computer systems.)

To an IBM display system, block graphics are considered text and are handled exactly like ordinary text characters. All of the text attributes are available to every character of block graphics, including all of the available text colors, highlighting, and inverse video characteristics.

Moreover, because block graphic displays are built in text mode, they can be pushed into video memory and onto the screen just as quickly as any other text—which is fast indeed. Block graphics are, in fact, the fastest graphics available on the PC.

On the other hand, block graphics offer the worst quality of the graphic display systems that PCs can use. The images made with block graphics are jagged and lumpy—in a word, blocky. Intricate shapes and fine details are impossible to create using large character blocks. Block graphic images are chunky, clunky, and otherwise aesthetically unappealing for most applications.

Then again, block graphics comprise the only graphics available on all IBM and compatible computer systems whether color or monochrome-equipped. They are the minimum graphic standard and the least common graphic denominator among IBM display systems.

Table 13.1 **IBM Block Graphic Characters**

ASCII	Character	ASCII	Character
169	⌐	170	¬
176	░	177	▒
178	▓	179	│
180	┤	181	╡
182	╢	183	╖
184	╕	185	╣
186	║	187	╗
188	╝	189	╜
190	╛	191	┐
192	└	193	┴
194	┬	195	├
196	─	197	┼
198	╞	199	╟
200	╚	201	╔
202	╩	203	╦
204	╠	205	═
206	╬	207	╧
208	╨	209	╤
210	╥	211	╙
212	╘	213	╒
214	╓	215	╫
216	╪	217	┘
218	┌	219	█
220	▄	221	▌
222	▐	223	▀

Bit-Mapped Graphics

One way to improve the poor quality of block graphics would be to make the blocks smaller. Smaller blocks would build an image with finer grain, which could show more detail. The smaller the blocks, the better the image. However, physical aspect of the display system impose a distinct and unbreakable limit on how small each block can be—the size of the individual dots that make up the image on the video screen. The sharpest and highest quality image that could be shown by any display system would individually control every dot on the screen.

These dots are often called *pixels,* a contraction of the descriptive terms *picture element,* like atomic elements, they are the smallest known building blocks from which reality can readily be constructed. The terms dot and pixel are often used as synonyms but their strict definitions are somewhat different. When a system operates at its limit, putting as many dots on the screen as it is physically capable of handling, the number of dots and the number of pixels are the same. Often, however, systems operate with somewhat less sharpness than they are capable; the result is that one pixel may be made from several on-screen dots.

Bit-Mapped Graphics

The most straightforward way of handling the information to be displayed on such a screen is to assign some part of memory to each pixel, just as two bytes are given over each character of a character-mapped display. In the IBM system, because the data controlling each pixel is stored as one or more memory bits, this kind of display system is often called *bit-mapped graphics.* Alternately, because each pixel or point on the video screen can be separately addressed through memory, this method of controlling the video display is often called *All Points Addressable graphics* or an *APA display.*

Bit-mapped graphics hold the potential for being much sharper than block graphics. More pixels means more detail. The number of dots on a screen and the ultimate number of pixels are many times the number of characters displayed on that same screen, from 64 to 126 times greater.

However, bit-mapped graphics imposes its own penalty—memory usage. Assigning a byte or two to each dot on the screen would take a prodigious amount of memory, even the lowest quality graphics display that IBM offers would require 128K of memory to assign one byte to each dot. Although by today's standards, 128K is not a lot of memory, it was at the time IBM introduced graphics for the PC. To keep the system affordable, IBM bequeathed only 16K of RAM to graphics information.

Fortunately, one byte per dot would be more lavish than necessary. A single pixel cannot make a pattern, so there's no need to code for anything but whether the pixel is viewable (illuminated on the screen) or invisibly dark. In simplest form, then, only one bit is needed to code each pixel and to indicate whether it glows; each bit of memory would then be used to map what is revealed on the video display. As you might have guessed, 16K amounts to the minimum possible memory for controlling every dot on a screen that shows 640 dots horizontally and 200 vertically (the measurements of the minimum quality IBM video display).

Graphic Attributes

What's lacking from this system is contrast and color. All bits are treated the same and their associated pixels look about the same, either on or off. The result is a single-hued picture with no variation or shading, essentially the same sort of an image as a line drawing. While that may be sufficient for some purposes like the display of a chart or graph that mimics the monochrome look of ink-on-paper for example, color and contrast can add impact.

The way to add color to bit-mapped images is much the same as adding color to character-based displays, adding attribute information. Additional memory is devoted to storing the attribute of each bit. The bit-mapped system works somewhat differently from the character-based mode, however. All of the memory devoted to a bit is used to describe it—not a byte needs to be devoted to identifying a character or pattern for each picture element because each one is essentially a featureless dot.

A single bit per pixel results in what graphics folk call a two-color system much like the two-state digital system. All pixels are either on or off, white or black.

Color Planes

Adding a second dot per pixel doubles the number of possible displayable colors. (Shades, degrees of darkness or light, are considered different colors in the terminology of computer graphics.) Every additional bit assigned to each pixel likewise doubles the number of possible colors, hence with n bits, 2^n colors are possible.

In computer graphics, the number of bits that are assigned to coding color information is sometimes described as the number of *color planes*. This term relates to the organization of display memory. The memory map of the graphic image can be visualized much like a Mercator projection of the world with latitude and longitude lines corresponding to the different positions of the bits corresponding to pixels in the image. Additional bits per each pixel add a third dimension, layers of maps stacked atop one another, a series of flat planes containing the color information.

Color planes are related to memory banks but are not exactly the same thing, for example, to map more memory into the limited address space reserved for video under the IBM standard, more advanced IBM video adapters used bank switching techniques to move video memory bytes in and out of the address range of the host microprocessor. In some video modes, these banks correspond exactly to the color planes used by the video adapter. In other modes, several planes of video information may be stored in each bank.

Resolution

The number that quantifies the possible sharpness of a video image is called *resolution*. It indicates how many individual pixels can be resolved across the screen. Because the quality of the electrical form of an image is independent of the screen that it is displayed upon, physical measurement play no part in a resolution measurement. Hence, resolution is expressed without reference to units of linear measurement—resolution is expressed as pixels or dots rather than dots per inch.

Memory to Screen

Images are loaded into video memory by the microprocessor, either with direct commands to move byte to specific memory locations or through calls to the BIOS, which handles the detail work. Presumably, the application software you run on your computer generates the necessary code to make the microprocessor dump the appropriate bytes into video memory.

Getting those bytes from memory to screen is a much more complex matter because the resemblance between the memory map and the on-screen image is only metaphoric. The bytes of video information are scattered between eight or more memory chips and must somehow become organized and find their way to the monitor. In addition, the monitor itself must be brought under the control of the computer.

These are the job of the *video controller,* generally a special VLSI chip designed specifically for the task of turning memory bytes into video. IBM has used a number of video controllers, which compatible makers have duplicated in their designs.

The first IBM color and monochrome adapters relied on an off-the-shelf chip, the 6845, to handle its displays. More recently IBM has switched to custom-designed and manufactured chips.

The data must be serialized. That means the information that's so nicely laid out in the memory map must be converted to a long train of data that's suitable for driving the electron gun in the monitor. Addresses in the memory map are simply read off in sequential order. However, the video controller must mix with the stream of data a host of synchronizing and control signals.

Images on most video displays are traced out by a single beam of electrons that sweeps across the face of the picture tube, often called a *Cathode Ray Tube* or *CRT* because its electron beam is shot from a cathode (an electron emitter) to the phosphors of the screen.

When display systems not based on CRTs are used—for example, the flat-panel *Liquid Crystal Displays* or *LCD* of most laptop computers, data for the display may not actually be serialized, but still must be manipulated into a format that can be handled by the display.

Retrace

The beam traces a nearly horizontal line across the face of the screen and then, in an instant, flies back to the side of the screen from which it started but lower by the width of the line it already traced out. This quick zipping back is termed *retrace,* and, although quick, it cannot take place instantly because of the inertia inherent in electrical circuits. Consequently, the smooth flow of bytes must be interrupted briefly at the end of each displayed line (or else the video information would vanish in the retrace). The video controller must take each retrace into account as it serializes the image.

In addition, another variety of retrace must occur when the electron beam reaches the bottom of the screen when it's finished painting a screen-filling image. The beam must travel as quickly as possible back up to its starting place, and the video controller must halt the flow of data while it does so.

Blanking

During retrace, should the electron beam from the gun in the tube be on, it would paint a bright line diagonally across the screen as the beam returns to its proper position. To prevent the appearance of this distracting line, the beam is forcibly switched off not only during retrace but also during a short interval on either side to give the beam time to stabilize. The interval in which the beam is forced off and cannot be turned on by any degree of programming is called *blanking* because the electron beam can draw nothing but a blank on the screen.

Vertical Interval

The period during which the screen is blanked during the vertical retrace is called, appropriately, the *vertical interval*. Its physical manifestation is the wide black horizontal bar that's visible between image frames when your television screen or computer monitor picture rolls and requires adjustment of the vertical hold control.

Synchronizing Signals

The electron beam in the monitor is swept across the screen by a combination of magnetic fields; one field moves the beam horizontally, and another vertically. Circuitry in the monitor supplies a steadily increasing voltage to two sets of *deflection coils* to control the sweep of the beam. These coils are electromagnets, and the increasing voltage causes the field strength of the coils to increase and deflect the beam farther. At the end of the sweep of a line, the field that controls the horizontal sweep of the electron beam is abruptly switched off, returning the beam to the starting side of the screen. Likewise, when the beam reaches the bottom of the screen, the field in control of the vertical sweep switches off. The result is that the electron beam follows a tightly-packed zig-zag path from the top of the screen to the bottom.

The primary difference between the two sweeps is that several hundred horizontal sweeps take place for each vertical one. The rate at which the horizontal sweeps take place is called the *horizontal frequency* of the display system. The rate at which the vertical sweeps take place is called the *vertical frequency* or *frame rate* of the system because one complete image frame is created every time the beam sweeps fully down the screen.

The electronics generating the sweep frequencies used by a monitor are inside the monitor itself. However, the signals themselves must be synchronized with the data stream coming from the computer so characters appear at their proper positions on the screen. Lose sync, and the ordinarily orderly screen display takes on the countenance of the Tower of Pisa, or the present day appearance of the Colossus at Rhodes.

To keep things organized, the video controller sends out special synchronizing signals: *Horizontal sync* before each line is sent to the display; and *vertical sync* before each frame.

Raster and Vector Graphics

This form of video display system, which organizes the screen into a series of lines that's continually scanned dozens of times a second, is termed a *raster* display. Although workable and the basis of all PC and PS/2 displays, as well as today's television and video systems, it's not the only way to put a computer image on a monitor. A completely different technique does not regularly scan the screen at all, instead, it precisely controls the circuitry operating the horizontal and vertical deflection yokes. It doesn't trace scan lines but instead draws figures the same way you would a series of strokes of a paintbrush. To keep the screen lit, it constantly retraces the figures.

Because the signals controlling the monitor drive the electron beam in the CRT is a series of vectors, this image-making technique is termed *vector graphics*. Alternately, this kind of display system is sometimes called a *stroker* because of the kinship to drawing brushtrokes. Although not used on PCs, the term pops up occasionally in the descriptions of expensive computerized workstations.

Graphics Coprocessors

Just as numeric coprocessors can help your PC crunch through transcendental functions faster, a graphics coprocessor can accelerate the performance of your system in drawing images of your monitor. Complementing the speed is often a dramatic improvement in video quality because graphics coprocessors are capable of dealing with huge amounts of graphics information—hundreds of thousands of pixels—in a fraction of the time it would take your computer's native microprocessor to ponder them. Today two graphics coprocessor chips, the Intel 82796 and the Texas Instruments TMS34010, are finding their ways into high performance video systems. IBM also offers a complete graphics coprocessor system as its 8415A board.

These chips are the fodder of high-end video boards, products that have floated above the graphics mainsteam. As with numeric coprocessors, graphics coprocessors require special software to take advantage of their advanced features and speed. In addition, they often require more expensive monitors than their more mundane counterparts.

Graphic Operating Environments

The software problem can be solved by using a *graphics operating environment* such as Microsoft Windows or Digital Research GEM when running under DOS or Presentation Manager when using OS/2. These operating environments serve as software bridges between your applications and advanced video systems, including those based on graphics coprocessors.

They work much like your system's BIOS by providing software routines called *hooks* that programs can use to elicit certain images on the video display. The operating environment translates the hook commands into the language understood by the graphic coprocessors or other video innovation. Application writers need only concern themselves with the operating environment hooks. The operating environment designers, on the other hand, match their products to as many of the competing non-standard video systems as they can.

For example, a program may want to blank the video screen so it sends Windows the appropriate command without concern for the hardware that's connected to the computer. Windows, however, knows how the particular video system that it is using blanks the screen, and sends the appropriate command to the hardware. Windows, as with most graphic operating environments, learns about its hardware environment through a software driver that you install in your computer's CONFIG.SYS file. If you change the video hardware attached to your system, you only need change the one driver used by Windows to match *all* your applications to the new display system.

Graphic Development Systems

If you strip the graphic operating environment of its user interface, you'll end up with a set of software hooks that help applications match to hardware. Several such products, termed *graphic development systems,* are available to application developers. These are wonderful products because you don't have to worry about them. The programmer uses the software tools supplied by the development system to make his job of writing flashy code easier and broaden the market for his product across a wide range of hardware. You, as the user of the application, don't have to fret about complications other than loading the appropriate driver when you start your system.

Without the operating environment or use of a development system and its drive, the only way you can take advantage of a graphic coprocessor (or other advanced video system) is through applications written specifically for it. Some programs support a wide array of video systems. Some manufacturers of video systems include special software drivers to make their hardware compatible with a limited number of very popular applications (almost invariably including Lotus 1-2-3 and AutoDesk AutoCAD).

Note that compatibility issues are important only for graphic applications. In general, programs written only to use text mode will work on nearly any video system.

High-Level Commands

One of the biggest bottlenecks in the performance of a high speed computer, such as one based on the Intel 80386 chip, is the continual need of the microprocessor to handle all the calculations and pixel-manipulating functions generating images for the video display requires. Such time-consuming complications can be avoided by severing the direct link between display and microprocessor by passing the chore of handling the display and computing graphics functions over the graphics coprocessor.

Although a coprocessor handles the screen much in the same way as the normal PC-video controller, it remains memory-mapped. However, the microprocessor no longer must handle pixel-level calculations or moving bytes into the appropriate locations in video memory, instead, it sends out high-level commands to the coprocessor to indicate what kind of image to draw, and the coprocessor in turn executes them. In effect, the computer takes on a degree of parallel processing with two brains working at once.

The microprocessor issues high-level instructions to the graphic coprocessor to carry out whatever action is necessary to put the proper image on the screen. For example, instead of dealing with the calculation required for drawing a circle, solving a formula, then generating the set of points that must be lit on the screen, the microprocessor merely passes the command to draw a circle to the graphics coprocessor. The high-level commands, which comprise instructions to make the basic lines and shapes of the graphic coprocessor's repertory, are termed graphic or drawing *primitives*. From them any image that the system will display can be made.

While the microprocessor does, in fact, control what is on the screen, it no longer needs to deal with how that image is effectuated. The microprocessor operates like a manager, delegating the day-to-day (or microsecond-to-microsecond) responsibilities for operating the display to the coprocessor, and this saves valuable microprocessor time.

Because these graphics coprocessors are optimized for one particular task—handling the display image—they can change the contents of display memory faster than the microprocessor itself can, which speeds screen updates and system performance even further.

Even though they work in the same manner, the two coprocessors represent two entirely different approaches to the coprocessing problem. The 82786 supplies a set of hardware functions designed to handle the bulk of the chores involved in operating the display much like a glorified 6845. It is an evolutionary device that advances on earlier graphics chips. The TMS34010 is an innovative break with past designs. It is effectively a free-standing microprocessor that has been optimized for manipulating graphics, and as with any microprocessor, it can do nearly anything. Its exact function is determined by software programming.

Both chips, however, work differently from IBM's standard equipment video systems. Even the IBM VGA chip used in the Micro Channel models of Personal System/2 is a gate array rather than true coprocessor. Its only innovation is the ability to handle more pixels and produce higher on-screen resolution. At a functional level, however, VGA operation is not too different from that of the 6845 chip. VGA display processing is carried out in an entirely conventional manner, mediated by the main microprocessor in the system.

8514/A Application Interface

Only the IBM 8514/A video board operates as if it were a true graphic coprocessor—besides putting additional pixels on the screen, it also incorporates its own set of higher level functions called the *Application Interface.*

The IBM Application Interface comprises a set of commands that allow for bit-block transfer (moving a block of video information with one command), line drawing, area filling, pattern generation, color mixing, and scissors-style editing. In addition, it provides text support that includes proportionally-spaced fonts and alphanumeric operations based on the those of the IBM 3270 terminal. Commands to the Application Interface are used like BIOS function calls except they are entered through CALL instructions rather than software interrupts.

The 8514/A Application Interface provided the graphic industry with a needed standard, and many hardware developers are creating products that function with the same instruction set. These video adapters may themselves be implemented with graphics coprocessors like the Intel 82786 or Texas Instruments TMS34010.

The Intel 82786

Intel's 82786 acts like a cross between a true graphic coprocessor and an ordinary video controller. It handles both deeds of computing figures from high-level commands and handling the normal housekeeping required to put images on the screen. Although at its best when image sharpness is on par with that of IBM's now standard VGA system, it adds several special hardware features and can push image clarity skyward.

Coprocessor Functions

The true coprocessor functions of 82786 include a small but useful repertory of high level drawing functions built into its hardware. It draws lines, polygons, and circles and moves text into video memory under command of high level language instructions. Although it still relies on its host microprocessor to handle some of the calculations required in drawing on-screen images, the 82786 hardware routines can eliminate some of the most common and time-consuming of those calculations.

Display Controller Functions

The display controller part of the 82786 controls a hardware cursor, allows pixel level zooming, and can even add color borders to windows. In some modes, it supports hardware windows, a feature which can considerably accelerate the performance of graphic operating environments.

The 82786 is designed to work with either standard dynamic RAM (DRAM) chips and special video RAM (VRAM) chips. When VRAM is used, the chip (and the entire video system) can operate more quickly because DRAM video memory cannot be updated when the image it contains is being scanned to the screen. VRAM can be updated at any time while DRAM can be updated only for the short time between screen refreshes.

The 82786 handles DRAM and video processor functions only at resolutions of 640 × 480 × 8 (or the equivalent with another video depth). At higher resolutions, VRAM must be used with the 82786. Moreover, many of its advanced features, such as hardware windowing, must be foregone at higher resolutions.

Display speed is achieved at higher resolutions only through the high processing speed of the 82786, about 24 megabits per second, that translates to about 1/24th of a second being needed to move a complete 1024 × 1024 screen.

Part of the 82786 called the bus interface unit allows the chip to communicate with the host computer bus, including the microprocessor and its RAM, and the video memory. In addition, this bus interface allows the microprocessor itself to directly address the video memory.

Hardware Supported Functions

The 82786 hardware also supports a number of graphics functions that are usually handled by software including clipping, mouse support, bit-plane masking, logical operations and character-set support.

Hardware clipping allows the 82786 to draw partial sections of complete figures without wasting the time needed to generate the entire image.

The mouse support minimizes the intervention of the host microprocessor when the pointing devices is used to select an on-screen object.

The microprocessor can generate an interrupt when an object is selected, so the microprocessor only needs to intervene after the selection is completed.

The 82786 can support an almost unlimited number of character sets because they can be stored in and read from RAM. The only limit is the amount of memory available. Proportional spacing is built into each character set and allows not just more uniform spacing of letters but also true kerning (squeezing characters like A and V tightly together).

Hardware Windowing

From the user's point of view, the most appealing feature of the Intel 82786 is its ability to operate *hardware windows*.

In a conventional windowing system, software controls the display of each window. The layout of the screen is calculated, and the proper values for each pixel are plugged into the appropriate locations in the memory map. The image is generated by reading each memory location in sequence, and using the information it contains, to control the intensity of the electron beam in the display as it sweeps down the screen. Every memory location is scanned sequentially in a rigid order.

Hardware windowing works by slicing up the memory map. Although each dot on the screen has one or more bits of memory assigned to it, the map no longer needs to be an exact representation of the screen. The video chip no longer scans each memory location in exact sequential order as the video beam traces down the screen, instead, the memory scanned to control the beam is indicated by pointers, which guide the scan between different memory areas. Each memory area pointed to represents an on-screen window.

Each window can be individually manipulated. The memory used by a window can even be mapped into the address range of the system microprocessor, perhaps used conventionally as a monochrome or CGA display, while the rest of the screen is handled separately by the graphics coprocessor.

Intel elaborates on this scheme by allowing each window to effectively operate in a different video mode. Each window may have a different video depth, or number of memory bits assigned to each pixel. As a consequence, most of the calculating normally required to change a window is eliminated and therefore screen updates can be speeded up substantially.

Texas Instruments' TMS34010

The Texas Instruments TMS34010 differs from the Intel 82786 in that instead of operating as a glorified video controller, it is essentially a microprocessor that's been optimized for handling graphics. Even when compared to the best of today's microprocessors, the TMS34010 is a formidable chip, one with awesome horsepower. It has the equivalent of 31 registers 32 bits wide—that is twice as many 32-bit registers as the 68000 microprocessor used in the Macintosh, and nearly four times as many as used in Intel's 80386 microprocessor.

In graphics, the large number of registers is particularly valuable because they permit the many parameters often used in graphics manipulation to stay inside the processor instead of being shifted continually between the chip and memory. The pointless swapping of information out of the processor and into memory and back again is called *thrashing* and is deadly to performance.

Because of its microprocessor base and its many registers, the TMS34010 can handle pixel calculation tasks better than any other single chip currently in existence. It combines the best features of the general purpose microprocessor such as programability, mathematical and logical functions, with specialized graphics functions, such as the ability to move blocks of pixels.

Although it may be somewhat slower using software to handle the functions that are built into the hardware of the 82786, the TMS34010 is still two to ten times faster than letting the host microprocessor in the computer handle all display chores, and the TMS34010 earns the same speed advantage over the Intel chip in carrying out functions not intrinsic to the 82786 hardware.

In fact, the TMS34010 is so powerful in itself that an entire graphics computer could be built around it without the need for any other processor. However, the TMS34010 chip does not manage the scanning of the display, instead it relies on other graphics controllers—possibly the 82786.

The TMS34010 lacks Intel's sophisticated bus interface and so operates entirely separately, but under the control of, the host microprocessor. Screen manipulations are carried out with high-level commands rather than memory manipulation.

Because it is fully programmable, video systems built around the

TMS34010 can mimic other standards. One obvious application is the implementation of boards compatible with the 8514/A Application Interface or just about any other standard.

14

VIDEO
ADAPTERS

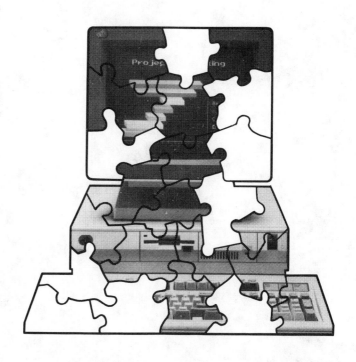

In the beginning, there was one—one model of IBM Personal Computer and one display type. You had one choice of screen color, green, and no options. Your screen showed text or crude block graphics, but that was all. One thing was certain, however: You didn't have any trouble making up your mind about what sort of video system you wanted to plug into your PC.

Since then, choices and confusion have grown apace with technology. Video is better than ever, and almost continually getting better. And the headaches of decision-making are getting ever-worse. You've got dozens of video adapters to choose from, half a dozen "official" video standards, and dozens of better ideas—the proprietary display systems that tip-toe around the prevailing standards.

Leading all these changes have been a flurry of video standards that, with but one exception, formed around the video adapters that IBM tucked inside its personal computers. From the eerie green screen to today's colorful high-resolution displays, the progress has been steady—and almost fast enough to keep up with the deterioration of your eyesight.

The Monochrome Display Adapter

In that all of the other IBM video standards have become known by their initials, the *Monochrome Display Adapter* has earned the nickname *MDA* mostly by default even though its official name is the Monochrome Display and Parallel Printer Adapter.

As with most lengthy compound names, the MDA's epithet is quite descriptive. The "monochrome" in its name reveals the most important characteristic of the MDA. It is designed to work with single-color displays, in particular the virulent green screen that sits atop a huge number of all IBM systems.

The "display adapter" part of the name is a functional description.

This board adapts the signal on the PC bus into a form that can be digested by a video system. The parallel printer adapter is a bonus, providing a connection for a printer without sacrificing another expansion slot.

Technically, the MDA is a character-mapped system with no provision for graphics other than the IBM extended character set. It was the first display adapter offered by IBM and, until recently, it was the best for text processing because it yielded up the sharpest character of any pre-PS/2 display system.

Text was the design purpose of the system. IBM must never have imagined anyone wanting to draw pictures on his display.

MDA Dot Box

For legibility on par with terminals used with larger computer systems, IBM set the character box for the MDA at 9×14 pixels with a typical character using a 7×9 matrix in the box. The extra dots space individual lines apart for greater readability, something that's most appreciated when it's not available.

To put this character box on the screen in the default arrangement used by most VDTs, 80 columns and 25 rows, requires 720 pixels horizontally and 350 vertically, a total of 252,000 dots on every screen.

Table 14.1 **6845 Video Controller Registers**

Reg. No.	Description	Prog. Unit	Read/Write
R0	Horizontal total	Character	Write Only
R1	Horizontal displayed	Character	Write Only
R2	Horizontal sync position	Character	Write Only
R3	Horizontal sync width	Character	Write Only
R4	Vertical total	Row	Write Only
R5	Vertical total adjust	Scan line	Write Only
R6	Vertical displayed	Row	Write Only
R7	Vertical sync position	Row	Write Only
R8	Interlace mode	None	Write Only
R9	Maximum scan line address	Scan line	Write Only
R10	Cursor start	Scan line	Write Only
R11	Cursor end	Scan line	Write Only
R12	Start address (High)	None	Write Only
R13	Start address (Low)	None	Write Only
R14	Cursor (High)	None	Read/Write
R15	Cursor (Low)	None	Read/Write
R16	Light pen (High)	None	Read Only
R17	Light pen (Low)	None	Read Only

MDA Frame Rate

IBM compromised in how to display all those dots. At a high-frame rate, displaying that amount of information would require a wider bandwidth monitor than was available (at least inexpensively) when the PC was introduced. IBM instead slowed down the frame rate to 50 Hz. and compensated for whatever flicker might develop by using long persistence phosphors in its standard monochrome display.

The lower-frame rate gave the horizontal sweep of the scanning electron beam extra time to cover each line of the image. However, even with the lower frame rate, the dot density of the IBM monochrome standard demanded a higher horizontal frequency than was used by popular video monitors (and television sets), 18.1 kHz versus 15.525 kHz.

6845 Video Controller

The essence of the MDA is the *6845 video controller* and four kilobytes of dual-ported static RAM used for holding character-mapping video information. That memory is sufficient only for a single video page.

The 6845 is a completely programmable device that's controlled through a series of registers. (Table 14.1 lists the registers of the 6845 chip.)

The Cursor

The flashing cursor on the screen is created by the 6845-video controller. Its flashing rate is set by system hardware and cannot be changed. However, flashing can be switched off and the size of the cursor can be altered by loading values into the registers of the 6845-video chip.

Interfacing

Not only does the MDA use different frequencies than most garden-variety monitors, it also uses an connection scheme that was odd for monitors, but, because of the IBM influence and ubiquity of the PC, has become commonplace. Sometimes called *direct drive,* the signals from the MDA are fourfold, a drive signal for the electron gun, an intensity bit (which causes highlighted dots and characters to glow more brightly), horizontal, and vertical synchronizing signals. All are directly connected to the part of the display circuit that handles them without the need for decoding, hence the name.

Figure 14.1 **MDA pin-out**

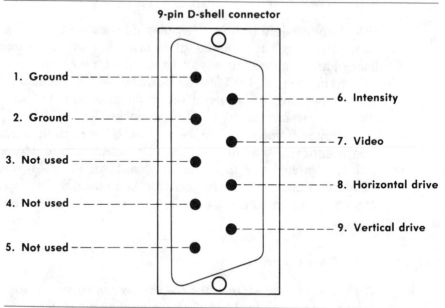

9-pin D-shell connector

1. Ground ————————— •
                              • ————————— 6. Intensity
2. Ground ————————— •
                              • ————————— 7. Video
3. Not used ————————— •
                              • ————————— 8. Horizontal drive
4. Not used ————————— •
                              • ————————— 9. Vertical drive
5. Not used ————————— •

These signals are assigned pins on a female nine-pin D-shell connector on the retaining bracket of the MDA. (The pin-out of this connector is shown in Figure 14.1.)

Monitors compatible with the MDA are sometimes termed direct-drive, alternately they may be called TTL because the signal generated by the MDA are at the levels used by TTL logic. Such displays are also occasionally simply called digital because they use digital inputs instead of the analog inputs used by composite displays. The MDA is completely incompatible with a composite display.

The Color Graphics Adapter

The first bit-mapped display adapter that IBM developed for the PC was the *Color Graphics Adapter* or *CGA*. Introduced as an alternative to the MDA, its first images dazzled a world accustomed to plain green computer screens. It boasted the ability to show 16 bright, pure colors (a total which misleadingly includes black, dark grey, light grey, and white). It also featured a host of graphics modes with several different levels of resolution.

As the name implies, the CGA system is designed to put graphics on a color screen. However, it also features text modes and will work with monochrome displays as well—but not the IBM Personal Computer Display that's designed for the MDA board. It will work with both monochrome and color composite monitors and even features an output for a modulator for use with a television set. (You cannot plug a television directly into the CGA board unless, of course, the television features a composite video input.) In addition, it also supports a light pen.

The CGA is a multi-mode display adapter. It can use both the character-mapped and bit-mapped display techniques, and allows several options under each. It includes 16 kilobytes of memory, which is directly accessible by your system's microprocessor.

CGA Character Modes

Operated in character-mapped mode, its boot-up default, the CGA operates much like the MDA. The chief difference between the two is that the MDA was designed to work with a proprietary monitor with nonstandard horizontal and vertical frequencies to produce a sharper image. The CGA opts for more standard frequencies—those used by composite displays—endowing it with compatibility with the greatest range of monitors but resulting in lesser on-screen quality.

To fit its operation under the confines of a 15,525 Hz horizontal rate and 60 Hz vertical rate, the CGA divides the display into a pixel array numbering 640 horizontally and 200 vertically. To put the same 2000 text characters on the screen in the same 80 × 25 arrangement used by the MDA allows only a dot box measuring 8 × 8 pixels.

The 16 kilobytes of memory on the CGA is sufficient to handle four pages of text. Normally, only a single page, the first one, is used in text mode. The others are, however, accessible by programs and you through both the BIOS and directly through the mode register on the CGA.

CGA Character Quality

In the CGA system, each character is allocated a 7 × 7 matrix with one dot reserved for descenders and one for letter spacing. Obviously, a descending character will occupy the full height of the dot box and thus bump into an ascending character on the line below with no separation. The fewer dots means that on-screen text will otherwise look more crude and less pleasing than that made by the MDA.

Forty-Column Text

Even those rudimentary characters are more than can be imaged sharply on a standard color television set. On most televisions, lines of text 80 characters wide appear blurry if not indecipherable because of the resolution limits of both the signals inside the set and the picture tube. To allow adequate text renderings on color televisions, IBM added a special low-resolution text mode that cuts the number of columns of text from 80 to 40. The number of rows, 25, is left the same as for other displays because it is not a problem for televisions.

Characters in 40-column text mode are made within the same 8 × 8 dot box used in 80-column mode, and they suffer the same quality limitations. They look rough but they may be more legible than 80-column characters because they are wider.

Although 40-column mode is rarely used in serious computing, many programs (particularly utilities) make allowance for it by generating lines of text no wider than 40 characters each. That's why some of their displays look so odd most of the time. The 40-column mode is the least common denominator of IBM text-display systems.

Text Colors

In any text mode, the IBM system of attributes allows up to the full 16-color palette to be displayed on the screen at once. Any character of text can be any one of the 16 colors allowed.

The background of the character—the dots in the 8 × 8 box that are not part of the character shape—can be separately set to one of those same 16 colors with one limitation. In the default operating mode of the system, only eight background colors are possible because the bit in the attribute byte which controls the brightness or intensity of the background color is assigned a different task. It controls the blinking of the character.

A register on the CGA alters the definition of this attribute bit. By loading values into this register, you or a program can toggle its function between blinking and high-intensity background colors. Note, however, that this register affects all text on the screen. You cannot have both blinking characters and a high-intensity background on the screen at the same time.

The CGA forces programmers to directly manipulate this register. More advanced IBM display adapters add an extra BIOS routine that handles this function.

Border Color

Another register on the CGA controls the *border color*. The screen border is the screen area outside of the active data area in which text appears. The default colors of the CGA display (white text on a black background) hide the matching black border circling the screen. Change the background color of the text, and the border will appear, with an obnoxious sharp demarcation between it and the edge of the perimeter characters in the text display.

The setting the CGA register for a border color, which can be any of the 16 colors displayable by the CGA system, makes for a more pleasant on-screen image. This register is called the *color select register* and is available at the I/O port 03D9(Hex). The lower four bits of this register control the border color.

Flicker and Snow

One of the most notable, and to many people the most obnoxious characteristics of the CGA system is its tendency to flash the text display off and on when the display scrolls in high-resolution text mode. This tendency is called *flicker,* (different from the flicker of slow frame rate and interlaced displays) and is a direct result of the sorry, slow processing speed of the PC and XT.

Scrolling the screen requires that every byte used by the display must be moved because every character on the screen (and its associated attribute) must change position. The IBM display system is designed so information is written to the screen only during the brief period called *vertical retrace,* when the scanning electron beam travels back from the bottom of the screen at the end of one frame, to the top for the beginning of the next. During vertical retrace, the electron beam is *blanked,* switched off, so no matter what is sent to it, nothing gets on the screen.

If the CGA memory is changed some other time, when the beam is not blanked, the system may scan through video memory while it is being changed and all sorts of odd pulses may be picked up and sent to the screen. The result is a flurry of bright dots that can appear anywhere on the screen, video noise called *snow* because the randomly placed dots look somewhat like a snowstorm (if you have enough imagination).

The CGA card provides a status bit which indicates when vertical retrace is occurring. This is a "coast is clear" signal that programs or that the BIOS can query to see when it is okay to write to the screen. The vertical retrace period only provides enough time for a few lines to be updated, however, so to avoid snow, the scrolling must take place slowly, in chunks, during several retrace periods or snow may occur. IBM sidestepped this issue by turning off the electron beam for the whole time that the screen is being updated during a scroll. Instead of momentarily going black during the invisible vertical retrace, the screen turns black for a substantial and readily visible, fraction of a second. This whole-screen blanking causes the flicker.

With a CGA adapter, the trade-off is flicker for snow. Other video adapters use faster memory that can be entirely updated within a single retrace period or different types of memory which can be updated while being read to eliminate both problems.

Graphics Modes

The CGA standard allows for graphics at three different levels of resolution appropriately named low, medium, and high. In each case, the number of on-screen dots is traded off against the number of displayable colors. The 16K of memory on the CGA severely restricts the number of bits that can be used for storing the attributes of each dot on the APA display.

Low Resolution

The lowest resolution graphics mode of the CGA, which is not supported by IBM, breaks the screen into a display of 160 lines each 200 dots wide. Because this display requires 32,000 pixels, only half a byte is available for the storing attributes, allowing four color planes, enough for 16 colors. All of the 16 colors possible with the CGA system can be put on a single screen in low-resolution mode, but displays are so chunky that this mode is little-used.

Medium Resolution

As a compromise between color and sharpness, IBM created medium-resolution mode. Based on displays of 320 lines, each 200 dots wide, the medium resolution standard allows for two color planes that permit up to four simultaneous colors to be displayed.

The four colors cannot be chosen at random, however. IBM allows four possible palettes to chose from: red, green, brown, and black; white, magenta, cyan, and black (or a selected background color); and the previous two but in high intensity colors. The palette to be used is selected using a special I/O port located at address 03D9(Hex) bit, 5 at this port address selects between the red/green palette (set at 0) and magenta/cyan palette (set at 1). This port has other functions too. Bit 4 selects the intensity—0 for dim, 1 for intensified. Bits 0 through 3 select the background color. The default values, set by the BIOS, are for the intensified magenta/cyan palette with a black background.

High Resolution

The highest resolution mode of the CGA assigns one bit to each pixel on the screen, allowing for individual control of an array of pixels 640 horizontally and 200 vertically. Because no additional memory is available on the CGA for storing attribute information, all pixels must be the same color and intensity. You can, however, choose what color you want them to be with the color-select register.

CGA Memory Arrangement

In graphics mode, the CGA uses an unusual storage arrangement. It stores even-numbered scan lines, starting with zero, one after the other starting at absolute memory location 0B8000(Hex). The odd-numbered scan lines are stored in sequence starting at an address 2000(Hex) higher. The unusual arrangement was chosen for entirely practical hardware-design reasons.

When multiple bits are assigned to an individual pixel, they are stored as sequential bits in a given byte of storage, four pixels per byte in medium-resolution mode. (See Figure 14.2.) The strange arrangement should not bother you because all graphic software and language automatically takes it into account.

Outputs

You can connect your video display to the CGA through one of three different connectors. The one that you choose depends on the kind of display you want to connect.

The preferred display is an IBM 5151 Personal Computer Color Display which uses TTL digital inputs through a nine-pin D-shell connector. Separate on-and-off digital signals are provided for each of three color guns (red, green, and blue), an intensity bit (which brightens

Figure 14.2 CGA medium resolution graphics data storage arrangement

In medium resolution graphics mode, each byte encodes four on-screen pixels; the two-bit pattern encodes four colors, one background or one of three foreground colors:

Bit 1	Bit 2	Bit 3	Bit 4	Bit 5	Bit 6	Bit 7	Bit 8
Fourth Pixel		Third Pixel		Second Pixel		First Pixel	

These bytes are arranged sequentially across a scan line. Scan lines then alternate across two storage areas, even lines getting stored in the lower 8K bank, odd lines in the higher 8K bank, as shown below:

FUNCTION:	ADDRESS BOUNDARY:
	———— B8000(Hex)
Even Scan Lines (0, 2, 4, ... 198) 8,000 Bytes	
	———— B9F3F(Hex)
Unused memory	———— BA000(Hex)
Odd Scan Lines (1, 3, 5, ... 199) 8,000 Bytes	
	———— BBF3F(Hex)
Unused memory	———— BBFFF(Hex)

all three guns simultaneously), horizontal sync, vertical sync, and ground. (The pin-out is shown in Figure 14.3.)

All of these signals are positive-going, in other words, a digital high turns on the appropriate gun or indicates a synchronizing pulse—with the exception of vertical sync. When this style of connection was first becoming popular, this arrangement caused untold problems for developers because horizontal sync is normally negative-going. IBM's signal thus appears upside down.

The composite output of the CGA is provided both on an RCA-style pin jack on the retaining bracket of the card and as part of a header on the surface of the board. The signal provided at the RCA jack are compatible with both color and monochrome displays that follow the NTSC standard.

The composite output provided on the card itself is meant to operate a *modulator* that converts the CGA in to a standard television signal.

Figure 14.3 **CGA RGB interface pin-out**

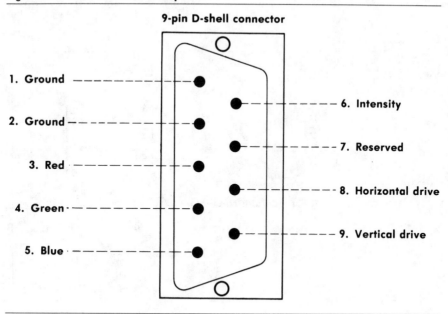

9-pin D-shell connector

1. Ground

2. Ground

3. Red

4. Green

5. Blue

6. Intensity

7. Reserved

8. Horizontal drive

9. Vertical drive

Other pins of this single-row header supply the voltage needed to operate the modulator. (See Figure 14.4.)

Black-and-White Mode

When a monochrome composite monitor is connected to the CGA, the screen will sometimes shift to an eye-straining jumble of vertical lines and shadings instead of solid color; text can be almost impossible to read. This odd display is caused by the color subcarrier that's part of the composite-video signal. It limits the bandwidth of the video signal and interferes with monochrome information, creating the odd patterns on the screen.

You can clear up the problem by switching to *black-and-white* mode, which turns off the color subcarrier. Although you can control this by loading values into a CGA register, the MODE command supplied with DOS does the job more easily. Just type:

    MODE BW

to switch off the color subcarrier.

Figure 14.4 **CGA modulator output pin-out**

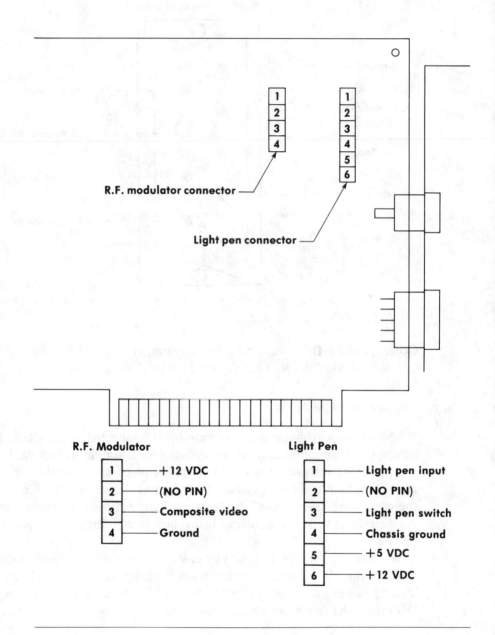

R.F. Modulator

1	+12 VDC
2	(NO PIN)
3	Composite video
4	Ground

Light Pen

1	Light pen input
2	(NO PIN)
3	Light pen switch
4	Chassis ground
5	+5 VDC
6	+12 VDC

Hercules Graphics

Although a step in the right direction, CGA had two major drawbacks: It wasn't particularly sharp, and it required the purchase of both a video adapter and a new monitor. The latter was particularly galling if you had just invested in a monochrome system or had no need for color. Adding a second display for graphics when a system already had a perfectly good, and sharp, text-based imaging system appeared counterproductive (at least to those not in the business of selling CGAs and color displays).

Hercules Computer Technology, Inc., headed by Kevin Jenkins, developed a seeming perfect solution, one that worked so well that it has become the only nearly universal video standard not first unleashed by IBM.

The *Hercules Graphics Card* or *HGC* was the obvious solution, adding bit-mapped graphics to the character-mapped MDA, but Hercules had the forethought to obtain support from Lotus Development Corporation in *1-2-3,* at the time (and long afterward) the most popular program for the PC. *1-2-3* graphics were in themselves justification for the purchase of the HGC.

HGC Compatibility

The foundation for the HGC was complete emulation of the MDA. From a functional standpoint, the two boards worked exactly alike in text mode, operated at the same frequencies with exactly the same cabling and displays. Characters were formed in the same 9 × 14 pixel dotbox on a screen with a full-screen resolution of 720 × 350 pixels, a horizontal sync frequency of 18.1 kHz and a 50 Hz frame rate. All attributes of the IBM MDA—underline, blink, high-intensity, and inverse video—are supported by the HGC. The HGC even included a parallel printer port with a base address of 03BC(Hex), same as the MDA.

While the HGC is compatible with MDA hardware and its text-mode software, it is not compatible with any IBM graphic standard. Applications must be specially written with support for the HGC. Programs written for the CGA and other IBM graphic standards will not properly execute on the HGC unless they also have HGC support.

HGC Memory

The point of departure for the HGC was its memory. Instead of the mere four kilobytes of the MDA, the HGC was equipped with a full 64K, functionally arranged in two contiguous 32K banks with base addresses of 0B0000(Hex) and 0B8000(Hex).

The various video modes supported by the HGC allowed the use of this memory for several purposes: In text mode, it could be devoted to numerous text pages—up to 16. In graphics mode, it even was sufficient for two full-screen pages.

Memory Overlap

One problem with the Hercules monochrome system was that its 64K was too large to fit into the space reserved for monochrome memory. It overlapped into the color area, potentially conflicting with CGA boards plugged into the same system.

The Hercules solution was to offer degrees of compatibility controlled by a software switch. In default, boot-up mode, the HGC would activate only half of its memory, 32K starting at the 0B0000(Hex) base, eliminating the conflict. By poking a value into the software configuration switch register located at I/O port 03BF(Hex), the HGC would convert the use of both banks of its memory. Poking zero into the second bit (Bit 1) of the register at this port disables the second bank of memory. Poking a one enables the second bank.

A special program was supplied with the board, appropriately termed *HGC.COM*. Running this program with its FULL option put the full memory of the HGC into use. The HALF option switched off the upper bank. Later software incorporated this switching procedure in software drivers designed for use with Hercules graphics.

Hercules Graphics Standards

In its graphic modes, the HGC slightly alters its on-screen resolution to 720 × 348. One bit is assigned to each pixel, allowing no attributes (other than the pixel being off or on). Eight contiguous on-screen bits are assigned each byte, 90 bytes to each 720 pixel line. The most significant bit of each byte corresponds to the leftmost on-screen pixel stored in the byte.

Lines are not stored in memory in the same order that they are displayed on the screen, however. Contiguous lines in memory display four lines apart on the screen. In effect, the screen is divided into four fields, and one line from each field in sequence is fitted into memory, then the second line from each field, and so on.

Switching to graphics mode is accomplished by poking a bit into the software-configuration switch register. The first bit at this register, located at I/O port 03BF(Hex), controls the mode. Poking a zero here disables graphics mode; a one enables graphics mode.

The Enhanced Graphics Adapter

By 1984 the shortcomings of the CGA system had become obvious—if just from the skyrocketing white cane sales to the people who were using it regularly. The hard-to-read text displays and coarse graphics probably generated more eyestrain than anything since the insurance industry invented two-point type.

The answer as a system based on a new video adapter called the *Enhanced Graphics Adapter* or *EGA*. The enhancements wrought by the new system were severalfold: It increased on-screen resolution; it brought the possibility of graphics to monochrome screens such as the venerable green IBM Personal Computer Display; and it added new BIOS routines that augmented and extended the existing ROM-based video support built into the PC and XT.

EGA Resolution

The most obvious change appeared was visible on the screens of the new Enhanced Graphics Display that matched the EGA: resolution was pushed up to 640 × 350 pixels. Characters were formed in dot boxes measuring 8 × 14. Although the box was a dot narrower than that used by the MDA, characters were formed from the same 7 × 9 matrix. More importantly, enough extra space was available so descenders and ascending characters on adjacent rows did not touch. Color text was finally as readable as monochrome.

The 640 × 350 resolution was also extended to graphics. All previous IBM-supported graphics modes were also included in the capabilities of the VGA so that it was entirely downwardly compatible with CGA graphics.

EGA Frequencies

To accommodate the additional on-screen information required under the EGA standard, a larger bandwidth signal operating at higher frequencies is required. Instead of the 15,525 Hz of the CGA, the EGA ups the horizontal scanning frequency to 22.1 kHz. The vertical scanning frequency (or frame rate) is maintained at about 60 Hz. Because of the higher operating frequency of the EGA standard, it is incompatible with standard NTSC devices such as television sets requires its own displays or multisync-style displays for proper operation.

EGA Colors

Even more notable was the increase in color capability brought by the EGA standard. By altering the adapter-to-display interface, the possible palette in the EGA system was increased to 64 different hues (again, counting black and various shades of grey as separate colors). In addition, the greater memory capabilities of the EGA standard meant that the wider rainbow was possible at higher resolution levels. At its maximum resolution and maximum memory endowment, the EGA could spread 16 different shades from its 64 color palette on a 640 × 350 screen at one time.

EGA Monochrome Graphics

The EGA was also designed to eliminate the two-standard system that reigned in the IBM universe. The EGA adapter was equally adept at handling color and monochrome displays. By setting DIP switches that were cleverly arranged to be accessible through a cut-out in the card retaining bracket without popping the top off your PC, the EGA could be adapted to any standard IBM display. (Note, however, that this clearly does not include composite monitors—the EGA has no composite output. Then again, IBM never made a composite display for its personal computers.)

More importantly, the support of monochrome displays extended to graphics. The EGA provided IBM's first monochrome graphics standard. Note, however, that IBM went its own direction and did not accommodate the graphics standard used by the Hercules Graphics Card. Instead, it substituted its own standard, one compatible with EGA color graphics so that no extra effort was required to write programs compatible with both EGA monochrome and color graphics. Adopting the Hercules standard would have required programmers to develop separate code for color and monochrome graphics on the EGA.

EGA Memory

By the time the EGA was introduced, many applications had been written that moved bytes directly to video memory rather than endure the sluggishness of using IBM's primitive BIOS routines. Changing the memory arrangement used by the EGA would have made the adapter incompatible with those existing applications.

The EGA designers faced another problem—more colors and resolution automatically requires more memory. This would not be a problem except that only a finite range of addresses were reserved out of the 8088 microprocessor's range for holding video information.

The IBM solution was to make the EGA a bank-switched memory card. Its video memory was divided into four planes that could alternately be switched into the address range of the 8088.

In standard (minimal) configuration, the EGA was equipped with 64 kilobytes of RAM, split into four 16K banks. To the host system the adapter looked like a CGA board as long as the advanced EGA modes and their bank-switching was not brought into play.

This 64K was not sufficient for the wide palette, high resolution modes of the EGA, therefore IBM provided expansion up to 256K through a memory expansion daughter card. Expansion EGA memory was allotted equally among the banks on the card, so the maximum configuration gave four banks of 64K each.

The memory of the EGA board can be switched to either the base address of the CGA or MDA to achieve compatibility with programs that write directly to video memory. In EGA modes, however, the base address of the board's memory is shifted downward to 0A0000(Hex).

EGA Interface

The EGA retained the digital signal format used by the MDA and CGA before it. To accommodate its additional color capabilities, the CGA wiring scheme was altered slightly by redefining one connection and adding two new ones. Each color gun was given two signals, essentially the individual drive signals as used on the CGA and individual intensity signals. Instead of all three guns being controlled by a single intensity

Figure 14.5 **EGA pin-out**

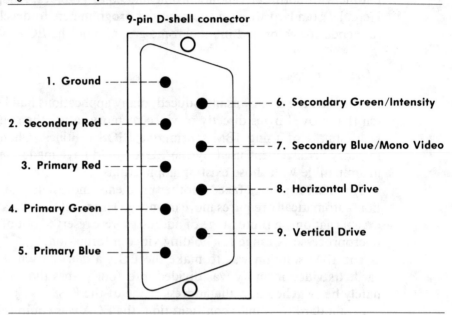

9-pin D-shell connector

1. Ground
2. Secondary Red
3. Primary Red
4. Primary Green
5. Primary Blue

6. Secondary Green/Intensity
7. Secondary Blue/Mono Video
8. Horizontal Drive
9. Vertical Drive

signal, each gun could be brightened by itself. The two-bit digital code given to each gun allowed it four intensities—off, bright, and two intermediary levels. The combination of four levels per gun times three guns allows up to 64 hues to be displayed from the various combinations.

For compatibility with all IBM monitors, the EGA used the same connector as previous video boards, a nine-pin, female D-shell connector. The definitions of its signal pins were controlled by the setup DIP switches depending on the type of monitor that was to be connected to the board. Both the monchrome and CGAcompatible color schemes corresponded exactly with the MDA dn CGA standards to allow complete compatibiltiy. For EGA displays, the CGA intensity pin was used for the intensity signal for the green gun. Additional intensity signals were added for the red and blue guns. (See Figure 14.5 for the pin-out.)

EGA Monitor Compatibility

Because the EGA adapter cannot determine which variety of display that it is connected to, you must be certain to properly match its setup to your display or risk damage to your monitor. Supplying the wrong sychronizing signals to a monochrome IBM Personal Computer Display for more than a short period can permanently damage the monitor.

At the other end of the connection, matters are just as critical with IBM color and monochrome displays introduced before the EGA. The IBM enhanced Color Display can determine whether it is connected to an EGA or CGA display and adjust itself to accommodate the correct synchronizing frequency. Rather than determine the frequency of the signal, however, the EGA display examines the polarity of the horizontal synchronizing signal. If the horizontal sync is positive, the monitor operates with a 15,575 Hz sync frequency. If the horizontal sync is negative-going, the display switches to a 23.1 kHz sync frequency.

EGA Compatibility With Other Display Adapters

In the IBM scheme of things, you are allowed to connect one monochrome, one color, or one of each sort of display to a system, but you can never connect more than one of each. You could, for example, add both a CGA and MDA to your computer, but you could never use two CGAs at once. That's because both CGAs would try to locate their memories at the same addresses. Monochrome and color systems use different memory addresses, however.

The EGA follows this philosophy. If you set up an EGA to operate a color display, then it will happily co-reside with a MDA board. If you setup your EGA as a monochrome adapter, then you can also add a CGA to your system. You cannot, however, add two EGAs—even if one is set up as monochrome and one as color—because their BIOS codes and memory assignments would conflict. While a jumper on the EGA board allows you to alter its base address, the alternate address is not supported by the IBM EGA BIOS code.

Addressing the EGA

In its compatibility modes, the EGA looks to your system as if it were an MDA or CGA, depending on how you have it set up. It even sets the equipment flags appropriately to match the location assigned to its memory so your programs might never know that they are working with an EGA. You can write simple assembly (or higher level) language procedures that directly address video memory, and they will work properly with the EGA *provided you operate within its compatibility modes*.

In the EGA's advanced graphics modes, however, you're in for surprises because you can address only one of its four pages unless you toggle the page register. Fortunately, the EGA BIOS and most application software takes care of that automatically.

The Video Graphics Array

The IBM policy of making a display an option to its personal computers has both logical and illogical bases. It makes sense because some video systems are suited better to particular applications than are others. Detached video lets you adopt a mix-and-match approach. It also opens up a huge market for add-on video products from third party vendors and fosters an upgrade market. Separate display adapters can be pulled out and replaced as new standards evolve and budgets allow.

Built-in video is the logical choice in a number of applications, too. Portable computers, like the PC Portable (which does not actually have its display system built into its system board) and laptop Convertible (which essentially does) demand complete integration of the display and computer system just for the convenience of moving one box around. The ready-made approach also offers the advantage of no-thought convenience. The system comes as a unit in one big box (maybe two, but at least all in one shipment) that would require no decision-making or technical expertise. Moreover, the included-video approach is also likely to be cheaper because there is no need for expansion boards, interface circuitry, or added development costs. IBM's first low-end attempt, the PCjr, included its own video as part of its system board.

The middle ground is the compromise—video on an expansion board that's included in the purchase price of the system. Most personal computers are sold that way. PS/2s, however, broke with this strategy.

In the PS/2 line-up, IBM chose to capitalize on the best of both strategies. As with other video-included systems, building video circuitry into all of its PS/2 line as part of the planar board lowers overall cost and ends match-up worries. The specific design chosen by IBM does not ride roughshod over the advantage of separate video, however. The PS/2 display circuitry is specifically designed to be extensible. Build-in provisions for linking to new display systems are part of its design. More importantly, the on-board circuitry can work co-operatively with add-ons, potentially reducing the cost of the support needed for displays that are better than the out-of-the-box systems.

The centerpiece of this strategy is the *Video Graphics Array* or *VGA* that's built into all Micro Channel PS/2s. Non-Micro Channel machines, like the Models 25 and 30, use a degraded form of VGA called the *Memory Controller Gate Array* or *MCGA,* which incorporates only part of the

VGA philosophy. Sometimes this same abbreviation is interpreted as *Multi-Color Graphics Array*.

The VGA name is derived from a VLSI chip used in the implementation of the PS/2 line. Most of the circuitry of the EGA board (including emulation of Motorola's 6845 video chip) was engineered into this one logical gate-array chip, which IBM dubbed with the "video graphics array" name. The chip name quickly became the label for the entire system, probably because of the resemblance of its abbreviation to those of its predecessors, CGA and EGA. The new name seemed like an logical outgrowth.

In fact, VGA itself is a logical outgrowth of IBM's previous video standards. It incorporates all previous video modes and extends them into new, more colorful, higher resolution territory.

Yet VGA is neither the best possible video system nor does it rank as anything revolutionary. Third party video systems available even before the VGA was introduced displayed sharper or more colorful images or both.

VGA Graphics Resolution

As with previous IBM products, the VGA standard incorporates several resolution levels in a variety of modes, but the VGA offers more modes than ever before, a total of 17. Unlike previous IBM video systems, however, the top resolution offered for text and graphic modes are different.

Of the graphics modes, the sharpest bit-mapped color images made by the system achieve a resolution of 640 × 480 pixels while displaying 16 simultaneous colors selectable from a palette of 256K. This same level of resolution is also available in a two-color (white on black) mode.

While 640 × 480 pixel resolution appears to be a trifling improvement over the 640 × 350 pixels offered by the EGA adapter, the new standard has its strong points—the obvious strength is sharpness. The VGA standard allows for sharper, more colorful images than ever before.

For graphics programmers, the four-to-three relation of horizontal to vertical pixels is a blessing because it mirrors the four-to-three aspect ratio of most video monitors. The net result is square pixels—every dot is a square mosaic tile in the on-screen image—which relieves the programmer of needing to include extra steps to allow for oblong pixels and the otherwise resultant oddly-shaped figures.

VGA Text Resolution

Text resolution under the VGA standard is even sharper than that available in graphics modes. The spec calls for 720 × 400 pixels in either 16 colors or shades of grey in monochrome. Characters in this mode are more detailed than ever before, each constructed from a 9 × 16 matrix of on-screen dots, two dots taller than MDA and a dot wider than EGA.

Strangely, a 40-column mode survives, even though the VGA standard precludes the use of a television set as a display. The reason underlying this throwback mode is compatibility with older software. Programs written for 40-column displays will work on VGA systems as well as all previous display standards. In addition, a brand-new 40-column mode is available with 360 × 400 16-color text mode.

Two other new text modes allow for 30 rows of text on the screen instead of the more common 25 by maintaining the maximal resolution making minor alterations to the operating frequencies of the system.

VGA Colors

While more pixels mean more detail, other VGA modes also improve over previous standards by giving greater color capabilities. These wider spectrum available on the VGA system allows for greater realism to computerized image-making.

At its most colorful, the VGA standard supports up to 256 hues on the screen at one time, with the colors selectable from a total palette of 262,144. In this mode, resolution is limited to 320 × 200 pixels, the same as medium-resolution color mode on the original Color Graphics Adapter which only allowed for four simultaneous hues from a palette of 16.

The displayable colors are selected from the palette of possibilities through mapping. The number of displayable colors represent the limits of VGA memory—the limit on the number of discrete values that could be stored in pixel location in video memory. The codes that are stored in each video memory location are sent to the part of the VGA processing system which matches the value to the address of one of a number of registers (one for each of the displayable values stored in memory). Each register, in turn, holds a different value drawn from the 256K possibilities. The VGA circuitry then substitutes the value stored in the register for the one that was stored in video memory, then sends it along its way to the display.

VGA Signals

Achieving this wide color palette required a major change in IBM display technology. Where previous IBM systems had used digital signals, the VGA system is built around analog. Only IBM's Professional Graphics Controller, which was never intended as a mainstream PC product, used analog signals in the PC environment.

In an analog system, the brightness of the on-screen image is determined by the voltage level of the video signal. In a digital system, image brightness is determined by a digital code as expressed as a pattern on several separate wires.

One reason for switching to analog was simple logistics. The more colors that a digital system has to display, the more control signals are required (unless, of course, the system uses serial data, which would complicate both display and adapter to an extraordinary degree). The necessary number of signals increases geometrically. For example, the 16-color palette of the CGA (that is, 2^4 colors) required four separate signals (red, green, blue, and intensity). The 64-color palette of the EGA (2^6 colors) was built around six signals.

To support the 262,144 colors of the VGA system—that's 2^{18} (two to the eighteenth power) colors—would require 18 signals in a purely digital system, six signals per color. Instead of such a multiplicity of signals and wires to carry them, the VGA standard substitutes a diversity of voltage levels on three conductors. One signal on one wire is assigned to each primary color, and each signal corresponds to one of the electron guns in the cathode ray tube of the monitor. The strength of the signal controls the intensity of the beam.

The analog approach does more than just save on cabling. It makes the circuitry of the monitor quite a lot simpler. Even in a digital system, the power going to the electron beam would have to be converted from digital to analog form to be displayed, anyway. The VGA standard just puts the converter on the video card instead of in the monitor.

Digital-to-Analog Conversion

Despite the analog nature of the VGA signals, they still must originate in the digital form that can be manipulated by the circuits of a computer. Moving between the digital and analog realms requires a special interface circuit called a *Digital-to-Analog Converter* or *DAC*. Although the conversion can be accomplished with discrete circuits, in keeping with the large-scale of the integration in the PS/2 (and current technology), IBM chose to use a one-chip DAC known as the *Inmos 6171S*. Like the 6845 of the CGA and MDA, this chip has become ubiquitous in VGA-compatible display adapters as card makers seek to obtain the greatest possible compatibility with IBM's designs.

The DAC used by the VGA system does more than just convert digital signals to analog. It's actually three DACs in one—one for each color. In addition, it contains the *color look-up table* for the color mapping process which assigns one of the 262,144 colors possible under the VGA system to each of the 256 values that can be stored in memory in the VGA 320 × 200 color-graphics mode. The look-up table values are stored in 256 registers inside the DAC chip itself.

VGA Frequencies

As with previous new IBM video standards, taking full advantage of VGA requires an entirely new kind of monitor that operates at substantially higher synchronizing frequencies than those used by previous IBM systems.

Because each of its higher resolution images is made from a greater number of scan lines, each of those line must be drawn more quickly. The VGA standard requires a horizontal frequency of 31.5 kHz, almost exactly double the roughly 15 kHz rate of the CGA standard and about 50 percent higher than the 22 kHz of the EGA standard.

For more stable images, the vertical refresh or frame rate of the VGA system was also increased over previous IBM standards. The VGA frame rate is 70 Hz in most display modes, although the high-resolution VGA graphics modes operate at 60 Hz to squeeze more data on the screen. As a result of the faster frame rate, flicker should be less apparent in text modes. Faster phosphors can be used, which can mean less image lag and less chance of encountering the lingering ghosts endemic to most IBM monochrome screens.

VGA Memory

Storing 640 × 480 graphics in 16 colors (which take six dot-planes) requires a great deal of memory, roughly 230K. The VGA system built into PS/2 system boards is equipped with the next even memory multiple up, 256 kilobytes. VGA circuitry permits mapping this memory in several ways—at a base address of 0B0000(Hex) or 0B8000(Hex) to achieve compatibility with the MDA and CGA adapters or at a base address of 0A0000(Hex) for EGA and VGA.

The full 256K is divided into four 64K banks, controlled by the Map Mask Register, located at 03C5(Hex) when the index at the sequencer register port 03C4(Hex) is set at 02. This register controls whether the system microprocessor can write to one or more of the banks at a given time.

Addressing within each bank is linear in VGA modes. In other words, the memory arrangement puts on-screen pixels and lines into memory in the same order they appear on the screen.

VGA Compatibility

The VGA system boast extremely good software compatibility with previous standards and negligible hardware compatibility. The higher synchronizing frequencies and analog signals used by the VGA system require an entirely new kind of monitor. Old displays cannot be adapted to the VGA standard with but one exception. Many, but not all, multisync-style displays (discussed in the next chapter) have a wide enough tolerance for synchronizing frequencies and analog inputs so that they can accept the signals made by previous video standards, VGA, and even higher resolution standards. Unless you have a multisync-style display with analog inputs, however, you'll need a new monitor to take advantage of VGA.

Software is another matter entirely. Even with the new standard, IBM has endowed the VGA system with nearly complete compatibility with software written for previous video standards. The VGA system supports all past IBM video modes down to the lowest resolution levels, albeit occasionally in a form and format that's slightly different from the original. For example, in the old-fashioned 200-line video modes (320×200 and 640×200 graphics), the displays are double-scanned at a 400-line rate, making on-screen characters look sharper but just as chunky as on a 200-line display.

All of the 200-line modes of previous video adapters are *double-scanned* by the VGA system. That is, each horizontal line is duplicated on the screen, producing a display of 400 lines. This simple expedient of duplicating each line allows the twice-speed VGA to easily mimic its slower predecessor, however, it does not increase the sharpness of the images made in 200-line compatibility modes.

BIOS Versus Register Compatibility

The software compatibility of video adapters comes in two flavors. *BIOS compatibility* indicates that a particular board reacts identically to the original that it is copied from when it receives a software command to its on-board firmware. The video BIOS then does the dirty work, poking the appropriate values into the registers on the display adapter. The video BIOS thus isolates software from the video hardware. The EGA and IBM video boards designed after it was introduced add their own BIOS code to the host system in which they are installed, and the BIOS takes responsibility for matching software commands to the hardware. This degree of compatibility assures that the code of one video adapter will work the same as another—at least at the level of commands sent to the BIOS.

Although IBM's intention was that the BIOS level of compatibility should be sufficient, programmers often don't heed the rules that IBM laid down. Sometimes to gain extra performance, programmers write software that takes direct control of video hardware. Such programs write directly to video memory and may even poke values into registers that control the functions of the video system. For programs written at this level to function properly, all the registers of a video board must work exactly like those of the prototype that they are copying. When perfect, this *register-level compatibility* assures that all programs written for one video board will work on the so-called compatible board.

IBM's VGA system maintains register-level compatibility with EGA boards and BIOS-level compatibility with CGA and MDA. This is all the compatibility that need be expected from the products of a third-party vendor. If such a product lacks register-level compatibility with either EGA or VGA, you face the prospect of programs crashing or not running at all.

VGA Auxiliary Video Connector

For third-party manufacturers making VGA boards for PC-bus computers, true hardware compatibility with the VGA standard goes beyond the register level. It also requires one additional item, duplication of IBM's *VGA auxiliary video connector*. This special connection permits add-on accessories to share signals and control with VGA circuitry. Add-ons can even overpower the VGA and switch it off, claiming the video output as their own.

The VGA auxiliary video connector takes two forms. In Micro Channel PS/2s, it is available as a bus extension, an extra part of the connector in one 16-bit expansion slot that makes the video system available to expansion cards. On IBM's *PS/2 Display Adapter,* an expansion board for PC-bus machines that upgrades them to VGA performance, the VGA auxiliary video connector takes the form of a series of contacts on the card edge at the top of the board.

VGA Color and Monochrome Integration

While previous IBM video standards have drawn a hard line between monochrome and color, the VGA is designed to accommodate both. This is the culmination of gradual IBM progress to unite the two-in-one product. The MDA and CGA were completely incompatibility standalone systems. The EGA was capable of performing duties (and then some) of either but required that its DIP switches be properly setup—or else you risk display damage. The VGA standard allows one output to be interchangeably plugged into monochrome or color VGA displays without fear of damage and with a guaranty of proper operation.

The secret is a special extra signal added to the VGA interface. This extra signal is simply feedback from the display that tells the VGA circuitry whether it's plugged into a color or monochrome display. VGA monitors are designed to send out the proper signal.

VGA Monochrome Operation

When the VGA circuitry detects a monochrome display, instead of sending out three separate signals for each color gun in the display (monochrome only has one gun), it instead sends out only the green signal, which the display uses to control the intensity of the display. Of course, the color repertory of the VGA system is compromised by this operation, but the VGA compensates by translating the colors into up to 64 shades of grey, a result of the green signal being capable of handling 2^6 discrete intensities, limited by the 6-bit green channel of the DAC.

VG Vertical Gain

The VGA system creates displays that may have one of three possible line counts—350 (for MDA and EGA-compatible modes), 400 (for double-scanned CGA modes), and 480 (for new VGA modes). All else being equal, a display made out of fewer lines will be shorter in that the lines stay a constant width (or high, depending on your perspective). The result would be that EGA-style displays would look more than 25 percent too short on the screen—in other words, all scrunched up.

IBM displays compensate for this height difference by changing their vertical gain depending on the mode of the signal being received from the VGA. To relieve the display from the responsibility of figuring out the video mode from its signals alone, the VGA sends the display a code to indicate what number of vertical lines it is sending in each frame. The code is contained in the polarities of the vertical and horizontal synchronizing signals.

The code specifies 480 line operation is both sync signals are negative-going. For 400-line mode, vertical sync is negative-going and horizontal is positive-going (as it is in CGA displays, which 400-line mode mimics). For 350-line mode, the code is vertical sync positive-going and horizontal sync negative-going. The remaining combination, both sync signals positive-going, is reserved.

IBM provides two methods for dealing with the differing times spent on each horizontal line when the number of lines change. Two dot-clocks

Figure 14.6 **VGA pin-out**

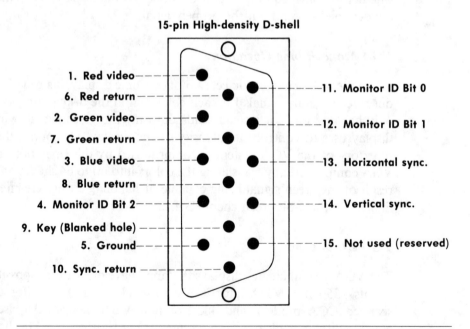

15-pin High-density D-shell

1. Red video
6. Red return
2. Green video
7. Green return
3. Blue video
8. Blue return
4. Monitor ID Bit 2
9. Key (Blanked hole)
5. Ground
10. Sync. return

11. Monitor ID Bit 0
12. Monitor ID Bit 1
13. Horizontal sync.
14. Vertical sync.
15. Not used (reserved)

Table 14.2 **15-Pin, High-Density (VGA) Connector Suppliers**

Male, in-line (cable) connector, crimp-type installation
    AMP part no. 748364-1

Female, in-line (cable) connector, crimp-type installation
    AMP part no. 748565-1

AMP Inc.
Harrisburg, Penn.
800-624-2177

71325-series connectors

Molex Incorporated
2222 Wellington Court
Lisle, Illinois 60532
312-969-4550

(oscillators) are available, one each for 350 and 400-line modes. The 480-line graphics mode slightly lower the normal VGA 70 Hz frame rate to 60Hz, allowing extra time for more lines.

VGA Connectors

Because the signals generated by the VGA are so different from those of previous IBM display systems, IBM finally elected to use a different, incompatible connector so the wrong monitor wouldn't be plugged in with deleterious results. Although only nine connections are actually needed by the VGA system (11 if you give each of the three video signals its own ground return as IBM specifies), the new connector is equipped with 15 pins. It's roughly the same size and shape as a nine-pin D-shell connector but before IBM's adoption of it, this so-called *high-density 15-pin connector* was not generally available.

(Figure 14.6 shows the signal assignments to this connector.)

In that the same connector is now used by all of IBM's PS/2 display systems as well as by a large number of compatible manufacturers, it is becoming more available. (Two sources are given in Table 14.2.)

Although many multisync-style displays will work with VGA signals, many such displays use nine-pin connectors compatible with the EGA standard. To plug one of these displays into an IBM-standard VGA connection, you'll need an adapter cable. (The wiring of such a cable is shown in Figure 14.7.)

Figure 14.7 **9-to-15 pin adapter cable for VGA**

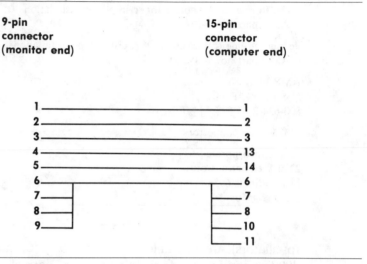

The Memory Controller Gate Array

The lesser PS/2s like the Models 25 and 30 presented IBM with a number of problems, one of them being video. This equipment was designed to be low cost even to the extent that IBM skimped on the Model 25 memory quota by giving it 512K instead of the DOS maximum 640K. However, including VGA graphics, with its demand for 256K of RAM, would be antithetical to the cost-driven goal. However another monitor standard, or a backstep to a previous standard, would undercut the promotion of VGA as the next standard.

The compromise was to compromise, to offer some VGA hardware compatibility while slicing away three-quarters of the memory and much of the functionality. The result was a video half-breed, better than before but not as good as VGA. Its heritage is a mixture of previous IBM standards—registers arranged like those of the EGA, video modes carried over from the MDA and CGA, and hardware and two modes like that of the VGA. For lack of a better name, this system has earned the label *Memory Controller Gate Array* or *MCGA*. Note that the PS/2 Model 30 286 upgraded the original Model 30s UCGA circuitry to full VGA capabilities.

MCGA Text Modes

As with the CGA, two text modes are provided by the MCGA system, one with 40-column character and one with 80-column characters. Text resolution is superior to that of the CGA because resolution was driven up to 640 × 400 pixels to match with the VGA hardware standard. Characters are formed in a 8 × 16 dot box in which every on-screen dot is addressed. A total of 16 different on-screen colors can be displayed simultaneously, drawn from the full VGA palette of 256K because MCGA circuitry uses the DAC chip as VGA.

To your software, however, MCGA text looks like that of the CGA. The video buffer is assigned a base address of 0B8000(Hex), just as is the CGA.

MCGA Graphic Modes

The MCGA system offers four distinct text modes, two roughly compatible with the CGA standard and two with the VGA standard.

The CGA-compatible modes allow medium or high-resolution CGA graphics. Both the 320 × 200 and 640 × 200 modes are double-scanned to produce 400 on-screen lines for compatibility with VGA equipment. As with other systems, however, double-scanning does not increase the sharpness of the image.

In medium resolution, CGA-compatible mode, four simultaneous colors are available, but they can be draw from the full 256K color VGA palette. Just as with the CGA, an alternate palette can be selected (through the same register), but this alternate palette can be filled with colors of your choice drawn from the full VGA repertory. In high-resolution CGA mode, foreground and background colors (the only two allowed) can be drawn from the full 256K VGA palette.

The VGA-compatible high-resolution graphics mode suffers most from the reduced memory of the MCGA system. With only 64K bytes available, the color choice at the 640 × 480 resolution level necessarily had to be sacrificed, resulting in the support of a single color plane. The color mapping abilities of the system allow a choice from the full 256K palette for both the foreground and background color, but that is all.

The MCGA system does support fully the VGA's 320 × 200, 256 color mode, including full color mapping from the 256K VGA palette.

MCGA Software Compatibility

BIOS support provided by the MCGA system is negligible, the same level supplied by the CGA system. About the most the BIOS can do is to put strings of characters on-screen in teletype mode. MCGA does support both standard IBM CGA graphics modes, and is thus compatible with all software that sticks to IBM's rules.

The register structure of the MCGA system is quite similar to the VGA system to support its two VGA graphics modes. The differences arise because of the fewer modes and possibilities allowed by the MCGA circuitry.

MCGA Hardware Compatibility

From the hardware side, the MCGA system uses VGA-style displays and VGA connectors. The system can detect color or monochrome displays and reset its output accordingly. It also uses the same synchronizing signal polarity code to indicate whether it is operating in a 400 or 480-line mode. An MCGA system can thus use the same monitors as a VGA system, including IBM's PS/2 display line, VGA-compatible displays, and even VGA-compatible multisync-style displays.

Upgrading MCGA to VGA

The design of the Model 25 and the original Model 30 allows you to upgrade either system to full VGA graphics by adding an expansion board. When a VGA adapter is installed in either computer, the system-board video circuitry is automatically switched off, and the expansion board becomes the sole video output of the computer. Because the system board video connector is inactivated, you must plug in your display to the connector on the VGA adapter board. Either the IBM Personal System/2 Display Adapter or its third-party equivalent is a suitable upgrade for either the Model 25 or 30.

EGA Plus

From a graphics standpoint, VGA appears like a trifling improvement over the EGA standard—350 vertical lines giving way to 480 lines while horizontal resolution stays the same. In the face of the new VGA, third-party vendors of display hardware did IBM one better and developed their own pseudo-standard.

Generally termed *EGA Plus,* it pushes far beyond VGA to a resolution level of 800 × 600. For the most part it is just an expansion on the EGA standard, and allows the same basic memory arrangement as EGA. With 256K of RAM on most boards, four simultaneous colors are supported at highest resolution. A few boards with greater memory push the high resolution color capabilities to 16. Not only EGA boards but also VGA-compatible boards feature the EGA Plus resolution level. Boards with either or both TTL and analog outputs at the 800 × 600 level are available.

The limiting factor on these EGA Plus boards is not in their own electronics. Rather, they were created to exploit as best they could the capabilities of a certain popular style of monitor that could accommodate a wide range of synchronizing frequencies. EGA Plus pushes these monitors to their limits to get the best possible quality on-screen with almost no additional cost—the memory would be on the EGA board anyway and the higher resolution capability was already built into the displays. EGA Plus looked like a great way of getting the most for your money.

The only problem with the EGA Plus system is its lack of official sanction. Although it has not proved to be a winner with software developers, a growing number are incorporating software drivers for the 800 x 600 mode into their products. In addition, many board-makers include drivers with their products to make the highest resolution modes useful. In general, support is included for Lotus 1-2-3 (of course), AutoDesk's AutoCAD (the most popular engineering drawing program), and at least one of the two popular graphic operating environments, Digital Research GEM and Microsoft Windows.

EGA Plus is a bonus if you use one of the supported software packages, if you have a multisync-style monitor, and if you were going to buy such a video board anyway. Otherwise, it remains an interesting curiosity, a mode with which to toy.

8514/A

8514/A Memory

One-half megabyte of memory is standard equipment on the 8514/A, which is more than enough for a 1024 × 768 image four bits deep. The memory is arranged into four bit-planes, each comprising a megabit of storage, allowing 16 simultaneous on-screen colors.

This arrangement leaves 128K of memory to spare, 256 kilobits in each of the bit-planes. The memory used for the display takes up the lowest portion of that storage, and the rest is put to work as auxiliary storage for functions such as area-filling and holding loadable character sets. Although it can be addressed directly by the host microprocessor just like the rest of the memory of the 8514/A, this ability is not supported by IBM. This means that writing to it may destroy information the 8514/A has stored there for another purpose.

In its VGA-compatible mode, the 8514/A divides up its half-megabyte into eight 1024×512 bit planes arranged in two independent banks four bit-planes deep. The hardware design of the 8514/A does not allow combining these planes into one 8-bit plane.

8514/A Memory Expansion

A half-megabyte expansion option is available for the 8514/A as a daughter card. This additional memory increases the color capability of the display adapter, increasing its spectrum to eight bit-planes and 256 simultaneous on-screen colors. In addition, both VGA-mode maps of the 8514/A also gain 8-bit depth and a full range of 256 simultaneous color.

8514/A Frequencies

The signals used by the 8514/A display adapter pack so much information that they require almost twice the bandwidth of those of the VGA standard, 44.90 MHz versus 25.17 MHz. Were it not for the clever use of interlacing (discussed in the next chapter), the bandwidth needs would be even greater. The 8514/A adapter uses a horizontal scanning frequency of 35.52 kHz (versus 31.47 for VGA) and a vertical scanning frequency of 43.48 Hz (versus 59.94 for VGA). Interlacing prevents the relatively low vertical frequency from causing the screen to flicker, effectively doubling the speed at which the screen is scanned downward to nearly 88 timers per second.

Dual Screen Operation

The 8514/A operates independently of the VGA circuitry built into its computer host. Operations that change the memory of one will not necessarily change that of the other. When the 8514/A is in its VGA mode,

Table 14.3 **VGA and 8514/A Sync Code**

Mode number	1	2	3	4
Mode function	EGA	VGA text or CGA compatibility	VGA graphics	8514/A
Lines on screen	350	400	480	768
Horizontal sync polarity	Positive	Negative	Negative	Positive
Vertical sync polarity	Negative	Positive	Negative	Positive

Display code signals:

DISPLAY TYPE	8503 (Mono)	8513	8512	8514
ID BIT:				
0	N/C	0 V.	0 V.	0 V.
1	0 V.	N/C	N/C	N/C
2	N/C	N/C	N/C	0 V.

the two VGA systems duplicate one another. However, some operations (such as loading a palette or changing modes) may affect the 8514/A screen differently, revealing incorrect colors or a skewed greyscale. When the 8514/A is in its native mode, the two screens can be used independently. Typically, you will put text displays on the VGA screen while the 8514/A makes drawings.

8514/A Connections

The 8514/A display adapter shares the same high-density 15-pin D-shell connector with the VGA standard. Pin assignments are somewhat different. In addition to the separate signal leads provided for each color and its return, and horizontal and vertical sync, three additional leads replace the one devoted to identifying the display attached to the adapter. (See Figure 14.7.)

The monitor identification signals provide feedback to the 8514/A board so it knows what kind of display with which it is working. These signals prevent the 8514/A from sending a high resolution/interlaced image to a fixed-frequency VGA display that might be plugged into its connector. This feedback scheme assures that the display and adapter function properly together and avoids the problems that might be encountered plugging a monochrome display into a CGA adapter.

(Table 14.3 lists how the polarities of the synchronizing signals code different display types.

Display Adapter Setup

In the original IBM design, no feedback was provided from display to the host computer. Many programs needed to know what kind of display and adapter were connected to the system, if just to know the correct block of memory to write display information to.

PC and XT Switch Settings

To let the host computer know what sort of displays and adapters were connected to it, the original PC and XT required that you set a pair of DIP switches. The switch setting determined where the computer would send video information. If the switches are set improperly, the computer will boot up with an invisible error message. You'll get an error because the switch settings are improper but you won't be able to see it because the computer doesn't know the correct base address for the display adapter. All you will see is a cursor slowly flashing on the screen (because the cursor is generated by the display adapter independent of the rest of the computer).

The same switches also determine whether systems equipped with color displays boot up in 40-column mode or 80-column mode. Another setting is used if an EGA or VGA board is used with the computer. (The settings of the PC and XT display switches are shown in Figure 14.8.)

The Primary Display

In the original PC and XT scheme of things, you could connect either an MDA or CGA adapter and display one or both. If you connected one of each kind of adapter, the one for which the DIP switches were set would be the *primary display* and the boot message and most other image would appear on that display. You could switch between displays using the MODE utility supplied with DOS.

The AT Switch

By the time IBM had introduced the AT, the DIP switches used for setting up the computer had been simplified and repackaged as the Setup program that accompanied the system. One problem remained, however. If the computer did not know what kind of display was attached, it might use the wrong memory area when attempting to run the Setup program.

Figure 14.8 **PC and XT display switch settings**

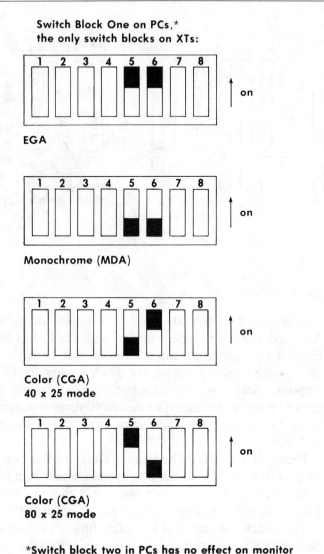

Switch Block One on PCs,*
the only switch blocks on XTs:

EGA

Monochrome (MDA)

Color (CGA)
40 x 25 mode

Color (CGA)
80 x 25 mode

*Switch block two in PCs has no effect on monitor
settings

To let the AT know what kind of display is connected to the system, or which of the displays is primary, IBM incorporated a single slide switch on the AT system board to select monitor type. (Figure 14.9 shows the proper positions of this switch for use with color and monochrome displays.)

Figure 14.9 **AT display adapter switch settings**

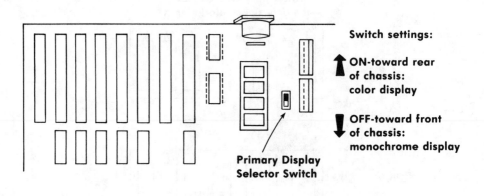

EGA Switches

The BIOS of the EGA takes over the video sections of the BIOS of the PC, XT, and other computers in which the board is installed. It has the capability of operating either monochrome or color displays. Although sync-polarity coding allows the EGA to handle CGA and EGA-style displays with impunity, its switches must be set to reflect color or monochrome operation. The reason is simple—either color monitor expects display memory in the same place, while the monochome area is different.

Because the EGA can be setup as either a color or monochrome display adapter, it is possible to install it in conjunction with other video adapters. When the EGA is in its color mode, it will co-reside with a MDA; when the EGA is in monochrome mode, it will co-reside with a CGA.

The switches on the rear accessible through the cut-out in the EGA retaining bracket must be set properly to reflect the type of monitor with which it is connected and whether it is co-residing with another display adapter. (The settings of these switches are shown in Table 14.4.)

Most third-party EGA adapters use a similar switch scheme. Those that have but four setup switches usually use exactly the same settings as the IBM EGA. Those with a greater number of DIP switches usually use a superset of the IBM settings.

Table 14.4 **EGA Switch Settings**

To use the monitor connected to the EGA adapter as the primary display:

EGA Operating Mode	Other Display Adapter	Sw 1	Sw 2	Sw 3	Sw 4
40 × 25 Color	Monochrome (MDA)	On	Off	Off	On
80 × 25 Color	Monochrome (MDA)	On	Off	Off	Off
EGA Emulation*	Monochrome (MDA)	Off	On	On	On
High Res. EGA	Monochrome (MDA)	Off	On	On	Off
Monochrome	CGA 40 × 25	Off	On	Off	On
Monochrome	CGA 80 × 25	Off	On	Off	Off

To use a monitor connected to the EGA as the secondary display:

EGA Operating Mode	Other Display Adapter	Sw 1	Sw 2	Sw 3	Sw 4
40 × 25 Color	Monochrome (MDA)	On	On	On	On
80 × 25 Color	Monochrome (MDA)	On	On	On	Off
EGA Emulation*	Monochrome (MDA)	On	On	Off	On
High Res. EGA	Monochrome (MDA)	On	On	Off	Off
Monochrome	CGA 40 × 25	On	Off	On	On
Monochrome	CGA 80 × 25	On	Off	On	Off

*EGA emulation mode means the EGA maps 5 × 7 (in 8 × 8 box) CGA characters to 7 × 9 (in 8 × 14 box) EGA characters.

VGA Setup

By the time IBM released the VGA system, DIP switches were a thing of the past. IBM's VGA adapter, and most of those that are hardware-compatible with it, uses no switches because it automatically configures itself for a color or monochrome display. The host system is prepared for a VGA adapter the same as it would be for an EGA.

Note that only one VGA board can be used in a system and that it cannot co-reside with other video adapters, so settings for such operation are not needed. The 8514/A does co-reside with a VGA adapter, but provisions for cooperative operation are built into the 8514/A.

15

COMPUTER DISPLAYS

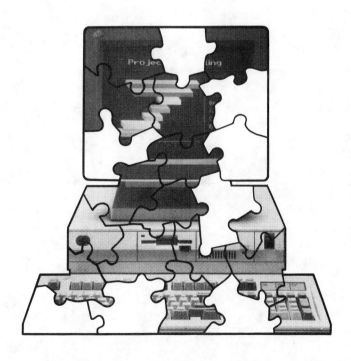

You cannot see data. The information that your computer processes is nothing but ideas, and ideas are intangible no matter whether in your mind or your computer's. While you may be able to visualize your own ideas, you cannot peer directly into the pulsing digital thought patterns of your computer. You probably have no right to think that you could—if you can't read another person's thoughts, you should hardly expect to read the distinctly non-human circuit surges of your PC.

Although most people (at least those not trained in stage magic) cannot read thoughts per se, they can get a good idea of what's going on in another person's mind by carefully observing his external appearances. Eye movements, facial expressions, gestures, and sometimes even speech can give you a general idea about what that other person is thinking, although you'll never be privy to his true thoughts. So it is with computers. You'll never be able to see electrons tripping through logical gates, but you can get a general idea of what's going on behind the screens by looking into the countenance of your computer, its *display*. What the display shows you is a manifestation of the results of the computer's thinking.

The display is your computer's line of communication to you, much as the keyboard lets you communicate with it. Like even the best of friends, it doesn't tell you everything, but it does give you a clear picture, one from which you can draw your own conclusions about what the computer is doing.

Since the display has no direct connection to the computer's thoughts, the same thoughts—the same programs, can generate entirely different on-screen images while working exactly the same way inside your computer. Just as you can't tell a book's contents from its cover, you cannot judge the quality of a computer from its display.

What you can see is important, however, because it influences how well you can work with your computer. A poor display can lead to eyestrain and headaches, making your computer literally a pain to work with. A top quality display means clearly defined characters, sharp graphics, and a system that's a pleasure to work with.

Monitors Versus Displays

Although the terms are often used interchangeably, a display and a monitor are distinctly different. A display is the image-producing device itself, the screen that you see. The monitor is a complete box that adds support circuitry to the display. This circuitry converts the signals set by the computer (or some other device, such as a videocassette recorder) into the proper form for the display to use. Although most monitors operate under principles like those of the television set, displays can be made from a variety of technology including liquid crystals and the photon glow of some noble gasses.

Because of their similar technological foundations, monitors to a great extend resemble television sets. Just as a monitor is a display enhanced with extra circuitry, the television is a monitor with even more signal conversion electronics. The television has incorporated into its design a *tuner* or *demodulator* which converts signals broadcast by television stations or a cable television company, into about the same form as those signals used by monitors. Beyond the tuner, the television and monitor work in much the same way. Indeed, some computer monitors will work as television as long as they are supplied the proper signals.

Computer displays and monitors use a variety of technologies to create visible images. A basic bifurcation divides the displays of desktop computer and those of laptop machines. Most desktop computers use systems based on the same cathode ray tube technology used in most television sets. Laptops chiefly use liquid crystal displays. Occasionally a desktop or portable system may be equipped with a gas-plasma display, but these are unusual and costly.

Cathode Ray Tubes

The oldest electronic image-generating system still in use is the cathode ray tube. Its name is purely descriptive. The device is based on a special form of vacuum tube, a glass bottle that's been partially evacuated and filled with an inert gas at very low pressure. The *cathode,* another name for a negatively electrode, of the tube shoots a beam or ray of electrons toward a positively charged electrode, the *anode.* (Electrons, having a negative charge, are naturally attracted to positive potentials.) Because it works like a howitzer for electrons, the cathode of a CRT is often called an *electron gun.*

At the end of the short flight of the electrons, from the gun in the neck of the tube to the inside of its wide, flat face where lies a layer of a phosphors compound with a wonderful property—it glows when struck by an electron beam. To move the beam across the breath of the tube face (so that the beam doesn't light just a tiny dot in the center of the screen), a group of powerful electromagnets arranged around the tube called the *yoke* bend the electron beam in the course of its flight. The magnetic field set up by the yoke is carefully controlled and causes the beam to sweep each individual display line down the face of the tube.

Convergence

The three electron beams inside any color monitor must converge on exactly the right point on the screen to illuminate a single set of phosphor dots or pixel. If a monitor is not adjusted properly, or if it is not designed or made properly, the three beams will not converge properly to one point. Poor convergence will result in images with rainbow-like shadows and a loss of sharpness and detail on color screens.

Because the electron beam inside the display tube is bent most sharply to reach the corners of the screen, convergence problems show up most obviously in the corners of a display.

Phosphors

The image you see in a CRT is the glow of the electrically-stimulated phosphor compounds. Not all of the phosphorous compounds used in CRTs (usually just called *phosphors*) are the same. Different compounds and mixtures glow various colors and for various lengths of time after being struck by the electron beam.

A number of different phosphors are used by PC-compatible monitors. (Table 15.1 lists some of these and their characteristics.)

Persistence

CRT Phosphors also differ in *persistence,* the word used to describe how long the phosphor glows after being struck by the electron beam. Most monitors used short persistence phosphors.

Persistence becomes obvious when it is long. Images take on a ghostly appearance, lingering for a few seconds and slowly fading away. Although the effect may be bothersome, particularly in a darkened room, it's meant to offset the effect of another headache-producer, *flicker.*

Table 15.1 **Phosphors and Their Characteristics**

Type	Steady-state Color	Decay Color	Decay Time (ms.)*	Uses or Comments
P1	Yellow-Green	Yellow-Green	15	oscilloscopes, radar
P4	White	White	.1	display, television
P7	White	Yellow-Green	unavail.	oscilloscopes, radar
P11	Blue	Blue	.1	photography
P12	Orange	Orange	unavail.	radar
P16	Violet	Violet	sh	ultraviolet
P19	Orange	Orange	500	radar
P22R	Red	Red	.7	projection
P22G	Yellow-Green	Yellow-Green	.06	projection
P22B	Blue	Blue	.06	projection
P26	Orange	Orange	.2	radar, medical
P28	Yellow-Green	Yellow-Green	.05	radar, medical
P31	Yellow-Green	Yellow-Green	.07	oscilloscope, display
P38	Orange	Orange	1000	radar
P39	Yellow-Green	Yellow-Green	.07	radar, display
P40	White	Yellow-Green	.045	med. persist. display
P42	Yellow-Green	Yellow-Green	.1	display
P43	Yellow-Green	Yellow-Green	1.5	display
P45	White	White	1.5	photography
P46	Yellow-Green	Yellow-Green	.16	flying spot scanners
P55	Blue	Blue	.05	projection
P56	Red	Red	2.25	projection
P101	Yellow-Green	Yellow-Green	.125	display
P103	White	White	.084	P4 w/bluish background
P104	White	White	.085	high efficiency P4
P105	White	Yellow-Green	100+	long persistence P7
P106	Orange	Orange	.3	display
P108	Yellow-Green	Yellow-Green	125	P39 w/bluish backgr.
P109	Yellow-Green	Yellow-Green	.08	high efficiency P31
P110	Yellow-Green	Yellow-Green	.08	P31 w/bluish backgr.
P111	Red/green	Red/green	unavail.	voltage penetration
P112	Yellow-Green	Yellow-Green	unavail.	ir lightpen doped P39
P115	White	White	.08	yellower P4
P118	White	White	.09	display
P120	Yellow-Green	Yellow-Green	.075	P42 w/bluish backgr.
P122	Yellow-Green	Yellow-Green	.075	display
P123	Infrared		unavail.	infrared
P124	Yellow-Green	Yellow-Green	.130	yellow part of P4
P127	Green	Yellow-Green	unavail.	P11+P39 for light pens
P128	Yellow-Green	Yellow-Green	.06	ir lightpen doped P31

Table 15.1 (continued)

Type	Steady-state Color	Decay Color	Decay Time (ms.)*	Uses or Comments
P131	Yellow-Green	Yellow-Green	unavail.	ir lightpen doped P39
P133	Red to green	Red to green	varies	current-sensitive
P134	Orange	Orange	50	European phosphor
P136	White	White	.085	enhanced contrast P4
P137	Yellow-Green	Yellow-Green	.125	high efficiency P101
P138	Yellow-Green	Yellow-Green	.07	enhanced contrast P31
P139	Yellow-Green	Yellow-Green	70	enhanced contrast P39
P141	Yellow-Green	Yellow-Green	.1	enhanced contrast P42
P143	White	Yellow-Green	.05	enhanced contrast P40
P144	Orange	Orange	.05	enhanced contrast P134
P146	Yellow-Green	Yellow-Green	.08	enhanced contrast P109
P148	Yellow-Green	Yellow-Green	unavail.	lightpen applications
P150	Yellow-Green	Yellow-Green	.075	data displays
P154	Yellow-Green	Yellow-Green	.075	displays
P155	Yellow-Green	Yellow-Green	unavail.	lightpen applications
P156	Yellow-Green	Yellow-Green	.07	lightpen applications
P158	Yellow	Yellow	140	medium persistence
P159	Yellow-Green	Yellow-Green	unavail.	enhanced contrast P148
P160	Yellow-Green	Yellow-Green	.07	data displays
P161	Yellow-Green	Yellow-Green	.07	data displays
P162	Yellow-Green	Yellow-Green	.1	data displays
P163	White	White	2	photography
P164	White	Yellow-Green	.1	displays
P166	Orange	Orange	unavail.	ir lightpens
P167	White	White	.075	display
P168	Yellow-Green	Yellow-Green	.075	projection
P169	Yellowish	Yellowish	1.5	display
P170	Orange	Orange	unavail.	enhanced contrast P108
P171	White	Yellow-Green	.2	display
P172	Green	Green	unavail.	lightpen displays
P173	Infrared		unavail.	lightpen
P175	Red	Red	.6	display
P176	Yellow-Green	Yellow-Green	.2	photography
P177	Green	Green	.1	data displays
P178	Yellow-Green	Yellow-Green	.1	displays
P179	White	White	1	displays
P180	Yellow-Orange	Yellow-Orange	.075	displays
P181	Yellow-Green	Yellow-Green	unavail.	color shutter displays
P182	Orange	Orange	50	displays
P183	Orange	Orange	unavail.	lightpen displays

Table 15.1 (continued)

Type	Steady-state Color	Decay Color	Decay Time (ms.)*	Uses or Comments
P184	White	White	.075	displays
P185	Orange	Orange	30	enhanced contrast P134
P186	Yellow-Green	Yellow-Green	25	displays
P187	Yellow-Green	Yellow-Green	unavail.	lightpen P39
P188	White	White	.05	White displays
P189	White	White	unavail.	White displays
P190	Orange	Orange	.1	displays
P191	White	White	.12	White displays
P192	White	White	.2	White displays
P193	White	White	.08	White displays
P194	Orange	Orange	17	displays
P195	White	White	.125	inverse displays

*Approximate time in milliseconds for display to decay to 10 percent of its emission level.

This flicker is the quick flashing of the screen image caused by the image decaying before it gets re-scanned again by the electron beam. The persistence of vision (a quality of the human visual system) makes rapidly flashing light sources appear continuously lit. Fluorescent lights, for example, seem to glow uninterruptedly even though they switch on and off 120 times a second (twice the nominal frequency of utility-supplied electricity).

The lingering glow of long persistence phosphors bridges over the periods between passes of electron beam when they stretch out too long for human eyes to blend them together. Long persistence phosphors are thus often used in display systems that are scanned more slowly than usual. The IBM Monochrome display, perhaps the most notorious user of long-persistence green phosphors, is scanned 50 times a second instead of the more normal (and eye-pleasing) 60 or higher.

Long-persistence phosphors need not be green, however. Long-persistence color systems are also available for use in applications where flicker is bothersome. Most often, long-persistence color phosphors are used in interlaced systems which are scanned more slowly than non-interlaced displays.

Interlaced systems use a trick developed for television to help put more information on a screen using a limited bandwidth signal. Instead of scanning the image from top to bottom, one line after another, each *frame* of the image is broken in half into two *fields*. One field consists of the odd-numbered lines of the image, the other the even-numbered lines. The electron beams sweeps across and down, illuminating every other line, then starts from the top again and finishes with the ones it missed on the first pass.

What this technique achieves is an apparent doubling of the frame rate. Instead of sweeping down the screen 30 times a second (the case of a normal television picture), the top-to-bottom sweep occurs 60 times a second. While a 30-frame per second rate would noticeably flicker, the 60-frame per second rate does not. At least not to most people under most circumstances. Some folks' eyes are not fooled, so interlaced images have earned a reputation of being flickery.

Interlacing is used on computer display signals to keep the necessary bandwidth down. A lower frame rate lowers the required bandwidth of the transmission channel. Of all the prevailing standards only the original high-resolution operating mode of IBM's 8514/A display adapter uses interlacing.

Persistence and Light Pens

Long persistence phosphors also frustrate *light pens,* which depend on detecting the exact instant a dot of phosphor lights up. Because of the lingering glow, several dots will appear to most light pens to be lit simultaneously. The pen cannot zero in on a particular dot position on the screen.

Phosphor Color

The type of phosphor determines the color of the image on the screen. Several varieties of amber, green, and whitish phosphors are commonly used in monochrome displays. Color displays use three different phosphors that are each one of the additive primary colors—red, green, and blue. The primary colors are created by individually hitting the dots associated with that color with the electron beam. Other colors can be made by illuminating combinations of the primary colors. By varying the intensity of each primary color, an infinite spectrum can be generated.

Monochrome Phosphor Colors

Monochrome displays have their CRTs evenly coated with a single, homogenous phosphor so wherever the electron beam strikes, the tube glows in the same color. The color of the phosphors determine the overall color that the screen glows. Three colors remain popular for monochrome computer displays amber, green, and white. Which is best is a matter of both preference and prejudice; various studies have supported the superiority of each of these colors.

Green

Green screens got a head start as IBM's choice for most of its terminals and the first PC display. It is a good selection for use where ambient light levels are low, part of its heritage from the days of oscilloscope and radar screens (most of which remain stubbornly green). Over the last few years, however, green has fallen from favor as the screen of choice.

Amber

Amber screens have risen in popularity at the same time because they are, according to some studies, easier on the eyes and more readable when the surrounding environmental light level is bright. Amber was also selected as a de facto European standard.

White

Once white screens were something to be avoided, if just from their association with black-and-white televisions. A chief reason was that most early monochrome displays used a composite interface and gave low on-screen quality.

Apple's Macintosh and desktop publishing forced the world to re-evaluate white. White is the color of the paper executives have been shuffling through offices over the ages. White also happens to be among the most readable of all color combinations. IBM added impetus to the conversion of the entire world to white with the introduction of the VGA and its white-screen monochrome display.

There's no good dividing line between ordinary white and *paper-white* displays. In theory, paper-white means the color of the typical bond paper you type upon, a slightly warmer white than the blue-tinged glow of most "white" monitors. But "paper-whiteness" varies with who is giving the name.

Background Color

Often ignored yet just as important to screen readability as the phosphor colors is the background color of the display tube. Monochrome screen backgrounds run the full range from light grey to nearly black. Darker screens give more contrast between the foreground text and the tube background, making the display more readable, particularly in high ambient light conditions.

Phosphor Colors in Color Displays

In color displays, the three phosphors are spread across the screen arranged in triads, a triplet of three dots of phosphor, one of each of the additive primary colors—red, green, and blue.

Matrix Color

The area on a color screen in between the phosphor dots, the *matrix,* does not illuminate. Its color determines what the screen looks like when the power is off—pale grey, dark green-grey, or nearly black. Darker and black matrices gives an impression of higher contrast to the displayed images. Lighter grey matrices make for purer white. The distinctions are subtle, however, and unless you put two tubes side-by-side, you're unlikely to be able to judge the difference.

Color Guns

Most color CRTs have three electron guns, each one of which targets the phosphor dots of a specific color. This trio of guns is arranged either as a triangle or in a straight line, the latter often termed *in-line guns.* In theory in-line guns should be easier to setup, but as a practical matter excellent performance can be derived from either arrangement. The three guns in a color CRT emit their electrons simultaneously, and the three resulting beams are steered together by the yoke.

Individual adjustments are provided for each of the three beams, however, to assure that each beam falls exactly on the same triplet of color dots on the screen as the others. In that these controls help the three beams converge on the same triplet, they are called *convergence* controls and the process of adjusting them is usually termed *alignment.*

IBM and many other display makers now claim that their products are converged for life. While this strategy should eliminate the need to adjust them (which should only be done by a skilled technician with the correct test equipment), it also makes it mandatory to test your display before you buy it. You don't want a display that's been badly converged for life.

The Shadow Mask

Just pointing the electron beams at the right dots is not enough because part of the beam can spill over and hit the other dots in the triplet. The result of this spillover is a loss of color purity—bright hues become muddied. To prevent this effect and make images as sharp and colorful as possible, all color CRTs used in computer displays and televisions alike have a *shadow mask,* a metal sheet with fine perforations in it, located inside the display tube and a small distance behind the phosphor coating of the screen.

The shadow mask and the phosphor dot coating on the CRT screen are critically arranged so the electron beam can only hit phosphor dots of one color. The other two colors of dots are in the "shadow" of the mask and cannot be seen by the electron beam. (CRTs with in-line guns, such as Sony's pioneering Trinitron, use slots rather than holes in the mask but accomplish the same end.)

The spacing of the holes in the shadow mask to a great degree determines the quality of the displayed image. For the geometry of the system to work out, the phosphor dots on the CRT screen must be spaced at the same distance as the holes in the mask. Because the hole spacing determines the dot spacing, it is often termed the *dot-pitch* of the CRT, the term for slotted tubes is *slot-pitch.*

The dot-pitch or slot-pitch of a CRT is simply a measurement of the distance between dots or slots. It is an absolute measurement, independent of the size of the tube or the size of the displayed image.

If you look closely at the screen of a color monitor, you can see the shadow mask lurking behind. If you can see the holes in the mask, they are most likely .40 millimeter or larger; if you can't see the holes, they're likely .31 mm or smaller.

Bandwidth

Perhaps the most common specification that is usually listed for any sort of monitor is bandwidth, which is usually rated in megahertz.

In theory, the higher the bandwidth, the higher the resolution and sharper the image that can be displayed. In the case of color displays, the dot-pitch of the display tube is the biggest inherent limit on performance. Usually convergence problems are the primary limit on sharpness.

In a monochrome system, however, bandwidth is a determinant of overall sharpness. The IBM display standards do not demand extremely wide bandwidths—extremely large bandwidths are often superfluous.

The bandwidth necessary in a monitor is easy to compute. A system ordinarily requires a bandwidth wide enough to address each individual screen dot plus an extra margin to allow for retrace times. (Retrace times are those periods in which the electron beam moves but does not display, for instance, at the end of each frame when the beam must move from the bottom of the screen at the end of the last line of one frame, back up to the top of the screen for the first line of the next frame.)

A TTL monochrome display operating under the MDA standard shows 252,000 (or 720 × 350) pixels 50 times per second—12.6 million pixels per second. A composite display shows 128,000 (or 640 × 200) pixels 60 times per second—7.68 million pixels per second. A VGA display, 288,000 (or 720 × 400 in text mode) pixels 70 times per second—20.16 million pixels per second.

Allowing a wide margin of about 25 percent for retrace times, it can thus be seen that for most PC applications, a bandwidth of 16 MHz is acceptable for TTL monitors, and 10 MHz of bandwidth is sufficient for sharp composite video displays, figures well within the claims of most commercial products. For VGA, 25 MHz is the necessary minimum. The 8514/A standard requires 45 MHz, although lesser quality displays may work adequately.

(Table 15.2 summarizes the bandwidth required by the various IBM display standards.)

Screen Curvature

Most CRTs have a distinctive shape—a narrow neck, which contains the electron gun or guns and fits inside the deflection yoke, a funnel-like flaring that allows the bending electron beam to sweep across the inner surface of the wide face of the tube, and the rectangular face itself, often (but becoming much less so) a spherically curving surface.

The common spherical curve makes sense for a couple of reasons: It makes the distance traveled by the electron beam more consistent at various points on the screen, edge to center to edge. A truly flat screen would require the beam to travel farther at the edges than at the center

Table 15.2 **Dot-clocks (Bandwidths) of IBM Video Standards**

Video Standard	Dot-Clock
MDA	16.3 MHz
CGA	14.3 MHz
EGA	16.3 MHz
PGC	25 MHz
VGA	
(350- or 480-line mode)	25 MHz
(400-line mode)	28 MHz
8514/A	44.9 MHz

Because in real-world applications the worst-case display puts an illuminated pixel next to a dark one, the actual (as opposed to theoretic) bandwidth required by a display system is half the dot-clock plus system overhead.

and would require the beam to strike the face of the screen obliquely, resulting in image distortion. Although this distortion can be compensated for electrically, the curving screen helps things along.

In addition, the CRT is partly evacuated, so normal atmospheric pressure is constantly trying to crush the tube. The spherical surface helps distribute this potentially destructive force more evenly, making the tube stronger.

Screen curvature has a negative side effect. Straight lines on the screen appear straight only from one observation point. Move your head closer, farther away, or to one side, and the supposedly straight lines of your graphics images will bow this way and that. The effect, noticeable in photographs, occurs because your eyes accommodate the curves and interpret things back into the straight lines it expects.

Technology has made the reasons underlying spherical curved screens less than compelling. The geometry of in-line guns simplifies tube construction and alignment sufficiently that cylindrically curved screens are feasible, and they have fewer curvilinear problems because they warp only one axis of the image.

In the last few years, the technical obstacles to making genuinely flat screens have been surmounted. A number of manufacturers now offer flat-screen monochrome displays, which are relatively simple because compensation for the odd geometry is required by only one electron beam.

The first color flat screen was Zenith's *flat tension-mask* system. The tension-mask solves the construction problems inherent in a flat screen color system by essentially stretching the shadow mask. Its flat face and black matrix make for very impressive images, only the case of the monitor itself is bulky and ugly to look at, and an internal fan made the first model as much a pain for the ears as the screen was a pleasure for the eyes.

Screen Size Versus Image Size

Most computer displays are rated by their screen size. As with television sets, the measurement of the cathode ray tube (CRT or picture tube) in a computer monitor is made diagonally across its face, thus the active display area of a 12-inch monitor may measure somewhat less than nine by seven inches.

Two monitors with the same size screens may have entirely different on-screen image sizes. Composite monitors are often afflicted by *overscan;* they attempt to generate images that are larger than their screen size, and the edges and corners of the active display area may be cut off. (The overscan is often designed so that as the components inside the monitor age and become weaker, the picture shrinks down to normal size—likely over a period of years.) *Underscan* is the opposite condition, the image being smaller than nominal screen size.

Underscan may be perfectly normal—designed into a particular display—and does not necessarily indicate any underlying problems. Image geometry is easier to control nearer the center of the screen than it is at the edges. Pulling in the reigns on the image can assure that straight lines are actually displayed straight. Excessive underscan can be intimidating and counterproductive. If underscan is excessive, you're actually getting a smaller display than you're paying for. Actual image size that is displayed rather than screen size should be taken into account when comparing monitors.

Aspect Ratio

Today the shape of the screen of nearly every monitor is standardized as is that of the underlying CRT that makes the image. The screen is 1.33 times wider than it is high, resulting in the same 4:3 aspect ratio used in television and motion pictures before the wide-screen phenomenon took over.

The electronics of monitors separate the circuitry that generates the horizontal and vertical scanning signals and results in their independent control. As a result, the relationship between the two can be adjusted, and that adjustment results in an alteration of the aspect ratio of the actual displayed image. For example, by increasing the amplification of the horizontal signal, the width of the image will be stretched, raising the aspect ratio.

Normally you should expect that the relative gains of the horizontal and vertical signals will be adjusted so that your display shows the correct aspect ratio on its screen. A problem develops when a display tries to accommodate signals based on different standards. This mismatch is particularly troublesome with VGA displays because the VGA standard allows images made with three distinct line counts—350, 400, and 480.

All else being equal, an image made from 350 lines will be less than three-quarters the high of a 480-line image. A graphic generated in an EGA-compatible mode shown a VGA display would thereby look quite squashed. A circle drawn on the screen would look like an ellipse; a orange would more resemble a watermelon.

IBM monitors compensate for such obtuse images with the sync-polarity detection scheme. The relative polarities of the horizontal and vertical sync signals instruct the monitor in which mode and line count the image is being set. The monitor then compensates by adjusting its vertical gain to obtain the correct aspect ratio no matter the number of lines in the image.

Unfortunately, not all monitors take advantage of the IBM-sync signaling system. Shifting display modes with such a monitor can lead to graphics displays that looks crushed.

Image Controls

A few (far from a majority) monitors make coping with underscan, overscan, and odd aspect ratios simply a matter of twisting controls. These displays feature horizontal and vertical size (or gain) controls which allow you to adjust the size and shape of the image to suit your own tastes. With these controls—providing they have adequate range—you can make the active image touch the top, bottom, and sides of the screen bezel or you can shrink the bright area of your display to a tiny (but geometrically perfect) patch in the center of your screen.

The size/gain control should be accompanied by *position controls* which will allow you to move the active display area right-and-left and up-and-down on the screen.

Most displays also carry over several controls from their television progenitors. Nearly every computer monitor has a *brightness* control, which adjusts the level of the scanning electron beam, which in turn makes the on-screen image glow brighter or dimmer. The *contrast* control adjusts the linearity of the relationship between the incoming signal and the on-screen image brightness. In other words, it controls the brightness relationship that results from different signal levels—how much brighter high-intensity is. In a few displays, both the brightness and contrast function are combined into a single "picture" control. Although a godsend to those who might get confused by having to twiddle two knobs, the combined control also limits your flexibility in adjusting the image to best suit your liking.

Other controls ubiquitous to televisions are usually absent from better computer monitors because they are irrelevant. Vertical hold, color (saturation), and hue controls only have relevance to composite video signals, so they are likely only to be found on composite-interfaced displays. The vertical-hold control tunes the monitor to best decipher the vertical synchronizing signal from the ambiguities of composite video signals. The separate sync signals used by other display standards automatically removes any ambiguity. Color and hue only adjust the relationship of the color subcarrier to the rest of the composite video signal and have no relevance at all to non-composite systems.

Anti-Glare Treatment

Most mirrors are made from glass, and glass tries to mimic the mirror whenever it can. Because of the difference between the index of refraction of air and that of glass, glass is naturally reflective. If you make mirrors, that's great. If you make monitors—or worse yet, use them—the reflectivity of glass can be a big headache. A reflection of a room light or window from the glass face of the CRT can easily be brighter than the glow of phosphors inside. As a result, the text or graphics on the display tends to "wash out" or be obscured by the brightness.

Anti-glare treatments are supposed to reduce or eliminate reflections from the face of the CRT. Several strategies are used, with varying degrees of success:

Mesh

The lowest tech and least expensive anti-glare treatment is simple a fabric mesh, usually nylon. The mesh can either be placed directly atop the face of the screen (the Amdek 310A is a good example of this treatment) or in a removable frame that fits about half an inch in front of the screen. Each hole in the mesh acts like a short tube, allowing you to see straight in at the tube but cutting off light from the sides of the tube. Your straight-on vision gets through unimpeded while glare that angles in doesn't make it to the screen.

As simple as this technique is, it works amazingly well. The least expensive after-market anti-glare system use mesh suspiciously similar to pantyhose stretched across a frame.

Mechanical

Glare can be reduced by mechanical means—not a machine that automatically intercepts glare before it reaches the screen but mechanical preparation of the screen surface. By lightly grinding the glass on the front of the CRT, the face of the screen can be made to scatter rather than reflect light. Each rough spot on the screen resulting from the mechanical grinding process reflects light randomly, sending it every which direction. A smooth screen reflects a patch of light all together, like a mirror, reflecting any bright light source into your eyes. Because the light scattered by the ground glass is dispersed, less of it reaches your eyes and the glare is not as bright.

Coating

Glare can be reduced by applying coatings to the face of the CRT. Two different kinds of coatings can be used: One forms a rough film on the face of the CRT; this rough surface acts in the same way as a ground-glass screen would, scattering light.

The screen can also be coated with a special compound like magnesium fluoride. By precisely controlling the thickness of this coating, the reflectivity of the surface of the screen can be reduced. The fluoride coating is made to be a quarter the wavelength of light (usually of light at the middle of the spectrum). Light going through the fluoride and reflecting from the screen thus emerges from the coating out of phase with the light striking the fluoride surface, visually canceling out the glare. Camera lenses are coated to achieve exactly the same purpose, the elimination of reflections.

Polarization

Light can be polarized, that is, its photons can be restricted to a single plane of oscillation. A polarizing filter allows light of only one polarization to pass. Two polarizing filters in a row can be arranged to allow light of only one plane of polarization to pass—by making the planes of polarization of the filters parallel—or the two filters will stop light entirely when their planes of polarization are perpendicular.

The first filter lets only one kind of light pass, the second filter lets only another kind of light pass. Because none of the second kind of light reaches the second filter, no light gets by.

When light is reflected from a surface, its polarization is shifted by 90 degrees. This physical principle makes polarizing filters excellent reducers of glare.

A sheet of polarizing material is merely place a short space in front of a display screen. Light from a potential source of glare goes through the screen and is polarized. When it strikes the display and is reflected, its polarization is shifted 90 degrees. When it again reaches the filter, it is out of phase with the filter and cannot get through. Light from the display, however, only needs to go through the filter once. Although this glow is polarized, there's no second screen to impede its flow to your eyes.

Every anti-glare treatment has its disadvantage. Mesh makes an otherwise sharp screen look fuzzy because smooth characters are broken up by the cell structure of the mesh. Mechanical treatments are expensive and tend to make the screen appear to be slightly "fuzzy" or out of focus because the same is true of coatings that rely on the dispersion principle. Optical coatings, Polaroid filters, and even mesh suffer from their own reflections because the anti-glare material itself may add its own bit of glare. In addition, all anti-glare treatments, and polarizing filters in particular, tend to make displays dimmer. The polarizing filter actually reduces the brightness of a display to one-quarter its untreated value.

Even with their shortcomings, however, anti-glare treatments are amazingly effective, they can ease eyestrain and eliminate the headaches that come with extended computer use.

Resolution Versus Addressability

The *resolution* of a video system refers to the fineness of detail that it can display. It is a direct consequence of the number of individual dots that make up the screen image and thus is a function of both the screen size and the dot-pitch.

Because the size and number of dots limit the image quality, the apparent sharpness of screen images can be described by the number of dots that can be displayed horizontally and vertically across the screen. For example, the resolution required by IBM's Color Graphics Adapter is 640 dots horizontally by 200 vertically. The 8514/A Display Adapter produces an image 1024 by 768 dots in its highest resolution mode.

Sometimes, however, the resolution available on the screen and that made by a computer's display adapter are not the same. For example, a video mode designed for the resolution abilities of a color television set hardly taps the quality available from a computer monitor. On the other hand, the computer-generated graphics may be designed for a display system that's sharper than the one being used. You might, for instance, try to use a television in lieu of a more expensive monitor. The sharpness you actually see will then be less than what the resolution of the video system would have you believe.

Actual resolution is a physical quality of the video display system—the monitor—that's actually being used. It sets the ultimate upper limit on the display quality. In color systems, the limit on resolution is purely physical—the dot-pitch of the tube. In monochrome systems, which have no quality-limiting shadow masks, the resolution is limited by the *bandwidth* of the monitor, the highest frequency signal with which it can deal. (Finer details pack more information into the signals sent from computer system to monitor. The more information in a given time, the higher the frequency of the signal.)

A few manufacturers persist in using the misleading term *addressability* to describe the quality of their monitors. Addressability is essentially a bandwidth measurement for color monitors. It indicates how many different dots on the screen the monitor can point its electron guns at. It ignores, however, the physical limit imposed by the shadow mask. In other words, addressability describes the highest quality signals the monitor can handle, but the full quality of those signals won't necessarily be visible to you on the screen.

Required Dot-Pitch

It's easy to compute the pitch necessary for a resolution level in a computer system. The screen size is merely divided by the number of dots required to be displayed.

For example, a typical IBM-PC text display comprises 80 columns of characters which are each eight dots wide, for a total of 640 dots across the screen. The typical twelve-inch (diagonal) monitor screen is roughly 9.5 inches or 240 millimeters across. Hence to properly display an IBM-PC text image, the dot pitch must be smaller than .375 (or 240/640) millimeter, assuming the full width of the screen is used for display. Often a monitors image is somewhat smaller than full-screen width and such displays require even finer dot pitch. The larger the display, the coarser the dot-pitch can be for a given level of resolution.

IBM Monitor Types

The world of IBM-standard monitors is marked by a profusion of confusion. In order to be certain that you talking about the right type of display, you must describe it with specificity. Stipulating color or monochrome is not enough for you must also indicate the signal standard to which the monitor must abide. The standard is dictated by the video adapter that's used by the monitor, but some monitors work with different adapters and many adapters are flexible in regard to your monitor choice. However, certain terms are in general use to describe and distinguish particular monitor types:

Monochrome

Monochrome means exactly what its root words say—"mono" means one and "chrome" indicates color. Monochrome monitors show their images in one color, be it green, amber, white, puce, or alizarin crimson. Monochrome does not describe what sort of display adapter the monitor plugs into. Among the monitors available, you have three choices that give you long odds at finding the right combination by chance. A fourth, the multiscanning monochrome display, accepts almost any monochrome signal.

TTL Monochrome

The original display type offered by IBM, the one that plugs into the Monochrome Display Adapter, is distinctly different from any monitor standard made for any other purpose. It uses *digital* input signals and uses separate lines for both its horizontal and vertical synchronizing signals.

Its digital signals match the level used by integrated circuits of the *Transistor-Transistor Logic* family or *TTL* family. These chips operate with tightly defined voltage ranges indicating a logical one or zero. (Five volts is nominally considered a digital one, although that's the input voltage level of TTL chips. The maximum level TLL signals ever reach is about 4.3 volts.) Because of their use of TTL signals, such monitors are often called *TTL monochrome* displays. They can only be plugged into MDA or compatible display adapters (including the Hercules Graphics Board.

Composite Monochrome

A monitor bearing no other description other than merely "monochrome" is most likely a composite monochrome monitor. This type of monitor offers the lowest resolution of any monochrome system available for PCs, the same level as a CGA color display but without the redeeming virtue of color. Because the composite monochrome monitor uses the same signal as home and professional video systems, it is as ubiquitous as it is hard on the eyes. Designed for the mass market, the composite monochrome monitor is likely to be the least expensive available. It can only be plugged into a CGA or compatible display adapter. The built-in display of the Portable Personal Computer is actually a composite monochrome monitor.

VGA Monochrome

As with TTL monochrome monitors, VGA monochrome monitors follow a proprietary IBM standard, but unlike IBM's Personal Computer Display, the Monochrome VGA display quickly won acceptance and spawned a number of compatibles. These all are incompatible with other video standards but plug into any VGA-style output.

Multiscanning Monochrome

Unlike the other three monochrome display types, which are designed to operate at certain fixed frequencies, the multiscanning monochrome display adapts to the signals sent to it within a wide range of frequencies. Usually, this kind of monitor can handle any standard monochrome signal, from composite to VGA. It offers no advantage over the fixed-frequency displays except an impunity from errors. You can shift it between monochrome-equipped computer systems no matter what standards they follow.

Color Monitor Types

Five types of color display are generally available for connecting to PCs and PS/2s; among these are composite color, RGB (or CGA), enhanced RGB (or EGA), VGA, and mulitscanning monitors.

Composite Color

Generic video monitors, the kind you're likely to connect to your VCR or video camera, use the standard NTSC composite video signal. This signal is also available from the CGA, many compatible display adapters, and built-into the PCjr. The 3.58 MHz color subcarrier specified by the standard limits color sharpness, however, so the best you can expect is readable 40-column text. Compensating for the poor quality is the low price. As with monochrome, the mass market has driven the prices of composite color monitors way down.

RGB

The original color display for the IBM PC, the Personal Computer Color Display, IBM model 5151, used three discrete digital signals for each of the three primary colors. From these signals, the display type earned the nickname RGB from the list of additive primary colors: (one more time) Red, Green, and Blue. To be completely accurate, of course, this style of monitor should be termed RGBI, with the final "I" standing for intensity, per the CGA standard.

Except for the interface signal, the RGB monitor works like a composite color monitor, using the same frequencies, but substituting digital signals for analog. Because there's no need for the NTSC color subcarrier, bandwidth is not limited by the interface, and RGB monitors appear much sharper than composite monitors, even though they display the same number of lines. RGB monitors work with the CGA, EGA (in its degraded CGA mode), and compatible display adapters as well as the PCjr.

Enhanced RGB

Moving up to EGA quality requires a better display, one able to handle the 22.1 kHz horizontal synchronizing frequency of the EGA standard. In addition, its interface is somewhat different. While still digital, it must accommodate intensity signals for each of the three primary colors. The EGA signals require a matching EGA connection on the display.

VGA Displays

VGA displays were introduced by necessity with the PS/2s. They use analog inputs and a 31 kHz horizontal synchronizing frequency to match with the VGA standard.

Multiscanning Color Displays

Color multiscanning displays were introduced even before the monochrome models. At the time, at least two competing IBM color standards were in use while only one monochrome standard was popular. Among the first color multiscanning systems was NEC's *Multisync,* a monitor so successful that any monitor in this entire class is often erroneously referred to as being a "multisync."

Multiscanning displays don't lock their horizontal and vertical synchronizing frequencies to any particular standard. Instead, they try to match the sync pulses sent to them by your computer system. By automatically adjusting themselves to the available signal, color multiscanning displays can work with just about any video standard.

The range of frequencies that they can latch on to is limited, however. For example, a manufacturer might specify that a display can handle horizontal sync frequencies from 48 to 60 Hz. Such a display would not be able to cope with the 70 Hz signals used under the VGA standard.

Most multiscanning displays are designed to be able to handle signals even beyond the VGA standard. EGA Plus cards were initially created to capitalize on this potential. After IBM introduced its 8514/A display adapter, many manufacturers extended the range of their system to make them compatible with that standard.

Multiscanning Matching

Normally, a multisync-style display automatically switches its input designations to accommodate either CGA or EGA signals. Some displays, however, require that you explicitly set their inputs to reflect whether they are to use CGA or EGA signals. These switches, usually located on the rear panel near the input connector, are often labeled with one of two designations, 4-bit/6-bit or 16-color/64-color. The CGA mode is the former in each case—*4-bit* or *16-color* mode. The CGA interface uses four signals, each one representing a bit in the data stream, and produces a maximum of 16 colors. The EGA system, which uses six signals and produces at most 64 colors, is represented by the *6-bit* or *64-color* designations.

Inputs and Connectors

Monitors can be grouped by the display standard they support, mostly based upon the display adapter card that they are designed to plug into. One basic guide will help you narrow down the compatibility of a display just by inspecting its rear panel is the input connector used by the monitor. After all, if you cannot plug a monitor into your computer, odds are it won't be much good to you.

Three styles of connectors are shared by the video standards promulgated by IBM. By name, these three connectors are the RCA-style pin jack, the nine-pin D-shell, and the 15-pin "high-density" D-shell.

Three is just short enough of the number of major IBM video standards (four) that you can get into serious trouble—plugging the wrong kind of monitor into a display adapter connector into which it seemingly fits can result in fatal damage to your monitor. Obviously, you'll want to get to know which is which and what is fatal.

Pin Jacks

The bull's eye jack used on stereo and video equipment is used by IBM for the composite video connections available from the Color Graphics Adapter. Although a wealth of monitors and television sets made by innumerable manufacturers also use this connector, no display made by IBM does. However, this concession connector does give you a wealth of choices for alternate displays—that is, if you don't mind marginal quality.

Composite monitors (those dealing with the composite video and NTSC color only) rank among the most widely available and least expensive in both color and monochrome. Even better quality television sets have such jacks available.

While you can use any composite video display with a CGA or compatible color card, the signal itself limits the possible image quality to okay for monochrome, acceptable for 40-column color, and unintelligible for 80-column color. Nevertheless, a composite video display, already a multipurpose device, becomes even more versatile with a computer input.

Daisy-Chaining

A side benefit of pin plug/composite video displays is that most have both input and output jacks. These paired jacks allow you to daisy-chain multiple monitors to a single video output. For example, you can attach six composite video monitors to the output of your computer for presentations in the classroom or boardroom.

In many cases, the jacks just loop through the display (that is, they connect together). The display merely bridging the input video signal and alters it in no other manner. You can connect a nearly unlimited number of monitors to these loop-through connections with no image degradation. Some monitors, however, buffer their outputs with a built-in video amplifier. Depending on the quality of the amplifier, daisy-chaining several of these monitors can result in noticeable image degradation.

Discovering Buffer Amplifiers

One way to tell the difference is by plugging the output of the display into the output of your computer. Most amplifiers don't work backwards, so if the display has a buffering amplifier nothing will appear on the screen. If you do get an image comparable to the one you get when plugging into the input jack, the signal just loops through the display.

Analog Voltage Level

The specifications of composite monitors sometimes include a number describing the voltage level of the input signal. This voltage level can be important when selecting a composite display because all such monitors are essentially analog devices.

In analog monitors, the voltage level corresponds to the brightness which the electron beam displays on the screen. A nominal one volt peak-to-peak input signal is the standard in both the video and computer industries and should be expected from any composite monitor. IBM's VGA and 8514/A requires a slightly different level—0.7 volts.

Termination

For proper performance, a composite video signal line must be terminated by an impedance of 75 ohms. This termination assures that the signal will be at the proper level and that aberrations will not creep in because of an improperly-matched line. Most composite input monitors (particularly those with separate inputs and outputs) feature a *termination switch* which connects a 75 ohm resistor across the video line when turned on. Only one termination resistor should be switched on in any daisy-chain, and it should always be the last monitor in the chain.

If you watch a monitor when you switch the termination resistor on, you'll notice the screen get dimmer. That's because the resistor absorbs about half the video signal. Because composite video signals are analog, they are sensitive to voltage level. The termination cuts the voltage in half and consequently dims the screen by the same amount. Note that the *dim* image is the proper one. Although bright might seem better, it's not. It may overload the circuits of the monitor or otherwise cause erratic operation.

Composite monitors with a single video input jack and no video output usually have a termination resistor permanently installed. While you might try to connect two or more such monitors to a single CGA composite output (with a Y- cable or adapter), doing so is unwise. With each additional monitor, the image will get dimmer (the signal must be split among the various monitors) and the CGA adapter will be required to send out increasing current. The latter could cause the CGA to fail.

Nine-pin D-Shell Connectors

Three different IBM video standards share the nine-pin D-shell connector: monochrome, standard RGB, and enhanced RGB. To confuse things further, many monitor makers also use the same connector for VGA and proprietary display systems.

Nine-pin Mismatch

Because of the huge potential for confusion, your must follow one important rule—know what kind of display adapter you're about to plug into. Making the wrong choice can be fatal to your display, particular should you try to plug an IBM Monochrome Display into a CGA adapter. The mismatch of synchronizing frequencies will lead to the internal components of the display overheating and failing.

A mismatch is easy to spot because you simply can't make sense out of the image on the screen. You may see a Venetian-blind pattern of lines, the screen may flash, or it may look like the vertical hold failed in a dramatic way. Should you observe any of these patterns or hear a high-pitched squeal from your display and see nothing on the screen, immediately turn off your display. Hunt for the problem while life of your monitor is not ticking away.

Fifteen-pin High-Density D-shell Connectors

The only monitors you'll likely to find 15-pin high-density D-shell connectors are those that are VGA-compatible, whether dedicated to that purpose or multiscanning.

So far, IBM has done a good job of insuring that problems like the nine-pin mismatch won't occur with these connectors. While both monochrome and color displays use the same connectors, the VGA circuit can sense which is connected and handle either one properly.

IBM's 8514 display and 8514/A display adapter also use the same connector even though they at times use different signals. Again, however, IBM has incorporated coding in the signals to assure that problems won't arise. The 8514/A adapter can sense the type of display that is connected to it, and won't send out conflicting signals. The 8514 monitor will operate happily with VGA signals, so problems won't occur if its plugged into an ordinary VGA output.

Audio Inputs

A steadily declining number of monitors, particularly those with composite inputs, have audio as well as video capabilities. This facility can be useful in at least two cases—to take advantage of the new voice synthesis and voice digitization options now becoming available for PC systems, and to amplify the three-voice audio output of the PCjr. Most monitor audio amplifiers, even those with modest specifications (limited audio frequency bandwidth and output powers less than a watt), can handle either job adequately.

None of the IBM line-up of personal computers have been designed as music makers. Although you can add accessories to transform the musical mission of your PC, you'll also want to add better quality audio circuitry than you'll get with any PC. A patch cord to connect the add-on accessories to your stereo system will do just fine.

16

PARALLEL PORT

The term *parallel port* is almost synonymous with "printer port." The parallel port is the easiest, most foolproof way of connecting a printer to your PC. Just plug it in, and odds are that your printer will work flawlessly—or whatever flaws in its operation do appear won't have anything to do with the interconnection. The parallel port is one of the few truly plug-and-play connections in PC-dom.

Well, almost: some printers (thankfully a minuscule and dwindling number) react negatively to the IBM parallel port convention, negatively enough that they may forever cease to function.

In addition, while IBM has elected to follow the single standard set by one once-prominent manufacturer, Centronics, IBM has chosen its own direction for parallel port connectors. In almost every case, you'll need a special adapter cable to plug your printer into your PC. Fortunately, the ubiquity of PCs has made the odd adapter cable a standard accessory. (If you dare to make your own, Table 16.1 lists the proper connections.)

A further problem occurs not when mating printer to the port, but the port to your PC. Parallel ports come standard in many video adapters, multifunction products, and computers. It's easy to mysteriously find a number of parallel ports in a computer to which you have not intentionally tried to add ports. You might even exceed the official IBM parallel port maximum of three, or try to make two ports think they are the same one, with confusing and crashing consequences.

Parallel Information Transfer

If nothing else, parallel ports are aptly named. They send information out one byte at a time using eight separate conductors, one for each bit of the byte of data. The bits all move at essentially the time and (unavoidably) at the same rate down the individual conductors.

Table 16.1 **IBM Parallel Printer Cable**

Connect these:	To these:	Connect these:	To these
25-pin connector	36-pin connector	25-pin connector	36-pin connector
1	1	16	31
2	2	17	36
3	3	18	19–30,33
4	4	19	19–30,33
5	5	20	19–30,33
6	6	21	19–30,33
7	7	22	19–30,33
8	8	23	19–30,33
9	9	24	19–30,33
10	10	25	19–30,33
11	11		
12	12		
13	13		
14	14		
15	32		

Parallel Port Strong Points

Because eight paths are available, the data can potentially move eight times faster than down a single wire. Because data moves through the port in essentially that same parallel fashion that it courses through the 8-bit bus arrangement inside PCs, the circuitry necessary for building a parallel port is relatively simple and inexpensive.

Parallel Port Weaknesses

On the other hand, parallel ports use expensive cables. Instead of the two wires used by telephones and serial computer circuits, a parallel port typically requires a cable with 25 conductors in it. Although only eight data lines are used, control signals require their own conductors and most signals are equipped with their own, matching ground return leads.

Crosstalk Problems

The parallel nature of the parallel port is also its undoing from an electrical standpoint. In addition to the eight data signals, a variety of control signals also course through the parallel connection. By itself, that's no problem. Parallel ports do, in fact, work well. However, the multiple signal paths tend to react with one another as they travel down the parallel cable that connects the port on your computer to the one on your printer and signals from one lead tend to leak into others, a problem called *crosstalk*. (In telephone systems, the same tendency causes the talk in conversations in one circuit to cross over into others.)

The longer the cable, the greater the leakage. Most manufacturers recommend that parallel connections be kept under ten feet in length to prevent problems.

Computers and printers vary in their sensitivity to parallel-port crosstalk. Some systems will work with lengthy parallel connections, fifty feet long; others will balk with anything over ten feet.

If you have a long printer cable, or use an extension cable, keep your printer more than ten feet from your computer and you can't get your system to work properly, try connecting the printer with a shorter cable. Keeping parallel cable lengths short will prevent problems.

Parallel Communications

Your computer communicates with each of its parallel ports through three input/output ports. These ports allow your machine to send data out the port or receive it from the port.

In all machines before the PS/2 series, IBM considered the parallel port to be essentially a unidirectional device. The parallel port could send data to a printer but, with the exception of monitoring the status of some port conditions, it could not receive information from the port.

This one-way nature was a result of the electrical design of the port. The port was not designed to be able to supply a significant level of current. Grounding one of the data lines of the port, which might happen when sending data to it, could be destructive to the circuitry of the port. By disallowing any equipment from altering the port outputs (in effect, discouraging sending information to the port), IBM effectively precludes using the parallel port for data acquisition or reception. The parallel ports used by PS/2s were redesigned to allow bidirectional operation.

Using PC Parallel Ports Bidirectionally

The parallel port support built into all models of IBM personal computer does, in fact, permit reading of the various data lines. As long as care is taken to keep from grounding the data lines (for instance, controlling them through resistors to keep currents low), it is possible to use PC parallel ports bidirectionally. In that the IBM design allows the system to source 2.6 milliamps, resistors of 2.2 kilohms are sufficient. PC parallel ports can sink (absorb) up to 24 milliamps.

Port Assignments

The IBM-standard assigns up to three triads of input/output ports to communicate with parallel ports. These I/O port triplets are assigned base addresses of 03BC(Hex), 0378(Hex), and 0278(Hex). In any system, these I/O addresses must be uniquely assigned. Two parallel ports may not use the same base address.

The first of these, 03BC(Hex) was originally reserved for the parallel port that was installed on the IBM Monochrome Display Adapter card. Because the MDA card cannot be used with PS/2s, which have their own built-in display adapters, this same set of addresses was assigned to the standard equipment parallel port in each PS/2. The other two starting addresses are available for additional parallel ports.

PC-, XT-, and AT-compatible computers (including 80386-based ATs) equipped with built-in parallel ports do not normally assign the standard equipment port to 03BC(Hex) because there's a good chance a MDA video adapter may be plugged into the system. Instead, they usually provide for a base address of 0378(Hex) and some provision for reassigning the address used by the port, typically jumpers or DIP switches.

Device Names

In the IBM system, the special device names LPT1, LPT2, LPT3 are reserved for the three parallel ports the systems support. (Think of LPT as an abbreviation for *L*ine *P*rin*T*er.) The device name PRN is equivalent to LPT1.

These logical names do not necessarily match with a given set of I/O port addresses, however. At boot-up, the system searches for parallel ports at each of the three supported base addresses. The search is always performed in the order listed above: first 03BC(Hex), then 0378(Hex), and then 0278 (Hex). The first parallel port that is found in the system is assigned the name LPT1; the second, LPT2; the third, LPT3. If you have a monochrome display adapter or a PS/2 with built-in parallel port, that port will always be LPT1.

As a consequence of this allocation scheme, you are assured of having a LPT1 (and PRN) device in your system no matter the I/O ports assigned to your parallel ports providing you have at least one parallel port! If, however, you have two ports assigned to the same base I/O addresses, your system will assign both ports the same name and neither is likely to work.

Parallel Port Signals and Connections

The parallel port uses a multiplicity of connections to carry out its seemingly trivial function. Table 16.2 lists where each connection is assigned on the 25-pin connector IBM uses for parallel ports. The function of each of these connections is as follows:

Data Lines

The information that's to be sent to the printer to become hardcopy is first loaded onto eight data lines, one for each bit of a byte of ASCII code. The signals are at standard TTL voltage, nominally a "high" or five volts indicating a digital one; a "low" or zero volts indicating a logical zero.

Strobe Line

Just loading bits onto the data lines is not sufficient to indicate to the printer that it should print a character. The data bits are constantly changing, and there's no assurance in the system that all eight will simultaneously pop to the right value—and even if it did, the printer would have no way of knowing that it should (or should not) print the same character twice or more. Some way is required to signal that the

Table 16.2 **IBM Parallel Cable Pin Assignments**

25-pin connector	Function	25-pin connector	Function
1	Strobe	16	Initialize printer
2	Data bit 0	17	Select input
3	Data bit 1	18	Ground
4	Data bit 2	19	Ground
5	Data bit 3	20	Ground
6	Data bit 4	21	Ground
7	Data bit 5	22	Ground
8	Data bit 6	23	Ground
9	Data bit 7	24	Ground
10	Acknowledge	25	Ground
11	Busy		
12	Paper end (Out of paper)		
13	Select		
14	Auto Feed		
15	Error		

computer is finished loading bits onto the data lines and that a character can be printed. The Strobe line serves this purpose.

The strobe signal in the IBM parallel scheme is negative going. When data bits are *not* to be read, it is high. When a byte of data is to be transmitted, it goes low.

The timing of the data signals and the strobe signal is critical. All data lines must be at their proper value *before* the strobe signal is triggered so that the printer circuits have adequate time to assume the proper values. About one-half microsecond is required. The strobe signal should last for a full microsecond (long enough for the printer to realize that it's there!), and the data signals should persist slightly (another half microsecond) after the completion of the strobe. The overlap helps assure against errors.

Busy Line

This data-strobe-and-data process allocates a minimum of two microseconds per character. At that rate, the parallel interface could dump 500,000 characters per second into some poor, defenseless printer. The printer needs a way to fight back, to tell the computer that it's busy blasting a character onto the paper. The *busy* signal, sent from printer computer, accomplishes this task. It's a hold-your-horses signal.

As soon as the printer receives the strobe and starts the process of printing a character (be it only to shove the data into an internal buffer), it trips the busy signal, sending it to a logical high state.

The busy signal stays high as long as it takes the printer to prepare to receive the next byte of data. This busy condition can persist momentarily as the byte is loaded into a buffer or for an extended period during which the printer would be unable to accept another character for printing. For example, the buffer may fill up, the ribbon could jam, or the printer might not have been fully initialized after being turned on.

Acknowledge Line

While the busy line is a negative signal it commands "Don't send data"—another parallel port line is used for positive flow control. The *acknowledge* line carries a signal from the printer to your computer that indicates the previous character has been properly received and dashed to paper and that the printer is ready for the next character. As with the strobe signal, acknowledge is normally a logical high that shifts low to indicate that the printer is ready for the next character. Typically, this negative-going pulse lasts about eight microseconds.

Parallel Port Performance

Together, the pulsing of the strobe and acknowledge lines are sufficient for normal parallel-port flow control. With system timing set for the minimal lengths of these signals, a complete character transmission cycles requires about ten microseconds, which is a speed sufficient to move 100,000 bytes in a second. That's the ultimate speed limit for a parallel port and one that's unlikely to be ever achieved.

The characters being sent have to come from somewhere, and they have to go somewhere. Processing overhead at both ends of the connection slow the orderly parallel flow substantially. The computer, for example, must receive the acknowledge signal, then run through a BIOS routine to understand it, then load the next character into the parallel port, and finally send the strobe signal out the port. Even if the printer is equipped with its own buffer, it must go through an equivalent electronic ritual each time a character is received.

With an ordinary PC pumping characters directly into a buffer, you can expect data rates about the same as those you'd get with a serial port running at its top 9600 bit per second speed. That's an effective throughput of nearly 1,000 characters per second—although a tiny fraction of the top parallel speed, it's faster than any printer you're likely to connect to your PC can churn out paper.

Printer Feedback

The parallel interface does more than just move data. Dedicated lines in the parallel circuit are used by the printer to signal various aspects of its condition to the host computer. The signals tell the computer that the printer is ready, willing, and able to do its job. In effect, they endow the computer with a modicum of remote sensing abilities.

Select

The *select* line indicates that the printer is "selected." This means it is in its on-line condition, ready to receive information. The select line acts exactly like the on-line light on the front panel of the printer; but instead of being visible to your eyes, it's registered through the parallel port.

The select line goes high when the printer is on-line. If the select line is not high, the parallel port will not transmit data.

Paper Empty

The most common problem encountered during a printjob is running out of paper. When that happens, your printer could just run the busy signal high, which would effectively stop your computer from pouring data into it. In fact, most printers do exactly this. However, they do more, too, to give you some idea of what's going on (in case you can't see the printer or don't realize your paper pile has been depleted).

To indicate to you the exact nature of its problem, your printer pulls the *paper empty* line high. Again, it operates just like the paper out light on the printer, but supplies its signal in a form your computer can understand.

Fault

One further signal is used as a catch-all for other printer problems, *fault*. This signal indicates to your computer that something is wrong without indicating exactly what there aren't enough wires in a cable to indicate all possible printer problems. For example, fault could indicate that the lid to the printhead chamber is open, the printhead has jammed, the printhead won't index (maybe the drive belt broke), or whatever other error conditions your printer can detect on its own.

The fault signal is negative-going. It's normally held high. When an error occurs, it goes low.

Many printers don't use a single-barreled defense. When something goes wrong, all the flags are raised. Busy, select, and fault all go to their warning states.

Computer Control

In the IBM parallel port-scheme, three additional signals are used to control various aspects of the printer through hard-wired port connections. These initialize the printer, switch it to an on-line condition (when the printer allows such a remote-controlled change), and line feeding.

Initialize Printer

The computer and printer are two separate organisms that can grow and change independently. This is, you can send commands to the printer to change its operation, to set new fonts, change character pitch, and so on. On its own, your computer does nothing to keep track of the commands it sends to your printer—the printer could turn into a monster that would dump the next 47 pages of your monthly report as a amorphous blob in graphics mode, and your computer wouldn't know the difference.

The printer always starts at the same point, however, with fonts, pitches, and modes all sent in a predetermined way. You can reset the printer to this condition by turning it off and then on, initializing all of its important operating parameters. The *initialize printer* or *input prime* is an alternate means of accomplishing the same end. It's like a reset button for the printer. Drive this line low from its normal high condition, and the printer initializes itself, running through it own boot-up operation.

Select Input

Some printers are designed to be switched on and off line by their computer hosts. The signal used for commanding the switch is called by IBM *select input*. When this signal is low, printers will accept data;

when high, they will not. Many printers allow you to defeat this control by operating a DIP switch that causes the machine to always hold this line low.

Auto Feed XT

The lowly carriage return can be a confusing thing. Some printers assume that a carriage return should automatically advance paper to the beginning of the next line; others think a carriage return merely swerves the printhead back to the beginning of the line currently being printed. Most printers give you a choice—a DIP switch determines how the printer will react to carriage returns.

The *auto feed XT* signal gives your computer the choice. By holding this signal low, the printer is commanded to automatically feed one line when it detects a carriage return. Make it high, and a line-feed character is required to roll the paper up to the next line.

17

PRINTERS

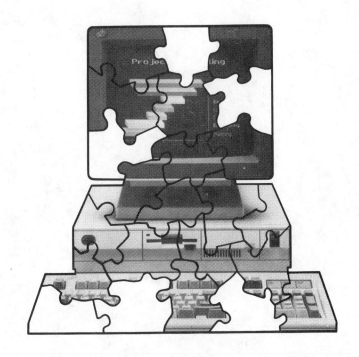

The most popular peripheral that's connected to the personal computer is the printer. Little wonder, considering that all the wonders that the machine can work would otherwise be locked inside. The printer extends the reach of your computer to the material world, putting its work on paper to enlighten and confound posterity.

The term printer is perhaps the broadest in the language of data processing. Printers can use any one of a large variety of technologies, operate at speeds from lethargic to lightning-like, and look like anything from Neolithic bricks to Buck Roger's nightmares. Some are better than typewriters at making sharp, legible text. Others rival plotters in their abilities to chart out graphics. Some may make a two-year-old's handiwork look professional.

Printers can be classified by their quality, speed, technology, purpose, weight, color, or any other of their innumerable (and properly pragmatic) design elements.

A definitive discourse on all aspect of printer technology would be a never-ending tale because the field is constantly changing: New technologies arise; new innovations are incorporated into old machines; and seemingly obsolete ideas recur again and again.

Printer Mechanics

Obviously the term "computer printer" is a general one that refers not to one kind of machine but several. Even looking at the mechanical aspects of the job of smudging paper with ink, there is more than one way to put a computer's output on paper, just as there are multiple methods of getting your house cat to part with its pelt.

Impact and Non-Impact Printers

One of the most evident demarcations between printer technologies is whether anything mechanical actually makes impact with the paper on which you want to print. Impact printers beat your paper to death.

Non-impact printers cuddle and squeeze it—perhaps even electrocute it—but never slam it hard. The practical differences between these technologies has little to do with what happens to the paper, however. Rather, it can determine output quality, reliability, cost, and even the quiet or lack of it that rewards you as your paper streams from the machine.

Typewriter Technology

Currently, the most likely printer to be lounging next to your home computer is the impact machine. All impact printers are direct descend-ants of the original office typewriter, and they are perhaps best understood by examining their aged forefather.

Although an old-fashioned typewriter is a mechanical complexity (as anyone knows who has tried putting one back together after taking it apart), its operating principle is quite simple. Strip away all the cams, levers, and keys, and you'll see that the essence of the typewriter is its hammers.

Each hammer strikes against an inked ribbon which in turn is pressed against a sheet of paper. The *impact* of the hammer against the ribbon shakes and squeezes ink onto the paper. Absorbed into the paper fibers, the ink leaves a visible mark or image in the shape of the part of the hammer that struck at the ribbon, typically a letter of the alphabet.

One way or another, all impact printers rely on this basic typewriter principle. Like Christopher Sholes first platen-pecker, all impact printers smash a hammer of some kind against a ribbon to squeeze ink from the ribbon onto paper, making their mark by force. In fact, if there is any difference between an impact printer and a typewriter at all, it's the directness of the linking of the typists fingers and the on-paper output. The typewriter directly lines your fingers to the mechanism that does the printing. A printer, on the other hand, inserts your personal computer between you mind and printed word.

Typewriter Conversion

The extreme case illustrating the similarity of typewriters and computer printers is the convertible typewriter, a machine that can take orders from fingers or printer port. In the earliest days of personal computers, before typewriter makers were sure that PCs would catch on and create a personal printer market, a number of companies adapted typewriters to computer output chores. The Bytewriter was typical of the result—a slow, plodding computer printer with full typewriter keyboard. It could do double-duty as fast as your fingers could fly, but, alas, no match for the computer's output.

One device, short-lived on the marketplace, even claimed to let you turn your typewriter into printer merely by sitting a box on the keyboard. The box was filled with dozens of solenoids and enough other mechanical parts to make the Space Shuttle look simple. The solenoids worked as electronically-controlled "fingers," pressing down each key on command from the host computer. Interesting as it sounds, such machines tread the thin line between the absurd and surreal. More than a little doubt exists as to whether these machines, widely advertised in 1981, were ever actually sold.

Impact Advantages

As with typewriters, all impact printers have a number of desirable qualities. Owing to their heritage of a century and a quarter of engineering refinement, they represent a mature technology. Their designs and functions are relatively straightforward, easy-to-understand, and reassuringly familiar.

Most impact printers can spread their output across any medium that ink has an affinity for, including any paper you might have lying around your home, from onion skin to thin cardstock. In addition, they are easily capable of making multiple copies using carbon paper or "carbonless" multi-copy sets. The impact goes right through the complete set and smashes ink from the carbon paper as easily as from the normal ribbon.

Impact Noise

Impact printers reveal their typewriter heritage in another way. The hammer bashing against the ribbon and paper makes noise, a sharp staccato rattle that's high in amplitude and rich in high-frequency components, penetrating and bothersome as a dental drive or an angry horde of giant, hungry mosquitoes. Typically, the impact printer rattles and prattles louder than most normal conversational tones, and it's more obnoxious than an argument.

Non-impact Designs

The obvious opposite to impact technology is non-impact printing. A number of other ways of putting images on paper sans the typewriter-like hammer impact have been developed through the application of new technologies and a good deal of imagination. The three leading non-impact technologies are the *ink jet,* the *thermal printer,* and the *laser printer*.

Ink-jet Printers

If the term "ink jet" conjures up images of the Nautilus and giant squid or a B-52 spraying out blue fluid instead of a fluffy white contrail, your mind is on the right track. Ink-jet printers are electronic squids that squirt out ink like miniature jet engines fueled in full color. They spray tiny drops of ink from several equally tiny nozzles onto the paper rather than hammering it on.

Thermal Printers

The equivalent of a wood-burning set on a much smaller scale, the thermal printer uses heat to make its mark. Rather than burning its image onto paper, however, it relies on a specially treated medium that it wipes tiny pin-like styli across. Upon the application of heat, the paper treatment discolors to form an image.

A more recent development, *thermal transfer printers* (sometimes called *thermal-wax printers*) use special wide ribbons and coated with a wax-based ink. The heat from the printhead melts the wax and transfers it to paper where it cools and sticks. The machines currently yield some of the brightest, most colorful, and sharpest image available from your PC's parallel output.

Laser Printers

An outgrowth of electrostatic copier technology, laser printers make their images on paper indirectly using a single tiny laser beam. The output of a semiconductor laser is modulated by the image to be printed. The laser beam is focused onto a special optically sensitive drum, a rotating mirror assembly forcing the beam to rapidly scan across the drum. The coating reacts to the laser impact by converting its light to an electrostatic charge. The drum is then dusted with pigment which clings electrostaticly to the charged area of the drum, the rest of the powder is removed. Paper is wrapped around the drum, then heat is applied to fuse the pigment to paper. Finally, the paper is pulled from the drum and pushed from the printer, with the pigmented image fused to it.

Although the mechanism is complex, the laser can be sharply focused to yield high quality and it can be scanned quickly to give high speed. Sales volume and competition have driven down the price of this technology to the point at which it is quite competitive with more traditional designs.

Image-Forming Methods

The terms "impact" and "non-impact" describe the sort of devilry involved in getting any marks at all to appear on paper. But the method of making those marks is independent of what they are and how they are shaped. While differing printing technologies have some affect on the quality of the image and what the printer is used for, other considerations are just as important in regard to image quality. Among the most important among them is the character-forming method used by the printer.

Fully-formed Character Printers

The original typewriter and all such machines made through the 1970's were based on the same character-forming principal as Gutenberg's original printing press. Every letter was printed fully-formed from a complete, although reversed, image of itself. The character was fully formed in advance of printing. Every part of it, from the boldest stroke to the the tiniest serif, was printed in one swipe of the press or clash of the typewriter hammer. The hammer (or piece of type for the printing press) acts like a mold for the letter to be produced.

Computer printers that make their characters by the same means are termed *fully-formed character* printers, although they often go by a number of different names. Among them are *letter-quality printers* and *daisy-wheel printers*. As the former epithet implies, these machines produce top-quality output, suitable for business correspondence because it resembles the work of the typewriter that is *de rigueur* in such work.

Nearly all of the fully-formed character printers that you are apt to be connected to a personal computer use the impact principle to get their ink on paper. Rather than having a separate hammer for each letter, however, the characters are arranged on a single separate element that is inserted between a single hammer and the ribbon. The hammer, powered by a solenoid that's controlled by the electronics of the printer and your computer, impacts against the element. The element then squeezes the ink off the ribbon and on to the paper. To allow the full range of alphanumeric characters to be printed using this single-hammer technique, the printing element swerves, shakes, or rotates each individual character that is to be formed in front of the hammer as it is needed.

Most often the characters are arranged near the tips of the spokes of a wheel. These machine earn the term ''daisy-wheel'' because the hubs resemble flower petals.

Hold the daisy horizontally and bend those petals upward, and the printing element becomes the thimble (or what you might call a ''tulip-wheel'') that's used by NEC's *thimble* printers.

Quality Advantage

The trademark of the fully-formed character printer is top quality output. The standard by which all other printing is measured is made by a type of non-impact, fully-formed character printer call the *photo-typesetter* or photocomposer. This class of machine is used to make the master plates for printing newspapers, magazines and books. These machines work photographically. The characters are fully-formed on longer strips of film negative. Each needed character is shuttled in front of a light beam in turn and its image is projected onto a sheet of photosensitive paper. The result is row after row of picture perfect characters.

Other fully-formed character printers produce text nearly as good. In fact, the chief limitation is not the printing technology but the ribbon that's used. Some daisy-wheel printers when equipped with a Mylar film ribbon can give results almost on-par with the work of the photo-typesetter.

Fully-formed Character Printer Disadvantages

Printing speed is one of the chief drawbacks of most commercially-available fully-formed character printers. They are *comparatively* slow. Budget-priced machines peck along at a lazy 12 to 20 characters per second—quick compared to the work of your own nimble fingers on the typewriter but truly turtle-like when compared to alternate technologies. Higher prices fully-formed character printers may push those rates up to 40 to 90 characters per second, quicker but still one-third to one-sixth the speed available with other character-forming technologies in the same price range.

Fully-formed character printers also limit you to a few typefaces. You can only print the type faces—and font sizes—that are available on the image-forming daisy-wheels or thimbles. Moreover, fully-formed character printers don't do graphics very well. Most won't do graphics at all.

Dot-matrix Printers

The alternative to fully-forming each character is making each one on the fly. The raw material for characters on paper is much the same as it is on the video screen—dots. A number of dots can be arranged to resemble any character that you want to print. To make things easier for the printer (and its designer), printers that form their characters from dots usually array those dots in a rectilinear matrix like a crossword puzzle grid. Because characters are formed from dots placed within a matrix, it's only natural to call such machines *dot-matrix printers*.

The prototypical dot-matrix printer is an impact machine. It uses a *printhead* that shuttles back and forth across the width of the paper. A number of thin *printwires* act as the hammers that squeeze ink from ribbon to paper.

Impact Dot-matrix Operation

In most dot-matrix printers a seemingly complex but efficient mechanism controls each of the printwires. The printwire is normally held away from the ribbon and paper, and against the force of a spring, by a strong permanent magnet. The magnet is wrapped with a coil of wire that forms an electromagnet, wound so its polarity is the opposite of that of the permanent magnet. To fire the print wire against the ribbon and paper, this electronmagnet is energized (under computer control, of course), and its field neutralizes that of the permanent magnet. Without the force of the permanent magnetic holding the print wire back, the spring forcefully jabs the print wire out against ribbon, squeezing ink onto the paper. After the printwire makes its dot, the electromagnet is de-energized and the permanent magnet pulls the printwire back to its idle position, ready to fire again.

The two-magnets-and-spring approach is designed with one primary purpose—to hold the printwire away from the paper (and out of harm's way) when no power is supplied to the printer and the printhead. The complexity is justified by the protection it affords the delicate printwires.

The printhead of a dot-matrix printer is made from a number of these printwire mechanisms. Most first generation personal computer printers and many current machines use nine wires arrayed in a vertical column. To produce high quality, an increasing number of newer impact dot-matrix printers use even more wires, typically 18 or 24. These are often arranged in parallel rows with the printwires vertically staggered, although some machines use different arrangements.

To print a line of characters, the printhead moves horizontally across the paper, and each wire fires as necessary to form the individual characters, its impact precisely timed so it falls on exactly the right position in the matrix. The wires fire on the fly—the printhead never pauses until it reaches the other side of the paper.

A major factor in determining the printing speed of dot-matrix machine is the time required between successive strikes of each print wire. Physical laws of motion limit the acceleration of each print wire can achieve in ramming toward the paper and back. Thus the time needed to retract and re-actuate each printwire puts a physical limit on how rapidly the printhead can travel across the paper. It cannot sweep past the next dot position before each of the print wires inside it is ready to fire. If the printhead travels too fast, dot positioning (and character shapes) would become rather haphazard.

To speed up operation, some impact dot-matrix machines print *bi-directionally,* rattling out one row from left to right then the next row right to left. This mode of operation saves the time that would ordinarily be wasted when the carriage returns to the left side of the page to start the next line. Of course, the printer must have sufficient memory to store a full line of text so it can be read out backwards.

Dot-matrix Character Quality

Characters made by a dot-matrix printer often look much rougher than fully-formed characters because the individual dots may stand out. The quality of the characters printed by a matrix printer is primarily determined by the number of dots in the matrix. The denser the matrix (the more dots in a given area), the better the characters look.

Often even bidirectional printers slow down to single-direction operation when quality counts. To increase dot density, they retrace each line two or more times, shifting the paper half the width of a dot vertically, between passes, filling in the space between dots. Unidirectional operation helps insure accurate placement of each dot in each pass.

A matrix measuring 5 × 7 (horizontal by vertical) dots is just sufficient to render all the upper and lower case letters of the alphabet unambiguously—and rather unaesthetically. The dots are big and they look disjointed. Worse, the minimal matrix is too small to let descending characters ("g," "j," "p," "q" and "y") droop below the general line of type and thus makes them look cramped and scrunched up. The minimum matrix used by most commercial dot-matrix printers measures 9 × 9 dots, a readable arrangement but still somewhat inelegant. But dot-matrix printing does not have to look bad. Laser printers actually use dot-matrix technology. However, they pack tiny dots very densely, 300 per inch. A single character may be formed in a 30 × 50 matrix. The latest generation of impact dot-matrix printers approaches that quality level.

As with computer displays, the resolution and *addressability* of dot-matrix printers are often confused. When resolution is mentioned, addressability is meant. A printer may be able to address any position on the paper with an accuracy of, say, 1/120 inch. However, if a printwire is larger than 1/120 inch in diameter, the machine will never be able to render detail as small as 1/120 inch. The big dots made by the wide printwires will blur out the detail. Better quality impact dot-matrix printers have smaller as well as more printwires. Laser printers generally use dots the same size as their resolution, about 1/300 inch.

Dot-matrix Advantages

Although the letters and numbers made by matrix printers look rougher than those of fully-formed character printers, matrix machines hold a big advantage over the competition. The dot patterns that make up individual characters are computer-controlled and can be changed and varied by your computer (or the computer-like control electronics built into the printer) without your needing to make any mechanical adjustments to the machine. A daisy-wheel, fully-formed character printer may allow you to shift from Roman to Italic typeface or from Pica to

Elite type size by merely swapping printing elements (the daisy-wheels themselves), but matrix printers make the switcheroo even easier and the repertory wider. Just send a computerized instruction to the printer, and you can change the typeface in mid-line, double the height of each character, squeeze type to half its width, or shift to proportionally-space script.

Block Graphics

In addition, dot-matrix printers excel at drawing graphics. Many dot-matrix printers have extra built-in character sets called "block graphics" which permit you to draw pictures out of building blocks of simple shapes such as squares, rectangle, triangles, horizontal and vertical lines, and so on. Each of these shapes is electronically coded and recognized by the printer as if it were a letter of the alphabet, and the printer merely lays down line after line of these block characters to make a picture, like filling in each square on a piece of graph paper with different shapes. The pictures look a little chunky because the building blocks are big, just a little under 1/8 inch across.

All Points Addressable Graphics

Most matrix printers even allow you to decide where to place individual dots on the printed sheet using a technique called *all points addressable graphics* or *APA graphics*. With the appropriate instructions you can draw graphs in great detail or even make pictures resembling the halftone photographs printed in newspapers. The software built into the printer allows every printable dot position to be controlled—specified as printed (black) or not (white). An entire image can be built up like a television picture, scanning lines several dots wide (as wide as the number of wires in the printhead) down the paper.

This graphics printing technique takes other names, too. Because each individual printed dot can be assigned a particular location or "address" on the paper, this feature is often called *dot-addressable graphics*. Sometimes that title is simplified into *dot graphics*. Occasionally it appears as *bit-image* graphics because each dot is effectively the image of one bit of data.

As with text-quality, the sharpness and clarity of the printed all-points-addressable picture can range from mediocre to very good. True resolution (rather than addressability) indicates how sharp the printed detail can be and varies from 72 to 300 or more dots per inch. The more dots per inch of resolution, the better the graphics image will look.

Downloadable Character Sets

Besides addressing each dot on the paper individually, some dot-matrix printers even allow you to determine the dot patterns for an entire alphabet of character. The character shapes you define can be used as a normal type font. Each letter pattern is printed just by sending one an ordinary alphanumeric character from your computer. This feature is called a *downloadable character set* because the information necessary for forming the patterns are loaded down from your computer into the memory of your printer.

Font Cartridges

Some dot-matrix printers offer another way of adding more fonts to their repertories. The dot patterns for forming alternate character fonts are stored in ROM chips that are held inside special *font cartridges*. The cartridge itself merely provides a housing for the chip and a connector that fits a mate in the printer. By sliding in a cartridge, you add the extra memory in the cartridge to that in the printer. Many impact and laser dot-matrix printers have been designed to use font cartridges.

Note that each manufacturers' cartridges are different and incompatible (sometimes the cartridges of two models of printer made by the same manufacturer are incompatible), although several laser printer makers are making their machines compatible with Hewlett-Packard laser printer cartridges.

Laser Memory

Most dot-matrix printers accept dot-addressable graphics on the fly. That is, data bytes are sent to them and either as soon as the bytes are received or after at most a full line has been accepted, the printer obediently rattles them to paper.

Lasers can't work so quickly. They work a page at a time, digesting an entire sheet of graphics before committing a dot to paper. The laser mechanism is tuned to run at exactly one speed, and it must receive data at the proper rate to properly form its image. In addition, many lasers recognize higher level graphics commands to draw lines and figures across the entire on-paper image area. To properly form these images, the laser needs to get the big picture of its work.

For these and other reasons, lasers require prodigious amounts of memory to buffer full-page, *bit-mapped images* in their highest resolution modes. (Most lasers operate in a *character-mapped mode* when rendering alphanumerics, so memory usage is not as great.) A full page at 300 dot per inch resolution requires nearly a megabit of storage (90,000 bits per square inch times about 80 inches of image area per page). Lasers also require some memory area for housekeeping and may require more for downloaded fonts.

The typical standard memory of many laser printers, 512K, is clearly inadequate for full-page, top-resolution graphics. As a result, you'll need at least a full megabyte of memory to make a laser a worthwhile graphics engine else you'll have to settle for lower full-page resolution (usually 150 dots per inch) or a smaller high-resolution image area.

Multicolor Output

A growing number of applications demand color output. A number of impact dot-matrix printers allow you to add color to both the alphabets and graphics they put on paper. A few have two color ribbons (like old-fashioned typewriters) and special software instructions to control shifting between them.

Most color printers now use ribbons soaked with three or four colors of ink and can achieve seven colors on paper by combining color pairs. To switch colors that they print out, they merely shift the ribbon up or down. (A few machines use multiple ribbons, each one a different color, to achieve the same effect.)

While adding color to a printer used to add substantially to its price, current technology has severely cut costs. The ribbon-shifting mechanism is built into some printers. In others, it may add only about $100 to the price.

Non-impact matrix printers excel at color, however. Inkjets are well suited to the task because their liquid inks can actually blend together on the paper before they dry. Most thermal-wax matrix printers are particularly designed for color output. They achieve on-paper color mixing by using transparent inks that allow one color to show through another. The two hues blend together optically.

The only problem with color printers is that they need special software to bring their rainbows to life. Absent having the right software, you have to understand computer programming to take advantage of multi-color capabilities.

Paper Handling

If shuffling the printhead back and forth were a printer's sole goal in life, all your printouts would be long, thin documents exactly one line long. The printer must advance the paper line by line just as a typewriter does when you slam the carriage back. The various schemes developed to help printer and operator deal with this chore—the way the printout paper is handled and the kind of paper that can be handled—must be carefully considered to match a printer to your needs.

Friction Feed

The old-fashioned typewriter moved paper through its mechanism by squeezing it between the large rubber called a *platen* and smaller rollers. The paper is additionally held around the platen above the area where the hammers strike it by a *bail arm,* which usually pivots out of the way when you load paper. The friction between the platen, smaller rollers, and bail arm keeps the paper from slipping as it is rolled past the printhead so this paper feeding system is often called *friction feed*.

In most cases, friction feed implies that loading paper is a manual operation—you have to pull out the bail arm, insert each individual sheet, line it up to be certain that it is square (so that the printhead doesn't type diagonally across the paper), lock it and the bail arm down, and finally signal to the machine that all is well. Easier said than done, of course—and more tedious, too, should you decide to print a computerized version of the *Encyclopaedia Britannica*. Worse yet, you have to stand by and give the machine your undivided attention, constantly shuffling in a fresh new sheet of paper every time the printer finishes one.

On the positive side, however, most friction feed mechanisms will handle any kind of paper you can fit through the mechanism, from your own engraved stationery to pre-printed forms, from W-2s to 1040s, envelopes and index cards.

Automatic Sheet Feeder

Anything you can do, someone can design a machine to do, too. Whether the machine can be made affordably is another matter. Feeding paper through a friction-fed printer is no exception. A device, quite logically termed the *automatic sheet feeder* (although occasionally called *bin-feed*) can relieve your tedium and tantrums by loading most standard size forms and plain papers into your printer without your intervention or attention. Unfortunately, sheet feeders have been among the most complex accessories you can add to your computer system, many of them being much akin to the inventions of Rube Goldberg. Price rises with complexity, and sheet feeders tend also to be expensive, quite capable of ripping a multiple hundred dollar hole in your pocket. Most sheet feeders are designed for single-layer paper, which means two separate printings of separate sheets (no carbons), as a result, your printing project can run into double and triple time when you need more than one copy.

Roll Feed

One way to reduce the number of times you've got to slide a sheet of paper into the friction-feed mechanism is to make the paper longer. In fact, you could use one, long continuous sheet. Some systems do exactly that, wrapping the long sheet around a roll (like toilet paper). The printer just pulls the paper through as it needs it. By rigidly mounting a roll-holder at the back of the printer, the paper can be kept in reasonable alignment and skew can be eliminated.

The shortcoming of this system is, of course, that you end up with one long sheet. You have to tear it to pieces or carefully cut it up when you want traditional $8\frac{1}{2}$ by 11 output.

Pin-Feed and Tractor-Feed

While roll-fed paper could be perforated at eleven-inch intervals so that you could easily and neatly tear it apart, another problem arises. Most friction mechanisms are not perfect. The paper can slip so that gradually the page breaks in the image and page breaks at the perforations no longer correspond. In effect, the paper and the image can get out of sync.

By locking perforations in the edge of the paper inside sprockets that prevent slipping, the image and paper breaks can be kept in sync. Two different paper-feeding systems use sprocketed paper to avoid slippage. *Pin-feed* uses drive sprockets which are permanently affixed to the edges of the platen roller. Consequently, the pin-feed mechanism can handle only one width of paper, the width corresponding to the sprocket separate at the edges of the platen. *Tractor-feed* uses adjustable sprockets that can be moved closer together or farther apart to handle nearly any width paper that will fit through the printer.

As the names imply, a *uni-directional* tractor only pulls (or pushes) the paper through in a single direction (hopefully forward). The *bi-directional* tractor allows both forward and backward paper motion, which is often helpful for graphic, special text functions (printing exponents, for example) and lining up the top of the paper with the top of the printhead.

Push and Pull Tractors

The original tractor mechanism for printers was a two-step affair. One set of sprockets fed paper into the printer and another set pulled it out. For the intended purpose of tractor feeding, however, the two sets of sprockets is one more than necessary. All it takes is one set to lock the printer's image in-sync with the paper.

A single set of sprockets can be located in one of two positions, either before or after paper wraps around the platen in front of the printhead. Some printers allow you to use its single set of tractors in either position. In others, the tractors are fixed in one location or the other.

Push tractors are placed in the path of the paper before it enters the printer. In effect, they push the paper through the machine. The platen roller helps to ease paper through the printer while the push tractor provides the principal force and keeps the paper tracking properly. This form of feeding holds a couple of advantages. You can rip the last sheet of a printout off without having to feed an extra sheet through the printer or rethread it. The tractor also act bidirectionally with relative ease, pull the paper backwards as well as pushing it forward.

Pull tractors are located in the path of the paper after it emerges from the printmaking mechanism. The pull tractor pulls paper across the platen, and the paper is held flat against the platen by its friction and the resistance of pulling it up through the mechanism. The pull tractor is simpler and offers less to go wrong than push designs.

Although most pull tractors operate only unidirectionally, they work well in high speed use on printers with flat metal (instead of round rubber) platens. Because of their high speed operation, typically several pages per minute, the machines naturally tend to be used for large print job during which the waste of a single sheet is not a major drawback.

Paper Control

Printers differ to a great degree in how precisely they can move paper through their mechanisms. Some are designed to allow exacting tolerances and move each sheet in increments of the tiniest fractions of an inch (as small as 1/216 inch). A few still cling to their typewriter heritage and restrict you to shifting paper to one line (or half-line) at a time.

The trend has been to more precise control because it allows more format versatility in printing text—for instance, you can change line spacings from six lines per inch for manuscripts to eight per inch for business letters or add a few extra inch-fractions to each line to stretch ten pages into a twelve page when you have a tough essay assignment—and more accuracy in printing graphics.

Printers also vary in the control they afford in the other direction, the horizontal movement of the printhead across the paper. A few primitive machines still stick with the mechanical cog of the typewriter. Most modern machines, however, let you vary the character pitch in text mode and the spacing of dots and speed of printing in graphics modes. This versatility is necessary for the rendering of proportionally-spaced text and for printing multiple graphic densities.

Smart and Dumb Printers

A printer is not just a brute-force paper-pounder. It's got to have brains, too. Even the cheapest impact dot-matrix printer has to be smart enough to know the one exact instant it must trigger each of its printwires to ram one dot of the image on exactly the right spot on the paper. Lasers must match each character in their font cartridges with the proper on-paper position and possibly flick their light beams seven million or more times for each sheet that rolls through. Daisy-wheel machines time their hammer blows to the exact instance the right character on its spinning wheel is lined up properly. Behind the scenes, all printers must sort embedded commands from printed characters to carry out advanced operations such as printing bold characters or changing fonts.

Printers vary substantially in their native intelligence. While many printers operate as little more than slaves, taking orders and carrying them out, many printers have much greater abilities. Some can go so far as to format the data as they print it.

The old-line printer, typified by the classic all-mechanical teletype, was so *dumb* that it didn't even know when it came to the edge of the paper. It would gladly perforate its platen with the text of an entire novel if the data it was sent wasn't broken into short lines with the appropriate carriage return and line feed characters mixed in with the text. Many of today's printers have brains almost equally as primitive and rely on the computer and its software to tell them exactly what to do. Some computer programs, like word processors designed to be used with specific printers, may include special printer drivers software that adds in all sorts of extra ASCII code symbols to the data stream. Every fractional-inch movement of the printhead between proportionally-spaced characters, every character to be pecked, every roll of the platen, is specifically indicated by the computer program and sent to the printer.

On the other hand, *smart* printers can take over these same text processing functions on their own. They can accept a nearly completely unformatted string of text, break it into proportionally-spaced lines, and leave the proper margins at the top and bottom of the page. To handle these and other chores, even inexpensive printers nowadays have their own built-in microprocessors. The internal microbrain helps the printer position the proper petal of the daisy-wheel in front of the print hammer or calculate when to fire the wire of a dot-matrix printhead.

Horizontal and Vertical Tabbing

One place the intelligence of a printer can be put to use is optimizing printhead motion, making every movement of the printhead the most efficient possible. The internal microprocessor in a printer can look ahead in the memory and see what's coming up next and optimize the positioning of the printhead or print wheel by finding the shortest difference between consecutive lines. The goal is to move between printhead positions as quickly as possible. Often called *logic seeking* printers, these machines use a number of techniques to optimize printhead movement. Using *horizontal tabbing* they can breeze over oceans of blank space in each line without dwelling on the each individual space and deciding what not to print. With *vertical tabbing* they can be equally adept at skipping blank lines on the page. Both techniques, combined with bidirectionally printing, will allow a printer so blessed to type normal documents faster than machines with the same characters-per-second speed rating that lack these features.

Printer Control

Smart or dumb, a printer often requires guidance from the host computer and the program it runs to tell it exactly how to make a printout look. The computer must send the printer a series of instructions, either to control the most intimate operation of the dumb printer or to coax special features from the brainy machine.

The instructions from the computer must be embedded in the character stream because that is the only data connection between the printer and its host. These embedded instructions can take on any of several forms.

Control Characters

Some of the most necessary instructions are the most common, for example, to backspace, tab, or even underline characters. In fact, these instructions are so commonplace that they were incorporated into the ASCII character set and assigned specific values. To backspace, for instance, your computer just sends your printer a byte with the ASCII value 08, the backspace character. Upon receiving this character, the printer will backspace instead of making a mark on the paper. The entire group of these special ASCII values are termed *control characters*.

Escape Sequences

The number of ASCII characters available for printer commands are few, and the number of functions that the printer can carry out are many. To sneak additional instructions through the data channel, most printers use special strings of characters called *escape sequences*.

An escape sequence is simply a series of ASCII characters that begins with a special code symbol assigned the ASCII value of 27. This special character is often called *escape* by programmers, and is abbreviated ESC.

In most commands, the escape character by itself does nothing and it serves only as an attention getter. It warns the printer that the ASCII character or characters that follow should be interpreted as commands rather than printed out.

ANSI Escape Sequences

The *American National Standards Institute* has defined as standard set of escape sequences for controlling printers. (A partial listing of these *ANSI escape sequences* is given in Table 17.1.)

Table 17.1 **ANSI Control Characters**

ASCII value	Control Value	Mnemonic	Function
0	ˆ @	NUL	Used as a fill character
1	ˆ A	SOH	Start of heading (indicator)
2	ˆ B	STX	Start of text (indicator)
3	ˆ C	ETX	End of text (indicator)
4	ˆ D	EOT	End of transmission; disconnect character
5	ˆ E	ENQ	Enquiry; request answerback message
6	ˆ F	ACK	Acknowledge
7	ˆ G	BEL	Sounds audible bell tone
8	ˆ H	BS	Backspace
9	ˆ I	HT	Horizontal tab
10	ˆ J	LF	Line feed
11	ˆ K	VT	Vertical tab
12	ˆ L	FF	Form feed
13	ˆ M	CR	Carriage return
14	ˆ N	SO	Shift out; changes character set
15	ˆ O	SI	Shift in; changes character set
16	ˆ P	DLE	Data link escape
17	ˆ Q	DC1	Data control 1, also known as XON
18	ˆ R	DC2	Data control 2
19	ˆ S	DC3	Data control 3, also known as XOFF
20	ˆ T	DC4	Data control 4
21	ˆ U	NAK	Negative acknowledge
22	ˆ V	SYN	Synchronous idle
23	ˆ W	ETB	End of transmission block (indicator)
24	ˆ X	CAN	Cancel; immediately ends any control or escape sequence
25	ˆ Y	EM	End of medium (indicator)
26	ˆ Z	SUB	Substitute (also, end-of-file marker)
27	ˆ [	ESC	Escape; introduces escape sequence
28	ˆ \	FS	File separator (indicator)
29	ˆ]	GS	Group separator (indicator)
30	ˆ ˆ	RS	Record separator (indicator)
31	ˆ __	US	Unit separator (indicator)
32		SP	Space character
127		DEL	No operation

Table 17.1 (continued)

ASCII value	Control Value	Mnemonic	Function
128		Reserved	Reset parser with no action (Esc])
129		Reserved	Reset parser with no action (Esc A)
130		Reserved	Reset parser with no action (Esc B)
131		Reserved	Reset parser with no action (Esc C)
132		IND	Index; increment active line (move paper up)
133		NEL	Next line; advance to first character of next line
134		SSA	Start of selected area (indicator)
135		ESA	End of selected area (indicator)
136		HTS	Set horizontal tab (at active column)
137		HTJ	Horizontal tab with justification
138		VTS	Set vertical tab stop (at current line)
139		PLD	Partial line down
140		PLU	Partial line up
141		RI	Reverse index (move paper down, backwards, one line)
142		SS2	Single shift 2
143		SS3	Single shift 3
144		DCS	Device control string
145		PU1	Private use 1
146		PU2	Private use 2
147		STS	Set terminal state
148		CCH	Cancel character
149		MW	Message writing
150		SPA	Start of protected area (indicator)
151		EPA	End of protected area (indicator)
152		Reserved	Function same as Esc X
153		Reserved	Function same as Esc Y
154		Reserved	Function same as Esc Z
155		CSI	Control sequence introducer
156		ST	String terminator
157		OSC	Operating system command (indicator)
158		PM	Privacy message
159		APC	Application program command

Some of the above are also implemented as standard *Escape Sequences* for use in seven-bit environments. Some of these are as follows:

Esc D	Index
Esc E	Vertical line
Esc H	Set horizontal tab
Esc Z	Set vertical tab
Esc K	Partial line down
Esc L	Partial line up

Table 17.1 (continued)

ASCII value	Control Value	Mnemonic	Function
Esc M		Reverse index	
Esc N		Single shift 2	
Esc O		Single shift 3	
Esc P		Device control string	
Esc [		Control sequence introducer	
Esc \		String terminator	
Esc]		Operating system command	
Esc ^		Private message	
Esc __		Application program command	

Characters shown as implemented by Digital Equipment Corporation

De Facto Command Standards

As is so often the case with personal computer products, the standard escape sequences aren't that standard. The ANSI list is chiefly designed to handle the printing of text using fully-formed character printers. Many printers have advanced graphics and other functions that transcend the ANSI design. Consequently, nearly every printer manufacturer has broadened, adapted or ignored the standard to suit the special needs of its own printer.

Whatever standards that do exist among printers are *de facto*, after the fact, earning their status as standards simply because lots of people follow them. Usually the codes and commands used by a large manufacturer with a top-selling product will be followed by smaller companies making compatible products.

Daisy-Wheel Commands

Initially the market for fully-formed character printers was dominated by two companies, the Diablo division of Xerox and Qume, owned by the ITT conglomerate at the time the PC was introduced. (The company has changed hands several times since then.) The commands used by the printers manufactured by those two companies have emerged as compatibility standards among letter-quality printers. Most such machines boast either Diablo or Qume-compatibility.

The two command sets are very similar, differing only in a few instructions. (A condensed listing of the two command sets is given in Table 17.2.)

Table 17.2 **Diablo and Qume Control Codes and Escape Sequences**

Control Codes

ASCII Value	Control Value	Mnemonic	Function
1	^ A	SOH	Perform user test continuously
2	^ B	STX	Perform user test once
5	^ E	ENQ	Halt continuous user test
7	^ G	BEL	Sounds audible bell tone
8	^ H	BS	*Backspace
9	^ I	HT	*Horizontal tab
10	^ J	LF	*Line feed
11	^ K	VT	*Vertical tab
12	^ L	FF	*Form feed
13	^ M	CR	*Carriage return
27		ESC	Return to normal mode
31		US	Program mode carriage motion
127	DEL		*No operation

Escape Sequences

Escape Sequence	Function
Esc BS	*Backspace 1/120 inch
Esc LF	*Negative (backwards) line feed
Esc SO	Shift to primary mode
Esc SI	Return to normal mode
Esc RS n	*Define vertical spacing increment as n-1
Esc US n	*Set horizontal space increment to n-1
Esc VT n	*Absolute vertical tab to line n-1
Esc HT	*Absolute horizontal tab to column n-1
Esc SP	Print special character position 004
Esc SUB I	Initialize printer
Esc SUB SO	Terminal self-test
Esc CR P	Initialize printer
Esc 0	*Set right margin
Esc 1	*Set horizontal tab stop
Esc 2	*Clear all horizontal tab stops
Esc 3	*Graphic on 1/60 inch
Esc 4	*Graphics off
Esc 5	*Forward print
Esc 6	*Backward print
Esc 8	*Clear horizontal tab stop
Esc 9	*Set left margin
Esc .	Auto line feed on

Table 17.2 (continued)

Escape Sequences

Escape Sequence	Function
Esc ,	Auto line feed off
Esc <	Auto bi-directional printing on
Esc >	Auto bi-directional printing off
Esc +	Set top margin
Esc −	Set bottom margin
Esc @ T	Enter user test mode
Esc #	Enter secondary mode
Esc $	*WPS (proportional spaced printwheel) on
Esc %	*WPS (proportional spaced printwheel) off
Esc (n	Set tabs at n (n can be a list)
Esc) n	Clear tabs at n (n can be a list)
Esc /	Print special character position 002
Esc C n m	Absolute horizontal tab to column n
Esc D	*Negative half-line feed
Esc E n m	Define horizontal space increments
Esc F n m	Set form length
Esc G	*Graphics on 1/120 inch
Esc H n m l	Relative horizontal motion
Esc I	Underline on
Esc J	Underline off
Esc K n	Bold overprint on
Esc L n n	Define vertical spacing increment
Esc M n	Bold overprint off
Esc N	No carriage movement on next character
Esc O	Right margin control on
Esc P n	Absolute vertical tab to line n
Esc Q	Shadow print on
Esc R	Shadow print off
Esc S	No print on
Esc T	No print off
Esc U	*Half-line feed
Esc W	Auto carriage return/line feed on
Esc V n m l	Relative vertical paper motion
Esc X	Force execution
Esc Y	Right margin control off
Esc Z	Auto carriage return/line feed off
Esc e	Sheet feeder page eject
Esc i	Sheet feeder insert page from tray one
Esc x	Force execution

Qume Sprint 11 Commands shown; * indicates commands shared by Diablo 630

Epson and IBM Nine-Wire Commands

The closest to de facto standards that exits in dot-matrix printers are the code and commands used by IBM and Epson. These are closely related if simply because the first IBM Graphics Printer was based on the Epson MX-80. The chief differences between the two were their character sets. IBM used the upper half of the 256 ASCII values for a variety of special symbols, the *IBM extended character set,* while Epson used those values for italics. The commands used by these two printers have become a *de facto* standard for nine-wire dot-matrix printers. (A condensed table of these commands is given in Table 17.3.)

Epson 24-wire Commands

When dot-matrix technology advanced from nine-wire printers to 24-wire designs, graphics commands needed to be augmented to take additional print modes into account. Again, the commands for Epson's 24-wire series of printers have become as close to a standard as exists in the personal computer industry. (The 24-wire extensions to the Epson command set is listed in Table 17.4.)

Table 17.3 **Epson Control Characters and Escape Sequences**

		Control Codes	
ASCII Value	Control Value	Mnemonic	Function
7	^G	BEL	Sounds audible bell tone
8	^H	BS	Backspace
9	^I	HT	Horizontal tab
10	^J	LF	Line feed
11	^K	VT	Vertical tab
12	^L	FF	Form feed
13	^M	CR	Carriage return
14	^N	SO	#Turns enlarged print mode on
15	^O	SI	#Turns condensed print mode on
17	^P	DC1	#Select printer
18	^R	DC2	Turns condensed print mode off
19	^S	DC3	#Deselect printer
20	^T	DC4	Turns enlarged print mode off
24	^X	CAN	Cancel line
127		DEL	No operation

Escape Sequences

Escape Sequence	Function
Esc SO	#Turns enlarged print mode on
Esc SI	#Turns condensed print mode on
Esc EM	#Cut sheet feeder control
Esc SP	#Select character space
Esc !	#Selects mode combinations
Esc #	#MSB mode cancel
Esc $	#Set absolute horizontal tab
Esc %	#Selects active character set
Esc :	#Copies ROM to user RAM
Esc &	#Defines user characters
Esc /	#Set vertical tab
Esc \	#Move printhead
Esc <	Turn unidirectional (left-to-right only) printing on
Esc >	#MSB set (MSB = 0)
Esc =	#MSB reset (MSB = 1)
Esc @	#Initialize printer

Esc - n	Underline mode
	    n = 1 or 49, turns underline mode on
	    n = 0 or 48, turns underline mode off

Esc * n	#Select bit-image mode (data follows n)
	    n = 0, normal density
	    n = 1, dual density
	    n = 2, double-speed dual density
	    n = 3, quadruple density
	    n = 4, CRT graphics
	    n = 6, CRT graphics II

Esc ^	Nine-pin graphics mode
Esc 0	Set line spacing at 1/8 inch
Esc 1	Set line spacing at 7/72 inch
Esc 2	Set line spacing at 1/6 inch
Esc 3 n	Set line spacing at n/216 inch (n between 0 and 255)
Esc 4	#Turns alternate character (italics) set on
Esc 5	#Turns alternate character (italics) set off
Esc 6	*Select character set 1 #Deactivate high-order control codes
Esc 7	*Select character set 2 #Restores high-order control codes
Esc 8	Turns paper-end detector off
Esc 9	Turns paper-end detector on

Table 17.3 (continued)

Escape Sequences

Escape Sequence	Function
Esc A n	Set line spacing at n/72 inch (n between 0 and 85)
Esc B	#Set vertical tab stop
Esc C n	Sets form length to n lines (n between 1 and 127)
Esc C 0 n	Sets form length to n inches (n between 1 and 22)
Esc D	Set horizontal tab stop
Esc E	Turns emphasized mode on
Esc F	Turns emphasized mode off
Esc G	Turns double-strike mode on
Esc H	Turns double-strike mode off
Esc I	#Control code select
Esc J n	Tentative n/216-inch line spacing
Esc K	Normal-density bit-image data follows
Esc L	Dual-density bit-image data follows
Esc M	Elite-sized characters on
Esc N n	Set number of lines to skip-over perforation n = number of lines to skip between 1 and 127
Esc O	Turn skip-over perforation off
Esc P	#Elite mode off/Pica-sized characters on
Esc Q n	#Sets the right margin at column n
Esc R	*Return to default tabs
Esc R n	#Select international character set
	n = 0, USA
	n = 1, France
	n = 2, Germany
	n = 3, England
	n = 4, Denmark I
	n = 5, Sweden
	n = 6, Italy
	n = 7, Spain
	n = 8, Japan
	n = 9, Norway
	n = 10, Denmark II
Esc S n	Superscript/subscript on mode
	n = 0 or 48, superscript mode on
	n = 1 or 49, subscript mode on

Table 17.3 (continued)

Escape Sequences

Escape Sequence	Function
Esc T	Turns superscript/subscript off

Esc U n	Unidirectional/bidirectional printing
	   n = 0 or 48, turn bidirectional printing on
	   n = 1 or 49, turn unidirectional printing on

Esc W n	Enlarged (double-width) print mode
	   n = 1 or 49, enlarged print mode on
	   n = 0 or 48, enlarged print mode off

Esc X	*Set margins
Esc Y	Double-speed, dual-density bit-image data follows
Esc Z	Quadruple-density bit-image data follows
Esc a	#Justification
Esc b	#Set vertical tab

Esc e n	Set tab unit
	   n = 0 or 48, sets horizontal tab unit
	   n = 1 or 49, sets vertical tab unit

Esc f n	Set skip position setting
	   n = 0 or 48, sets horizontal skip position
	   n = 1 or 49, sets vertical skip position

Esc g	#Select fifteen width
Esc i	#Immediate print (typewrier mode)
Esc j	#Immediate temporary reverse paper feed
Esc k	#Select family of type styles
Esc l n	Sets the left margin at column n

Esc m n	Special character generator selection
	   n = 0, control codes accepted
	   n = 4, graphics characters accepted

Esc p n	Proportional printing
	   n = 0 or 48, turn proportional printing
	off
	   n = 1 or 49, turn proportional printing
	on

Esc s	Half-speed printing
	   n = 0 or 48, turn half-speed printing off
	   n = 1 or 49, turn half-speed printing on

Esc z	Select letter quality or draft

Includes codes used by many printers
* IBM command only
# Epson command only

Table 17.4 **Epson 24-Pin Graphics Commands**

Generalized Command Form:

Exc * m c1 c2 [graphics data]

where m is the code number from the table below, and c1 and c2 specify the number of columns to use for graphics.

25-Pin Graphics Mode Codes

Mode	Pins	Code	Density Dots/in.
Single-density	8	0	60
Double-density	8	1	120
High-double density	8	2	120
Quadruple density	8	3	240
CRT I	8	4	80
CRT II	8	6	90
Single-density	24	32	60
Double-density	24	33	120
CRT III	24	38	90
Triple-density	24	39	180
Hex-density	24	40	360

Computing c1 and c2:

The values of c1 and c2 specify the number of columns dots to use for the graphics display. Since one byte can code only 256 values, a second byte is used to code encompass the total number of dot-columns possible. The c1 value is least significant. To determine the proper values, divide the desired number of graphic columns by 256. The quotient is the value of c2; the remainder is c1.

Graphics data:

Each 24-pin column of data in a line is encoded with three separate bytes; the first byte code the top eight wires, the second codes the middle eight, the last codes the bottom eight. The least significant bit in each byte codes the bottom dot of the octet associated with that byte; the most significant bit codes the top dot of the octet. A value of one indicates a dot will appear on paper.

Postscript

Laser printers are more than mere printers. Most have the brains of a complete computer. Many are smarter than the computers that they are plugged into. The instructions that they understand reflect this intelligence. Rather than mere commands, the software controls for laser printers are more like programming languages.

Two standards are emerging. One is the Hewlett-Packard Laserjet command set, used by that company's line of laser printers. It functions like an elaborate printer command set, with length strings of characters initiating the various Laserjet functions. Although the Hewlett-Packard commands include several higher level instructions (for example, for drawing lines and leaders on paper), it works primarily in a bit-image mode that requires your computer to send every data for every dot that is to be printed. Your computer does the bulk of the image manipulation.

The alternative is Adobe Systems' *Postscript* page description language. Postscript comprises a group of commands and codes that describe graphic elements and indicate where they are to appear on the printed page. Your computer sends high-level Postscript commands to your laser printer, and the printer executes the commands to draw the image itself. In effect, the data processing load is shifted to the printer which, in theory, has been optimized for implementing such graphics commands. Nevertheless, it can take several minutes for the printer to compute a full page image after all the Postscript commands have been transferred to it. (Older Postscript printers might take half-an-hour or more to work out a full page of graphics.)

The advantage of Postscript is its versatility. For example, while Hewlett-Packard printers need to have font cartridges or downloaded fonts for every type style *and size* that they are to print, Postscript machines can compute almost any necessary character size. Postscript allows much more intimate control of the image inside the printer.

18

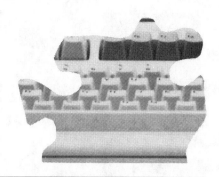

SERIAL
PORTS

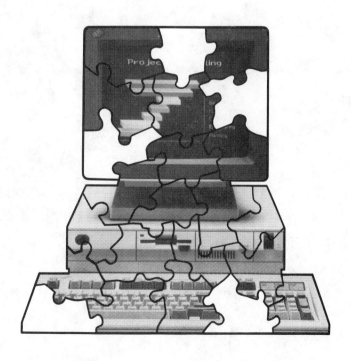

T he only two-way access to the outside world provided by all PCs that was officially recognized by IBM until the release of the PS/2 series was the asynchronous data communications port, known also as the async port, serial port, or "comm" port. Because this port operates under the EIA (Electronics Industry Association, a trade group) RS-232C standard, it's often also classified as an RS-232 port.

No matter the name, all IBM serial ports are the same, at least functionally. They take the eight (or more) bits at a time data words and turns them on end, changing them from a broadside of digital blips into a pulse chain that can walk a plank, single-file. Because of the bits of information are transferred as a long series, this form of data exchange is called serial.

In a perfect world, a single circuit—nothing more than two wires, a signal line and a ground—would be all that was necessary to move this serial signal from the one place to another without further ado. The world is, of course, not perfect, and the world of computers even less so. For example, a computer has no guarantee that it will always catch exactly the first bit in a series when it starts listening to the march of a serial signal; one mistake, and every byte that follows will be in error.

Synchronous and Asynchronous Communication

Two chief serial transmission methods are used to avoid such problems. In one of these, the sending and receiving systems are synchronized using some kind of auxiliary signal so that both ends of a connection are always in step. This *synchronous* communication technique is used primarily in mainframe systems.

The alternative is to provide markers in the data train to indicate where every distinguishable block of data begins and ends. The receiving system can then sort out the proper beginning and avoid confusion without any synchronization. Such systems are described as being *asynchronous* and are the operating basis of personal computer serial ports.

411

In most asynchronous systems, the data is broken up into small pieces, each roughly—though not exactly—corresponding to one byte. Each of these chunks is called a *word,* and may consist of five to eight data bits. The most widely used word lengths are seven and eight bits, the former because it accommodates all upper and lowercase text characters in ASCII code; the latter because each word corresponds exactly to one data byte.

As serial data, the bits of a word are sent one-at-a-time down the communication channel. As a matter of convention, the least significant bit of the word is sent out first. The rest of the bits follow in order of their increasing significance.

Added to these data bits is a very special double-length pulse called a *start* bit, and it indicates the beginning of a data word. One more *stop* bit indicates the end of the word. Between the last bit of the word and the first stop bit a *parity* bit is often inserted as a data integrity check. Together the data bits, the start bit, the parity bit, and the stop bits make up one data *frame.*

Five kinds of parity bits can be used in serial communication, two of which actually offer error detection. This error detection works by counting the number of bits in the data word and determining whether the result is even or odd. In *odd parity,* the parity bit is set on when the number of bits in the word is odd. *Even parity* switches on the parity bit when the bit total of the word is even.

In *mark parity* the parity bit is always on, regardless of the bit total of the word. *Space parity* always leaves the parity bit off. *No parity* doesn't even leave space for a parity bit.

All of these bits are sent down the serial line as *negative-going* pulses superimposed on the normal positive voltage on the data line. That is, the presence of a bit in a serial word will be a negative pulse. Compared to normal logical systems, RS-232 standard data looks upside down. There's no particularly good reason for the inversion except that it's the way things have always been done and, when it comes to communications, things work best when everybody sticks to the same standard.

Serial signals are also described by the nominal rate at which the bits in the serial train are sent. The standard form of measurement is amazingly simple—the number of bits per second that are sent—with the standard unit being one bit per second or bps.

For somewhat arbitrary reasons, bit rates are enumerated in a rather odd increment. The usual minimum speed is 300 bps, although slower submultiples of 50, 100, 150 bps are available. Faster standard speeds merely double the preceding rate, so the sequence runs 600, 1200, 2400, 4800, 9600, to 19,200, the fastest speed IBM supports in its fastest personal computers, the PS/2 Models 50 and above.

Even the fastest of these speeds are not the limit of serial hardware. In fact, third-party developers offer software that drives IBM hardware to much higher speed—today 115,200 bps appears to be the limit. At the unsupported speeds above 19,200 bps, the doubling increment no longer applies, and most developers allow a 19,200 bps gaps between the higher speeds they support. The 9600 and 19,200 bps limits enforced by IBM represent the maximum operating speed of the parts once the overhead of the serial port BIOS routines are taken into account. Programs that run faster than the IBM limit do so by avoiding these slow BIOS routines.

UARTS

IBM relies on a special type of integrated circuit to transform the parallel signals inside the computer into a serial train of pulses. Called a *Universal Asynchronous Receiver/Transmitter* or *UART,* this chip accepts eight data lines as a parallel input and provides a serial output. From the name, you can tell that it's designed to work both ways, and can convert serial signals into the parallel kind that your PC wants to work with.

Three different types of UART are used in the IBM family of computer. The original PC and XT used a chip numbered the 8250 that was installed on IBM's Asynchronous Communications Adapter card. Most aftermarket vendors adapted this same chip to their communications and multifunction boards. It is also used in many internal modems.

The 8250 was not highly regarded even at the time the PC was introduced. IBM improved on it with the introduction of the AT by upgrading to the 16450 UART, a compatible and improved version of the 8250. With the PS/2 series, IBM upgraded the standard UART, now found on the system board, to the higher performance 16550. Despite performance differences, these chips are all seen similarly by your computer, and they all work in the same manner.

Besides data transmissions, the UART also creates and reacts to other signals which control its operation and how the serial conversation it engages in is managed. Control is afforded through several registers that are access by your computer through I/O ports. For example, to change the speed at which the serial port communications, you merely need to load a register with the proper number. The conversation control is handled by voltages that appear or are received on the serial port connectors on the rear panel of your PC or PS/2.

Flow Control

Public speakers know that no matter how eloquent their delivery, it will have not effect if no one is listening. Computers run into exactly the same problem. They may shovel out data and have it disappear into the ether unused. Even when the connection is good, the receiving equipment may be otherwise engaged and not able to give its attention to the serial information being delivered to it. Or the serial data may arrive at such a high speed that it exceeds the capacity of the receiving system to do anything with it on the fly—even saving the information for later inspection. Consequently, some means is needed for the receiving system to signal the sending system to hold on and wait until it is ready to acquire data. Several techniques for controlling the flow of serial data have evolved, all generally classed as methods of *handshaking,* called that because it signifies the agreement to the terms of the transmission method.

The easiest solution is to use a special wire as a signal line that the receiving system can use to indicate that's it is actually ready to receive. Because this method used extra hardware—the flow control wire—it is termed *hardware* handshaking. This is the default flow control method used by IBM personal computers.

Some communications channels do not allow the use of an extra signal wire. For instance, the telephone connection used by modems (the prototypical serial communications device) only provide the two wires necessary for carrying data; consequently flow control systems based on characters embedded in the data being transmitted are often used. Because these flow control characters can be added through special programming of the sending system, it is often called *software* handshaking.

In most software handshaking methods, the receiving system uses two distinct characters to tell the sending system when it is ready to receive a data transmission and when it can no longer accept more data at least temporarily.

Two methods of software handshaking are commonly used: One, called *ETX/ACK,* uses the control code represented by the ASCII hexadecimal character 03(hex) (also called ETX or Control-C) to indicate that it requires a pause in data transmission, and the ASCII character 06(hex) (ACK or Control-F) to indicate that it's okay to resume. More common among PC products today is XON/XOFF handshaking, which uses the ASCII characters 13(hex) (also called DC1, XOFF, or Control-S), and 11(hex) (or DC3, XON, or Control-Q) to ask for pauses or resumptions of data flow.

Although most PC peripherals that used a serial connection offer the option of software handshaking, without special driver software, they will not work properly with an IBM personal computer product or a compatible. The computer doesn't even listen for the flow control characters, so it will never act upon them. The result is data overflow and characters lost from the transmission. For example, if you use a serial printer and the handshaking does not work, characters, words or whole paragraphs may mysteriously disappear from your printouts.

Software flow control is, however, built into many application programs, such as communications products. Many multiuser or multitasking operating systems such as OS/2 and PC MOS/386 also come with special drivers that allow you to use the software handshaking through your system's serial ports without special applications.

Connectors

You can identify serial ports on an IBM standard computer by the connectors that they use. IBM PCs, XTs, and PS/2s all use 25-pin connectors for their serial ports. ATs use nine-pin connectors. In either case, the connectors are called male miniature D-shell connectors. They can be identified by having two parallel rows of pins, one row one pin longer than the other. IBM parallel ports, which also used 25-pin miniature D-shell connectors, and MDA/CGA/EGA monitors, which use nine-pin D-shell connectors can be distinguished because they are female, in other words, the connectors show holes instead of pins.

Except for ATs, few (almost no) serial devices in the IBM realm use nine-pin connectors. In fact, the principal virtue of the nine-pin connector is that it is smaller and would fit on an expansion-card retaining bracket when paired with a parallel port. Not all 25 pins in a serial connector are actively used in the IBM scheme, allowing the uses of the shorter connectors, while the parallel port uses all of its pin allotment. Obviously, the serial port was the likely candidate for this size reduction.

In that most serial cables are equipped with 25-pin connectors at either end, an adapter is usually required to convert the AT's nine-pin

Figure 18.1 **Wiring for 9-to-25 pin serial port adapter**

25-pin connector	9-pin connector
2	3
3	2
4	7
5	8
6	6
7	5
8	1
20	4
22	9

connection to 25. Commercial adapters are generally available, or you can make your own. (Figure 18.1 shows the proper wiring of an IBM 9-to-25 pin serial converter.)

Serial Device Types

To understand how serial ports are supposed to work requires taking a giant step backward to the dark ages when huge lizards roamed the earth and personal computers were not to be found anywhere. Original-ly, RS-232 ports were designed to connect data terminals with modems to connect the terminals to a giant mainframe computer in some far-off city. The connection scheme was based on a typical division of labor that was near-ubiquitous in a world that had only semi-miniaturized electronics. The terminal reduced keystrokes to digital pulses and con-verted other pulses to characters on the screen. The modem transformed the digital signals from the terminal into analog signals that could be transmitted over telephone lines. The serial port linked them together.

In the RS-232 system, certain tightly-defined names were assigned to the devices at either end of the connection. The terminal earned the epithet *Data Terminal Equipment* or *DTE*. The modem was called *Data Communication Equipment* or *DCE*. The difference between the two is more than just the names. Communication between the two is mediated by a very elaborate hierarchy of query signals and responses. The two behave differently and are wired differently.

No matter whether it's a DTE or DCE, the serial port on a device must function as a two-way street. Information is allowed to flow in both directions so both ends of the connection must be able to operate as both sending and receiving devices. Every connection has two ends. One may be the terminal and modem first considered. Those devices may talk to a computer, another terminal, or a printer, always using another modem. No matter which end of the connection it is attached to, as long as the modem is DCE and the terminal/computer/printer is DTE, everything will work fine.

Because of the complication of both ends both sending and receiving data, oftentimes simultaneously, a single communication circuit is not sufficient to implement a true RS-232 connection. Thus, to prevent serial devices from becoming confused by hearing—and reacting to—their own transmissions, the standard serial connection uses separate wires for sending and receiving. (Modems avoid the need for separate wires by using two different signals on the same wire link.)

This use of separate wires for sending and receiving signals leads to a problems. The wire one system uses for sending must be the wire the other system uses for receiving, and vice versa. If both devices sent down the same wire, no one would be listening, and no communications would take place.

By convention, the connector pins numbered 2 and 3 are used for the two communication signals. Ordinarily, DTE devices use pin 2 to send and pin 3 to receive, and DCE use pin 3 to send and pin 2 to receive. The nine-pin equipped AT is an exception, however. Although considered DTE, it uses pin 3 on its DB-9 connector to send and pin 2 to receive. The normal 9-to-25 pin adapter supplied by IBM converts the AT to a standard 25-pin DTE-style connection. The one important point about the sending and receiving pins of serial ports is that when a normal *straight-through* cable is used, one in which the pins at one end are directly connector to the pins with the same number at the other end, DTE devices must always be connected to DCE devices, and DCE devices will only work when connected to DTE devices.

Serial Connections

The RS-232 assigns particular functions to the wires in a serial cable. Besides the two conductors used for data, several others are required for hardware handshaking and to make everything work properly. (The various connections and their names on standard 25-pin and 9-pin IBM serial connectors are shown in Table 18.1.)

The most important of all these assignment is number seven, *Signal*

Table 18.1 **IBM Serial Port Pin-outs**

25-pin connector:

Pin	Function	Mnemonic
2	Transmit data	TXD
3	Receive data	RXD
4	Request to send	RTS
5	Clear to send	CTS
6	Data set ready	RTS
7	Signal ground	GND
8	Carrier detect	CD
20	Data terminal ready	DTR
22	Ring indicator	RI

Current loop connections (only on IBM Async Adapter, now obsolete)

9	Transmit current loop return	
11	Transmit current loop data	
18	Receive current loop data	
25	Receive current loop return	

9-pin (AT-style) connector:

Pin	Function	Mnemonic
1	Carrier detect	CD
2	Receive data	RXD
3	Transmit data	TXD
4	Data terminal ready	DTR
5	Signal ground	GND
6	Data set ready	DSR
7	Request to send	RTS
8	Clear to send	CTS
9	Ring indicator	RI

Ground. This wire provides the necessary return path for both the data signals and the handshaking signals, and it must be present in all serial cables.

Signal ground is separate and completely different from pin one, *Chassis Ground.* The pin in the serial connector corresponding to this wire is connected directly to the metal chassis or case of the equipment much as the third prong of a three-wire AC cable is. In fact, this connection provides the same safety function as the electrical ground: It insures that the outside metal parts of the two serial devices are at the same electrical potential. It prevents you from getting a shock by touching the two devices at the same time. It carries whatever electricity might flow between the two units instead of letting you body do it (and potentially electrocuting you).

Proper Grounding

This connection is not always necessary, however, and not always desirable. It's not necessary when both devices in a serial link-up are already grounded together through their AC cables. It may not be desirable when the two serial devices are separated by a great distance and derive their power from different sources. Electrical ground potentials vary (because of differing resistances that are present in every ground return path), and it is entirely possible that grounded AC cables could put the two devices at widely different potentials. The chassis ground circuit might then carry substantial current as a *ground loop*. If the current in the loop is great enough, it can cause electrical interference. A small chance exists that it might be large enough to melt the chassis ground conductor and start a fire.

The best strategy is to follow these rules: If both serial devices in a connection are grounded through their AC cords, you do not need the chassis ground wire. If only one is grounded through its AC wire, the best bet is to ground the other device through its AC wire, too. Otherwise, you should use the chassis ground connection in your serial port.

Normal Serial Protocol

Trying to engage in serial communication would be fruitless if one or the other device at an end of the connection were turned off. Without a second device to listen, information from one would pour down the serial line and vanish into the ether, wasted. Consequently, the RS-232 specification includes two wires dedicated to revealing whether a device is attached to each end of the connection and turned on.

The signal on pin 20 is called *Data Terminal Ready* or simply *DTR*. It is a positive voltage sent from the DTE device to indicate that the device is plugged in, powered up, and ready to begin communication.

The complementary signal appears on pin 6. Called *Data Set Ready* or *DSR,* a positive voltage on this line indicates that the DCE is turned on and ready to do its job.

In a normal RS-232 serial connection, both of these signals must be present before anything else happens. The DTE sends the DTR signal to the DCE, and the DCE sends the DSR signal to the DTE. Both devices then know that the other device is ready.

Normal modem hardware handshaking is implemented on two entirely different conductors. The DCE puts a positive voltage on the connection on pin 5, which is called *Clear to Send* or *CTS,* to indicate whether it is all right to send data to the DCE. In effect, it signals to the DTE that the coast is clear. At the other end of the connection, the DTE puts a positive voltage on pin 4, called *Request to Send* or *RTS* to indicate to the DCE that wants to receive information, too.

The important rule to remember is that unless both CTS and RTS have positive voltages on them, no data will flow in either direction. If no positive voltage is on the CTS wire, the DTE will not send data to the DCE. If no positive voltage is on RTS, then the DCE will not send data to the DTE.

The DCE issues one further signal that can affect the flow of data. Called *Carrier Detect* or sometimes Data Carrier Detect, abbreviated *CD* or DCD, a positive voltage on this conductor indicates that the DCE modem has a carrier signal from the modem at the other end of the connection. If no carrier is detected, then the serial signal may likely be nothing but the garbage of line noise. The CD signals helps the DTE know when to be on its guard. In some cases, when CD is not positive, the DTE will refuse to accept data.

The signal on pin 22 is called *Ring Indicator* or *RI* and is used by a DCE modem to signal to the DTE terminal to which it is attached that it has detected ringing voltage on the telephone line. In other words, a positive voltage on RI alerts the terminal that someone is calling the modem. In most serial communications systems, this can be regarded as an optional signal because its absence usually will not prevent the flow of serial data.

A normal serial communication session follows a very particular protocol. Before anything else can happen, the hardware at both ends of the connection must be turned on and ready to go. The DTE, your computer, will assert its DTR signal and the DCE, your modem, will assert its DSR. When a telephone call awakens the modem from its lethargy, it will send a RI to the computer, which may trigger a message on the screen. Once the modem negotiates the connection with the other modem at the distant end of the call, the local modem will send a CD signal to your computer. If they were not already on during the wait before the call, your computer will assert its RTS and the modem will assert its CTS.

Type something at the computer keyboard to send to the modem or send some data from a file, and if the modem can send the bytes out fast enough to keep up, it will drop its CTS signal to tell your PC to hold off for a while. When it again makes CTS positive, your computer will resume sending data to it.

If data rolls in from the modem and your computer needs to take care of something more important—such as saving part of the transmission to disk—it will drop its RTS signal, and the modem will stop dumping data to it. When your computer finishes with its disk chores, it will assert RTS again, and data will again flow from the modem.

Non-Standard Serial Connections

As long as you want to connect a computer serial port that functions as DTE to a modem that functions as DCE, this serial connection scheme will likely work flawlessly the first time you try it. Simply sling a cable with enough conductors to handle all the vital signals between the computer and modem, and voila! Serial communications without a hitch. Try it, and you're likely to wonder why so many people complain about the capricious nature of serial connections.

A problem occurs, however, when you want to connect something besides a modem to a serial port. Other common serial devices include printers, plotters, mice, digitizing pads, even video display terminals. Many of these devices are not set up to be DCE but are themselves DTE, patterned after the first computer printers that did double-duty as terminals.

Connect two DTE devices together with an ordinary serial cable and the result will be that you have two serial devices tied together with a cable—you will not have a communications system at all. The two DTE units won't even listen to one another because each will listen on the line that the other is listening on and talk on the line that the other talks on—if they even get that far. Lacking proper voltages on their DSR pins, they won't even try to talk.

All IBM standard computers (except the very special case of ATs with nine-pin serial connectors) are DTE. Modems and most mice are DCE and can be directly connected to IBM-style 25-pin serial ports. Serial printers, operate as DTE, however, and present problems, as do many plotters and other peripherals.

The simple solution to connecting one DTE device to another, and

Figure 18.2 **Generalized crossover cable**

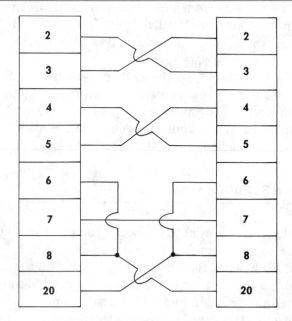

having it work, is to reverse pins 2 and 3 somewhere between the two ports. Special cables called *cross-over cables* do exactly that. In addition, most cross-over cables also swap the DTR and DSR leads as well as the RTS and CTS leads. In this way, the two DTE devices talk and listen to each other. The DTR signals from each device tell the other that it is ready, and the RTS signals act as flow control. (A typical cross-over cable is shown in Figure 18.2.)

In the best of all possible worlds, such a cross-over cable between two DTE devices would work just as well as an ordinary straight-through cable between DTE and DCE. The real world is different.

The first problem you may encounter is that the CD line has no corresponding match—the DTE device sends out nothing similar to a CD signal. Without the CD signal, the DTE device may be inhibited from ever sending out data.

The simple solution to do is to create a CD from something that's already at hand. Both CD and CTS has to be present for the DTE to send data out. They could be tied together, and the DTE would never know the difference. When CTS is asserted, the DTE would see CD at the same time and would know it was safe to transmit.

A variation on this theme makes the system easier to wire and more

Figure 18.3 **Crossover cable for NEC and similar printers**

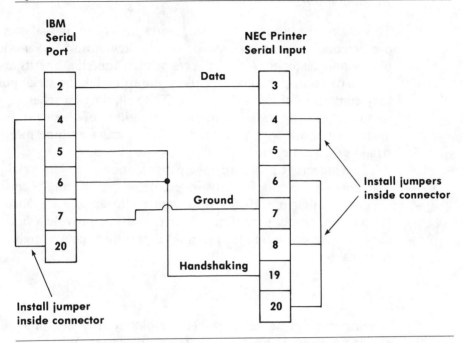

reliable. In that a DTE device must be turned on if it is going to produce any signal—let alone the DTR and RTS, which are flipped into DSR and CTS, to let the other DTE that's party to the connection know it can send—the RTS can serve both functions. Thus one signal, RTS, through a cross-over cable can control three at the other end—DSR, CTS, and CD. These wires can actually be bridged together within the connector attached to a serial cable. In a great many cases, this cable will allow two DTE devices communicate with one another.

This specialized cross-over cable does not work in all circumstances because not all DTE devices are wired the same. Some printers, for instance, are designed with the intention of connecting them to the serial outputs of computers that function as DTE. Consequently, they use a special flow control pin on their serial connectors that differs from DTR, but works in the same way. Perhaps the most common of these, used by Digital Equipment Corporation and NEC on some of their printers, devotes pin 19 to flow control. While DTR from the computer is used to control the other device by pulling its DSR, CTS, and CD high, pin 19 on these printers does the same thing. (A cross-over cable that works with many such serial printers is shown in Figure 18.3.)

Adaptable Ports

This entire confusion of crossing wires and rerouting signals can be prevented when serial ports themselves allow you to tinker with their philosophic leanings. A few makers of multifunction boards and some makers of multi-port adapters allow you to define the serial ports that they contain as either DTE or DCE. By flipping switches or moving jumpers, you can reassign the pin definitions of these products and make them work with many serial devices using nothing more than a straight-through cable.

These indecisive ports are not a panacea, however. The serial printers that posed problems for cross-over cables by defining themselves as DTE and using pin 19 for flow control thwart the elegance of this strategy. A properly configured DCE will not provide working flow control when connected to such a DTE port through a straight-through serial cable.

One-way Serial Communications

When connecting a serial printer or plotter to a computer, it's not always necessary to have two-way communication. When you use hardware handshaking, the printer has nothing more to say to its computer host other than twitching the flow control wires. Consequently, you can often get by with three conductors in a printer cable—one for data on TXD, a Signal Ground, and a handshaking line.

The reason for making such a slimmed-down cable are several. Because there are fewer connections to make, there are fewer things to go wrong. And when you're trying to get a system to work and you must resort to the brute force method of trial-and-error, the three wires technique can greatly simplify your experimentation. (Figure 18.4 shows two possible three-wire cables for such connections, straight-through and cross-over.)

Software Handshaking

The simple solution to all of these wiring problems might seem to be avoidance of troublesome hardware handshaking and exploiting the XON-XOFF software-flow control available on most serial devices. Although a good idea, it can also cause hours of headscratching when nothing works as it should or nothing works at all.

Figure 18.4 **Three-wire serial cables**

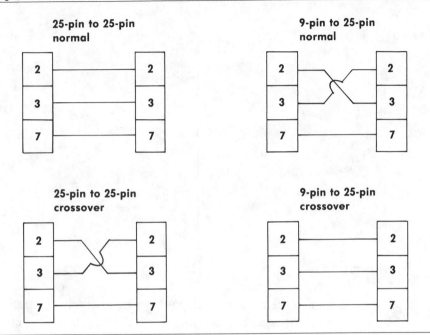

25-pin to 25-pin normal

9-pin to 25-pin normal

25-pin to 25-pin crossover

9-pin to 25-pin crossover

Nothing happening is a common occurrence. Without the proper software driver, your PC or PS/2 has no idea that you want to use software handshaking. It just sits around waiting for a DSR and a CTS to come rolling in toward it from the connected serial device.

Moreover, switching to software-flow control does nothing to change the sending and receiving connections of DTE and DCE. If you plan on connecting a DTE computer to a DTE printer, plotter, or whatever, you'll still need a cross-over cable even if you use software handshaking.

Software handshaking does free you from many of the other concerns about serial connections, however. By using local voltages, you can fool a serial port into believing that it's getting what it wants from the distant end of the cable. For example, you can substitute the positive voltage that the PC itself provides as the DTR signal to make it believe it has received the full complement of DSR, CTS, and CD signals by wiring the four pins together inside your serial connector.

A cable or adapter that provides this tomfoolery (usually in both directions, to both ports that it is connected to) is sometimes called a *Null Modem*. This term has, however, lost much of its specificity. Ask

Figure 18.5 **Wiring of a true null modem (a loopback connector)**

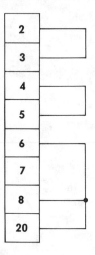

for a null modem cable and you're just as likely to receive a simple cross-over cable, a cable with all of the handshaking circuits wired together, or a combination of the two that flips the data pair (pins 2 and 3) and connects the handshaking lines together. (Figure 18.5 shows the wiring of a true null modem.)

The only way to ensure that such a cable is wired properly is to make it yourself. Even that may be no guarantee that the cable will work, particularly if you are unskilled in soldering. Therefore, thoroughly scrutinize a cable wiring diagram or cable description before making your purchase.

PC-Based Serial Ports

In IBM and compatible computers, serial ports are simple extensions to the circuitry of the machine. Data from memory or a microprocessor register is simply moved into the UART, which makes the necessary conversion from parallel to serial data. The output of the UART is than channeled through a *serial line driver* integrated circuit which converts the five volt logic used by the computer to the bipolar, higher voltage system specified by the RS-232 standard.

Each serial port in an IBM standard uses one I/O port to move data to and from the microprocessor. The address assigned to each port is read during the computer's self-test and is stored as a two-byte value in absolute memory locations starting at 400(hex). Although the PC, XT, and AT only support two serial ports, eight bytes are available at this location for storing serial port assignments. PS/2s use all eight bytes. Port addresses are stored with the least-significant byte first.

When DOS initializes itself, it scans these bytes and assigns the port it finds in the first two bytes starting at 400(hex) as COM1; the next two become COM2. In PS/2, it continues up to COM4.

Bytes are thereafter simply moved into the appropriate port using the OUT microprocessor instruction and pulled from the port with the IN instruction.

The registers of the UART chip are also directly accessible through other I/O ports to control the various functions of the serial port. Data to be transmitted or received occupy separate registers located at the base address of the serial port. The next six addresses are used by other serial port registers, in the following order: the Interrupt Enable Register, the Interrupt Identification Register, the Line Control Register, the Modem Control Register, the Line Status Register, and the Modem Status Register. Another register, called the Divisor Latch, shares the base address used by the Transmit and Receive registers and the next higher register used by the interrupt enable register. It is accessed by toggling a setting in the line control register.

Registers not only store the values used by the UART chip but also are used to report back to your system how the serial conversation is progressing. For example, the line status register indicates whether a character that has been loaded and is waiting to be transmitted has actually been sent. It also indicates when a new character has been received.

Although you can change the values stored in these registers manually using Debug or your own programs, for the most part you'll never tangle with these registers. They do, however, provide flexibility to the programmer.

Instead of being set with DIP switches or jumpers, the direct addressability of these registers allows all the vital operating parameters to be set through software. For example, by loading the proper values into the line control register, you alter the word length, parity, and number of stop bits used in each serial word.

To determine its operating speed, the IBM Asynchronous Communication Adapter uses its own on-board crystal as a time base. This crystal sets a serial board clock speed of 1.8432 MHz. All bit rates are set by dividing down this clock. For example, a 1200 bit per second rate is set by dividing the clock by 1536; a 9600 bit per second rate by dividing by 192. The serial card allows programs to set the bit rate by loading a number into the Divisor Latch register. The number in the latch is multiplied by 16 to determine the actual clock speed divisor.

As a result of this division-by-sixteen process, the maximum possible speed at which a PC serial port can operate is 1/16 the clock speed of the board, 115,200 bits per second. Although IBM does not support speeds higher than 9600 bits per second on the Async card, this speed is used by programs designed to move data quickly in and out of serial ports, such as Traveling Software's LapLink and the White Crane Software's Brooklyn Bridge (programs that allow portable computers to dump data into desktop machines).

Diagnosing Serial Communication Problems

Is the Port the Problem?

All to often we blame problems on the wrong party. What may seem to be a serial port problem could be a device disaster or cabling catastrophe. The first step in diagnosing any serial communication problem is to zero-in on the area of trouble.

The chore is made easier if you already have one serial circuit that works properly. You can switch ports and see if the problem stays with the device you are trying to use or moves with the port assignment. Check for this by moving the connection of a working serial device over to the reluctant port by moving the cable connector that's directly plugged into the port (*not* the one plugged into the serial device). If the serial device that you've moved works with the otherwise unwilling port after you've altered the software to address the port being used, odds are that your serial port is working just fine, but you have a problem with the cabling or device attached to it.

Another preliminary check to make is whether the serial device you want to use is designed to operate as a DCE or DTE device. The cable you use will depend on the device type. When connected to an IBM-standard computer, a DCE device should work with a straight-through cable. A DTE device connected to a PC or PS/2 will require a special cable of some kind. If the cable and device type don't match, no data will flow. If the lack of alignment of sending and receiving signals doesn't let it get lost, the lack of handshaking will prevent either device from transmitting so much as a bit.

Dueling Ports

If you do have the luxury of more than one port but none of them work, or they don't work in pairs, the problem could be a conflict in their port assignments. You may have two ports that are both trying to be COM1, for example. With two different pieces of hardware responding to each of your computer's commands, neither you nor your software will have any idea which of the pair is responding at any given time. Your system may behave intermittently or not at all.

You can easily walk into the dual port trap when your system comes equipped with a standard equipment serial output built into its system board, and you add an internal modem, multifunction board, or some mouse adapters. Because neither the computer nor the add-in product has made you specifically tangle with a serial port, you can easily forget about one of them. If it happens, as it usually does, that serial systems have chosen the same port assignment, confusion will reign until you sort it out.

The first step in analyzing any serial problem, consequently, is counting the number of ports in your system. Add-in serial boards, multifunction products with built-in ports, internal modems, standard-equipment system board serial ports, and mouse adapter boards that use a serial connection all count.

If you count more than two and have a PC, XT, or AT, you'll have to do some thinking. If one of them is an internal modem, odds are you'll be able to assign it as "COM3," which is the proper thing to do. Many communication packages—presumably including the one that may have been included with the internal modem—will recognize this COM3 as a legitimate port assignment. DOS and your PC will not recognize this port, so you won't be able to use the DOS Mode command to make it accessible as a printer port. Because you're unlikely to manipulate your modem directly through DOS, you probably won't miss it.

Similarly, the driver software that accompanies the mouse-and-adapter board combination should allow you to assign the mouse interface to a series of ports that won't collide with your regular serial communications.

If you still end up with more than two ports, you'll have to disable the excess.

One-Port-Only Systems

When you don't have the luxury of having a serial port and accessory that's been proven to work, you'll have to resort to more exhaustive and exhausting testing. You can check the port by trying a known-to-be-functional serial device with it.

The best piece of test equipment is probably a Hayes-compatible modem and a known-good straight-through connecting cable. Plug the modem into the port and see if it works. If it does, you've narrowed down the problem areas to the other serial device and its cabling. If the modem doesn't work, perhaps because it was the device you were originally trying to connect to the recalcitrant circuitry, you've have to dig deeper.

If you don't have a known-to-be-good serial device or the one you have fails to work, the next step is to examine how the port has failed. Actually, you've already done this in discovering the port doesn't work, but instead of throwing up your hands in disgust, note how the failure occurred and the condition the failure left your system in.

The most common problem encountered with serial ports is that they don't work. Trying to send data to a serial port results in nothing happening and perhaps the loss of the control of your computer, with rebooting the only medicine that will bring it back to life.

The most basic problem is that you may not have a serial port even though you think you do. You've plugged in what you think is a serial card and it isn't. Or it is a serial card but it doesn't work.

The first step is to make certain your system recognizes the serial port. You can do so by checking the port assignments in memory using the DOS diagnostic Debug. The Dump command (simply the letter D) in Debug will display on the screen data that are stored in memory. The particular locations of interest are those beginning at absolute address 400(hex). In PCs, XTs, and ATs, the first four bytes at 400(hex) store the port assignments of the two serial ports that these computer support. PS/2 uses the first eight bytes to store the four port assignments that they support. As with most PC-based data, these port assignments are stored least significant byte first.

To display the serial port assignments of your system, run Debug, then at the hyphen prompt enter the command:

```
-d 40:0
```

(which means to dump the 128 bytes to the display starting at absolute memory location 400(hex).

For example, if your system has one serial port, you should get a display such as this:

```
-d                      40:0
```

```
0040:0000  F8 03 00 00 00 00 00 00-78 03 00 00 00 00 00 00   ........x.......
0040:0010  63 42 F0 C0 02 00 00 80-00 00 2A 00 2A 00 20 39   cB........*.*. 9
0040:0020  34 05 30 0B 3A 27 30 0B-0D 1C 09 0F 0B 25 66 21   4.0.:'0......%f!
0040:0030  64 20 65 12 62 30 75 16-67 22 0D 1C 64 20 01 80   d e.b0u.g"..d ..
0040:0040  43 00 00 00 00 00 00 09-02 03 50 00 00 10 00 00   N.........p.....
0040:0050  00 18 00 00 00 00 00 00-00 00 00 00 00 00 00 00   ................
0040:0060  07 06 00 D4 03 29 30 98-00 B3 09 04 F3 5F 0B 00   .....)0......_..
0040:0070  00 00 00 00 00 01 00 00-14 14 14 14 01 01 01 01   ................
```

The first two bytes indicate that this system has a single serial port assigned at port number 03F8(hex), exactly where it belongs.

Interrupt Conflicts

Some serial boards force you to assign serial ports and the interrupts that service them separately, perhaps through moving separate jumpers. If you receive the board with the port assignments for COM1 but its interrupt set for COM2 or accidentally set it up that way, the serial port may work intermittently or not at all.

Other peripherals might also attempt to use one of the interrupts that should be assigned to your serial port. For instance, a tape backup system or a bus mouse that purports not to use a serial port may try to steal interrupt three from your COM2 serial port.

One prime symptom of this condition is sporadic operation of the port; sometimes it works and sometimes it doesn't, depending on what other accessories you're using. Of course, another device may totally preempt the serial port and prevent its operating at all.

The obvious solution to this sort of problem is to insure that every port has its own interrupt, and reassign those that are in conflict—if you can. The PC and XT are notoriously short of hardware interrupts to assign to peripherals.

No Handshaking

If your serial port suffers no interrupt or address port conflicts and otherwise seems operable but fails to work with a specific serial device, the likely cause is a lack of handshaking. This problem is most likely when your serial port failure does not totally lock up your system but instead allows you to abort whatever you were trying to do with the serial port, perhaps by pressing Ctrl-Break or Ctrl-C. The likely cause is that the handshake wiring of this serial circuit is not arranged properly.

Remember, unless you have software that specifically nullifies the need, a PC, XT, AT, or PS/2 requires its handshaking demands be met before a byte leaves any serial port. In addition, mismatching DCE and DTE devices and their cables will invariably guarantee a failure of handshaking.

You can verify handshaking in two ways—testing and the empirical approach.

Testing requires a Volt-Ohm Meter (or VOM) or a digital logic probe. Simply dig into the connector attached to the serial port in question and measure the voltages or logic states at the DSR, CTS, and CD pins. If handshaking signals are present, you should measure a positive voltage, usually in excess of five volts, when you touch each of the three pins. The indicator of the logic probe should glow when touched to these pins.

Empirically, you can connect the DSR, CTS, and CD pins directly to DTR to insure that handshaking is present at least at the PC-end of the circuit. You can either solder the necessary wires in place (a messy solution, but one that works) or invest in a breakout box that will allow you to experiment. If after making this adjustment your PC acts differently, and if it has sent at least some characters to the serial device, you had a handshaking problem. (If your PC acts like it has sent out data and the serial device, such as a printer, acts as if it has received nothing, odds are your TXD and RXD lines need to be crossed, and what you thought was a DCE was a DTE device.)

Buffer Overflow

If your serial device seems to work okay but loses characters from whatever is sent to it, the likely cuase is a flow-control problem. Typically, a serial printer will rattle out characters that appear just fine until you try to read them. Characters, words, sentences, and whole paragraphs may disappear. Lines may ignore margin settings because carriage return and line feed characters get lost on their way from computer to printer, too.

The problem is caused by handshaking working too well. Instead of the handshake signal being interrupted when the receiving device has no room to work with incoming characters, the handshake signals are locked on. To your computer, your printer always looks as if it wants more, more, more, even though it is choking on what it has already received.

Check the connection used for flow control—it may be CTS or something totally unrelated (such as DEC and NEC's pin 19)—and insure that it is connected to DSR or CTS on your PC. In addition, verify that both devices in your serial system are using the same flow control protocol. If your computer is dumping characters under hardware control, your printer may be futilely sending XOFF after XOFF trying to stave the flow. If protocols don't match, you'll likely lose characters.

Premature Conclusions

If your serial printjobs finish before you think they should, for example, before the last page is printed, or if your serial print jobs suddenly stop with an error message like "Device Timeout Error," the cause is simply that you forgot to add the P parameter to the end of the Mode command you used to set up your computer's serial port parameters. The printer does not respond fast enough to satisfy your computer, so it thinks something is wrong.

Gibberish

If your serial system gives every indication of working except all that it produces is gibberish, you probably have not properly matched serial port parameters at the two ends of the connection. Your computer is sending characters at one bit rate, and the serial device is expecting to receive them at another. Similarly, you may have your computer set for odd parity when the other end of the connection is expecting even. The two devices are not speaking the same language, so it's natural that they would get confused. The solution to the problem is simply to match the communications parameters at both ends of the connection.

19

MODEMS

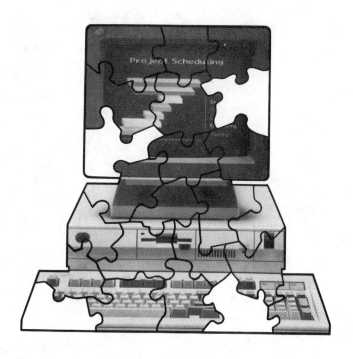

For some reason known but to God and the infidels who figure out the most profitable hardware packages to call computers, the modem—perhaps the most desired and used computer peripheral—remains an option in all but a random sampling of portable computers. The modem is the one computer feature that lets you display the personality of your personal computer to the outside world. It puts you in touch with on-line databases, remote computer systems, far-flung friends, and even those who are still flinging around the country.

The purpose and function of the modem seem almost absurd in their simplicity. The modem merely connects your computer to the telephone line. The need for the extra device seems so absurd because both computer and telephone use obstensibly the same stuff for making and moving messages—electrical signals. Were not the giant corporations specializing in computers and telephones (we won't name names) not such avowed rivals, you might suspect that they were in cahoots to foist such a contrived accessory on the computer marketplace.

Step back and look at what a modem does, however, and you'll gain new respect for the device. In many ways, the modern modem is a miracle worker. For instance, the best of today's modems can squeeze more than a dozen data bits through a cable where only one should fit. Even the least expensive generic modem operates like a specialized time machine that can bridge the century-wide chasm cutting between state-of-the-art computer and stone-age telephone technologies.

Far from the hatchlings of some plot by the military-industrial complex—or that even more sinister force, the telephone company—modems are a necessary bridge between digital and analog signals. The modern modem usually does much more than connect. Most are boxes chocked full of convenience features that can make using them fast, simple, and automatic. The best of today's modems not only make and monitor the connection but even improve it. They dial the phone for you, even remembering the number you want and trying again and again. They listen in until they're sure of good contact, and only then let you transmit across the telephone line. Some even have built in circuits to detect and correct the inevitable errors that creep into your electrical conversations.

Modem Operating Principles

A modem is a signal converter that mediates the communications between a computer and the telephone network. The very name "modem" indicates the role that it plays. The term is a foreshortening of the words *MO*dulator/*DEM*odulator. As a modulator, the modem converts the digital, direct current pulses used by the computer system into an analog signal containing the same information, a process called *modulation*.

Modulating and Demodulating

Modulation is necessary because the telephone system was designed even before electronics was invented and solid-state digital circuitry lay almost a hundred years off. The first pained words out of Dr. Bell's speaking telegraph were analog electrical signals, the same juice that flows through the receiver of your own telephone. Although strictly speaking, digital communications are older—the conventional telegraph predates the telephone by nearly three decades (Samuel F. B. Morse wondered what God had wrought in 1844)—current digital technology is only a recent phenomenon.

The telephone system was designed only to handle analog signals because that's all that speaking into a microphone creates. Over the years, the telephone system has evolved into an elaborate international network capable of handling millions of these analog signals simultaneously and switching them from one telephone set to another, anywhere in the world and possibly beyond. Although telephone companies are increasingly using digital signals to move trunk line communications between switching centers, the input and output ends of the circuit still end in conventional analog-based telephones.

Modulation, and hence modems, are necessary because these analog telephone connections will not allow digital, direct current signals to pass freely—or at all. The modulation process creates analog signals that code all the digital information of the computer original but can be transmitted through the voice-only channels of the telephone system.

Demodulation reverses the modulation process. At the other end of the connection, the modem as a demodulator receives that analog-coded signal and converts it back to its original digital form while preserving its information content.

The Carrier

The actual processor of modulation superimposes one signal on another. The modem as modulator starts its modulation process by generating a constant signal which is called the *carrier* because it carries or bears the load of the modulating information. In most systems, the carrier is a steady-state signal of constant amplitude (strength) and frequency, and coherent phase.

Modulation

The signal that's electrically mixed with the carrier to modify some aspect of it is given the same name as the process, *modulation*. Changes in the modulation result in a change in the carrier-and-modulation mix. The change in the modulation makes a corresponding change in the carrier but not necessarily a change in the same aspect of the carrier. For instance, in FM or frequency modulation, a change in the *strength* of the modulation is reflected as a change in the *frequency* of the carrier.

Modulation brings several benefits, more than enough to justify the complication of combining signals. Because electronic circuits can be tuned to accept the frequency of one carrier wave and reject others, multiple modulated signals can be sent through a single communications medium. This principle underlies all radio communication and broadcasting. In addition, modulation allows digital, direct-current-based information to be transmitted through a medium, like the telephone system, that otherwise could not carry direct current signals.

In demodulation, the carrier is stripped away and the encoded information is returned to its original form. Although logically just the complement of modulation, demodulation usually involves entirely different circuits and operating principles, which adds to the complexity of the modem.

Short-Haul Modems

Some so-called modems aren't even modems at all. The inexpensive *short-haul modems* advertised for stretching the link between your PC and serial printer, actually involve minimal circuitry, definitely not enough to modulate and demodulate signals. So little, in fact, that often it is entirely hidden inside the shell of a simple cable connector. All that the short-haul modem does is convert the digital output of a computer to another digital form that can better withstand the rigors of a thousand feet of wire.

Channel Limits

Like all great works of art, the modem is constrainted to work within the limits of its medium, the telephone channel. These limits are imposed by the characteristics of analog communications and the communications medium that's used (primarily unshielded twisted-pair wire).

Signal Bandwidth

All communications channels and the signals that travel through them have a characteristic called *bandwidth*. Bandwidth merely specifies a range of frequencies from the lowest to the highest that the channel can carry or are present in the signal.

An unmodulated carrier wave has a nominal operating frequency. For example, in radio broadcasting, it's the number you dial in when you tune in your favorite station. Without modulation, the carrier wave uses only that one frequency and has essentially zero bandwidth.

The modulation that's added to the carrier contains information that varies at some rate. Traditional analog signal sources—music or voice signals, for instance—contain a near-random mix of frequencies between 20 and 20,000 Hz. Although digital signals start off as DC, which also has no bandwidth, every change in digital state adds a frequency component. The faster the states change—the more information that's squeezed down the digital channel, as measured in its bit rate (bits per second)—the more bandwidth the signal occupies.

Sidebands

In the simplest modulation systems, a modulated carrier requires twice the bandwidth of the modulation signal. Although this doubling sounds anomalous, its the direct result of the combining of the signals. The carrier and modulation mix together and result in *modulation products* corresponding to the frequency of the modulation both *added to* the carrier together with the frequency of the modulation and *subtracted from* the carrier. The added result is often called the *upper sideband,* and the subtracted result is correspondingly called the *lower sideband.*

Because these upper and lower modulation products are essentially redundant (they contain exactly the same information), one or the other can be eliminated without loss of information to reduce the bandwidth of the modulated carrier to that of the modulation. (This form of bandwidth savings, termed *single sideband* modulation, is commonly used in broadcasting to squeeze more signals into the limited radio spectrum.)

Even with sideband squeezing, the fundamental fact remains that any modulated signal requires a finite range of frequencies to hold its information. The limits of this frequency range define the bandwidth required by the modulated signal.

Channel Bandwidth

The bandwidth of a communications channel defines the frequency limits of the signals that it can carry. This channel bandwidth may be physically limited by the medium used by the channel or artificially limited by communications standards. For example, the bandwidths of radio transmissions are limited artificially, by law, to allow more different modulated carriers to share the air waves while preventing interference between them.

In wire-based communications channels, bandwidth is often limited by the wires themselves. Certain physical characteristics of wires cause degradations in their high frequency transmission abilities. The *capacitance* between conductors in a cable pair, for instance, increasingly degrades signals as their frequencies rise to the point that a high frequency signal might not be able to traverse more than a few centimeters of wire. *Amplifiers* or *repeaters,* which boost signals so that they can travel longer distances, often cannot handle very low or very high frequencies, imposing more limits.

Most telephone channels also have an artificial bandwidth limitation imposed by the telephone company. To get the greatest financial potential from the capacity of their transmissions cables, microwave systems, and satellites, telephone carriers regularly limit the bandwidth of telephone signals. One reason bandwidth is limited is so that many separate telephone conversations can be stacked atop of one another through multiplexing techniques, allowing a single pair of wires to carry hundreds of simultaneous conversations. Although the effects of bandwidth limitation are obvious—that's why your phone doesn't sound as good as your stereo—the telephone company multiplexing equipment works so well that you are generally unaware of all the manipulations made on the voice signals as they are squeezed through wires.

Bandwidth Limitations

One of the consequences of telephone company signal manipulations is a severe limitation in the bandwidth of an ordinary telephone channel. Instead of the full frequency range of a good-quality stereo system, from 20 to 20,000 Hz, a telephone channel will only allow frequencies between 300 and 3000 Hz to freely pass. This very narrow bandwidth works well for telephones because frequencies below 300 Hz contain most of the power of the human voice but little of its intelligibility. Frequencies above 3000 Hz increase the crispness of the sound but don't add appreciably to intelligibility.

While intelligibility is the primary concern with voice communications (most of the time), data transfer is principally oriented to bandwidth. The comparatively narrow bandwidth of the standard telephone channel limits the bandwidth of the modulated signal it can carry, which in turn limits the amount of digital information that can be squeezed down the phone line by a modem.

Try some simple math and you'll see the harsh constraints faced by your modem's signals. A telephone channel typically has a useful bandwidth of about 2700 Hz (from 300 to 3000 Hz). At most a carrier wave at exactly the center of the telephone channel, 1650 Hz, and burdened by both sidebands, could carry data that varies at a rate of 1650 Hz. Such a signal would fill the entire bandwidth of the telephone channel without allowing for a safety margin.

Safety Margin

A safety margin is necessary, however, because the quality of telephone lines varies greatly, particularly when long distance connections are involved. Because poor connections can't handle the nominal 300 to 3000 Hz telephone bandwidth, it's ill-advised for a modem to try to take advantage of that entire frequency spread. If the connection is substandard, when the data rate reaches the fringes of the bandwidth, errors are likely to crop in.

Duplex

The usable bandwidth of a data communications channel through a modem is also limited because most modem communications are handled in *duplex* mode. The term "duplex"—often redundantly called *full-duplex*—describes the ability of a communications channel to simultaneously handle two signals, usually (but not necessarily) going in opposite directions. Using these two channels, a full duplex modem can send and receive information at the same time. Two carriers are used to simultaneously transmit and receive data. Using two carriers, of course, halves the bandwidth available to each.

Half-Duplex

The alternative to duplex communications is *half-duplex*. In half-duplex only one signal is used, and to carry on a two-way conversation a modem must alternately send and receive signals. It allows more of the channel bandwidth to be put to use but in practice slows data communications because a modem often must switch between sending and receiving modes after every block of data crawls through the channel.

Echoplex

The term "duplex" is often, and mistakenly, used to describe *echoplex* operation. In echoplex mode, a modem sends a character down the phone line, and the distant modem returns the same character thereby echoing it. The echoed character is then displayed on the originating terminal as confirmation the character was sent correctly. Without echoplex, the host computer usually writes the transmitted character directly to its monitor screen.

Guard Bands

Duplex does more than cut the bandwidth available to each channel in half. Separating the two channels is a *guard band,* a width of unused frequencies that isolate the active channels and prevent confusion between their separate carriers. The safety margin is, in effect, also a guard between the carriers and the varying limit of the bandwidth.

Once you add in the needs of duplex communication and the guard bands, the practical bandwidth limit for modem communications over real telephone channels that have an innate 2700 Hz bandwidth works out to about 2400 Hz. That leaves 1200 Hz for each of the two duplex channels.

Modem Modulation Methods

For the job of making modulation, a modem has several methods available to it much as AM and FM radio stations use different modulation methods. The different forms of modulation all are based on the characteristics of the carrier wave that can be changed to encode information.

Three of the primary carrier characteristics that might be used for modulation are its amplitude, its frequency, and its phase.

Amplitude Modulation

The amplitude is the strength of the signal or the loudness of a tone carried through the telephone wire. Varying the strength of the carrier in response to modulation to transmit information is called *amplitude modulation*.

One way that digital information could be coded with amplitude modulation is as two discrete strengths of the signal corresponding to the two digital states. In fact, the most rudimentary form of amplitude modulation—which has earned the special name *Carrier Wave* or *CW* transmission uses the two limits of carrier strength for its code: full power and zero power. The loudness of a telephone signal is its most likely characteristic to vary, however, with both changes in the telephone line and noise that might be picked up by the line. Consequently, pure amplitude modulation is not used by modems.

Phase Modulation

Another state of the carrier that can be altered to encode information is its phase. An unmodulated carrier is a constant train of identical waves that follow one after another precisely in step. If one wave were delayed for exactly one wavelength, it would fit exactly atop the next one. The peaks and troughs of the train of waves flow by at constant intervals.

By delaying one of the waves without altering its amplitude or frequency, a detectable state change called a *phase shift* is created. The onset of one wave is shifted in time compared to those that preceded it.

Information can be coded as *phase modulation* by assigning one amount of phase shift from the constant carrier to a digital one and another to a digital zero. Although this form of modulation is useful in modem communications, it is most often used in combination with other modulation techniques.

Frequency Modulation

The other alternative modulation technique alters the frequency of the carrier is response to the modulation. For example, a higher amplitude of modulation might be made to cause the carrier to shift upward in frequency. This technique, called *frequency modulation*, is commonly used in radio broadcasting by familiar *FM* stations.

Frequency Shift Keying

In the most rudimentary digital form of frequency modulation, a digital one would cause the carrier wave to change from one frequency to another. In other words, one frequency would signify a digital one and another discrete frequency a digital zero. This form of modulation is called *frequency shift keying* or *FSK* because information is encoded in (think of it being "keyed to") the shifting of frequency. The keying part of the name is actually left over from the days of telegraphy when this form of modulation was used for transmitting Morse code and the frequency shift came with the banging of the telegraph key. Frequency shift keying is used in the most rudimentary of popular modems, the once-ubiquitous 300 bit per second modem that operated under the Bell 103 standard.

Baud Rates

With such modems one bit of data causes one corresponding change of frequency in the carrier wave. Every change of frequency or state carries exactly one bit of information. The unit of measurement used to describe the number of state changes taking in place in one second is the *baud.* In the particular case of the FSK modulation, one change of state per second—one baud—conveys exactly one bit of information per second.

Depending on the number of states used in the communication system, a single transition—one baud—can convey less than or more than one bit of information. For example, several different frequencies of tones might be used to code information. The changing from one frequency to another would take place at one baud, yet because of the different possible changes that could be made, more than one bit of information could be coded by that transition. Hence, strictly speaking, one baud is *not* the same as one bit per second, although the terms are often, and incorrectly, used interchangeably.

The number of bits that can be coded by baud varies by the inverse logarithm of the number of available states (tones, voltage or phases). Most 1200 bit per second modems operate at 600 baud with four different states available, and most 2400 bit per second modems operate at 600 baud with 16 different states.

(In case you're interested, the term "baud" was named after J.M.E. Baudot, a French telegraphy expert. His name is also used to describe a 5-bit digital code used in teletype systems.)

FSK Modems

This 300 bit per second rate using the simple FSK technique requires a bandwidth of 600 Hz. The two 300 baud carriers (which require a 1200 Hz bandwidth, two times 600 Hz) and a wide guard band fit comfortably within the 2700 Hz limit.

Under the Bell 103 standard, which is used by most 300 bit per second modems, the two carrier frequencies are 1200 and 2200 Hz. Space modulation (logical zeros) shifts the carrier down by 150 Hz, and mark modulation pushes the carrier frequency up by and equal amount.

Because the FSK modulation technique is relatively simple, 300 baud modems are generally inexpensive. Because they don't push out to the limits of the available bandwidth, they are generally reliable even with marginal connections.

Using the same simple modulation technique and exploiting more of the 2700 Hz bandwidth of the typical telephone line, modem speeds can be doubled to 600 baud. Beyond that rate, however, lies the immovable bandwidth roadblock.

Modems Faster Than 300 Bits Per Second

A data communications rate of 300 bits per second is slow—slower than most folks can read text flowing across the screen. Even the slowest PC can absorb information at least 32 times faster, limited by the maximum serial port speed that IBM supports. Were long distance communications limited to the 300 bit per second rate, the only people who would be happy would be the shareholders of the various telephone companies. Information could, at best, crawl slowly across the continent.

By combining several modulation techniques, modern modems can achieve much higher data rates through ordinary dial-up telephone lines. Instead of merely manipulating the carrier one way, they may modify two (or more) aspects of the constant wave. For instance, today's most popular 1200 and 2400 bit per second modems combine frequency and phase modulation to achieve faster data flow.

Quadrature Modulation

These more complex forms of modulation add no extra bandwidth (remember, that's a function of the communications channel) but they take advantage of the possibility of coding digital data as changes between a variety of states of the carrier wave. For example, the carrier wave can be phase modulated so that it assumes one of four states.

In the *quadrature modulation* (a form of phase modulation) used by most 1200 bit per second modems, each state of the carrier differs from the unmodulated carrier wave by a phase angle of 0, 90, 180, or 270 degrees—while operating at 600 baud.

Group Coding

The four different phase states are sufficient to encode the four different patterns of two digital bits. Each baud can hold two bits of data, thus, a quadrature-modulated 600-baud modem can communicate at its data rate of 1200 bits per second. This bit-packing is the key to advanced modulation techniques. Instead of dealing with data one bit at a time, bits of digital code are processed as groups. Each group of data bits is encoded as one particular state of the carrier.

The ultimate speed of the mode is determined by the number of states that are available for coding. The relationship is not linear, however. As the number of bits in the code increases by a given figure (and thus the potential speed of the modulation technique rises by the same figure), the number of states required increases to the corresponding power of two. Twice as fast requires four states; four times faster requires 16 states; eight times as fast requires 256 states; and so on. Data rates of 2400 bps can be achieved by using an even more complex modulation that yields 16 discrete states while still operating at 600 baud. Each state encodes one of the 16 different patterns of four digital bits. One blip on the telephone line carries the information of four bits going into the modem.

More complex methods of modulation allow even higher modem speeds—dial-up modems operating at 4800 bps and beyond are already available. Most higher speed modems—for example, today's 9600 bps products—get an extra boost by foregoing duplex transmission and alternate between sending and receiving.

High Speed Modems

Modems that operate at data rates in excess of 2400 bits per second are generally classed as *high speed modems*. The distinction is as qualitative as it is quantitative: Above 2400 bps, squeezing more information into the confines of the telephone line becomes increasingly difficult, requiring inventive modulation techniques quite unlike those used at lower rates.

According to the free lunch principle, this system of seemingly getting something for nothing using complex modulation must have a drawback. With high speed modems the problem is that the quality of the telephone line becomes increasingly critical as the data rate is increased. Moreover, as modem speeds get faster, each phone line blip carries more information, and a single error soon can have devastating effects.

Leased-Line Modems

One way to coax higher speed from a modem is to forego the one part of the connection that imposes the severe bandwidth limitation—the telephone line. Special high-grade circuits can be rented from telephone companies to whisk data from point to point at almost unbelievably high data rates (from ten thousand to millions of bits per second). The special lines are semi-permanently installed and stretch directly from one location to another, never allowed to venture through the rigors of the telephone switching system. Because these special lines are leased by the month (or other period), they are called *leased lines* and the modems that use them are termed *leased-line* or *dedicated-line* modems. They usually lack the dialing and answering features of dial-up modems, and are meant for continuous connections.

Dial-Up Modems

In contrast, the modems that you are likely most familiar with—the ones that tie into the telephone switching system—are distinguished as *dial-up* modems. They face the constraints of the telephone system and must be capable of dealing with its special problems and shortcomings. However, they are the most useful because they can reach nearly anyone, anywhere—as long as the modems at the two ends of the call are compatible with one another.

Line Compensation

Although a long distance telephone connection may sound unchanging to your ear, its electrical characteristics vary by the moment. Everything from a wire swaying in the Wichita wind to the phone company's automatic rerouting of the call through Bangkok when the direct circuits fill up can change the amplitude, frequency, and phase response of the circuit. The modem then faces two challenges—not to interpret such changes as data and to maintain the quality of the line to a high enough standard to support its use for high speed transmission.

Switching Modems

Perhaps the biggest limit imposed on high speed modem communications is the use of full duplex communications. Because a complete duplex modem circuit is essentially two complete channels, each can have (at most) only half the telephone line's bandwidth available to it. Most of the time, however, communications go only in one direction. You key in commands to a remote access system, and only after the commands are received does the remote system respond with the information that you seek. While one end is sending, the other end is more than likely to be completely idle.

To make better use of the available bandwidth so-called *switching modems* are designed to make use of the full bandwidth of the telephone channel, switching the direction of the signal as each end of the line needs to send data. Such modems are able to achieve a doubling of data rate without adding any complexity to their modulation. In remote mainframe access situations, where the protocol of the call fits the mold of the two ends of the connections taking turns using the phone line, switching modems can give a genuine boost to the cross-country through-put of a modem system.

Asymmetrical Modems

Switching doesn't always work, however. The change of direction of communication isn't instantaneous. The modem has no way of knowing when to switch other than listening for a pause in the data stream. Some delay to recognize such a pause must be built into the system. Further, when the direction of the call changes, the modem may be called to adjust for line differences (the characteristics of a telephone connection are not necessarily the same in both directions because the two directions of communication may take entirely different paths). In all, switching the direction of the data movement can take a full second.

While a second pause may not be burdensome when you're simply sending characters and watching a response on the screen, it can be overwhelming when transferring a file. Most file transfer protocols (for example, XMODEM and Kermit) are designed to send a small block of data to the remote system, which then checks it for accuracy and finally sends a brief return message that the data was received intact or that it was bad. A switching modem may require a full second or more for each turn-around and confirmation. In that some protocols use blocks only 256 or 512 bytes long between confirmations, sending a file amounts to the classic hurry-up-and-wait syndrome. The modems blast a block across the line, then lolly around for a much longer period awaiting a confirmation.

In an attempt to get the best of both worlds, *asymmetrical modems* cut the waiting by maintaining a semblance of two-way duplex communications while optimizing speed *in one direction only* by shoehorning in a low speed (typically 300 bps) channel in addition to the high speed one. As with a switching modem, asymmetrical modems can flip-flop the direction of the high speed communications. They rely on algorithms to determine which way is the best way. Typically, the high speed channel is used for transferring blocks of data while the confirmations trickle back on the lower speed channel.

Fallback

Most modems use, at most, two carriers for duplex communications. These carriers are usually modulated to fill the available bandwidth. Sometimes, however, the quality of the telephone line is not sufficient to allow reliable communications over the full bandwidth expected by the modem. In such case, most high speed modems incorporate *fallback* abilities. When the top speed does not work, they attempt to communicate at lower speeds that are less critical of telephone line quality. The pair of modems might first try 9600 bps and be unsuccessful; they might then try 4800, then 2400, and so on until reliable communications are established.

Multiple-Carrier Modems

While most modems rely on a relatively complex form of modulation on one or two carriers to achieve high speed, a few (notably the Telebit Trailblazer) use instead relatively simple modulation on multiple carriers. One of the chief advantages of this system used by these *multiple-carrier modems* comes into play when the quality of the telephone connection deteriorates. Instead of dropping down to the next incremental communications rate, generally cutting data speed in half, the multiple-carrier modems just stop using the carriers in the doubtful regions of the bandwidth. The communication rate may fall off only a few percent in the adjustment. (Of course, it could dip by as much as a normal fallback modem as well.)

Data Compression

Although there's no way of increasing the number of bits that can cross a telephone line beyond the capacity of the channel, the information handling ability of the modem circuit can be increased by making each bit more meaningful. Many of the bits that are sent through the telecommunication channel are meaningless or redundant—they convey no additional information. By eliminating those worthless bits, the information content of the data stream is more intense, and each bit is more meaningful. The process of paring the bits is called *data compression*.

The effectiveness of compression varies with the type of data that's being transmitted. One of the most prevalent data compression schemes encodes repetitive data—eight recurrences of the same byte value might be coded as two bytes, one signifying the value, and the second the number of repetitions. This form of compression is most effective on graphics, which often have many blocks of repeating text. Other compression methods may strip out start, stop, and parity bits. Modem manufacturers often claim that their proprietary data compression methods might reduce the number of bits that need to be transferred by 50 percent, effectively doubling communications speed.

Error-Checking

Because all higher speed modems operate closer to the limits of the telephone channel, they are naturally more prone to data errors. To better cope with such problems, nearly all high speed modems have their own built-in *error-checking* methods. These work like communications protocols—grouping bytes into blocks and sending cyclical redundancy checking information. They differ from the protocols used by communications software in that they are implemented in the hardware instead of your computer's software. That means that they don't load down your computer when it's straining at the limits of its serial ports.

It can also mean that software protocols are redundant and a waste of time. As mentioned before in the case of switching modems, using a software-based communications protocol can be counterproductive with many high-speed modems, slowing the transfer rate to a crawl. Most makers of modems using built-in error-checking will advise against using such software protocols.

Modem Control

Besides its basic purpose of converting digital data into modulated audio signals, the modem is often called upon to handle other chores of convenience. For example, it may be called upon to automatically dial or answer the phone or report the condition of the telephone line. These features of the modem must be able to be controlled by your computer, and the modem must be able to signal your computer about what it does and what it finds out.

Dual Modes

Most modems operate alternately in one of two modes. In *command mode,* the modem receives and carries out instructions sent by your computer. In *communications mode,* it operates as transparently as a modem can, merely converting data.

Changing modes is mostly a matter of sending control characters to the modem. The characters can only be received and processed in command mode. In communication mode, they would be passed along down the telephone line.

Hayes Command Set

Today, most modems use a standardized set of instructions called the *Hayes command set,* after Hayes the modem manufacturer (which was, in turn, named after Dennis Hayes, its founder). For the most part, the Hayes command set comprises several dozen modem instructions that begin with a two character sequence called *attention characters.* The sequence is almost mnemonic—the letters AT, which must be capitals. Other characters specifying the command follow the attention character. Because the AT is part of nearly every command, the Hayes command set is also termed the *AT command set,* most often by Hayes' competitors that don't want to give the competition credit. A modem that understands the Hayes command set (or the AT command set) is said to be *Hayes-compatible.* (The basic Hayes command set is listed in Table 19.1.)

Most AT commands follow the attention characters with one letter that specifies the family of the command and another character that indicates the nature of the command. For example, H stands for Hook. H0 means put the phone "on the hook" or hang up. H1 indicates that the modem should take the phone off the hook, that is, make a connection to the line.

Several commands and their modifiers can be combined on a single line after an initial attention command. For example, to command a Hayes or Hayes-compatible modem to dial information on a tone-dialing line, the proper sequence of commands would read: ATDT15511212. The AT is the attention signal, D is the Dial command, the T tells the modem to use tones for dialing, and the 15511212 is the number of the telephone company information service.

All AT commands must be followed by a carriage return. The modem waits for the carriage return as a signal that the computer has sent the complete command and that the modem should start processing it.

At first it would appear that shifting into communications mode would be a one-way street for the modem, particularly were it only able to receive instruction in command mode. Fortunately, the Hayes command set allows the modem to react to exactly one command in

Table 19.1 **Hayes Extended Command Set**

Command	Function
AT	Attention (used to start all commands)
ATIn	Request product code and ROM checksum
	0 = modem sends its 3-digit product code
	1 = request numeric checksum of firmware ROM
	2 = request OK or ERROR state of ROM checksum
A/	Repeat last command (No AT or Return)
A	Answer without waiting for ring
Bn	Bell mode—set 1200 bps protocol compatibility;
	0 = CCITT v.22/v.22bis
	1 = Bell 212A
Cn	Carrier state;
	0 = off
	1 = on
Dn	Dial telephone number n

Special dialing commands:

P	Pulse dialing
R	Reverse mode (use answer frequencies when originating a call)
S	Dial stored number
T	Tone dialing
W	Wait (for second dial or access tone)
@	Wait for quiet answer
,	Pause (a delay in dialing sequence)
!	Flash (on-hook for 1/2 second)
;	Return to command mode after dialing
En	Echo modem commands;
	0 = no
	1 = yes
Fn	Full or half duplex operation;
	0 = half
	1 = full
Hn	Hook;
	0 = on hook (hang up)
	1 = off hook

Table 19.1 (continued)

Command	Function
Ln	Loudness or speaker volume; 0 = low 1 = low 2 = medium 3 = high
Mn	Mode of speaker operation; 0 = = off; 1 = on; 2 = always on; 3 = disable speaker when modem receives a carrier signal while modem is dialing
On	On-line state; 0 = modem returns to the on-line state 1 = modem returns on-line and retrains equalizer (2400 bps mode only)
Qn	Quiet command for result codes; 0 = commands are sent 1 = commands are not sent
Sn = x	S-register commands; n = S-register number x = value to set register to
Sn?	Display value of S-register n
Vn	Verbose mode for result codes; 0 = use digits 1 = use words
Xn	Enable extended result code and mode setting; 0 = basic (300 bps); 1 = extended (no dialtone or busy signal detection) 2 = extended (detects dialtone but not busy signals) 3 = extended (no dialtone detect but detects busies) 4 = extended (detects both dialtones and busies)
Yn	Long space disconnect 0 = disabled 1 = enabled; disconnects after receiving 1.6 sec break

Table 19.1 (continued)

Command	Function
Z	Fetch configuration profile from non-volatile memory
&Cn	Data Carrier Detect handling; 0 = modem keeps DCD (RS-232 pin 8) always on 1 = DCD tracks data carrier detected by modem
&Dn	Data Terminal Ready handling; 0 = modem ignores DTR line (RS-232 pin 20) 1 = modem assumes asynch command state when DTR goes off 2 = DTR off switches modem off hook, out of answer mode and back to command state 3 = DTR switching off initialized modem
&F	Fetch factory configuration profile from ROM
&Gn	Guard tone selection; 0 = no guard tones 1 = 550 Hz guard tone 2 = 1800 guard tone
&Jn	Telephone jack selection; 0 = RJ-11/ RJ-41S/ RJ-45S 1 = RJ-12/ RJ-13
&Ln	Leased-line or dialup line selection; 0 = dialup operation 1 = leased-line
&Mn	Asynchronous/Synchronous mode selection; 0 = asynchronous 1 = synchronous mode 1—async dialing, then switch to synchronous operation 2 = synchronous mode 2—stored number dialing 3 = synchronous mode 3—manual dialing
&Pn	Pulse dial make/break pulse length selection; 0 = 39% make, 61% break (US and Canada standard) 1 = 33% make, 67% break
&Rn	Request to Send/Clear to Send handling (sync mode only); 0 = CTS (RS-232 pin 5) tracks RTS (pin 4) 1 = modem ignores RTS and turns CTS on when ready to receive synchronous data

Table 19.1 (continued)

Command	Function
&Sn	Data Set Ready handling;
	0 = modem forces DSR on whenever modem is turned on
	1 = DSR (RS-232 pin 6) operates accong to EIA specs
&Tn	Test mode
	0 = terminate any test in progress when last command on a line
	1 = initiates local analog loopback test
	3 = initiate local digital loopback
	4 = conditions modem to perform remote digital loopback when requested by another modem
	5 = prohibits remote digital loopback
	6 = initiates remote digital loopback with another modem
	7 = initiates remote digital loopback with self-test
	8 = initiates remote digital loopback with self-test
&W	Write active configuration profile to memory
&Xn	Select synchronous transmit clock source (sync mode only);
	0 = modem generates timing and sends through pin 15
	1 = modem's host computer generates timing and sends it to modem on pin 24, which modem routes to pin 15
	2 = modem derives timing from incoming signal and supplies it to pin 15
&Zn	Store telephone number
	n = string of digits compatible with Dial command

communications mode, a command that instructs the modem to break off communications and shift back to command mode.

The tricky part of designing such a command it that it must be a character sequence that will never appear in the data that the modem is supposed to be communicating across the telephone line. Although it's impossible to guarantee that any command sequence will never appear in the normal progress of communications, the command in the Hayes set is specifically designed to be statistically unlikely. This command simply consists of a string of three "plus signs"—that is, + + + . To make the command stand out from data, the Hayes command set also specifies that the three plus signs be isolated from any other characters by at least one second, before and after. Such a pause followed by three specific characters, followed by a pause should never occur (well, almost) except when the command is really meant.

Extended Hayes Command Set

At the time the Hayes command set was developed, modems had relatively few special features. As modems became more sophisticated, they became more loaded with abilities and features. The original Hayes command set had to be extended to handle all the possibilities. Note that many Hayes-compatible modems recognize only the original command set. All of their features—if they have them—may not work with software that expects the extended Hayes set.

S-Registers

The extensions to the original Hayes command set include sufficient new functions that the command language would become ungainly and confusing. After all, there are only 26 letters in the alphabet that might be used for one-letter commands. Hayes added the facility of a special register or memory area called the *S-register* inside its modems that allows the setting of the modem's operating parameters. By setting the value contained by the S-register, a variety of modem functions can be controlled. (S-register settings are shown in Table 19.2.)

Response Codes

Commands sent to a Hayes-compatible modem by their very name and nature are one-way. Absent some means of confirmation, you would never know whether the modem actually received your command, let alone acted upon it. Moreover, you also need some means for the modem to tell you what it discovers about your connection to the telephone line. For example, the modem needs to signal you when it detects another modem at the end of the line—and when that connection is broken.

Part of the Hayes command set is a series of *response codes* which serve that feedback function. When the modem needs to tell you something, it sends back—via the same connection used to send data between your computer and modem—code numbers or words to appraise you of the situation. In the Hayes scheme of things, you can set the modem to send simple *numeric* codes, consisting solely of codes (which you can then look up in your modem manual, if you have one) or *verbose* responses, which may be one or more words long in something close to everyday English.

Table 19.2 **Hayes Modem S-Registers**

Register		Range	Units	Description	Default
S0		0–255	rings	answer on ring #	0
S1		0–255	rings	count number of rings	0
S2		0–127	ASCII	escape code	43
S4		0–127	ASCII	character used as return	13
S4		0–127	ASCII	character used as line feed	10
S5		0–32, 127	ASCII	character used as backspace	8
S6		2–255	sec.	time to wait for dial tone	2
S7		1–255	sec.	time to wait for carrier	30
S8		0–255	sec.	length of comma pause	2
S9		1–255	0.1″	response time, carrier detect	6
S10		1–255	0.1″	delay before hang up	7
S11				reserved	
S12		20–255	0.02″	escape code dead time	50
S13				reserved	
S14		bit-mapped	modem options	AA(Hex)	
	bit 0	reserved			
	bit 1	command	echo		
			0 = no echo		
			1 = echo		
	bit 2	result codes			
			0 = enabled		
			1 = disabled		
	bit 3	verbose mode			
			0 = short form result codes		
			1 = verbose result codes		
	bit 4	dumb mode			
			0 = modem acts smart		
			1 = modem acts dumb		
	bit 5	dial method			
			0 = tone		
			1 = pulse		
	bit 6	reserved			
	bit 7	originate/answer mode			
			0 = answer		
			1 = originate		
S15				reserved	
S16		bit-mapped	modem test options		0
	bit 0	local analog loopback			
			0 = disabled		
			1 = enabled		
	bit 1	reserved			

Table 19.2 (continued)

Register	Range	Units	Description	Default
bit 2	local digital loopback 0 = disabled 1 = enabled			
bit 3	status bit 0 = loopback off 1 = loopback in progress			
bit 4	initiate remote digital loopback 0 = disabled 1 = enabled			
bit 5	initiate remote digital loopback with test message and error count 0 = disabled 1 = enabled			
bit 6	local analog loopback with self test 0 = disabled 1 = enabled			
bit 7	reserved			
S17			reserved	
S18	0–255	seconds	test timer	0
S19			reserved	
S20			reserved	
S21	bit-mapped		modem options	0
bit 0	telco jack used 0 = RJ-11/ RJ-41S/ RJ-45S 1 = RJ-12/ RJ-13			
bit 1	reserved			
bit 2	RTS/CTS handling 0 = RTS follows CTS 1 = CTS always on			
bit 3,4	DTR handling 0,0 = modem ignores DTR 0,1 = modem to command state when DTR goes off 1,0 = modem hangs up when DTR goes off 1,1 = modem initializes when DTR goes off			
bit 5	DCD handling 0 = DCD always on 1 = DCD indicates presence of carrier			

Table 19.2 (continued)

Register	Range	Units	Description	Default
bit 6	DSR handling			

0 = DSR always on
1 = DSR indicates modem is off-hook and in
    data mode

bit 7	long space disconnect			

0 = disabled
1 = enabled

S22	bit-mapped		modem option register	76(Hex)

bit 0,1 speaker volume

0,0 = low
0,1 = low
1,0 = medium
1,1 = high

bit 2,3 speaker control

0,0 = speaker disabled
0,1 = speaker on until carrier detected
1,0 = speaker always on
1,1 = speaker on between dialing and carrier detect

bit 4,5,6

result code options

0,0,0 = 300 baud modem result codes only
1,0,0 = modem does not detect dialtone or busy
1,0,1 = modem detects dialtone only
1,1,0 = modem detects busy signal only
1,1,1 = modem detects dialtone and busy
other settings undefined

bit 7	make/break pulse dial ratio			

0 = 39% make, 61% break
1 = 33% make, 67% break

S23	bit-mapped		modem option register	7

bit 0   obey request from remote modem for remote digital loopback
        0 = disabled
        1 = enabled

bit 1,2 communication rate

0,0 = 0 to 300 bps
0,1 = reserved
1,0 = 1200 bps
1,1 = 2400 bps

Table 19.2 (continued)

Register	Range	Units	Description	Default
bit 3	reserved			
bit 4,5	parity option			
		0,0 = even		
		0,1 = space		
		1,0 = odd		
		1,1 = mark/none		
bit 6,7 guard tones				
		0,0 = disabled		
		0,1 = 550 Hz guard tone		
		1,0 = 1800 Hz guard tone		
		1,1 = reserved		
S24			reserved	
S25	0–255	0.01 ″	delay to DTR	5
S26	0–255	0.01 ″	RTS to CTS delay	1
S27	bit-mapped	modem options register	40(Hex)	
bit 0,1 transmission mode				
		0,0 = asynchronous		
		0,1 = synchronous with async call placement		
		1,0 = synchronous with stored number dialing		
		1,1 = synchronous with manual dialing		
bit 2 dialup or lease-line operation				
		0 = dialup line		
		1 = leased-line		
bit 3	reserved			
bit 4,5 source of synchronous clock				
		0,0 = local modem		
		0,1 = host computer or data terminal		
		1,0 = derived from received carrier		
		1,1 = = reserved		
bit 6	Bell or CCITT operation			
		0 = CCITT v.22 bis/v.22		
		1 = Bell 212A		
bit 7	reserved			

Typical responses include "OK" to signify that a command has been received and acted upon, "CONNECT 1200" to indicate that you've linked with a 1200 bit per second modem, and "RINGING" to show

Table 19.3 **Hayes Response Codes**

Numeric code	Verbose code	Definition
0	OK	Command executed without error
1	CONNECT	Connection established (at 300 bps)
2	RING	Phone is ringing
3	NO CARRIER	Carrier lost or never detected
4	ERROR	Error in command line or line too long
5	CONNECT 1200	Connection established at 1200 bps
6	NO DIALTONE	Dialtone not detected in waiting period
7	BUSY	Modem detected a busy signal
8	NO ANSWER	No silenced detected while waiting for a quiet answer
10	CONNECT 2400	Connection established at 2400 bps

that the phone at the other end of the connection is ringing. (Hayes response codes are listed in Table 19.3.)

Note that because the response codes flow from your modem to your computer as part of the regular data stream, you may accidentally confuse them with text being received from the far end of your connection.

Modem Features

The broad term "features" describes various subtle—and some not-so-subtle—ways in which modems differ from one another. For the most part, the features of a modem taken together determine how easily and conveniently you can put it to work. A no-frills modem, for example, may require that you spin the dial of your phone with your index finger or answer incoming calls before turning them over to your computer system when you hear the carrier tone of the modem at the other end of the line. Many people are willing to put up with such petty inconveniences to save on the price of a modem.

Although none of the tasks that features-deficient modems foist upon you will tax your mind or constitution, a no-frills modem shortchanges the capabilities of your computer. With a full-featured modem, your PC can dial the phone faster and with fewer errors and can handle the chore automatically when you're not around. Or with the latest memory-resident communication software, your PC can dial the full-featured modem and collect your messages while you are in the midst of browbeating data into shape with another program.

Actually, nearly every modem made today—including the lowest budget models made in obscure foreign lands—has all the standard features that you might normally want. Once you start integrating features into circuit chips, adding a few more features is not an arduous process. The only time you're likely to run into a modem deficient in today's convenience features is when you try to make do with one manufactured to yesterday's standards—the modem you inherit from some corporate higher-up, one that you find lying face-down in the gutter and you nurse back to life, one that you buy used from a shady-looking character in a trench coat on a deserted street corner.

Of the various features of a state-of-the-art modem, the ones you should expect in any new product that you buy include:

Auto-Answer

An auto-answer modem is capable of detecting incoming ringing voltage (the low-frequency, high-voltage signal that makes the bell on a telephone ring) and seizing the telephone line as if it had been answered by a person. Upon seizing the phone line, the auto-answer modem sends a signal to its host computer to the effect that it has answered the phone. The computer then can interact with the caller.

An auto-answer modem allows you or others to call into your computer system without anyone being present to answer the telephone and make the connection to your computer.

Auto-Dial

An auto-dial modem is capable of generating pulse-dial or DTMF (dual-tone modulated frequency or touch-tone) dialing signals independent of a telephone set.

An auto-dial modem can dial the telephone under computer command, for example, after hours when you're asleep and phone rates are low. Without auto-dial, you would have to dial the phone yourself, listen for the screech of the far-end modem's answer, plug in your modem, and finally hang up the phone.

Automatic Speed Sensing

Before a connection is made, you may have no way of knowing at what speed a distant modem will be operating. Most of today's modems can automatically adjust for the speed of the distant modem—if it is within the speed range that can be handled. High speed modems usually negotiate the highest possible shared speed to operate at using proprietary protocols.

Many modems also attempt to adjust to the speed at which you send them data—again if it is within the range of speeds that the modem can handle. The attention code of the Hayes command set conveys enough data that a modem can lock into the data and appropriately match its operating speed to that of the information flow.

CCITT Compatibility

A branch of the United Nations, the CCITT, which roughly translated from the original French means "Cooperative Committee for International Telephony and Telegraphy," has created a number of communications standards that have won great worldwide acceptance. Many of these standards apply to modems. For example, many modems boast of *CCITT compatibility* with the v.22 standard, which describes operation at a data rate of 2400 bits per second. At higher speeds other CCITT standards are gaining popularity, such as v.32 for 9600 bit per second modems.

In theory, the adoption of the CCITT standard is good news for people who want to communicate overseas (where the Bell standards may be illegal). The principal value of the CCITT standards is, however, that many manufacturers are taking them to heart and designing products to match, increasing compatibility and eliminating marketplace confusion.

Acoustic Couplers

Really vintage modems made no electrical contact with telephone lines at all. That's because years ago hooking your modem directly to the phone line was neither practical or legal. It wasn't practical before the now-common modular telephone plug-and-jack arrangement allowed anyone to plug in telephone equipment without fear of embarrassment or electrocution. It wasn't legal because telephone company regulations dating long before the AT&T telephone monopoly was split up did not permit individuals to directly connect modems to their telephone lines.

Instead of electrical connections, vintage modems sent their signals to telephones as sound waves. A device called an *acoustic coupler* was used to convert the tone-like analog signals made by the modem into sounds which are then picked up the the microphone in the telephone handset and passed through the telephone network again as electrical signals. To make the sound connection a two-way street, the acoustic coupler also incorporated a microphone to pick up the squawks emanating from the earpiece loudspeaker of the telephone handset, convert them into electrical signals, and supply them to the modem for demodulation.

Acoustic couplers can take many forms. In early equipment, the acoustic coupler was integral to the modem—a special cradle in which you lay the telephone handset. Today you're more likely to see couplers made from two rubber cups designed to engulf the mouthpiece and earpiece of a telephone handset. This latter form of acoustic coupler persists because it allows modems to be readily connected and disconnected from non-modular telephones—those that you cannot unplug to directly attach a modem. This connectability is especially important for roving computers that may be called upon to tie their internal modems into non-modular pay station and hotel room telephones.

Direct-Connect Modems

Modems that directly plug into the electrical wires of the telephone system are called, quite logically, *direct-connect* modems. Almost in tribute to the acceptance of the modular telephone wiring system, nearly every modem that you can buy today is direct-connect.

Asynchronous Modems

Almost any modem that you buy for normal use with your PC will feature *asynchronous transmission*. This odd-sounding term describes a method of exchanging information between two different computer systems that operate completely independently and do not share any timing information.

Normally, the time at which a pulse occurs in relation to the ticking of a computer's system clock determines the meaning of a bit in a digital signal, and the pulses must be synchronized to the clock for proper operation. In asynchronous transmissions, however, the digital pulses are not locked to the system clock of either computer. Instead, the meaning of each bit of a digital word is defined by its position in reference to the clearly (and unambiguously) defined start bit. Because the timing is set within each word in isolation, each word of asynchronous signal is self-contained and essentially independent of any time relations beyond its self-defined bounds.

The signals of modems that use the telephone system are generally asynchronous because it is more expensive and difficult to synchronize signals through the telephone system through which signals may be rerouted at any time without any warning.

Synchronous Modems

Most dedicated-line modems use a special communication technique often used among mainframes called *synchronous transmission*. In this method of transmitting data across phone lines, the two ends of the channel share a common time base and the communicating modems operate continuously at substantially the same frequency and are continually maintained in the correct phase relationship by circuits that constantly monitor the connection and adjust for the circuit conditions. Higher speed modem—2400 bits per second and beyond—often use synchronous transmissions.

In synchronous transmissions the timing of each bit independently is vital, but framing bits (start and stop bits) are unnecessary, which makes this form of communication a bit—actually two or three bits—faster. One problem in using it is that before information can be exchanged, not just the two ends of the connection must be synchronized, but also the link between the modem and computer must be synchronized. Autodialing features usually won't work in synchronous mode because without a connection being made there's nothing to synchronize to—and the connection cannot be made without dialing.

Autosynchronous Modems

Hayes solved the dialing problem for synchronous communications by adding an *autosynchronous* feature to their newest higher speed modems. This special mode allows the connection between PC and modem to operate asynchronously. The modem translates those signals into synchronous mode before sending them down the telephone line. It also works the other way and translates synchronous signals from the far end of the line into asynchronous for sharing with the host computer. The autosynchronous features can help PCs talk to mainframe and other computers that use synchronous communication as easily as they communicate with other PCs.

Modem Packaging

Perhaps the biggest choice you have in buying a new modem is whether it installs inside your PC as an *internal modem* or connects outside your PC through a cable as an *external modem*. Internal modems are like any other expansion cards that plug into a vacant slot inside your PC. External modems are additional boxes to find a place for on your desk.

In many cases when you have to choose between actual products, physical appeal may be the best guiding factor because exactly the same circuitry is often available in the different packages.

There are a few practical reasons for preferring one style of modem packaging over another. External modems offer the advantage of portability. You can move your external modem between different computer systems (even those that are not IBM compatible) simply by pulling the plug. Moving an internal modem requires popping the lid off your PC and the recipient and all the folderol that follows.

Additionally, internal modems can restrict you to certain computer systems. Some internal modems are built as full-length expansion cards, which means you can only install them in full-size PCs, XTs, ATs, and hardware compatibles. You'll need a different modem for a foreshortened computer (like the Tandy 1000). When you make the move from PC to PS/2 architecture, you'll also have to shell out the cash for a new internal modem. Most laptops and the PCjr can use only internal modems that were specifically designed for their proprietary expansion buses.

If you have a PC with its original, minimal 63.5-watt power supply, adding an internal modem—an older, full-length modem card in particular—may limit the number of other expansion boards that you can plug into your system. Such modems are notoriously power-hungry and may leave few watts for other cards, such as hard disks and EMS boards.

On the other hand, internal modems tend to be a few dollars cheaper than external models because the internal units don't need extra packaging or power supplies (although they need some extra signal circuitry). You can also forego the cost of a serial cable, which might cost you $30 or more from a local dealer. With an internal modem, you don't have to deal with a tangle of cords, plugs or transformers vying for the few holes in your wall outlet, extra boxes on your desk, or another thing to switch off when you put your system to sleep at night.

Port Assignments

Other than matters of power supply, the impact on your system resources will be the same no matter the style of modem you choose. While external modems require a serial port and cable, internal modems also require the use of a serial port address—which means you still lose the use of that address by a serial port, COM1 or COM2 (or COM3 or COM4 in PS/2s and the latest DOS versions). If you use versions of DOS before 3.3, you'll only be able to add one serial port in addition to the port or address used by either an external or internal modem. While some internal modems can have their addresses to be set as COM3 or COM4, you must be sure that the communications software that you choose can control the ports beyond COM2.

If there is any general rule, it's that you should choose an external modem for its flexibility and its ability to move to new and different computer systems; choose an internal modem for its neatness and lower overall cost.

Other Modem Considerations

Selecting one modem from the hundreds of products currently available is no small task. However, it can be made more tractable by making four separate judgments about each particular modem's performance, compatibility, features, and price.

Over a perfect telephone line, nearly all modems function perfectly—without errors. However, perfect telephone lines are impossible to find, and even getting an acceptable one nowadays seems to require bribing an operator. The performance differences between modems appear as line quality goes down. Better modems are better able to cope with bad connections. They work with worse circuits and can pull data through with fewer errors.

One of the critical parameters of the telephone line is the amount of noise it contains in relation to the strength of the signal it carries. This relationship is usually termed the signal-to-noise ratio of the line. The higher this ratio is, the better the connection.

The signal-to-noise ratio is often expressed in decibels (one tenth of a measurement unit called the Bel, which is named after Alexander Graham Bell, by the way) which form a logarithmic measurement scheme—that is, a signal-to-noise ratio that is twice as good will only appear three decibels better.

The compatibility of a modem refers to software and not its hardware connection. Controlling all the features of an advanced dial-up modem requires that commands be sent to it from the computer that it is connected to. These commands are usually sent invisibly by the communications program that is actually in control. More compatible modems recognize the commands of a wider range of software packages.

Obviously, to be useful communications software must know the commands that the modem recognizes. Some communications programs let you define the modem commands yourself (usually during the installation process) and in theory will work with any modem. However, most communications programs are designed to accept a one or more standard sets of commands.

In dial-up modems, no command set has received official sanction as the one and only standard. Most modems today, however, follow a de facto standard, the Hayes or AT command set. Originally developed by Hayes Microsystems and used in the company's line of Smartmodems, the popularity of the hardware led to many software companies incorporating the commands in their products. Newer modems were adapted to accept the existing software, resulting in an acceptance of the standard. A modem that recognizes the Hayes command set will therefore work with the widest variety of software. Hayes-compatible modems are thus more versatile.

Note, however, that the Hayes standard is not immutable. As new modem features and capabilities are developed, the commands set becomes richer. Moreover, varying degrees of Hayes compatibility exist. Some modems only recognize the most rudimentary of commands, for example, using ATDT to initial the dialing sequence. Others more elaborately mimic the operation of Hayes products and incorporate the same registers as used by Smartmodems, which permit, for example, setting the number of rings required before the modem answers.

Unless you have masochistic tendencies or software that is specifically designed for another modem command set, the safe bet is selecting a modem that's as Hayes compatible as possible.

The price difference between different manufacturers dwarfs the difference between the internal and external modems of any given manufacturer. Exactly how much you should spend depends on what you're looking for and what you're willing to settle for. As with any other PC product, you should carefully consider every aspect of your modem purchase before making your decision—select the one that you're absolutely sure you want, then settle for the one you can afford.

Connecting and Using a Modem

Unlike other common peripherals, modems often are not plug-and-play devices, external modems particularly. Perhaps that's to be expected because they plug into ornery serial ports.

Modem Cabling

The easiest part of installing a modem is hooking up the cable. Modems connected to the serial ports used by PCs and PS/2s use "straight-through" cables. Only AT-style serial ports with nine-pin connectors require adapters to match them to most modems.

The problems begin with software. In the interactions various communications packages make with modems, a number of serial port control lines are brought into play. Some communications programs, such as PC-Talk III make minimal use of the indications modems provide. Others monitor every connection. Consequently, the number of control lines that must be connected—and thus the number of wires that must be available in the cable that links your modem to your computer—depends on the communications software you plan to use. In some situations the minimal triad—pins 2, 3 and 7—will suffice. Other programs require the full complement of ten connections. The moral to be drawn from this story is that should you not know the type of cable required by your modem, use a straight-through serial cable equipped with at least ten conductors.

Modem Switch Settings

Modems themselves can be programmed to treat their various connections in different ways to match the needs of software. For example, some programs require that the modem keep them abreast of the connection through the Carrier Detect signal. Other programs couldn't care less about carrier detect but carefully scrutinize Data Set Ready. To accommodate the range of communications applications, most modems have setup switches that determine the handling of their control lines. In one position, a switch may force Carrier Detect to stay on continually, for example. The other setting might cause the status of Carrier Detect to follow the state of the modems' conversations.

These switches take two forms, mechanical and electrical. Mechanical

Table 19.4 **Hayes Smartmodem DIP Switch Settings**

Switch	Name	Function	Equiv. Command
1	DTR Recognition On/Off	Up—Modem recognized DTR signal; computer can make modem hang up or not answer with DTR lead (RS232 pin 20) Down—Modem ignores DTR	
2	Result Code Select	Up—Verbose result codes (Codes send as English words) Down—Numeric result codes	ATV1 ATV0
3	Result Code On/Off	Up—Result codes are sent to computer Down—Result codes are sent	ATQ1 ATQ0
4	Character Echo On/Off	Up—Modem echoes commands it receives in command mode Down—Modem does not echo characters unless in half-duplex mode and on-line	ATE1 ATE0
5	Autoanswer On/Off	Up—Modem automatically answers calls on first ring Down—Modem will not answer incoming calls	ATSO = 1 ATSO = 0
6	Carrier Detect On/Off	Up—Modem sends signal to computer to indicate character detected (RS232 pin 8) Down—Modem does not change status of pin 8 to reflect detected carrier. Defaults to making carrier always appear present	
7	RJ11/ RJ12 Select	Up—Modem connected to single line RJ11 telephone jack Down—Modem connected to multi-line service using RJ12 or RJ13 jack. This setting will make in-service indicators illuminate on multi-line phones when the modem goes "off-hook."	
8	Command Recognition	Up—Disables Smartmodem 1200 command recognition Down—Enables Smartmodem 1200 command recognition	

switches are generally of the DIP variety. In the prototypical modem, the original Hayes Smartmodem 1200, these switches are hidden behind the front panel of the modem. (To get to them, carefully pry up the trailing ears of the sides of the bezel, first one side, then the other of the black front panel of the modem. Then pull it forward and off.)

Most commercial modems that use DIP switches are patterned after the Hayes Smartmodem 1200. (Its DIP switch settings are shown in Table 19.4.)

Table 19.5 **Hayes Smartmodem 2400 Setup Commands**

These commands for the Smartmodem 2400 (which has no DIP switches) duplicate the functions of the DIP switches of the Smartmodem 1200.

Switch	Name	Substitute Command
1	DTR Recognition On/Off	On—Make bit 3 of S-register 21 equal 1; bit 4 equal 0 Off—Make bits 3 and 4 of S-register 21 equal to 0.
2	Result Code Select	Verbose codes—Send command ATV1 to modem Numeric codes—Send command ATV0 to modem
3	Result Code On/Off	On—Send command ATQ1 to modem Off—Send command ATQ0
4	Character Echo On/Off	On—Send command ATE1 to modem Off—Send command ATE0 to modem
5	Autoanswer On/Off	On—Send command ATS0 = 1 to modem Off—Send command ATS0 = 0
6	Carrier Detect On/Off	On—Set bit 5 of S-Register 21 to a value of 1 Off—Set bit 5 of S-Register 21 to a value of 0
7	RJ11/ RJ12 Select	RJ11—Set bit 0 of S-Register 21 to a value of 0 RJ12—Set bit 0 of S-Register 21 to a value of 1
8	Command Recognition	Dumb—Set bit 4 or S-Register 14 to a value of 1 Smart—Set bit 4 of S-Register 14 to a value of 0

The other kind of switch is electrical, exemplified by the Smart-modem 2400. Made from EEPROM memory, these switches are set by sending commands to the modem from your computer. Because of their EEPROM nature, they retain their settings even when the modem is turned off or unplugged.

Other modems may follow this pattern exactly or may use another memory technology—for example, battery backed-up dynamic RAM. A few don't make any effort toward removing the volatility. Such modems require you to reprogram their settings every time you turn them on. While you can't do much to make modem memory non-volatile when it's not, you can make life easier using disk memory. Simply add the modem settings you wish to enforce to the setup strings that many communications software packages send to the modem before they begin to make a connection.

(The setup commands for the industry-standard Smartmodem 2400 are shown in Table 19.5.)

20

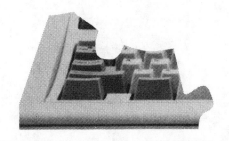

MAGNETIC
AND
MASS
STORAGE

M ass storage is an electronic closet, the place where you put information that you don't immediately need but don't want to throw away, either. As with the straw hats, squash rackets, wallpaper tailings, and all the rest of your dimly remembered possessions that pile up out of sight behind the closet door, retrieving a particular item from mass storage can take longer than when you have what you want at hand. And if you don't keep it organized, you may never find what you're looking for—or the whole horde my crash down upon you.

Personal computers use several varieties of mass storage, among them floppy disks, hard disks, streaming tape, and cassette tape. All of these share the defining characteristics of mass storage. They deal with data *en masse* in that they store thousands and millions of bytes at a time. They also store that information off-line. Instead of being held in your computer's memory where each byte can be directly accessed by your system's microprocessor, mass storage data require two steps to use. First, the information must be moved from the mass storage device into your system's memory, then it can be accessed by the microprocessor.

Moving bytes from mass storage to memory determines how quickly stored information can be accessed. In practical systems, the time required for this access ranges from 0.01 second to 1000 seconds, spanning a range of 100,000 or five orders of magnitude.

Various mass storage systems span other ranges as well. Storage capacity reaches from as little as 160 kilobytes to nearly a million kilobytes. Costs run from under $100 to more than $10,000.

In today's practical mass storage systems, however, one design factor unites them all. Uniformly, they are based on magnetic storage technology.

Introduction to Magnetic Media

Magnetic media has long been the favored choice for computer mass storage. The primary reason is that magnetic storage is *non-volatile,* at least when compared to electronic or solid-state storage.

Magnetism

Magnetic fields have the wonderful property of being static and semi-permanent. On their own, they don't move or change. The electricity used by electronic circuits is just the opposite. It's constantly on the go and seeks to dissipate itself as quickly as possible.

The semi-permanence of magnetism is important to making working storage systems. If it were permanent and unchangeable, it would present no means of recording information. If it couldn't be changed, nothing about it could be altered to reflect the addition of information. It would be the equivalent of trying to carve cuneiform in an invincible diamond using a banana as your only tool. You could never make your mark on any facet of posterity.

Magnetic fields work as a storage medium because they can be changed, and once they have been changed, they tend to retain those changes until altered again by the imposition of another force. Magnetic fields are changed by the effects of other magnetic fields. (Yes, some permanent magnets can be demagnetized simply through heating them sufficiently, but the demagnetization is actually an effect of the interaction of the many minute magnetic fields of the magnetic material itself.)

Magnetism is itself a manifestation of the same elemental force as is electricity. Both are electromagnetic phenomena. One result of that commonality makes magnetic storage particularly desirable to electronics designers. Magnetic fields can be created by the flow of electrical energy. Consequently, evanescent electricity can be used to create and alter semi-permanent magnetic fields.

Once set up, these fields are self-sustaining. They require no energy to maintain because they are fundamental, a characteristic displayed by the minute particles that make up the entire universe (at least according to current physical theories). On the submicroscopic scale of elemental particles, the fields that make magnetism are, for the most part, unchangeable and unchanging. Nothing is normally subtracted from them—they don't give up energy even when they are put to work. They can affect other electromagnetic phenomena, for instance, diverting the flow of electricity. In such a case, however, all the energy in the system comes from the electrical flow.

The magnetic fields we are more concerned with are those large enough to measure and effect changes on things that we can see. This magnetism is the macroscopic result of the sum of many microscopic magnetic fields. Magnetism is a characteristic of submicroscopic particles. (Strictly speaking, in modern science magnetism is made from particles itself, but we don't have to be quite so particular for the purpose of understanding magnetic computer storage.)

Magnetic Materials

Three chemical elements are magnetic—iron, nickel, and cobalt. The macroscopic strength as well as other properties of these magnetic materials can be improved by alloying them, both together and with non-magnetic materials, particularly rare earths like samarium.

Many particles at the molecular level have their own intrinsic magnetic fields. At the observable (macroscopic) level, they do not behave like magnets because their constituent particles are organized—or disorganized—randomly so that in bulk the cumulative effects of all their magnetic fields tend to cancel out. In contrast, the majority the minute magnetic particles of a permanent magnet are oriented in the same direction. The majority prevails, and the material has a net magnetic field.

Some materials have the ability to be magnetized. That is, their constituent microscopic magnetic fields can be realigned so that they reveal a net macroscopic magnetic field. For example, by subjecting a piece of soft iron to a strong magnetic field, the iron will become magnetized.

Magnetic Storage

If that strong magnetic field is produced by an electromagnet, all the constituents of a magnetic storage system become available. Electrical energy can be used to alter a magnetic field, that can be later detected. Put a lump of soft iron within the confines of an unenergized electromagnet. Any time you return, you can determine whether the electromagnet has been energized in your absence merely by checking for the presence of a magnetic field in the iron. In effect, you've stored exactly one bit of information.

To store more, you need to be able to organize the information. You need to know the order of the bits. In magnetic storage systems, information is arranged physically the way data travel serially in time. Instead of being electronic blips that flicker on and off as the milliseconds tick off, magnetic pulses are stored like a row of dots on a piece of paper, a long chain with both beginning and end. This physical arrangement can be directly translated to the temporal arrangement of data used in a serial transmission system just by scanning the dots across the paper. The first dot becomes the first pulse in the serial stream, and each subsequent dot follows neatly in the data stream as the paper is scanned.

Instead of paper, magnetic storage systems use one or another form of media—generally either a disk or long ribbon of plastic tape—covered with a magnetically reactive mixture. The form of medium directly influences the speed at which information can be retrieved from the system.

Digital Magnetic Systems

Computer mass storage systems differ in principle and operation from tape *systems* used for audio and video recording. Because most audio and video systems use analog systems (this is, of course, changing in audio with the popularity of Compact Discs and Digital Audio Tape and likely to similarly change in video), they record analog signals on tape. That is, the strength of the magnetic field written on the tape varies in correspondence with the signal being recorded. The intensity of the recorded field can span a range of more than six orders of magnitude.

Saturation

Digital recordings, on the other hand, ignore the strength variations of magnetic field strength. They just look for the unambiguous "it's either there or not" style of digital pulses of information. Analog systems achieve their varying strengths of field by aligning the tiny molecular magnets in the medium. A stronger electromagnetic field causes a greater percentage of the fields of these molecules to line up with the field, almost in direct proportion to the filed strength, to produce an analog recording. Because digital systems need not worry about intermediate levels of signal, they can simply lay down the strongest possible field that the tape can hold. This level of signal is called *saturation* because much as a saturated sponge can suck up no more water, the particles on the tape cannot ever produce a stronger magnetic field.

Although going from no magnetic field to a saturated field would seem to be the widest discrepancy possible in magnetic recording—and therefore the least ambiguous and most suitable for digital information—this contrast is not the greatest possible. Nor is it easy to achieve.

Magnetic systems attempt to store information as densely as possible, trying to cram it in so every magnetic particle holds one data bit. Magnetic particles are extremely difficult to demagnetize—but the polarity of their magnetic orientation is relatively easy to change. Digital magnetic systems exploit this ability to change polarity and record data as shifts between the orientations of the magnetic fields of the particles on the tape. The difference between the tape being saturated with a field in one direction and the tape saturated with a field in the opposite direction is the greatest contrast possible in a magnetic system, and is exploited by nearly all of today's digital magnetic storage systems.

Coercivity

One word that you may encounter in the description of a magnetic medium is *coercivity* which is simply the measure of how strong a magnetic field a particular medium can store. Stronger stored fields are better because the field stands out better against the random background noise that is present in any storage medium. As a physical corollary, a higher coercivity requires a more powerful magnetic field to be maximally magnetized. Equipment must be particularly designed to take advantage of its great intrinsic magnetism.

With hard disks, which characteristically mate the medium with the mechanisms for life, matching the two is permanently handled by the manufacturer. Removable media devices—floppy disks, tape cartridges, cassettes, and other removable media devices—present more of a problem. Obtaining optimum performance requires that changes in media be matched by hardware upgrades. Even when better media are developed, they may not deliver better results with existing equipment.

Smaller storage devices are generally accompanied by improvements in media. For example, the coercivity of new DC2000 tape cartridges is much higher than that of older DC600 designs. The better media allows more information to be squeezed into the tighter confines of the newer cartridges.

Retentivity

Another term that appears in the descriptions of magnetic media is *retentivity,* which measures how well a particular medium retains or remembers the field that it is subjected to. Although magnetic media are sometimes depended upon to last forever—think of the master tapes of phonograph records—the stored magnetic fields begin to degrade as soon as they have been recorded.

A higher retentivity assures a longer life for the signals recorded on the medium. No practical magnetic material has perfect retentivity, however. Even the best hard disks slowly deteriorate with age, showing an increasing number of errors as time passes after data has been written. For that reason, magnetically-stored records should be periodically refreshed. Although noticeable degradation may require several years— perhaps a decade or more—you may not want to depend on media written that long ago.

As a practical matter, refreshing a disk or tape means backing it up, reformatting the storage medium if necessary, then restoring the data again, effectively rewriting everything stored there. In the case of hard disks, low level reformatting is required because the address marks put on the disk during the low level format process also deteriorate with age. This deterioration can lead to Sector Not Found or similar errors that make data impossible to recover.

Flux Transitions

The ones and zeroes of digital information are not normally represented by the absolute direction in which the magnetic field is oriented, but by a change from one orientation to another. These changes are called *flux transitions* because the magnetic field or flux makes a transition between each of its two allowed states. In the simplest systems, the occurrence of a flux transition would be the equivalent of a digital 1; no transition, a digital 0.

Of course, the system must know when to expect a flux transition, or it would never know that it had missed one. Somehow the magnetic medium and the recording system must be synchronized with one another so the system knows the point at which a flux transition should either occur or not.

Data Coding

While the obvious magnetic recording method would be to assign a single flux transition the job of storing a digital bit, the obvious solution is rarely the optimal one. For instance, to prevent errors, a direct one-to-one correspondence of flux-to-data would require that the pulse train on the recording medium be exactly synchronized with the expectations of the circuitry reading the data, perhaps by carefully adjusting the speed of the medium to match the expected data rate.

Asynchronous recording eliminates the need for exact speed control or other physical means of synchronizing the stored data. All popular magnetic recording systems store data asynchronously. However, asynchronous recording also imposes a need for control information to help make sense from the unsynchronized flux transition pulse train.

Single-Density Recording

In one of the earliest magnetic digital recording schemes called *Frequency Modulation,* or *FM* recording, the place where a flux transition containing a digital bit was going to occur was marked by an extra transition called a *clock bit*. The clock bits form a periodic train of pulses that enables the system to be synchronized. The existence of a flux change between those corresponding to two clock bits indicated a digital 1, and no flux change between clocks indicated a digital 0.

The FM system requires a reasonably loose frequency tolerance. That is, the system could reliably detect the presence or absence of pulse bits between clock bits even if the clock frequency was not precise. In addition, the bandwidth of the system is quite narrow, so circuit tolerances are not critical. The disadvantage of the system is that two flux changes were needed to record each bit of data, the least dense practical packing of data on disk.

Initial digital magnetic storage devices used the FM technique, and for years it was the prevailing standard. After improvements in data packing were achieved, FM became the point of reference, often termed *single-density* recording.

Double-Density Recording

Single-density almost automatically implies that there's something better, and that something is called *Modified Frequency Modulation* recording (or *MFM*) or *double-density*.

The most widely used system in disks in today's PCs, double-density recording eliminates the hard clock bits of single-density to pack information on the magnetic medium twice as densely.

Instead of clock bits, digital 1's are stored as a flux transition and 0's as the lack of a transition within a given period. To prevent flux reversals from occurring too far apart, an extra flux reversal is always added between consecutive 0's.

Run Length Limited

Even though double-density recording essentially packs every flux transition with a bit of data, it's not the most dense way of packing information on the disk. Other data coding techniques can as much as double the information stored in a given system compared to double-density recording.

This seemingly extraordinary data packing ability is a result of the various artificial limits enforced in most data storage systems. Until recently, most storage devices were designed for double-density recording, and they followed tightly defined interface standards for the connections between themselves and their control electronics.

The real limit on data storage capacity is the spacing of flux transitions in the magnetic medium. The characteristics of the magnetic medium, the speed at which the disk spins, and the design of the disk read/write head together determine the minimum and maximum spacing of the flux changes in the medium. If the flux changes are too close together, the read/write head might not be able to distinguish between them; too far apart and they cannot be reliably detected.

By tinkering with the artificial restraints on data storage, more information can be packed within the limits of flux transition spacing in the medium.

Run-Length Limited or *RLL* recording uses a complex form of data manipulation to fit more information in the storage medium without exceeding the range limits of its ability to handle flux transitions. RLL translates the incoming binary code into its own, different digital code of 1's and 0's, which will be sent to the disk. This translation is not made at the bit level but one step higher: each incoming byte is assigned a new code pattern 16 bits long.

Digital information is handled not as individual bits but as groups. Hence, an early form of this recording scheme used by IBM in mainframe tape systems and at one time by Tallgrass Technologies in hard disks, was called *Group Coded Recording* or *GCR*.

At first, this translation might seem like a backward step, requiring double the number of bits to store information. Moreover, only a tiny fraction of the total number of 16-bit codes would be needed to unambiguously store all the possible 8-bit codes. That's the key to how RLL (and GCR) works. 8-bit codes are translated only into the 16-bit codes that are easiest to record magnetically.

In today's most common RLL system, the translation is set up so there always will be between two and seven digital zeroes between each digital one in the resulting 16-bit data stream. The limits of two and seven give this system its name, *2,7 RLL*. The 16-bit code patterns that do not enforce the 2,7 rule are made illegal and never appear in the data stream that goes to the magnetic storage device.

Although the coding scheme requires twice as many bits to encode its data, the pulses in the data stream better fit within the flux transition limits of the recording medium. In fact, the 2,7 RLL code insures that flux transitions will be three times farther apart than in double-density recording because only the digital ones cause flux changes, and they are always spaced at least three binary places apart. Although there are twice as many code bits in the data stream because of the 8 to 16-bit translation, their corresponding flux transitions will be three times closer together on the magnetic medium while still maintaining the same spacing as would be produced by MFM. The overall gain in storage density achieved by 2,7 RLL over MFM is thus 50 percent.

The penalty of the greater recording density of RLL is that much more complex control electronics and wider bandwidth electronics in the storage device are required to handle the higher data throughput.

Advanced RLL

A more advanced RLL coding system improves not only on the storage density that can be achieved on a disk, but is also more tolerant of old-fashioned disks. This newer system differs from 2,7 RLL in that it uses a different code that changes the bit pattern so that the number of sequential zeros is between three and nine. This system, known for obvious reasons as *3,9* RLL or *Advanced RLL* still uses an 8 to 16-bit code translation, but it insures that digital ones will never be closer than every 4 bits. As a result, it allows data to be packed into flux transitions four times denser. The net gain, allowing for the loss in data translation, amounts to 100 percent. Information can be stored about twice as densely with 3,9 RLL as with ordinary double-density recording techniques.

Sequential and Random Access Media

The original magnetic storage system was tape, actually a thin strip of paper to which a layer of refined rust had been glued. Later, the paper gave way to plastic, and the iron oxide coating give way to a number of improved magnetic particles based on iron, chrome dioxide, and various mixtures of similar compounds.

Tape Recording

The machine that recorded upon these ribbons was the Magnetophone, the first practical tape recorder, made by the German company Telefunken. From this World War II vintage device, able to capture only analog sounds, tape recording gradually gained the ability to record both video and digital data. Today both data cassettes and streaming tape system are based on the direct offspring of the first tape recorder.

These tape media have a very straightforward design. The tape simply moves from left to right past a stationary read/write head. When a current is passed through an electromagnetic coil in this head, it creates the magnetic field needed to write data onto the tape.

When the tape is later passed in front of this head, the moving magnetic field generated by the magnetized particles on the tape induces a minuscule current in the head. This current is then amplified and converted into digital data. The write current used in putting data on the tape overpowers whatever fields already exist on the tape, both erasing them and also imposing a new magnetic orientation to the particles representing the information to be recorded.

Sequential Media

A fundamental characteristic of tape recording is that information is stored on tape one-dimensionally—in a straight line across the length of the tape. This form of storage is called *sequential* because all of the bits of data are organized one after another in a strict sequence, like those paper-based dots. In digital systems, one bit follows after the other for the full length of the tape. Although the width of the tape may be put to use in multi-track and the helical recording used by video systems, conceptually these, too, store information in one dimension only.

In the Newtonian universe (the only one that appears to make sense to the normal human mind), the shortest distance between two points is always a straight line. Alas, in magnetic tape systems, the shortest distance between two bits of data on a tape may also be a long time. To read two widely separated bits on a tape, all the tape between them must be passed over. Although all the bits in between are not to be used, they must be scanned in the journey from the first to second bits. If you want to retrieve information that's not stored in order on a tape, the tape must shuttle back and forth to find the data in the order that you want it. All that tape movement to find data means wasted time.

In theory, there's nothing wrong with sequential storage schemes—depending on the storage medium that's used, they can be very fast. For example, one form of solid-state computer memory, the all electronic "shift register," moves data sequentially at nearly the speed of light.

The sequential mass storage systems of today's computers are not so blessed with speed, however. Because of their mechanical foundations, most tape systems operate somewhat slower than the speed of light. For instance, while light can zip across the vacuum of the universe at 186,000 miles per second (or so), cassette tape crawls along at 1 7/8 inches per second. While light can get from here to the moon and back in a few seconds, moving a cassette tape that distance would take about ten billion times longer, several thousand years.

Although no tape stretches as long as the 238,000 mile distance to the moon, sequential data access can be irritatingly slow. Instead of delivering the near-instant response most of today's impatient power users demand, picking a file from a tape can take as long as ten minutes. If you had to load all your programs and data files from tape, you might as well take up crocheting to tide you through the times you're forced to wait.

Random Access Media

On both floppy and hard computer disks, the recorded data are organized differently to take advantage of the two dimensional aspect of the flat, wide disk surface. Instead of being arranged in a single straight line, disk-based data are spread across several concentric circles like lanes in a circular race track or the pattern of waves rolling away from a splash.

Tracks

The mechanism for making this arrangement is quite elementary. The disk itself moves in one dimension under the read/write head, which scans the tape in a circle as it spins and defines a *track,* which runs across the surface of the disk much like one of the lanes of a racetrack. In most disk systems the head, too, can move—else the read/write head would be stuck forever hovering over the same track and the same stored data, making it a sequential storage system that wastes most of the usable storage surface of the disk.

In today's disk systems, the read/write head moves across a radius of the disk, perpendicular to a tangent of the tracks. The read/write head can thus quickly move between the different tracks on the disk. Although the shortest distance between two points (or two bytes) remains a straight line, to get from one byte to another, the read/write head can take short cuts across the lanes of the racetrack. Once the head reaches the correct track, it still must wait for the desired bit of information to cycle around under it. However, disks spin relatively quickly—300 revolutions per minute for most floppy disks and 3600 rpm for most hard disks—so you only need to wait a fraction of a second for the right byte to reach your system.

Because the head can jump from byte to byte at widely separated locations on the disk surface and because data can be read and retrieved in any order or at random in the two-dimensional disk system, disk storage systems are often called *random access* devices, even though they fall a bit short of the mark with their need to wait while hovering over a track.

The random access ability of magnetic disk systems makes the combination much, much faster than sequential tape media for the mass storage of data. In fact, disks are so superior and so much more convenient than tapes that tape is almost never used as a primary mass storage system. Usually tape plays only a secondary role as a backup system. Disks are used to store programs and files that need to be loaded on a moment's notice.

Sectors

Tracks are usually broken down into smaller segments called *sectors*. The number of sectors on each track varies from eight on some floppy disks to 34 on ESDI hard disks. On IBM disks, the number of sectors is the same on all tracks, even though information has to be squeezed in more tightly on the tracks nearer the center of the disk because the track diameter is smaller. The normal sector size in the IBM scheme of things is 512 bytes.

Each sector is unambiguously identified with special magnetic markings on the disk. These sector identifications are part of the format of the disk. Figure 20.1 shows the contents of a typical sector identification.

Figure 20.1 **Typical sector ID markings (ST5061412 controller)**

occurs once per track	Repeats for each sector, 17 times per track:				occurs once per track
		10 FIELD	GAP 2	DATA FIELD GAP3	
GAP 1 16 x 4-E(Hex)	SYNC 13 x 00(Hex)	ID PAD 13 x 00(Hex)		DATA PAD 15 x 4-E(Hex)	GAP 4 Pod of 4-E(Hex)

GAP 1 occurs at the start of each track before first sector

13 Bytes of sync (digital zeros) occur at the beginning of each track

The next two bytes are the ID field address marks, always A1(Hex) followed by FE(Hex).

This byte identifies the cylinder on which the sector occurs. On drives with more than 256 cylinders, this byte contains the eight least significant bits of the cylinder number

The five least significant bits identify the head number of this sector. The three most significant bits are the most significant bits of the cylinder number.

This byte identifies the sector number on the track.

These bytes, nominally 15, all of 4-E(Hex) pad out the sector to the proper length.

Write splice of 3 bytes of 00(Hex)

Two cylical redundancy check bytes for error detection within the data field.

512 bytes of data

Data field address mark comprises two bytes: A1(Hex) followed by F8(Hex)

ID Pad of 13 bytes of 00(Hex) pad out the length of the ID field and allow the phase lock oscillator to synchronize with the data field

Write splice of 3 bytes of 00(Hex)

Two cylical redundancy check bytes to detect errors in the ID field.

Clusters

DOS rarely deals with individual disk sectors. Instead, it uses groups of them called *clusters,* sometimes called *allocation units.* Each cluster is an interchangeable unit of a standard size which can vary from 512 to 8096 bytes depending on disk type, its format and the DOS version that you use.

To store a file on disk, it is broken down into a group of clusters, perhaps hundreds of them. Each cluster can be drawn from anywhere on the disk. Sequential pieces of a file do not necessarily have to be stored in clusters that are physically adjacent.

Early versions of DOS follow a simple rule in picking which clusters are assigned to each file. The first available cluster, the one nearest the beginning of the disk, is always the next one used. Thus on a new disk, clusters are picked one after another, and all the clusters in a file are contiguous.

When a file is erased, its clusters are freed for reuse. These newly freed clusters, being closer to the beginning of the disk, will be the first ones chosen when the next file written to disk. In effect, DOS first fills in the holes left by the erased file. As a result, the clusters of new files may be scattered all over the disk.

The early versions of DOS use this strange strategy because they were written at a time when capacity was more important than speed. The goal was to pack files on the disk as stingily as possible.

Starting with Version 3.0, DOS doesn't immediately try to use the first available cluster closest to the beginning of the disk. Instead, it attempts to write on never-before-used clusters before filling in any erased clusters. This helps assure that the clusters of a file will be closer to one another, a technique that improves the speed of reading a file from the disk.

File Allocation Table

To keep track of which cluster belongs in which file, DOS uses a *File Allocation Table* or *FAT,* essentially a map of the clusters on the disk. When you read to a file, DOS automatically and invisibly checks the FAT to find all the clusters of the file; when you write to the disk, it checks the FAT for available clusters. No matter how scattered over your disk the individual clusters of a file may be, you—and your software—only see a single file no matter how the clusters are scattered.

Device Controllers

Mass storage systems usually consist of three parts, which are sometimes combined together. The actual drive or *transport* (complete with its own internal electronics) handles the medium itself, spooling the tape or spinning the disk. The *controller* electronics generate the signals that control the transport from commands given by the host computer system. And the *host adapter* converts the signals generated by the host computer—for our purposes, the signals that travel on the PC bus or Micro Channel—into those that are compatible with the controller.

Primeval Controllers

Before the appearance of the IBM XT, most controllers for mass storage devices were most often free-standing circuit boards that were often installed in the same housing as the hard disk drive itself. A separate host adapter card would convert the signals of the host computer to those of the standard favored by the controller. The host adapter and controller were linked by a kind of glorified parallel port. Control functions were distributed in three places—the host adapter inside the computer, the controller itself which was typically mated in the cabinet with the mass storage device, and the transport electronics which were part of the mass storage device itself.

Many early add-ons for PCs, such as hard disks and tape backup systems, used this separate controller-adapter-disk drive system. The manufacturers of these products had good reason to do this. This design allowed mass storage equipment to mate with virtually any computer system simply by substituting a different host adapter. Off-the-shelf controllers could be designed so that they could be matched to any computer system, giving them the widest possible market. After all, before the PC there was no such thing as a truly universal bus standard. When incompatible computers of unlike designs were sold in quantities of dozens and hundreds (unlike the millions of standardized IBM-style machine sold today), this technique opened large enough markets to make the manufacture of mass storage systems economically feasible.

Moreover, there was a good, practical reason for separating the host adapter and controller. The combination of controller and host adapter circuitry would likely consume more board space than would fit into an ordinary PC expansion slot.

Combined Host Adapter-and-Controller

Although neither the PC bus nor the Micro Channel qualify as universal standards, their huge user bases easily justify the manufacture of products designed exclusively for them. As the success of the first IBM Personal Computer began to prove such acceptance was coming, controller manufacturers began to integrate the host adapter and storage system controller electronics onto a single expansion board. Today, most mass storage systems use this approach, mating with the storage device on one end and the PC bus or Micro Channel on the other. This single board is also called a *controller* because that's its primary function, and its combination nature is taken for granted.

The IBM XT hard disk subsystem heralded the change from the the host adapter-controller system. The XT controller unified the host adapter and controller functions on a single, dense circuit board. This pioneering controller, initially made for IBM by Xebec Corporation, set the pattern for the next generation of devices. The great majority of hard disk controllers follow this two-in-one pattern.

Embedded Controllers

An increasing number of manufacturers are taking the next step, integrating or *embedding* the controller function in their storage devices. In the PC environment, embedded control functions don't make sense because they still require the use of an expansion slot to connect the drive to the system, and the slot could just as well be filled with a controller as a cable to run to the drive. However, the PS/2 line is taking great advantage of this technology.

For example, newer Micro Channel PS/2s such as the various Models 70 incorporated a dedicated expansion slot, physically separate from the Micro Channel slots, to plug the system hard disk into. This slot is electrically identical to the other Micro Channel slots. The interface and control circuitry for the hard disk drive is held on the drive itself. Because of this design, the interface technology is guaranteed to match the drive. It's entirely possible to design non-standard super-high-performance interfaces for these systems without drive compatibility worries.

Integrated Hard Disk Cards

Embedded controllers also make sense when all three functions (host adapter, controller, and storage device) can be mated together and dropped into a standard expansion slot (as opposed to the dedicated slots in PS/2s). Of course, this strategy is only effective when you don't require access to the medium used by the mass storage device, characteristic only of hard disks. Such hard disk/controller/host adapter combinations are called *hard disk cards* and are discussed in Chapter 22.

Device Interfaces

The whole purpose of the controller is to link a disk or tape drive with its computer host. So that the widest variety of devices can be connected to a controller, the signals in this connection have been standardized.

Floppy Disk Interface

Floppy disks follow a standard that's simply referred to as the *floppy disk interface*. This connection scheme is also used by a number of inexpensive tape backup systems. In operation, it's much like a glorified serial port that's had a few new command lines added to it to handle the particular functions associated with the floppy disk drive.

Among hard disks and high performance tape drives, the most common interface standard in PC hard disk systems is *ST506/412,* which is used both in IBM's XT and AT systems. ST506 specifies a data transfer rate of five million bits per second (MHz). Newer interfaces, such as the *Small Computer System Interface* or *SCSI* and the *Enhanced Small Device Interface* or *ESDI* allow higher performance and greater ease and flexibility in configuring systems.

ST506/412

The original hard disk interface used in the IBM XT, AT, and some models of PS/2 computers followed an industry standard called *ST506/412.* This connection scheme is classified as a *device-level interface* because it connects at the device level, that is, directly to the hard disk or tape transport.

As with the floppy disk interface, ST506 transfers data to and from the disk drive in serial form. Bits are read as flux transitions off the disk and delivered in original form to the controller. The *data separator* in the controller then figures out which bits are meaningful data and which are formatting or sector identification information.

The stream of actual data bits then goes to a *deserializer* circuit, which converts the serial train of bits into parallel data compatible with the bus of the host computer. As the same time, the data is checked for errors and most of the errors corrected.

Unlike the floppy disk interface, the ST506 interface uses two cables—a wide *control cable* with 34 connections and a smaller *data cable* with twenty. Table 20.1 shows the functions assigned to each of these connections.

ESDI

Basically an upgrade to the ST506 standard, ESDI permits much higher data transfer speeds. Many of the first ESDI products transferred data between transport and controller at 10 MHz, although the interface standard permits faster and slower speeds as well.

This higher speed has some important implications. To make information move faster while maintaining the same spin rate as ST506 drives (3600 revolutions per minute), the typical ESDI hard disk drives must pack twice as much data onto each track to be read during each revolution. Most ESDI drives thus lay 34 sectors on each track, doubling data density as well as transfer rate. ESDI tape drive manufacturers can either increase tape speed or linear data density.

As with the ST506 standard, the ESDI is a device-level interface. Its connections are fundamentally made directly to the device that's to be connected to the system. In the case of hard disks, ESDI goes beyond ST506 by allowing configuration and bad track information to be stored on the drive itself. Instead of requiring the host computer to know what kind of disk drive is connected through the interface (either through a BIOS extension, as on the XT, or through configuration memory, like the AT and some PS/2s) each ESDI drive tells the controller how many tracks, cylinders, and such it has. Instead of requiring that you test for and type in all the bad tracks on the drive, it lets the manufacturer test the disk, flag the bad tracks, and store that information on the disk in a standardized form that the controller can directly access.

Table 20.1 **ST506/421 Cable Pin-out**

Control cable:

Pin	Function	Pin	Function
1	Head select 8	2	Ground
3	Head select 4	4	Ground
5	Write gate	6	Ground
7	Seek complete	8	Ground
9	Track 0	10	Ground
11	Write fault	12	Ground
13	Head select 1	14	Ground
15	Reserved	16	Ground
17	Head select 2	18	Ground
19	Index	20	Ground
21	Ready	22	Ground
23	Step	24	Ground
25	Drive select 1	26	Ground
27	Drive select 2	28	Ground
29	Drive select 3	30	Ground
31	Drive select 4	32	Ground
33	Direction in	34	Ground

Data cable:

Pin	Function	Pin	Function
1	Drive selected	2	Ground
3	Reserved	4	Ground
5	Reserved	6	Ground
7	Reserved	8	Ground
9	Reserved	10	Reserved
11	Ground	12	Ground
13	MFM write data +	14	MFM write data −
15	Ground	16	Ground
17	MFM read data +	18	MFM read data −
19	Ground	20	Ground

The added speed and convenience of ESDI make a good match in the PC environment. When performance counts, ESDI is becoming the interface of choice in personal computer systems. For instance, Compaq has chosen ESDI for its highest capacity, highest performance Deskpro 386 hard disk drives, and IBM is using the ESDI (often in the form of embedded controllers) in its higher performance PS/2 drives.

Table 20.2 **ESDI Cable Pin-out**

Control cable:

Pin	Function	Pin	Function
1	Head select 3	2	Ground
3	Head select 2	4	Ground
5	Write gate	6	Ground
7	Config/Status data	8	Ground
9	Transfer acknowledge	10	Ground
11	Attention	12	Ground
13	Head select 0	14	Ground
15	Sector/Addr mark found	16	Ground
17	Head select 1	18	Ground
19	Index	20	Ground
21	Ready	22	Ground
23	Tranfer request	24	Ground
25	Drive select 1	26	Ground
27	Drive select 2	28	Ground
29	Drive select 3	30	Ground
31	Read gate	32	Ground
33	Command data	34	Ground

Data cable:

Pin	Function	Pin	Function
1	Drive selected	2	Sector/Address mark found
3	Seek complete	4	Address mark enable
5	Reserved for step mode	6	Ground
7	Write clock +	8	Write clock −
9	Cartridge changed	10	Read reference clock +
11	Read reference clock −	12	Ground
13	NRZ write data +	14	NRZ write data −
15	Ground	16	Ground
17	NRZ read data +	18	NRZ read data −
19	Ground	20	Index

ESDI uses similar connections to those of the ST506 interface, including the same two-cable system. The two interfaces are not compatible, however. You cannot plug an ESDI drive into an ST506 interface and expect the system to work. Nor will an ST506 drive work through an ESDI connection.

(The pin-out of the ESDI connection scheme is shown in Table 20.2.)

SCSI

Pronounced "scuzzy" by much of the computer industry (but sometimes "sexy" by its staunchest advocates), SCSI is unlike either ST506 or EDSI in that it is a *system-level interface*. It attaches mass storage devices (or nearly anything else) at the system level, that is, when data is in a form that can be used by the host system. In effect, SCSI provides what is essentially its own expansion bus to plug into peripherals. In the PC and PS/2 environment, for instance, SCSI works like a sub-bus. Other interfaces, such as ESDI, may actually plug into a SCSI interface much as they plug directly into the PC bus.

As a system-level interface, SCSI requires that some controller functions be embedded in the disk drive circuitry, for instance, the data separator and deserialization functions are embedded into SCSI transports. In some ways, embedding these functions can be redundant, particularly when two devices are connected to one SCSI port. In an ESDI system, one data separator and deserializer could serve both drives; a SCSI connection duplicates this circuitry.

But SCSI earns favor for its greater data integrity (raw data need not course through a lengthy and vulnerable serial interface) and much greater flexibility. Not only can a variety of device types be connected to a SCSI port, but a number of them can be mixed through a single port connection. Up to eight SCSI devices can be daisy-chained to one SCSI port. All the devices function independently, under the control of the host system through the SCSI adapter.

In addition, SCSI also provides a speed increase over the ST506 interface. As with ESDI, the designer has a greater degree of freedom for choosing the optimum transfer rate for his system. Unlike the other interfaces, SCSI uses a parallel connection between the device and the SCSI adapter, giving it greater ultimate potential than the other connection schemes. Only a single cable—albeit one with a wealth of conductors—is needed for a SCSI link up. (Its pin-out is listed in Table 20.3.)

Power Connections

Besides control signals, all mass storage devices need power to operate their circuits and motors. This power is generally derived directly from the system's power supply. Most power supplies include two to four special power connectors which provide both regulated five and twelve volt power for mass storage devices.

You (or the factory that made your computer) will have to attach one

Table 20.3 **SCSI Cable Pin-out**

Pin no.	Function	Pin no.	Function
1	Ground	2	Data line 0
3	Ground	4	Data line 1
5	Ground	6	Data line 2
7	Ground	8	Data line 3
9	Ground	10	Data line 4
11	Ground	12	Data line 5
13	Ground	14	Data line 6
15	Ground	16	Data line 7
17	Ground	18	Parity line (data)
19	Ground	20	Ground
21	Ground	22	Ground
23	Ground	24	Ground
25	No connection	26	Terminator Power
27	Ground	28	Ground
29	Ground	30	Ground
31	Ground	32	Attention
33	Ground	34	Ground
35	Ground	36	Busy
37	Ground	38	Acknowledge
39	Ground	40	Reset
41	Ground	42	Message
43	Ground	44	Select
45	Ground	46	C/D
47	Ground	48	Request
49	Ground	50	I/0

of these connectors to each mass storage device in your system. These connectors are polarized so that you cannot inadvertently connect them upside-down or backwards. (The wiring of this connector is shown in Figure 10.2.)

PCs and some compatible computers are decisively frugal with their power connectors, supplying only two outlets. Powering more than two drives will require a Y-adapter that splits the power lines two-ways. A better idea is to replace the meager PC power supply with one that can supply more current, because the factory standard supply really doesn't have the capacity for operating multiple mass storage devices other than their standard two-floppy endowment.

Physical Aspects of Mass Storage Devices

When you buy a complete computer system, you don't have to worry about interfaces, controllers, and the like. The manufacturer has done all the work and properly matched everything for optimum operation. Adding a new drive to enhance a system or replacing one that has failed provides several interesting challenges. Not only must the prospective product be electrically matched to your system, but also it must be physically matched.

Form Factors

Disk drives come in a variety of heights and widths. The basic unit of measurement of the size of a drive is the *form factor*. A form factor is the volume of a standard drive that handles a particular medium. There are three form factors regularly used in personal computers: the 8-inch, the 5 1/4-inch, and the 3 1/2-inch form factors.

A full-size drive, one which defines the form factor and occupies all of its volume, is usually a first generation machine. If the drive is a reasonable size and proves particularly—successful successful enough that other manufacturers eagerly want to cash in, too—others follow suit and copy the dimension of the product, making it a standard. Dimensions of the various accepted form factors are shown in Figure 20.2.

Device Heights

The second generation of any variety of hardware results in some sort of size reduction. Cost cutting, greater precision, experience in manufacturing, and the need to put more in less space leads to smaller dimensions. The result of the downsizing process is a variety of fractional size devices, particularly in the 5 1/4-inch form factor. Drives that are full-height, two-thirds-height, half-height, and quarter-height have all been manufactured at one time or another. The 3 1/2-inch form factor is so new that drives have yet to shrink. The 3 1/2-inch drives used by all PS/2s, for example, are full-height devices.

Only two sizes of 5 1/4-inch drives have been used in IBM equipment. The original PC, the Portable PC, and XT used full-height devices.

Figure 20.2 **Standard form factors**

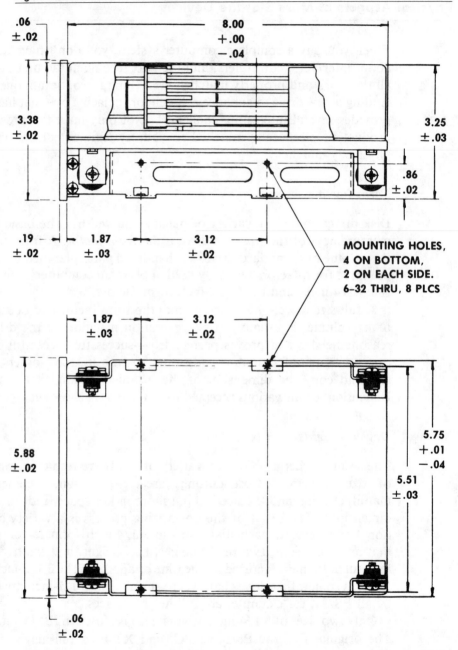

a) typical 5¼ inch form factor hard disk

Figure 20.2 **(continued)**

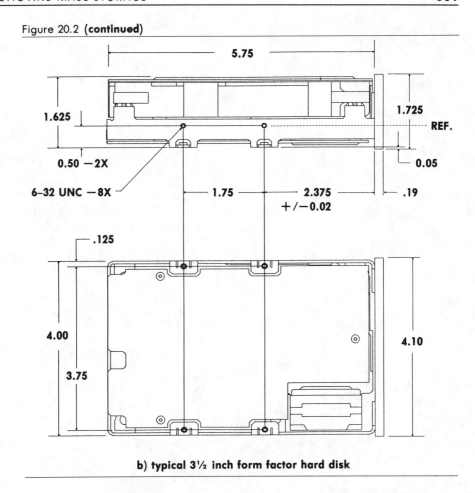

b) typical 3½ inch form factor hard disk

First to use half-height drives was the PCjr. The AT and later machines were also equipped with half-heights.

Although they have become rare, a few 5 1/4-inch devices that measure two-thirds-height can be found, often at bargain prices. While these units can be fitted to a standard full-height drive bay, their appearance in such an installation will most likely be unpleasant. You'll be left with a hole one-third the height of the bay that you'll have to fill.

A few quarter-height 5 1/4-inch floppy disk drives have been offered. Many of them found homes in early lunchbox-style portable computers, mostly machines unleashed before the 3 1/2-inch form factor proved its popularity. If you could find them, you could stick two of these drives into a single half-height drive bay. However, the severely restricted height of these drives has caused centering problems and damage to diskettes.

21

FLOPPY
DISKS

Everyone bemoans the floppy disk, using the same adage usually reserved for kids, spouses, and governments: "You can't live with them, and you can't live without them." The floppy disk provides a means of information interchange, data storage, file archiving, and endless frustration. They're convenient and easy to use; but they're slow and don't hold enough data—facts you quickly discover once you take your first spin on a hard disk. Floppies, like taxes, are something that everyone lives with and no one likes.

Floppies are actually part of a system that involves not just the disks themselves, called the *media,* but also the floppy disk drive mechanism, floppy disk drive controller, and the disk operating system software. All four elements are essential for the proper operation of the system.

Floppy Disk Media

The term "floppy disk" is one of those amazingly descriptive terms that abound in this age of genericisms. Inside its protective shell, the floppy disk medium is floppy, that is flexible, and is a wide, flat disk. The disks are stamped out from wide rolls of the magnetic medium like cutting cookies from dough.

The wide rolls look like hyperpituitary audio or video tape—and that's no coincidence. The floppy disk's composition is the same as that of recording tape, a plastic substrate on which a magnetic oxide is bound. Unlike tape, however, all floppy disks are coated with magnetic material on both sides.

Single-Sided Disks

Even single-sided disks have this double-coating of magnetic material. Either side of a single-sided disk can be used for reading and writing data. By convention, the bottom surface of the disk is used in single-sided floppy disk drives.

The only difference between single and double-sided disks themselves is the testing. Double-sided disks are tested and verified on both sides; single-sided disks are tested only on one side. Both types of disks may be made from the same batch of magnetic medium.

If you're willing to play quality-control expert, you can save substantially when buying floppies. Buy single-sided disks even when you have double-sided drives and do the testing yourself. You bear the cost of the rejected disks. These disks still should be usable as single-sided media. For instance, you can hand a copy of one of your data files to a friend.

Disk makers will tell you that their testing is more thorough and critical than what you can accomplish with your disk drives, and they are right. But your application may not be so crucial that it requires the certainty of factory testing.

High-Density Disks

Not all magnetic media are the same. Different manufacturers have their own secret formulae for the right magnetic coatings to spread on the disk. One of the differences is in the size of magnetic particles that remember the data. So-called *high-density* disks use a magnetic medium with a notably finer grain, allowing the disk to pack more information into a smaller space. In general, you should always use high-density media in drives that require it. Otherwise, the time you waste on disk errors will quickly erase any savings you make in using cheaper disks.

Disk Sizes

Floppy disks have been made in sizes from twelve inches down to two inches with untold variety in between. Only three of these have acquired acceptance in the PC community: 8-inch, 5 1/4-inch, and 3 1/2-inch diameters.

Bigger came first. Introduced in 1971, the 8-inch disk became a standard among small computer systems before it was a decade old. It had a number of features going for it. It was small—at least compared to the ream of paper that could hold the same amount of information—convenient, and standardized. Above all, it was inexpensive to produce and reliable enough to depend on. From the computer hobbyist's standpoint, it was a godsend for its speed, at least when compared to the only affordable alternative, the cassette tape.

By the time IBM introduced its first PC, other computer makers had moved to the 5 1/4-inch floppy, a size that was introduced in 1976. IBM's adoption of the smaller disks was remarkable, however. Negative remarks included that it introduced yet another medium into the arsenal of IBM products. That it brought yet another disk format to a world plagued by multiple, incompatible 5 1/4-floppy disk formats. (Over 50 different data formats were used by various manufacturers at one time or another.) And that the disk held less data—originally only 160 kilobytes— compared to the megabyte capacity of the 8-inch disk. On the other hand, the new disk was more compact. Its drives, too, were smaller, which allowed the PC itself to be smaller.

Portable laptop computers forced the issue of still smaller disks on the world even before the introduction of the PS/2 series made them standard across the IBM product line. Besides being compact, the 3 1/2-inch floppy medium also boasts more storage capacity (owing to oxide advances and a precision design) and greater ruggedness (because of the tough plastic shell.)

The 5 1/4-Inch Disk

The 5 1/4-inch disk is a sandwich in which the balogna is the disk itself. Appropriately named, the disk itself is 5 1/4 inches across; the shell it fits into extends to a full 5 1/2 inches square. The layout of a 5 1/4-inch floppy disk is shown in Figure 21.1.

The shell is molded from a tough plastic and is usually sonically welded together. Inside the shell is a layer of non-woven cloth, the *liner,* that reduces the friction of the disk spinning against the shell and sweeps contaminants off the disk.

The large hole in the center of the shell allows the drive hub of the disk drive to fit through. The hole that is cut out in the outer shell of the disk allows the drive mechanism to clamp onto the disk and spin it without slippage. The liberal lateral and longitudinal play of the disk in its shell allows it to be precisely centered on the hub.

The hub clamp is shaped like a truncated cone. The narrower portion slips into the hub hole of the disk and as it is forced down against the drive hub itself to clamp the disk, its increasing diameter forces the disk into the proper position. The clamp holds the disk against the hub by pressing down against a narrow (about 1/16 inch) circle of disk around the hub hole.

This area of the disk is the most prone to wear and damage. Center-

Figure 21.1 **Layout of 5 1/4-inch floppy disk**

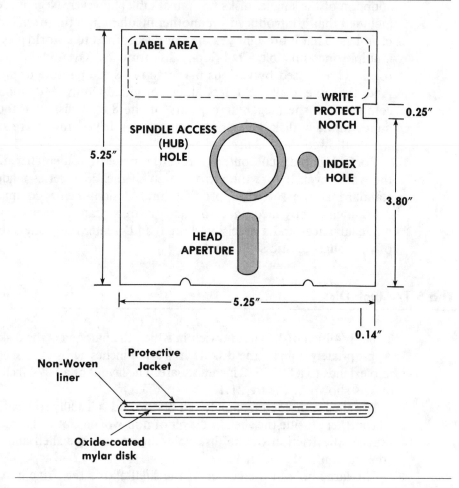

ing can warp and tear it; the disk spinning before clamping can wear it down. To forestall damage, many disks are equipped with protective *hub rings* which reinforce this vital center area of the disk. Some disks have rings on both sides; others have only one, which should be on the bottom where the most wear takes place. Some disks don't have any.

A number of aftermarket suppliers offer kits to add them yourself. In the long run, however, you're probably better off (you'll save time in installation and the cost of the kit) by copying and replacing any disks that begin to show wear at the hub.

Index Hole

A smaller hole in the floppy shell not far from the hub hole is designed to allow mechanical indexing of the disk. If you rotate a 5 1/4-inch disk inside its shell (spread your fingers inside the hub hole to rotate it without touching the magnetic surface), eventually you can make a small hole in the disk itself line up with the one in the disk shell. This is the *index hole*.

Hard and Soft-Sectors

Some disks, rare today, may have multiple index holes. Designed to be sensed by a light shining on a photocell, the many holes allow the disk drive to always find the right radial position on the disk, so that it can know where the data on the disk begins.

Disks that rely on such mechanical cues to locate information are termed *hard-sectored* because the sectors that hold information are fixed in place by the hardware mechanism. The IBM PC floppy disk system does not use the index hole but instead relies on magnetically-coded digital information written on the disk to identify sectors of information, the sector identification marks. Such disks are called *soft-sectored*.

Ignoring holes is a lot easier than making do without them, so disk drives based on soft-sectoring can use disks designed for hard or soft-sectoring. Systems designed for hard-sectoring cannot use soft-sectored disks, however.

Sector Count

The actual format of data on soft-sectored floppy disks varies under the control of the software that you use. IBM's original DOS 1.0 knew only one floppy disk format that puts 40 tracks on one side of a disk only, each track divided into eight sectors. The total capacity of such a disk was 160 kilobytes. When double-sided disk drives and a new version of DOS became available, the capacity of each disk doubled.

DOS 2.0 brought additional formats. The operating system was adjusted to put 9 sectors on each of 40 tracks. This version of DOS was compatible with the earlier versions and would let any double-sided drive read, write, or format disks with one or two sides and eight or nine sectors per track.

Figure 21.2 **Double versus high-density floppy disk heads**

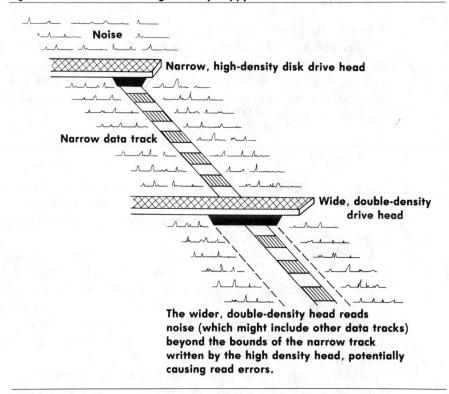

The wider, double-density head reads
noise (which might include other data tracks)
beyond the bounds of the narrow track
written by the high density head, potentially
causing read errors.

The high-density disks introduced with the AT and DOS 3.0 gained
their extra storage space by increasing the density of data in both directions. Under the new DOS with high-density drives, 80 tracks were laid
on each side of the disk with 15 sectors per track.

High-Density Incompatibility

To achieve that greater number of tracks, the read/write head of high-
density floppy disk drives was made narrower. The result of this change
is an incompatibility in writing and formating double-density disks.
Although a high-density drive can read, write, and format any IBM
5 1/4-inch floppy disk format, the disks it makes may not be readable on
a double-density drive. The narrow head doesn't fill the entire track
with magnetic data, and whatever magnetic fields are left outside the
range of the narrow head may confuse the wider head of a double-
density drive. See Figure 21.2.

In general, if you format a double-density disk in a double-density drive, the data that a high-density drive puts on that disk will also be readable by the double-density drive. However, if you write anything on a disk with a double-density drive and write over it using a high-density drive, that disk will likely be unreadable by a double-density drive (although the high-density drive may have no trouble reading back what it has written).

Head Access Aperture

The large oval hole or slot—it's shaped like an elongated racetrack—in both sides of the disk shell allows the read/write head(s) of the floppy disk drive to contact the disk surface. Two rules govern this slot, termed the *head access aperture.* One: The end of the disk closest to this hole goes into the disk drive first. Two: Never touch the disk surface, which can be seen through this hole. Those two rules are about all you need to know to operate a floppy disk drive successfully.

Write-Protect Notch

The shell surrounding the disk is generally square except for a notch near one corner. Called the *write-protect notch,* this cutout is sensed by a switch inside the disk drive. If the slot is found, then you have *write access* to the disk, enabling you to read, write to, or format the disk. If the notch is covered with a *write-protect tab* or a piece of tape, the disk drive sensor won't find it. The drive will then report to your computer that the disk is *write-protected,* and you will not be able to write to or format the disk.

Eight inch disks also have write-protect notches, but they work just the opposite. The absence of a notch indicates to the drive that you can write on the disk. Uncovering the notch write-protects the disk.

The scheme used by 5 1/4-inch disks has several advantages. If you insert a disk upside down, the write-protect notch will be in the wrong place, and the drive won't be able to find it. It effectively prevents you from trying to write to an upside down disk, possibly destroying valuable data. Special disks without notches can be made that can never be written to (disk duplicating machinery does not have to obey the notch rule). With these special notchless disks, distribution copies of software can be protected from accidental erasures or alterations.

You cannot override the physical write-protection afforded by the notch through software. Even though you may get the message ''Abort,

Retry, Ignore?'' (or, with newer versions of DOS, "Abort, Retry, Fail?'') after a write-protect error, telling the system to "Ignore" won't override the protection. You can, however, remove the write-protect tab or carefully cut the disk shell to make your own notch.

If you like to live dangerously, you could also cut the wire from the switch that senses the write-protect notch in the disk drive. Shortly thereafter, after you make your first mistake and destroy your only copy of a program or data file, you'll discover how valuable hardware write-protection can be.

Flippy Disks

The write-protect notch is the one thing that prevents you from flipping over a 5 1/4 double-sided disk in a single-sided disk drive to use both sides. (Although single-sided disk drives haven't been shipped inside PCs since the 64K system board was abandoned, somewhere out there, someone is happily using the 160K wonders.) So called *flippy disks* sidestep the issue by putting a write-protect notch on two edges of the disk. That way, you can flip the disk over and use the other side when one side is full.

Practical experience has shown the flippies are not a flawless or long-term solution. When a disk is flipped over, it turns in the opposite direction. In doing so, it bends the nap of the liner in the disk shell in the opposite direction and tends to dislodge the dirt that has collected and scatters it all over the disk again, severely shortening the life of the magnetic coating on the disk.

Sometimes software is distributed on flippies—one side holding IBM PC information, the other, Apple data. Because IBM doesn't recognize the Apple disks (and vice versa), your computer thinks such a flippy is just a single-sided disk. Unless you have two computer systems, one matching each standard, you won't be tempted to flip that flippy over. If you do, you should guarantee the life of the programs it contains by making yourself a duplicate copy and putting the flippy safely away.

5 1/4-Inch Disk Care

The rules governing the care of floppy disks are all based on the prevention of damage. Two forces can impair the function of floppies: physical damage and magnetism.

Magnetic Enemies

Magnetism is the more insidious. Invisible magnetic fields can alter or erase the data you have stored on your floppy disk. For instance, if the File Allocation Table of the disk is damaged, you may never be able to recover information from your disk even though it's still written on the disk.

Sources of potentially damaging magnetism abound in the office. For instance, the ringers inside old-fashioned telephones—the Bell telephones that have ringing bells inside them—are operated by powerful electromagnets. Whenever the phone rings, it sets up a magnetic field that can erase disks that are near or underneath the telephone. The field is not too strong, however, and keeping your disks a few inches from the phone should be sufficient.

Other common disk-damaging devices include magnetized scissors, paper-clip holders with ring magnets at the top to hold the clips in readiness, and even the motorized playthings found on some executives' desks. Even some monitors may exude magnetic fields from their power supplies or degaussing coils.

Physical Dangers

Physical damage includes anything that may alter the surface or substrate of the floppy disk. Any alteration—be it a coating of dust, oily fingerprints, or a physical tear or crease—is enough to interfere with the proper operation of the disk.

Writing on a disk label with ballpoint pen, a commonly cited problem, creases the disk. When the head scrapes over the disk, the crease causes a slight, temporary loss of contact with the disk. The data that might be read during that period are lost, resulting in a disk error. Folding or creasing the disk, even within its protective shuck, causes the same problem.

Dirt and fingerprints are cumulative and work slowly, wearing out the disk and your disk drive mechanism. They can combine together to literally gum up the works. Loose labels and write-protect tabs can come free and also damage your disk or drive mechanism.

Disk Care Recommendations

The best way to prevent disk problems is to take good care of your disks. Always keep them in their protective sleeves when they are not being actively used. Before you switch off your computer, remove the disk from the drive and put it away. Although IBM computers offer little risk of damaging a disk when they are powered down, even inside the machine a disk can collect potentially destructive dust on its surface. It's much less likely to inside its sleeve.

Keep your disks organized in a disk file cabinet. Although most are made from plastic and thus offer no magnetic shielding, they automatically put your disks far enough away from most magnetic sources that magnetic damage is minimized. Just don't put your magnetized scissors inside with the disks. The file cabinet also protects the disks from physical damage besides keeping you organized.

Radical Recovery

The protective (generally black) plastic shell of the 5 1/4-inch floppy disk deflects most woes that might afflict your data. Sometimes, however, it becomes the problem rather than the solution. When one of your floppy disks suffers some tremendous indignity—say from being trod upon by the local high school cross-country team wearing their cleats—the damage done to the shell may be all that stands between you and reading your data from the disk. The shell might get so bent it won't fit into the drive slot or so corrugated that the disk won't turn inside it. If you've got data on such a disk, all is not lost—at least not yet.

Radical surgery can give you a chance to see what's left on the disk. Using the radical recovery technique, you may be able to save your data, though your disk has met its demise.

Radical recovery merely means separating the disk from its shell for one last spin in your disk drive. To get the disk out of its shell, you can either break the sonic welds holding the shell closed (more difficult than it sounds) or slice off one edge of the shell with a scissors or paper cutter.

Once you have opened the shell, carefully slide the disk out, touching its surface as little as possible. With most disk drives, you can gently insert this naked disk right into the slot, watching carefully as you operate the level to lower the head that the centering hub actually engages the center hole of the vulnerable disk.

Some floppy disk drives have an anti-head crash lock that prevents you from lowering the head without a disk *in its shell* being present in the drive. If that's the case for yours, you'll have to sacrifice a second, good quality disk. Slice the new disk open, pull out the disk itself, and reinsert the disk from the corrupted shell.

Once you have your bad floppy in a disk drive, copy its contents to a new disk to substitute for the old. You should be able to get more than a few spins from your reconstituted disk. You stand a good, though hardly perfect, chance of recovering the information stored on it.

Note that some companies—notably Polaroid—offer a free data recovery service for their warrantied disks. If the disks that you use are covered by such a warranty, do not try the radical recovery because it will likely void the warranty. Instead, let the disk manufacturer dig out your data. The disk maker stands a better chance of getting back your data, and you'll suffer fewer heartaches and headaches.

3 1/2-Inch Floppies

Portable computers and downsized machines like Apple's Macintosh drove the need for still smaller floppy disks. A variety of abortive attempts, including a miniaturized 5 1/4-inch system that had two inches of diameter loped off, finally led to the near-universal acceptance of the demonstrably superior 3 1/2-inch system originally promulgated by Sony. In their favor, 3 1/2-inch disks are convenient critters, exactly shirt-pocket size, and they are tough and reliable enough to be tossed around with impunity. The layout of a 3 1/2-inch floppy disk is shown in Figure 21.3.

Tough Shell

The 3 1/2-inch system embodies several improvements over the veteran 5 1/4-inch design. Most notable is its hard shell, which is tough and only slightly flexible. The hard shell protects the fragile disk while allowing you the freedom of carrying out such crimes, forbidden with 5 1/4-inch disks, as writing on an already-applied disk label with a ballpoint pen. Unlike the bigger disks, which leave a large head-access swath of the disk vulnerable to dirt, dust, and fingerprints, the 3 1/2-design covers the vulnerable access area with a spring-loaded sliding metal shield or shutter. It opens automatically only when you insert a disk into a drive. This protection means that 3 1/2-inch disks don't need the protection of a sleeve or shuck.

Figure 21.3 **Layout of 3 1/2-inch floppy disk**

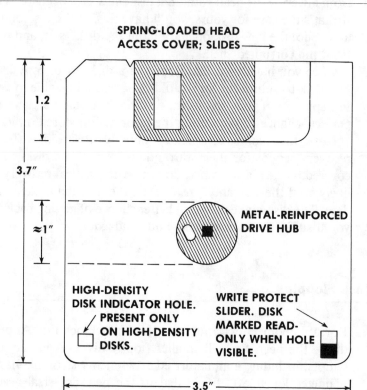

SPRING-LOADED HEAD ACCESS COVER; SLIDES ⟶

1.2

3.7"

≈1"

METAL-REINFORCED DRIVE HUB

HIGH-DENSITY DISK INDICATOR HOLE. PRESENT ONLY ON HIGH-DENSITY DISKS.

WRITE PROTECT SLIDER. DISK MARKED READ-ONLY WHEN HOLE VISIBLE.

3.5"

Insertion Key

Unlike 5 1/4-inch disks, the 3 1/2 is designed to prevent improper insertion. One corner is truncated so that a disk will only fully engage in a disk drive when correctly oriented.

Write-Protection

Instead of a write-protect notch and tab, the 3 1/2-inch design uses a hole and a plastic slider. When the slider blocks the hole, you can read, write on, and format the disk. When the slider is moved back to reveal the hole (or is entirely absent, as it is on many software distribution disks) the disk is write-protected.

More Tracks

The storage capacity of the 3 1/2-inch disk proves that less can be more. Although less than half the surface area is available for recording on a 3 1/2-inch disk compared to a 5 1/4 disk, the standard format of the little disk actually can pack in more data, up to 1.44 megabytes. The larger capacity results from the use of a more finely grained medium with better magnetic properties and greater precision. The old problem of disk centering is reduced by the 3 1/2-inch disk's metal hub, which allows easier, more positive mechanical action with less chance of damage or wear. Instead of 48 or 96 tracks per inch, the 3 1/2-inch design squeezes in 135 per inch. Because of the cramped quarters, however, only 80 of these narrow tracks fit on a disk.

Sector Count

The lower-capacity IBM 3 1/2-inch drives of the IBM Convertible and some compatible computers use the same physical and logical layout as ordinary double-sided, double-density disks—512 byte sectors arranged nine per track—and increase capacity solely by doubling the number of tracks per disk side (up to 80 tracks) to obtain 720K per disk. The high-density disks used by the PS/2 line double the density of the data in each track (to fit 18 sectors per track) to achieve their 1.44 megabyte limit. Single-sided 3 1/2-inch disks are not supported in the IBM universe.

Your disk drive can tell whether you've put a normal-density or high-density floppy disk into it. An extra *high-density notch* marks the disks with greater capacity.

Floppy Disk Drives

As computer equipment goes, floppy disk drives are simple devices. The essential components are a *spindle motor,* which spins the disk, and a stepper-motor that drives a metal band in-and-out to position the read/write heads, an assembly that is collectively called the *head actuator.* A manual mechanism is provided for lowering a hub clamp to center and lock the disk in place and to press the heads against the surface of the disk. In all except the single-sided drives of the original PC, two heads are used that pinch together around the disk to read and write from either side of the medium.

Speed Control

All of the electronics packed onto the one or more circuit boards attached to the drive unit merely control these simple operations. A servo system keeps the disk spinning at the correct speed. Usually an optical sensor looks at a stroboscopic pattern of black dots on a white disk on the spindle assembly. The electronics counts the dots that pass the sensor in a given period to determine the speed at which it turns, adjusting it as necessary. Some drives use similar sensors based on magnetism rather than optics, but they work in essentially the same way—counting the number of passing magnetic pulses in a given period to determine the speed of the drive.

Head Control

Other electronics control the radial position of the head assembly to the disk. The stepper motor that moves the head reacts to voltage pulses by moving one or more discrete steps of a few degrees (hence the descriptive name of this type of motor). Signals from the floppy disk controller card in the host computer tell the disk drive which track of the disk to move its head to. The electronics on the drive then send the appropriate number of pulses to the stepper motor to move the head to the designated track.

The basic floppy disk mechanism receives no feedback on where the head is on the disk. It merely assumes it gets to the right place because of the number of steps the actuator makes. Because the drive does its best to remember the position of the head, hard reality can leave the head other than in its expected place. For instance, you can reach in and manually jostle the head mechanism. Or you might switch off your computer with the head halfway across the disk. Once the power is off, all the circuitry forgets, and the location of the head becomes an unknown.

Note that the stepper motors in most double-density floppy disk drives sold today are capable of tracing out all 40 tracks used by the IBM floppy disk format. Some earlier computers did not require all 40 tracks. Consequently some drives made for these computers—usually those drives closed out at prices that seem too good to be true—may not have a full 40-track range. Caveat emptor!

Head Indexing

So that the head can be put in the right place with assurance, the drive resorts to a process called *indexing*. That is, it moves the head as far as it will go toward the edge of the disk. Once the head reaches this index position, it can travel no farther, no matter how hard the actuator tries to move it. The drive electronics just make sure that the actuator moves the head a sufficient number of steps (a number greater than the width of the disk) to ensure that the head will stop at the index position. After the head has reached the index position, the control electronics can move it a given number of actuator steps and know exactly where on the radius of the disk the head is located.

DOS Requirements

Functionally, there's no difference between the full and half-height 5 1/4-inch units. They run exactly the same with all software; however, half-height drives should not be used with DOS 2.0 or earlier. Because of the slower mechanism of the smaller drives, IBM increased a few time constants in DOS 2.1, which was made available at the same time as the PCjr (which introduced half-height drives to IBM personal computers).

Not only do DOS 3.0 and later versions take into account the requirements of half-height drives, these later versions of DOS also support high-density (1.2 megabyte) 5 1/4-inch drives. You must use DOS 3.0 or later with 1.2 megabyte floppy disks.

The first DOS version to support 3 1/2-inch drives was DOS 3.2, which supports only the 700K drives used by the PC Convertible. The high-density 3 1/2-inch drives with 1.44 megabyte capacity used by the PS/2 series require either DOS 3.3 (or later) or OS/2.

Floppy Disk Controllers

Although operating a floppy disk drive seems simple, it's actually a complex operation with many levels of control. When you press the Save button while running an application program, your button press does not connect directly to the drive. Instead, the keystroke is detected by your computer's hardware and recognized by its BIOS. The BIOS, in turn, sends the appropriate electronic code to your application program. The program then probably makes one or more requests to DOS to write something to the disk. DOS sends instructions to the BIOS, and the BIOS sends codes to ports on the disk control hardware. Finally, this hardware tells the drive where to move its head and what to do once the head gets where it's going.

The penultimate piece of hardware in this chain is the *floppy disk controller*. It has two purposes in operating your system's floppy disks. One is to translate the logical commands from your computer system, which are usually generated by the BIOS, into the exact electrical signals that control the disk drive. The other function is to translate the stream of pulses generated by the floppy disk head into data in the form that your computer can deal with.

The best way to understand the operation of the floppy disk controller is to examine the signals that control the floppy disk drive and those that the drive sends to its computer host.

Only a few signals are required to control the two floppy disk drives normally attached by a single cable to the controller.

Drive Select A and *Drive Select B* are used to individually select either the first or second drive, A or B. (In four-drive systems, the signals for A in the second cable control drive C, and those of B control D.) If the signal assigned to a particular drive is not present, all the other input and output circuits of the drive are deactivated, except those that control the drive motor. In this way, two drives can share the bulk of the wires in the controller cable without interference. However, this control scheme also means that only one drive in a pair can be active at a time. You can write to drive B at the same time as you read from drive A. That's why you must transfer the data held on a disk (or file) from one drive into memory before you can copy it to another drive.

One wire is used for each drive to switch its spindle motor on and off. These are called, individually, *Drive Select A* and *Drive Select B.* Although it is possible to make both motors spin simultaneously, rules laid down by IBM admonish against activating these two lines to make both floppy disk drive motors run at the same time. This saves power in the severely constrained PC system and is a moot issue in the single-drive XT system. Of course, the two drives in your PC may run simultaneously for brief periods due to a delay built into most drives that keeps their motors running for a few seconds after the Motor Enable signal stops.

Two signals control the head position. One, *Step Pulse,* merely tells the stepper motor on the drive to move one step—that's exactly one track—toward or away from the center of the disk. The *Direction* signal controls which way the pulses move the head. If this signal is active, the head moves toward the center.

To determine which of the two sides of a double-sided disk to read, one signal, called *Write Select,* is used. When this signal is active, it tells the disk drive to use the upper head. When no signal is present, the disk drive automatically uses the default (lower) head.

Writing to disk requires two signals. *Write Data* comprises the information that's actually to be written magnetically onto the disk. It consists of nothing but a series of pulses corresponding exactly to the flux transitions that are to be made on the disk. The read/write head merely echoes these signals magnetically. As a fail-safe to preclude accidentally writing over valuable data, a second signal called *Write Enable* is used. No write current is sent to the read/write head unless this signal is active.

The controller receives four signals back from the floppy disk drive.

Two of these help the controller determine where the head is located. *Track 0* indicates to the controller when the head is above the outermost track on the disk so the controller knows from where to start counting head-moving pulses. *Index* helps the drive determine the location of each bit on a disk track. One pulse is generated on the Index line for each revolution of the disk. The controller can time the distance between ensuing data pulses based on the reference provided by the Index signal.

The *Write-Protect* signal is derived from the sensor that detects the existence or absence of a write-protect tab on a diskette. If a tab is present, this signal is active.

The *Read-Data* signal comprises a series of electrical pulses that exactly matches the train of flux transitions on the floppy disk.

In its control function, the floppy disk controller must convert the requests from the BIOS or direct hardware commands that are couched in terms of track and sector numbers into the pulses that move the head to the proper location on the disk. For the most efficient operation, the controller must also remember where the head is located, index the head as necessary, and report errors when they occur.

In its translation function, the floppy disk controller must make sense from the stream of unformatted pulses delivered from the drive. It first must find the beginning of each track from the Index pulse, then mark out each sector from the information embedded in the data stream. Once it identifies a requested sector, it must then read the information it contains and convert it from serial to parallel form so that it can be sent through the PC bus. In writing, the controller must first identify the proper sector to write to, which is a read operation, then switch on the write current to put data into that sector before the next sector on the disk begins.

Most of the hard work of the controller is handled by a single integrated circuit, the 765 controller chip. The 765 works much like a microprocessor. It carries out certain operations in response to commands that it receives through registers connected to your computer's I/O ports.

This programmability makes the 765 and the IBM floppy disk controller extremely versatile. None of the essential floppy disk drive parameters are cast in stone or the silicon on the controller. The number of heads, tracks, and sectors on a disk are set by loading numbers into the registers of the 765. Usually, the normal IBM operating values are loaded into the controller when you boot up your computer. You ordinarily don't have to worry about them after that.

Special software can reprogram your controller to make it read, write to, and format floppy disks that differ from the IBM standard. Two types of software perform this reprogramming. Copy-protection schemes may alter vital drive parameters by misnumbering sectors, adding extra sectors, or a similar operation, which cannot be duplicated using normal IBM parameters. Disk compatibility software alters the controller programming to make the floppy disk drives in your system act like those used by other computers such as those that use the CP/M operating system.

Note, however, that although the IBM system is flexible, it cannot handle all possibilities, such as Commodore or Apple disks. These computers use entirely different drive control hardware which the 765 cannot mimic.

IBM Floppy Disk Controllers

IBM has used three distinct styles of floppy disk controllers. The original design used in the first PC was also adopted by the XT and Portable PC. The PCjr used a separate design. The floppy disk controllers of the AT and XT Model 286 were combined with the hard disk controller. All PC/2 models have their floppy disk controllers built into their system board circuitry.

Compatible computer manufacturers have adopted all of these designs except for that of the PCjr. In the case of the AT, manufacturers use a nearly identical controller to that used by IBM, even made by the same principle manufacturer, Western Digital Corporation. Besides PS/2 clones, many XT and AT compatibles are equipped with system board floppy disk controllers.

The PC and XT Controller

One distinguishing characteristic of the orginal PC controller that is often not carried over to the boards used in other brands of computer is its ability to control up to four floppy disk drives. In addition to the edge connector on the card, which allows two drives to be attached to a single cable, a second, 37-pin connector is provided on the card option retaining bracket. All the signals necessary for running a third and a fourth floppy disk are available there. This connection is perfect for adding a third external floppy disk, perhaps a 3 1/2-inch unit to facilitate the transfer of files between different disk formats.

Installing Floppy Disk Drives

As is the case with anything mechanical, floppy disk drives can go bad unexpectedly. The prices of aftermarket drives has fallen so low that it is often less expensive to replace a failed or failing floppy disk drive with a new or rebuilt one than it is to have repairs made. You might also want to replace a disk drive to add a new format of floppy disk to your system or to build an entire system from the chassis up.

Replacing and installing a floppy disk drive is quite easy with most computers, particularly those made by IBM. That's stands to reason. If they were difficult for you to install, they would be difficult for the manufacturer to install; hence, installation would be costly. and that would be a costly proposition.

The first step in making a replacement of a floppy disk drive is to ensure the product you want to use is compatible with the system that you have. The broad issue of compatibility covers serveral topics, including the compatibility of the disk format with your hardware and the physical compatibility of a drive unit with the chassis of your computer.

Format Compatibility

All computers in the IBM PC and PS/2 families (as well as completely compatible computers) support standard double-density, double-sided floppy disk drives. These drives are the only truly universal storage systems across the PC product line, making their media the one format with the widest range of compatibilities.

High-density 5 1/4-inch drives with 1.2 megabyte data capacity are supported by IBM hardware only in AT and later computers (including the XT Model 286). The BIOS of earlier machines—PCs, XTs, Portable PCs, and the PCjr—is unable to handle the larger number of tracks used by these drives.

Similarly, 3 1/2-inch drives are not supported by the hardware machines earlier than the PS/2 series, with the exception of the Convertible, whose initial versions were only capable of handling 700K drives.

These hardware shortcomings are correctable, however, by the installation of driver software. The program *DRIVER.SYS,* included with DOS Versions 3.2 and later, allows the use of any standard IBM drive with any standard IBM computer that it can be physically connected to. The only shortcoming of using DRIVER.SYS is it does not allow you to boot your computer from more advanced media than your machine was designed to handle.

In general, compatible computers introduced more than a few months after the PS/2 series was brought to market have built-in support for 3 1/2-inch drives. Machines that do not can be made compatible with the DRIVER.SYS program.

Physical Compatibility

Not only must floppy disks match the BIOS of your computer, but they must physically fit inside it. Although external drives are available (even from IBM), they tend to be much more expensive than the minimally priced install-it-yourself internal variety (especially those from IBM).

For the most part, physical limitations on drive installations are obvious. Since a small chassis PS/2 (for instance, the Models 30 and 50) has no room for 5 1/4-inch disk drives, plugging one in is not a simple matter. But problems also arise in less obvious situations. For instance, you'll face unexpected difficulties should you want to plug a new half-height drive or a pair of them into a PC, XT, or PS/2. In its wisdom, IBM designed its first personal computers to accommodate only full-height devices. You'll find that the drive mounting tray only provides an area for attaching a full-height drive or, at best, one half-height drive in the bottom of a full-height bay. Big chassis PS/2s present a similar problem; their rail mounting scheme offers a place to plug in only one half-height drive in the bottom of the bay.

If you only want to install one half-height drive, the problem is easily solved. Just screw the drive into place in the bottom of the slot. But putting a single half-height drive in a full-height bay may defeat your purposes, which are likely the need of extra mass storage expansion. The easy solution is buying or making adapter plates to tie together two drives into a single unit.

Half-Height Adapter for PCs

To make your own, slice or saw thin sheet metal to approximately the dimensions shown in Figure 21.3. Add four holes for attaching the drives, then duplicate your efforts so you have one adapter for either side of your drive stack.

Screw your assembly together using hardware with the lowest possible profile, such as flat headed screws (which you can lower further by beveling the screw holes you cut into your adapters). Make sure your drives fit together with, at most, only about 1/16-inch distance between them and no excess adapter extends above or below the drive units themselves. Once you're satisfied that everything fits together properly, remove the screws from one side of the bottom drive.

Now attempt to fit the entire assembly into the waiting drive bay of your computer. If the hardware you used was slender enough, the assembly should slide into place without a problem. Then just fit in the pair of screws you previously removed to hold the assembly in place. (The IBM mounting scheme affords no support on the other side of the floppy disk bay.)

If your assembly does not fit, it's likely the screw heads are too thick and they bump into the slides of the drive bay opening. The only alternative you have is to remove all the screws from one side, insert the assembly, then reassemble it within the confines of the bay. If the adapters and associated hardware on just one side of the drive interfere with the installation of the assembly, you'll have to put the whole adapter plate together inside the drive bay, which will likely involve removing the device in the other drive bay.

Adapting 3 1/2-inch Drives to PCs and ATs

Fitting 3 1/2-inch drives into a 5 1/4-inch bay also requires an adapter, but one that is better bought. Most makers of 3 1/2-inch drive products offer such adapters that convert the little drives to fit a 5 1/4-inch form factor.

The problem of installing the drive then becomes the same as fitting in any other half-height 5 1/4-inch device.

With 3 1/2-inch drives, you may also have to adapt the miniature edge connector on the drive to match the larger connectors used by bigger drives. Most 3 1/2-inch drive adapter kits include the necessary adapter, which is why you would be better off getting a commercial product.

Cabling Considerations

Drive Select Jumpers

The cable used in a floppy disk subsystem apparently presumes that a drive attached to it already knows whether it is supposed to be drive A or B in your system. However, for compatibility reasons, all floppy disk drives are created equal with a common design for all drive letters. In order that a given floppy disk drive can assume the identity of A or B, drive manufacturers equipped their products with DIP switches or jumpers to select the appropriate appellation. Termed drive select jumpers, most floppy disk drives allow you to select one of four potential identities.

For reasons related to their function—they essentially switch some of the connections delivered by the cable—drive select jumpers can usually be found on a drive near the edge connector onto which you attach the cable. Usually you'll be faced with an array of jumpers or switches, each labelled with a not-too-meaningful combination of two or three letters and numbers. The drive select jumpers can be identified (when they are labelled) by their two-character prefix DS. From there, different disk drive manufacturers go in two directions. Some start numbering the drive select settings with one and count up to four; others start with one and venture only as far as three.

Drive Select Settings

With IBM products, drive select settings have no relevance. All floppy disk drives in an IBM-style computer are set to be the second drive in the system. A special twist to the floppy disk connecting cable sorts out the proper disk drive's identity.

To configure a floppy disk drive for installation in an IBM-style system, you should invariably set it as the second drive, paying no attention to whether it will be A or B. With drives with which the drive select jumpers are numbered starting with zero, all floppy disk drives should be set as one. With drives with which the number of the drive select jumpers begins with one, all drives should be set as two.

Drive Cabling

The special twist that sorts out the drive identities is a group of five conductors in the floppy disk cable that are twisted in the run to one of its connectors. This twist reverses the drive select and motor control signals in the cable as well as rearranges some of the ground wires in the cable (which effectively makes no change). (See Figure 21.4.)

Because all drives are setup as the second drive, this reversal makes the drive attached to the cable after the twist the first drive, drive A. In other words, drive A is attached to the connector at the end of the cable, the one where the wire twist takes place. Drive B is attached to the connector in the middle of the length of the cable. The third connector, at the end of the cable with no twist, goes to the floppy disk controller.

Single Drive and Straight-Through Cables

With hard disk drives, you can use a straight-through cable—one without the twist near the last connector—to operate a single disk drive by moving the drive select jumper of the connected hard disk to the first drive position. This tactic *will not work* with floppy disk drives. The twisted part of the cable moves not only the drive select conductor but also the motor control conductor. Therefore, you cannot use a straight-through cable with a single floppy disk drive in your computer system.

If you make your own floppy disk cable to handle a single drive, you'll have to abide by the IBM drive select numbering scheme. You have to make a twist in the conductors, as indicated in Figure 21.4.

Terminating Resistor Networks

In the floppy disk system used by IBM and compatible computer makers, there is one physical difference between drives A and B. Drive A always has a *terminating resistor network* installed. Drive B always

Figure 21.4 **Two-drive floppy disk cable**

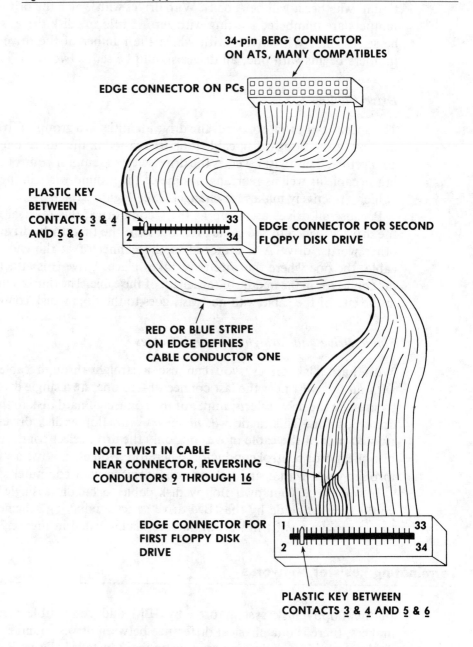

34-pin BERG CONNECTOR
ON ATS, MANY COMPATIBLES

EDGE CONNECTOR ON PCs

PLASTIC KEY
BETWEEN
CONTACTS 3 & 4
AND 5 & 6

1   33
2   34

EDGE CONNECTOR FOR SECOND
FLOPPY DISK DRIVE

RED OR BLUE STRIPE
ON EDGE DEFINES
CABLE CONDUCTOR ONE

NOTE TWIST IN CABLE
NEAR CONNECTOR, REVERSING
CONDUCTORS 9 THROUGH 16

EDGE CONNECTOR FOR
FIRST FLOPPY DISK
DRIVE

1   33
2   34

PLASTIC KEY BETWEEN
CONTACTS 3 & 4 AND 5 & 6

does not. In three or four floppy disk drive systems, drive C always has a terminating resistor. Drive D does not.

Purpose

The terminating resistor is used to absorb the excess current that flows through the connection between the floppy disk controller and the drive electronics. The circuits are designed so that a specific current is expected to flow through them. The terminating resistor network forces the proper current to flow so that no excess is left in the system. Without the terminating resistor, the signal going to the floppy disk drive would be mismatched and might bounce back and forth through the circuitry before finally decaying, possibly resulting in errors. By absorbing the excess, the terminating resistor prevents these potential errors.

Two terminating resistors—for instance, having a resistor network installed on both disk drives in a system—would cause too much current to flow, which can lead to the premature failure of the circuits themselves. The terminating resistor network is always located on the last drive that's physically connected to the cable because that's where the signal reflections would occur.

Identification

Terminating resistors usually take on one of two forms. They are either housed in a single in-line package or, more usually, in a dual in-line package that looks like an ordinary integrated circuit, except that it's sometimes blue or amber instead of black and may be shinier. Single in-line packages usually resemble small oblong blocks, about an inch long, 1/8 inch thick, and 1/2 inch high. Nine separate leads, at 1/10 inch spacing, project from the bottom of the network and into a socket or directly through the printed circuit board of the floppy disk drive electronics.

Although terminating resistor networks made by different manufacturers use different nomenclature for their printed-on identifications, they can usually be recognized by their resistance value, nominally 150 ohms. The capital Greek letter Omega stands for Ohms.

In most contemporary floppy disk drives, the termination resistor stands out because it's the only socket-mounted device on the circuit board. Figure 21.5 illustrates common terminating resistor types.

Figure 21.5 **Terminating resistors**

(can be black, blue, or opaque amber)

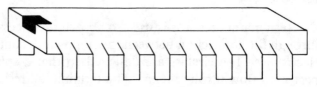

1. **Dual in-line package; usually has eight** *pairs* **of "legs".**

(usually black)

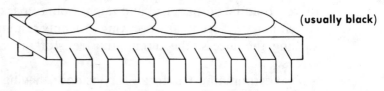

2. **Sometimes the dual in-line package appears "lumpy".**

(usually black)

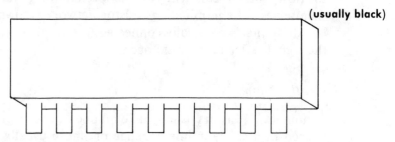

3. **Single in-line package generally has nine "legs".**
   Sometimes it, too, appears lumpy.

Location

The terminating resistor network in most floppy disk drives is found adjacent to the edge connector to which you plug in the drive. Because the network must be removed from a generic drive in roughly half its installations, the resistor network is generally accessible near the rear edge of the printed circuit board holding the electronics of the drive. Usually it is near or adjacent to the drive select jumpers or switches.

Removal

For the most part, when you need to make a floppy disk drive either drive B or drive D, you only need pull out the resistor. SIP networks should be removable just by pulling them firmly away from their sockets. DIP networks may require the use of a chip puller, or you can pry them up with a small screwdriver.

Soldered-In Networks

Lately a few low-budget manufacturers have been skimping on parts when it comes to making floppy disk drives by omitting the socket for the terminating resistor network. In such cases, the networks are soldered directly to the circuit board, making them much more difficult to remove.

The best—and often least practical—way of removing soldered-down terminators is by de-soldering them. Heat up the connections, suck away the excess solder with a wick or bulb, and remove the network. De-soldering risks damage to the disk drive. The alternative is to clip off the network leads with diagonal cutters. Don't worry about destroying the network because one with gimpy legs won't be much good anyhow. That's a problem you'll have to live with. After you clip its resistor network off, a floppy disk drive is eternally confined to status as B or D.

Double-Termination

The other alternative is, of course, living with two resistor networks in your floppy disk subsystem or removing the network from drive A. The former case, double-termination, is the more likely; it befalls nearly everybody one time or another as he forgets this part of the drive installation process.

Either situation is not likely to be fatal to the operation of your system. As a practical matter, everything works fine with zero, one, or two termination resistor networks in the system, with the single resistor installed in drive A or B. The only problem is that it's not the right way of doing things and that something potentially could go wrong. Odds are you won't encounter an extraordinary number of disk errors if your system's terminations are wrong. You could skimp by ignoring termination matters, but it's better to do things by the book and postpone if not prevent disasters.

22

HARD DISKS

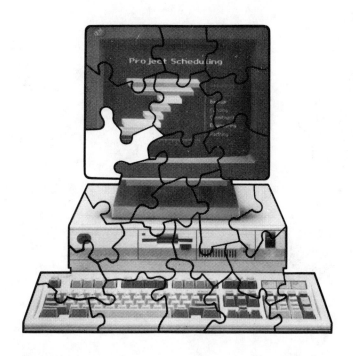

Hard disks resemble the personal computers in which they operate in that most people don't realize how much they need or will use one until they have it. Suddenly the seeming luxury of having such a device transforms itself into necessity and a strong dependency grows.

The evolution of the PC echoes and emphasizes the changed perception of the hard disk. The first PC made no provision for a hard disk. The XT brought hard disk capabilities. The AT put the emphasis on hard-disk performance. Micro Channel PS/2s made the hard disk standard equipment. And OS/2 makes a hard disk mandatory.

Once you have a hard disk, you'll wonder how you got along without it. After you've used a hard disk, a personal computer won't seem like a computer to you unless it is equipped with one.

The hard disk puts the bulk of your programs and data at your fingertips, ready for instant access. It can speed up everyday work by loading programs in a fraction of the time required by floppy disks. By storing and sorting through data very quickly, it will make many of your programs seem to run faster. The hard disk will even make the rest of your computer system seem more responsive.

Depending on your needs and demands, hard disks can be expensive or cheap. They come in various sizes and speed ratings. And they can be a pleasure or a pain to use or install.

Naming Conventions

The name *hard disk* distinguishes such drives from the other familiar mass storage device, the floppy disk. While the floppy disk has a flexible carrier for its magnetic medium, the hard disk uses a rigid, or hard, substrate. The name is merely descriptive.

Winchester Disk Drives

Hard disks can be difficult to discuss because several appellations have been applied to them. Often hard disks are termed *Winchester* disk drives because of the technology they use. The underlying principle of Winchester technology is the flying read/write head. That is, the head is attached to a slight airfoil like an airplane wing. The spinning hard disk creates air motion which flows across the airfoil and creates enough lift to pull the head away from the disk by a distance of a dozen or so microinches (millionths of an inch).

Winchester Origins

The name Winchester is a carry-over from the original disk drive that used this technology. Built by IBM, it was once code named the *"3030"* because it had two sides, each of which could store 30 megabytes. Because this designation recalled the famous Winchester 3030 repeating rifle that, according to legend, won the West, the name Winchester carried over to the like-numbered disk drive. The moniker not only stuck but was generalized to the flying head technology upon which the drive was based.

Another story holds that the name Winchester was derived from the flying head technique being developed in an IBM laboratory in Winchester, England. When queried in 1987, however, IBM officially supported the rifle story as the origin of the Winchester designation. According to IBM, substantial development work on the technology was carried out at the IBM United Kingdom Laboratories at Hursley Park, Winchester, but the lab location had nothing to do with the drive name.

Whitney Technology

Not all hard disks are Winchesters any more, however. A new head technology, called *Whitney*, results in much smaller, faster, and sturdier assemblies that are replacing the Winchester head design.

Bernoulli Technology

Iomega Corporation's *Bernoulli Box* removable media drives turn Winchester technology upside down. Instead of using the airflow generated by the spinning disk to lift the head above a rigid disk, these drives use a flexible disk that bends around the head under the force of the air pressure. The advantages of this system are that the spinning disk has much lower mass and is more resistant to head crashes. The disadvantage is that the medium is constantly flexed and eventually wears out.

Fixed Disks

IBM, and just about no one else, calls the hard disk a *fixed disk* because, unlike floppy disk drives, the recording media cannot be removed from a hard disk. Strictly speaking, the disk of a hard disk is not fixed—it rotates faster than IBM can turn a buck. Moreover, a few hard disk drives use removable media.

No matter the terminology—hard disk, Winchester, or fixed disk— the technology is the same, as are your concerns in installing, using, and taking advantage of one.

Understanding Hard Disks

Not all hard disks are created equal. Different hard disk models are made from different materials using different technologies and under different standards. As a result the performance, capacities, and prices of hard disks cover a wide range from a few hundred dollars to tens of thousands. Understanding these differences will enable you to better judge the quality and value available in any disk product. You'll also better understand what you need to do to get one running and keep it that way.

The hard disk is actually a combination device, a chimera that's part electronic and part mechanical. Electrically, the hard disk performs the noble function of turning evanescent pulses of electronic digital data into more permanent magnetic fields. As with other magnetic recording devices, from cassette recorders to floppy disks, the hard disk accomplishes its end using an electromagnet, called a read/write head, to align the polarities of magnetic particles on the hard disks themselves. Other electronics in the hard disk system control the mechanical half of the drive and help it properly arrange the magnetic storage and locate the information that is stored on the disk.

Drive Mechanism

The mechanism of the typical hard disk is actually rather simple, comprising fewer moving parts than such exotic devices as electric razors and pencil sharpeners. The basic elements of the system include a stack of one or more *platters*, the actual hard disks themselves, that are covered with a magnetic *medium* on which data can be recorded. Together the platters rotate as a unit on a shaft, called the *spindle*. Typically the shaft connects directly to a *spindle motor* that spins the entire assembly. Most hard disks use servo-controlled spindle motors, which constantly monitor their own speed using optical or magnetic sensors and automatically compensate for any variation.

Constant Spin

Typically, hard-disk platters spin at about 3600 rpm, about ten times faster than floppy disks. Unlike floppy disk drives, the hard-disk platters are kept constantly spinning (at least while the disk drive is powered up) because achieving a stable spin of the massive stack of platters at their relatively high speed may require 10 to 30 seconds. This constant spin earns the hard disk one of its two biggest benefits—the data recorded on it are nearly instantly accessible. Floppies, on the other hand, require you to wait a half-second or so until they get spinning up to speed.

The higher rotating speed of hard-disk platters also means that data can be written to and read from them faster. The quicker spin means more of the disk holding more information passes the point at which the data on the platter is read or written in a given period. By itself, faster rotation earns the hard disk a performance advantage in reading and writing large blocks of data of more than a factor of ten. Newer hard-disk technologies that pack more information into a given area of the hard disk further increase this advantage.

Multiple Platters

One of the major factors in determining the storage capacity of a hard disk is the number of platters that the drive uses. Simply put, the more surface area that a drive has for recording data, the more storage capacity it will have. Given the same media type and the same actuator design, a drive with more platters will store more. In fact, to achieve a line of hard-disk models of various capacities, many manufacturers simply use the same mechanism equipped with a different number of platters.

Platter Composition

Typically, the platters of a hard disk are made from an aluminum alloy that's precisely machined to an extremely fine tolerance measured in microinches. The aluminum serves as a *substrate* to which a *magnetic medium* is affixed either with a binder or mechanically.

Oxide Media

The first magnetic medium used in hard disks was made from the same materials used in conventional audio recording tapes, ferric or ferrous oxide compounds—essentially fine grains of rather exotic rust. As with recording tape, the oxide particles are milled in a mixture of other compounds, including a glue-like *binder* and often a lubricant. The binder also serves to isolate individual oxide particles from one another. This mud-like mixture is then coated onto the platters.

The technology of oxide coatings is old and well developed. The process has been evolving for more than 40 years, and now rates as a well-understood, familiar technology. In computer terms, most of the bugs have been worked out. In addition, many sources of supply are available. Consequently, oxide coatings are a safe bet for disk makers.

Oxide particles are not the best storers of magnetic information, however. Oxides tend to have lower coercivities and their grains tend to be large when compared to other, newer media technologies. Both of these factors tend to limit the storage density available with oxide media. The slight surface roughness of the oxide medium also requires the hard disk read/write head to fly farther away from it than other media, which also reduces maximum storage density. In addition, oxide coatings are generally soft and are more prone to damaging head crashes.

Thin-Film Media

The competing technology is thin-film magnetic media. As the name implies, a thin-film disk has a microscopically skinny layer of a pure metal, or mixture of metals, mechanically bound to its surface. These thin-films can be applied either by *plating* the platter much the way chrome is applied to automobile bumpers or by *sputtering*, a form of vapor plating in which metal is ejected off a hot electrode in a vacuum and electrically attracted to the disk platter.

Thin-film media hold several special advantages over oxide technology. The thinness of thin-film media allows data to be packed more tightly onto the disk, and that means more megabytes per platter. Tracks and data are closer together, so the read/write head need not move as far between random bytes, fractionally improving disk performance.

One reason that thin-film disks can be so thin and support high-recording densities is that, as with chrome-plated automobile bumpers and faucets, plated and sputtered media require no binders to hold their magnetic layers in place. As with chrome plating, the thin-films on Winchester platters are genuinely hard, many times tougher than oxide coatings.

Because plated platters are harder than most read/write heads, they are less susceptible to some forms of head crashes. Typically, head crashes on oxide-coated platters harm the disk rather than the head—the head actually plows a small furrow in the soft oxide coating, uprooting data along the way. The head merely bounces off most plated media.

Read/Write Heads

The only other moving part in most hard disk drives is the head system. In nearly all drives, one *read/write head* is associated with each side of each platter and flies just above or below its surface. Each of these read/write heads is flexibly connected to a more rigid arm, which supports the flying assembly. Usually several of these arms are linked together to form a single moving (usually pivoting) unit.

Altitude Effects

The height at which the read/write head of a hard disk flies is one factor in determining the ultimate storage capacity of the drive. Magnetic fields spread out with distance, so the farther the head is from the disk the larger the apparent size of the field generated by a flux transition on the disk. Moving the head closer shrinks the apparent size of the flux transitions, allowing them to be packed closer together on the disk surface and increasing the capacity of the disk.

Head Actuator

Each read-write head scans the hard disk for information. Were the head nothing more than that, fixed in position as is the head of a tape recorder, it would only be able to read a narrow section of the disk. The head and the entire assembly to which it is attached must be able to move in order to take advantage of all the recordable area on the hard disk. The mechanism that moves the head assembly is called the *head actuator*. Usually the head assembly is pivoted and is swung across the disk by a special head actuator solenoid or motor.

Modern head actuator designs also help increase hard disk capacity. This increase is achieved by precision. One of the most important limits on the density of data storage in a disk system is the ability of the mechanism to exactly and repeatably locate a specific location on the disk surface that will store a bit of information. The more precise the mechanism, the tighter it can pack data. The better actuators (along with the dimensional stability of the rigid platters themselves) used in the hard disk for a more stable, more precise storage environment that can reliably pack information at a greater density.

Head Actuator Types

The head actuator is part of an electro-mechanical system, which also includes the electronics that control the movement of the head. Two distinct types of electronic systems are commonly used in hard-disk designs, *open-loop actuators* and *closed-loop actuators*. Specific mechanisms are associated with these two design techniques, and the most common realizations of these design techniques are the band-stepper and servo-voice coil actuators for the open and closed-loop systems, respectively.

Whether the "loop" is open or closed merely indicates whether direct feedback about the head position is used in controlling the actuator. An open-loop system gets no direct feedback; it moves the head and hopes that it gets to the right place.

Band-Stepper Actuators

The most common open-loop actuator system is called the *band-stepper actuator*. The band-stepper actuator uses a *stepping motor* to generate the force to move the head, the same mechanism used to move floppy disk heads. A stepping motor is a special direct current motor that turns in discrete increments in response to electrical pulses from the control electronics instead of spinning. The electronics of the band-stepper system send out a given number of pulses and assume the stepper motor rotates that number of steps. The *band* of the band-stepper is simply a thin strip of metal that couples the rotating shaft of the motor to the linear travel of the head. Each pulse from the control electronics thus moves the head across one track of the hard disk. The speed at which this form of actuator can operate is limited by the rate at which pulses can reliably be sent to the motor.

Servo-Voice Coil Actuators

The closed-loop system gets a constant stream of information regarding the head position from the disk, so it always knows exactly where the head is. The system determines the location of the head by constantly reading from a special, dedicated platter—the *servo surface*—in the disk mechanism on which a special pattern that identifies each disk location is written.

The most common of the closed-loop actuator systems uses a voice coil mechanism that operates like the voice coil in a loudspeaker—hence its name, the *servo-voice coil actuator*. A magnetic field is generated in a coil of wire (a solenoid) by the controlling electronics, and this field pulls the head mechanism against the force of a spring. By varying the current in the coil, the head mechanism is drawn farther from its anchoring spring and the head moves across the disk.

The most common form of this actuator connects the voice coil mechanism directly to a pivoting arm which also supports the read/write head above the platter. The varying force of the voice coil swings the head radially in an arc across the platter surface.

Because of its closed-loop nature, the servo-voice coil system need not count out each step to the disk location it needs to travel to. It can quickly move to approximately the correct place, and in milliseconds, fine tune its location based on the servo information.

For better performance, the servo-voice coil system trades off the use of one side of a platter and the need for more complicated control electronics. In general, high-performance hard disks use servo-voice coil actuators. Lower-performance drives use the less-expensive band-stepper arrangement.

Platter Speed Effect

The number of platters inside a hard disk also influences the speed at which data stored on the hard disk can be found. The more platters a given disk drive uses, the greater the probability that one of the heads associated with one of those platters will be above the byte that's being searched for. Of course, the more heads in an assembly, the more massive it will be. This additional mass tends to slow things down, but it can be compensated for with a more powerful actuator.

Hard Disk Vulnerabilities

The strengths of the hard disk also have their down side. For instance, the constant spin of the hard disk platters extracts its own penalty. The spindle motor continuously consumes enough power to preclude the use of most hard disk drives in computers with modest power supplies, such as the paltry 62.5 watts of the IBM PC or the 35 watts of the PCjr.

Head Crashes

The precision mechanism of the hard disk is also vulnerable to environmental damage. Shock can cause the flying hard disk head to impact on the media on the platters. Or contaminants such as dust or air pollution particles on the media surface can strike the head and upset its flight. The head touching and damaging the media may result in a *head crash*, which not only destroys the storage ability of the media in the area struck by the head but also loosens particles of media that can, in turn, cause further head crashing.

Landing Zone

Hard disks are most vulnerable to head crash damage when they are turned off. As soon as you flick the off switch on your computer, the platters of its hard disk must stop spinning, and the airflow that keeps the heads flying stops. Generally, the airflow decreases gradually, and the head slowly progresses downward, eventually landing like an airplane on the disk media.

In truth, however, any head landing is more of a controlled crash and holds the potential for disk damage. Consequently, most hard disks have a dedicated *landing zone* reserved in their media in which no data can be recorded. This landing zone is usually at one edge of the other of the actual data storage area.

Park-and-Lock

Usually a software command is necessary to bring the head to the landing zone and hold it there while the disk spins down. This process is called *head parking*. Some drives are designed so that whenever their power is switched off, the head automatically retracts to the landing zone before the disk spins down. Such drives are termed *automatic head parking*.

Even when the read/write head touches down in the proper landing zone when the power to the disk drive is turned off, potential problems can still arise. An impact or other shock to the system can jar the head out of the landing zone, in the process bouncing it across the vulnerable medium. To guard against such disasters, a growing number of hard disks lock their read/write heads in place at the landing zone when power is removed. This feature is generally termed automatic *park-and-lock*.

Hard Disk Vent

The microinches that the head flies above the disk surface are tiny, indeed, compared to much of the gunk that floats around in the air everywhere but the clean rooms like those in which hard disks are made. A dust particle looks like a boulder on a microinch scale; it looms like a freight train. A flying head bumping into such obstacles may have its otherwise flat trajectory upset with the result of a head crash. To guard against contamination of the platter surface with dust, hair, and other floating gunk, most hard disks keep all their vulnerable parts in a protective chamber. In fact, this need to avoid contamination is why nearly all PC hard disks use non-removable media, sealed out of harm's way.

The disk chamber is not completely air tight. Usually a small vent is designed into the system to allow the air pressure inside the disk drive to adjust to changes in environmental air pressure. Although this air exchange is minimal, a filter in this vent system traps particles before they can enter the drive. Microscopic pollutants, such as corrosive molecules in the air, can seep through the filter, however, potentially damaging the disk surface. Although the influx of such pollutants is small—the hard disk vent does not foster airflow, only pressure equalization—it is best not to operate a hard disk in a polluted environment. You wouldn't want to be there to use it, anyhow.

Removable Media Drives

So-called *removable hard disks* put the hard disk platter (or platters) in a plastic cartridge that can be withdrawn from the disk drive mechanism and separately stored. Other platters can be inserted in the drive and interchanged, much like floppy disks.

Sealing these removable platters from the atmosphere is practically impossible. As a consequence, removable media drive manufacturers often use very tough plated media in their products to make them more resistant to head crash damage. Usually, they suck the air—and, they hope, the contaminants—out of the cartridge before they allow the platters to begin to spin.

In addition, the head actuator of the removable media drive must be toughened up and some means must be found to move the head from a great distance from the platters (so that the platters can be safely removed or inserted into the drive) to a tiny distance (so they can fly the proper distance from the platter). These robust mechanisms are inherently slower than the fastest hard disks, imposing a penalty on the average access times of such products.

To circumvent such difficulties, a new product area puts the entire drive mechanism in a removable cartridge form—motor, platter, head, actuator, and protective chamber are fashioned into one removable unit. Such removable drives have all the security advantages of other removable media devices. In addition, they can be built more like hard disks, with fewer contamination and crash worries and greater speed. Currently, their sole drawback is a higher price.

IBM Disk Formats and Capacity Limits

A combination of the hard disk mechanism, its controller, and the software operating it all dictates the manner in which data is arranged on the platter. Unlike floppy disks, which are often interchanged, hard disks need not fit any particular standard because their media are never at large, always sealed inside the drive mechanism. Because platters cannot be removed from drives (at least safely) they have no need of interchangeability.

The physical layout of the data on disk is thus left to the imagination of the disk's designer. He's not given free reign, however, because of one overriding necessity: compatibility with DOS and the IBM hardware standard. Certain disk parameters must be arbitrarily set at values true compatibility requires.

The most important ramification of these arbitrary design considerations are the limits they put on disk capacity. Understanding these limits—and how to break them—entails an understanding of the disk mechanism, disk geometry, and the inner workings of DOS.

Tracks

No matter the type of magnetic media or style of head actuator used by a disk, the read/write head must stop its lateral motion across the disk whenever it reads or writes data. While it is stationary, the platter spins underneath it. Each time the platter completes one spin, the head traces a full circle across its surface. This circle is called a *track*.

Cylinders

Each head traces out a separate track across its associated platter. Because the combination of all the tracks traced out at a given head actuator position forms the outline of a solid cylinder, this vertical stack of tracks is called a *cylinder*.

Typical PC hard disks have between 312 and 1024 cylinders (or tracks per platter). The number is permanently determined by the number of steps made by the stepper motor or magnetic pattern on the servo surface (which you cannot alter) of the disk having them.

The 1024-Cylinder Limit

For personal computer models up to the first generation of ATs and their compatibles, the maximum possible cylinder count for a hard disk was 1024. This limit was imposed by a number of factors, including DOS and the hard disk controller. Although hard disks with larger cylinder counts might be used in such systems, only the first 1024 cylinders were accessible because neither DOS nor the controller could count higher.

Strictly speaking, the 1024-cylinder maximum does not limit the capacity of hard disks that can be used in PCs. Instead of increasing the cylinder count, drives can be made larger by adding platters and heads. The cylinder limit does, however, restrict the maximum density at which information can be stored on the disk. Higher densities require greater cylinder counts. Increasing data density is one of the primary means of increasing drive capacity because technical progress in magnetic media has progressively increased the possible storage density of information. The 1024-cylinder limit thwarts such efforts at capacity increases.

Although software drivers can compensate for the inability of early versions of DOS (before 3.3) to handle greater cylinder counts, the controllers of all PCs and XTs limit the addressability of cylinders beyond 1024. This hardware limit also applies to ATs and compatibles that use the Western Digital WD1002-series of controllers or those designed to be exactly compatible with them. Starting with the WD1003-series, however, this limit was removed. To take advantage of larger disks with such controllers, you'll still need a driver or more recent version of DOS.

Sectors

Most hard disks systems further divide each track into short arcs termed sectors, usually 17 of them. Sectors are merely marked magnetically (using a low-level format program) and their number is somewhat arbitrary. The sector count varies depending on the interface used for connecting the disk. For instance, when the disk is formatted for 2,7 Run Length Limited recording, 26 cylinders are often used. Enhanced Small Device Interface controllers usually use 34 sectors per disk track.

In the standard hard disk configuration of any DOS or OS/2 version, each hard disk sector holds 512 bytes of data. This sector size is arbitrarily defined. Some software that extends the hard disk capacities accessible by DOS stretches sector size. Typically, the sector size is increased from 512 by a power of two.

The 32-Megabyte Addressing Limit

This sector size indirectly results in a restriction of standard DOS volumes under all versions of DOS before 4.0 to 32 megabytes or less. This limit was imposed not by any physical characteristic of the disk itself but by an arbitrary factor in the design of DOS.

DOS normally divides files into clusters of four sectors. It keeps track of which clusters are part of which file using the *File Allocation Table*. The number of clusters that DOS can address is limited by the overall size of the File Allocation Table and the size of each entry in the table.

In versions of DOS before 3.0, each entry in the File Allocation Table was a byte and a half—that is, 12 bits—allowing a maximum of 4096 clusters to be identified. In these early versions of DOS, clusters were made from eight sectors, totaling 4096 bytes each. Under this scheme, the maximum size for a standard DOS volume would be 16 megabytes.

Starting with DOS Version 3.0, each File Allocation Table entry was allowed to be either 12 or 16 bits, depending on disk capacity. With disks smaller than about 16 megabytes, 12-bit allocation units are used. Larger disks get the 16-bit File Allocation Table entries, permitting a total of 65,536 entries. With the larger number of allocation table entries, cluster size was reduced to four sectors or 2048 bytes.

Not all of those entries are useful, however, because versions of DOS from 3.0 to 3.32 (and, for compatibility reasons, OS/2 version 1.0) limit the size of the File Allocation Table itself to 16,384 entries. That number of entries coupled to the cluster size of four sectors results in the *32-megabyte addressing limit* of DOS. Larger disks are not possible using this scheme because no space is available for recording more than 16,384 File Allocation Table entries.

DOS 4.0 breaks the 32-megabyte limit by allocating the 65,536 bytes to the File Allocation Table. This change alone effectively quadruples the maximum hard disk capacity to 128 megabytes. This limit is also imposed by the 16-bit size of File Allocation Table entries.

Using the standard DOS structure, larger disks may not seem possible. The simple expedient of enlarging the size of a cluster will increase the addressable capacity of a disk, however. Doubling the cluster size doubles the maximum addressable capacity. Even before DOS 4.0, hard disk management programs resorted to this technique to break the 32-megabyte limit. Some such programs worked a bit more deviously and increased the disk sector size from 512 bytes to another arbitrary value. The effect was the same; the size of a cluster was increased.

The problem with this technique is that it can be wasteful. Disk space is divvied up in units of a cluster. No matter how small a file (or a subdirectory, which is simply a special kind of file) may be, it occupies at minimum one cluster of disk space. Larger files take up entire clusters, but any fractional cluster of space that's left over requires another cluster. On average, each file on the disk will waste half a cluster of space. The more files, the more waste. The larger the clusters, the more waste. Unless you work exclusively with massive files, increasing cluster size to increase disk capacity is a technique to avoid whenever possible.

Write Precompensation

The division of each disk track into the same number of sectors, notwithstanding the distance of the track from the spindle, has a dramatic result. Sectors are shorter the closer they are to the spindle, requiring data to be packed into them more tightly and squeezing the magnetic flux reversals on the platter ever closer. The ability of many magnetic media to hold flux transitions falls off as the transitions are packed more tightly; pinched together, they produce a feebler field and induce a lower current in the read/write head.

One way of dealing with this problem is to write on the disk with a stronger magnetic field as the sectors get closer to the spindle. By increasing the current in the read/write head when its writes nearer the center of the disk, the on-disk flux transitions can be made stronger. They can then induce stronger currents in the read/write head when that area of the disk is read.

This process is called *write precompensation* because the increased writing current compensates for the fall-off in disk responses nearer its center at a place logically *before* the information is stored on the disk.

Disk Parameters

Taken together, the number of platters (or heads), the number of cylinders, and the point at which write precompensation begins make up the set of *disk parameters*. These three numbers are required by the disk drive controller to properly operate a disk drive.

In early model computers, such as the IBM XT and early add-on disk subsystems, the disk parameters were permanently encoded into the ROM firmware of the disk controller itself. Using this technique, every controller had to be matched to the disk drive model that it was to operate.

A few aftermarket suppliers had a better idea. They recorded the disk parameters on the disk itself in a place that would be reachable in the same way across many different models of disk drive. As part of the boot-up process, the disk drive would be commanded to read back its identifying information, loading it into the controller. Thereafter, the controller could properly run the drive.

With the IBM AT, a new method of getting disk parameters to the controller was developed. The parameters were stored in the CMOS setup memory of the computer. The controller read the parameters from the CMOS and could then properly run the drive. This same technique is used by the PS/2 series of computers.

ESDI and SCSI drives permit the drive parameters to be embedded in the system. For instance, ESDI drives can record their parameters on the disk itself because the location and means of accessing this information is standardized. (Nevertheless, some computers require knowing the disk parameters of ESDI drives.) Because SCSI is a system level interface, the issue doesn't even arise. The controller electronics are part of the drive and there is no chance of mismatch.

(Table 22.1 lists the essential drive parameters of most of the commonly available hard disks that may be used in ATs and similar computers.)

Disk Performance Issues

The principal variables in hard disks relate to their speed and capacity, and these qualities are directly related to design choices in making the mechanism. The head actuator has the greatest effect on the speed at which data can be retrieved from the disk; the number of platters has a smaller effect. Capacity of the hard disk is influenced by the number of platters, the magnetic material on the platters, and the head assembly.

Average Access Time

Unlike microprocessor performance, disk speed is not a simple issue controlled by one or two variables, nor can it be quantized in discrete levels. For instance, most mortals believe that there are but two levels of hard disk performance: AT-standard and XT-standard. Those specifications are just guidelines. IBM requires that drives for the AT have an *average access time*, which specifies the length of time how long it takes the mechanism to find any random byte of data on the disk be less than 40 milliseconds. An XT-speed drive may take more than twice as long to find the same random byte. (The IBM XT specification for hard disk average access time is 85 milliseconds, although some of the equipment supplied by the company is slower than that.) Actual hard disk access times, however, stretch across a wide continuum, from less than 15 to as long as 150 milliseconds.

Although the often-quoted average access time of a hard disk does in-

Table 22.1 **Parameters for Common Hard Disks**

ATASI

Model Number	Cylinders	Heads	Sectors	Write Precomp	Landing Zone	Capacity
3046	645	7	35	323	644	81
3051	704	7	35	352	703	88
3051 +	733	7	35	368	732	92
3085	1024	8	17	None	1023	71

CDC

Model Number	Cylinders	Heads	Sectors	Write Precomp	Landing Zone	Capacity
9420x-51	989	5	35	0	989	89
9415x-21	697	3	35	0	697	37
9415x-36	697	5	35	0	697	62
9415x-48	925	5	35	0	925	83
9415x-57	925	6	35	0	925	99
9415x-67	925	7	35	0	925	116
9415x-77	925	8	35	0	925	133
9415x-86	925	9	35	0	925	149
94166-101	969	5	34	None	968	84
94166-141	969	7	34	None	968	118
94166-182	969	9	34	None	968	152
94186-442	1412	15	34	None	1411	369
94186-383	1412	13	34	None	1411	320
94186-383H	1224	15	34	None	1223	320
94186-324	1412	11	34	None	1411	270

CMI

Model Number	Cylinders	Heads	Sectors	Write Precomp	Landing Zone	Capacity
CM-6426	615	4	35	300	615	44
CM-6640	615	6	35	300	615	66

FUJITSU

Model Number	Cylinders	Heads	Sectors	Write Precomp	Landing Zone	Capacity
M2241AS	754	4	35	375	754	54
M2242AS	754	7	35	375	754	95
M2243AS	754	11	35	375	754	149

Table 22.1 (continued)

HITACHI

Model Number	Cylinders	Heads	Sectors	Write Precomp	Landing Zone	Capacity
DK511-3	699	5	35	300	699	63
DK511-5	699	7	35	300	699	88
DK511-8	823	10	35	400	822	147
DK521-5	823	6	35	None	822	88

LAPINE

Model Number	Cylinders	Heads	Sectors	Write Precomp	Landing Zone	Capacity
Titan20	615	4	35	None	615	44

MAXTOR

Model Number	Cylinders	Heads	Sectors	Write Precomp	Landing Zone	Capacity
XT1085	1024	8	35	None	1023	147
XT1105	918	11	35	None	1023	181
XT1140	918	15	35	None	1023	247
XT2085	1224	7	35	None	1223	154
XT2140	1224	11	35	None	1223	241
XT2190	1224	15	35	None	1223	329
XT1120	1024	8	26	None	1023	109
XT1240	1024	15	26	None	1023	204
XT4170E	1224	7	35	None	1223	154
XT4380E	1224	15	35	None	1223	329
XT8380E	1632	8	52	None	1631	348
XT8760E	1632	15	52	None	1631	652

MICROPOLIS

Model Number	Cylinders	Heads	Sectors	Write Precomp	Landing Zone	Capacity
1302	830	3	17	None	829	22
1303	830	5	17	None	829	36
1304	830	6	17	None	829	43
13x3	1024	4	35	None	1023	73
13x3A	1024	5	35	None	1023	92
13x4	1024	6	35	None	1023	110
13x4A	1024	7	35	None	1023	128
13x5	1024	8	35	None	1023	147
1556-11	1224	11	35	None	1223	241

Table 22.1 (continued)

MICROPOLIS

Model Number	Cylinders	Heads	Sectors	Write Precomp	Landing Zone	Capacity
1557-12	1224	12	35	None	1223	263
1557-13	1224	13	35	None	1223	285
1558-14	1224	14	35	None	1223	307
1558-15	1224	15	35	None	1223	329
1653-4	1249	4	35	None	1248	90
1653-5	1249	5	35	None	1248	112
1654-6	1249	6	35	None	1248	134
1654-7	1249	7	35	None	1248	157

MICROSCIENCE

Model Number	Cylinders	Heads	Sectors	Write Precomp	Landing Zone	Capacity
HH-325	615	4	35	None	615	44
HH-825	615	4	17	None	615	21
HH-830	615	4	26	None	615	33
HH-1050	1024	5	17	None	1023	45
HH-1060	1024	5	26	None	1023	68
HH-1075	1024	7	17	None	1023	62
HH-1090	1314	7	17	None	1313	80
HH-1095	1024	7	26	None	1023	95
HH-1120	1314	7	26	None	1313	122
HH-2120	1024	7	35	None	1023	128

MINISCRIBE

Model Number	Cylinders	Heads	Sectors	Write Precomp	Landing Zone	Capacity
3425	615	4	17	128	656	21
3438	615	4	26	128	656	33
3650	809	6	17	300	852	42
3675	809	6	26	300	852	65
3053	1024	5	17	512	1023	45
3085	1170	7	17	512	1169	71
3130E	1250	5	35	None	1249	112
3180E	1250	7	35	None	1249	157
6032	1024	3	17	512	1023	27
6053	1024	5	17	512	1023	45
6074	1024	7	17	512	1023	62
6085	1024	8	17	512	1023	71
6128	1024	8	26	512	1023	109

Table 22.1 (continued)

MINISCRIBE

Model Number	Cylinders	Heads	Sectors	Write Precomp	Landing Zone	Capacity
8051A	745	4	28	300	744	43
8425	615	4	17	128	663	21
8438	615	4	26	128	663	33
9230E	1224	9	35	None	1223	197
9380E	1224	15	35	None	1223	329

MITSUBISHI

Model Number	Cylinders	Heads	Sectors	Write Precomp	Landing Zone	Capacity
MR522	612	4	35	300	612	44
MR533	977	3	35	None	976	53
MR535	977	5	35	None	976	88

NEC

Model Number	Cylinders	Heads	Sectors	Write Precomp	Landing Zone	Capacity
D5124	309	4	35	None	664	22
D5126	612	4	35	None	664	44
D5146	615	8	35	None	664	88

NEWBURY

Model Number	Cylinders	Heads	Sectors	Write Precomp	Landing Zone	Capacity
NDR320	615	4	35	None	615	44
NDR340	615	8	35	None	615	88
NDR1085	1024	8	35	None	1023	147
NDR1105	918	11	35	None	1023	181
NDR1140	918	15	35	None	1023	247
NDR2190	1224	15	35	None	1223	329

PTI

Model Number	Cylinders	Heads	Sectors	Write Precomp	Landing Zone	Capacity
PT238R	615	4	26	410	614	33
2PT251R	820	4	26	544	819	44
PT357R	615	6	26	410	614	49

Table 22.1 (continued)

PTI

Model Number	Cylinders	Heads	Sectors	Write Precomp	Landing Zone	Capacity
PT376R	820	6	26	544	819	65
PT4102	820	8	26	544	819	87
PT225	615	4	17	410	614	21
PT234	820	4	17	544	819	29
PT338	615	6	17	410	614	32
PT351	820	6	17	544	819	43
PT468	820	8	17	544	819	57

PRIAM

Model Number	Cylinders	Heads	Sectors	Write Precomp	Landing Zone	Capacity
V130	987	3	35	None	987	53
V150	987	5	35	None	987	88
V170	987	7	35	None	987	124
V185	1166	7	35	None	1165	146
519	1224	15	35	None	1223	329

QUANTUM

Model Number	Cylinders	Heads	Sectors	Write Precomp	Landing Zone	Capacity
Q520	512	4	35	256	512	37
Q530	512	6	35	256	512	55
Q540	512	8	35	256	512	73

RODIME

Model Number	Cylinders	Heads	Sectors	Write Precomp	Landing Zone	Capacity
RO203	321	6	35	132	321	35
RO204	321	8	35	132	321	46
RO202E	640	4	35	0	640	46
RO203E	640	6	35	0	640	69
RO204E	640	8	35	0	640	92
RO3055	872	6	17	650	871	46
RO3065	872	7	17	650	871	53
RO3075R	750	6	26	650	871	60
RO3085R	750	7	26	650	871	70
RO5090	1224	7	17	None	1223	75

Table 22.1 (continued)

RODIME

Model Number	Cylinders	Heads	Sectors	Write Precomp	Landing Zone	Capacity
RO5125E	1224	6	34	None	1223	128
RO5130R	1224	7	26	None	1223	114
RO5180E	1224	8	34	None	1223	170

SEAGATE

Model Number	Cylinders	Heads	Sectors	Write Precomp	Landing Zone	Capacity
ST213	615	2	17	300	615	11
ST225	615	4	17	300	615	21
ST125	615	4	17	None	615	21
ST138	615	6	17	None	615	32
ST412	306	4	17	128	305	11
ST251	820	6	17	None	820	43
ST4026	615	4	17	300	615	21
ST4038	733	5	17	300	733	32
ST4038M	733	5	17	None	977	32
ST4051	977	5	17	None	977	43
ST4053	1024	5	17	None	1023	45
ST4096	1024	9	17	None	1023	80
ST138R	615	4	26	None	615	33
ST157R	615	6	26	None	615	49
ST238R	615	4	26	300	615	33
ST251R	820	4	26	None	820	44
ST277R	820	6	26	None	820	65
ST4077R	977	5	26	None	977	65
ST4144R	1024	9	26	None	1023	123
ST250R	667	4	31	None	667	42

Type 16 — (handwritten, next to ST4051)

TANDON

Model Number	Cylinders	Heads	Sectors	Write Precomp	Landing Zone	Capacity
TM262	615	4	35	None	615	44
TM755	981	5	35	None	981	88
TM362	615	4	35	None	615	44
TM703	695	5	35	None	695	62
TM705	962	5	35	None	962	86
TM702AT	615	4	35	None	615	44
TM703AT	733	5	35	None	733	66

Table 22.1 (continued)

TOSHIBA

Model Number	Cylinders	Heads	Sectors	Write Precomp	Landing Zone	Capacity
MK-53F	830	5	35	512	830	74
MK-54F	830	7	35	512	830	104
MK-56F	830	10	35	512	830	149

TULIN

Model Number	Cylinders	Heads	Sectors	Write Precomp	Landing Zone	Capacity
TL226	640	4	35	None	640	46
TL326	640	4	35	None	640	46
TL240	640	6	35	None	640	69
TL340	640	6	35	None	640	69
TL238	640	4	35	None	640	46
TL258	640	6	35	None	640	69

dicate a general level of performance, such figures do not accurately or completely reflect the response of the disk system in actual use. Average access time is, for the most part, a function of the drive alone, but the hard disks are just part of a complete system that also includes the disk controller and the software that controls the drive.

Moreover, average access time indicates only one aspect of hard-disk speed. Once a byte or record is found on the disk, it must be transferred to the host computer. Another disk system specification, the data transfer rate, reflects how fast bytes are batted back and forth, effectively how quickly information can shuttle between microprocessor and hard disk.

Access time is chiefly determined by mechanical factors in hard-disk design and construction, specifically the type of head actuator and the number of platters used in the disk. The head actuator is the actual moving force that positions the read/write heads over the exact area of the hard disk platter that contains the desired information. The faster the actuator can move the head, the faster an individual record can be located on the disk.

Data Transfer Rate

Other hardware design factors can influence the speed at which information can be moved from a hard disk to the electronics of your computer, however. The ultimate data moving speed is controlled by the data transfer rate of the hard disk subsystem, although other considerations often limit the actual throughput of information to a much lower rate than this data transfer speed.

The primary controlling factor in data transfer rate is the type of interface used in connecting the disk drive to its host computer. Standards organizations recognize several hard disk interfaces and tightly define their interconnection specifications. The old ST506 interface is the slowest currently in use. Although both RLL and Advanced RLL help speed it up, SCSI and ESDI hold greater potential.

But the interface is only part of the data transfer speed issue. Laggardly ST506 worked fine in XTs because it was able to dish out data faster than the host computer could process it. More modern systems turn the tables on ST506, however.

One bottleneck was the 8-bit bus of the XT. Data could be moved to the controller at five megabits per second, but could not get from the controller to the rest of the system at anywhere near that speed. The faster performance of the AT meant that it could accept data faster. The 16-bit interface of the AT disk controller and the AT's 16-bit BIOS mediated transfer abilities boost data throughput substantially over that of the XT and put it more in line with the microprocessor's abilities.

Sector Interleave

Among other things, the low-level format determines the *sector interleave* used by a hard disk, the order in which sectors are arranged on each track. A low-level format program will often ask you for the sector interleave to use in the formatting process.

Sector interleaving is used because data can be written to and read from hard disks faster than most computers can handle it. In effect, sector interleaving is used to slow down the disk so that the computer can catch up.

Sector interleaving works by forcing the disk drive to skip a given number of sectors when DOS tells it to read consecutive sectors. For instance, DOS may instruct the drive to read sectors one and two. The hard disk system reads sector one, then skips the next six sectors, and reads the next one. Because the same number of sectors are skipped during writing and reading, the disk system never gets confused. In fact, when numbers are applied during the low-level format operation, they follow the skipping order so that sequential sector numbers may be several physical sectors apart.

The ratio of the length of a sector to the distance between the start of two logically consecutive sectors is termed the *interleave factor*. Because the length used for measuring interleave is one sector, often only the righthand factor in the ratio is used to describe the interleave. Thus, a disk in which no sectors are skipped would be said to have an interleave factor of 1:1 or simply one. If five sectors are skipped between each one that's used, the interleave factor would be 1:6 or six.

This interleaving helps the computer catch up because after one sector is read, the computer has time to catch its breath before the next burst of data from the next sector is dumped on it. For instance, consider an XT that's equipped with a hard disk with an interleave factor of six. For every six sectors that the disk rotates, only one sector is written or read. Writing or reading a whole track of data, ordinarily comprising 17 sectors, would thus require five spins of the disk. Because each turn of the disk requires 1/60 of a second at 3600 rpm, gleaning a full track takes 8.33 milliseconds, about 1/12 second, all else being equal. Without interleaving, reading the same data would require merely the time its takes the disk to make one full revolution, 1/60 second.

Although on the surface, it appears that interleaving will only degrade performance, it can actually make systems work more quickly because it helps match speeds—at least when the interleave is set optimally.

In practice, however, it often is not. IBM, for instance, was overly conservative in specifying interleave factors for the XT and AT hard disks, specifying six and three respectively. Lower interleaves often speed disk operation, although making the interleave too low can have more detrimental performance effects than making it slightly too large (and hence, probably IBM's conservatism).

The interleave of a hard disk is set during the low level formatting process and cannot be altered without reformatting the disk and thereby erasing all the data it contains.

Track Buffering

A growing number of hard disks use a 1:1 interleave factor, among them most ESDI drives as well as a few older units operated with controllers that incorporate *track buffering*. These controllers read from the disk one entire track at a time, storing all the data in memory, and only sending the sector data requested by DOS along to the host computer.

Cylinder Skewing

Although a 1:1 interleave factor sounds like the most desirable, it is not without its own problems. After the disk drive head finishes reading one track, it must be repositioned slightly to read the next. As with any mechanical movement, repositioning the head requires a slight time. Although brief, this repositioning period is long enough that should the head try to move from the end of one track to the beginning of another, it will get there too late. Consequently, you have to wait while the whole track passes below the head until it is ready to read the beginning of the second track.

This problem is easily solved by the simple expedient of not aligning the starting points of all tracks along the same radial line. By offsetting the beginning of each track slightly from the end of the preceding track, the travel time of the head can be compensated for. Because the beginning of the first sector of each track and cylinder do not line up and are somewhat skewed, this technique is called track skewing or *cylinder skewing*.

Configuring a Hard Disk

Adding a first or second hard disk to any computer system is a task that is inherently simple that manufacturers have gone to great lengths to make confounding.

The first step is to determine whether the system that's to receive the disk transplant is already equipped to handle it. Three needs must be met by any prospective host: enough space of the correct dimensions must be available to hold the disk, the system must be able to provide sufficient power to operate the disk, and the system must have a hard disk controller. None of these three conditions presents an insurmountable obstacle, but you must be prepared to cope with the deficiencies of your system.

Space Considerations

It should be obvious that your drive must fit where you want to put it. It must have a form factor that matches one of the available drive bays in your computer or, if it's smaller, you need an adapter kit to fit it in.

Mounting a hard disk is much the same as installing a floppy. Unlike floppy disk drives, however, hard disks have no controls, knobs, or removable media that require user attention. Consequently, hard disks do not require front panel access and can thus be buried inside your computer without sacrificing anything other than a glance at the drive activity indicator LED on the front of most hard disks.

The issue is moot with early PCs, XTs, and compatibles because all their drive bays have front panel access. Starting with the AT, IBM and compatibles makers began to design internal drive bays aimed specifically at housing hard disks. The AT provides for one and a half 5 1/4-inch form factors' worth of this buried drive space. The half-height internal bay, located below the two floppy disk bays, can also be used for a full-height hard disk by sacrificing the half-height floppy disk bay above it. With that floppy bay vacant, a second hard disk can be normally installed in the bottom righthand bay.

The PS/2 Model 50 (and newer models with the same size chassis) allows one 3 1/2-inch internal hard disk bay; the floor-standing PS/2 computers, such as the Models 60 and 80, incorporate two 5 1/4-inch full-height drive bays.

If you don't have sufficient space inside your computer for disk expansion, two alternative strategies are available to you. You can opt to move the disk drive outside the chassis, in which case your expansion opportunities are essentially unlimited. External drives with capacities up to a gigabyte are available. Alternately, if you have a PC or AT-bus computer you can opt for a *hard disk card*, a small hard disk combined with its own controller that fits into an expansion bus slot instead of a disk drive bay. Both external disks and hard disk cards are discussed below.

Hard Disk Power

Power is a problem with every hard disk—including the tiniest hard card—that's installed in factory issue IBM PCs. The 63.5 watt power supply with which these machines are equipped is marginally able to run the system when it's fully expanded, let alone handle the additional load imposed by a hard disk. A typical hard disk card which draws in the vicinity of 13 watts, will cut the power available in the PC by almost one-quarter. A full-size, high-capacity hard disk can draw 30 watts or more. Then again, some new 3 1/2-inch hard disks draw as little as 3 to 5 watts.

In most cases, trying to operate even a low-power hard disk card in a

63.5 watt PC is marginal and ill-advised. If you want to try to skimp by, the rule of thumb is that an ordinary PC can supply two of the following expansion options: a hard disk card, an internal modem, and full memory expansion. Any additional expansion cards (not counting the floppy disk controller) will further reduce the chances of successfully operating a hard disk card.

The 135-watt power supply of the XT and the larger power supplies of later IBM computers should be able to deal with most hard disks. Most compatible computers are rated at greater than 130 watts because the power deficiencies of the PC became known early, while compatible designs were still on the drawing board. A few compatibles have 100-watt supplies, however, and may not be able to power the largest, fastest hard disks.

In a 63.5 watt PC, hard disk cards with lower power requirements are always the best choice. However, the power requirements specified by most hard disk card vendors tend to be optimistic. Many such vendors list the power requirements of the combined hard disk and controller system as being less than what the manufacturer of the hard disk specifies for that one part of the system alone.

The best strategy is not to try to sneak by because insufficient power inevitably results in the system crashing—irrevocably locking up—either when you first turn it on or unexpectedly any time thereafter. The crash will wipe out all your current work and, should it happen at a particularly inpropitious time, it may scramble the file allocation table of the hard disk and make all the data you have stored inaccessible and unusable.

The best way to avoid such problems is to ensure your system has an adequate power supply. If you have a 63.5 watt PC, replace the power supply with one that has more energy. Or you can opt for an external disk with its own source of power.

Disk Controllers

A hard disk must also electronically match the computer in which it is to be used. For instance, while the controller of an XT can handle a second disk drive, that drive must use the same disk parameters as the first. ATs allow more freedom, but the disk parameters of the drive must be within the range supported by the computer's setup procedure. (Some specialized software lets you sidestep this issue by recording the disk parameters on the disk and reading them into the computer as they are needed.)

If you want to install a hard disk in a PC or XT-compatible computer that has not had a hard disk before, you'll require a hard disk controller as well as a drive. In such a case, you're better off buying a complete drive-and-controller kit so that you do not have to worry about disk parameters. They will either be permanently encoded into the controller ROM or some other provision will be made for them.

The AT and most compatible computers are equipped with combined floppy-and-hard disk controllers. If the computer has a floppy disk drive, you should be able to add a hard disk without the cost of an additional controller. Be careful. A few AT-compatibles don't strictly follow the AT scheme and floppy-only models may require the addition of a hard disk controller.

Micro Channel PS/2s all come with hard disks. For the most part, upgrading them is simply a matter of swapping disks without a worry about the controller, providing the parameters of the new disk are supported by the system.

Changing to a new interface requires a new controller in most computer systems. The latest IBM drives and a growing number of third-party hard disks simplify this matter by embedding the controller on the hard disk itself. For instance, the 60 megabyte ESDI hard disk of the Model 50Z and 70 has an embedded controller. To install it, you remove the old drive and its old controller, and slide the new drive and an adapter card into place.

Once you have your new drive and controller in place, you must attach its cable, setup up your system to accept it, then format the drive.

External Hard Disks

External chassis units were once, and briefly, the only hard disks that you could attach to your PC. They simultaneously solved two problems with the first PC: inadequate space and inadequate power. Another advantage often cited by the manufacturers of these devices is they added no heat to the inside of your PC. The external chassis also allows you to use very large drives—8-inch and larger disks—with your PC.

Complete Subsystems

Where still available, the external chassis hard disk subsystem comprises the disk drive, a case with a built-in power supply, and a host adapter card. Early units packaged the drive controller in the external chassis and used a simple host adapter. More recent units combine the function of host adapter and disk controller into a single printed circuit board that mounts in an expansion slot of your computer.

External Disadvantages

The disadvantages of external mounting are numerous. It is inherently more expensive. All external units require a chassis and a case of some kind, as well as their own power supply, all of which are unnecessary with an internal drive. The costs of these items can increase the price of an external drive by $100 to $500 or more.

Most often external drives are assembled by system houses, companies that buy raw disk drives, controller electronics, and the other hardware needed to make a complete system and put everything together into one "no-hassles" package. While the system integrator is one level removed from the original disk drive manufacturer and adds his own profit to the price you have to pay, the bargain is not necessarily bad. The system integrator not only assembles the complete unit, saving you the trouble, but also the integrator usually tests the finished product, adding one degree of quality control and eliminating a degree of worry.

External drives can be inconvenient, however. In general they take up more of your deskspace sitting next to the already too-large computer chassis. A few don't sacrifice desk space, however. Instead, large, tower-like floor-standing units swallow up floor space. A few small units mount either under your monitor or next to it and thus occupy no additional desktop space at all, providing you jack up your monitor or slide it to one side of the top of your computer.

External Cables

In any case, the external chassis must be connected to your computer by a cable of some kind. The FCC provides a tremendous incentive for manufacturers to make these connecting cables as short as possible; shorter cables are less likely to radiate interference, so getting FCC certification for external drives with shorter cables is easier. But short cables can severely restrict your flexibility in positioning the drive where you want it. You might be forced to put the unit to the left of your computer and have to rearrange you desk around the needs of the disk drive.

Regardless of the length of the cable, it's also one more thing to get in the way. And it's one more thing to go wrong. Connectors are the most troublesome part of any circuit and one of the elements most likely to fail.

On the other hand, external drives can be somewhat easier to install. For the most part, you won't have to deal with nuts, bolts, and screws because the external chassis is usually supplied to you completely assembled. Instead, you only need to plug the host adapter into an expansion slot inside your computer, then link the external chassis and the adapter with the cable supplied by the manufacturer.

External Choice

Choose external mounting when your present computer cannot accommodate the drive that you want to use, either because your system lacks internal expansion room or because you want more capacity than you have any right to hope will fit inside a PC. For those greedy for gigabytes, some suppliers offer disk subsystems with capacities nearing one billion bytes using drives with platters as large as 14 inches in diameter. These humongous drives themselves dwarf a PC chassis, so you have little help of mounting one inside your machine.

Hard Disk Cards

In 1985, the hard disk makers at Quantum Corporation hit upon an idea with so much promise that they created a new company to develop and promote it. The company was Plus Development Corporation; the idea, the *Hardcard*, essentially a hard disk on a standard-size PC expansion card. This all-in-one package eliminated all the hardware worries in installing a hard disk. It required no cables, no bloody knuckles, and no worries about an errant touch on a delicate circuit causing a $100 per hour repair job. In addition, the Hardcard was a perfect fit for systems that had no drive bays available for adding another disk.

The Hardcard

The original Hardcard used a proprietary disk controller and a special low-power, low-profile disk drive, all manufactured by Japan electronics giant Matsushita Industrial Corporation. It was a modest device. Its capacity was 10 megabytes, and its performance only on par with the ordinary XT hard disk. And it was expensive, priced at about three times the level of do-it-yourself hard disk systems of equivalent performance and capacity. Nevertheless, it was enough to prove the viability of the combined hard disk on an expansion board idea, now generally termed the hard disk card.

The worth of a product idea can be best gauged by the number of imitators it spawns and the speed at which it does so. Few developments have swept through the PC industry as quickly as hard disk cards. Dozens of Hardcard imitators appeared within a few months, everything from slick commercial preparation from major suppliers to cobbled-together concoctions from garage-based mail order suppliers.

All were helped along by a stroke of luck just shy of being coincidental. The standard 3 1/2-inch form factor disk package proved just the right size for sideways installation in a PC expansion slot. Prospective hard disk card makers did not have to invest heavily in special compact hard disks to usher their products onto the market.

Hard Disk Card Advantages

Hard disk cards are not just for PCs that lack fast mass storage. They also make an ideal supplement to the meager byte capacity of standard 10-megabyte XT hard disks. Most will also work in ATs and compatible computers, even those based on the 80386 microprocessor. Compared to the standard equipment AT hard disks, however, the little disk cards don't work very well. Few hard disk cards are able to deliver the performance that IBM specifies for AT hard disks (40 milliseconds average access time). In addition, no hard disk card takes advantage of the 16-bit data bus of the AT, thus, hard disk cards can move data to and from a host AT only half as fast as a genuine AT disk. These performance deficiencies are readily perceptible during use.

The PS/2 series is a mixed bag when it comes to hard disk cards. Micro Channel Architecture expansion slots are slimmer than those used by PCs. A 3 1/2-inch hard disk won't fit in such slots. Moreover, the PS/2 muscle machines, Models 50 and up, all come with standard hard disks, a disincentive for prospective creators of hard disk cards for them. To date, no such Micro Channel hard disk cards have been developed.

The low-end PS/2s are a different story. They use conventional size PC slots and most of the machines lack factory-installed hard disks. Moreover, because their two drive bays are designed particularly for small floppy disk drives, the hard disk card provides the only practical and convenient means for upgrading the speed and capacity of these machines. Some PC-style hard disk cards will function in these PS/2s unmodified. In a number of cases, however, manufacturers supply separate hard disk card models for PCs and PS/2s. The differences are mechanical and in some memory assignment. In other words, be certain that product you buy will work with the computer you have.

Hard Disk Card Components

All that is required to make a hard disk card is a small disk drive, a disk controller (usually an expansion board half the length of a PC expansion slot), and some form of sheet metal assembly to hold everything together. With a hand brake and a hacksaw, you could make one in a couple of hours, but your efforts would not be rewarding. Generic hard disk cards are now priced at about the same level as their open market component cost, so you would save nothing by doing it yourself.

All hard disk cards are not created equal, however. Besides the expected differences in speed and capacity characteristic of any hard disk, they also differ in physical size, mounting versatility, and power requirements. Selecting the right hard disk card may actually require more forethought than finding a suitable conventional hard disk.

Hard Disk Card Size

Physical size is perhaps the most perplexing problem. Only one line of hard disk cards is compact enough to fulfill the original aspiration of fitting inside a single PC expansion slot. Only the Plus Development series of Hardcards are slender enough (8/10 of an inch thick) to slide into a single slot, a virtue attributable to the proprietary hard disk subassemblies used by the products.

Other hard disk cards bulge as if they have goiter because the standard 3 1/2-inch form factor hard disk package is almost twice as thick as an expansion slot. Additionally, Plus Development has legally protected its design, making efforts at duplicating the Hardcard style of package financially risky. Consequently, most hard disk cards specify installation in 1 1/2-expansion slots.

The 1 1/2-slot package is designed to be narrow at the end nearest its expansion card retaining bracket and thicker at the far end (near the front of the PC once the card is installed). The thin area is occupied by the disk controller, the fat end by the hard disk itself. This form of packaging allows a "short card," an ordinary PC expansion card five inches long or less, to fit in the slot adjacent to the hard disk card. In the eyes of the hard disk card manufacturers, this package thus requires only 1 1/2-expansion slots.

By hanging the fatter hard disk off the left side of the hard disk card package, some manufacturers also allow a form of single slot installation. You are instructed to move the loudspeaker in your PC from its normal mounting area at the left side of the chassis to a location next to the drive bays. When you installed this style of hard disk card in the left slot in your PC chassis, the wider part of it then spreads into the area formerly occupied by the speaker instead of another expansion slot. Effectively, then, this card only requires a single expansion slot. Note, however, that the extra effort involved in the installation of this sort of product erases the easy installation benefit of the hard disk card. It will actually require more work than installing a conventional hard disk.

Hard Disk Card Power Options

Two different methods are used by hard disk cards to suck electricity from your PC. Many get all the current they need through the bus connector at the bottom of the expansion slot they are installed in. Other hard disk cards require that you run a separate small wiring harness to directly tap into your PC's power supply.

This power option does not affect how much power a hard disk card consumes, but it may influence how conveniently you can install the drive. Because PCs that are equipped with two floppy disk drives have no spare power connectors to devote to a hard disk, hard disk cards that require a special power cable won't have a power source to draw from. In such cases, you'll need a Y cable to provide the necessary power connection. Usually, but not always, such a cable is supplied with hard disk cards that require a direct power tap. You can also make such a cable if you can find a source for the proper connectors. Of course, this additional length of forked cable will also add to the snarl of wires nesting in your PC.

Although opinions differ, the most complex separate power cable style of installation may be the better alternative. It eliminates the need to route a great deal of 12-volt-power through the PC expansion bus, which was not designed to channel current for disk drives. However, the through-the-bus method makes for easier installation and less clutter.

Hard Disk Card As Second Drive

Although a hard disk card makes an excellent choice as the second hard disk drive in a system, such installations are not trouble-free. When you try to install more than one hard disk in a system, particularly with separate hard disk controllers, incompatibilities can arise. For instance, should two disk controllers try to occupy the same memory address, it's likely neither will work properly. Most, but not all, hard disk cards allow you to reassign the base address of their controller-based BIOS extension code. If you're planning on installing a hard disk card as a second drive in your system, be sure that this code can be appropriately reassigned (usually by altering jumpers or DIP switches).

Some hard disk cards allow you to take advantage of the abilities of their controllers to simultaneously operate two hard disks. The hard disk card controllers use the same designs and techniques as freestanding disk controllers because they are essentially ordinary controllers with extra hardware (the disk itself) strapped onto them. If you plan on operating another hard disk with the disk card controller, ensure that the second drive conforms to the standards used by the first. Most use the standard ST-506 interface, although the SCSI interface has appeared on a few models. Most hard disk cards use MFM data coding. A growing number take advantage of RLL to increase capacity.

Hard Disk Cabling

Once you've selected a hard disk (and are sure that it will work with your system), you must physically install it. The most important aspect of the physical installation is properly connecting the various cables that provide the disk drive with its control signals and power and allow data to move between it and your computer.

For proper operation, all standard IBM personal computer hard disks require three separate cable connections: a power cable, a control cable, and a data cable. Both ST506 and ESDI drives use this arrangement. The SCSI interconnection system used by some aftermarket products differs, however, and combines the data and control cables into one.

The purposes of the three standard hard disk cables should be self-explanatory. The power cable supplies the hard disk with its lifeblood of electricity. The control cable enables the host computer to tell the disk drive where to move its head. And the data cable transfers what has been read from the disk to the host computer or sends information to the disk for writing.

The Power Cable

The power cable is the most rudimentary, and the same style of cable and connectors is shared by drives that use any of the three popular interfaces (ST506, ESDI, and SCSI). Generally it consists of four separate wires, two of which are redundant. The wires even follow a standardized color code, although exceptions exist. A red wire carries five volts of direct current for operating the disk drive logic and control circuitry. An orange wire moves the 12 volts that is used to power the disk drive spindle motor. And a black wire (and often a yellow one) provides the return path, the ground, for the other two voltages.

In the PC environment, the disk drive power connector is a standardized white nylon connector with removable pins. The female connector is used as a power input jack on the disk drive. This connector, generally made from translucent white nylon, is molded so that it is inherently polarized and cannot inadvertently be plugged in backwards or upside down.

Both male and female forms of these connectors are designed to have their pins crimped onto the wires to which they are attached using a special crimping tool. Once the pin is crimped onto the wire, it is pushed into the back end of the connector with the wire trailing. Fin-like tabs on the pin then snap positively into the connector shell, effectively locking the pin in place. The pin can be later removed with a special tool that compresses the tabs.

Should you choose to make an extension cable for disk drive power—or make a Y cable to supply power to more devices than your computer's power supply allows for—you should use 18 gauge or heavier wire because of the moderate to high current demands of disk devices.

The Data Cable

In the ST506 and EDSI environment, the hard disk data cable is also quite straightforward. Usually a ribbon cable, it comprises twenty conductors. On the disk drive end, the cable terminates in a female edge connector. To provide the keying that prevents inadvertent reversal, a plastic insert is often placed between the second and third rows of pins in this edge connector, and the mating circuit board edge on the disk drive is slotted between the matching contacts.

Because ribbon cables are polarized and generally marked with a colored leader corresponding to the number one conductor, you should have no problem properly orienting a hard disk data cable even if the plastic key is absent. The colored leader on the edge of the cable that indicates the location of conductor number one always goes to the side of the hard disk contact, the edge of which is closest to the keying slot. (See Figure 22.1.)

The other end of the cable generally features a header connector that slips over the golden pins of a circuit board header. This end of the cable usually is not keyed, although sometimes a header pin is removed and the corresponding hole in the connector is plugged. Usually the circuit board on which the header is mounted is stenciled with a legend identifying a few pin numbers. The keying stripe on the cable is always oriented toward pin one or pin two, away from pins 19 and 20.

Most hard disk controllers provide headers for plugging in two data cables, one for each disk drive that the controller is capable of operating. Usually these headers are labeled as J3 and J4, and the lower number jack is meant for the first hard disk.

Plugging the data cable into the wrong disk drive controller header is not a fatal error. While the disk drive system will not operate properly, no damage is likely to result. Symptoms of this condition include the drive seeming to operate properly, rattling its head around and lighting its activity indicator (because the control cable in the proper position ensures the drive does what it is supposed to do). But error messages will appear on screen because the controller is not receiving data on the pins that it expects to. Moving the cable to the correct header will bring the disk drive to life, barring other problems.

The Control Cable

The signals from the controller that specify what the hard disk drive is supposed to do are relayed through a 34-conductor cable. Much like floppy disk cables, the hard disk control cable is designed to daisy-chain two devices: One end of the cable plugs into the controller, and two connectors are provided for attaching to individual disk drives.

IBM's hard disk daisy-chain scheme is reminiscent of that used by floppy disks, and the hard disk control cable is very similar to the floppy disk control-and-data cable. For instance, both cables have several

Figure 22.1 **ST506 and ESDI cables**

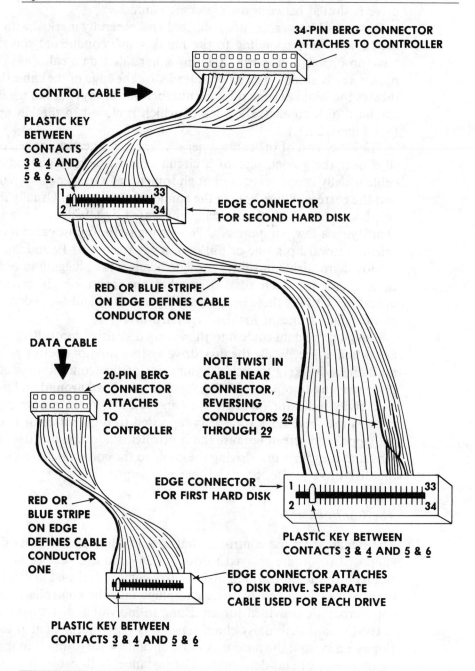

34-PIN BERG CONNECTOR ATTACHES TO CONTROLLER

CONTROL CABLE

PLASTIC KEY BETWEEN CONTACTS 3 & 4 AND 5 & 6.

EDGE CONNECTOR FOR SECOND HARD DISK

RED OR BLUE STRIPE ON EDGE DEFINES CABLE CONDUCTOR ONE

DATA CABLE

20-PIN BERG CONNECTOR ATTACHES TO CONTROLLER

NOTE TWIST IN CABLE NEAR CONNECTOR, REVERSING CONDUCTORS 25 THROUGH 29

EDGE CONNECTOR FOR FIRST HARD DISK

RED OR BLUE STRIPE ON EDGE DEFINES CABLE CONDUCTOR ONE

PLASTIC KEY BETWEEN CONTACTS 3 & 4 AND 5 & 6

EDGE CONNECTOR ATTACHES TO DISK DRIVE. SEPARATE CABLE USED FOR EACH DRIVE

PLASTIC KEY BETWEEN CONTACTS 3 & 4 AND 5 & 6

conductors twisted near the first disk drive connector, that is, the connector that is plugged into what DOS recognizes as drive C:. The connector in the middle of the cable—without the twist—gets plugged into drive D:.

Despite the similarity of the cable twist, hard disk control cables and floppy disk control-and-data cables *are not the same*. Each of these two species of disk drive cables twists different conductors in the ribbon cable. Substituting one for the other will *not* be successful.

If you have a number of loose, uninstalled floppy control-and-data hard disk control cables, to avoid confusion you should plainly identify the nature of each one. One good strategy is to use an indelible ink marker to label the drive connectors with the proper identifying letters: A and B for floppy cables and C and D for hard disk cables. Or mark on the ribbon cable itself "floppy" or "hard disk."

Drive Select Jumpers

Every hard disk must be uniquely definable by the system that it is resident in. While DOS uses drive letters, such as the familiar C:, the drive letter is only a logical identification. The hardware of your system also requires a unique physical identification for each drive. Every hard disk is thus assigned a device number or a *drive select* number, much as floppy disks are. Device numbers generally are selected by jumpers or DIP switches located on the hard disk itself.

No matter the drive letter that DOS assigns to a hard disk, the IBM hard disk scheme requires that each hard disk be set up as the *second* hard disk drive. For hard disks that start numbering with device one, an IBM hard disk must be number two. For hard disks that start numbering with zero, an IBM hard disk must be set as number one.

Both drives in a system are thus set with *the same device number*. The control cable takes care of distinguishing one drive from another. The twist in the cable makes the drive plugged into the connector at the end of the cable appear to the system as the first drive. The other disk, set up as the second drive and connected by a length of cable without a twist, appears exactly as it should, as the second drive.

No hard and fast rule says you must obey the IBM scheme. As long as you know what you're doing, you can use a straight-through or twisted cable. The secret to success is knowing how to set the drive select jumpers on your hard disk for your particular configuration.

To use a straight-through control cable to connect a single hard disk to your IBM standard controller, you must set the drive select jumper on the disk drive to reflect it being the *first* drive in your system. To daisy-chain two hard disks on a single control cable that does not have a twist before the last connector on the cable, set the drive you want to be recognized as C: as the lowest drive select number in your system and the drive to be recognized as D: as the second-lowest drive select.

More Than Two Hard Disks

Most hard disks support drive select values in excess of two. The IBM scheme never uses these settings. Instead, the system favored by IBM and most compatible makers uses separate disk drive controllers for each pair of hard disks. The hard disks attached to each controller are assigned drive select numbers in exactly the same way. With standard IBM cabling (a twist in the control cable near the connector for drive C:), both drives connected to each controller are "jumpered" as the second physical hard disk in the system.

The different drive select numbers assigned to each hard disk, either through jumpers or the cable twist, merely serve to distinguish the two units at the controller. Drive letter assignments are actually issued by DOS.

DOS follows a strict order in assigning drive letters, starting by giving the letter C: to the first hard disk (or other device) it finds in its logical search. This search begins with reading through the system BIOS and then progresses through the device drivers in the system's CONFIG.SYS file.

The BIOS search involves not just the firmware contained in the system or planar board ROM but also the code in add-in peripheral expansion boards including any hard disk controllers. Most disk controllers assign a memory address of C8000(hex) to the start of the code they contain; most also allow you to set an alternate address of D8000(hex). Memory is searched sequentially, so the drives attached to the controller with the lower starting address—C8000(hex) in this case—will be detected first and eventually assigned the first hard disk drive letters. When the controller using memory starting at the D8000(hex) address are found, they will be assigned the next available drive letters, regardless of their drive select settings. Note that when only a single disk controller is present and it is assigned the secondary base address of D8000(hex), it will be the first to be recognized. The drive or drives connected to it will be issue DOS assignments starting with C:.

The general rule is that drive select jumpers (and cable twists) distinguish the hard disks attached to a given controller, and base memory addresses distinguish controllers.

Hard Disk Setup

Once a drive is physically installed and cabled in place, you must let your computer know what you've done. With PCs, XTs, and third-party systems with disk parameters encoded into firmware, you needn't do anything. The firmware sends the proper message to the system and lets it know what's going on. With ATs and later computers, however, you must take positive steps to setup your system for a new hard disk.

AT Drive Types

Starting with the AT (and the XT Model 286), IBM increased your hard disk choices by storing disk configuration information in a different way. Fifteen configurations are built into the hard disk BIOS, and half of a byte of CMOS storage is used as a pointer to indicate which set of parameters are to be used. These configurations are in the same form as disk parameters, and they should match the parameters of the disk you choose to use.

When you run the AT Setup program, you're inserting the proper information for the disk drive you have into this special memory location. Each of the two drives that the standard IBM controller supports can be any of the drive types in the list. Mixing drive types is permitted.

Later IBM computers have expanded the number of different configurations that are predefined in the memory of the controller and has necessarily expanded the CMOS pointer storage to a full byte. The XT Model 286 and PS/2 lines of IBM machines use this byte-size hard disk indicator. These systems, too, allow you to connect two different drive types to a single controller.

IBM is generally consistent about what numbers it assigns to each drive type. The first 15 types used by the AT retain their numbers even in the wider collections available in later machines. The IBM drive number assignments for different hard disk configurations are given in Table 22.2.

While compatible computer manufacturers usually copied IBM for the first 15 drive type choices, many makers went in their own directions for the later extrapolations. Indeed, many began to offer a wider choice of hard disk types even before IBM. (A list of some of these variations is given in Table 22.3.)

AT and PS/2 style systems make adding a second hard disk a breeze. Getting proper control is as simple as typing the proper number during

Table 22.2 **IBM Drive Number Assignments**

AT supports types 1–15
XT Model 286 supports types 1–24
PS/2s support types 1–32

Type	Cylinders	Heads	Write Precomp	Landing Zone	Capacity (Mbytes)
1	306	4	128	305	10
2	615	4	300	615	21
3	615	6	300	615	32
4	940	8	512	940	65
5	940	6	512	940	49
6	615	4	None	615	21
7	462	8	256	511	32
8	733	5	None	733	32
9	900	15	None	901	117
10	820	3	None	820	21
11	855	5	None	855	37
12	855	7	None	855	52
13	306	8	128	319	21
14	733	7	None	733	44
15	0	0	None	0	0
16	612	4	All	663	21
17	977	5	300	977	42
18	977	7	None	977	59
19	1024	7	512	1023	62
20	733	5	300	732	32
21	733	7	300	732	44
22	733	5	300	733	32
23	306	4	None	336	10
24	612	4	305	663	21
25	306	4	None	340	10
26	612	4	None	670	21
27	698	7	300	732	85 [ESDI]
28	976	5	488	977	85 [ESDI]
29	306	4	All	340	10
30	611	4	306	663	42 [ESDI]
31	732	7	300	732	89 [ESDI]
32	1023	5	None	1023	89 [ESDI]

Note: Capacities based on ESDI drive having 34 sectors per cylinder; other drives assumed to have 17 sectors per cylinder. RLL capacities can be higher.

the setup procedure. Of course, not all possible drive parameters are covered in the abbreviated IBM (or other manufacturer) tables. Although IBM does make a provision for the use of such unsupported drives

Table 22.3 **Compatible Manufacturer Drive Number Assignments**

A. Drive number assignments used by Advanced Logic Research, FlexCache 25386 implementation:

Type	Cylinders	Heads	Write Precomp	Landing Zone	Capacity (Mbytes)
1	306	4	128	305	10
2	615	4	300	615	21
3	615	6	300	615	32
4	940	8	512	940	65
5	940	6	512	940	49
6	615	4	None	615	21
7	462	8	256	511	32
8	733	5	None	733	32
9	900	15	None	901	117
10	820	3	None	820	21
11	855	5	None	855	37
12	855	7	None	855	52
13	306	8	128	319	21
14	733	7	None	733	44
15	0	0	None	0	0
16	612	4	0	663	21
17	977	5	300	977	42
18	977	7	None	977	59
19	1024	7	512	1023	60
20	823	10	None	823	137 [EDSI]
21	733	7	300	732	42
22	971	5	None	971	61 [26 sec]
23	820	6	None	820	40
24	-	-	Not used	-	-
25	615	4	0	615	20
26	1024	4	None	1023	34
27	1024	5	None	1023	42
28	1024	8	None	1023	68
29	615	4	612	615	31 [26 Sec]
30	1160	7	None	1160	103 [26 Sec]
31	989	5	128	989	41
32	1020	15	None	1024	127
33	1024	9	None	1024	76
34	966	9	None	966	144 [ESDI]
35	966	8	None	966	128 [ESDI]
36	1024	5	512	1024	42
37	1024	5	None	1024	65 [26 Sec]

Table 22.3 (continued)

A. Drive number assignments used by Advanced Logic Research, FlexCache 25386 implementation:

Type	Cylinders	Heads	Write Precomp	Landing Zone	Capacity (Mbytes)
38	611	16	None	612	300 [63 Sec]
39	925	9	None	925	69
40	615	8	128	664	41
41	917	15	None	918	114
42	1023	15	None	1024	127
43	823	10	512	823	68
44	1024	8	None	1024	104 [26 Sec]
45	1024	8	None	1024	68
46	1024	7	None	1024	91 [26 Sec]
47	966	5	None	966	60 [25 Sec]

B. Drive number assignments used by AST Research, AST Xformer/286 implementation. Note: Types 1-19 conform to those used by IBM.

Type	Cylinders	Heads	Write Precomp	Landing Zone	Capacity (Mbytes)
1	306	4	128	305	10
2	615	4	300	615	21
3	615	6	300	615	32
4	940	8	512	940	65
5	940	6	512	940	49
6	615	4	None	615	21
7	462	8	256	511	32
8	733	5	None	733	32
9	900	15	None	901	117
10	820	3	None	820	21
11	855	5	None	855	37
12	855	7	None	855	52
13	306	8	128	319	21
14	733	7	None	733	44
15	0	0	None	0	0
16	612	4	0	663	21
17	977	5	300	977	42
18	977	7	None	977	59
19	1024	7	512	1024	62
20	733	5	300	733	32
21	733	7	300	733	44
22	782	4	None	782	43

Table 22.3 (continued)

B. Drive number assignments used by AST Research, AST Xformer/286 implementation.
Note: Types 1-19 conform to those used by IBM.

Type	Cylinders	Heads	Write Precomp	Landing Zone	Capacity (Mbytes)
23	805	4	None	805	43
24	907	9	None	908	142
25	968	5	0	969	84 [ESDI]
26	968	7	0	969	118 [ESDI]
27	1023	7	None	1024	125 [ESDI]
28	1223	7	None	1224	149 [ESDI]
29	1223	11	None	1224	234 [ESDI]
30	1223	13	None	1224	279 [ESDI]
31	989	5	0	989	43
32	968	9	0	969	152 [ESDI]
33	1023	5	0	1024	89
34	1223	15	None	1223	317 [ESDI]
35	1024	9	1024	1024	80
36	745	4	None	745	41 [28 Sectors]
37	830	10	None	830	72
38	823	10	256	824	72
39	1631	15	None	1632	576 [ESDI]
40	615	8	128	664	43
41	917	15	None	918	120
42	1023	15	None	1024	134
43	776	8	None	776	105 [33 Sec]
44	820	6	None	820	43
45	1024	8	None	1024	71
46	925	9	None	925	72
47	1024	5	None	1024	45

C. Drive number assignments used by Dell Computer Corporation

Type	Cylinders	Heads	Write Precomp	Landing Zone	Capacity (Mbytes)
0			No drive installed		
1	306	4	17	11	
2	615	4	17	21	
3	615	6	17	32	
4	940	8	17	65	
5	940	6	17	49	

Table 22.3 (continued)

C. Drive number assignments used by Dell Computer Corporation

Type	Cylinders	Heads	Write Precomp	Landing Zone	Capacity (Mbytes)
6	615	4	17	21	
7	462	8	17	32	
8	733	5	17	32	
9	900	15	17	118	
10	820	3	17	21	
11	855	5	17	37	
12	855	7	17	52	
13	306	8	17	21	
14	733	7	17	45	
15			<< Reserved >>		
16	612	4	17	21	
17	977	5	17	43	
18	977	7	17	60	
19	1024	7	17	62	
20	733	5	17	32	
21	733	7	17	45	
22	733	5	17	32	
23	306	4	17	11	
24	830	10	17	72	
25	1024	9	17	80	
26	918	7	17	56	
27	1024	8	17	71	
28	918	11	17	88	
29	1024	4	17	36	
30	820	6	17	43	
31	969	9	34	152	
32	615	8	17	43	

Drive types 33 and higher are reserved.

D. Drive number assignments used by generalized AMI BIOS:*

Type	Cylinders	Heads	Write Precomp	Landing Zone	Capacity (Mbytes)
1	306	4	128	305	10
2	615	4	300	615	21
3	615	6	300	615	32

Table 22.3 (continued)

D. Drive number assignments used by generalized AMI BIOS:*

Type	Cylinders	Heads	Write Precomp	Landing Zone	Capacity (Mbytes)
4	940	8	512	940	65
5	940	6	512	940	49
6	615	4	None	615	21
7	462	8	256	511	32
8	733	5	None	733	32
9	900	15	None	901	117
10	820	3	None	820	21
11	855	5	None	855	37
12	855	7	None	855	52
13	306	8	128	319	21
14	733	7	None	733	44
15	0	0	None	0	0
16	612	4	0	663	21
17	977	5	300	977	42
18	977	7	None	977	59
19	1024	7	512	1023	62
20	733	5	300	732	32
21	733	7	300	732	44
22	733	5	300	733	31
23	306	4	0	336	10
24	925	7	0	925	54
25	925	9	None	925	69
26	754	7	754	754	44
27	754	11	None	754	69
28	699	7	256	699	41
29	823	10	None	823	69
30	918	7	918	918	54
31	1024	11	None	1024	94
32	1024	15	None	1024	128
33	1024	5	1024	1024	43
34	612	2	128	612	10
35	1024	9	None	1024	77
36	1024	8	512	1024	68
37	615	8	128	615	41
38	987	3	987	987	25
39	987	7	987	987	58
40	820	6	820	820	41

Table 22.3 (continued)

D. Drive number assignments used by generalized AMI BIOS:*

Type	Cylinders	Heads	Write Precomp	Landing Zone	Capacity (Mbytes)
41	977	5	977	977	41
42	981	5	981	981	41
43	830	7	512	830	49
44	830	10	None	830	69
45	917	15	None	918	115

*Many machines with BIOS written by American Megatrends use these drive type definitions.

through its AT option 15—parameters unspecified—this option does not support the hard disk as a boot device.

Unsupported Drives

You can work around this lack of support, perhaps with some loss of disk capacity, by matching as closely as possible, telling your system your drive is smaller than it really is. Although wasteful, giving up capacity is generally a better idea than tossing out an entire hard disk.

The secret to using such an unsupported drive is to use the drive type number for a unit with fewer cylinders than the drive you have. For instance, if you have a drive with 1224 cylinders, choose an AT drive type with 1024. The other 200 cylinders will not be accessible on your system (the space will be wasted) but the drive will work.

You can also specify fewer heads than your system actually has, but in such a case you're likely to give up much more capacity to make a match. Do this only as a last resort.

If you're adding a hard disk to a PC or XT class computer that's never before had one, you'll need to get a disk controller to go along with it.

Constant Glow

If you're installing a new hard disk into an AT, you may notice a particular odd occurrence the first time you turn the computer on with the disk inside. The disk activity light on the front of the drive will constantly glow. There is nothing wrong with your system. The constant glow is a result of the IBM AT hard disk design.

All IBM computers with internal hard disk mounting allow for a front panel drive activity indicator. In every case, the signal that controls this indicator is derived from the hard disk controller and not the disk drive itself, so it reflects what the controller tells the drive to do and not what the drive is actually doing. The controller makes the drive think that it is constantly selected and active, causing the constant glow of its light. If a red light inside your computer bothers you, you can often disconnect the LED on the drive or clip one of its leads.

Hard Disk Formatting

A new hard disk is blank. Although its cylinders are predefined, either by the steps of its stepper motor head actuator or by the servo tracks on the servo platter of a voice-coil actuated drive, the sectors that slice up each cylinder and provide convenient pigeonholes for plugging data are nowhere to be seen or sensed. Before data can be written on the disk, the sectors must be defined to serve as markers so that the information can later be found and retrieved.

Low-Level Formatting

The process by which sectors are defined on the hard disk is called *low-level formatting*. Despite its similar name, low-level formatting is completely distinct from DOS formatting. It has nothing to do with the program FORMAT which accompanies DOS, but instead requires separate software.

IBM has chosen to isolate users from the low-level formatting process by supplying all hard disks in its systems already low-level formatted. Anyone who sticks to the official IBM scheme may never have to deal with the process—except when you want to ensure the integrity of the data on your drive by refreshing its magnetic fields every few years.

Compatible computer manufacturers often supply their systems and hard disks without low-level formats. Instead, they usually bundle their systems with a version of MS-DOS, which includes a low-level formatting program with a name such as LLFORMAT or HDPREP.

With IBM, the function that these programs carry out is accomplished by routines included with the Advanced Diagnostics programs that are optionally available for PC and AT systems.

PS/2 Low-Level Format

A low-level formatting program accompanies the machines in the PS/2 series, but is hidden on the Reference diskette. IBM provides instruction for neither using nor even finding the program.

The program is located on the *Reference Diskette* that accompanies each machine. To use the format program, boot up your PS/2 from its Reference Diskette. At the first screen, where you are asked to type Enter to continue, press the Enter key. You should then see the *Main Menu*, which offers you seven menu selections that you can use with the program. Ignore them. Instead, press the Ctrl and letter A keys (Ctrl-A) simultaneously. Your machine will then load its Advanced Diagnostics. You can choose the low-level format routine from its two selection menus.

Third-Party Disk Formatting

Many of the manufacturers of aftermarket hard disk controllers include the necessary program for low-level formatting a hard disk, which is connected to their product in the controller's ROM firmware. These routines are normally executed through the Go command of the DOS DEBUG program. For instance, a number of these routines are accessed by typing the following instruction at the DEBUG hyphen prompt:

```
G=C800:5
```

If you try this with your controller and it doesn't work, you'll likely lock up your system. If it works, you'll be prompted on the screen. The built-in low-level formatting rountines of some vary a few bytes in position in their add-in BIOSs. You may want to try starting execution at C800:6 or C800:8 if the first example does not work. Other than locking up your computer, you won't do any damage to anything. In particular, you won't hurt any data on a new hard disk because there's nothing there to begin with!

Bad Sectors

In the manufacture of hard disk platters, defects occasionally occur in the magnetic medium. These defects will not properly record data. Sectors in which these defects occur are called *bad sectors*; the tracks containing the sectors are called *bad tracks*.

Your computer can deal with bad sectors by locking them out of normal use. During the low-level formatting process, the sectors that do not work properly are recorded and your system is prevented from using them. The only ill effect of reserving these bad sectors is that the available capacity of your hard disk may diminish by a small amount.

Some low-level formatting programs require that you enter bad sector data before you begin the formatting process. Although this seems redundant (the format program will check for them anyhow) it's not. Factory checks for bad sectors are more rigorous than the format routine. This close scrutiny helps minimize future failure. Tedious as it is, you should enter the bad sector data when the low level format program calls for it. The listing of bad sectors is usually on a sheet of paper accompanying the disk drive or on a lable affixed to the drive itself.

Track 0 Bad

The only time a bad sector is detrimental is when it occurs on the first track of the disk. The first track, *Track 0*, is used to hold partition and booting data. This information must be located on the first track of the disk. If it cannot be written there, the disk won't work.

Should you get a hard disk with Track 0 bad, return it to the dealer from whom you bought it. If you reformat a disk after a head crash and discover Track 0 bad during the format process, you need a new disk.

Partitioning

Once the low-level format is in place on a hard disk, you must partition it. Partitioning is a function of the operating system. It sets up the logical structure of the hard disk to a form that is compatible with the operating system.

The IBM program for partitioning is called FDISK. After low-level formatting your disk, you must run FDISK before you can do anything else with the disk using the DOS (or OS/2) operating system.

DOS Formatting

The final step in preparing a disk for use is formatting it with the operating system you intend to use.

Note that IBM operating systems are backwardly compatible but not forwardly compatible. If you format a hard disk under DOS 3.3, you may not be able to use it under DOS 2.1. You will either get an error message or see strange things on your screen, such as file names consisting of odd combinations of numbers and smiling faces. Never write to a hard disk using a version of DOS from a previous generation to the format that's on the disk. If you do, the disk will be irreparably damaged.

23

TAPE

T ape was the first magnetic mass storage system, harking back to the last days of World War II. Although first used for voice and music, tape soon invaded the computer world, first as a convenient alternative to punched cards and punched paper tape, the primary storage system used by mainframe computers. Later, information transfer became an important use for tape. Databases could be moved between systems as easily as carting around one or more spools of tape. After magnetic disks assumed the lead in primary storage, tape systems were adapted to backing them up.

Personal computers have benefited from the evolution of tape in the mainframe environment. Never considered as primary storage—except in the nightmare of the original designers of the first PC, who thoughtfully included a cassette port on the machine for its millions of users to ignore—tape started life in the PC workplace as a backup medium. Only in exceptional circumstance is tape used as an interchange medium. For years, that application has seemed near fruition, but it has yet to catch on.

Tape Design

As a physical entity, tape is both straightforward and esoteric. It's straightforward in design, providing the perfect sequential medium: a long, thin ribbon that can hold orderly sequences of information. The esoteric part involves the materials used in its construction.

Tape consists of two essential layers, the *backing* and the *coating*. The backing provides the support strength needed to hold the tape together while it's flung back-and-forth across the transport. Progress in the quality of the backing material has mirrored developments in the plastics industry. The first tape was based on paper. Shortly after the introduction of commercial tape recorders at the beginning of the 1950's, cellulose acetate (the same plastic used in safety film in photography for three decades previously) was adopted. The state of the art plastic is polyester, of double-knit leisure suit fame.

Coatings also have evolved over the decades, as they have for all magnetic media. Although most tapes are coated with doped magnetic oxides, coatings of pure metal particles in binders and and even vapor-plated metal films have been used for tape.

Media Matching

While all magnetic media must be matched with the transports they are used on for optimal operation, matching is more critical with tape because it is by its nature a removable medium. Removability brings with it the chance of media mismatches, that the wrong kind of tape will be used with a particular device. Much as metal tape won't sound very good when used in a stereo is not "metal ready," the wrong tape in a data system can result in an unacceptably high error rate. In particular, some tape will not support high-density recording. If you value your data, do not attempt to use a tape not certified for the data density that your system uses.

Three major types of tape systems (as well as a few out-of-the-mainstream technologies) are sometimes used in personal computer systems, all of which were originally designed for other purposes. These include open-reel tape, cassettes, and data cartridges.

Open-Reel Tape

The classic computer tape medium uses individual tape spools termed *open-reel tape* because the spools are not kept inside protective shells, as are other computer tape formats. All of the Big-Brother-style computer films of the Fifties and early Sixties used the jerky, back-and-forth movement of big open reel tape transports, which are a symbol of the vast computer power of the age. At the time, the big reels of tape were the primary storage systems of those computers, and the back-and-forth rocking of the tape was the machine's quest to find a given record. As you can imagine, put to such purposes, the average access time of the tapes was measured in seconds and could stretch for an eternity, particularly when the right tape was not mounted on the transport.

Nine-Track Tape

From a diversity of formats, one standard quickly evolved in open-reel tape. The tape, nominally one-half inch wide, is split into nine parallel tracks, each running the full length of the tape. One track is used for each bit of a byte of data, the ninth track containing parity-checking information. Every byte is recorded in parallel, a lateral slice across the tape. Because of these physical characteristics of the medium, open-reel tape is often termed *half-inch* or *nine-track* tape.

Individual reels of tape can be of almost any diameter larger than the three-inch central hole. The most common sizes are 7 and 10 1/2 inches in diameter. Tape lengths vary with reel size and with the thickness of the tape itself. A 10-inch spool holds 2500 to 3600 feet of tape.

Storage Density

As open-reel technology has evolved, the distance between each byte has been gradually reduced, packing an increasing amount of information on every inch of tape. Originally, open-reel tapes were recorded using FM signals, packing 800 bytes on every linear inch of the tape. Advancing to MFM doubled the capacity to 1600 bpi. This density is now the most common in open-reel tape. More exotic transports push data densities up to 3200 or even 6250 bpi.

Inter-Block Gap

Data are recorded on open-reel tape in distinct blocks, each separated by a stretch of blank tape called the *inter-block gap*. The length of this gap can vary from a fraction of an inch to several inches, depending on the characteristics of the overall system (involving such factors as how quickly the host computer can send and receive information from the tape subsystem). Together, the tape length, data density, and inter-block gap determine the capacity of a single reel of tape. The common 1600 bpi density and a reasonable inter-block gap can put about 40 megabytes on a 10-inch reel.

Open-Reel Disadvantages

Although once considered great, that 40 megabytes isn't much by today's PC storage standards. It takes very large reels to pack a workable amount of information. And that's the chief disadvantage of open-reel tape. Tape reels are big and clumsy, and the drives match. When a single reel is more than 10 inches across, fitting a drive to handle it inside a 5 1/4-inch drive is more than difficult. Ten-inch reels themselves are massive, and spinning (and stopping) them requires a great deal of torque, which means large, powerful motors—again something incompatible with the compact necessities of the PC. In fact, most open-reel tape transports dwarf the typical PC. Some look more like small refrigerators.

Open-reel drives also tend to be expensive because they are essentially low-volume yet precision machinery. Even the least expensive open-reel system costs more than a good, high-speed PC: $3000 and up.

Open-Reel Advantages

On the positive side, age and mass can be virtues when it comes to system and data integrity. Because of the low density used in recording, each flux transition on an open reel tape involves a greater number of oxide particles, making it potentially more resistant to degradation (all other oxide characteristics being equal). The big, heavyweight drives are generally sturdy, designed for industrial use, and should last nearly forever when attached to a PC.

As a backup system alone, open reel tape is not much of a bargain, however. Other tape systems, particularly the various cartridge formats, are less expensive and—according to their design specifications—as reliable or even more reliable. For most people, cartridges are also easier to use.

Open-reel tape excels as a data-interchange medium, however. Almost any 1600 bpi tape is readable on almost any open-reel transport. Although block lengths and inter-block gaps may vary, these differences are relatively easy to compensate for. Consequently, open-reel remains the medium of choice for shifting information between mainframe and minicomputers. For instance, most mailing lists are delivered on open-reel tapes. The Internal Revenue Service has allowed corporations to file their taxes on open-reel tapes. An open-reel transport opens this world to the personal computer, allowing the interchange of megabytes of information with virtually any other system. Although most open-reel systems for PCs concentrate on the interchangeability of the tapes, they also include provisions for making open-reel backups. Think of the back-up ability as a bonus rather than the reason for buying an open-reel system.

3480 Cartridges

Operators of mainframe computers endured the inconveniences of open-reel tape for more than 20 years before an accepted successor appeared on the scene. A new tape system that is essentially a cross between cartridges and open-reel is replacing old-fashioned open-reel tapes in its role of backup storage. Because of its newness, however, the system has not yet proven a successor to open-reel tape as an interchange medium.

Termed *3480* after the model number of the first IBM machine that used the new media, the system is based on cartridges that are little more than open-reel tapes stuffed into a protective shell. The tape is still half an inch wide, and it runs through the drive much like open-reel tapes. The drive mechanism pulls the tape out of the cartridge, winds it onto a tape-up spool, shuttles it back and forth to find and write data, and rewinds it back into the cartridge when it is done. In effect, the cartridge is little more than an all-enclosing reel that doesn't itself rotate.

The 3480 system holds a bigger advantage over open-reel than just convenience in mounting tapes, however. The upgrade to 3480 also brings double the number of tracks, and IBM promises more doubling in the future. In IBM's current implementation, these eighteen tracks are written in two parallel sets of nine tracks simultaneously, which doubles the data transfer speed and throughput of the system. In addition, the recording density is higher than open-reel tapes, increasing both capacity and the data speed of the system. The result of this redesign is that a cartridge with less than a quarter of the volume of an open-reel tape (3480 cartridges measure 4 1/4 × 4 1/4 × 3/4 inches) can hold hundreds of megabytes.

The price of these innovations is the price. All 3480 tape transports that are currently available are big ticket ($20,000-plus) products designed for the mainframe market.

Several companies are working at adapting the 3480-style cartridge into systems that would be practical (and affordable) for PC applications. However, these new 3480-style cartridge systems use different data formats than the true IBM 3480 tape drive, chiefly to cut price tags down to size. Although effective repositories for multiple hundreds of megabytes, tapes that veer away from the IBM 3480 standard lack the big advantage of open-reel tape: its ability to exchange information with mainframes. Although not currently available as products to attach to your PC, prices of systems designed to use 3480 cartridges are expected to be in the $1000 to $2000 range.

Cassette Tape

Introduced originally as a dictation medium, cassettes grew both up and down: up into a stereophonic music recording medium that spawned a market for equipment sometimes costing thousands of dollars and down into the realm of cheap, portable recorders costing $10 to $20. These low-end machines represent the cheapest way to magnetically record any information created. The low prices and ready accessibility made cassettes the choice of early computer hobbyists for recording data and pushed cassettes into the commercial market as a distribution medium for computer software, mostly for inexpensive home-style computers.

When the PC was first brought to market, the cassette was a viable storage alternative, at least among the home computer and computer hobbyists markets. Consequently, IBM elected to build a port for attaching a cassette machine into every PC. Little more than a year later, the PC had established its business purpose and the incongruence of that application and cassette technology. The cassette port was dropped from the XT and all subsequent IBM computers. Even the home-oriented PCjr lacked one. Among PCs, the cassette as a primary data storage device is mostly of historical interest only.

In the last few years, the cassette mechanism has proven a compelling platform, however. Teac developed a new, high-speed cassette transport aimed particularly at data storage. It abandoned the audio cassette standard used by earlier systems and pegged its performance on par with higher priced cartridge-based backup systems. These data-only cassettes now represent a viable secondary storage technology.

The Cassette Mechanism

Developed and patented by the Dutch Philips company, the audio cassette was just one of many attempts to sidestep the biggest complaint against open-reel tape systems: The tapes were difficult to handle and hard to thread through the recording mechanism. The idea did not originate with Philips. An earlier attempt by RCA which used a similar but larger cassette package failed ignobly in the marketplace. The Compact Cassette, as it was labeled by Philips, was successful because it was more convenient and did not aspire so high. It was not designed as a high-fidelity medium, but grew into that market as technology improved its modest quality. While the RCA cartridge was about the size of a thin book, the Compact Cassette fit into a shirt pocket and was quite at home when it was on the go in portable equipment. Size and convenience led to its adoption as the autosound medium of choice, then the general high-fidelity medium of choice. Even before the introduction of the Compact Disc, cassettes had earned the majority of the music market.

The basic cassette mechanism simply takes the two spools of the open-reel tape transport and puts them inside a plastic shell. The shell protects the tape, because the tape is always attached to both spools, eliminating the need for threading.

The sides of the cassette shell serve the purpose of the side of the tape reel—holding the tape in place so that the center of the spool doesn't pop out. This function is augmented by a pair of Teflon slip sheets, one on each side of the tape inside the shell, that help to eliminate the friction of the tape against the shell. A clear plastic window in either side of the shell lets you take a look at how much tape is on either spool and how much is left to record on or play back.

The reels inside the cassette themselves are merely hubs that the tape can wrap around. A small clip that forms part of the perimeter of the hub holds the end of the tape to the hub. At various points around the inside of the shell, guides are provided to assure the tape travels in the correct path.

The shell is thickened at the edge that is open to allow the record/playback head and the drive puck to be inserted against the tape.

Write-Protection

The cassette also incorporates protection against accidental erasure of valuable music or information. On the rear edge of the cassette, away from where the head inserts, are a pair of plastic tabs protecting hole-like depressions in the shell. A finger from the cassette transport attempts to push its way into this hole. If it succeeds, it registers that the cassette is write-protected. Breaking off one of these tabs therefore protects the cassette from accidental erasure. To restore recordability, the hole only needs to be covered up. Cellophane or masking tape—even a

Band-Aid or file folder label—works for that purpose. There are two such tabs, one to protect each side of the tape. The tab in the upper left protects the top side of the cassette. (Turn the cassette over and the other side becomes the top—and the tab for the other side appears in the upper left.)

Audio Tape Types

More recent audio cassettes may have additional notches on the rear edge to indicate to automatic sensing cassette decks the type of tape that's inside the cassette shell. Audio tape comes in four varieties which require different settings on the cassette recording for optimal operation.

For recording computer data, the type of tape you use doesn't make much difference as long as it is a kind your cassette recorder can handle. Most computer applications use simple battery-operated recorders in which cheap Type I cassettes operate best.

High Speed Tapes

Teac's high-speed cassette system requires special cassettes designed to match its magnetic and mechanical requirements. These cassettes are uniquely marked by a deep notch near the center of their backbone. The high-speed machines will not accept ordinary cassettes that lack this notch.

Cassette Formats

The original Philips specification for Compact Cassettes allowed for both monophonic and stereophonic tapes, each having two sides. Monophonic tapes used two tracks, one for each direction. Stereophonic tapes use four tracks, two in each direction. The track arrangement puts the two stereo tracks for a specific direction in the same space used by a single monophonic track in the same direction, allowing stereo tapes to be played back on a mono machine (and vice versa). Four-track open-reel audio systems did not provide this facility.

Computer data is recorded on cassette tape as a modulated audio signal, much like that made by a modem. Because the data flow on the tape serially, only one channel is necessary. A monophonic recorder (i.e., the cheap portable unit) suffices nicely. You can actually use a stereo cassette recorder for the job by ganging together the right and left channels as you record. The resulting tapes will also be readable on monophonic machines. If you should fill up one side of a cassette with data, you can simply flip it over and use the other side.

The Teac system uses two tracks for recording in both directions. However, the mechanism is bidirectional and automatically uses both sides. You cannot flip over a tape in the Teac system. In fact, the asymmetrical placement of the identifying notch absolutely precludes the use of the wrong side of a tape.

Audio-Data Cassette Systems

The first PC made a floppy disk drive (and a single-sided, 160K unit at that) entirely optional. Without one, the only mass storage available to the PC was a cassette drive.

The software required for using a cassette system is built into the ROM-based DOS that's part of every PC. Cassettes could thus be used without DOS or any other program. Turn on an original PC without a DOS disk in its floppy drive, and the system boots up in BASIC, ready to read and write to the cassette.

The only things you have to add are the cassette deck and a connecting cable, neither of which is available from IBM.

The cassette deck is the easy part. Almost any remote controllable cassette drive will work. Battery-powered portables are most easily adapted.

The only remote control facility that's required is a motor on/off switch. Most portable cassette decks provide this facility as a small jack on the machine, usually appropriately labeled as "Remote." The cheap external microphones most often used with these units often include a switch that closes these contacts to allow you to control the cassette recorder from the microphone. The PC duplicates the function of this switch, switching on the cassette drive motor as it is needed to copy files to tape.

Note that the computer has only this on/off power. It cannot change the operating mode of the cassette. You must punch it into play and have the tape threaded before the place you want to use before you give the computer control.

The cassette recorder also requires a signal connection with your PC—actually, two of them: one for the output from the computer to be recorded, and one from the recorder to the computer so that tapes can be read back. The recorder-to-PC connection simply plugs into the recorder's headphone jack. The PC-to-recorder signal often gives you a choice of two connections: the Mic or microphone input (nominally 75 millivolts) or a line-level input (nominally 680 millivolts). The difference between these two is critical. A line-level signal will overload a microphone input causing distortion and errors in the data stream. A microphone connected to a line input is not powerful enough to effect a good recording.

The Cassette Output Level Jumper

IBM allows for both types of cassette inputs. A jumper on the system board selects the output level of the signal bound for the cassette recorder through the jack on the rear panel of the PC. You only need to adjust this jumper to reflect the sort of cassette input you want to use. For microphone inputs, use the "M" position (for Microphone), which bridges the two jumper pins on the left. For high level inputs, use the "A" position (for Auxiliary) by moving the jumper to the pair of pins on the right. (See Figure 23.1.) If one setting doesn't work, try the other.

The required cable is available from Radio Shack. It's the same as those used by the Tandy Model 100-200 line and a number of other Tandy computers. Or you can make your own cable, as shown in Figure 23.2. Data from the computer to the cassette recorder travels on Pin 4; from the cassette to the computer, it uses Pin 5. Pins 1 and 3 provide a normally open relay circuit to control the cassette motor—the relay closes to complete the circuit and run the cassette motor. This contact is rated at 1 amp, 6 volts, and Pin 3 is considered the switched contact. Pin 2 is grounded.

High Speed Cassette Connections

The Teac high-speed cassette backup system requires its own dedicated interface and its own host adapter.

Cartridge Tape

The quarter-inch tape cartridge appears to be based on the same principles as the cassette: Put two reels in an easy-to-handle plastic box. But in function, operation, and construction, the two ideas are very dissimilar. The quarter-inch tape cartridge was invented by and patented in 1971 by Robert von Behren of the 3M Company.

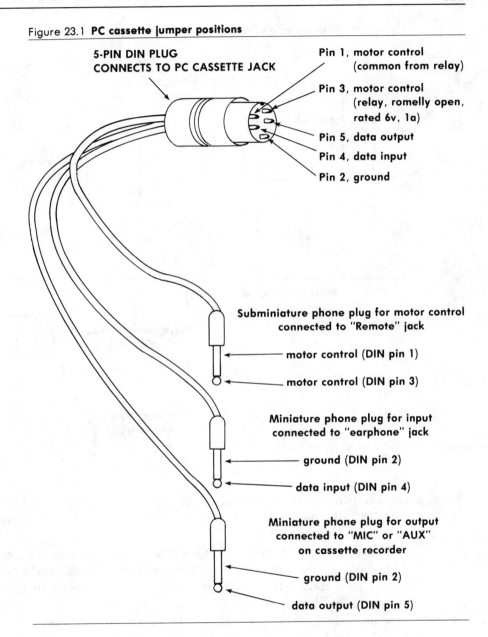

Figure 23.1 **PC cassette jumper positions**

The Quarter-Inch Cartridge Mechanism

Instead of using the capstan drive system like cassettes, the quarter-inch cartridge operates with a belt drive system. A thin, isoelastic belt stretches throughout the cartridge mechanism, looping around and making

Figure 23.2 **PC-to-cassette cable**

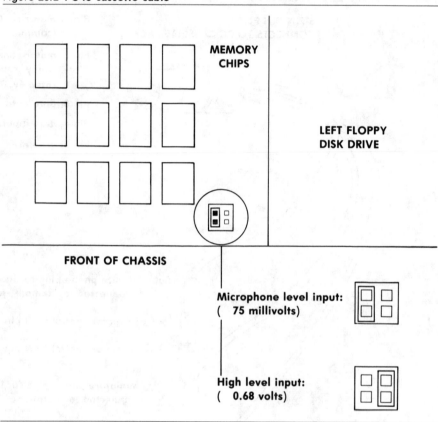

contact with both the supply and takeup spools on their outer perimeters. The belt also passes around a rubber drive wheel, which contacts a capstan in the tape drive.

The capstan moves the belt but is cut away with a recess that keeps it away from touching the tape. The friction of the belt against the outside of the tape reels drives the tape. This system is gentler to the tape because the driving pressure is spread evenly over a large area of the tape instead of pinching the tape tightly between two rollers. In addition, it provides for smoother tape travel and packing of the tape on the spools. The tape is wound and the guide and other parts of the mechanism arranged so that the fragile magnetic surface of the tape touches nothing but the read/write head. (See Figure 23.3.)

Figure 23.3 **Quarter-inch cartridge mechanism (DC-600 style cartridge shown, DC2000 similar but smaller)**

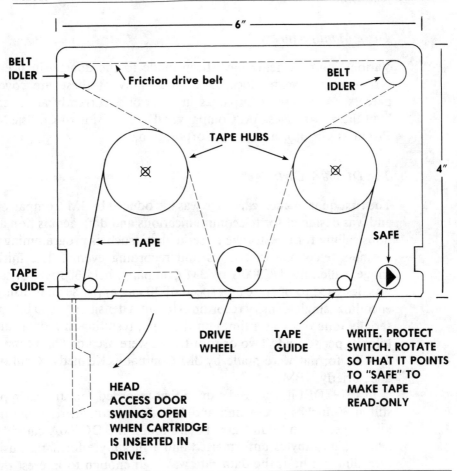

For sturdiness, the cartridge is built around an aluminum baseplate. The rest of the cartridge is transparent plastic, allowing the condition of the tape and the mechanism to be readily viewed.

The essence of the design is that the cartridge itself acts as the tape drive. It contains the tape guides, the tape, and the tape moving mechanism. While this means that the data cartridge is somewhat more expensive to make, drives are less expensive because they essentially need only a motor and a head. The design also ensure the best possible consistency of alignment of the tape and minimizes the need for adjustments to the drive.

Three Manufacturers

Various improvements have been made to the quarter-inch cartridge system in the years since 1971, and many of these are covered by patents. Only three companies in the world currently are licensed to built these cartridges: 3M Company, DEI (a division of Carlisle Memory Products Group), and Sony Corporation.

The DC300A Cartridge

The first quarter-inch cartridge was introduced by 3M Company in 1972 and was designed for telecommunications and data acquisition applications calling for the storage of serial data, such as programming private business telephone exchanges and recording events. The initial cartridge, called the DC300A by 3M Company, held 300 feet of tape and was designed to operate at a speed of 30 inches per second, using phase encoding (single-density recording) to put a density of 1600 bits per inch serially (one track at a time) on the tape, resulting in a data rate of 48 kilobits per second. Two or four tracks were used one at a time. Drives for this format were made by 3M Company, Kennedy, Qantax, DEI, and, briefly, IBM.

In 1979, DEI introduced a drive that recorded four tracks in parallel, still at 30 inches per second and 1600 bits per inch, resulting in a 192 kilobit per second data rate. Even though the DC300A cartridge only held 1.8 megabytes unformatted and 1 megabyte formatted using this recording method, the data rate was high enough to interest the computer industry.

A year later, another four-track drive for the DC300A cartridge was introduced. The capacity of the system was increased to about 15 megabytes by shifting to MFM recording and a data density of 6400 bits per inch. Although the 192-kilobit-per-second transfer rate and 30 inch per second speed were maintained, data was transferred serially, one track at a time, in start-stop mode. In 1988, this drive was still in production, although it was no longer used in mass market PC products which were being superseded in those applications by higher capacity systems.

Start-Stop Tape

All of these original drives operated in *start-stop* mode. That is, they handled data one block at a time, and wrote it to tape as it was received. Between blocks of data, the drive would stop moving the tape and await the next block.

Streaming Tape

In 1981, DEI and Archive introduced the first quarter-inch cartridge *streaming tape* drives. These products were capable of accepting data and writing it to tape continuously without needing to stop. Because the tape did not have to stop between blocks, the system could accept data faster. It also lowered the cost of the drive because it did not have to accelerate the tape quickly or brake the motion of the tape spools so a lighter weight mechanism could be used. The first streamers were still four-track drives, however, and they benefited from the introduction of 450 foot cartridges, the *DC300XL*.

The DC600 Cartridge

Since then, tape lengths have again been increased to a now-standard 600 feet in a cartridge designated DC600. Current implementations of cartridge technology using cartridges the same size and shape as the 3M originals are now generally termed DC600 systems. Cartridge lengths of 1000 feet were expected by the end of 1988.

The Quarter-Inch Compatibility Committee

In 1982 a number of tape drive manufacturers including DEI, Archive, Cipher Data, and Tandberg met together at the National Computer Conference in Houston and formed a working group to develop standards so that a uniform class of products could be introduced. The group took the name Quarter-Inch Compatibility (sometimes rendered as Quarter-Inch Cartridge) or QIC committee.

The QIC committee was formed primarily of drive manufacturers who do not sell directly to the PC market, and initially concerned itself with physical standardization. Data formats were left for system integrators to develop—and, in general, each one designed his own. With time, the committee has developed into a trade association and it recognized the need for format standardization, too. Today, it promulgates standards at all levels of the application of tape.

The first standard developed by the committee to reach the marketplace in a commercial product was *QIC-02*, a 9-track version of a DC300 tape drive. The first units were shipped in 1983.

As of 1988, quarter-inch cartridge standards specified up to 32 tracks recorded at 12,500 flux transitions per inch, using a drive that operates at 120 inches per second. Standards allowing for both 300 and 600 megabyte systems have already been developed, and products using them were expected in 1988.

DC600-Style Cartridges

The most popular of today's machines that use cartridges based on the original 3M design stream tape at 90 inches per second and can cram 60 or 120 megabytes on nine tracks onto the 600 feet of oxide-coated film in each DC600 cartridge.

Serpentine Recording

In most current implementation of these DC600-based systems, information is written individually and serially to the nine tracks across the width of the tape. These systems course through the various tracks using a method called *serpentine recording*. The data bits are written sequentially, in one direction, on one track at a time, continuing for the length of the tape. When the end of the tape is reached, the direction of its travel is reversed, and the read/write head cogs down one step to the next track. At the end of that pass, the process is repeated until all nine tracks are filled.

DC600 Advantages

One of the biggest advantages of DC600-style cartridge systems is that they are fast. With data transfer rates identical to those of most PC hard disks—5 MHz—the fastest commercial DC600 systems backup throughput of over 3 megabytes per minute when installed in high performance computers of the AT class or better.

DC600 Manufacturers

A number of companies manufacture DC600-style drives, including Archive, Cipher, Kennedy, Tandberg, and Wangtek. Nearly every major system integrator selling into the PC market offers a system based on one of these drives. In 1988, the lengthy list of suppliers includes Alloy, AST Research, Core International, Emerald Systems, Emulex, Micro Design International, Mountain Computer, Sysgen, Tallgrass Technologies, and Tecmar.

The price of these DC600 systems varies with how and from whom you buy. Mail order units are regularly available in the $600 to $800 range. Complete name brand systems may cost upwards of $1500.

DC600 Compatibility

If DC600 systems have a problem, it is compatibility. Until recently, cartridges written on one manufacturer's DC600-based system could not be read on a system sold by another manufacturer.

Although the drives from different manufacturers vary in how they load the cartridges—some require you twist a lever, others you merely shove the cartridge fully into a slot—the drives of different manufacturers deliver similar performance (which is a tribute to the QIC committee). The principal difference between systems is the software that's used for controlling them. The software determines the features and ease of each system's use. The software also determines the data format that's used on the tape. Two different drives running with the same software potentially can make interchangeable tapes. Two identical drives with different software probably will not.

DC2000 Cartridge Systems

Another of the biggest shortcomings of the the DC600 system is that the cartridges are, in fact, big. A DC600 cartridge is almost the size of a paperback book: a full 6 × 4 × 5/8 inches. Shoehorning a drive that can handle such bulky cartridges into a 5 1/4-inch form factor PC drive bay, which is itself six inches wide, offers a considerable engineering challenge. Fitting a drive for those cartridges into one of the 3 1/2-inch form factor drive bays of a PS/2 is patently impossible.

The most straightforward way to make something smaller is to make it smaller, and the *DC2000* cartridge represents the result of applying that strategy to the DC600. Similar to the DC600 in both construction and operating principle, the DC2000 was cut down with the simple expedient of reducing its tape capacity. The DC2000, trimmed to under 3 1/4 × 2 1/2 × 5/8 inches, holds 205 feet of tape of the same quarter-inch nominal width of that in the DC600.

Less tape means lower capacity. While today's DC2000 cartridges won't hold as much as their larger forebears, current systems are more than adequate, able to pack 40 megabytes on one of these tiny cartridges. New systems with 60- and even 80-megabyte capacities are coming on the market.

DC2000 Cartridge Manufacturers

Currently three companies hold licenses to use this technology and make cartridges: The 3M Company, which originally developed the system, DEI (Data Electronics, Inc.), and Hewlett-Packard, which currently does not sell cartridges in the retail market.

DC2000 Standardization

One way in which DC2000 cartridges differ from the DC600 style is standardization. While the recording standards used by DC600-based systems evolved over more than a decade, culminating in a confusion that finally led to a special industry committee to hammer out some sort of consistency among drive manufacturers, DC2000 systems have been standardized almost from the start.

Two new standards for DC2000 systems adopted by the QIC committee have already become popular: QIC-40 and QIC-100.

QIC-40

The QIC-40 system is designed primarily to be a low-cost backup medium for DOS and OS/2-oriented systems. To keep user expenses under control, it connects to a conventional floppy disk controller. In most cases, neither special controller nor cable is required. In fact, many QIC-40 drives simply slide into the floppy drive bays of PS/2s.

The QIC-40 Format

Under the QIC-40 standard, 20 tracks are arrayed across the width of the tape; and each holds roughly two megabytes of data. Each track is divided into 68 segments of 29 sectors. Each sector holds 1024 bytes each. Modified frequency modulation (MFM) recording is used for QIC-40 at a density of 10,000 bits per inch.

Sectors are assigned to files much in the same way that disk space is allocated. Each tape has the equivalent of a file allocation table that lists the bad sectors contained on the tape so that no bytes are risked on bad or marginal media. Data on the tape are specifically structured under the QIC-40 format. (See Figure 23.4.)

Under QIC-40, tape drives run at either 25 or 50 inches per second when writing data, depending on the data transfer rate of the floppy disk controller in command of the unit. Normal double-density drives (XT-style) operate with a data transfer rate of 250 kilobits per second; AT-style high-density (1.2 megabyte) and PS/2-style 3 1/2-inch drive controllers operate at 500 kilobits per second. Data bits are transfered to tape at the same rate they would be written to floppy disk.

QIC-40 Error Correction

One-third of the possible 60 megabyte capacity of a DC2000 tape under the QIC-40 format is devoted to identifying the format structure of the tape and to data error-correction. Two methods of error correction are used: cyclical redundancy checking and a Reed Solomon code (an efficient error-correction algorithm that's used, among other places, in interplanetary communications). The resulting error rate is extremely low—one in 10^{14}—one bad bit in 100 trillion. That should ensure that less than one tape in two hundred thousand has a single bit error. That is actually substantially fewer errors than you could expect to achieve with a typical disk drives.

Because the tape format is so closely tied to the disk formats used by DOS and OS/2, QIC-40 appears aimed most directly at the PC market. The QIC-40 standard also supports Unix as well.

QIC-40 Speed Problems

The chief disadvantage of QIC-40 is time. Using QIC-40 can sometimes be an exercise in patience. Because of the use of the floppy disk interface, data transfers are limited to floppy disk speeds. As a practical

Figure 23.4 **QIC-40 logical structure**

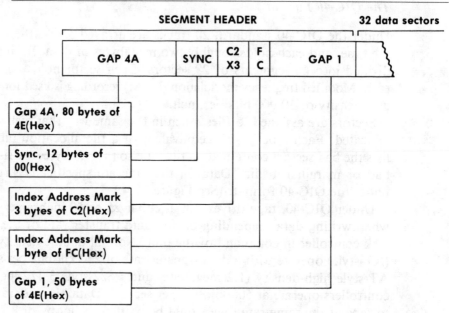

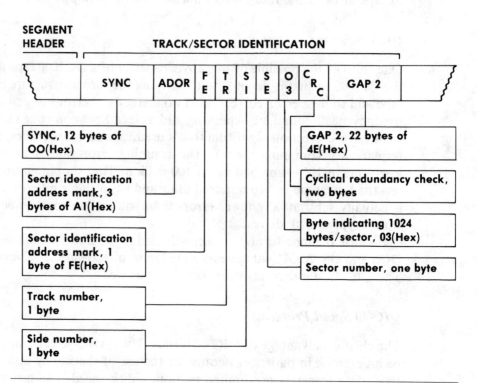

Figure 23.4 (continued)

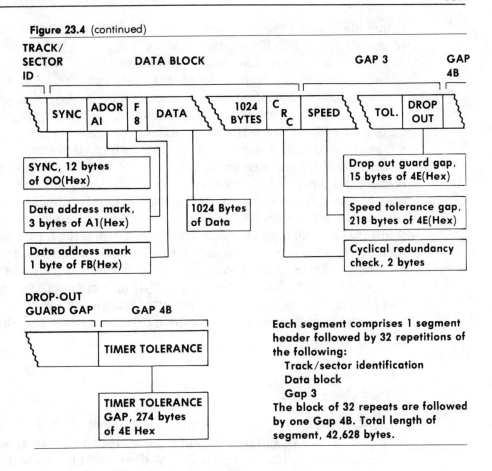

TRACK/
SECTOR
ID

DATA BLOCK

GAP 3

GAP
4B

SYNC, 12 bytes
of OO(Hex)

Data address mark,
3 bytes of A1(Hex)

Data address mark
1 byte of FB(Hex)

1024 Bytes
of Data

Drop out guard gap,
15 bytes of 4E(Hex)

Speed tolerance gap,
218 bytes of 4E(Hex)

Cyclical redundancy
check, 2 bytes

DROP-OUT
GUARD GAP   GAP 4B

TIMER TOLERANCE

TIMER TOLERANCE
GAP, 274 bytes
of 4E Hex

Each segment comprises 1 segment
header followed by 32 repetitions of
the following:
    Track/sector identification
    Data block
    Gap 3
The block of 32 repeats are followed
by one Gap 4B. Total length of
segment, 42,628 bytes.

matter, that slows hard-disk backups to about one-half the speed of
DC600 systems.

More of a bother is the need of the precision QIC-40 drives to index
their read/write heads to find the edge of the tape so that they will properly position themselves over the very narrow tracks on the tape. This
indexing process takes between fifteen seconds and a minute, depending
on the drive, and is unavoidable even when doing such trivial tasks as
reading a tape directory or a single short file near the beginning of the tape.

QIC-40 Tape Formatting

As with floppy disks, QIC-40 tapes must be formatted before they can
be used. Because the tapes have much greater capacity than disks, the
formatting process takes commensurately longer—up to an hour for 40
megabytes. That means the best strategy is to start the format process

before lunch or leaving work for the day. Not all of the tape must be formatted for a QIC-40 cartridge to work.

To save formatting time, many manufacturers of QIC-40 systems allow you to partially format a tape to a lower capacity, often in two megabyte increments representing a single track.

The alternative to spending hours formatting tapes is buying *preformatted cartridges*, which the manufacturers of QIC-40 systems claim are available at only a slight premium over unformatted tapes.

The formatting requirement of QIC-40 is not all bad. Along with the bother come a number of benefits. For example, during the format process, bad sectors can be reserved. Because the tape is formatted with a file allocation table, individual tape sectors can be accessed randomly. While the tape still must be shuttled to any given spot, the format allows each sector to be unambiguously identified without reference to its neighbors. That means you don't have to read through the whole tape just to find a single file. As a result, a QIC-40 tape can mimic the operation of a floppy disk. In addition, formatted tapes make appending files to a partially used tape easy because the system can quickly find where it left off writing to the tape.

QIC-40 Compatibility

The QIC-40 standard promises interchangeability of DC2000 tapes between tape drives of different manufacturers. If this were true, a tape backed up on one manufacturer's QIC-40 drive could be restored from a different manufacturer's products.

QIC-40 falls a bit short of that goal, however. The QIC-40 standard stops short of actually specifying the exact arrangement of the tape file structure. That's left to the individual software developer who makes the backup program to run the QIC-40 system. As a result, while tapes are interchangeable between different drives and can be read without regard to the equipment used, you might not be able to make sense of the results. Because there's no compatibility of file structure, you can read every byte on a tape in any system, but all you might end up with is a big pile of data; files can run into one another and even intermingle.

Compounding this compatibility problem are manufacturers who offer DC2000-based systems that are close to the QIC-40 standard but are not completely compatible with it. The bottom line is that while the QIC-40 standard for DC2000 cartridges goes deeper than those applied to DC600 tapes, the end result is the same. Often cartridges remain captive to the manufacturer and model of the system making them.

QIC-100

Where QIC-40 aims for low cost, the QIC-100 standard is more oriented toward performance. By using its own controller rather than sharing one with floppy disk drives, QIC-100 allows for the option of higher data transfer rates. Of course, the additional cost of the controller also means that QIC-100 systems will tend to be more expensive than those based on QIC-40.

As with QIC-40, under the QIC-100 standard, the data to be written to the tape is divided into blocks. However, QIC-100 is a looser standard and permits the system manufacturer to define the block length to be used.

The QIC-100 Format

Blocks are written across the tape serially, using 12 or 24 tracks of serpentine recording. Data bits are recorded at a density of 12,000 flux reversals per inch. The actual data density is somewhat less because the specification calls for Group Coded Recording, which uses five flux reversals to encode each four-bit nibble of data.

As with QIC-40, the tapes used by QIC-100 must be formatted prior to their use. In that the block length is undefined, the precise tape format is left to the discretion of the system manufacturer. Of course, the drawback of the formatting requirements of QIC-100 are the same as those for QIC-40.

For error protection, QIC-100 requires that every block of data feature a special Cyclic Redundancy Code block, which reveals data errors. In addition, the standard does not specify but allows the use of error correction.

QIC-100 Compatibility

Because it is a looser standard, QIC-100 does less to ensure the compatibility of tape between drives of different manufacturers than does QIC-40. Commercially, the QIC-100 standard has not won general acceptance as has QIC-40, despite its higher performance potential.

Nonstandard Tape Systems

A number of tape systems go in their own directions, obeying no generally agreed standard but instead making their own. Such a strategy is not necessarily bad (after all, following an industry standard still does not guarantee compatibility) and may prove advantageous. Nonstandard systems can excel in one or more characteristics, such as price, performance, capacity, or convenience. A wide variety of these tape systems are in use or soon will be. Among them are DC1000 cartridges, VHS and 8-millimeter videotape, spooled tape, and digital audio tape.

DC1000 Cartridges

Out of the mainstream, but aiming at getting in, are several other tape formats. DC1000 cartridges, about the same size as DC2000s, use 150 mil (thousandths of an inch) wide tape the same width as audio cassette tape—and hold 10 to 20 megabytes. Tape systems based on the DC1000 cartridge have proven to be popular mostly because of their low prices. In fact, when interfaced through a floppy disk controller, DC1000 systems are among the least expensive tape systems available for small computer systems. One manufacturer is dominant in the DC1000 industry, Irwin Magnetics, and has essentially set its own standard for such products.

As with QIC-40, the floppy disk interface used by these systems tends to limit their performance. The various commercially available systems rank among the slowest tape drives that can be connected to a PC. For most people, however, a slower tape drive is better than no tape drive and price is the deciding factor in the purchase.

Spooled Tape

Spooled tape systems, primarily offered by Interdyne Company, Milpitas, CA, are based on an unusual cross between quarter-inch cartridges and open-reel tape. Using techniques similar to that of IBM's 3480 tape drives, the plastic-cased spool of quarter-inch tape is put in the drive, which automatically threads it onto an integral tape up spool. Although the first of these systems were slow, relying on floppy disk controllers, a new generation of drives with much higher speed potentials is promised soon.

Videotape Backup Systems

Of all media that can be directly recorded upon by consumers, ordinary videocassettes currently have the greatest capacity. A single tape might hold the equivalent of several gigabytes of digital data.

While capacity alone should make the VCR an intriguing backup device, videos and computers don't get along well. The reason is the familiar incompatibility faced by the modem. Video signals are analog, while computer signals are digital.

Two different companies have taken the modem approach to videotape and have produced digital storage systems based on standard videotapes and recorders. Alpha Microsystems offers a backup system called *Videotrax* that's based on an rather ordinary VHS videocassette recorder. Emerald Systems offers a system called the *VAST device* which is based on Sony's 8-millimeter videotape system.

Videotrax

In the Videotrax backup system, a single expansion card in the host computer converts hard-disk or other system data into NTSC (National Television Standards Committee) video signals, which can then be backed up and stored on a conventional videocassette recorder. Although either a VHS or a Betamax machine (or even a professional-caliber U-matic) can be used, Alpha Micro offers commercial systems based on VHS recorders.

The Videotrax system combines Alpha Micro's proprietary digital-to-video conversion board with a specially modified VHS machine that can be remotely controlled by a PC. The host computer can take command of tape travel during the backup or you can run the system manually.

Redundancy Against Errors

One problem faced by the Videotrax or any similar system is that videocassettes generally have more dropouts than certified computer data cartridges. Dropouts, minute lapses in the magnetic medium, can cause the recorded signal and the data it encodes to disappear. Alpha Microsystems ensures against dropout-related problems by writing multiple copies of data to tape, a procedure called *redundancy* that is successful because it is statistically unlikely each of the copies will suffer dropout degradation.

According to Alpha Microsystems, this error protection scheme results in the Videotrax system being one of the most secure forms of information storage available. However, because of the duplication of all the redundant information, at present the total capacity of a single two-hour video tape is limited to about 80 megabytes.

Videotrax Speed

The Videotrax system also ensures data integrity by verifying the on-tape signal by playing it back and analyzing it to detect errors. In effect, each backup copy can be certified as correct before it is depended upon. This verification process and the duplication of backups to eliminate dropouts slows down the backup process, however. The Videotrax system creeps along at a rate of about 13 megabytes every 10 minutes, substantially slower than today's streaming tape systems.

One of the prime advantages of the Videotrax system and using conventional consumer-quality components for data storage is cost. Both the equipment and supplies for video recording are mass-produced and readily available at low prices, as low as $5 for 80 megabytes. Streaming tape data cartridges cost about five times more. The hardware price of videotape backup can be lower, too, because you can make use of the video recording hardware that you already own. If you have a VCR, the only hardware you'll need is the Alpha Micro data-to-video conversion board, currently $595.

The VAST Device

Instead of merely converting the video signals, Emerald Systems has reworked the entire 8-millimeter video system to create the VAST device. Although it's as easy to load as a VCR, the VAST device cannot function as one. It's designed solely to be a storage and backup instrument.

Eight-millimeter cartridges are substantially smaller than those used by VHS or Beta machines by design. As the name implies, 8-millimeter cartridges use a magnetic ribbon that's exactly 8 millimeters wide compared to the half-inch of VHS cartridges. Up to 346 feet of the tape can be packed into a single cartridge, which is about the size of an audio cassette, albeit somewhat thicker.

Using a modified videocassette tape transport and its own electronics, the VAST device stores up to 2.2 gigabytes on a single cartridge. (Cartridges with intermediary capacities—250, 500, and 1000 megabytes—are also available.)

Using the same spinning head/helical recording technique used by all video cassette recorders, the VAST device lays down thousands of skewed tracks, each three inches long and 0.00098 inches wide, diagonally across the tape. Each one holds about 12K, yielding storage for 8K of data. The rest of the track is used for the error correction code and servo (control) information. While the tape travels at only 0.43 inches per second, the rapidly spinning head (1800 RPM) results in an effective writing speed of 148.4 inches per second.

To assure data integrity, the VAST device uses a three-head system. One head writes data to the tape and a second head reads it back shortly thereafter for true read-after-write verification. This technique ensures that all information that the system thinks that it wrote on the tape actually appears on it. The third head is used for servo information, which locks the rotation rate of the head to the data on the tape. The combination of read-after-write verification and ECC results in an overall data error rate of one in ten trillion. The odds are that one bit might go bad in every 500 fully recorded tapes.

Other than the unusual medium and overwhelming capacity, the VAST system works like other Emerald backup systems because it shares the same software. It provides all the expected backup and restore options and works either under menu or command control. It features a "learn" mode that will help you quickly and almost effortlessly build an automatic backup system for your gigabytes.

The one problem that the VAST device hasn't licked is moving gigabytes. The hardware-software system moves megabytes at a prodigious rate, up to nine megabytes per minute, on par with other backup systems. But filling a whole VAST cartridge at that rate would take four hours. Rather than a coffee break, you'll probably have time for a 16-course feast while your backup runs.

Tape Backup Systems

No one backup system rates best for everyone. Each has its own combination of features, which can recommend it for a given host PC environment.

For most people, the most important factor in guiding their backup choice is cost. In general, more buys more—speed, capacity, compatibility, and convenience.

The most expensive systems for PCs today are those that use nine-track open-reel tapes. They earn their keep by giving your data the utmost security as well as providing a portal through which you can access and exchange data with other computer systems.

Next in the price spectrum are the various cartridge disk systems. For their somewhat steep prices (which seem particularly high when compared to conventional hard disks), you get random access speed and convenience, the ability to serve as primary mass storage, and unlimited off-line capacity.

Of the available formats of cartridge tape, the DC600 is the fastest and most expensive system. While some DC2000 systems with dedicated controllers can rival the speeds of larger cartridges at less cost, those that operate through floppy-disk controllers (and are consequently slower) are the least expensive.

Of today's first-generation DC2000 implementations, however, only a few deliver performance that may be acceptable to the anxious AT user. Some floppy disk-based backup systems are actually faster.

In removable media systems, the price of tapes or disks can be a major factor in overall cost. For instance, you may be able to buy an entire tape drive for the price of a couple Bernoulli cartridges.

For most backup scenarios, you will want sufficient media capacity to hold a minimum of three complete backups. For greater peace of mind or more elaborate backup rituals, such as keeping a separate backup for each day of the week, your media needs increase. Most people actively use between 6 and 10 tapes in their regular backup routine.

You should also figure in the cost of periodically replacing any media that can wear out. All tape media and all disks except for cartridge hard disks will eventually wear out.

The exact amount of life to expect from a particular medium depends on your own personal paranoia. According to one major media manufacturer, DEI, DC600-style cartridges should last 5000 to 6000 passes across the read/write head. On the other hand, cautious mainframe managers may routinely replace open-reel tapes after they've been used as few as 50 times. A good compromise, according to DEI, would be annual replacement of your backup tapes.

When you look beyond backing up, other considerations can overrule the price differences between systems. For instance, when you absolutely need access to mainframe tapes or want to interchange information, you'll have to bite the bullet and budget for an open-reel tape drive.

The best backup system is the one that you're most likely to use—and use routinely. No matter how good or expensive it may be, a backup system is worthless if you never bother to put it to work. The backup system that's easiest and most convenient to operate is the one least likely to be ignored—and the one most likely to help when disaster strikes.

No matter the backup hardware you choose, you still need a backup system. That system requires more than just hardware, even more than software. To make it work, you must adhere to a strict backup routine after you make one overall backup of all the files on your hard disk.

The absolute best backup system is one in which you make a duplicate copy of each file as soon as it is made. Finish a worksheet and immediately copy it to your backup medium.

For this kind of backup system, your best choice is a random access backup system: floppy disks, a duplicate hard disk, a cartridge disk, or a tape system that attempts to emulate a disk device. Random access will speed the backup process so you can quickly make your copy and get on to something else.

If you don't like the bother of constantly making copies, you may want to investigate Tallgrass Technologies' BackTrack software, now supplied by all of the company's backup hardware. BackTrack runs in the background and constantly monitors your disk. When it finds a file that has not been backed up, it duplicates it on the backup disk or tape drive. A similar, newer system called Nonstop Backup is sold by Digital Storage Systems.

The second major backup system is one with which the file copies are made at regular intervals. For instance, every day at an appointed time you duplicate all the files that have changed that day by copying them onto the backup medium. This sort of routine is the backup choice in systems where data is really important; most mainframes are backed up on such a daily schedule.

Large capacity media are often best for this kind of backup because the number of files to backup may be great and you won't want to stick around the whole time shuffling floppy disks in and out of the disk drive.

Traditionally tape systems have been the choice for these regular backups, although there is no reason that cartridge or duplicate hard disks can't be used. Removable cartridge media (tapes or disks) are usually preferred because they permit storing several copies of the entire system setup for recovery when the worst disaster befalls you.

Streaming tape is the traditional medium of choice, and among PC and minicomputer users, the DC600-style cartridge is particularly favored. Of course, DC2000, open-reel tapes, or DC1000 cartridges are also suitable (usually in that order). Although the media are somewhat more expensive, disk cartridges can also be used.

The best backup system is the one that enforces the routine that you're most likely to follow. A backup system that does not get used (or used often) is not a backup system at all.

In general, two DC600-style backup techniques have evolved: image and file-by-file backups. Manufacturers have developed their own format standard for their own tapes.

Image Backups

The image backup is a bit-for-bit copy of the original disk. Bytes are merely read from the disk and copied on tape without a glance at their content or structure. Because little processing overhead is involved, these image backups can be fast.

File-by-File Backups

File-by-file backups add structure to the information as it is backed up. Although processing overhead tends to slow down file-by-file systems, finding files within the structure (and hence, individual file restoration) is easier.

These two techniques are tending to merge. File-by-file backups are becoming faster, and smarter restoration software can make sense of the inherent structure of image backups so that individual file restorations can be made from them.

The current trend is toward faster file-by-file backups. Among such systems the compatibility situation is improving, and a standard is emerging: the on-tape data format used by the backup software product, SY-TOS, which is published by Sytron Corporation, Marlboro, MA. The format gained credibility when IBM adopted the format (and software) for its own line of PC tape cartridge backup systems. Now several manufacturers offer systems using the same format.

Either image file-by-file backups can make a workable system. When your hard disk is nearly filled to capacity—less than 10 percent to 15 percent of its free bytes free—and you want to back everything up all the time (recovery is faster when all files are on the same tape), image backups are usually faster. When your disk is far from full or you demand the utmost in file recovery flexibility, file-by-file backups are the better choice.

In either backup mode, the ability to append several backups or files on one previously used tape will save on cartridge costs.

If you plan on overseeing all of your backups as they happen, the fastest backup system is always the more endurable. But if your time is valuable and you don't mind leaving your PC running overnight (and have the faith that it will, indeed, continue to run overnight), you can take advantage of the automatic backup programs offered by several manufacturers (including Alloy, Sysgen, and Tallgrass). This software will copy disk files to tape per your instructions but without your intercession at a designated hour, even on a designated day.

INDEX

1167, 75
16-color, 359

2,7 RLL, 485

3,9 RLL, 485
3030, 536
32-megabyte addressing limit, 547
3480, 593
386 Max, 95
3M Company, 598

4-bit, 359
40-column mode, 330
4004, 43

6-bit, 359
64-color, 359
6502, 11, 14
6800, 15
6845 video controller, 297

80-column mode, 330
8008, 43
80186, 47
80188, 47
80286, 48
80287, 70, 71
80386, 51
80387, 70, 72
80387SX, 70, 72
8080, 12, 44
8085, 44
8086, 15, 44
8087, 70
8088, 15, 45
80C86, 47
80C88, 47
82284, 185
82385, 91
8253, 182
8259, 190
8259A, 191, 192, 194
8514/A, 354

ABIOS, 176
Abort
  Retry, Ignore, 512

Access time, 90
Accumulator, 58
Acoustic couplers, 465
Active cooling, 221
Adapter Description File, 175
Adapter plate, 228
Address bus, 42
Address decoder logic, 89
Address Enable, 121
Address Latch Enable, 120
Address Lines, 120
Addressability, 354, 387
Adobe Systems, 407
Advanced BIOS, 176
Advanced Logic Research, 135
Alexander Graham Bell, 469
Alignment, 345
All points addressable, 388
All Points Addressable graphics, 278
Allocation units, 490
Alpha Microsystems, 613
Amdek, 352
American Megatrends, 159
American Megatrends Inc., 106
American National Standards Institute, 397
AMP, 254
Amplification, 40
Amplifiers, 441
Analog, 40
Anode, 338
ANSI escape sequences, 397
APA, 388
APA display, 278
APL, 17
Apple, 13
Apple Computer, 9, 11, 258
Apple DOS, 11
Apple II, 11
Application Interface, 287
Arbitrate/Grant, 150
Arbitration Bus Priority Levels 0 through 3, 150
Ashton-Tate, 97
Assemblers, 59
Assembly language, 58
AST Research, 97
Asynchronous transmission, 466
Attribute bytes, 273
Audio, 144

August Dvorak, 247
Auto feed XT, 376
Auto-answer, 464
Auto-dial, 464
AutoCAD, 285, 327
AutoDesk, 285, 327
Automatic head parking, 544
Autosynchronous modems, 467
Average access time, 550
Award Software, 159

Bad sectors, 584
Bad tracks, 584
Bail arm, 391
Band-stepper actuator, 541
Bandwidth, 354, 440
Bank-switching, 96
Base memory, 93, 95
BASIC, 17
Basic Input/Output System, 17, 34, 159
Baud, 445
Bell 103, 445, 446
Bernoulli Box, 536
Bi-directional tractor, 393
Bidirectionally, 386
Bin-feed, 392
Binary coded decimal, 70
Binder, 539
Binders, 590
BIOS, 34, 159
BIOS compatibility, 320
BIOS data area, 169
Bit, 84
Bit-image graphics, 388
Bit-mapped, 390
Bit-mapped graphics, 11, 278
Black-and-white mode, 305
Blackouts, 210
Blanked, 301
Blanking, 145, 282
Block Graphics, 277
Boca Raton, 9
Border color, 301
Brightness, 351
Brooklyn Bridge, 428
Burning, 87
Burst, 150
Bus, 23
Bus mice, 263
Bus-oriented computer, 19, 23
Busicom, 43
Byte Enable Bits, 148
Bytewriter, 381

Capacitance, 441
Capacitors, 84
Capacity, 213
Card Data Size 16, 148
Card Data Size 32, 148
Card selected, 122
Card Selected Feedback, 147
Card Setup, 147
Carrier, 439
Carrier Wave, 444
Cassette BASIC, 168
Cathode, 338
Cathode Ray Tube, 281
CBIOS, 176
CCITT, 465
Central Arbitration Control Point, 150
Centronics, 367
CGA, 298
Channel, 24
Channel Check, 147
Channel Ready, 147
Channel Ready Return, 147
Character box, 271
Character mapping, 271
Character-mapped, 390
Character-mapping, 18
Chicklets, 245
Chips, 41
CHMOS, 51
Christopher Sholes, 380
Clamping speed, 210
Clamping voltage, 210
Clock, 120
Clock bit, 483
Clocked logic, 181
Clusters, 490
CMOS, 46
Coercivity, 481
Color Graphics Adapter, 298, 354
Color look-up table, 318
Color planes, 280
Color select register, 301, 303
Command set, 41
Commodities, 26
Compaq, 134, 135, 495
Compatibility BIOS, 176
Complementary Metal Oxide Semiconductor, 46
Composite video, 359
Computer terminal, 269
Conductors, 39
Control cable, 494
Control characters, 396
Controller, 491, 492

Convergence, 345
Coprocessor, 67
Coprocessors, 34
Cordless keyboards, 246
CP/M, 12, 44
Crosstalk, 369
CRT, 281
Crystal, 182
CW, 444
Cycle time, 90
Cylinder, 546

DAC, 317
Daisy-wheel printers, 383
Data bus, 42
Data cable, 494
Data Lines, 120
Data separator, 494
Data Size 16 Return, 148
Data Size 32 Return, 148
Daughterboards, 23
DC1000 cartridges, 612
DC2000, 606
DC300XL, 603
DC600, 603
DEBUG, 165, 584
DEC, 10, 13
Deflection coils, 282
Demodulating, 438
Demodulation, 438
Demodulator, 338
Dennis Hayes, 453
Deserializer, 494
Deskpro 386, 495
Device-level interface, 493
Diablo, 399
Diagnostic code modules, 176
Dial-up, 449
Digital, 40
Digital Equipment Corporation, 10, 423
Digital Research, 327
Digital-to-Analog converter, 145, 317
DIP, 100
Direct-connect, 466
Direct-connect modems, 466
Direct drive, 297
Direct Memory Access, 91, 182, 194
Discrete chips, 99
Disk parameters, 549
Display, 337
DisplayWriter, 17
DMA, 128, 194
DMA Acknowledge, 122

DMA Request, 121
Doping, 39
DOS, 330
DOS Memory Area, 95
Dot graphics, 388
Dot-addressable graphics, 388
Dot-matrix printers, 385
Dot-pitch, 346
Double-density recording, 483
Double-scanned, 319
Double-sigma, 54
Downloadable character set, 389
Dragging, 258
DRIVER.SYS, 524
DTMF, 464
Dual In-line Pin, 100
Dual-ported memory, 101
Dual-tone modulated frequency, 464
Dumb terminal, 270
Duplex, 443
Dvorak-Dealey, 247
Dynamic memory, 84

Echoplex, 443
EEMS, 97
EGA, 309
EGA Plus, 327
Electron gun, 338
Embedded controllers, 492
Emerald Systems, 613
EMS, 96
EMS Version 4.0, 98
Enable Sync, 145
Enhanced Expanded Memory Specification, 97
Enhanced Graphics Adapter, 309
Enhanced Graphics Display, 309
Enhanced Small Device Interface, 493
Entry Systems Division, 9
EPROM, 87
Equipment flag, 80
Equipment flags, 169
Erasable Programmable Read-Only Memory, 87
Escape sequences, 396
ESDI, 493
ESYNC, 145
Everex Systems, 135
Expanded memory, 96
Expanded Memory Manager, 97
Expansion boards, 24
Expansion bus, 11
Extended memory, 95
External modem, 468

FAT, 490
FCC Class A, 220
FCC Class B, 220
FDISK, 585
Federal Communications Commission, 220
Ferrite beads, 220
Ferroresonant transformer, 211
File Allocation Table, 490, 513, 547
Fixed disk, 537
Flags, 95
Flat tension-mask, 349
Flicker, 301, 339
Flip-top case, 225
Floating-point numbers, 68
Floating-point processors, 68
Floppy disk controller, 519
Floppy disk interface, 493
Flux transitions, 482
Flying read/write head, 536
FM, 445, 483
Font cartridges, 389
Form factor, 499
Fort's Software, 97
Frame rate, 283
Frequency modulation, 445, 483
Frequency shift keying, 445
Friction feed, 391
FSK, 445
Full-duplex, 443
Fully-formed character printers, 383

GCR, 484
GEM, 327
Gigabyte, 49
Glass-epoxy, 23
Graphic development systems, 285
Graphic operating environments, 284
Group Coded Recording, 484
Guard bands, 443

Half-duplex, 443
Hard disk card, 561
Hard disk cards, 493
Hard errors, 110
Hard sectored, 509
Hardcard, 565
Hardware windows, 289
Hayes Microsystems, 470
Head access aperture, 511
Head actuator, 517, 541
Head crash, 585
Head crashes, 537, 540, 543

Head parking, 544
Hercules Computer Technology, 307
Hercules Graphics Board, 356
Hercules Graphics Card, 307
Hewlett-Packard, 265, 389, 407
HGC, 307
HGC.COM, 308
High density notch, 517
High-density, 506
High-density 15-pin connector, 323
Higher level languages, 59
Hoff, 43
Hooks, 284
Horizontal frequency, 282
Horizontal tabbing, 395
Host adapter, 491
Hub rings, 508

I/O 16-bit Chip Select, 125
I/O Channel Check, 120, 147
I/O Channel Ready, 121, 127, 147
I/O Read Command, 121
I/O Support Gate Array, 188
I/O Write Command, 121
IBM, 259
IBM extended character set, 402
IC, 41
IDR Systems, 133
IEEE, 72
Index hole, 509
Indexing, 518
Initialize printer, 375
Ink jet, 382
Inmos 6171S, 318
Input prime, 375
Input range, 212
Institute of Electrical and Electronic
    Engineers, 72
Instruction set, 51
Insulators, 39
Integrated circuit, 41
Intel, 15
Interlace, 342
Interleaved memory, 92
Internal modem, 468
Interrupt Request, 122
Interrupt sharing, 192
Interrupt vectors, 93, 162
Inverter, 212
Iomega Corporation, 536
ITT, 399

J.M.E. Baudot, 446

Kevin Jenkins, 307
Keyboard buffer, 95
Keytops, 245

Landing zone, 544
LapLink, 428
Laser printer, 382
Laser printers, 387
Latch, 85
LCC, 62
LCD, 281
Leadless Chip Carrier, 62
Leased-line modems, 448
Letter-quality printers, 383
Light pen, 264
Light pens, 343
Linear power supplies, 201
Linear voltage regulator, 202
Liner, 507
Liquid Crystal Displays, 281
Logic gates, 40
Logic seeking, 395
Logitech, 259
Lotus 1-2-3, 285, 327
Lotus-Intel-Microsoft Expanded
    Memory Specification, 96
LPT, 370

Machine language, 58
Macintosh, 9, 258
Magnetism, 478
Magnetophone, 486
Main Menu, 584
Mantissa, 69
Mask ROM, 86
Masks, 48
Mass storage, 83
Master, 128
Matched Memory, 148
Matched Memory Command, 148
Matched Memory Cycle, 148
Matched Memory Cycle Request, 148
Matrix, 345
MCGA, 314, 324
MDA, 295
Mechanical mice, 259
Medium, 538, 539
Memory, 34
Memory 16-bit Chip Select, 125
Memory Address Enable 24, 148

Memory caching, 90
Memory Controller Gate Array, 314, 324
Memory map, 93
Memory modules, 99
Memory Read, 127
Memory Read Command, 120
Memory Write, 127
Memory Write Command, 120
Memory/Input-Output, 147
MFM, 483
Microcode, 41
Microprocessor, 11, 34, 39
Microsoft, 259, 327
Mini-AT cases, 225
MODE, 330
Model 5100, 14
Model Byte, 169
Modified Frequency Modulation, 483
Modified square waves, 214
Modulating, 438
Modulation, 438
Modulation products, 440
Monochrome Display Adapter, 295
Motherboard, 23
Motorola, 15, 315
Mouse, 258
Mouse port, 258
MSC Corporation, 262
Multi-Color Graphics Array, 315
Multisync, 358

N-channel Metal Oxide Semiconductor, 46
NEC, 358, 384, 423
NMI, 122
NMI Mask Registers, 122
NMOS, 46
Non-Maskable Interrupt, 122, 150, 189
NTSC, 357, 360
Null modem, 425
Numeric coprocessors, 68

OEM, 25
Open-loop actuators, 541
Optical mice, 259
Ordinate, 69
Original Equipment Manufacturers, 25
OS/2, 415
Oscillator, 119, 181
Overscan, 349
Overvoltage, 209
Oxide media, 539

P9, 56
Page-mode, 101
Page-mode RAM, 92
Parallel port, 367
Parity Check 1, 89
Parity Check 2, 89
Parity check bit, 89
Park-and-lock, 544
Passive convection, 221
PC Designs, 133
PC MOS/386, 415
PC's Limited, 119, 134
PC-1, 25
PC-2, 25
Persistence, 339
PGA, 61
Phase modulation, 445
Phoenix Technologies, 159
Phoenix Technology, 106
Phosphors, 339
Phototypesetter, 384
Pin Grid Array, 61
Pin-feed, 393
Pixels, 278
Planar, 24
Platen, 391
Plating, 540
Platters, 538
PLCC, 62
Plus Development Corporation, 565
POS, 146, 175
Position controls, 350
Postscript, 407
Power On Self-Test, 111
Power-Good, 204, 214
Power-On Self-Test Error Message Files, 176
Pre-empt, 150
Pre-fetch cache memory, 52
Preformatted cartridges, 610
Primary display, 330
Primary storage, 83
Primitives, 286
Printhead, 385
Printwires, 385
PRN, 370
Programmable Option Select, 146, 175
Programmable Read-Only Memory, 87
PROM, 87
Protected mode, 50
PS/2 Display Adapter, 321
Pulse-width modulation, 202
Push tractors, 393

QIC-02, 604
QIC-100, 611
QIC-40, 606
Quadram, 97
Quadrature modulation, 447
Qualitas Software, 95
Quantum Corporation, 565
Qume, 399
QWERTY, 246

Radio frequency interference, 220
Radio Shack, 11, 14, 256
RAM, 83, 87
Random access media, 487
Read-Only Memory, 86
Read-Write Memory, 86
Read/write head, 540
Real mode, 49
Rectifiers, 201
Reference Disk, 106, 146
Reference Diskette, 176, 584
Refresh, 85, 129
Register, 58
Register-level compatibility, 320
Registers, 15, 41
Regulation, 211
Relay, 85
Removable hard disks, 545
Repeaters, 441
Reset Driver, 120
Resolution, 280, 354
Response codes, 458
Response time, 210
Retentivity, 481
Retrace, 281
Reverse-engineering, 48
RFI, 220
Robert von Behren, 598
Rolm Corporation, 13
ROM, 86
ROM BASIC, 168
Run Length Limited, 484

S-100, 117
S-Register, 458
Sags, 210
Samuel F. B. Morse, 438
Saturable reactor, 211
Saturation, 480
SCSI, 493
Second source, 48
Sector Not Found, 482

Sectors, 488
Segments, 45
Select input, 375
Semiconductors, 39
Sequential, 486
Sequential media, 486
Serial mice, 263
Serpentine recording, 604
Servo surface, 542
Servo-voice coil actuator, 542
Setup, 330
Shadow mask, 346
Shadow memory, 88
Short haul modems, 439
Sidebands, 440
SIMM, 103
Sine wave, 214
Single In-line Memory Modules, 103
Single In-line Pin, 100
Single In-line Pin Package, 103
Single-board computer, 11, 23
Single-density recording, 483
Single-sided disks, 505
SIP, 100
SIPP, 103
Slot Eight, 122
Slot-pitch, 346
Small Computer System Interface, 493
Small footprint computers, 225
Smart terminal, 270
Smartmodem, 470
Snow, 301
Soft errors, 110
Soft-sectored, 509
Software interrupts, 162
Solid-state, 40
Sony, 346
Spikes, 210
Spindle, 538
Spindle motor, 517, 538
Spooled tape, 612
Sputtering, 540
Square waves, 214
ST506/412, 493
Standby power system, 211
Start bit, 466
Start-stop, 603
Static electricity, 105
Static memory, 85
Static-column, 101
Static-column RAM, 92
Status Bit One, 147

Status Bit Two, 147
Stepping motor, 541
Streaming tape, 603
Stroker, 283
Submodel Byte, 169
Substrate, 539
Surges, 210
Switching power supplies, 201
Synchronizing, 119
Synchronous transmission, 467
Synchronously, 69
System board, 24
System Bus High Enable, 125
System Identification Bytes, 169
System integrators, 26
System Support Gate Array, 188
System-level interface, 497

Tallgrass Technologies, 484
Tandy, 468, 598
Tandy Corporation, 12
Taps, 211
Telebit Trailblazer, 451
Telefunken, 486
Teletype, 18, 269
Teletype display, 270
Teletype interface, 12
Terminal Count, 121
Terminate-and-stay-resident programs, 162
Terminating resistor network, 527
Termination switch, 361
Texas Instruments, 15
Thermal printer, 382
Thermal transfer printers, 382
Thermal-wax printers, 382
Thimble, 384
Thin film media, 539
Thrashing, 290
Touch screen, 265
Touch-tone, 464
Traces, 23
Track, 487, 546
Track 0, 585
Tractor-feed, 393
Transformer, 201
Transients, 210
Transistor, 39
Transistor-Transistor Logic, 356
Transport, 491
Traveling Software, 428
Trinitron, 346
TRS-DOS, 12

TSR, 162
TTL, 356
TTL monochrome, 356
Tuner, 338
Typewriting Behavior, 248

UART, 413
Underscan, 349
Uni-directional tractor, 393
Uninterruptible power system, 211
Universal Asynchronous
    Receiver/Transmitter, 413
UPS, 211

V-EMM, 97
V20, 47
V30, 47
Varistor, 210
VAST device, 613, 614
VDT, 269
Vector graphics, 283
Vertical frequency, 283
Vertical interval, 282
Vertical retrace, 301
Vertical tabbing, 395
VGA, 314
VGA auxiliary video connector, 320
Video Data Terminals, 269
Video Graphics Array, 314
Video memory, 101
Video pages, 274

Videotrax, 613
Virtual 8086 mode, 53
Virtual memory, 49
Volatility, 86
Voltage regulators, 211

Wait states, 89
Weitek Corporation, 75
Weitek WTL 1167, 75
White Crane Software, 428
Whitney technology, 536
William L. Dealey, 247
Winchester, 536
Winchester disk drives, 536
Windings, 211
Windows, 327
Write access, 511
Write precompensation, 549
Write-protect notch, 511
Write-protect tab, 511
Write-through caches, 91

Xerox, 399

Yoke, 339

Z80, 12, 14, 44
Zenith, 349
Zero Wait State, 127
Zig-zag In-line Pin, 100
ZIP, 100